Black Psychology

BLACK PSYCHOLOGY

edited by *Reginald L. Jones*

University of California at Riverside

Harper & Row, Publishers

New York, Evanston, San Francisco, London

To

Julie
Angie
Cindy
And to the memory of Edward Allen Henry
(1947–1969)

CONTENTS

Preface   xi

PART VI

Perspectives on Racism 309

PART VII

Psychology and Psychologists in the Community 357

Biographical Sketches 407

Index 423

Black psychologists and other black social scientists insist, these days, on speaking for themselves. They perceive the need to move away from pathology oriented notions about the behavior of black people toward creating, interpreting, and reinterpreting the psychological literature on blacks. That blacks feel the need for outlets for their research and writing was indicated by several black psychologists who responded to a questionnaire about the need for a journal of black psychology.[1] They wrote:

I am convinced that there is a black and nonblack view of human behavior, growth and potential for development. All theoretical orientations must be examined and made viable within the phenomenological field of blacks' experiences.

The basic assumptions underlying much of the research on black people should be questioned. The journals in which such studies are published are not likely to accept publications oriented toward making these basic assumptions explicit and examining their validity.

I feel that black psychologists interested in the broad specialty of black psychology—that is, intelligence, personality development, family functioning— meet an adverse bias in seeking publication of material. This broad field is my interest and my success at publication has suffered because of it.

... We need a forum for sifting the research re black by black psychologists. We need to know in a handy and reliable way what's happening re black psychology that is useful in our work and research in this field. It would be enormously refreshing. ...

The present volume is designed to bring together in a single place writings by the new black psychologists and other black social and behavioral scientists. Such a volume can be expected to point to the range of activities in this new area, to highlight needed reinterpretations and clarification of the psychological literature on blacks, and to be instructive both to black and to white professional behavioral scientists and to students in behavioral science disciplines.

A range of writings will be found in the volume—from the empirical to the philosophical. No attempt has been made to restrict or confine authors in either content or style. In a sense the volume is a showcase of the range of perspectives

[1] R. L. Jones, Feasibility of developing a journal of black psychology. Unpublished paper presented at the Annual Meeting of the Association of Black Psychologists, Miami Beach, 1970.

held by black psychologists. The papers include previously published and unpublished writings. A number of individuals have been invited to prepare specific articles for the volume, and an intensive search of the literature has been made for work that complements these writings. In addition, relevant bibliographies which supplement the content of individual papers have been prepared in some instances.

The readings are organized into seven sections. In the first, "Black Psychology: Perspectives," a variety of viewpoints on psychology as applied to blacks are presented, including considerations leading to the development of black psychology as a discipline. Issues associated with the psychological assessment of blacks are taken up in Part II, including recommendations for the use of such tests with blacks in school settings. Problems of personality and motivation in blacks are dealt with in Part III. Several provocative reinterpretations and theoretical notions about black behavior are presented. A variety of points of view on the counseling and education of blacks are presented in Parts IV and V, while psychological perspectives on racism are presented in Part VI. A number of problems and issues in the application of psychology in the community, including the role of the black psychologist as professional in the community, and psychological interpretation and recommendations of a variety of community based behaviors are taken up in Part VII.

Four themes will be apparent in writings included in this volume. The first theme is a deemphasis upon deficiency-based hypotheses about black behavior, and second, a concurrent emphasis upon the positive aspects of black behavior which have permitted survival—though not without scars—in a racist society. Too often in interpreting black behavior the emphasis is upon what blacks do not possess that would make them white. A third theme is the rejection of white normative values as the basis for assessment and understanding of black behavior. This emphasis has been one of the significant constraining millstones around the necks of black Americans. A fourth theme is a quest for explanations of black behavior rooted not only in psychological phenomena but also in social and economic factors as well, which all serve to maintain the system which serves to subjugate blacks psychologically. Thus certain psychological states of blacks are described within the context of environmental forces which create and maintain them. It may appear that categorical black–white differences across social and personal domains are being made. Nothing could be further from the truth. To be certain, there are individual differences among blacks and there is some overlap in the behavior of blacks and whites. There are, however, forces operative in American society which shape and influence black Americans. Understanding the nature of these influences as they relate to the psychological development and functioning of black Americans is at the core of the volume.

It will become apparent that unanimity does not exist among authors of the papers in regard to the subject matter of Black Psychology or indeed, about whether a discipline Black Psychology should exist. No attempt has been made to secure definitional agreement among contributors about the term Black Psychology, or about its unique concerns. It is apparent, nevertheless, that the authors are of a single voice in their demand for change and reinterpretation of the psychological literature about blacks, that their concern is with problems affecting the psychological health and well-being of black Americans and, when necessary, with the development of new theories and alternative interpretations of research and writing in this area. If a definition of Black Psychology must be given, it is suggested that its parameters are those as defined above, and those identified in the four themes characterizing papers presented in this volume; its architects are black social and behavioral scientists.

As with any product of this nature, I am indebted to many persons for its birthing: as always, to my family who endured; to the many contributors who met deadlines, revised papers, and provided the creative and seminal flow that made the volume possible; to Ruby Tapia Miller, with the project from its inception, who kept track of authors, typed manuscripts, and did research; to Eddi Knopf who did more of the same; and to Peter Ekeh for his comments about African philosophy.

In preparation of the volume, an autocratic hand was maintained throughout, and thus what is in this volume and what is not has been my own doing; and I must, therefore, accept responsibility for it.

R. L. J.

Partial support for the publication of this book came from a grant from the Maurice Falk Medical Fund. The Fund, however, is not the author, publisher, or proprietor of the material presented here and is not to be understood, by virtue of its grant, as endorsing any statement made or expressed herein.

Black Psychology: Perspectives

Part I presents a forum for the diverse views of black social and behavioral scientists on the psychological nature of blacks in contemporary America, and explores the possibilities of developing a discipline of Black Psychology, which would be devoted solely to these matters. All contributors agreed that there is a need to seek alternative explanations of black behavior, but there was no agreement on the aims or specific subject matter of such efforts; one writer rejected the development of any discipline which might be labeled Black Psychology.

In the first paper, "Black Studies or the Study of Black People?" Cedric Clark presents the philosophical underpinnings of a black psychology. A key distinction is made between black studies and the study of black people drawing analogies from Aristotelian and modern scientific points of view. In this conception, black studies derives its interpretive framework from the nature of black people, whereas the study of black people has as its interpretive framework the nature of nonblack people. Clark makes several points about the distinctive black-studies approach to black behavior:

that it cannot be value free but must be directed to the specific end of creating an "alternative framework within which black behavior may be differently described, explained, and interpreted"

that it is positive with respect to black behavior and not just negative as regards white behavior

that its focus be on "the understanding of phenomena and on the communication of that understanding to those who are desirous of it"

Key tasks for building the discipline are identified and certain propositions from psychohistory and the philosophy and history of science are used as cornerstones.

Wade Nobles, in "African Philosophy: Foundations for Black Psychology," sees as the task of Black Psychology the understanding of the behavioral definition of African philosophy, and the documentation of its modification over time. Presumably, once the operation of such variables is understood it will be possible (1) to demonstrate how these orientations affect the behavior of black Americans and (2) to validate the explanatory potency of this class of variables as opposed to others.

Any discipline which would seek to understand the nature of black behavior must of course take into account experiences which shaped that behavior. It is not surprising then that Africa should be turned to in the quest for understanding the values, attitudes, and customs of black Americans. This point of view represents the thesis of Nobles's paper. He outlines various elements of African

1

philosophy that presumably have relevance to black Americans (e.g., unity, death and immortality, and kinship) and documents their presence in contemporary black American life.

The papers by Clark and Nobles outline certain potential philosophical foundations of a Black Psychology and point to its parameters. Neither would assert his discussion to be exhaustive. Each, however, suggests directions for activity.

The papers by Doris Mosby and Joseph White point to the precise subject matter dictating the need for a Black Psychology. Mosby, in "Toward a New Specialty of Black Psychology," makes the case for qualitative differences in the life experiences of blacks which lead to differences in developmental, social, personal, intellectual, educational, and family functioning. Black Psychology would account for the differences. Mosby demonstrates the fallacy of using a white frame of reference (i.e., white test-standardization groups) in explaining deviancy in blacks. When such frames of reference are used, the meaning of the findings for blacks is, of course, unknown. Indeed, a real question is whether the meaning of such results for blacks can be known. Understanding the context in which responses occur is, Mosby points out, a critical task for Black Psychology.

White, in a well-known paper, "Toward a Black Psychology," gives compelling reasons for developing a Black Psychology: Principles and theories developed by white psychologists to explain the behavior of white people simply do not have sufficient explanatory power to account for the behavior of blacks. White presents alternative conceptions of black family life, black dialect, black paranoia, and black life styles in general, which provide the meat of a Black Psychology.

The first four selections in Part I all indicate in one fashion or another that alternative perspectives and alternative explanations are required if valid theories of the behavior of black people are to be developed, and that black social and behavioral scientists should be the architects of these changes. The writings are atheoretical in that no particular school of behavior theory is espoused. The paper by William Hayes, "Radical Black Behaviorism," is an exception. He too calls attention to the need for understanding black behavior, but he rejects a discipline of Black Psychology as the vehicle that would accomplish this goal. Hayes's objections are based upon the fact that great variations exist among subdisciplines within "American psychology," and that beyond a common core of black experience, great variations exist in the training of black psychologists inasmuch as such training was received at white institutions. Hayes urges that a discipline of Radical Black Behaviorism be established. Such a discipline would be limited to the study of behaviors that can be observed, measured, and reproduced. Explanations are those that produce and maintain the behavior to be explained. He demonstrates that the conceptualization offers interpretations of black behavior which provide an alternative to conventional mentalistic dynamic explanations.

CEDRIC CLARK

Black Studies or the Study of Black People?

I

Modern conceptions of science are in many respects quite similar to those held by the ancient Greek philosophers, Aristotle in particular. We do not normally think of Aristotle as a scientist, but this is because we are victims of our own current linguistic patterns and particular modes of thought. The word *scientist* is less than one hundred years old, but the activities of science are ancient, having their origins in the great civilizations of North Africa, thousands of years before the founding of the Greek city-states. Aristotle, who was influenced heavily by the thinkers of North Africa—Ptolemy in particular—was very much a scientist: He was not only thoroughly conversant with, but in many cases the architect of, the disciplines we now refer to as the sciences of chemistry, botany, zoology, physiology, and astronomy. Aristotle excelled in all of these, plus several others. Yet he is usually referred to as a philosopher, not a scientist. Why should this be so? Primarily because "science," at that time, was not divided into the various subbranches we know today. All of the "hard" sciences we are acquainted with were considered during Aristotle's time to be a part of "natural philosophy."

Because Aristotle's natural philosophy to a large extent made possible the formation of the various sciences available to us now, it is perhaps not surprising that his thinking still pervades much contemporary scientific activity. Yet few scientists would consider it flattering to be described as "Aristotelian" in their mode of activity. As is so often the case with the thinkers of the past, we tend to be much more familiar with the differences which separate ourselves from them than with the similarities which bind us together. We tend to associate newness with "goodness" or "freshness" and old things with "irrelevancy."

Aristotle, like the modern scientists of today, believed that the chemical processes going on inside animals (the organic world) were essentially similar to those going on inside nonanimals (the inorganic world). This is not to say, however, that since Aristotle's time there has been an uninterrupted and undisputed train of thought on this matter. Indeed, the fields of Organic Chemistry and Inorganic Chemistry were created to handle what in the nineteenth century were considered to be major and substantial differences between man (organic)

Preparation of this paper was facilitated by faculty release time granted by the Department of Psychology, the Department of Communications, and the Afro-American Studies Department, Stanford University. Portions of this paper are taken from the author's monograph, *The psychological dimensions of the black experience.* Reprinted by permission of the author.

3

and matter (inorganic). This division was chiefly a reflection of the theory of the dualism (separate existence) of man and matter, which the French mathematician and philosopher Descartes popularized within the scientific community.

Advances in science during the twentieth century, beginning first with Einstein's formula equating matter and energy, and elaborated upon by Heisenberg's "principle of uncertainty," however, have shown that Aristotle was fundamentally right—that "matter" and "nonmatter" are essentially the same.

Why, then, we may ask, was this fundamental tenet of Aristotle so bitterly rejected during much of the period which characterized the development of European science from the sixteenth century on up to (and, in part, including) the modern day? The answer is that, while Aristotle drew the same conclusions as do contemporary physicists, he interpreted them quite differently. Instead of building his interpretive framework around the reactions of inorganic "reality" and explaining organic or physiological processes in terms of these—as we do today—he took the development of organic "reality" as his basic paradigm and attempted to fit his observations into this scheme.

Thus we see that there are at least two different ways of interpreting the same basic "reality." Neither is necessarily right or wrong; they are simply different. One way asks one set of questions, derived from its paradigm, and gets one set of answers; the other way asks a different set and acquires a different set of answers. In modern physics, for example, one scientist may hypothesize that light is a *particle* and ask a set of questions (which will preclude his acquiring answers to a different set), while another scientist may hypothesize that light is not a particle, but a *wave* and, accordingly, pose a different set of questions and acquire a different set of answers. Which set of questions and answers represents "truth"? In fact, *both* do or, if one is totally monistic in his conception of reality, *neither* does. This is the heart of the "uncertainty principle" in modern science. And its relevance to the study of man has yet to be fully appreciated.

It may have already occurred to the reader that a similar phenomenon exists between two different modes of thought involved in the study of black behavior. That these two modes of thought exist, there seems little doubt; the title of this book indicates as much. What we appear to be less certain about, however, are the major dimensions which characterize and differentiate the two modes of thought. Are they as radically different as some would have us believe, or are they "fundamentally" the same as many others claim? It would appear that one of the first steps in the development of Black Studies as a distinctive scientific approach would be to answer this fundamental question. To some it might seem that efforts directed toward this end would be "wasted" in a system that needs drastic and immediate overhauling. How, some may ask, can answers to such philosophical questions be made relevant to today's black man? From one point of view, however, all scientific activity is relevant to somebody at some point in space and time. (It is important not to confuse "relevant" with "beneficial," or else we would be placed in the awkward position of claiming to a Vietnamese peasant that war-related research in the United States is "irrelevant" to him.)

My main purpose in this paper is to attempt to differentiate between two modes of approaching the study of black behavior. It is an attempt (perhaps overly ambitious) to lay the groundwork for a "wave-particle" theory of black behavior. I shall work on the assumption that most interpretations of black behavior have, traditionally, been of a "particle" variety and that what differentiates (or should differentiate) *Black Studies* from the *Study of Black People* is a conscious effort to promote the reality of a wave theory. The tasks for Black Studies, as I see it, then, is to describe the nature and limitations of "classical" social science and, at the same time, develop a framework within which "modern" social science can develop and hopefully flourish.

It may have appeared to the reader that I already specified one characteristic distinctive of a Black Studies approach to black behavior: Such an approach should not be, or pretend to be, value-free. It must consciously direct itself to a specific end, which represents a particular goal or value. This end, as I have indicated, is the creation of an alternative framework within which black behavior may be differently described, explained, and interpreted. Of course, we must recognize that, strictly speaking, the pursuit of a particular end does not in and of itself differentiate Black Studies from the Study of Black People. All scientific enterprises have some goal or value, if none other than to be impartial. Impartiality is as much a value as partiality (1).

The major difference, then, involves the extent to which Black Studies is conscious of its goals and articulates them unashamedly. (Although many blacks have reduced the amount of personal shame associated with their physical appearances, many others are still ashamed of their mental activities. Increases in black consciousness, however, seem to be eradicating these last vestiges of a slave mentality.)

This problem of a slave mentality brings us to a point more directly concerned with Black Psychology. If the creation of an alternative framework is considered to be the major general aim of Black Studies what should the particular aim of Black Psychology be?

I propose that it should be nothing more, or less, than *the liberation of the black mind.* Again, there is nothing to be ashamed of in promoting such a goal, for science involves precisely that: freeing people from irrational fears and superstitions. The achievement of mental liberation does not merely involve putting in new information, it also involves getting rid of old information. Only by so doing can the mind be truly opened.

Getting rid of old information is often a much more difficult task, for many of our very questions can only be phrased using language associated with the old information. The questions we ask today concerning the movement of celestial bodies, for example, could not have been asked during pre-Copernican times. The necessary concepts were not yet available. Similarly, the questions of today's Quantum Physics could not have been asked before Einstein's time. Man is always limited in what he *can* know by what he *does* know, even though he may not know (be conscious of) what he knows (2).

When I suggest that the aim of Black Psychology should be "no more than" or "less than" the liberation of the black mind, I mean to put as much stress on the former phrase as on the latter. Science is not only limited in what it can do, it is also limited in what it should do. That is, it should not attempt to do too much. Science is a disciplined activity, although it need not be restricted to the study of disciplines. For science knows no disciples other than those involved in the search for truth, which is itself the acknowledgment and acceptance of uncertainty. In the language of contemporary social psychology, science should seek to arouse dissonance, not reduce it. For the reduction of dissonance is ignorance; the path to knowledge involves the deliberate introduction of uncertainty or doubt (3).

To be a "disciplined doubter," then, sets definite limits on what one should do, even when one's charge is as broad as the liberation of black minds. But these limits are not proscriptive, in the sense of setting dictums about what should not be done, but prescriptive, in the sense of setting dictums about what should be done. That is, its approach is positive, not negative.

This, then, is another distinguishing feature of Black Studies—as contrasted with the Study of Black People—*viz.*, its approach is positive with respect to black behavior and not just negative with respect to white behavior (4).

I must hasten to add that, in some areas of psychology, the two are not easily separated. This is particularly true in those areas where an apparent dialectical process governs the nature of black–white interaction. The psychology of self-esteem seems to be one such area. It is generally acknowledged, for example, that many blacks have "low" self-esteem; it is also generally acknowledged that many whites have "high" self-esteem. Indeed, most studies comparing whites and blacks show these patterns very clearly (5). What is not frequently examined, let alone acknowledged, however, is the possibility that perhaps a high self-esteem among whites depends upon blacks having a low self-esteem. I am not talking about the purely statistical artifacts which might be involved; I am referring to a causal law relating the two phenomena in the following way:

"*If* the self-esteem of whites is high,
then, the self-esteem of blacks will be low."

As it happens, this is precisely the major point of much of the essayist James Baldwin's writings. He claims that because American whites, unlike their European counterparts, do not possess a long cultural history, they have been forced to forge their identity around the mythology of nonwhite peoples they came into contact with or, as was the case with the Native Americans, conquered. This identity was forged by means of the following dialectic type of reasoning:

"Everything good that I (white American) am,
is everything that you (nonwhite American) are not;
and everything bad that you are, I am not."

The self-identity of whites, according to Baldwin, thus emerged from a dialectic of separateness which was later so firmly rooted in American institutional life—particularly during slavery—that it persists still today (even though some of the legal foundations have been destroyed). In short, Baldwin was arguing—with, incidentally, considerable theoretical support in social psychology—that the concept of a self grows out of particular types of interactions with others. While blacks and whites may be geographically segregated, they are not so psychologically—at least not with respect to conceptions of self. What one has gained in terms of a self-conception, the other has lost. Neither psychological state would be possible without the other. Self-esteem is thus akin to a psychological *resource* in the context of a zero-sum game being played by white and black cognitive systems (6).

This particular problem of black self-esteem to the contrary notwithstanding, it is possible in many cases to take a positive approach to black behavior without necessarily advancing a negative approach to white behavior.

It might be valuable at this point to refer again to Aristotelian conceptions of science. The major difference between Aristotle and most modern scientists, it will be recalled, was that Aristotle took as his interpretive framework the nature of organic processes, while scientists today take as their framework the nature of inorganic processes. In like manner, we might say that whereas Black Studies takes as its interpretive framework the nature of black people, the Study of Black People takes as its framework the nature of nonblack people. Such differential frames of reference have characterized the history of science, often in bitter conflict (as was the case with Ptolemy and Copernicus), but frequently in a state of peaceful coexistence (as is the case now between the wave and particle conceptions of the nature of light).

What does it mean, then, to take as an interpretive framework the "nature of black people" as opposed to the "nature of nonblack people?" It certainly could not be argued that there are no differences between the behavior of blacks and whites, for we have too much published evidence to refute such a claim. The question is, then, what are the differences, and which should be made the building blocks of an alternative framework? Or, in other words, what is the core of the black experience which differentiates itself clearly from the core of the white experience?

I suggest *slavery*. I am not claiming that this is the only difference separating the black experience from the nonblack experience, but that it is a major one. Moreover, it has, more than any other single event, shaped the mentality of the present-day black American. It is, in a word, the most relevant event in the history of black Americans (7).

Some psychologists might be disturbed by my selection of slavery as an experiential foundation, not because they hold any particular brief for slavery or because they do not consider it a valid area of scientific study. What they will object to, primarily, is that it happened "too long ago" to be of much relevance today. What is relevant, they would argue, is what is happening today, right now. One can again sympathize with this view and recognize its merits. Yet, we should examine carefully the foundation of this belief. It seems to have its origins in nineteenth-century conceptions of science, articulated by the British philosophers Locke and Hume, and practiced by that scientific giant of his time, Isaac Newton. In the Newtonian scheme of things, "a body at rest remains at rest unless acted upon by some external force." The behavior (movement) of things was thought to be the consequence of some antecedent and external event. Because any single event might be preceded by a number of preceding events, it was thought necessary not only to observe, but also to control, the nature of the immediately preceding events. This gave rise to experimentation as a basic scientific method. (The earlier scientists, the African astronomers, could only observe the phenomena they were interested in; they could not manipulate them. Indeed, they thought it more likely that the things they were observing, i.e., the heavens, were controlling or influencing *them*. Hence, no distinction was made between astrology and astronomy [8].)

Also important in the Newtonian conception of the universe were the notions of absolute time and space. Space had to be absolute for Newton or else the axioms of Euclidian geometry were wrong. And no scientist seriously questioned Euclidian geometry during Newton's time. More important for our purposes, time also, according to Newton, had to be absolute and finite. If it were not, we could never be sure when one event preceded another. And if this could not be known, the entire (deterministic) view of the universe as being governed by causal laws would break down. The fact is that it did break down (and with it the sacredness of Euclidian geometry), with the introduction of quantum theory. This issue is less important for our purposes than the fact that much of contemporary psychology (behaviorism in particular) is still in the conceptual grips of nineteenth-century Newtonian thinking.

In particular, Newtonian conceptions of absolute time and space have so conditioned many of us that it is impossible for us to conceive of (let alone believe in) such phenomena as ESP (which are made not at all impossible given the basic tenets of modern physical theory). More relevant to our present concerns, Newtonian thinking has led us to believe that events that have occurred "long in the past" (e.g., slavery) could not *conceivably* have as much effect in determining present behavior as those events of relatively "recent" occurrence.

The point is that "long in the past" and "recent" are highly misleading terms when we recognize that space and time are not absolute but relative. In other words, in terms of a relative universe, the occurrence of slavery might be as near in succession as the time it took you to finish reading this sentence. Time and space are not absolute, but infinite. The life of *Homo sapiens* on this planet is infinitesimally short (like a snap of your fingers) compared with the time it would take man to visit even the closest star in our immense universe (9).

What, then, is to prevent us from conceiving of slavery as happening "only yesterday" and, therefore, just as relevant as any of "yesterday's" events?

Aside from having a firm scientific foundation, the consideration of slavery as a dominant experiential aspect of black Americans has also to commend it a potentially strong capacity for enabling us to better understand the behavior of blacks (as well as whites).

This is not to suggest, however, that Black Psychology should consist solely of black psychohistory, concerned only with events that took place in the (again, not so remote) past. We should use this event, that is, slavery, as a starting point, not an end point. That is, the past is useful in understanding the present (and future), though not always for the prediction and control of the same.

This raises another factor distinguishing Black Studies from the Study of Black People: In the latter case, the goal of scientific inquiry is taken to be the prediction and control of future behavior. In contrast, the goal of Black Studies should place its primary emphases, not on prediction and control but on understanding phenomena and communicating that understanding to those who wish to understand.

Very few psychologists today would subscribe to such a goal; indeed, another legacy of nineteenth-century scientific thinking is the virtual equation made between science and prediction. But, as I have indicated, this, a very recent notion in scientific thinking, is still largely confined to psychology as studied in Western nations.

The conception of science as prediction and control vs. science as understanding apparently had its origins in the intellectual separation of man from nature. This separation between animal (or organic) and nonanimal (or inorganic) phenomena reached its heights in Greek philosophy, particularly in the writings of Plato. However, during the same time, on the continent of Africa, scholars very much retained their belief in the essential unity of *all* things, organic and inorganic (10). Practitioners of the most highly developed of the African sciences (i.e., alchemy) insisted that spiritual forces (e.g., incantations) were just as much a part of reality as were the chemicals with which they were working. This belief later held force even in some parts of Europe, France in particular, and was later transported to American with the slave trade. Even today, in many parts of the West Indies and southern United States, there is variant of alchemy practiced, called Voodoo or Hoodoo (11).

And, just as man's mind was considered inseparable from terrestial reality (where the alchemists focused on precious metals), it was also considered inseparable from celestial reality (where the astrologers focused on the divine heavens). Thus, as I have indicated, astrology was firmly believed in, even by such African scientists as Ptolemy. Whereas in the northern part of Africa man saw his destiny tied in with his observations of the heavens, in the southern part he saw it tied up with the forest and rivers. In both cases, as well as in many parts of the eastern and southern American world, man did not see himself separated from nature and, significantly, from other men.

What, then, made the intellectual climate in Plato's Athens receptive to the idea that man and nature were two different realms of being? There are several answers to this question, but perhaps most relevant for our present concerns is the fact that the Greek political state was a *slave* state. Even the most noble of the Greek thinkers, Aristotle, saw fit to justify the existence of slaves in Greek society.

It seems not too far fetched to suggest that the slave-owning Greeks felt it conceptually necessary, for psychological reasons, to distinguish themselves from other people. Plato's promotion of the philosopher-king and the totalitarian state epitomized this belief. In separating themselves from other men, the Greeks, of necessity, separated themselves from nature as well—for man was, even in the early Greek legends, considered to be an integral part of nature. One could not divorce himself from other men and still maintain a personal involvement with nature. But such a divorce did take place in the minds of the influential Greek thinkers, and such a division is the cornerstone of contemporary Western scientific thinking (12).

What is important for present purposes is the answer to the following question: "What kind of scientific approach would the Greek *slaves* have taken were they permitted to do so?" The answer to this question, it seems to me, would provide an indication of how the descendants of American slaves ought to proceed in constructing their scientific *Weltanschauung*. Of one thing we can be reasonably certain: The conceptions of the world held by the slave-master and the slaves are likely to be quite different. The task of Black Psychology thus seems clear: to specify the dimensions of this "slave" conception of reality and, by so doing, provide a basis for understanding the slave mentality. Through such understanding, the freeing of the mind might become possible.

II

How are we to proceed? What knowledge do we now possess? And how valid is that knowledge? Taking our lead from the African scientists, much of whose valuable work has been lost due to a reliance on oral tradition and the failure of many Greeks to understand Arabic, we might begin by questioning the Cartesian duality of mind and matter. This at once frees our mind *to conceive of the possibility* that there might be some validity in the thinking of the so-called Occult Sciences. The distinction between magic and science has never taken a firm root in the minds of many black people. For that matter, even some of the otherwise "average" Americans (e.g., the Christian Scientists) still refuse to make a clear demarcation between "mind" and "matter" (13). Indeed, the term *occult* is now virtually synonymous with "non-European," even though its literal meaning is "hidden" or "secret."

We need to be extremely cautious, however; to conceive of a possibility is not the same as to assert its actuality. This difference is what separated Freud and Jung, and the conflict between the two serves to illustrate the distinctive scientific paths open to contemporary black scientists. Freud never doubted that there could be something valid about occult reality; but never in his most penetrating analyses of dreams would he claim that indeed there was. Jung, however, was (to use Freud's perspective) much less cautious in this regard. While Jung's concept of *synchronicity* is perhaps no less fanciful than Newton's concept of *gravity* (i.e., both can not be seen and have to be accepted on faith), the range of phenomena to which it was applied strained the credibility of Jung's contemporaries. And to be conceived of as *incredible*, means, to most scientists, that one is "mystic" at best and "foolish" at worst.

While both were trained as "hard" (i.e., nonsocial) scientists, Freud and Jung were a generation apart in their ages. Freud, the older of the two, grew up in a scientific *Zeitgeist* which did not question the existence of Newton's deterministic universe. Thus, Freud's psychodynamic system, for all its modern flavor, had a critical defect: It was conceived of as a *closed* system. Jung, however, reached intellectual maturity during the post-Einsteinian period, when nineteenth-century Newtonian conceptions were relegated to what we now term *classical* (as opposed to *modern*) physics. He was quite at home in the probabilistic, field-dominated universe of open systems, which is characteristic of contemporary science.

The point is that while Freud was and is frequently misunderstood, Jung seems not to be understood at all. It would indeed be one of those supreme ironies in the history of science if Jung, alleged to be a consultant to the Nazi regime, were to find himself laying the foundations for a psychology relevant to black mental liberation.

I am of course not suggesting that Black Psychology become a branch of the psychic sciences; that would probably sound its death knell on most contemporary college campuses. Its foundations are already shaky enough without blindly accepting as "real" the unverified pronouncements of the occult enthusiasts. It is the adoption of an open mind I am advocating; for unless one's own mind is open to begin with, how is it possible to undertake the liberation of other minds?

This brings us to a consideration of an issue implicit throughout this article: Black Studies ought also to involve itself deeply and systematically with philosophical pursuits, particularly the philosophy of knowledge itself, or *epistemology*. To be sure, the study of philosophy is today considered retrogressive and unscientific, but this is a peculiar attitude, particularly given the fact that the science of physics, which most psychologists still take as a pattern for theoretical development, is itself very much concerned with philosophical matters. Physicists are not startled when they see a book entitled *Physics and Philosophy*; they know precisely what the contents of such a book are likely to be (14). In short, they (or at least the best of them) are more or less conscious of the issues involved. This does not appear to be at all the case with respect to the science of psychology. To many, if not most, psychologists, philosophical issues were settled with the dualism of Descartes. Recent attacks on the dualistic conception, not only by modern physicists themselves, but also by large segments of the educated public, seem to have had little effect on much current thinking in psychology (15).

The concept of Black Studies raises some fundamental questions with regard to the objectivity of social knowledge. Despite efforts by Berger and Luckman, Mannheim, Merton, and others, the relevance of epistemology to the ongoing activities of science (i.e., the "sociology of knowledge") remains a relatively underdeveloped area of American psychology (16).

Black Studies seems to take a consistent, although often unarticulated, position with regard to such issues. The basic proposition is that *all knowledge is rooted in social relations, particularly as these are determined by racial classifications*. In other words, what the individual perceives as "truth" or "valid knowledge" is a function of the racial group he belongs to—particularly when he is studying race-related phenomena.

Our philosophical heritage—that is, what is taught to us in our public schools—is firmly grounded in European conceptions of reality. The dualistic conception of Descartes, as refined by the British Empiricist thinkers, particularly Hume, Locke, and Mill, still stands as the scientific foundation of contemporary psychology. The only "truth" that matters, according to these thinkers, is that which is given to us by our sensory experience with things. The mind may exist, but it is totally independent of matter, and "what matters" (i.e., is important) is the reality of matter. Matter is sense; the mind is non-sense, or would result in nonsense if one philosophized on it too long. It was, I think, the historian of psychology, Boring, who claimed that the science of psychology "first lost its *soul*, then its *consciousness*." At least one contemporary writer has since added that "psychology threatens to go out of its *mind* completely." There are good reasons for this, if one is operating within a European frame of reference; but there are very good reasons for reversing this trend if one is operating within an African frame of reference.

Of the five sensory organs from which, according to Empiricism, all of our "valid" knowledge emanates, only one, the sense of sight, has been emphasized. Thus, what can be observed (not merely "sensed") is what most traditional psychologists would accept as valid knowledge. While one need not accept in its entirety McLuhan's thesis that the introduction of the printing press in European culture had a profound effect in further accentuating the visual mode of perception, one can agree with him that these effects have not always been beneficial or conscious (17).

The apparent lack of development of the other major sensory receptors (particularly the ear, or sound) among Europeans may be traced as much to philosophical biases as to technological achievements (although, of course the two are usually related). In any case, it seems apparent that aural deficiency is one of the major characteristics differentiating European culture from African culture. Black Americans, of course, partake of both European and African culture and thus the balanced development of the visual and aural senses is probably greater for them than for those influenced predominantly by one or the other. The extent to which this has had a distinctive effect on black behavior, in relationship to both other blacks and whites, is a question for systematic research. What seems relatively certain, however, is that the philosophical foundations associated with the British Empiricist tradition have been narrowly conceived and need to be closely examined if appropriate questions are to be raised about black behavior (18).

To conclude this brief and oversimplified discussion of the relevance of philosophical issues to Black Psychology, it is perhaps worthwhile to report a personal experience.

A California research institute recently consulted me about research concerning the effectiveness of some federally supported educational programs in the local black community. As an example of the epistemological issues differentiating Black Studies from the Study of Black People, I have reproduced the institute's conceptions of the basic problems along with those I suggested might emanate from a different set of philosophical premises.

TABLE 1

Definitions of Black Community Problems

Study of black people defined	Black studies defined
1. Black apathy and lack of communication with school officials	1. Failure of school officials to provide community with needed educational-concepts strategies, and tactics for successful black adaptation to a (hostile) environment
2. Pessimism about future black opportunities	2. Realistic appraisal of opportunities open to black people in America
3. Lack of knowledge about and interest in goals of schools	3. Black reluctance or refusal to accept the goals of white-oriented schools that are irrelevant or detrimental to the black culture
4. Lack of educationally relevant models	4. Failure of school officials to recognize the "educational relevance" of such black models as Huey Newton, Malcolm X, Muhammad Ali, Marcus Garvey, et al.
5. Alienation and isolation from middle-class white institutions	5. Experiences of exploitation with white middle-class institutions, and the failure of school officials to accord recognition and respect to the black culture

It may be unnecessary to note that the incorporation of these different conceptual definitions of problems into measurement instruments will lead to the collection of quite different data and the generation of quite different propositions concerning educational effectiveness. The point, again, is not that one set of definitions is "right" and the other "wrong," but that the selection of one represents a particular observer-observed interaction pattern (i.e., culture) while the other represents a different pattern.

To heighten these issues further, let us consider for a moment an example taken from contemporary American psychology, that concerning "Negro intelligence." While it is tempting to claim that this concept is irrelevant to the issue of Black Psychology, it would, I think, set a dangerous precedent if we were to react to pseudoscience with nonscience. The stakes surrounding the nature of "Negro intelligence" are extremely high, and simply because such research is conducted primarily by white South Africans and North Americans is no reason to dismiss the findings as "irrelevant."

We can begin an examination of any aspect of reality by asking four basic questions:

1. Where did it come from? (genetic properties)
2. What is it? (formal properties)
3. How does it behave? (behavioral properties)
4. Why does it behave? (functional properties)

Inevitably, inquiries into any given phenomena involve a mixture of these four approaches, although one usually predominates.

Traditional psychology has, in general, adopted the first two approaches with respect to intelligence, and its epistemology has generated such questions as "Which is more important in determining the nature of intelligence: heredity or environment?" and, "Of what general and specific factors is intelligence composed?"

Black, or African, psychology, it seems to me, ought to focus its attention on the latter two approaches. To give a concrete example of an answer to each of these questions, consider the following propositions:

1. Black intelligence manifests itself in a decision to run zigzag down an alley (as opposed to straight) when a policeman pulls his gun on you.
2. The purpose of this behavioral manifestation is to increase the probability of personal survival.

This example is not presented facetiously; it represents a real and concrete behavioral event, which most readers of this volume would immediately recognize as having considerable temporal-spacial generality (19). This temporal-spatial generality was epitomized in a statement concerning "Negro intelligence" made by Marcus Garvey at the turn of the century:

When the Colonists of America desired possession of the land they saw [that] a weak aboriginal race was in their way. What did they do? They got hold of them, killed them, and buried them underground. This is a fair indication of what will happen to weaker peoples of the world in another two or three hundred years when the stronger races will have developed themselves to the position of complete mastery of all things material. They will not then as they have not in the past, allow a weak and defenceless race to stand in their way, especially if in their doing so, they will endanger their happiness, their comfort, and their pleasures . . . the illiterate and shallow-minded Negro who can see no further than his nose is now the greatest stumbling block in the way of the race. He tells us that we must be satisfied with our condition; that we must not think of building up a nation of our own, that we must not seek to organise ourselves racially. . . . This is a dangerous policy. (20)

Implicitly throughout, and explicitly on occasion, Garvey gives the following answers to the questions indicated above:

1. Black intelligence should be viewed as the ability of blacks to defend themselves against their environment in general, and white people, in particular; and
2. The purpose of such intelligent behavior is to insure the survival of the race.

Thus we see that in the very conception of intelligence there lies a hidden interpretation. We cannot pose a question without providing some answers (to unposed questions). These "answers of the first instance" set the parameters within which "answers of the second instance" must fall. The process, because it is largely unconscious, is far more subtle than asking the question, "When did you stop beating your wife?" but it partakes of the same general principle. To ask the question, "Are Negroes equal in intelligence to whites?" is effectively to preclude the possibility that they may be *superior* in intelligence to whites.

We have thus returned essentially to the issue that began this paper: Observers may agree on the existence of given phenomena (e.g., lack of black intelligence; the basic similarity between organic and inorganic processes), but they will frequently disagree on the interpretations made of them. One group might claim that black intellectual development should and does pattern itself after white intellectual development, while another group might claim it is precisely this which is the cause of low black intelligence in the first place. Again, the question is not which is "right" or "valid." The question, rather, is which would better advance the type of understanding (not control) one is interested in gaining.

While it is true that Black Studies has been late in beginning the scientific advancement of black people, we may note, in closing, that perhaps it is better not to have advanced at all than to advance without purpose or in directions where the correlation between psychological knowledge and mental liberation have been all too low—for black people in particular, and the human race in general.

Notes and References

1. Kwame Nkrumah, in his greatest philosophical work, *Consciencism* (London: Panaf, 1968), discusses the value behind "value-neutrality" in considerable detail.
2. For a brief, but excellent discussion of the cultural limitations in science, see T. S. Kuhn, *The structure of scientific revolutions* (Chicago: University of Chicago Press, 1962).
3. For the relevant psychological literature, see L. Festinger, *The theory of cognitive dissonance* (Stanford, Calif.: Stanford University Press, 1957) and compare with D. Berlyne, *Conflict, arousal and curiosity* (New York: McGraw-Hill, 1964). See also, D. Fiske and S. Maddi, *The functions of varied experience* (Homewood, Ill.: Dorsey Press, 1961). Another valuable work dealing with the same issues at a more general level is J. Z. Young, *Doubt and certainty in science* (Oxford: Clarendon Press, 1953).
4. I am arguing here on behalf of a principle, not for total and complete commitment. There is some need for the critical analysis of white behavior in relation to blacks. Why, for example, is there so much current concern over the size of the black population? Is there any relationship between this concern and the general fear many whites have of blacks? These are legitimate questions for psychological research, and I do not mean to suggest that they, and other aspects of white behavior, should not be systematically studied. See C. Clark, General systems theory and black studies: Some points of convergence, in C. Thomas (ed.), *Boys no more: A black psychologist's view of community* (Beverly Hills, Calif.: Glencoe Press, 1971).
5. See H. Proshansky and P. Newton, The nature and meaning of Negro self-identity, in M. Deutsch et al. (eds.), *Social class, race, and psychological development* (New York: Holt, Rinehart, & Winston, 1968). See also, W. C. Kvaraceus et al., *Black self-concept* (New York: McGraw-Hill, 1965).
6. I have discussed these issues regarding the black self-concept more thoroughly elsewhere. See C. Clark, Competency and legitimacy as organizing dimensions of the black self-concept, paper presented to the Self-Concept Work Group, Social Science Research Council, 1971. The article will appear in a book to be published during 1972. The theoretical works relevant to Baldwin's conception include, G. H. Mead, *Mind, self, and society* (Chicago: University of Chicago Press, 1934); L. Festinger, A theory of social comparison processes, *Human Relations*, 1954, 7, 117–140; and R. D. Laing, *Self and others* (New York: Pantheon, 1969).

7. Nor do I mean to suggest that the attitudes of American whites toward blacks were first formulated during the period of slavery. Antiblack attitudes were in existence much earlier than this and, in fact, helped make slavery possible. See W. Jordan, *White over black: American attitudes toward the Negro, 1550-1812* (Chapel Hill: University of North Carolina Press, 1968).

8. This unwillingness of the African scientists to distinguish between astrology and astronomy was related to their general unwillingness to separate man (the observer) from nature (the observed). They were thus much closer to the modern physicist's conception of the universe than were the Greeks during the time of Aristotle—a point I will take up again in subsequent paragraphs.

9. An additional implication of the philosophy of the "new (Quantum) physics" is that it throws into question our entire notion of linear causality. If time and space are infinite and relative, then what might appear to one observer as time t might appear to another, differently located, observer as time $t + 1$. The logical conclusion to this is the recognition that "consequences" can precede "causes"! When, additionally, this conclusion is seen in the context of "traditional" African cosmology, we are forced to entertain the possibility that "primitive" modes of thought are extremely modern. See J. Mbiti, *African philosophy* (New York: Anchor, 1970) and C. Levi-Strauss, *The savage mind* (London: Weidenfeld & Nicholson, 1962).

10. Interestingly enough, there seems to be a negative correlation between an African philosopher's distance from Greece and the extent to which he still retained a belief in the essential unity of man and nature. Alchemy, for example, was much more extensively practiced in the kingdoms of the Sudan than in Alexandria. And, further to the south, in the forest regions of Africa, the idea of the separation of man and nature did not arise until the beginnings of Christianity and, concommitantly, of European colonialization. Further, it is likely that the spread of Islam in the northern part of the continent also propelled beliefs in the separateness of man and nature because, as did Christianity, Islam promoted monotheistic conceptions of God. See S. Toulmin and J. Goodfield, *The architecture of matter* (Middlesex, England: Penguin, 1962) and Okot p'Bitek, *African religions in Western scholarship* (Nairobi, Kenya: East African Literature Bureau, 1970).

11. See J. d'Argent, *Voodoo* (Los Angeles: Sherbourne Press, 1970) and W. B. Seabrook, *The magic island* (New York: Harcourt Brace Jovanovich, 1929).

12. Strictly speaking, of course, it was the philosophy of Descartes, several centuries later, that established much of the philosophical foundations for contemporary European science. Descartes, however, was strongly influenced by the philosophy of Plato, particularly by the latter's emphases on syllogistic reasoning. In any case, it seems certain that, without his deference to Greek (Aristotelian) thought, Descartes' work would have never received the attention it did. This seems particularly true when we also take into account the fact that Descartes was a devout Catholic, and his philosophical differentiation between the "soul" of man and the "body" of man confronted the Church with theological difficulties he sought to mitigate as much as possible.

13. See *A century of Christian Science healing* (Boston: Christian Science Publishing Society, 1966).

14. Cf. W. Heisenberg, *Physics and philosophy* (New York: Harper & Row, 1958).

15. See, for example, A. Koestler, *The ghost in the machine* (New York: Macmillan, 1967) and E. Schrodinger, *What is life? The physical aspect of the living cell* (Cambridge: Cambridge University Press, 1945).

16. See P. L. Berger and T. Luckman, *The social construction of reality* (New York: Doubleday, 1966); K. Mannheim, *Ideology and utopia* (New York: Harcourt Brace Jovanovich, 1936); R. Merton, *Social theory and social structure* (New York: Free Press, 1948).

17. See H. M. McLuhan, *Understanding media: The extensions of man* (New York: McGraw-Hill, 1964). See also, S. Steinberg, *Five hundred years of printing* (Middlesex, England: Penguin, 1955).

18. It appears that the emphasis on sight as the dominant perceptual mode has its origins in the considerable attention paid to the science of optics during the seventeenth and eighteenth centuries in Europe. The invention of the telescope and microscope seems to have firmly entrenched visual observation as the only legitimate scientific method. What I am arguing in this paper is that perhaps this reliance on the visual mode has been overextended and that we ought to pay at least as much attention to our other senses. The culture of black Americans is distinctive for its reliance on senses in addition to the visual. These are as yet unexplored senses and are worthy of serious attention in Black Psychology. Perhaps future books regarding black behavior ought to be *recorded* as well as *written* (note 19).

19. This example is taken from a poem recited by a group of black poets in an album entitled "The Last Poets" (produced by East Wine Associates, n.d.; distributed by Pip Recording Co., 850 Seventh Avenue, New York).

20. M. Garvey, *Philosophy and opinions of Marcus Garvey, or Africa for the Africans* (London: Frank Cass, 1923), pp. 146–147.

WADE W. NOBLES

African Philosophy: Foundations for Black Psychology

Black Americans derive their most fundamental self-definition from several cultural and philosophical premises which we share with most West African "tribes" (1). In exploring the character of these premises, which are basic conceptions of the nature of man and his relation to other men and his environment, we hope to establish a foundation upon which a Black Psychology can be constructed. Thus, it will be contended that Black Psychology is something more than the psychology of the so-called underprivileged peoples, more than the experience of living in ghettoes or of having been forced into the dehumanizing condition of slavery. It is more than the "darker dimension" of general psychology. Its unique status is derived not from the negative aspects of being black in white America, but rather from the positive features of basic African philosophy which dictate the values, customs, attitudes, and behavior of Africans in Africa and the New World.

The notion of common experience or common ethos seems almost fictional if one accepts uncritically the research findings of many so-called Africanists who argue that the territory of the western region of Africa held and still does hold within its boundaries many different "tribes," each having its own language, religion, and customs. However, one must note the orientation of these many Africanists whose incidental whiteness colors much of what they have to say. One must, therefore, be conscious of the inherent social dialectic. That is to say, while most foreign students of Africa have maintained that the western "tribes" have little shared experience because each has a distinct language and religion and many unique customs, they have overlooked "the similarities of the forest for the differences *between* the trees." In this view, it is suggested that the overemphasis given tribal differences by white investigators is the anthropological or scientific version of the imperialist strategy of "divide and conquer." Hence, it is likely that many white ethnographers are predisposed by conscious or unconscious racist assumptions to focus upon superficial differences and are thus "blinded" to underlying similarities in the experiential communality of African peoples. Fortunately, however, this anthropological analog of the "divide and conquer" strategy has been redressed by black (and even by a few white) scholars (Mbiti, 1970; Herskovits, 1958). These scholars maintain that "tribal" differences in Africa were minor compared to the binding quality of their communality. This author suggests that what supported this regional communality was a set of guiding beliefs—an ethos. Closer examination of the region indicates that the ethos determined two operational orders. The first is the

Reprinted by permission of the author.

notion that the people were part of the natural rhythm of nature: They were one with nature. The second order is the notion of the survival of one's people—that is, the "tribe." Hence, the African experience defines man's place (role) in nature's scheme.

However, unlike a written constitution, the ethos is more akin to a spiritual disposition and probably could best be described as collective unconsciousness. Although the ethos cannot be scientifically (i.e., empirically) examined with current methodology, it is believed that one way to understand the essential and pervasive nature of the African (black) ethos is to explore and understand African philosophy (2). It follows therefore that insofar as the African (black) ethos is distinct from that of the prevailing white ethos (upon which traditional psychology is founded) then a Black Psychology based upon the black ethos must also be uniquely different from white psychology. It is this principle that allows African philosophy to take its place as the foundation for Black Psychology.

African Philosophy

Religion and Philosophy

John Mbiti (1970) defines African philosophy as "the understanding, attitude of mind, logic, and perception behind the manner in which African peoples think, act, or speak in different situations of life." What is central to Brother Mbiti's definition is the "spiritual disposition," the "collective consciousness,"—in a word, the ethos. At this point, it should be made very explicit that when talking about the ethos one is talking about it in the context of African philosophy. In a sense, the ethos can be considered the operational definition of African philosophy. More specifically, this "collective consciousness" can be described as a *vital attitude*. That is to say, a kind of faith in a transcendental force and a sense of vital solidarity.

Examination of preslavery Africa suggests that there were hundreds of African peoples, or tribes, and some would suggest that each had its own philosophical system. More sophisticated scholarship indicates that for West Africa in general, philosophy was the essence of the people's existence, and that the many tribes shared one overriding philosophical system. It was through religion, however, that this philosophical system was expressed. In this sense religion and philosophy are the same phenomenon. Hence, to understand the essence of these peoples' existence one must examine their religion, proverbs, oral traditions, ethics, and morals—keeping clearly in mind that underlying the differences in detail is a general philosophical system which prevailed in Africa. Religion, however, is the more observable phenomenon and as such it permeated every aspect of the African's life. It was, in a very real sense, not something for the betterment of the individual, but rather something for the community of which the individual was an integral part. For the traditional African, to be human was to belong to the whole community (Mbiti, 1970, p. 5). Curiously enough, many African languages did not have a word for religion as such. Religion was such an integral part of man's existence that it and he were inseparable. Religion accompanied the individual from conception to long after his physical death.

As most scholars of African religion will attest, one of the greatest difficulties in studying African religion and philosophy is that there are no sacred scriptures or texts. A great number of beliefs and practices were and can be found in African society. However, these beliefs and/or traditions were handed down from father to son for generation upon generation. As such, and in accordance with the prevailing *oral tradition*, the beliefs were corporate and the acts were communal. Traditional religion in Africa was not proselytized. The people were their religion. Thus, individuals could not "preach" their religion to "others." As was noted above, religion was the observable phenomenon and, for the most part, the tribes seemingly were observably different. For instance, the Dogon conception of the universe is based, on the one hand, on the principle of vibrations of matter, and on the other hand, on a general movement of the universe as a whole (Forde, 1954, p. 84). For the Dogon, proliferation of life was directed by a perpetual alternation of opposites—right–left, high–low, odd–even, male–female—all reflecting the principle of twinness (no mention of right–wrong). Like all creatures, these twin beings, living images of the fundamental principle of twinness in creation, were each (i.e., both opposites) equipped with two spiritual principles of opposites. That is, each of them was himself a pair. This notion of man's unity with the universe is reflected in the Dogon belief that "man is the seed of the universe" (Forde, 1954). Hence, the organization of the earth's system is reproduced in every individual. The Fon of Dahomey believed that at the beginning of the present world there were the pair (twins) Mawu–Lisa— Mawu the female, Lisa the male. They were "regarded as twins and their union was the basis of the organization of the world" (Forde, 1954, p. 219). The Mende, also of West Africa, believed that each parent gave to their offspring some aspect of its (the child's) unified constitution. For instance, the Mende believed that the physical part of an individual (i.e., bones, flesh, etc.) is provided by the father through the semen he puts into the mother. The child's spirit (Ngafa) is contributed by its mother. The Ashanti believed that the human being is formed from the blood (Mogya) of the mother and the spirit (Ntoro) of the father (Forde, 1954, p. 196). Both peoples nevertheless believed that the spirit and the physical body and blood unite as one in making the new human being. In this sense each tribe had its own religious (life) system, and for one to have propagated his religion would have involved propagating the entire life of the people concerned. However, the substance of each tribal life system was not different.

Traditional Africans made no distinction between the act and the belief. "What people do is motivated by what they believe, and what they believe springs from what they do and experience" (Mbiti, 1970, p. 5). Action and belief in traditional West African society were not separated. They belonged to a single whole. Accordingly, traditional beliefs made no concrete distinction between the spiritual and the physical. Note that the Mende perceived physical and spiritual components as uniting to make the human.

Life after death is found in all African societies. However, belief in the continuation of life after death did not represent a hope for the future or possibly a better life when one dies. For the African, once dead, there was neither Heaven to be hoped for nor Hell to be feared. Again, this reflects the idea of vital force.

The whole of one's existence was an ontological religious phenomenon. The African was a deeply religious being living in a religious universe (Mbiti, 1970). For him to live was to be involved in, to be part of, a religious drama. As noted, traditional African religion was a religious ontology. As such, the ontology was characteristically very anthropocentric—everything was seen in terms of its relation to man.

Notion of Unity

The anthropocentric ontology was a complete unity which nothing could break up or destroy. Everything was functionally connected; to destroy one category completely would cause the destruction of the whole of existence, including the Creator. God was viewed as the originator and sustainer of man. The spirits explained man's destiny. Man was the center of the ontology. The animals, plants, and natural phenomena constituted the environment in which man lived. In addition to the five categories, *there existed a force, a power, or energy which permeated the whole universe*. In this kind of natural order (i.e., unity), God was the source and ultimate controller of the energy, but the spirits also had access to it. A few human beings—the Shaman (i.e., medicine men, priest, and rainmakers)—possessed the knowledge and ability to tap, manipulate, and use to a limited degree this energy. For the Dogon the social order was projected in the individual. An indivisible cell which, on the one hand, is a microcosm of the whole, and on the other hand has a circumscribed function. Not only was a person the product of his institutions, he also was their motive power. Lacking, however, any special power in himself, he was the representative of the whole. The individual affected the cosmic order which he also displayed (Forde, 1954). As stated earlier, a prevailing belief (Dogon) was that the organization (unity) of the earth's system was reproduced in every individual. This notion of the unity of things was so ingrained that the Mende, for instance, had developed a sense of collective responsibility. Also ingrained in the notion of unity is a particular conception of time.

Concept of Time

African philosophy concerned itself with two dimensions of time—the past and the present; and this conception of time helped to explain the general life system of traditional Africans (3). The direction of one's life system was from the present dimension backward to the past dimension. For the people, time itself was simply a composition of past events. Very little concern was given to time in and of itself. It existed, but the African time concept was (is) very elastic. It encompassed events that had already occurred, those that are taking place, and those that will occur immediately (Mbiti, 1970). What had no possibility of occurring immediately or had not taken place fell into the category of "no time" (Mbiti, 1970). Time was reckoned by phenomena. "Actual time" was what (events) was present or past and, because time essentially moved backward rather than forward, the traditional African set his mind not on future things but chiefly on what had taken place. Thus, the West African's understanding of all things—that is, the individual, the tribe (community), and the five characters of the universe—was governed or dominated by these two dimensions (past and present) of time. In order to make sense, or be real, to the West African, time had to be experienced; and the way in which one experienced time was partly through one's own individual life and partly through the life of the tribe which went back many generations before one's birth. Because time was reckoned by phenomena, "instead of numerical calendars, there were what one would call phenomenon calendars, in which the events or phenomena which constituted time were reckoned or considered in their relation with one another as they take place" (Mbiti, 1970). The Mandingo for instance had (have) a distinct "seasonal" calendar which reflected the changing of the seasons. Hence, the phenomenal changes of the environment constituted time. For most Africans, time was meaningful at the point of the event and not at the mathematical moment. Thus, in traditional life, any period of time was reckoned according to its significant events.

Recognizing the associations and connotations that the English words *past*, *present*, and *future* have, Brother Mbiti uses two Swahili words (Sasa and Zamani) to represent present and past. Sasa has the sense of immediacy, nearness, nowness (Mbiti, 1970). It is the period of immediate concern for the people because that is *where* or *when* they exist. For Africans, it is the period of personal recollections of events and phenomena. The Sasa period is not mathematically or numerically constant. Each member of the tribe has his own and, hence, the older the person, the longer his Sasa period. Each tribe (society, nation) also has its own Sasa period.

The Zamani period is not limited to what Europeans call the past. It overlaps or encompasses the Sasa and the two are not separable. The Sasa feeds or disappears into the Zamani. However, before events become incorporated into the Zamani, they have to be realized or actualized within the Sasa dimension. Thus, events (people) move backward from the Sasa dimension to the Zamani dimension. In a sense, Zamani is the graveyard of time (Mbiti, 1970). The Sasa dimension binds individuals and their immediate environment together. As such, it determines the experiential communality, encompassing the conscious limits of the tribe. The Zamani dimension, however, encompasses the Sasa dimension in a sort of spiritual medium and thus gives a common foundation to the universal reality and binds together all created things. All is embraced within the Zamani.

Everything has its center of gravity in the Zamani period, with nothing ever ending. West African peoples expect human history to continue forever, because it is part of the natural rhythm moving from Sasa to Zamani. The Mende apparently have a belief in rebirth or reincarnation. Children are sometimes named after a particular ancestor, especially when they bear resemblance to him. This behavior inevitably seems to suggest that the Mende, like other West African peoples, have a notion that the life cycle is renewable. Human life is part of the rhythm of nature, and just as the days, months, seasons, and years have no end, there is no end to the rhythm of birth, puberty, initiation, marriage, procreation, old age, death, entry into the community of the departed (the living dead), and entry into the company of the spirits. Life is an ontological rhythm, and abnormality or the unusual is what disrupts the ontological harmony.

Death and Immortality

In many African tribes, a person was not considered a full human being until he had gone through the whole rhythmic process of physical birth, naming ceremony, puberty, initiation rites (sometimes in the firm of ceremonial rebirth), and finally marriage and procreation. Then, and only then, was one fully "born"—a complete person. Similarly, death initiated the systematic rhythmic process through which the person gradually was removed from the Sasa to the Zamani period. Hence, death and immortality have especial significance in West African traditions. After physical death, as long as a person was remembered and recognized (by name) by relatives and friends who knew him (i.e., remembered his personality, character, and words and incidents of his life), he would continue to exist in the Sasa period. When, however, the last person who knew him also died, then the former passed out of the horizon of the Sasa period and, in effect, became completely dead. He no longer had any claims to family ties. He entered the Zamani period; that is, he became a member in the company of spirits.

The departed person who was remembered (recognized) by name was what Brother Mbiti calls the living-dead. He was considered to be in a state of personal immortality. The Mende believed that a person survives after death and that his surviving personality goes to the land of the dead (Forde, 1954). Those in personal immortality were treated symbolically like the living. The cycle of an individual ancestor, the Mende believed, lasted as long as the dead person was remembered in prayers and sacrifices (Forde, 1954). Hence, they were respected, given food and drink in the form of libations, and listened to and obeyed.

Being remembered (recognized) and respected while in personal immortality was important for the traditional African, a fact which helps one to understand the religious significance and importance of marriage and procreation in West African societies. Procreation was the surest way to insure that one would not be cut off from personal immortality. In a kind of multiplicative fashion, polygamy reinforced one's insurance.

Inevitably, as stated earlier, the point was reached when there was no longer anyone alive who would recognize and give respect to the (living-dead) person.

At this point, the process of dying was completed. However, he did not vanish out of existence. He now entered into the state of collective immortality. Now in the company of the spirits, he had at last entered the Zamani period. From this point on, the departed became nameless spirits who had no personal communication or ties with human families.

In terms of the ontology, entrance into the company of the spirits is man's final destiny. Paradoxically, death lies "in front" of the individual; it is a "future" event of sorts. But, when one dies, one enters the state of personal immortality and gradually "goes back" into the Zamani period. It should be emphasized that the African ontology was endless; such a view of man's destiny should not be construed to mean an or the end. Nothing ever ends.

Kinship: Collective Unity

Before concluding this brief and cursory review of African philosophy, a few words should be devoted to West African kinship, especially because kinship tied together the personal life system. Before they had carved up and colonized West Africa, Europeans could not say where one tribe ended and another tribe began. The number of people who made up what might be considered a tribe varied greatly. Depending upon the enumerator or ethnographer, many tribes were classified as unique and distinctly separate or simply as one.

Studies of African religious beliefs and practices demonstrate that among the so-called many distinct tribes there were more similarities (communalities) than differences (Mbiti, 1970). This author contends that all tribes shared basic beliefs—in the "survival of the tribe" and in the fact that the tribe was an integral and indispensable part of nature. Belief in tribal survival, was reflected in and sustained by a deep sense of kinship—probably one of the strongest cohesive devices in traditional life. Kinship controlled all relationships in the community (Mbiti, 1970). It included animals, plants, and nonliving objects. In effect, kinship bound together the entire life system of the tribe.

The kinship system stretched laterally (horizontally) in every direction as well as vertically. Hence, each member of the tribe was related not only to the tribal ancestors (both living-dead and spirits) but also to all those still unborn. In addition, each was a brother or sister, father or mother, grandmother or grandfather, cousin or brother-in-law, uncle or aunt, or some relation to everybody else. Africans still have many kinship terms which define the precise relationship binding any two people. Knowledge of one's tribal genealogy, vertical and horizontal, was extremely important. It imparted a sense of sacred obligation to extend the genealogical line. Through genealogies, persons (individuals) in the Sasa period were firmly linked to those who had entered the Zamani period.

To summarize: "In traditional life, the individual did not and could not exist alone" (Mbiti, 1970). The individual owed his very existence to other members of the "tribe." Not only those who conceived and nourished him but also those long dead and still unborn. The individual did not exist unless he was corporate or communal; he was simply an integral part of the collective unity. Africans believed that the community (tribe) made, created, or produced the individual; thus, the existence of the community was not imagined to be dependent on individual ingression.

Unlike Western philosophical systems, the African philosophical tradition does not place heavy emphasis on the "individual." Indeed one might say that in a sense it does not allow for individuals. It recognizes that "only in terms of other people does the individual become conscious of his own being" (Mbiti, 1970). Only through others does one learn his duties and responsibilities toward himself and others. Most initiation rites were designed to instill a sense of corporate responsibility and collective destiny. Thus, when one member of the tribe suffered, the entire tribe suffered; when one member of the tribe rejoiced, all of his kinsmen—living, dead, and still unborn—rejoiced with him. When one man got married, he was not alone, nor did his wife "belong" to him alone. The children from all unions belonged to the collective body.

Whatever happened to the individual happened to the corporate body, the tribe, and whatever happened to the tribe, happened to the individual. A concept the Ashanti share with all other Akan peoples is that "the dead, the living, and those still to be born of the 'tribe' are all members of one family." A cardinal point in understanding the traditional African's view of himself; his self-concept, is that he believes: "I am because we are; and because we are, therefore, I am" (Mbiti, 1970).

Experiential Communality

Cultural Configuration

Any basic cultural anthropology text will give one a general feeling about why and how man began to live in groups. However, what is not discussed in most texts is the interaction between man—in the group—and man's particular environment. The notion of particular environment is an important one for this presentation because it determines the common elements of the group's living experiences. For instance, primitive people living in the Sahara Desert respond differently to their environment than inhabitants of the frigid zones or polar regions (4). And those living in the tropic regions of the Congo would respond still another way to the elements in their environment. A more pointed example is provided by the differences between people living in postindustrial and preindustrial environments.

It can be said that the uniqueness of one's environment determines the parameters of one's experience.

Experiential communality is defined here as the sharing of a particular experience by a group of people. It helps to determine what the people will ultimately be like, and, congruently, what ethos, or set of guiding beliefs, a people will follow. These guiding beliefs, in turn, dictate the creation and adoption of the values and customs which in the final analysis determine what social behavior a people will express in *common*—their cultural configuration. Thus is experiential communality important in determining society's fundamental principles—its beliefs about the nature of man and what kind of society man should create for himself.

The peoples of Africa have traditionally lived in units or clusters commonly referred to as "tribes." For centuries West Africa has characteristically consisted of rolling stretches of tall grassy plains with intermittent bush country and scattered tropical rain forest (Bohannan, 1964). Within this region, the traditional peoples (tribes) were closely related to each other, yet distinct. Each tribe had its own distinct language which was related to the languages of all the other tribes in the region. African languages have been classified as of the Sudanic family (Werner, 1930) and the Niger-Congo stock (Bohannan, 1964). The closely related Bantu languages, the most well known of the Niger-Congo group, ranged from the west coast to most of central and southern Africa (Bohannan, 1964). Clearly, just as there was a common geographical flavor to the region, so, too, did its inhabitants develop and maintain common behaviors (5).

The physical nature of the experiential communality is important mainly in that the more unique or distinct it is, the higher the probability that the physical boundaries hinder the influx of neighboring cultural elements. Likewise, it also allows for the development and protective maintenance of indigenous cultural elements. Just as important, however, is the interaction of communal man with his unique environment. The quintessence of this phenomenon is that it results in a set of guiding beliefs which dictate the values and customs the people adopt. Ultimately, this set (or sets) of values determines man's social behavior.

As was noted earlier, close examination of the African ethos suggests two operational orders—survival of the tribe and oneness with nature. It was also suggested then that the ethos is probably the focal point of Black Psychology. The remainder of this paper will be devoted to offering evidence pointing to the continuing functioning of an African ethos.

African Reality and Psychological Assumptions

Black Psychology is more than general psychology's "darker" dimension. African (Black) Psychology is rooted in the nature of Black culture which is based on particular indigenous (originally indigenous to Africa) philosophical assumptions. To make Black Psychology the dreaded darker dimension of general psychology would amount to distorting African reality so that it will fit Western psychological theories and/or assumptions. For example, a study of the history of general psychology reveals that the controversial mind-body problem stems from the set of early Greek myths known as the Orphic Mysteries. One myth recounts how Dionysus was killed by the *evil* Titans and Zeus saved Dionysus's heart and killed the Titans. Zeus then created man from the "evil" Titan ashes and Dionysus's heart. Hence, man has a dual nature: He is both *evil* and *divine*. However, the assumptions arising from these early myths caused a problem. There had to be an evaluation of what was "good" and what was "bad." Assuming a dichotomy of the mind and the body, the early philosophers suggested that the body was the "bad" and the mind was the "good"—beliefs accepted unquestioningly during the early period of general psychology's emergence as a "science." Not surprisingly, psychology chose the mind (good) as the domain of its inquiry.

The African concept of man is fundamentally different. Dogon, Mende, and Ashanti all assume man's dual nature but do not attempt to *divide* "mind" from "body" or refer to or imply an inherent good or evil in either aspect of the duality. The propositions of "the notion of unity," "one with nature," and "survival of the people" deny possibility of such an artificial and arbitrary dichotomy. What is seemingly dualistic is the concept of "twinness." However, as stated earlier, the twin components unite to make the unified man. For Africans, who believed that man, like the universe, is a complicated, *integrated*, unified whole, concerns such as the mind-body controversy would never arise and theoretical developments and/or analysis based solely on the explication of the "mind" or the "body" as separate entities would be useless.

Although the mind–body issue is a single example, it is believed sufficient to demonstrate how philosophical assumptions determined the scientific investigation of psychology. Certainly particular people cannot be meaningfully investigated and understood if *their* philosophical assumptions are not taken into account.

Toward Black Psychology

This brings us closer to Black Psychology's evolution from African philosophy. The remaining question is how does one know or how can one "prove" that Africans living in the Western world, and in contemporary times, still have or maintain an African philosophical definition. Black Psychology's development is contingent first upon analysis of the linkages between distinct experiential periods in the lives of Africans, and second upon the demonstration of the particular ways in which African philosophy, interacting with alien (particularly Euro-American) philosophies, has determined contemporary African (black) peoples' perception of reality.

On the Question of Proof

History is an endeavor toward better understanding, and, consequently, a thing in movement. To limit oneself to "describing science as it is," will always be to betray it. . . . (Bloch, 1953)

For Black Psychology—and the many other social science areas which are attempting to "Blackenize" themselves in order to "explain" contemporary African peoples—the question of proof centers around more than determining whether a particular cultural element (e.g., an artifact) has been retained. The focus must be on the philosophical-psychological linkages between Africans and Afro-Americans (or Americanized Africans).

To determine whether—and to what extent—the African orientation has persisted, one must ask "How could it have been maintained?" "What mechanism or circumstances allowed it to be maintained?" An orientation stemming from a particular indigenous African philosophy could only be maintained when its cultural carriers were isolated (and/or insulated) from alien cultural interaction and if their behavioral expression of the orientation did not openly conflict with the cultural-behavioral elements of the "host" society. If the circumstances of the transplantation of New World Blacks met one or both of these conditions, then it is highly probable that the African orientation was retained. This writer maintains that a factor that often facilitated the retention of the African orientation was the particular region's physical features. And the slaves' accessibility to Western indoctrination was probably directly related to the degree of the retention of the African orientation. The rigidly enforced isolation of blacks allowed New World Africans to retain their definition (orientation). Thus, the oppressive system of slavery indirectly encouraged the retention, rather than the destruction, of the African philosophical orientation.

Throughout the New World, large numbers of Africans lived, segregated in given areas. Lorenzo Turner (1958) notes that "wherever Negroes were in the majority, African cultural elements had a better chance of surviving. . . ." In the United States, the policy of racial segregation must have often aided in keeping alive the African influence. It is proposed here that a comparative historical analysis of such areas as Brazil, Jamaica, Dutch Guiana, the rural South, and the northern ghetto would reveal a striking and direct correlation between (a) ecological and geographic factors and accessibility of interaction with Westerners and (b) maintenance of the African orientation. Not until the television "explosion" of early 1950s did the African orientation come fully into contact with Western (Euro-American) styles of behavior and the American way of life.

Expressive behavior and cultural modalities are determined by philosophical definition. One can observe "Africanism" throughout the New World because the orientation that allows a people to develop or continue to utilize particular cultural elements was not interfered with. Thus, the statement "We are an African people" is valid because, for the most part, New World conditions did not permit the enculturation of the African orientation.

Considerations for Black Psychology

The experiential communality of African peoples can be subdivided into periods. For Africans living in the Western world, particularly in North America, the breakdown used here is (a) the African experience (prior to 1600), (b) the slavery experience (1600 to 1865), and (c) contemporary Black America (1865 to present).

However, rather than treat a few specific behavioral transitions, the discussion will focus on several major philosophical positions and correlative behavioral modalities. The first is survival of the people. From this philosophical position an extended definition of self evolved. That is to say, the self was by philosophical definition the "we" instead of the "I." Tribal membership became the most important identity. One's identity was thus rooted in being an Ashanti, or an Ibo rather than the person, Lodagaa Nyakyusi, who just happened to be an Igbira. Thrust into an alien culture, the "we" notion seemingly came under severe attack. Many scholars note, for example, the prevalent practice during slavery (second distinct experiential communality period) of purposely separating members of the same tribe in order to break down the collective reinforcement of a common definition. However, additional information suggests that in North America the system of slavery was extremely unstructured in its beginning. Nevertheless, the system eventually came to define itself in terms of black people. During this same period, the notion of tribe or peoplehood which is crucial to the "we" notion underwent a particular modification. Clearly, Africans recognized and respected the distinctions of the tribe. The understanding that one was an Igbira or an Ibo suggested many things. However, the philosophical position within each tribe was the set of guiding beliefs which prescribed the survival of the tribe as a first order. As the system of American slavery began to define slavery in terms of Africans, tribe was more broadly defined in the minds of the Africans. Hence, one sees Africans no longer giving the Ibo or Igbira distinction its former level of importance but rather adopting broader categories. Thus, as slavery was moving closer and closer to its final definition, the slaves themselves were moving closer to African or black as the final definition of tribe. Thus, the notion of survival of the tribe was not changed or modified during the slavery experience. In fact, one could suggest that the slavery experience allowed the underlying communality of West Africa to surface and define itself as African. Hence, in slavery, the cardinal point, "I am because we are; and because we are, therefore, I am," was not destroyed.

In contemporary times, one can note the prevalence of benevolent societies and the role of the Negro church as expressing clear concern for the survival of the tribe.

The second philosophical position that has survived the effects of different experiential periods is the idea of man being an integral part of the "natural rhythm of nature," or, one with nature. Clearly, this can be seen within the African experience in terms of the anthropocentric ontology. The expression of this natural rhythm in the initiation rites gave definition to many of the periods within a person's Sasa dimension. This notion of rhythm also was expressed in the "talking drums."

In traditional African society, the living setting was the community and the emphasis was placed on living in the community not living in a particular household. Even in contemporary times, the "community" seems to manifest this same perception. One could propose that seeing oneself as an integral part of a community is the contemporary definition of man being an integral part of the natural rhythm of nature.

The oral tradition has clearly been transmitted throughout the three experi-

ential periods. As indicated earlier, beliefs and traditions were handed down
from father to son for generations upon generations. This tradition gave tremendous importance to the mind or the memory (6). Remembering phenomenal events in one's Sasa period was very important if not crucial. The slavery
tradition seemingly allowed this tradition to continue. That is, because oral
communication was the only acceptable system—laws prohibited slaves from
being taught to read and write—slavery unknowingly permitted the cultural
transmission of the African traditional emphasis of oration and its consequent
effects on the mind or memory to remain pretty much in tact. Brother Dr.
Joseph White (1970) suggests that playing the "dozens" as part of the oral
tradition is a game used by black youngsters to teach themselves to keep cool,
think fast under pressure, and not say what is really on their minds. Things like
rapping and the dozens could also be viewed as *initiation rites* or possibly
instances where the "power" of the word is used to make the "individual"
psychologically feel better. For example, the Avogan and the Lobi Singi
(Herskovits, 1966) are ritualized orations and dance ceremonies where the of-
fended is afforded release of suppressed emotions by ridiculing another. The
Dogon have a very interesting circumstance in which certain relations are
characterized by exchanges of often obscene insults and gestures (Forde, 1954).
Is this the dozens in African form, or better yet are the dozens an African
tribalism that has been maintained throughout the different experiential communalities? Another aspect of the oral tradition is the naming ritual. In traditional times, a child was named after an ancestor to symbolize his (the ancestor's) return (Forde, 1954). Often the name typifies a special event in the
child's life. Hence, because a person acquired names as he associated with different special experiences, one person may have many names. One need only
examine the names of black people to reveal historical tenacity in this orientation—for example, Bojangles, Brown Bomber, Stepin Fetchit, Wilt-the-Stilt,
Muddy Waters, Iceberg Slim.

   With certain modifications, tribalisms have been transmitted in the form of
Africanisms throughout the New World experiential periods. Cooperative effort
(tribalism) was expressed in the slavery experience. The "Knights of Wise"
symbolized that notion and the notion of the survival of the tribe. Funerals in
contemporary black America are very symbolic of the custom of reaffirming the
bonds of kinship. Distinct motor habits also have been maintained up to the
present. Photographic analysis of a particular dance in the Ashanti Kwaside rite
illustrates a perfect example of the Charleston. Morality was taught in traditional
times via the use of animal tales. Parables were widely prevalent during slavery—
the most notable being the "Brer Fox, Brer Rabbit Tales." In contemporary
times, one simply notes the use of animal names to denote certain qualities. In
the black communities (villages) throughout this country, women and men are
referred to as "foxes," "cows," "bears," "buzzards," "dogs," and so forth. The
style of talking (dramatic pauses, intonation, and the like), are all reminiscent of
a people in tune with the natural rhythm of nature—in tune with the oneness of
nature.

   The concept of time clearly is illustrative. The attitude that time is phenomenal rather than mathematical can be demonstrated to persist throughout the suggested experiential periods. The notion of CPT (colored peoples' time) has been translated to mean thirty minutes to an hour later than the scheduled meeting time. However, in the minds of Africans (blacks), time is flexible and the event begins when one gets there. This author thus suggests that a more appropriate enunciation of CPT is "communal potential time."

Black Psychology must concern itself with the question of "rhythm." It must discuss, at some great length, "the oral tradition." It must unfold the mysteries of the spiritual energy now known as "soul." It must explain the notion of "extended self" and the "natural" orientation of African peoples to insure the "survival of the tribe." Briefly, it must examine the elements and dimensions of the experiential communalities of African peoples.

It is my contention, therefore, that Black Psychology must concern itself with the mechanism by which our African definition has been maintained and what value its maintenance has offered black people. Hence, the task of Black Psychology is to offer an understanding of the behavioral definition of African philosophy and to document what, if any, modifications it has undergone during particular experiential periods.

Notes

1. Like most words that refer to things African, the English usage of the word "tribe" has semibad connotations. In addition, one must recognize that the defining characteristic for a tribe was completely alien and arbitrary. As British and American anthropologists changed their definitions of what constituted a tribe, so changed the physical size of a tribe's membership.

   Although Africa can be considered a cultural entity, most black Americans came from West Africa. While there is diversity, the author assumes that there are unifying cultural themes. For a rather different point, however, see R. A. Lavine, Personality and change in J. N. Padden and E. W. Soja, *The African experience*, vol. 1 (Evanston, Ill.: Northwestern University Press, 1970).

   For present purposes, West Africa is seen as extending from Senegal to Angola.

2. Note that given African philosophy is for the most part unwritten and has no conceptual terms as we know them. The understanding of African philosophy is accomplished by analyzing the traditional structures reflected in tales, proverbs, myths, and such. It is these which in turn reflect the structural concepts of the philosophy.

3. Africa is a very large continent and there are some differences in the concept of time in different areas. For example, hunters have a different conception of time than those in farming communities. In the present paper, the author is making certain simplifying assumptions for purposes of exposition.

4. Primitive is used here in the original sense (without negative connotations)–that is, primary, first, early.

5. In this case, behavioral tools–that is, languages.

6. Not in the mind–body dichotomy tradition.

Bibliography

Abraham, W. E. *The mind of Africa*. Chicago: University of Chicago Press, 1962.

Bloch, M. *Historians craft*. Trans. Peter Putnam. New York: Knopf, 1953.

Bohannan, P. *Africa and Africans*. New York: American Museum of Science Books, 1964.

Forde, D. *African worlds*. London: Oxford University Press, 1964.

Gamble, D. P. *The Wolof of Senegambia*. New York: International Publications Service, 1957.

Herskovits, M. J. *The myth of the Negro past*. Boston: Beacon Press, 1958.

Jahn, J. *Muntu*. New York: Grove Press, 1961.

Kenyatta, J. *Facing Mt. Kenya*. London: Vintage Books, 1938.

Mbiti, J. S. *African religions and philosophies*. Garden City, N.Y.: Anchor Books, Doubleday, 1970.

McCall, D. F. *Africa in time-perspective*. New York: Oxford University Press, 1969.

Murdock, G. P. *Africa: Its peoples and their cultural history*. New York: McGraw-Hill, 1959.

Oliver, R., and Fage, J. D. *A short history of Africa*. Baltimore: Penguin, 1962.

Parrinder, G. *Religion in Africa*. Baltimore: Penguin, 1969.

Radcliff-Brown, A., and Forde, D. (Eds.) *African systems of kinship and marriage*. New York: Oxford University Press, 1967.

Taylor, J. V. *The primal vision*. Philadelphia: Fortress Press, 1963.

Temples, P. *Bantu philosophy*. Paris: Presence Africaine, 1959.

Turner, L. African survivals in the New World with special emphasis on the arts. In *Africa seen by American Negroes*. Paris: Presence Africaine, 1958.

Werner, A. *Structure and relationship of African languages*. London: Kegan Paul, 1925.

White, J. Guidelines for black psychologists. *The Black Scholar*, 1970, 1(5), 52–57.

White, J. Toward a black psychology. *Ebony*, August 1970, 25, 44–45, 48–50, 52(a).

DORIS P. MOSBY

Toward a New Specialty of Black Psychology

A danger is inherent in the very labeling of the black as different in behavior or in personality. For many persons, the term *different* may imply qualitative inferiority or the proposal that one is to be judged by different or less rigid standards. Even a large faction of blacks might resist such a label because many recent black movements are dedicated to demonstrating the proposition that: "A black is the same, no more or no less so, and equal to other people in all respects." But it is possible to infer and to document that qualitatively different experiences within the black's life make mandatory, qualitatively different adjustments in his life pattern and in the actualization of his needs. Therefore, it can be reasoned that if the mature personalities of the white and black child are to be roughly comparable, then the early life experiences have to be approximately alike in quantity and quality.

Another premise is that, granted that the quantitative experiences of blacks and whites differ (Lott and Lott, 1963), "there comes a point at which quantitative development *releases* qualitative change. . ." (Cox, 1965, p. 5). Therefore, it follows that, given the pervasive nature of quantitative pressures (mostly adversive) placed upon blacks in all areas of human functioning, qualitative differences in personality and general functioning are likely.

Given also that differences between whites and blacks may be qualitative, psychology in its research and application may have to accommodate to the fact that there are qualitative differences in people. Therefore, it is predicted that psychology will have to evolve a separate specialty area, broadly labeled "Black Psychology" (to assimilate the distinction in child, adolescent, and adult psychology). Black Psychology will have to reexamine personality development, family functioning, social relations, interracial relationships, intellectual achievement and functioning, education, and general developmental areas (i.e., physical, motor, genetic, etc.).

What are some of the current rumblings about and from this direction in psychology? Already, a moratorium on intelligence testing of blacks has been advocated until such tests can be shown to be *as* relevant to the black as to the white background. The issue of the adequacy and the level of black intelligence in relation to whites is debated (Jensen, 1969). Some researchers have shown that blacks may have a unique configuration of personality traits when factors of age, sex, socioeconomic class, and urban-rural backgrounds are controlled

Paper presented at a University-Wide Lecture, Prairie View A & M College, Prairie View, Texas, February 20, 1970. Sponsored by the American Psychological Association Visiting Scientist Program. Reprinted by permission of the author.

(Karon, 1958; Kardiner and Ovesey, 1953). Other researchers contend that differences in black personality reflect an interaction with the cultural restrictions of the geographic regions in which they live (Gynther, 1963; Mosby, 1965). Studies show that in general blacks scored at the "psychoses level" on objective personality tests in contrast to whites who score at the "neuroses" or normal level. And rather than concluding that blacks are severely emotionally disturbed, these researchers suggest that "separate norms should be devised for those tests for blacks" (McDonald and Gynther, 1962, 1963). Furthermore, differences found between black males and females on a host of variables are such that researchers contend that more than a separate study of blacks is needed. They advocate that black males should be considered in contrast to black females (McDonald and Gynther, 1963; Mosby, 1965).

Black behavior is being reevaluated by sociologists, especially the assumption that the matriarchal pattern in lower-class black families represents merely a "disorganized and disintegrating social pattern" (Ladner, 1969; Schulz, 1969). Rather, family structure within this group is seen to be a constructive adaptation to the reality of life conditions. Also, the life style of the ghetto resident, in general, is being reevaluated as a "culture of poverty," with the resident's behavior representing an attempt to deal with an exploitative society by being exploitative himself (Schulz, 1969).

Further, the entire educational experience as it impinges upon, relates to, and has practical meaning for blacks and their future life is being reevaluated. Circumvention to checkmate cultural and emotional "disadvantages" in preschool human development, a central consideration in child psychology and education, is one of the goals of the Head Start and Parent–Child Center programs of the Office of Economic Opportunity.

The vision of a new specialty of Black Psychology within the broad field of scientific psychological inquiry is of special importance to this writer. My dissertation study dealt with the consequences of the identification process for black adolescents. Interest in this area was fostered when, as a student, I noticed that the bulk of psychological inquiry generalized from the white middle-class situation. It was known all too painfully that this "average" situation was a rarity for blacks, the writer included. And I "felt" that there were peculiar differences in blacks. Besides, blacks talking among themselves verbalized that their experiences were "different." Therefore, it was logically reasoned that 20 million blacks cannot all be wrong.

In a three-year study 140 mother-child pairs and 1100 adolescents were used to investigate a variety of psychological variables manifested in blacks. The research data reported below summarize this study. These findings are offered to support the following thesis: A distinct specialty of scientific inquiry will evolve on the new frontiers of psychological research and application in the 1970s—one that is respectable, well-grounded in objectivity, with a blending of the subjective impressions which add a flavor of truth to living. Hopefully, this new field will be forged by black psychologists themselves. This discipline should be properly labeled Black Psychology, not The Psychology of Minority Groups, because blacks are distinctly different from both whites and other minority groups. Although other minority groups (e.g., Jews and Catholics) have been subjected to cultural restrictions, it is only for blacks that the restrictions have been all pervasive, with no alternatives of escape. For other minority groups, avenues to ascend and to assimilate within the "melting pot" tradition of America have been open.

The Effect of Cultural Devaluation on the Personality of Blacks

The search for identity, the evolution of a comfortable self-image, is a continuous process through which the individual passes from birth to maturity. Few experiences after maturity significantly alter the evolved self-image. However, during the developmental stages significant people, daily experiences, ordinary perceptions of reality, and inferred attitudes of others contribute to the final opinion one has of himself, his reputation, and his character. It defines for the individual his repertoire of assets and limitations, which in turn determines the type, amount, and quality of his overt actions. Crises, traumas, and adverse experiences can negatively affect development of self-identity whereas positive experiences, success, and achievement can steer development in a positive direction.

The effect of cultural opinions, particularly the cultural devaluation held of blacks, acts on black adolescents to produce a discontinuity in the identification process. The conflicting attitudes, values, and mores which impinge upon the black youngster in search of a comfortable realistic identity mandate a crisis of identity, self-esteem, and individual worth. Such varying opinions held within the adolescent's culture, school, family, and peer groups engender feelings of inadequacy, a negative self-image, and general ambivalence. Such conflicts maintain in the adolescent a demeanor of apology, reserve, and passivity.

Sources of identity trauma for the black American are several. The first is a conflict between the home and the national stereotypes. Tragically, the traditional and national image of "the Negro," that his black color is offensive, bad, and inferior, may be repeated in the home situation. Within the black family itself, acceptance may be calibrated on a scale of color. Often the light-skinned child commands more positive rewards, material goods, verbal encouragement than his darker-skinned siblings. Thus the attitude "to be light is something good and admirable in its own right" is often reinforced in the home. Until recently, the home tended to side with the national stereotype and as a result engendered severe emotional conflicts in darker family members. At present, however, a new movement reinforces the pride of blackness as a state of mind if not as a fact of color. Ancient heritage and physical traits are judged by new and different standards of merit. In some homes, staunchly civil-rights oriented, a new system of "spoils" is instituted, with the black child now enjoying more or as favorable privileges. In this turnabout situation, "black is better and white is now of questionable good." Forces within the black community challenge acceptance of what the national image, the majority stereotype, and the cultural-devaluation forces of white America offer blacks. As the basic orienting foundation for the black child, the home is beginning to challenge, confront, and condemn the previous negative cultural image of the black group. The home refutes the image of only negative traits, low intellectual interest or ability, self-effacement, impulsiveness, primitiveness, and inferiority. The home offers a new alternative grounded in fact.

The black movement, which originated in the community, seeks to preserve the basic identity of black America, to retain the basic cultural identity, to build decent black institutions in black communities. It seeks to foster the acceptance of a different image—to erase the previous negative image ascribed to the Negro. The black American seeks to be a person in his own right, not a flimsy caricature of the white middle-class model. He seeks to pronounce "I'm none of the things you say I am, I am me, socially free, individually autonomous. I cannot be like you and still be me. My folkways, mores, customs, speech, and dress are deeply ingrained too. To denounce them, to transform myself is to commit psychological suicide." Black consciousness, advocated so strongly by the subcultural environment of the black adolescent, conflicts with the cultural devaluation which historically the adolescent has met from the majority members. The black subculture feels black consciousness is the individual's right to keep; it is devoid of shame, unmarred by others' opinions. The youth hears "I may be black but I am somebody," throughout the black community; the cultural image says "Equality and self respect have to be earned, and will be given when you measure up." These conflicting views necessarily produce apprehension in the black adolescent.

In the school also the youth encounters conflict. The values taught as important to and necessary for the best operation of a middle-class community (e.g., thrift, control of sexual and aggressive impulses, duty over individual rights, honesty) are less important, less valued in the lower-class community of the black group. And in fact, principles and practices opposite to these may be the rule rather than the rarity. This conflict is so basic and intense that the lower-class child who accepts the values of the educational system becomes indoctrinated in middle-class thought and risks unpopularity with his peers, exclusion by his family, and rejection by his ghetto culture. He becomes an alien in familiar quarters, a misfit in his own group. Such potent subcultural processes are adverse enough to deter many a ghetto youngster from cultivating his native, creative, innovative, and intellectual abilities within the educational setting. He sees practicality in what is rewarded today rather than promised for tomorrow. The values, behavior, and rewards of the school are promised for a future he can view only with apprehension, a future of uncertain probability and content. His home experiences do not reinforce learning for the job of self-improvement as practical, relevant, or even beneficial for survival. Instead, he sees practicality and benefit in what he can see, hold, touch, wear, and eat. School, and the concepts it teaches, fails to satisfy these prerequisites.

The region of the country in which one lives also predisposes the black American to discontinuity in the identification process because the content and severity of the cultural devaluation may vary. As mentioned previously, Karon (1958) in his study of southern and northern blacks and whites, attributed his findings of greater emotional difficulties in southern blacks to their place of residence and the intensity of the caste sanctions. The all-powerful, pervasive restrictions of the southern caste system predispose blacks to problems which persist even after northern migration. Karon concluded, as did Kardiner and Ovesey (1949), that the emotional difficulties of northern blacks do not differ significantly from those of northern whites. Therefore, the black child in the South is bombarded by mostly negative images of himself. This fact increases his difficulty of discovering experiences or persons who present or reinforce a positive self-image or feelings of esteem. But the black who resides in a "borderline" state may find conflicts between policy and practice. He may experience covert rejection, degradation despite an overt policy of equalitarianism. This external confusion may create internal ambivalence and be reflected in ineffectual behavior.

And last, cultural evaluation may severely frustrate the individual in his drive toward self-actualization and productivity. At present, the aspiration level of the black is at an all time high. He wants many of the good things in life and the chance to live the good life. However, as his hopes have become more crystalized and have increased, he is faced with unyielding, unopening opportunities. Frustration results. His tolerance for tension has lessened. Patience has petered out, and the black refutes the patience of Job as a standard for his conduct. Impatience and restlessness set in and frequently explosiveness erupts.

Effect of Region on the Personality of Black Adolescents

Confused, the black person too often lacks a definite conceptualization of his worth or his rightful place in America. This confusion varies in intensity and effect upon the black personality, depending upon the region of America in which the black lives.

McDonald and Gynther (1962, 1963) compared the performance of southern black and white adolescents on the Minnesota Multiphasic Personality Inventory (MMPI). They reported that (a) black youth, female and male, show more deviance from normality on *both* personality and test-taking attitude measures than their white contemporaries and (b) black males show even more deviancy than black females on measures that differentiated blacks from whites. To date, this is the only published study of adolescent black–white differences on the MMPI, a widely used psychological test.

It was felt that McDonald and Gynther's work deserved replication and expansion on a northern black sample, including mothers of black adolescents. There are several significant questions. How stable are the reported personality differences between black and white adolescents? Do southern black adolescents differ from northern black adolescents? Among blacks do adolescent males and females differ in the adequacy of their personality functioning? What cumulative effect does the sex of the adolescent and the region in which he lives have on his test performance? Do mothers of northern black adolescents show characteristic MMPI patterns? Data bearing on these questions are discussed below.

Northern Black Adolescents and Their Mothers

The data summarized in Table 1 show that the sample of northern black male and female adolescents, in grades 9 through 12, achieved more deviant scores on MMPI personality scales than the normative group. Comparisons were based on norms given in the MMPI manual. Unfortunately, blacks were not included in the standardization population, which, of course, limits the applicability of the norms and any inferences about black-white differences drawn from them. This point will be reiterated throughout the remainder of the paper.

In the following discussion the data are treated as if the differences were real. In reality, given sex and racial differences, nothing could be further from the truth. However, the point of this section is to demonstrate the kinds of conclusions about pathology that would be reached if we relied upon normative data that did not include blacks as part of the standardization group.

Using the normative standards, scores that border on extreme deviancy in personality and incapacitation were noted more among the northern students than among their mothers. The mothers showed abnormal concern about bodily functions and were fearful of bodily ills (i.e., unduly worried about their health). Other personality measures were within normal limits. However, as a group the mothers were particularly prone to lie and to be defensive about admitting weaknesses or inadequacies in themselves.

The adolescents revealed more personality departure from "normality." All males (except for the tenth-grade group) were significantly deviant on (a) suspiciousness of others and their motives, and oversensitivity to personal slur and harm; (b) abnormal preoccupation with the body's functions and ills; and (c) preoccupation with unusual thoughts or the dominance of odd behaviors. The female group was normal on general personality functioning except that the ninth-grade female adolescents showed a predominance of conversion-type hysterical symptoms. This heightened interest may be expected when one considers age-appropriate inner struggles, bodily changes, new social pressures, and expectations. Of course, in the lower-class female group sampled, illegitimate pregnancy is also a constant plague.

As a group, the adolescents were more prone to depression than their mothers. Males were the most significantly depressed. Males particularly showed psychotic traits, deep inadequacy feelings, and self-dissatisfaction. The northern black adolescents generally viewed the father as inadequate, and identification with him, especially for males, was ambivalent (Mosby, 1965). Earlier, Sopchak (1952) had found a failure to identify with father to be associated with a "stronger psychotic triad" (cluster of extremely deviant attitudes and behaviors). This association was confirmed for the northern male adolescents.

TABLE 1 *White–Black, Male–Female, and Northern Black–Southern Black Comparisons Using White MMPI Normative Data*

Evaluation of personality pathology and test-taking attitudes	Southern sample				Northern sample			
	White males	White females	Black males	Black females	Black males	Black females	Mother of males	Mother of females
Normal	Most areas	Most areas	—	—	Most areas (grades 10)	—	All other areas	All other areas
Neurotic (anxious, depressed, compulsive)	—	—	Abnormal concern about body functions; Depression Fears and compulsive behavior	Withdrawal from social contacts	Abnormal concern about body functions (grades 9, 11, 12)	Conversion type hysterical symptoms (grade 9) Depression	Abnormal concern about body functions and health	Abnormal concern about body functions and health
Psychotic (bizarre ideas and/or behaviors)	—	—	—	—	Depression Suspiciousness, over-sensitivity (grades 9, 11, 12) Unusual thoughts and behaviors (grades 9, 11, 12)	—	—	—
Tendency to lie (L)	Normal	Normal	High	High	Highest	Higher	High	High
Invalid responses (F)	Normal	Normal	—	High	Highest	Higher	—	—
Defensiveness against psychological weakness (K)	Normal	Normal	High	—	Highest	Higher	High	High

Test-taking attitudes for the adolescents indicated high tendencies toward falsification, defensiveness, and invalidity. Males were particularly high on all these traits; females (like the mothers' group) were high on such traits but not as deviant as the males.

Black Versus White Adolescents

Results on the sample of Northern adolescents, like other MMPI studies, show greater personality deviance among black high-school students than among their white contemporaries when MMPI normative standards are utilized. McDonald and Gynther (1963) note that such consistently obtained deviant patterns may lead the psychologist to a "marked tendency to 'see' deviancy or pathology where such deviancy or pathology in terms of the proper reference group is not necessarily present" (p. 116). The same authors (1962) have proposed that separate norms be developed for black and white adolescents to assure a proper reference base. MMPI differences between races seem linked to "a different pattern of interests, values, and expectations," and the authors predicted that "the greater the integration between races, the smaller the differences of MMPI scales" (McDonald and Gynther, 1963, p. 116).

But at present, the races are differentiated in the areas of undue concern about one's health, depression, fears and compulsive behaviors, and the tendency to withdraw from social contacts. Blacks were generally neurotic and anxious. White adolescents were normal in most areas; they were not especially anxious, depressed or fearful. Nor were they defensive about their weaknesses or especially prone to place themselves in a good light. The black adolescents tended to lie, be defensive, and make conscious attempts to appear adequate, consistently more so than did whites.

Southern Black Adolescents

Differences between southern black male and female adolescents were noted by McDonald and Gynther (1962, 1963). Males obtained neurotic scores on (a) preoccupation, anxiety, and fears regarding body functions and ills; (b) depressions; and (c) fears and compulsive behaviors. Females were neurotic only on the tendency to withdraw from social participation and contacts. Hence, males showed the most neurotic behaviors and attitudes.

Some sex differences were noted in the attitude that defines taking a personality test. Southern black female adolescents tended to lie, be irrational, and not be serious to a greater extent than did their white contemporaries. Using current MMPI norms, compared to a white group, black males tended to lie more and to be more defensive about their personal weaknesses. Once more, males tended to show more of the general defensiveness and conscious attempts to give socially desirable answers than did black females.

Northern Versus Southern Black Male Adolescents

Northern black males were *similar* to males in the southern sample in that they were consistently more deviant from normality than were females (and the entire white adolescent sample) in all personality and test-taking attitude measures. They were particularly more deviant than females (and the white sample) on the showing of excessive concern and fear about health. Unlike southern males, northern males showed a dominant pattern of psychotic reactions rather than neurotic traits. Northern males achieved objectively deviant patterns, on all *personality and validity measures*, which were considerably higher than noted in southern males. Northern males were extremely anxious, fearful, depressed, suspicious, overly sensitive, rigid, and they had more unusual thoughts and/or odd behaviors. Yet, in taking the test they lied, were playful, were irrational, or guarded against exposing their personal weaknesses.

In summary, the data imply that there is either more personality disturbance in the northern black sample *or* that there are different base levels for "normal personality" which are characteristic of different locales. Hence, cultural influences may operate on a regional level and may be selectively different for the southern black versus the northern black.

The differences lead to the observation that conceptualizations of the black personality should be based separately on black males and black females. Also, separate norms, within sex divisions, for different locales and cultural situations (northern vs. southern) should exist. If we are to avoid generalizations that would place all blacks in neurotic and psychotic categories, individual personality assessment and measures for the adequacy of that assessment should be based on norms from groups comparable in sex, race, and culture.

To conclude, scientific psychological inquiry in the future will have to accept and to deal with the fact that "although all men are created equal," in dispositions and in behavior they are vastly different and that such differences may follow racial lines. Racially-different people are therefore a respectable target for separate scientific study.

References

Clark, K. B., and Clark, M. K. The development of consciousness of self and the emergence of racial identification in Negro pre-school children. *Journal of Social Psychology*, 1939, 10, 591–599.

Clark, K. B., and Clark, M. K. Emotional factors in racial identification and preferences in Negro children. *Journal of Negro Education*, 1950, 19, 341–350.

Cox, H. *The secular city.* New York: Macmillan, 1965, p. 5.

Criswell, J. H. A sociometric study of race cleavage in the classroom. *Archives of Psychology*, 1939, No. 235.

Crowne, D., and Stevens, M. Self-acceptance and self-evaluative behavior: A critique of methodology. *Psychological Bulletin*, 1961, 58, 104–121.

Graham, T. Doll play phantasies in Negro and white primitive school children. *Journal of Clinical Psychology*, 1955, **11**, 29–33.

Greenwald, H., and Oppenheim, D. Reported magnitude of self-misidentification among Negro children—Artifact? *Journal of Personality and Social Psychology*, 1968, 8(1), 49–52.

Jensen, A. How much can we boost IQ and scholastic achievement? *Harvard Educational Review*, Winter 1969, 39(1), 1–123.

Kardiner, A., and Ovesey, L. On the psychodynamics of the Negro personality, in C. Gordon and K. Gergen (Eds.), *The self in social interaction*. New York: John Wiley, 1968, pp. 259–267.

Karon, B. *The Negro personality*. New York: Springer-Verlag, 1958.

Kellogg, W., and Eagleson, B. The growth of social perception in different racial groups. *Journal of Educational Psychology*, 1931, **22**, 367–375.

Ladner, J. The Negro family revisited. Paper presented to the Association for the Study of Negro Life and History, Birmingham, October 1969.

Lott, A. J., and Lott, B. E. *Negro and white youth*. New York: Holt, Rinehart & Winston, 1963.

McDonald, R., and Gynther, M. MMPI norms for southern adolescent Negroes. *Journal of Social Psychology*, 1962, **58**, 277–282.

McDonald, R., and Gynther, M. MMPI differences associated with sex, race, and class in two adolescent samples. *Journal of Consulting Psychology*, 1963, **27**, 112–116.

Mosby, D. P. Maternal "identification" and perceived similarity to parents in adolescents as a function of grade placement. Unpublished doctoral dissertation, Washington University (St. Louis), copyright 1965.

Mowrer, O. Learning theory and identification: I. Introduction. *Journal of Genetic Psychology*, 1954, **84**, 197–201.

Parsons, T. Age and sex in the social structure of the United States. *American Sociological Review*, 1942, **7**, 604–616.

Schultz, D. *Coming up black*. Englewood Cliffs, N.J.: Prentice-Hall, 1969.

Seward, G. Learning theory and identification: V. Some cultural aspects of identification. *Journal of Genetic Psychology*, 1954, **84**, 229–234.

Sopchak, A. Parental "identification" and "tendency toward disorders" as measured by the MMPI. *Journal of Abnormal Social Psychology*, 1952, **47**, 159–165.

Trent, R. The correlates of self-acceptance among Negro children. Unpublished Ed.D. dissertation, Teachers College, Columbia University, 1953.

JOSEPH WHITE

Toward a Black Psychology

Regardless of what black people ultimately decide about the questions of separation, integration, segregation, revolution, or reform, it is vitally important that we develop, out of the authentic experience of black people in this country, an accurate workable theory of black psychology. It is very difficult, if not impossible, to understand the life styles of black people using traditional theories developed by white psychologists to explain white people. Moreover, when these traditional theories are applied to the lives of black folks many incorrect, weakness-dominated, and inferiority-oriented conclusions come about.

In all fairness it should be said that only a few white psychologists publicly accept the idea most recently advanced by Dr. Jensen (see Carl Rowan's review of Jensen's work in the May [1970] issue of EBONY Magazine) that black people, according to his research findings, are at birth genetically inferior to whites in intellectual potential. Most psychologists and social scientists take the more liberal point of view which in essence states that black people are culturally deprived and psychologically maladjusted because the environment in which they were reared as children and in which they continue to rear their own children lacks the necessary early experiences to prepare them for excellence in school, appropriate sex role behavior, and, generally speaking, achievement within an Anglo middle-class frame of reference. In short, we are culturally and psychologically deprived because our experiential background provides us with inferior preparation to move effectively within the dominant white culture.

A simple journey with the white researcher into the black home may provide us with some insight into how such important, but somewhat erroneous, conclusions are reached. During this visit to the black home the researcher may not find familiar aspects of the white culture such as Book-of-the-Month selections, records of Broadway plays, classics, magazines such as *Harpers*, the *Atlantic Monthly*, or the *New York Review of Books*. He also might observe a high noise level, continuously reinforced by inputs from blues-and-rhythm radio stations, TV programs, and several sets of conversations going on at once. This type of observation leads him to assume that the homes of black children are very weak in intellectual content, uninteresting, and generally confusing places to grow up. Somehow he fails to see the intellectual stimulation that might be provided by local black newspapers, informative rapping, *Jet*, *Ebony*, *Sepia*, and the Motown sound. Black children in these same homes who supposedly can't read (even

From *Ebony*, September 1970, 25(11), 44–45, 48–50, 52. Reprinted by permission of the author and the publisher.

preschoolers) can sing several rock and blues tunes from memory and correctly identify the songs of popular entertainers. These same researchers or educational psychologists listening to black speech assume that our use of nonstandard oral English is an example of bad grammar without recognizing the possibility that we have a valid, legitimate, alternate dialect.

As the white educational psychologist continues with what for him has become a standard analysis, the next step becomes one of setting up programs which provide black children with the kind of enrichment he feels is needed to overcome and compensate for their cultural deprivation. As a consequence of this type of thinking, in recent years from Head Start and New Horizons to Upward Bound, we have repeatedly witnessed the failure of compensatory and enrichment educational programs. Possibly, if social scientists, psychologists, and educators would stop trying to compensate for the so-called weaknesses of the black child and try to develop a theory that capitalizes on his strengths, programs could be designed which from the get-go might be more productive and successful.

Many of these same so-called culturally deprived youngsters have developed the kind of mental toughness and survival skills, in terms of coping with life, which make them in many ways superior to their white age-mates who are growing up in the material affluence of Little League suburbias. These black youngsters know how to deal effectively with bill collectors, building superintendents, corner grocery stores, hypes, pimps, whores, sickness, and death. They know how to jive school counselors, principals, teachers, welfare workers, juvenile authorities, and, in doing so, display a lot of psychological cleverness and originality. They recognize very early that they exist in an environment which is sometimes both complicated and hostile. They may not be able to verbalize it, but they have already mastered what existential psychologists state to be the basic human condition; namely that in this life, pain and struggle are unavoidable and that a complete sense of one's identity can only be achieved by both recognizing and directly confronting an unkind and alien existence.

The black family represents another arena in which the use of traditional white psychological models leads us to an essentially inappropriate and unsound analysis. When the black family is viewed from a middle-class frame of reference, which assumes that the psychologically healthy family contains two parents, one male and one female, who remain with the child until he or she becomes a young adult, the fact that the same black male is not consistently visible to the white observer of the black family leads to a conclusion that the black family unit has a matriarchal structure. Once the idea of the matriarchal family is accepted, it is very tempting to use Freudian psychological theories to explain why black children, especially black males, who are reared in this type of one-parent family with an absent father develop psychosexual and identity hang-ups. Even more damaging, the male and female offspring of the matriarchal family carry their hang-ups into the next generation, only to have the matriarchal cycle repeat itself. Indeed, one white social scientist in making the black family a case for national action took the view that the major problem confronting black people had to do with reorganizing our family into a two-parent unit.

A closer look at the black family might show that the matriarchal or one-parent view fails to take into consideration the extended nature of the black family. Looking at the number of uncles, aunties, big mamas, boyfriends, older brothers and sisters, deacons, preachers, and others who operate in and out of the black home, a more valid observation might be that a variety of adults and older children participate in the rearing of any one black child. Furthermore, in the process of childrearing, these several adults plus older brothers and sisters make up a kind of extended family who interchange roles, jobs, and family functions in such a way that the child does not learn an extremely rigid distinction of male and female roles. A case comes to mind of a young white social worker, who, after observing a teen-age black male going about the business of cooking, cleaning house, washing clothes, and obviously helping his mother care for the younger children in his family, wrote in her report that his masculine development might be harmed by such obviously feminine activities. What the social worker failed to see was that this particular black male teen-ager did not rigidly separate these male and female roles in his own mind, and more importantly he also helped out his mother with a part-time job, was a member of the track team at a local high school, an able student, had a very healthy sex life with some of the younger women in the neighborhood, and was respected by the street brothers of the gang culture when it came down to his abilities to "throw hands" when such activities were necessary.

If the extended family model proves to be more accurate than the matriarchal conception describing the black family, this means that we can turn our attention away from continuous description of the unhealthy psychosexual and social role conflicts in black children and young adults and move toward ways of strengthening the extended family, as opposed to some basic reorganization of the black family. Furthermore, if the concept of the extended family is accurate, our teen-agers and young adults may have potentially fewer identity conflicts than those who come from families who expose them to extremely rigid distinctions between male and female roles and duties. Maybe people who want to make the black a case for national action should stop talking about making the black family into a white family and instead devote their energies into removing the obvious oppression of the black community which is responsible for us catchin' so much hell.

These examples of the cultural-deprivation hypothesis and the matriarchal family model were used to illustrate the need for a psychological explanation and analysis of black life styles, which emerges from the framework of the black experience. Not only will the understanding of the black frame of reference enable us to come up with more accurate and comprehensive explanations, but will also enable us to build the kinds of programs within the black world which capitalize on the strengths of black people. This is especially critical in the field of education because the most successful educational models tend to capitalize on the experiences which the child brings to the classroom, as opposed to constantly reminding the child of his weaknesses. Not all traditional white psychological theory is useless. It has already been implied that the views of the existential psychologists, with their recognition of pain and struggle as an unavoidable condition, apply to the lives of black people. The views commonly advanced by a group of psychologists called self-theorists may be helpful because the self-theorists take the view that in order to understand what a person is and the way he views the world, you must have some awareness of his experiential background, especially as it might include experiences with the institutions such as the home, family, immediate neighborhood, and the agencies of both cultures which directly affect the person's life.

To continue our discussion, rather than argue that black people are totally psychologically unique, it would seem that our experience with—and management of—key psychological concepts, as it pertains to handling of contradictions, role of the hero, language systems, the meaning of work, and a healthy sense of suspiciousness, differs profoundly as we compare the black experience with the white Anglo experience.

In a feeling-oriented culture, apparent—and when examined closely, superficial—logical contradictions do not have the same meaning as they might have in the Anglo culture. A white psychology student became thoroughly confused when he was provided with the opportunity to observe a particular brother one Sunday in what the student thought to be three very different and contradictory sets. The student by prior arrangement was allowed to watch the brother interact within the context of a 1968-type black nationalist rally. The brother in question was a very active participant in the audience. He seemed to enjoy the antihonky rhetoric, shouted and clapped at appropriate moments, and gave the speakers repeated replies of "Right on." Immediately following the rally this same brother walked across the street to a black, storefront church-type revival, grabbed a tambourine, rocked with the sisters, called on the Holy Ghost, and sang an unsolicited solo entitled *Where Shall I Be When the First Trumpet Sounds?* Next, the brother walked to a bar a block away, drank more than a little gin, and began to hum and keep time with the lyrics of *Chain of Fools* by Aretha Franklin. During the interview which occurred in the bar, the white psychologist opened by asking, "Don't you see any basic contradiction between participation in a black nationalist rally, a storefront revival, and sitting in this bar drinking gin?" (and I might add popping his fingers). The brother replied to the question by stating that not only did he not see any contradiction but that he looked forward to all three sets every Sunday because he basically just "dug on it." What might have represented a contradiction to the white psychologist meant nothing to the brother in the sense that all three sets were part of the same experience for him at a feeling level. As part of the same experience pool, with unimportant surface differences, the brother felt equally at home during all three activities. Within the black experience the church can be seen as an arena of strength or as an escapist movement. What is important is that these two views do not negate each other and can exist within the same person side by side. Closely related to the easy style of handling contradictions, it can also be stated that black people have a greater tolerance for conflict, stress, ambiguity, and ambivalence. White psychologists fail to take this into consideration when they assume that because we have a lower-class background, black people are therefore more impulsive, emotionally immature, and have less tolerance for stress.

In terms of the role of the hero, the dominant white culture is steeped in the tradition of a hero who is infallible, scores his triumphs with godlike skill, follows all the rules, and finally retires undefeated. The whole psychology of the hero in black and white cultures is different. In the black culture the hero is by and large the brother who messes with the system and gets away with it. Black people on the whole could care less about a few political figures partying it up in the West Indies at The Man's expense. They can dig it and can identify with it. Whereas this same hero, according to the white psychologists, is interpreted as the villain. In literature the two hero themes come together in John O. Killen's novel *And Then We Heard the Thunder.* Solly Saunders, as the noble savage, is a black college graduate serving as an officer in the Army during World War II. He runs into a brother in his outfit who, as the villain, talks back to the officers, ignores the rules, and follows his own self-determination-oriented mind. Because of this bad brother, Solly goes through some changes and at the end of the book the "bad nigger" emerges as the hero. Nowadays the bad nigger is very much in vogue as the hero in the black community, yet white people continue to perceive this person as the villain and cannot understand why black folks are currently rejecting white people's favorite Uncle Toms. As a people we have to trust our own kinds of perceptions and not absorb white expectations of superheroes and villains.

Black people have a genuine understanding of brothers like Eldridge Cleaver. Eldridge became kind of a cultural hero in the United States. A lot of white people, including white radicals, were disappointed because he didn't stand trial. They said that he had let down his responsibility to his people and wasn't "a credit to his race." But anybody who had heard Eldridge, read his books, or knew anything about his life and where he had been, knew that he was not going to go back there again.

Heroes are also important because they serve as role models for children, and in children's books produced by white publishers the black role model is often notoriously absent. Black children in the process of growing up need to see themselves realistically reflected in books, movies, radio, TV, and the like. By seeing themselves reflected it confirms that they exist and provides them with identification figures and images. After a righteously profound rebuking by black educators, a few white publishers of children's literature and TV producers are slowly trying to correct the situation. Let us take a brief look at their efforts. A typical children's story might start out with some white boys playing baseball. At the beginning of the ball game a black child is on the sidelines watching. At about the middle of the game a white boy's mama makes him come home for lunch; the white players talk it over and finally invite the black youngster to join the ball game. The brother proceeds to strike out six people in a row, hits four home runs, picks a runner off at second base, and later wins the game by setting up a double play. Psychologically, what this story does is to project the image of a "supernigger" and implies that they are okay in ones and twos. On the other

hand, one does not have to be a super white boy to gain membership on the team
or a respectable position in life. The average everyday white boy sees himself
reflected throughout the white culture in pictures, books, films, radio, TV during the process of growing up. Whereas the black child has to settle for distorted
images—recently the supernigger image and prior to that images projecting the
noble savage, beast, Bojangles, and other clowns. From a black psychological
standpoint we have to work to make the kind of breakthrough that puts black
children into typical situations rather than into distorted unreal worlds.

With respect to the use of language, the oral tradition with its heavy rap, folk
tales, blues, spirituals, and down-home sermons has a vital impact within the
black experience. Historically speaking, any discussion of the black experience
with language is further complicated by the fact that words were used to express
and conceal at the same time. Certain ideas had to be conveyed to the brothers
and the same ideas had to be hidden from the white man. The slavemaster in the
antebellum South listening to the field "nigras" singing "Steal away, steal away
to Jesus, steal away home" were deceived into believing that the brothers and
sisters were thinking only about Heaven. The real message was about stealing
away and splitting up North. Black language is also very deep in hidden meanings, intuition, and nuances. A poem like *The Signifying Monkey* confuses even
the most hip revolutionary ofay, yet brothers who cannot read or write know
exactly what the poem means—it is foolish, if not suicidal, to fight a powerful
enemy on its own ground and to neutralize obvious advantages, the monkey
engages in effective trickery, deceit, and a black form of psychological warfare
known as "signifying." These same so-called illiterate brothers also intuitively
know when the white power structure is being dishonest, jiving, and otherwise
engaging in tricknology. As part of our oral tradition, the dozens, as a game of
one-upmanship in which clever remarks are exchanged about the mamas, aunties,
and grandmamas of the contestants, causes white psychologists and linguists
nothing but confusion. Assuming the dozens to be part of our matriarchal bag,
they literally think we want to have destructive sexual encounters with our
mamas. An alternate historical explanation from the black experience might be
that the brothers and sisters use the dozens as a game to teach them how to keep
cool and think fast under pressure, without saying what was really on their
minds. In translating black language forms into standard oral English, we should
remember that some of the meaning will automatically be lost because these
words and idioms are accompanied by a very rich background of gestures, body
motions, and voice changes. Despite the loss in translation, black educators
should continue with their efforts to write black language programs with standard English equivalents. Since black children are exposed to two cultures they
should be able to express themselves in more than one dialect of the English
language.

The folklore of white American culture repeatedly emphasizes the value and
virtues of hard work. Work is supposed to cleanse us, move us ahead economically, and allow us to advance to positions of higher prestige and authority. In a
sense, hard work pays off, and generations of Americans were reared to believe

in the idea that through personal effort one could go from rags to riches. Stokely Carmichael has repeatedly stated that if hard work was the key to advancement "Black people would be the richest people in the country." We have worked in the fields from sunup to sundown, laid rails, picked cotton, scrubbed floors, messed with chain gangs, reared other people's children and at the end of three centuries have very little to show for this monumental effort at hard work. Since hard work has not dramatically altered the future of black people, we have evidence to believe that what happens to a person is more related to luck or chance than it is to hard work. To plan with the belief in the future is to plan for disappointment and heartbreak. Hence black folk have done their best to deal with the concrete realities and needs of the present. This does not mean that black people are present oriented in the sense that they are impulse ridden or incapable of delayed gratification. What it means is that the benefits of the white dream of hard work have not paid off for us. That being the case, as a group, our management of time is not bound or guided by a future orientation and time is not measured in the work-unit values of the dominant white culture.

Part of the objective condition of black people in this society is that of a paranoid condition. There is, and has been, unwarranted, systematic persecution and exploitation of black people as a group. A black person who is not suspicious of the white culture is pathologically denying certain objective and basic realities of the black experience. The late sociologist E. Franklin Frazier touched on this very well in *Black Bourgeoisie*, and the authors of *Black Rage* discuss the value of healthy black paranoia. White psychiatrists and psychologists often have considerable difficulty working constructively with the hostility and suspiciousness of black patients. This is because their frame of reference tells them that excessive suspiciousness is psychologically unhealthy. If a white dude were to tell a white psychiatrist that people have been systematically picking on him from his front door clear to the White House, the psychiatrist would diagnose him as in a psychotic, paranoid state and hospitalize him. Using a black frame of reference with a black patient should not result in the same diagnosis, and possibly white psychiatrists should stop diagnosing us and spend some of their time working to change the system which persecutes black people.

A comprehensive theory of black psychology will have to explain in much greater detail the dynamics of the black home, family, hero, role models, language systems, work and time management, and the nature of suspiciousness. Many other areas will have to be included, and hopefully the challenge of excellence will be met by a younger generation of black students who are deeply committed to the development of a true psychological picture of the black experience.

One of the primary reasons why interracial group sensitivity encounters often fail to make adequate progress may be due to the fact that black people and white people have different priorities, expectations, ways of viewing the world, and life styles. When black people confront white people, what they primarily want is a legitimate acknowledgment of their point of view and a follow-up with appropriate actions. But when a white person is pushed up against a wall, the worst thing he can do is admit that the party who pushed him up there has a valid point of view. In a group encounter when black people escalate the verbal fireworks the white reaction is to feel angry, threatened, alienated, or guilty. Were whites to drop their defensiveness and acknowledge the legitimacy of the black point of view, they might be able to move from there to a more cooperative relationship. But the white culture is so deeply entrenched in the whole concept of face-saving, sin, and repayment for past wrong-doings, that it expects an Old Testament eye-for-an-eye type of retaliation.

On TV recently, NET showed a black/white encounter in which each group was forced to take the roles of the others. White masks were put on black people, and black masks were put on white people. While this was a short encounter, perhaps in the future for training people in the black experience we should have them try to be black for a longer time with some of their experiences taking place outside the protective setting of the group.

In closing, one further comment on group encounters might be considered. While white people in their group encounters with other white people may need to deal with the questions of sex, aggression, affection, tenderness, shame, and guilt, black people, especially black change agents, have a completely different set of priorities. In moving from one pattern to another and more rapidly from one crisis situation to another, if one is not careful, it is easy to slip into a state of psychological fatigue with the accompanying symptoms of depression and angry despair. In this state of mind, without realizing it, we begin to use words like revolution, liberation, Tomming, imperialism, agent-provocateur, and many others in a very general, undefined global way—sometimes more for self-affirmation than for real communication. Furthermore, in such a psychological state of fatigue it is very difficult to see clearly both the goals one is striving for and the relevance of the tactic to the immediate situation. We mix up rhetoric about change with the process of change itself. Rhetoric properly applied can make us psychologically conscious of what it means to be black. But we must not equate the imagery of this black consciousness with the actualities of concrete social progress. A carefully developed psychological group encounter conducted with change agents, coordinated by a black person with psychological training in the black experience, might facilitate the process of regeneration, self-renewal, and meaningful communication. Like any human endeavor, in order to continue to be creative and productive, the black struggle must construct models which will take care of the process of internal cleansing and meaningful reflection and as such serve as self-corrective guides.

WILLIAM A. HAYES

Radical Black Behaviorism

The clarion call for a black psychology rings out from young black students of psychology who have come to understand that traditional American psychology in all its varied forms has been insensitive to the needs of black people. As a discipline, it has contributed disproportionately to the justification of personal and institutionalized racism which characterizes America. The call for a black psychology, then, is an adaptive reaction by young scholars with a social conscience to the failures of American psychology.

While one can support the need for a discipline that goes beyond the efforts of American psychology, one can also question whether a black psychology holds any significant promise, or even if it is wise or possible to develop a discipline called Black Psychology. The present paper supports the thesis that it is both unwise and impossible to develop a unified discipline of knowledge called Black Psychology which will contribute significantly more to the understanding of black people than American psychology. It offers an alternative to the proposed Black Psychology with the hope that the alternative will be evaluated on its scientific merit and utility to black people in America.

Why Not a Black Psychology?

The call for a black psychology seems to be predicated on the assumption that a unified, internally consistent discipline of psychology exists. In reality, nothing is further from the truth. American psychology embraces approaches to the study of human behavior as disparate as parapsychology and the Experimental Analysis of Behavior. The basic assumptions, methodologies, and even definitions of behavior of these several approaches vary so widely that it is unlikely that the disparity will ever be reduced to the extent that American psychology will become a single discipline of knowledge.

A similar disparity of approaches exists among black psychologists—the presumed architects of the black psychology. While there is the common thread of black experiences, it is not clear that these common experiences are sufficiently binding to negate the influences of different approaches to psychology adopted, for the most part, during graduate training at white institutions. Thus, it seems reasonable to expect the same problems in a black psychology which characterize American psychology. If this be true, the consequence of attempts to develop a black psychology would be the emergence of several approaches to psychology from a black perspective with enough differences in basic assump-

Reprinted by permission of the author.

tions, methodology, and so forth to negate the possibility of developing a unified, internally consistent body of knowledge called Black Psychology.

The fact of disparity of approaches within psychology suggests that even the meaning of the word *psychology* has become so polluted that it cannot serve as the basis upon which to develop a discipline that seeks to explain the behavior of black people without bias. If an unbiased understanding of black behavior is to emerge, it must be radically different from previous explanations offered by psychology. In fact, to use the word *psychology* as a part of the label for the new discipline is to begin with a set of biases governed, not by the principles of the new discipline, but by one's orientation to American psychology.

The call for a black psychology is an ambitious call. It is difficult to conceive of a black psychology becoming anything other than a warmed-over version of traditional American psychology with as many orientations and problems. Perhaps a more reasonable alternative is to adopt the approach to psychology with the greatest potential for leading to a fair understanding of the behavior of black people. The approach must be capable of demonstrating internal consistency and of developing into a formal discipline according to an explicit set of rules designed to establish it as a science.

The new discipline, by whatever name it is called, must seek ultimately to go beyond the explanation and understanding of the behavior of black people; it must seek to become the science of human behavior that has the most potential for explaining the behavior of the largest number of people with the minimum amount of bias. One approach to psychology deserves special consideration from the architects of the new discipline. Because of its potential for becoming an unbiased science of human behavior, it is suggested that black psychologists adopt and expand upon the principles of radical behaviorism to create a science of black behavior called *Radical Black Behaviorism*.

American psychology has been detrimental to the well-being of blacks, not because its leaders do not understand the "black experience" or because it is not relevant to black people, but because it is not a science. Any approach to the understanding of human behavior short of a science leaves room for biased and racist orientations and interpretations which are not in the best interest of black people. Radical Black Behaviorism represents the most scientific approach to the study of human behavior. As such, it stands as the antithesis of the most damaging and oppressive components of American psychology. Among other things, Radical Black Behaviorism insists upon explanations rather than conceptualizations; it is intolerant of mentalistic interpretations and theories which often serve as the pseudoscientific justification for personal and institutional racism; and it focuses upon consequences of behavior rather than causes and motives underlying the behavior. More importantly, it has a utility for black people, which seems to have gone unrecognized.

Explanations Versus Conceptualizations

The so-called explanations of black behavior in the American psychological literature stand as the greatest monument to the need for an alternative. Psychological literature is replete with attempts to explain black behavior or "psychological phenomena" by resorting to hypothetical mental structures, presumed needs, attitudes, and the like. Because these so-called explanations go beyond observable events, they are conceptualizations of behavior rather than explanations of behavior. Conceptualizations are based more on one's theoretical orientation and/or implicit theories of people and behavior than upon the behavior and the events surrounding the behavior being explained.

The practice of conceptualizing rather than explaining behavior is often combined with case studies or anecdotes. An example is provided by Erikson (1950):

Consider, for example, the chances for a continuity of identity in the American Negro child. I know a colored boy who, like our boys, listens every night to Red Rider. Then he sits up in bed, imagining that he is Red Rider. But the moment comes when he sees himself galloping after some masked offenders and suddenly notices that in his fancy Red Rider is a colored man. He stops his fantasy. While a small child, this boy was extremely expressive, both in his pleasures and his sorrows. Today he is calm and always smiles; his language is soft and blurred; nobody can hurry him or worry him—or please him. White people like him. (p. 241)

In the same book Erikson further "explains" the problems of black identity:

Tired of his own caricature, the colored individual often retires into hypochondriac invalidism as a condition which represents an analogy to the dependence and relative safety of defined restriction in the South: a neurotic regression to the ego identity of the slave. (p. 242)

The above explanations may serve to illustrate three points. First, as late as the 1950s, anecdotal evidence was still very much a part of contemporary American psychology. It is interesting to note that Lloyd Morgan's canon in 1891 led to the elimination of the use of anecdotal evidence and mentalistic concepts in explaining animal behavior, but it is still quite acceptable among contemporary psychologists as explanations of the behavior of black people. While anecdotal evidence has taken the form of case studies and mentalistic explanations have donned the pseudoscientific cloak of intervening variables and hypothetical constructs, they are still unacceptable as explanations to a science of human behavior. Seldom is the reader informed of the number of cases the writer has encountered which did not conform to the particular theoretical position he is espousing. Without this information, one suspects that the writer entertains a conceptual position and is attentive only to behaviors and situations that support his position in fact or through elaborate interpretations. We can only conclude that such writers are more committed to their theoretical formulations than to a realistic understanding of black behavior.

Mentalistic explanations such as "neurotic regression to the identity of the slave" defy any attempt for observable support; thus they are not explanations. The use of such conceptualizations maximizes the probability that personal biases will be included. Given the same set of behaviors, different observers may arrive at very different, erroneous explanations of behavior. This is illustrated in a clever study by Haughton and Ayllon (1965). These investigators shaped the repetitive response of holding a broom using reinforcement techniques and a female patient in a psychiatric hospital. Baseline observations taken in an unobtrusive manner indicated that the patient spent 60 percent of her waking time lying in bed, approximately 20 percent sitting and walking, and the remainder in activities associated with meals, grooming, and elimination. Broom holding was shaped by reinforcing the patient with cigarettes while she held the broom. The broom-holding behavior was quickly developed to the point that the patient resisted having the broom taken away. Two psychiatrists were asked to observe and evaluate the patient from behind a one-way mirror. One psychiatrist gave the following evaluation:

> *Her constant and compulsive pacing holding a broom in the manner she does could be seen as a ritualistic procedure, a magical action. When regression conquers the association process, primitive and archaic forms of thinking control the behavior. Symbolism is a predominant mode of expressing of deep seated unfulfilled desires and instinctual impulses. By magic, she controls others, cosmic powers are at her disposal, and inanimate objects become living creatures.*
>
> *Her broom could be then:*
>
> *1. a child that gives her love and she gives him in return her devotion;*
> *2. a phallic symbol;*
> *3. the sceptre of an omnipotent queen. (Haughton and Ayllon, 1965, p. 98)*

The second psychiatrist gave a different evaluation; he saw the broom as "some essential perceptual element in her field of consciousness" and the behavior as a "stereotyped form of behavior such as is commonly seen in rather regressed schizophrenics" and "analogous to the way small children or infants refuse to be parted from some favorite toy, piece of rag, etc." (Haughton and Ayllon, 1965.)

One wonders how many mentalistic explanations or evaluations have been given to the detriment of black people. In spite of the fact that such evaluations have no scientific merit, they are continuously used.

It is unfair to suggest that mentalistic explanations are only espoused by white psychologists and psychiatrists. Black psychologists and psychiatrists adopt the methods and orientations of their white mentors; therefore, their explanations tend to be of the same kind but seasoned by the black experience. Grier and Cobbs, two black psychiatrists, provide illustrations in *Black Rage* (1968). Black mentalistic explanations of black behavior are no more acceptable than white mentalistic explanations.

Radical Black Behaviorism is limited to the study of behaviors that can be observed, measured, and reproduced. Similarly, its explanations of behavior are also in terms of events that can be observed, measured, and reproduced. Thus, Radical Black Behaviorism is never in the position of explaining behavior, an observable event, by the postulation of an unobservable event. Any explanation based upon hypothetical mental structures, dynamics, or presumed needs is considered invalid. Valid explanations are ones that specify the actual conditions that reliably produce and maintain the behavior to be explained (Reynolds, 1968). Consistent use of definitions governed by this requirement negates the possibility of confounding explanation and bias.

Consequences Versus Cause

The guiding principle of Radical Black Behaviorism states that people act upon the environment in such a way that the environment changes. The environmental change is the consequence of behavior. The nature of the consequence determines the probability that the same class of response will occur given similar environmental conditions.

Two important implications are inherent in this principle. First, it implies that the consequence of behavior is vital to its explanation. The focus on the consequence of behavior allows explanations based upon an individual's present environment rather than specifying causes in terms of events occurring prior to the behavior being explained. Attempts to specify causes inevitably lead to inward, unobservable characteristics of the individual, which mediate between the environment and behavior. Because events occurring at any time in the person's past history can be specified as a cause, it is highly probable that different psychologists will specify different causes of the behavior. Again, biased interpretations and assumptions can play a major role in the explanation. Moreover, a previous event can be specified as a cause of the behavior; that knowledge contributes little to the potential for changing behavior.

Knowledge of the consequence of behavior that controls the behavior leads immediately to the suggestion that behavior can be changed through manipulation of the consequences. Because consequences are observable, this focus is potentially more scientific and therefore more acceptable to a science of human behavior.

Clearly, black people have been the victims of explanations whose major focus was on cause rather than consequence. Blacks have higher absenteeism rates in industry *because* they are lazy and unmotivated; blacks do not perform well on achievement tests *because* they are intellectually inferior. Seldom are the differences in consequences (salaries, job offers, etc.) in working or academic behavior related to different rates of performance between whites and blacks in work and academic settings. Radical Black Behaviorism rejects the specification of previous life events as causing behavior as unscientific and harmful to the well-being of black people.

Focus on Individual

Black people in America are seen as a rather homogenous group by the lay public and professionals. While giving cursory recognition to individual differences, behavioral scientists continuously attribute group characteristics to blacks. Howard Odum (1910), in a work described as "an effort to contribute something toward the scientific knowledge of the Negro," described the social and mental traits of blacks. Among other things, Odum's study found blacks to be expressive in their abuse of others, liars, exaggerators and lovers of music; gregarious in their sexual morality, sociality, and conformity to law and the group; and, responsive to forceful circumstances and to emotions (pp. 272–273).

Conclusions from the above and other pseudoscientific investigations (Garrett, 1945; Jensen, 1969) have become a part of white America's perception of black people and result in white people's reacting to individual blacks as if they were unintelligent, immoral, and so on. Often these perceptions work to the detriment of blacks, as is suggested by the studies of Rosenthal and Jacobson (1968).

The focus on blacks as a group is given credibility by the use of the normal curve and sophisticated statistical analyses. True statistical tests demonstrate functional relationships, but the functional relationships are between selected variables or events and groups of people not between events and individuals. Thus, statistics have contributed more to making psychology a study of the behavior of groups than to understanding individual behavior. Psychology perpetuates the myth that its principles founded on grouped data are applicable to the individual. Consequently, decisions which affect the future and well-being of individuals in major ways are based upon tests and scales whose validity has been established and can *only* be established through the statistical analysis of scores from groups of subjects. For example, the validity of intelligence tests for a single individual has never been established, but the same tests are used as the basis upon which a child is placed in a special rather than a regular classroom in school. When questioned about the validity of the decision for the individual, the validity indexes, based upon so-called representative groups, are inevitably given as justification. Radical Black Behaviorism rejects not only such use of statistics, but also the concepts of intelligence and intelligence measurement.

Alternatives to statistical analyses of grouped data and statistical control have been established by contributors to the *Journal of the Experimental Analysis of Behavior* (EAB) (Skinner, 1966; Sidman, 1960). Experimental control and research paradigms based upon replications have been used to demonstrate functional relationships between individual behavior and its controlling conditions. It is the demonstration of functional relationships through manipulation of controlling conditions that differentiates the EAB's study with an N of 1 from traditional psychology's case study. Unlike traditional psychology, the methods and principles established in basic research laboratories are directly applicable to programs designed to change behavior in clinical, educational, or other settings.

Practical Utility of Radical Black Behaviorism

One of the most important criteria by which any alternative to contemporary American psychology must be judged is its practical utility to blacks in the struggle for equality. The black movement has been characterized in various ways. Some have called it an economic struggle, others call it a political struggle, while still others feel that morality plays the most important role. The elements common to all these perceptions are people and their behavior. A science of human behavior should have a lot to say about the nature of the problem, but it should also lead to concrete suggestions for the solution of the problem.

The focus on behavior as the primary element of the black struggle and white resistance is not an original contribution of Radical Black Behaviorism. Such a focus is implied in the popular conception of the problem as "colonization of the mind." The implication is that the minds of blacks have been colonized to the extent that they respond in a manner that is highly predictable and consistent with the wishes of the "colonizer." Familiar statements such as "His head is in the wrong place" and "You've got to get your head together" indicate the popularity of this conception among blacks. While the focus is on behavior, the behavior is controlled by the mind. Any changes in behavior must be preceded by changes in the mind.

This conceptualization has the same disadvantages as the use of mentalistic concepts in psychology. It suggests that the first task of blacks in the movement is to initiate and/or facilitate the necessary mental changes. The procedures to be used and the criteria for sufficient change or its measurement are not clear. Thus, this conception does not predict behaviors that are useful to the struggle. Perhaps this is why so much time and energy is spent developing "black pride."

Without rejecting the need for or the utility of developing black pride, Radical Black Behaviorism supports a different perception of the struggle. The control of black people's behavior is seen as the bone of contention over which blacks and whites struggle. White America struggles to maintain its control of black people's behavior, while blacks struggle to control their own behavior. Freedom, then, is seen as a true interdependence between races or equal amounts of control by both races over the others' behavior.

During slavery, whites maintained virtually complete control over the behavior of blacks through the use of aversive control. Slaves worked to avoid punishment. Whites were reinforced for maintaining the system, as goods were produced with minimal expense and profits were high. With the abolition of slavery, new methods of control were developed. In addition to continued aversive control by so-called hate groups, mechanisms of economic control were instituted. Blacks began to be paid for their work, but only under the reinforcement schedules defined by whites. Thus, meager pay was made contingent upon high rates of behavior in an environment almost completely controlled by whites. This system of economic dependence still serves as the basic mechanism by which the behavior of contemporary blacks is controlled. One can argue that the history of blacks in America supports the contention that the basis of the whites' struggle was to maintain economic superiority as much as it supports the contention that the control of blacks' behavior was the fundamental issue. The issue is placed in proper perspective when one realizes that the economic superiority of whites is contingent upon their ability to maintain control over black behavior.

Behavioral control is far from the sinister control over mind and body often projected by the entertainment media. Behavioral control refers to the systematic manipulation of certain environmental events in such a way that the observed effect occurs in a predictable manner. The resulting effect may be to accelerate, decelerate, or maintain the behavior upon which the event is made contingent. Behavioral control requires two conditions to be maximally effective. First, the controller must have significant control over the environment in which the controlled behaves. The greater the control the former has over the latter's environment, the greater the potential for realizing the desired effect. Second, the controlled must be experiencing a state of deprivation; otherwise aversive control mechanisms must be used.

The implications of the first condition for black people is clear. To maintain economic superiority, whites in America must maintain control over the behavior of blacks by any means necessary. The major institutions of the society, job sources, and regulating and enforcement bodies must remain in control of white people. Community control and separatism can not be tolerated unless there is some supramechanism by which whites can control the larger unit which results from such black unifications.

The second requirement mitigates against whites' giving equality to blacks out of the goodness of their hearts. To be economically superior, whites must control blacks; to control blacks in a manner that is reasonably consistent with the rhetoric of democracy, blacks must be kept in a state of deprivation. Because money is the chief reinforcer in our society, it is reasonable to expect blacks to remain economically deprived. From this perspective, the racial differences in income, which hold when amount of education is controlled, takes on a new meaning. Economic deprivation of blacks must be maintained to maintain behavioral control over blacks, while maintaining the myth of democracy. It is clear that as blacks increasingly gain control over their own behavior and therefore contribute proportionally less to maintaining white economic superiority, one can expect increasing amounts of overt, aversive control.

Radical Black Behaviorism must address the issue of behavioral control directly. It recognizes that humans' ability to control other humans' behavior via a variety of mechanisms is a reality. It must participate in the ongoing development of methods and principles of behavioral control, both in and outside of the experimental laboratory. It is only through knowledge of the principles of behavioral control that blacks will be able to resist white control and develop effective means of countercontrol.

Radical Black Behaviorism is offered as an alternative to the more diffuse black psychology currently being proposed. Radical Black Behaviorism embraces radical behaviorism (Skinner, 1964; Day, 1969) and the experimental analysis of behavior as the basis upon which a radically objective science of human behavior can be developed. As a potential science, it rejects the mentalistic concepts of contemporary psychology, is individualistic in its approach, and has immediate utility for meeting the needs of black people.

References

Day, W. F. Radical behaviorism in reconciliation with phenomenology. *Journal of the Experimental Analysis of Behavior*, 1969, **12**, 315-328.

Erikson, E. H. *Childhood and society*. New York: Norton, 1950.

Garrett, H. E. A note on the intelligence scores of Negroes and whites in 1918. *Journal of Abnormal and Social Psychology*, 1945, **40**, 344-346.

Grier, W. H., and Cobbs, P. M. *Black rage*. New York: Basic Books, 1968.

Haughton, E., and Ayllon, T. Production and elimination of symptomatic behavior. In L. P. Ullman and L. Krasner (Eds.), *Case studies in behavior modification*. New York: Holt, Rinehart & Winston, 1965, pp. 94-98.

Hayes, W., and Banks, W. M. The nigger box *or* a redefinition of the counselor's role. In this volume, pp. 225-232.

Jensen, A. R. How much can we boost IQ and scholastic achievement? *Harvard Educational Review*, 1969, **39**, 1-23.

Odum, H. W. *Social and mental traits of the Negro*. New York: Columbia University Press, 1910.

Reynolds, G. S. *A primer of operant conditioning*. Glenview, Ill.: Scott, Foresman, 1968.

Rosenthal, R., and Jacobson, L. F. *Pygmalion in the classroom: Teacher expectation and pupils intellectual development*. New York: Holt, Rinehart & Winston, 1968.

Sidman, M. *Tactics of scientific research*. New York: Basic Books, 1960.

Skinner, B. F. Behaviorism at fifty. In T. W. Wann (Ed.), *Behaviorism and phenomenology*. Chicago: University of Chicago Press, 1964, pp. 79-97.

Skinner, B. F. What is an experimental analysis of behavior? *Journal of Experimental Analysis of Behavior*, 1966, **9**, 213-218.

PART II

The Psychological Assessment of Blacks

The psychological assessment of black Americans has a long history. The primary concern has been with the assessment of black intelligence and black school achievement. Although not completely ignored, the areas of specific aptitudes, personality, and employment tests have received relatively little attention. Generalizations stemming from studies of black-white differences in intelligence and achievement are well known. Compared to whites, blacks generally score significantly lower on standardized measures in these areas. Some speculate, particularly with respect to the assessment of intelligence, that a genetic basis for the differences may exist.

There are, of course, striking exceptions to these generalizations, a number of which have been called to the writer's attention by Professor William Brazziel. Several major studies show blacks matching whites on mental tests. Some show blacks excelling whites on these tests. A partial list follows: Ginsburg (1960) showed blacks from two states excelling whites from several states on Armed Forces Tests. A Los Angeles School Board study (1969) showed a black school leading the city in IQ. A Virginia State Board of Education study (1971) showed a black school leading the state in reading. Tanser (1939) showed rural Ontario blacks matching their white counterparts in IQ. Mayeske (1971) grouped the Coleman Report data according to social class and found black-white comparability. Heber (Strickland, 1971) showed average and above average IQ scores in a five-year longitudinal experiment with black slum children. Englemann (USOE, 1968) showed average and above average IQ scores in a variety of projects with black slum children. Mercer (1971) found black-white comparibility in a study of 125,000 school children grouped according to social class. A National Merit Scholarship study of black recipients of its awards—more than 30 a year—showed that average ability scores exceeded the 93rd percentile on national norms (1969).

Great controversy surrounds research and writing about the nature of black-white differences in intelligence and achievement, and about the origin and consequences of the differences. It is unlikely that the issues can be resolved here. It is hoped, however, that perspectives on these problems will be made clear by papers presented in this section.

Edward Barnes, in the first paper in the section, "Cultural Retardation or Shortcomings of Assessment Techniques?" presents an overview of certain key issues in the testing of blacks, giving particular attention to shortcomings in tests which reduce their validity when used with blacks. Concerns include the concept of intelligence itself, problems of examiner-examinee interaction, test reliability

61

and validity, and failure barriers built into the assessment techniques. References concluding Barnes's article are particularly valuable for the future researcher.

Additional problems and concerns related to the use of psychological tests are presented by Robert Williams in "Abuses and Misuses in Testing Black Children." In addition to calling attention to definitional problems (i.e., the nature of intelligence) and scientific considerations (i.e., the tests' validity and reliability), as does Barnes, Williams takes up political, educational, legal, and economic considerations in the use of tests with blacks, and others. Heretofore, the consequences of test practices for blacks have not been treated in the broad perspective provided by Williams. Such an analysis is valuable indeed.

The papers by Barnes and Williams both point to the fact that black children are being harmed by tests standardized on white middle-class children. In its "Position Statement on Use of IQ and Ability Tests," the Bay Area Association of Black Psychologists suggests a moratorium on the testing of black children and offers guidelines for specific changes that need to be instituted in the evaluation and assessment of black children.

It should be noted that even if the attempt to secure a moratorium on the use of certain tests with black children is successful, several problems will remain, including the racism of teachers and others working with black children, and general expectations for low cognitive performance. Nevertheless, the moratorium may force the schools to look at data directly relevant to the black child's school learning—that is, his learning strategies, learning preferences, and learning styles.

The papers cited above focus on the use of individual intelligence tests in the public schools. Many of the same problems hold for group tests used beyond the high-school level. Particularly critical is the employment of such devices as the Scholastic Aptitude Test and others in predicting the success of black students in colleges. Robert L. Green's "The Black Quest for Higher Education: An Admissions Dilemma" summarizes significant literature in this area and highlights important issues. It frequently is argued that the admission of substantial numbers of blacks lowers admissions standards. Evidence presented by Green indicates that substantial numbers of students of all social classes are being terminated by universities for substandard performance. The issue Green notes is not the raising or lowering of admissions standards but the development and utilization of standards that take into account more than intellectual functioning as measured by tests of scholastic aptitude.

Black psychologists (and others) are concerned about several perhaps obvious dimensions of the (mis)application of psychological tests with blacks. Some are based on well-known, but often ignored, axioms—for example, testing should be applied only to groups and subclasses included in the standardization population; many instruments having sufficient reliability for group predictions may be inappropriate for individual predictions; validity data should be developed for the situations in which the tests would be used. These axioms, and others, are repeatedly violated in the testing of black Americans.

Guilford (1967) and Cronbach (1970) have unequivocably stated limitations of tests when used with various racial and cultural groups.

That there are differences in means of test scores among racial groups, no one can deny. The meanings of these differences are not easy to determine. It can be stated as a general principle, from all that we have considered with respect to conditions and their effects upon test scores, that difference among means reflect differences in needs and opportunities for the development of various kinds of abilities within the culture in which the individuals have their existence. (Guilford, 1967, p. 408)

In a related vein, Cronbach (1970) notes:

We must accept Liverant's . . . conclusion that to decide "what is or is not intelligent behavior involves a cultural value judgment" and that a person's variation in efficiency from task to task must be explained by examining his expectations and the rewards available. (p. 248)

Test misuse in the employment situation presents as many problems as test misuse in the schools. One investigation of 152 companies using tests to screen for employment revealed that only 7 percent reported that the instruments had been validated locally against on-the-job performance measures and that nearly 60 percent had validated none of their tests (Wallace, Kissinger, and Reynolds, 1966). Unquestionably, too many tests used to predict employability are heavily verbal and bear no relationship to the work to be performed. Repeated admonitions about this practice have, for the most part, been ignored.

A most disturbing feature of testing is its emphasis upon what has been learned—using white middle-class values—rather than what can be learned. The tests are too seldom diagnostic and too much historical. Green has summarized the results of studies which indicate that given proper environmental support in the form of counseling and tutorial assistance, students identified as poor risks perform satisfactorily in college. Similar results have been found in business and industry. One midwestern department store group devised an experimental training program for individuals who had failed the standard employment tests and were classified as unemployable. Following a 10-week special training program, all were subsequently employed; the performance of the 14 for whom records were available exceeded what was predicted by standard sales-aptitude tests. Some surpassed performance standards for new employees by unusually large margins.

Arguments supporting the use of intelligence and aptitude tests with blacks point out that—particularly in school settings—the tests predict as well for blacks as for whites. Such arguments miss the mark by failing to consider the context in which the test scores are both secured and used. Take this situation from the school setting. A black or a white child is referred for psychological testing—usually in connection with potential placement in a special class for the retarded or disturbed. First, there is every likelihood that regardless of race the child will be found to be of low ability—supportive of the original reason for referral (Hersh, 1969). If the child is black, his chances of being placed in special classes for the retarded are even greater, based on the possibility that white psychologists are more likely to have difficulty in establishing rapport with the black child. The child, thus, is not motivated to perform at his optimum level. Consider now Mercer's finding (1971) that while blacks and Mexican-Americans were referred for psychological testing in no greater numbers than their proportions in the school population, they were much more likely to be placed in special classes for the retarded than Anglos of comparable low IQ. Thus, while 52 percent of those eligible for placement in the special class were black or Mexican-American, 68 percent of those placed were from these groups. This means, of course, that significantly fewer Anglos were placed in the special classes.

Once the child is placed in a special class, the chances of his being exposed to less are increased considerably, a point underscored by Beez's laboratory study (1968) which demonstrated that children identified as slow learners were exposed to less subject matter and, not surprisingly, learned less. There is some evidence to suggest that this phenomenon operates in special classes for the retarded as well.

One bit of evidence somewhat more tangential may be relevant. Analysis during the 1969–1970 school year of a small number of children who had been identified as educationally handicapped revealed that 20 white students were placed back in regular classes while only 8 blacks had made a similar transition, this despite the fact that blacks comprised approximately 47 percent and whites approximately 42 percent of students in classes for the educationally handicapped (EH) in the San Francisco schools (Association of Black Psychologists, 1970). There seem to be grounds for hypothesizing that a study of children placed in classes for the education of retarded children would produce similar results.

Taken together the data suggest that the black child has a greater chance of being placed in a special class for the educable mentally retarded than an Anglo once both have been identified as potential candidates for such classes. Second, once placed, the likelihood that he (or his white counterpart) will remain is increased by the operation of negative expectancies for change held by teachers and by the fact that he is exposed to less academic matter. Finally, compared to Anglos of the same ability level, the black child's chance for return to the regular class may be reduced.

The entire issue of the low intellectual functioning of blacks and the presumed environmental and genetic bases of such differences has been reopened by Jensen in his now famous Harvard Educational Review *article. Leading psychologists have criticized Jensen's research. The final paper in Part II, William F. Brazziel's "A Letter from the South," touches on the more offensive and scientifically indefensible points made by Jensen. This scholarly rebuttal represents one of the earlier rejoinders to "Jensenism." A bibliography of additional items related to the Jensen controversy is presented at the end of Brazziel's contribution.*

References

Bay Area Association of Black Psychologists. Reply to San Francisco Unified School District report on special education classes. Unpublished paper, May 5, 1970.

Beez, W. V. Influence of biased psychological reports on teacher behavior and pupil performance. *Proceedings, Seventy-sixth Annual Convention of the American Psychological Association*, San Francisco, Calif., 1968, pp. 605–606.

Cronbach, L. J. *Essentials of psychological testing*. New York: Harper & Row, 1970.

Ginsburg, E. *The Negro potential*. New York: Columbia University Press, 1960.

Guilford, J. P. *The nature of human intelligence*. New York: McGraw-Hill, 1967.

Hersh, J. B. Influence of biased referral reports in a clinical testing situation. Unpublished manuscript, Indiana University, 1969.

Los Angeles School Board. *Test score reports*. 1969.

Mayeske, G. W. Minority achievement. Paper presented at the Annual Convention of the American Psychological Association, 1971.

Mercer, J. R. Institutionalized Anglocentrism: Labeling mental retardates in the public schools. *Race, Change, and Urban Society*, 1971, 5, 311–338.

Mercer, J. R. Minority IQ. Paper presented at the Annual Convention of the American Psychological Association, 1971.

National Merit Scholarship Corporation Research Reports. *Outstanding Negro high school graduates*. 1969.

Strickland, D. M. Can slum children learn: A report on Heber cradle schools. *American Education*, July 1971.

Tanser, H. A. *The settlement of Negroes in Kent County, Ontario*. Chatham, Ontario: Shepard, 1939.

U.S. Office of Education. *It works: A report on Illinois academic primary programs*. Washington, D.C.: U.S. Government Printing Office, 1968.

Virginia State Board of Education. *Test score reports, city and county districts*, 1971.

Wallace, P., Kissinger, B., and Reynolds, B. Proposed solutions to the problem of cultural bias in testing. In the author's *Testing of minority group applicants for employment*. Office of Research and Reports, Equal Employment Opportunity Commission. Washington, D.C.: U.S. Government Printing Office, 1966, pp. 9–22.

EDWARD J. BARNES

Cultural Retardation or Shortcomings of Assessment Techniques?

The intellectual status of the so-called disadvantaged is a topic of widespread interest, as judged by the considerable literature devoted to it (1). This body of data indicates that the disadvantaged are deficient in mental ability scores (Scholnick et al., 1968), linguistic performance (Deutsch, 1965), logical reasoning (Leach, 1963), sorting ability (Siller, 1957), abstract problem solving and conceptual learning (Jensen, 1969), abstraction (Findlay and McGuire, 1957), and reading achievement (Scholnick et al., 1968). No doubt, this list of deficiencies could be extended to include a number of other measured cognitive functions. The term *disadvantaged* is defined variously by different writers. It refers principally to those who are victims of social, economic, ethnic, and racial discrimination: black Americans, American Indians, Mexican-Americans, and Puerto Ricans (Beck and Sexe, 1965). Black Americans constitute by far the largest racial minority in this country, and in 1965, 53.5 percent of all black Americans were classified as poor (Billingsley, 1968). Thus the designation disadvantaged refers mainly to black Americans.

For many years the level of general intelligence of the black American has been the focus of attention of psychologists of various persuasions, ideologies, and orientations. It is now a subject with a vast literature (Dreger and Miller, 1960, 1968; Shuey 1958, 1966; Pettigrew, 1964). The great bulk of this research finds most blacks scoring lower on IQ tests than most whites. This finding holds for preschool, school, and college populations. The same trend is found on the Armed Forces Qualification Test for a large sample of black males between ages 18 and 26 (*U.S. News and World Report*, 1966).

It is noted that these findings are not confined to economically depressed blacks. Blacks not only have lower tested average IQ than whites, they also contribute disproportionately to the mentally retarded population. Heber (1968) found that IQs below 75 have a much higher incidence among black than among white children at every SES level (2).

Thus the fact of lower tested performance of black people seems established. The critical issue concerns the interpretation of this finding. Numerous explanatory hypotheses are adduced in the studies reported in the literature. These explanatory attempts fall into two classes which are not mutually exclusive: genetically and environmentally based hypotheses. The conflict between these

Paper presented at the Annual Convention of the Council on Exceptional Children, Denver, Colorado, April 1969. Reprinted by permission of the author.

two positions revolves around the relative contributions to intelligence of heredity, on the one hand, and environment, on the other.

An extreme hereditarian position, designated the "scientific racist" position
(Pettigrew, 1964, p. 102), is overtly held by a small fraternity of American
psychologists (Garrett, 1961; Shuey, 1958; McGurk, 1951; Tanser, 1939;
McGraw, 1931). Shuey's (1958) unhesitating interpretation of research showing
that most blacks score lower than most whites on IQ tests as evidence "for the
presence of some native differences between Negroes and Whites, as determined
by intelligence tests" (p. 318), is illustrative of this position. Jensen (1969), the
latest proponent of the "scientific racist" thesis, after a selective review and a
sophisticated analysis of relevant research, concludes that genetics contributes
80 percent of the variance between black and white groups on standard measures
of intelligence, while environment contributes about 20 percent.

Environmental explanatory hypotheses do not assume predetermined development nor do they assume that "intelligence will unfold 'naturally' with gene-
determined anatomical maturation, barring extreme interference from the
environment" (Pettigrew, 1964, p. 108). This position does not deny a strong
genetic contribution to intelligence, a fact accepted as well established by twin
studies. Pettigrew (1964) observes that this position

*views intelligence in much the same way longevity is now regarded. A strong
hereditary component is recognized in longevity. Consistently long or short
spans typify many families. Yet, despite this component the life expectancies
at birth of Americans have almost doubled in the past century. Better medical
care, better diets, and a host of other environmental factors converge to enable
Americans to make fuller use of their longevity potential. Likewise the modern
view of intelligence holds that we have not begun to expand our phenotypic
intelligence even close to our genotypic potentials. (p. 108)*

If environment means any influence that is not genetic, it covers a broad range
of phenomena indeed, influences operating before, during, and after birth. En-
vironmentalists vary greatly in terms of which environment is focused upon. The
research of Klineberg (1935) and others in the 1930s, which seriously questioned racial inferiority as the primary cause of poor average black performance
on IQ tests, popularized the explanation of such performance in terms of general
environmental disabilities. Such explanations emphasize patterns of environmental conditions as the cause for depressed IQ scores and ability to learn—
economic status, job discrimination, substandard housing, poor nutrition, parental apathy, paternal absence from the home, incomplete family, quality of early
mother-child interaction, and so forth. The most recent version of the environmental position subsumed under this general rubric is "cultural deprivation."

As Kenneth Clark (1965) observes, the cultural deprivation hypothesis is
seductive. It is consistent with the apparently ascendant trend of thinking in
contemporary social science, and it provides a strong argument against the racial
inferiority hypothesis. Nevertheless, the plethora of cultural deprivation theories

must be subjected to close scrutiny to determine whether they account for the depressed functioning of black people on tests of general intellectual ability. A critical consideration concerns the mechanism by which environmental variables are transformed into "cognitive deficits." If the level of hypothesizing remains at the level of the black individual, the black family, the black community, and so on, and does not begin to deal with the forces in the larger society responsible for creating these conditions, then, as Clark (1965) observes, contemporary social deprivation theories may merely be substituting environmental immutability for biologically determined unmodifiability.

It is the contention of this paper that another source of variance in test scores of disadvantaged individuals in general, and of black Americans in particular, has been largely overlooked or treated in a cursory fashion, and that this source of variance calls into question the validity of the data for which various theories are being called forth to explain. The two positions discussed above implicitly or explicitly assume that available tests provide a valid assessment of the "disadvantaged" person's ability at that point in time. The genetic position goes farther and states that these test results represent intellectual potential as well. But the environmental position maintains that the score reflects not fixed ability, but the individual's position, status, and life conditions in the society, and if he is provided the proper experience his tested ability can be raised.

This writer maintains that forces are at work which undermine the validity of these test results, assuming that the validity of an IQ test rests on its ability to predict criteria with some degree of accuracy. In other words, the test scores often do not reflect an adequate picture of present status or potential. An analysis of factors that adversely affect the test scores of the "disadvantaged" follows.

Factors Influencing Test Validity

Concept of Intelligence

The concept of intelligence on which a given test is constructed can be a basis for its invalidity. In large measure the concept determines the kinds of behaviors tapped by the various test items. If the concept is extremely narrow, it may omit behaviors that are predictive of or relate to performance on a given criterion. If the sample of behaviors encompassed in the test is related to a criterion, but behaviors not included are also related, and the sample favors one group over others, then the test may well predict accurately for the one group but not for the others.

Intelligence has been defined as the ability to learn, to profit from experience, to adapt to novel situations, to acquire new modes of responses, and to carry on abstract thinking (3). Definitions of intelligence may be placed on a continuum from narrow to broad. For example, there is a considerable difference between Binet and Simon's (1916) definition of intelligence as "the sum total of all those processes which consist in mental adaptation," and Wechsler's (1958) " . . . the aggregate or global capacity of the individual to act purposefully, to think rationally, and to deal effectively with his environment." A test based on the latter concept would tap a greater variety of behaviors than one built on the former, provided the various domains were adequately sampled. A larger sample of functions should insure a larger pool of experiences common to a more diverse collection of people, thereby increasing the probability of predicting accurately for a greater number of groups.

It is generally accepted that current IQ tests have a middle-class bias, meaning that the behaviors tapped and the content and/or style of items, or any combination of these dimensions, intersect to a greater degree with white middle-class experience. If this is the case, then these tests should be less successful in predicting criterial performance for the "disadvantaged" generally and for black Americans in particular, unless the criterion is infested with the same bias contained in the tests. It is also known that the American public education system contains a middle-class bias; thus IQ tests or tests of general ability should predict scholastic achievement fairly accurately for both advantaged and disadvantaged pupils. However, if a learning situation can be devised that does not encompass (take into consideration) the biases inherent in the tests and in the education system, then scores from these same tests should not predict performance in that learning situation for disadvantaged youngsters. What do we find? Intelligence test scores do predict scholastic achievement with fair accuracy for both middle-class white and poor black youngsters (approximately 25 percent better than chance). However, in a situation requiring associational learning (various forms of auditory digit memory, learning the serial order of a number of familiar objects or pictures memory, learning to associate pairs of familiar objects, the free recall of names of objects presented in random order, etc.), disadvantaged youngsters perform much better than their IQ test scores would predict. In fact, they do as well as white middle-class youngsters with superior tested intelligence (Semler and Iscoe, 1963; Zigler and DeLabry, 1962; Zigler and Kanzer, 1962). One investigator has found that disadvantaged children in the tested 60 to 80 IQ range "do markedly better than middle-class children who are in this IQ range. Above about IQ 100, on the other hand, there is little or no difference between social class groups on the learning tasks" (Jensen, 1969, p. 112). At the lower IQ range, the superior performance of the disadvantaged children over the middle-class white children on the learning task suggests that the formers' intellectual ability was underestimated by the test scores. Thus arises a seeming paradox: depressed mental ability scores without a corresponding deficiency in ability to learn.

It might be tempting to attribute this lack of predictive validity to the type of learning demanded: The simplicity of learning tasks may be responsible for failure to find a relationship between learning and mental ability scores. More complex or abstract tasks might reveal a relationship; conceptual learning and abstract problem solving are held by some to be the essence of intelligence (Jensen, 1969). A recent study by Scholnick et al. (1958) did not find a relationship between IQ and performance on a concept identification task for advantaged and disadvantaged five- and eight-year-olds. This study manipulated motivation by offering tangible rewards, and insured comprehension of instructions by providing a practice problem. The findings suggest that a test performance deficit may reflect a number of things other than inability or lack of necessary intellectual power to perform the necessary operations.

Typically, IQ tests emphasize what the testee can do rather than what he can learn. An implicit assumption in this position is that he and those with whom he is compared have had equal opportunities to learn, and that inability to perform a given task on an IQ test reflects inferior intelligence. Given the nature of the disadvantaged child's life conditions, perhaps IQ tests based on ability to learn rather than on what he can do at a given time would have greater predictive validity for him.

Test Reliability and Disadvantaged Minority Groups

Anyone experienced in the use of tests is aware of the importance of the reliability of test results. If a test does not differentiate reliably, its validity is assumed to be nonexistent. Yet little attention has been given to this issue—that is, to the possible contingency of test reliability upon the group's position and status in the social structure. Clearly, on many tests lower socioeconomic status children —most oppressed minority-group members fall in this cateogory—have a smaller spread of scores than middle-class children. The reliability coefficient of a test is strongly affected by, among other things, the spread of scores in the group for which the reliability coefficient is determined. If one attempts to make differentiations within a group with a more restricted range of scores than the norm group for which the reliability was determined, he will find that the effectiveness of the test to make discriminations will be lower than indicated by the reliability coefficient. Thus, when used with a disadvantaged black sample, reliability coefficients computed for a middle-class white sample may well lead to the foregoing problem (4). Publishers should ensure that separate reliability coefficients for disadvantaged minority groups are provided in test manuals.

Examiner-Examinee Interaction

The effects of the examiner on test scores seem to be significant at both the child and adult level, especially when the examiner is white and the examinee is black (Katz, 1964; Katz and Benjamin, 1960; Katz et al., 1964; Pasamanick and Knobloch, 1955; Canady, 1936; Katz and Greenbaum, 1963). While examiner effects are not simple (examinee effects interact with task instructions and nature) caution should be observed in the white examiner-black examinee situation because the general trend of these effects appears to be adverse to test performance. This may be a more significant variable today, given the mood of black people. Some research (Katz et al., 1964; Katz, 1967) suggests that when the administrator of an intellectual test is white or when comparison with white peers is anticipated, black subjects tend to become fearful of failure. It is hypothesized that anticipation of failure elicits feelings of being victimized and covert hostility toward the tester. Because overt expression of hostility toward white authority is fraught with danger, the impulse is suppressed and elicits emotional responses disruptive to the subject's test performance. These considerations call into question the findings of research studies utilizing white examiners with black subjects. They also coincide with those of the writer and two white colleagues. Repeated testing of a sample of 13 white and 12 black preteen males revealed a significant drop in average IQ score for the black youngsters when they were tested by the white examiners (5). The implication about test validity is obvious. Failure to provide the correct response when tested by the white examiners obviously did not reflect an inability to do so. In many instances, items passed earlier with the black examiner were failed with the white examiner.

Failure Barriers Built into Assessment Technique

When the disadvantaged individual is required to solve problems with unfamiliar tools, or with tools too advanced, his primary objective typically becomes escaping an uncomfortable situation. His performance is most likely characterized by guessing, random responses, skipping, hasty and unreflective responses, and ready capitulation to test items as too difficult. These behaviors reflect his anxiety in the situation. The middle-class bias of intelligence tests contributes to the unfamiliarity factor for disadvantaged individuals. Haggard (1954) developed a less middle-class oriented test, which when administered to disadvantaged youngsters led to a significant increase in performance. He attempted to manipulate motivation and familiarity by offering a tangible reward for doing well and by having the questions presented verbally as well as in writing. If such procedures were followed, the testing of disadvantaged minority-group children would yield more accurate estimates of their mental abilities.

Another approach to familiarity, relevance, and meaningfulness lies in devising new tests, taking into consideration style, content, behaviors sampled, and so forth. Attempts to develop culture-free–culture-fair tests have not been successful. Perhaps another approach lies in the development of a culture-specific IQ test for black youngsters. Such a test would enable us to make the same kind of predictions successfully made for white children. These predictions would relate primarily to the child's potential and to the type of training that would facilitate his development. Which children can be expected to progress rapidly with certain kinds of learning; which at normal rates? Which children can profit best from which kinds of remedial work? Which need specially tailored programs? In order to understand fully and to plan for each child's maximum development we need information about black children as individuals. They do not constitute a homogeneous group; individual difference in ability characterizes the disadvantaged and the poor black child just as it does children from every culture. Educational programs should not ignore the differences in these children's learning rates. True, the best use of such a test would be programming to fit the student's needs. But employing it to establish ability tracks would doubtlessly result in less injury than current practices of establishing tracks on the basis of tests of general ability that result in misclassification and misuse of talent (6).

The Single Determinant Concept

Misinterpretation of test results occurs when the test content is seen as reflecting some absolute factor or process regardless of the condition of measurement or of the group being observed. This view results in the error of assuming that the obtained score reflects only intellectual ability. Generally, test-taking motivation in a middle-class group allows scores to reflect actual differences in intellectual ability. Because middle-class students "have generally internalized their need to excel at such tasks, a high score within itself is a reward" (Pettigrew, 1964, p. 117). But studies suggest that lower-class students often require a tangible, external reward for motivation (Pettigrew, 1964; Scholnick et al., 1968). High-level motivation varies directly with high task relevance, interest, and meaningfulness.

In this instance, where test success may not be reinforcing, test performance may reflect motivation as well as the trait supposedly measured. Other factors which may affect test scores also, but which may have little relation to the criteria the test predicts, include speed (7), comprehension of instructions, test-taking skills, and anxiety. Thus, in interpreting test results of disadvantaged minority-group children, considerable caution and knowledge of social and cultural background factors are necessary, on the part of the examiner, in assessing the probable effects of these factors on test results.

Conclusions

At first blush, this analysis of the use of tests with disadvantaged minority groups may appear gloomy and pessimistic, and lead to strong doubts about their value with these populations. If the analysis appears grave, it is because the situation analyzed is grave. In this instance, strong skepticism is a healthy posture. For too long, tests have been used in a psychologically damaging way with disadvantaged, and especially poor black people. They have been used to exclude rather than include; they have been used to paint a picture of an inferior being, biologically or socially, or both. It matters little whether these were consciously intended effects.

Many black people believe that IQ testing should be eliminated. While the writer shares much of the feeling inherent in it, he does not advocate this extreme course of action. However, he agrees that the user of tests should be fully aware of their shortcomings when administered to minority-group members, and of the kinds of inferences that can be legitimately drawn from test results. Numerically identical scores may have different meanings for persons with different life experiences. If a decision affecting the person's life, or explanations having implications for action, expectations, attitudes are to be made, it is ethically and morally incumbent upon the user of the results to ponder what lies behind the scores.

In the educational setting, ideally, test scores would be used to devise programs that take into consideration the individual's strengths and weaknesses. Such use conceptualizes the test as an integral part of the instructional program, where test results can help to assess the degree to which instructional objectives are being approximated.

Special emphasis should be given to selection or development of tests that maximize differentiations related to a criterion and that minimize irrelevant discriminations. For example, what discriminations required by the SB or WISC (WAIS) predict criterial performance requiring conceptual learning and abstract problem solving? The global IQ does not provide this information. A "dimension of intellect" approach (recommended by Dreger and Miller, 1960) which would allow patterns of dimensions (e.g., spatial, verbal, numerical reasoning, etc.) to be related to the criterion, could reduce items that contribute irrelevant discriminations and maximize those making criterial differentiations.

Admittedly, the fact that a test differentiates between advantaged and disadvantaged groups does not make it invalid. This is, in fact, the case where such tests predict culturally unfair but important criteria, notably academic achievement in our racist educational system. A test that predicts attainments in this system must reflect the system's social inequities. An unbiased test would not predict successfully unless the biases in the system were eliminated. The problem is that the test users interpret the predictive validity (agreement between test scores and scholastic achievement) to mean that the test results and school achievement converge to demonstrate the inability of the disadvantaged minority-group child to learn.

The test user might claim that he has to utilize the test according to limitations built into it, that the concern about bias in criteria extends beyond testing, that it becomes a societal problem, one of social policy and amelioration. Nevertheless, this does not free him from moral concern about and consideration of the limitations of IQ tests with oppressed minority-group members. The test results he elicits, and their interpretation, may result in actions, opinions and beliefs having far-reaching consequences for disadvantaged minority-group members as well as for the society as a whole. To ignore the kinds of issues discussed in this paper results in the misuse of tests with members of oppressed minority groups, and such misuse constitutes a serious violation of professional ethics, as well as an affront to human dignity.

Summary

This paper has focused on selected shortcomings of assessment techniques when applied to minority-group members in general and to black Americans in particular. Even though the primary emphasis is placed on tests of mental ability, much of the analysis and conclusions is relevant to other assessment techniques: projective techniques, value, attitude, and interest scales, and the like.

The writer questions a great deal of the research regarding the performance of oppressed minority-group members on tests of general ability. He considers factors that contribute to the invalidity of test scores of this segment of the American population. These factors, conceptualized as potential contributors to shortcomings of assessment techniques, are:

1. nature of the concept of intelligence
2. test reliability and nature of group on which it is established
3. examiner–examinee interactions
4. failure barriers built into assessment techniques
5. the single determinant concept

Suggestions for improvements in and more appropriate use of these devices with members of oppressed minority groups are offered.

Notes

1. Intellectual status is used to refer to intellectual ability, intellectual development, and intellectual functioning.
2. The percentage of black retardates (below IQ 75) at SES levels 1, 2, 3, 4, and 5 was 3.1, 14.5, 22.8, and 42.9, respectively; the percentage of white retardates in these same SES categories was 0.5, 0.8, 2.1, 3.1, and 7.8, respectively.
3. "The ability of the organism to adjust itself adequately to new situations" (Stern, 1914).

   "The sum total of all those thought processes which consist in mental adaptation and self criticism as characterizing intelligence in action" (Stanford Binet Intelligence Scale Manual, 3rd revision, 1960).

   "The property of so recombining our behavior patterns as to act better in novel situations" (Wells, 1917).

   "The power of good responses from the point of view of truth or fact" (Thorndike, 1921).

   "The ability to undertake activities that are characterized by (1) difficulty, (2) complexity, (3) abstruseness, (4) economy, (5) adaptiveness to a goal, (6) social value, and (7) the emergence of originals, and to maintain such activities under conditions that demand a concentration of energy and a resistance to emotional forces" (Stoddard, 1943).

   "The degree of availability of one's experiences for the solution of his present problems and the anticipation of future ones" (Goddard, 1945).

   "The aggregate or global capacity of the individual to act purposefully, to think rationally, and to deal effectively with his environment" (Wechsler, 1958).
4. See A. Anastasi, *Differential psychology*, 3rd ed. (New York; Macmillan, 1958).
5. Unpublished paper, 1966.
6. The writer and a colleague are in the beginning stage of formulating a proposal for developing such a test, covering the age range $3\frac{1}{2}$ through 7 years in half-year intervals.
7. Anastasi, *op. cit.*, comments on the differential value placed on speed by black and white Americans.

References

Beck, J. M., and Saxe, R. W. (Eds.) *Teaching the culturally disadvantaged pupil.* Springfield, Ill.: Charles C. Thomas, 1965.

Billingsley, A. *Black families in white America.* Englewood Cliffs, N.J.: Prentice-Hall, 1968.

Binet, S., and Simon, T. *The development of intelligence in children.* Trans. E. S. Kite. Vineland, N.J.: Training School, 1916.

Canady, H. G. The effect of "rapport" on the IQ: A new approach to the problem of racial psychology. *Journal of Negro Education,* 1936, 5, 209-219.

Clark, K. *Dark ghetto.* New York: Harper & Row, 1965.

Dreger, R. M., and Miller, K. S. Comparative psychological studies of Negroes and whites in the United States, 1959-65. *Psychological Bulletin* (Monograph Supplement), 1968, 70, 1-58.

Deutsch, M. The role of social class in language development and cognition. *American Journal of Orthopsychiatry,* 1965, 35, 78-88.

Findlay, D. C., and McGuire, C. Social status and abstract behavior. *Journal of Abnormal and Social Psychology,* 1957, 54, 135-137.

Garrett, H. E. The equalitarian dogma. *Mankind Quarterly,* 1961, 1, 253-257.

Haggard, E. Social status and intelligence: An experimental study of certain cultural determinants of measured intelligence. *Genetic Psychology Monograph,* 1954, 49, 141-186.

Heber, R., Dever, R., and Conry, J. The influence of environmental and genetic variables on intellectual development. In H. J. Prehm, L. A. Hamerlynck, and J. E. Crosson (Eds.), *Behavioral research in mental retardation.* Eugene, Ore.: University of Oregon Press, 1968, pp. 1-23.

Jensen, A. How much can we boost IQ and scholastic achievement? *Harvard Educational Review,* 1969, 39, 1-198.

Kanner, L. *Child psychology.* 3rd ed. Springfield, Ill.: Charles C. Thomas, 1966.

Katz, I. Review of evidence relating to effects of desegregation on the intellectual performance of Negroes. *American Psychologist,* 1964, 19, 381-399.

Katz, I. Negro performance in the desegregated school. In M. Deutsch et al. (Eds.), *Social class, race and psychological development.* New York: Holt, Rinehart & Winston, 1968, pp. 254-289.

Katz, I., Epps, E. G., and Benjamin, L. Effects of white authoritarianism in biracial work group. *Journal of Abnormal and Social Psychology,* 1960, 61, 448-456.

Katz, I., and Greenbaum, C. Effects of anxiety, threat, and racial environment on task performance of Negro college students. *Journal of Abnormal and Social Psychology,* 1963, 66, 562-567.

Klineberg, O. Negro-white differences in intelligence test performance: A new look at an old problem. *American Psychologist,* 1963, 18, 198-203.

Leach, J. C. A study of intellectual and personality factors of Negro and white children with equal educational opportunities in a Western community in the United States. Unpublished master's thesis, Florida State University, 1963.

McGraw, M. A. A comparative study of group of southern white and Negro infants. *Genetic Psychology Monographs,* 1931, 10, 1-105.

McGurk, F. C. J. *Comparison of the performance of Negro and white high school seniors on cultural test questions.* Washington, D.C.: Catholic University of America Press, 1951.

Pasamanick, B., and Knobloch, H. Early language behavior in Negro children and the testing of intelligence. *Journal of Abnormal and Social Psychology,* 1955, 50, 401-440.

Pettigrew, T. F. *A profile of the Negro American.* New York: Van Nostrand Reinhold, 1964.

Scholnick, E. K., Osler, S. F., and Katzenellenboger, R. Discrimination learning and concept identification in disadvantaged and middle-class children. *Child Development,* March 1968, 39, 15-25.

Semler, I. J., and Iscoe, I. Comparative and developmental study of learning abilities of Negro and white children under four conditions. *Journal of Educational Psychology,* 1963, 54, 38-44.

Shuey, A. *The testing of Negro intelligence.* Lynchburg, Va.: Bell, 1958.

Shuey, A. *The testing of Negro intelligence.* New York: Social Science Press, 1966.

Siller, J. Socioeconomic status and conceptual thinking. *Journal of Abnormal and Social Psychology,* 1957, 55, 356-371.

Tanser, H. A. *The settlement of Negroes in Kent County, Ontario, and a study of the mental capacity of their descendants*. Chatham, Ontario: Shepherd, 1939.

U.S. News & World Report. Mental tests for 10 million Americans—What they show. October 17, 1966, pp. 78–80.

Wechsler, D. *The measurement and appraisal of adult intelligence*. 4th ed. Baltimore: Williams & Wilkins, 1958.

Zigler, E., and DeLarby, J. Concept switching in middle-class, lower-class and retarded children. *Journal of Abnormal and Social Psychology*, 1962, **65**, 267–273.

Zigler, E., and Kanzer, P. The effectiveness of two classes of verbal reinforcers on the performance of middle- and lower-class children. *Journal of Personality*, 1962, **30**, 157–163.

ROBERT L. WILLIAMS

Abuses and Misuses in Testing Black Children

If a tree is to be judged by its fruit, if the intelligence of a race
bears any relation to its accomplishments, it seems difficult to draw
any conclusion other than that the Black and Brown races are inferior
to the white race. . . . R. S. Ellis (1928, p. 284)

I. Current Status of the Problem

Before considering the major issues in the dispute over testing black children, it is important to take a quick glance at the current status of the problem involving abuse and misuse in testing black children.

The dispute over the intellectual inferiority of black people and the corresponding problem of measuring black intelligence has created more controversy than perhaps any other single issue in the field of psychology. Some of the central disputants have compromised on occasion, but essentially there has been produced a sharp cleavage of opinion about the intelligence of black people, and intelligence testing in general. In a word, opinion is split over whether or not lower scores by blacks on the traditional ability tests are attributed primarily to genetic heritage or biased intelligence tests. It is seriously questioned today whether traditional ability tests may serve as valid measures of black intelligence.

In preparing this response, the writer carefully examined a vast array of publications dealing with one phase or another of the continuing controversy over abuses and misuses in testing black children. The single, most salient conclusion is that traditional ability tests do systematically and consistently lead to assigning of improper and false labels on black children, and consequently to dehumanization and black intellectual genocide. This conclusion is neither new nor is it surprising. The information has been known for many years. It was not until the Association of Black Psychologists generated some heat in this area by calling a moratorium on the testing of black people, however, that the *real* issues began to surface.

First of all, the meaning of intelligence is rather diverse and although considerable attention and effort have been given this concept, it is still ill-used and poorly understood. The ambiguity and senselessness of the research on the nature of the concept of intelligence is exceeded only by the research on ESP. Definitions of intelligence are so diverse that it would be impractical to list all of

From *The Counseling Psychologist*, 1971, **2** (1), 62–73. Reprinted by permission of the author and the publisher.

them here. A few examples are given as representative:

(a) Intelligence is what the intelligence tests measure.
(b) Intelligence is defined by a consensus among psychologists. It is repertoire of intellec-
    tual skills and knowledge available to a person at any one period of time. (Humphreys,
    1969)
(c) Intelligence is the summation of the learning experiences of the individual. (Wesman,
    1968)
(d) Intelligence is the aggregate or global capacity of the individual to act purposely, to
    think rationally, and to deal effectively with his environment. (Wechsler, 1944)

It is clear from the preceding definitions that there is not only lacking a
consensus among psychologists regarding the meaning of intelligence, but there
is no absolute definition as well. Such confusion and ambiguity make for considerable difficulty in precise and accurate measurement.

Secondly, the most frequently accepted definition is that intelligence is based
on the solution of brief problems of various kinds and on the quality of one's
responses to a wide range of questions. The final, standardized test score, which
is called the *intelligence quotient*, or IQ, is usually computed so that it is given a
scale score for which the average of the reference population is about 100.
Jensen (1969) and Humphreys (1969) claim that, in the general population,
blacks are about 15 IQ points, or one standard deviation, below whites. Psychologists and educators incorrectly use IQ and intelligence interchangeably. The
intelligence quotient is a symbol which refers to a set of scores earned on a test,
nothing more. An IQ per se cannot be inherited. A review of the research on
comparing intellectual differences between blacks and whites shows the results
to be based almost exclusively on differences in test scores, or IQ. Since the tests
are biased in favor of middle-class whites, all previous research comparing the
intellectual abilities of blacks and whites should be rejected completely.

Bennett (1970), in responding to the Association of Black Psychologists' call
for a moratorium on the repeated abuses and misuses of psychological tests and
to Williams (1970a), dealt with such factors as test anxiety, amount of formal
education, and uniform testing procedures. Clemans (1970) and Sommer (1970)
give what appear to be the most frequent reactions to charges of abuse of ability
tests, i.e., it is the user of the test who labels the child. In this regard, Newland
(1970) joins in unison:

*Ability tests do not label any children or adults. The adults who use them do
that on the basis of scores earned on tests. Human beings do the labeling as
well as selecting of the tests used to obtain scores in terms of which any such
labeling is done. (p. 5)*

Similarly, Munday (1970) sees the criticism against tests as misdirected. Instead of criticizing the tests, Munday identifies counselors, teachers, advisors,
and admissions officers as perpetrators of the improper uses of test results. From
a black perspective, these critics are not dealing with the real issue.

Messick and Anderson (1970) perhaps came closer to the real issues than any
of the critics when they made a clear distinction between the scientific and
ethical considerations involved in testing black children. Many important issues
however have been omitted from discussions in the literature. This paper will

endeavor to bring to the surface from a black perspective some of the previously "overlooked" issues in ability testing, involving scientific, political, educational, legal, and economic considerations.

II. Scientific Considerations

Messick and Anderson (1970) point out that the same test may measure "different attributes or processes in minority/poverty groups than it measures in white, middle-class samples or for the same processes to be captured with a different degree of fidelity" (p. 82).

Translated, if this is true, then that test is invalid and should not be used in testing black children. In fact, not only is the validity of ability tests being called into question, but other such psychometric considerations of tests as reliability, objectivity, and standardization.

A. *Validity.* The validity of a test pertains to the extent to which it measures what it is intended to measure (Anastasi, 1968). More specifically, construct validity refers to the extent to which the test is measuring a theoretical construct such as intelligence. Does the traditional ability test measure the intelligence of black children? Current ability tests do not and cannot measure a black child's capacity "to deal effectively with his environment." The tests were never intended to do so. It is obvious enough that a black child engages in many intelligent behaviors which are not validated in white, middle-class society. For example, a black child might respond with, "My mother told me to hit 'em back if anybody hits me," to one of the standard IQ test questions. That answer actually represents "a summation of the learning experiences" for that particular black child in his black culture. The response also represents an *effective* way of dealing with *his* environment. It would be less than intelligent for the child to give responses which are opposite to or different from his environmental training or to the dictates of his cultural norms. One child is taught not to hit back; another is taught to hit back. It is a value judgment as to which is more intelligent teaching. Most tests take the philosophic frame of reference that white, middle-class standards are the correct ones.

B. *Reliability and objectivity.* The reliability of a test refers to the extent to which a person earns the same score or rank each time he is measured (Anastasi, 1968). One of the most common causes of unreliability of a test is the inclusion of items which are scored on the basis of subjective judgment, or, in this context, a white, middle-class norm. For example, persons from different cultural backgrounds will respond differently to the question, "What is the thing to do if you find a purse with ten dollars in it?" One child might respond with, "Try to find the owner"; another might respond with, "Keep it." Such items lack objectivity in scoring. They do not take cultural differences into account. Black children from certain socioeconomic levels would be penalized, and therefore the reliability of such tests would be low for measuring the intelligence of black children.

C. *Standardization.* A test must be representative of the group for whom it was designed (Anastasi, 1968). Two of the major ability tests (the Stanford-Binet and the Wechsler Intelligence Scale for Children) excluded blacks from the representative sample. If the purpose of standardizing a test is to make it useful for certain reference groups, then the WISC and Stanford-Binet are invalid for use with blacks.

III. Political Considerations

In addition to the scientific issues of testing, traditional psychologists have created a number of polemics which involve political issues. The literature is fraught with examples. For instances, take the case of Jensen (1969), who asked the question, "How much can we boost IQ and scholastic achievement?" For the next 123 pages, he proceeded to answer his own political question. The Jensen report, clearly a political document, was well known to the Nixon Administration when the budgets for compensatory education programs were being sharply reduced. Boosting IQ is not a real issue; it clearly is a straw man. Changes in test scores should not serve as the primary criteria by which educational programs are evaluated. If the goal and objective of Head Start, Project Follow Through, and other compensatory educational programs is that of "boosting IQ," then the goal is misput, inappropriate, and irrelevant.

I submit to Jensen and to others several methods for boosting IQs of black children:

(a) Teach them the answers to the ability tests; or
(b) Develop a black IQ test containing items drawn exclusively from the black world; or
(c) Standardize black responses to white-oriented tests as follows: What is the thing to do if you find a purse with ten dollars in it?" Correct answers: "Try to find the owner"; "Keep the money, return the purse."

A concern with producing increases in test scores is similar to that of a physician whose main concern is treating the *casualties* rather than the *causes*. We refer to this approach as "victim analysis." System-produced educational problems cannot effectively be changed by focusing exclusively on the victims. The system that produced the damage must be closely examined and modified.

A. Deficit vs. difference model. Bennett (1970) makes the point that traditional ability tests merely reveal the "detrimental consequences of substandard opportunity." He believes that it would be better to remedy the "cultural deficit" than to discredit the test measures. Similarly, Wilkoff (1970) argues that culture of blacks needs to be improved and enriched. For too long psychologists and educators have believed in the mythology that low scores on a test are in fact a weakness or a deficit in the mental ability of the black individual. It has not been made clear that the individual may possess abilities not measured by a particular test. The deficiency may well be in the weakness of the test to measure black children; in the tester but not in the testee. Black Americans do not have an inferior culture; it is, indeed, different, but it remains a highly enriched culture.

A review of the literature on the major issues involved in testing black children clearly reveals two general conceptual models. The first group is classified under the general heading of a "deficit" model, whereas the second group is classified under the heading of a "difference" model.

The deficit model assumes that black people are deficient when compared to whites in some measurable trait called intelligence, and that this deficiency is due to genetic or cultural factors or both. To support this notion, such terms as "heritability of IQ," "cultural deprivation," and "the disadvantaged" have been invented to perpetuate the myth. Proponents of this school of thought assume that the intellectual and educational deficits experienced by the so-called culturally deprived are clearly revealed by such psychological tests as the Stanford-Binet, Wechsler, Scholastic Aptitude Test, Stanford Achievement, Iowa Basic Skills, Graduate Record Examination and Miller Analogies tests. These tests are devised to measure one's capacity to learn, or, more specifically, what one has learned. The items are supposedly selected on the basis that individuals of the same age have had the same opportunity to become familiar with the content of the items. This assumption is not true. Two five-year-olds, one black and one white, from different cultural backgrounds, will answer quite differently questions such as "What is the thing to do if another child hits you?" or "What is the thing to do if you find a purse with ten dollars in it?" The deficit model assumes a set of acceptable, standard responses. If the black child gives a response that is not validated as acceptable by the norm, he is declared as deficient in his "ability to comprehend and to size up certain social situations," whereas the white child is considered adequate in his ability to make appropriate judgments.

If the black child scores lower on ability tests than the white child, the difference does not mean that the black child is actually inferior in intelligence; all it means is that the black child performed differently on the test from the white. Test inferiority is not to be equated with actual inferiority. In this connection, Jensen (1968) found that many disadvantaged children with IQs between 60 and 80 performed better on learning tasks than upper middle-class children having IQs in the same range. These findings suggest that the tests were a much better predictor of ability and capacity of middle-class children since these children performed at the "expected" level. The results suggest further that the tests underpredicted the performance of the disadvantaged children since these children performed at a higher than expected level.

The deficit model therefore engages in faulty reasoning: If a child scores low on a test, the assumption is that he lacks the capacity to compete with those children who scored at a higher level. Present ability tests do not measure one's capacity to do work. At best they measure a level of learning in certain areas. From these "measurements" inferences are made regarding his capacity to learn further. It is this kind of reasoning that is faulty.

Briefly stated, the cultural difference model asserts that the differences noted by psychologists in intelligence testing, family and social organizations, and the studies of the black community are not the result of pathology, faulty learning, or genetic inferiority. These differences are manifestations of a viable and well-delineated culture of the black American. The difference model also acknowledges that blacks and whites come from different cultural backgrounds which emphasize different learning experiences necessary for survival. To say that the black American is different from the white American is not to say that he is inferior, deficient, or deprived. One can be unique and different without being inferior. The model, therefore, makes a clear distinction between *equality* and *sameness*. Two pieces of fruit, e.g., an apple and an orange, may be equal in weight, in quality of goodness and marketability, but they are not the same. An apple cannot become an orange, and vice versa. Each must express its respective characteristics of "appleness" and "orangeness," yet both are fruit. Whereas the deficit model espouses a "Get like me" response, the difference model endeavors to increase the number of options as to what constitutes acceptable and non-acceptable responses. Instead of being confined by an egalitarian doctrine that confuses equality with sameness, the cultural difference model recognizes that this society is pluralistic in nature, where cultural differences abound.

B. *Language deficiency vs. language deficit.* Because of the vast cultural differences in black and white society, significant language differences are present. Differences in language and dialect may produce differences in cognitive learning styles, but a difference is not a deficiency. Linguists do not limit themselves to defining dialect as the way words are pronounced. "Dialect refers to the linguistic structure of a people. The dialect is a fully developed linguistic system" (Baratz and Baratz, 1969). Instead of calling black language wrong, improper, or deficient in nature, one must realize that the black child is speaking a well-developed language commonly referred to as nonstandard English. Intelligence is frequently based quite heavily on language factors. It is a common observation that black and white children do not speak alike. The differences in linguistic systems favor white children since standard English is the *lingua franca* of the tests and the public schools.

Take, for example, the Scholastic Aptitude Test (SAT) which contains a verbal and a numerical factor. The students who do not show high verbal or numerical ability score low on the SAT and are typically excluded from entering college. If this fact is true, then blacks have been routinely excluded from college due to the different dialect and language systems rather than weakness in verbal ability. It does not mean that black people do not have the intellectual ability to compete in college. For example, blacks typically are not inferior in verbal ability. The average black adolescent will know how to "play the dozens," and play them well. He will know from memory, "The Signifying Monkey," "Shine," "Mr. Boon," and many other indicators of verbal ability, but these factors do not get measured in the typical classroom. In fact, many black children can state bits of poetry and prose in iambic pentameter. A case in point is revealed in the following revision of a Mother Goose rhyme made by a black eight-year-old:

"Baa baa, Black Sheep, Have you any wool?"
"Yes sir, yes sir, two bags full;

One for the black man; one for the Jew.
Sorry, Mr. Charlie, but none for you."

C. The Commission on Tests report. A special Commission on Tests appointed by the College Entrance Examination Board indicated that the Board examinations taken by about 2,000,000 high-school students a year failed to recognize and assess a wide variety of talents, skills, and mental attributes (Report of the Commission on Tests, 1970). Over the years, many students, particularly black ones, have been grossly penalized. Basically, the Commission on Tests found the SAT, which measures fluency in English and ability to deal with mathematical and spatial concepts, to be discriminatory against certain minority groups. Although high verbal and numerical abilities are generally those required in traditional academic liberal arts and scientific education, the Commission found these indicators to be too narrow for application to all who might benefit from college. The Commission recommended that the tests gradually be replaced by a flexible assortment of other tests, measuring not only verbal and mathematical ability but many other dimensions of excellence. These dimensions included musical and artistic talents; sensitivity and commitment to social responsibility; political and social leadership; athletic, political, and mechanical skills; styles of analysis and synthesis; ability to express oneself through artistic, oral, nonverbal, or graphic means; ability to organize and manage information; ability to adapt to new situations; characteristics of temperament; and so on.

In a recent memo directed to school counselors, the Washington University Director of Admissions had these points to make regarding changes in admission procedures:

We believe that this university has a great deal to offer to a wide variety of students; the scholar and the singer, the debater and dancer, the athlete, the artist and the actor, the editor and the engineer. Accordingly, we urge you to recommend capable, interesting students, even if there is some slight "lopsidedness" in their records. Where there is need for compensating strength for lower SAT scores, for instance, we will trust you to point this out to us. It is impossible to overemphasize how highly we regard your evaluation as we search for an ever-widening array of talents and abilities.

The political impact of reports issued under the rubric of education is enormous. Many of these reports are used as political and scientific clout against the black cause. The Moynihan report on black families reportedly led to deemphasis by the Nixon Administration on welfare programs. Moynihan's "benign neglect" memo hurt the cause of black people. "The time may have come when the issue of race could benefit from a period of 'benign neglect.' The subject has been too much talked about. The forum has been too much taken over to hysterics, paranoids, and boodlers on all sides" (Moynihan, 1970).

The Jensen report (1969) led directly or indirectly to a number of changes in the President's program regarding Head Start Programs, Project Follow Through, and other compensatory educational programs. These and other reports must be considered political in nature. A few of the reports lead to positive change for black people while others are quite detrimental.

IV. Educational Considerations

In addition to the foregoing comments regarding education, it is clear from this discussion that ability and certain achievement tests play a major role in current educational procedures and consequently in determining what doors in life will be opened or closed to a black child. Tests are used to determine admission, grouping, selection, assignment to special classes and educational tracks. If the tests are unfair (biased), then it is clear that they place (misplace), label (mislabel) a certain portion of the population in general and the black population in particular. Throughout the country, a disproportionately large number of black children are being misplaced in special education classes. Many states legally define the educable mentally retarded as those children obtaining an IQ below 80.

A. The Association of Black Psychologists' statement on testing abuse. At its annual meeting in 1969, the Association of Black Psychologists called for an immediate moratorium on the administration of ability tests to black children. The Association charged that these tests:

1. Label black children as uneducable;
2. Place black children in special classes;
3. Potentiate inferior education;
4. Assign black children to lower education tracks than whites;
5. Deny black children higher educational opportunities;
6. Destroy positive intellectual growth and development of black children.

In other words, black psychologists translated the whole abuse of testing issue into one of intellectual genocide of black children. Tests do not permit the masses of black children to develop their full intellectual potential. The tests are used to sort and consequently to misplace black children in Special Education classes.

B. Composition of Special Education classes in St. Louis and San Francisco. In St. Louis, during the academic year 1968-1969, blacks comprised approximately 63.6 percent of the school population, whereas whites comprised 36.4 percent. Of 4,020 children in Special Education, 2,975 (76 percent) were black, only 1,045 (24 percent) were white. Thus, black children were being placed in classes for the educable mentally retarded about three times as frequently as their white counterparts. Again, children are placed in Special Education classes primarily on the basis of scores earned on biased intelligence tests.

In San Francisco, a group of black psychologists recently presented a document on testing abuses to the San Francisco Unified School District School Board. The document called for an immediate moratorium on ability testing of black children until better and more appropriate assessment techniques are made available. The document pointed out the following: that although black children comprise only 27.8 percent of the total student population in the San Francisco Unified Schools, they comprise 47.4 percent of all students in educationally handicapped classes, and 53.3 percent of all students in the educable mentally handicapped classes. The black psychologists pointed out that the consultants to the psychologists and psychometricians in the San Francisco Unified School District are not familiar enough with the black experience to serve as competent evaluators of black children. The document also pointed out that, of the psychologists and psychometrists who administered and interpreted the psychological tests, no black personnel were involved. The Association of Black Psychologists has recently reported that the San Francisco School District has honored the moratorium on testing, and that no psychological tests are now being administered to black children for placement in special classes.

It is reported that an IBM computer was incorrectly programmed, sending the "slow" students into the high track and the "bright" ones into the low track. About one year later, when the error was discovered, "slow" pupils were behaving as though they were "bright" and the "bright" pupils were behaving as if they were dull.

Thus, the black mother who gratefully and naively sends her children to school daily does not suspect the dangers lurking in the shadows of the educational institution. No one has told her that her little child probably will be required to take a psychological examination. She does not know that this exam will yield a so-called IQ label which will probably follow her child for the rest of his school life. The mother does not understand that the IQ will lead to the placement (or misplacement) of her child in a Special Education class or an educational tracking system. The mother does not know that these tests are violating her child's constitutional and civil rights and that she can sue the perpetrators for their transgressions.

V. Legal Considerations on Testing

It is clear that the continued administration of traditional ability tests to black children is a violation of the child's civil and constitutional rights under the provisions of the Fourteenth Amendment for equal protection under the law.

The following four court cases will be discussed to show where charges have been made of actual abuse of tests:

(a) Leary (1970) reports the case of *Diana et al.* v. *California State Board of Education*, which led to a decision in favor of a Mexican-American child whose intelligence had been woefully underestimated by the Binet.

(b) The Skelly Wright decision in the case of *Hobson* v. *Hansen* in Washington, D.C., set an early precedent. In that decision, the judge ordered the track system abolished since unfair ability tests were used in sorting the children into tracks.

(c) In Boston, the case of *Stewart et al.* v. *Phillips et al.* charges that children are being placed in special classes irrationally and unfairly.

(d) The case of *Armstead et al.* v. *Starkeville, Mississippi, Municipal Separate School District et al.* involved the case of the Graduate Record Exam (GRE) for employment and retention of black and white teachers.

The increasing number of criticisms in the literature and the possible large number of impending court cases regarding the abuse and misuse of testing black children strongly suggest that the cries of the black community be heard as so eloquently stated by Halpern (1970-1971).

Article XIV, Section 1 of the Constitution of the United States reads as follows:

All persons born or naturalized in the United States, and subject to the juris-diction thereof are citizens of the United States and of the state wherein they reside. No state shall make or enforce any law which shall abridge the privi-leges or immunities of citizens in the United States; nor shall any state deprive any person of life, liberty, or property, without the due process of law; nor deny to any person within its jurisdiction the equal protection of the laws.

A. Diana et al. v. California State Board of Education. One case is reported by Leary (1970) of an eight year-old Mexican-American girl who earned an IQ of 30 on the Stanford-Binet intelligence test, clearly placing her in the mentally defec-tive range of functioning. Diana's mother had the test readministered by a school psychologist, also of Mexican-American descent, who translated the test into Spanish. Diana's IQ increased 49 points. In fact, of nine Mexican-American chil-dren retested in Spanish, all but one increased to above the cutoff score of 79 used by the California school district to place children in the category of the educable mentally retarded or the educationally handicapped.

Another case of misjudging is reported by Witty and Jenkins (1935) of a black child with superior intelligence who had an IQ of 200. She was rated by her teacher as lower in intelligence than a child whose IQ turned out to be 100. When a misjudgment does occur, the result will be to place the child into a curriculum paced to his measured abilities, where he is likely to progress only at the speed provided by the teacher. In fact, many black children probably have higher native intelligence than their teachers. These teachers frequently see the gifted black students as "problem children," "hyperactive," "disruptive," when, in fact, the children are simply bored in the classroom. They are not being challenged by teachers who have only average to slightly above average intelli-gence.

B. Hobson v. Hansen. In a rather momentous decision in the United States District Court for the District of Columbia, United States Circuit Judge J. Skelly Wright issued a 182-page document in the case of *Hobson v. Hansen* in regard to abolishing the track system in the D.C. schools. Judge Wright stated: "It is further ordered, adjudged, and decreed that the defendants be, and they are hereby, permanently enjoined from operating the track system in the District of Columbia public schools." The D.C. educational track system was implemented in the high schools in 1956, and extended downward to the junior high and elementary schools in 1959. The track system proved to be nothing more than another way of resegregating blacks and whites within the individual school system. As the evidence in the case became clear, grouping children on the basis of test scores was clearly a denial of equal educational opportunity to the poor and the majority of blacks attending school in the nation's capital. The findings clearly showed that black children dominated the lower tracks. White and the more affluent students were found to be in the upper tracks. Thus, the judge decided that when a student is placed in a lower track, his future is being decided for him, i.e., the kind of job he gets is greatly shaped by the quality of education he receives.

The judge found the most important single aspect of the track system to be the process by which the school system grouped children in different tracks. The sorting process is the keystone of the entire track system. Children were placed in tracks based on such ability tests as the Binet and WISC. Thus, as the judge decided, when standard ability tests are given to low-income black children or disadvantaged children, they are less precise and less accurate, so it is virtually impossible to tell whether the test score reflects lack of ability or lack of opportunity.

The judge, looking very closely into side issues of psychological testing and placement of track systems, pointed out the following damages inherent in the system:

> *By consigning students to specifically designed curricula, the track system makes highly visible the student's status within the school structure. To the unlearned, tracks can become pejorative labels, symptomatic of which is the recent abandonment of the suggestive "Basic" for the more euphemistic "Special Academic" as the nomenclature of the lowest track. A system that presumes to tell a student what his ability is and what he can successfully learn incurs an obligation to take account of the psychological damage that can come from such an encounter between the student and the school, and to be certain that it is in a position to decide whether the student's deficiencies are true, or only apparent. The District of Columbia school system has not shown that it is in such a position. (*Hobson v. Hansen, p. 140)

The judge interpreted the testing and track system as a way of forcing the self-fulfilling prophecy, i.e., teachers acting under false assumptions because of low test scores will treat the black student in such a way as to make him conform to their low expectations. In concluding, the judge decided as follows:

> *As to the remedy with respect to the track system, the track system simply must be abolished . . . even in concept the track system is undemocratic and discriminatory. Its creator admits it is designed to prepare some children for white collar and other children for blue collar jobs . . . the danger of children completing their education wearing the wrong collar is far too great for this democracy. (*Hobson v. Hansen, p. 177)

Many cities have abolished the track system as a direct result of the decision rendered in the *Hobson* v. *Hansen* case. However, they have implemented other systems which are not called track systems but which are just as lethal; for example, in one city the tracking system has been officially abolished, but three levels have been substituted in its place: (A) Academic Curriculum, (B) Standard

Curriculum, (C) General Curriculum. It is clear from the inequality of education provided that educational tracking is one of the major aspects of the new system. In any event, psychological tests are used to determine who goes into the academic, standard, or general curriculum, each of which leads to different educational careers or futures. A rose is a rose by any other name.

C. Stewart et al. v. *Phillips and Massachusetts Board of Education.* In the United States District Court for the District of Massachusetts, another case has recently been cited, *Stewart et al.* v. *Phillips and the Massachusetts Board of Education.* This action was brought by the public-school students and their parents for damages against officials of the Boston school system and the Board of Education of the Commonwealth of Massachusetts. The action challenges the arbitrary, irrational, and discriminatory manner in which students in the Boston public schools are denied the right to an education by being classified as mentally retarded and placed in so-called special classes. The State of Massachusetts uses the 79 cutoff IQ on ability tests as a basis for placing children in Special Education classes. The major claim in this suit is that a numerical IQ of less than 80 is an inadequate basis for placing children in the Special Education classes, and that since the tests are unfair and biased against black children, the state deprives the children of the right to equal protection of the laws in violation of the Fourteenth Amendment. The seven plaintiffs on behalf of their children are suing for $20,000 each in compensatory and punitive damages. They are asking that a permanent injunction be issued declaring and enjoining that no child be placed or retained in a special class in the city of Boston unless and until the following procedures are met:

1. That a special, nine-member Commission on Individual Educational Needs be established;
2. That no child be placed in a Special Education class unless a fair test has been administered by a competent psychologist, the parents are given notice, and the placement in the special class is naturally related to the child's educational needs;
3. That the Commission specify a battery of psychological tests from which examiners select the appropriate one for administration;
4. That the Commission approve a cadre of local psychologists and mental health agencies qualified to administer the tests;
5. That all children in Special Education classes by reevaluated under the new procedures;
6. That all children found to be improperly labeled be provided with "transitional" programs designed to compensate for the educational loss experienced while misclassified;
7. That the Commission study the procedures for administering tests;
8. That no child be placed in a special class solely on the basis of a test score.

D. Armstead et al. v. *Starkville, Mississippi, Municipal Separate School District et al.* Another case of intended misuse of psychological tests was filed in the United States District Court for the Northern District of the Mississippi Eastern Division, where a suit was brought when the school system planned to use the Graduate Record Exam (GRE) for determining employment and retention of elementary and secondary teachers. Manning (1970) of the Educational Testing Service pointed out in an affidavit that the GRE is a national program of tests designed to assist undergraduate students in graduate schools in the process of transition from undergraduate to graduate study. Thus, the GRE would be inappropriately used if employed as a way of screening applicants for teaching positions in the state of Mississippi. It was clear that the Board of Education planned to use the GRE as a way of eliminating black teachers in the state's transition from segregated to desegrated schools. The GRE was simply an instrument to be used in that connection. Manning pointed out in his affidavit that the test would be perhaps less reliable for a group of teachers than for regular graduate students enrolled in study at the doctoral level, and that in using a test for purposes other than that for which it was designed would be to invalidate the use of that test.

Manning (1970) points out:

In my judgment the use of the GRE aptitude and advanced test for selection and retention of teachers in the Starkville School System . . . would be a blind use of these tests unless studies were first performed that would, as a minimum, establish the content validity and concurrent validity of these tests for the criteria of teacher effectiveness. (p. 22)

Manning's affidavit provided the context for assessing the question of the validity of using the GRE and specified cutoff scores of the test as criteria for employment of elementary- and secondary-school teachers in the Starkville schools. The same arguments may be used in regard to testing black children and placing them in Special Education classes. In his conclusions, Manning (1970) noted the following characteristics of aptitude and achievement tests of blacks and whites:

1. The test may contain items that are specifically germaine to the white, middle-class environment, thus placing black students at a disadvantage
2. Black students may be less familiar with test-taking strategies and will, because they are less skilled or "test-wise," be less able to compete successfully
3. The conditions under which students are required to take the tests are such that black students may feel anxious, threatened, and alienated, thereby impairing their ability to perform successfully on the test
4. Tests measure abilities that are developed as a consequence of educational, social, and family experience over many years. One consequence of poverty, segregation, and inequality of educational opportunities to which black students are more likely to have been subjected is reflected in lower scores on tests such as the GRE Aptitude and Advanced Test (pp. 31–32).

VI. Economic Considerations

Testing is a big industry. One of the major nonprofit testing organizations showed the following statement of income from tests for the year ending June 30, 1970:

	Actual, 1968–1969	Actual, 1969–1970	Projected, 1970–1971
Admissions Testing Program	$17,424,015	$17,688,007	$18,520,800
College Level Exam Program	157,285	179,739	449,500
Puerto Rico Testing Program	211,697	259,850	233,000
Advanced Placement Program	973,823	1,236,065	1,363,000

Messick and Anderson (1970) point out [that] the social consequences of *not* testing are extreme. The economic consequences of not testing are also quite extreme!

For many black children, the economic consequences of testing are quite extreme. As pointed out earlier, testing may determine which doors may or may not be opened to black children. Or, as Judge Wright in the *Hobson* v. *Hansen* case so aptly put it, the tests may determine that the child wear the "wrong collar" occupationally. As reported by Williams (1970b), 100 minority group postal employees were hired without the usual screening tests being administered. At the end of one year, by and large they received satisfactory ratings based on job performance. The employees were administered the usual screening tests at the end of a one-year period; they all failed. The tests certainly would have led to the unemployment of qualified persons. Lowering standards is not the issue; appropriate assessment is a vital issue, however.

Conclusions

Testing is a big business. The use of tests has become deeply imbedded in the American version of education. To some, testing represents an American dream; to others, it represents a horrible nightmare. Tests shape, in large measure, what is to be taught in schools. Teaching the test is not an uncommon phenomenon in American schools. Teachers prepare the student for the test to be taken. In many ways, the tests may shape teacher expectations. If this assertion is at all true, and some evidence exists to suggest that it is (Goslin, 1967), one strategy for improving or changing the educational system would be to change the content of the tests as a way of bringing about educational reforms in the system. Items relevant to the black experience would bring about similar changes in classrooms. This effort might bring about a greater similarity between the predictor (tests) and the criterion (scholastic achievement).

While Bennett (1970) and others continue to declare the intellectual inferiority of black people, the courts are reaching decisions which negate their allegations. Thus, it merely becomes an academic exercise to continue this "straw man" debate. Black professionals must be about the business of developing appropriate measuring instruments and black educational models for black children.

Court Cases

1. *Hobson* v. *Hansen*. Civil Action No. 82–66. United States District Court for the District of Columbia.
2. Winton H. Manning, An Affidavit of Winton H. Manning, cited in *Armstead et al.* v. *Starkville, Mississippi, Municipal Separate School District et al.* Civil Action No. EC 70-51-5.

3. *Stewart et al.* v. *Phillips and Massachusetts Board of Education.* Civil Action 70-1199F. United States District Court for the District of Massachusetts.

4. *Diana et al.* v. *California State Board of Education.* Cited by M. E. Leary, Children who are tested in an alien language: Mentally retarded? *The New Republic*, 1970, 162(22), 17-18.

Bibliography

Anastasi, A. *Psychological testing.* New York: Macmillan, 1968.

Baratz, S., and Baratz, J. C. Negro ghetto children and urban education: A cultural solution. *Social Education*, 1969, 33(34), 401-405.

Bennett, G. L. Response to Robert Williams. *The Counseling Psychologist*, 1970, 2(2), 88-89.

Clemans, W. U. A note in response to a request by the editor to comment on R. L. Williams' article. *The Counseling Psychologist*, 1970, 2(2), 90-91.

Ellis, R. S. *The psychology of the individual.* New York: Appleton-Century-Crofts, 1928.

Goslin, D. A. *Teachers and testing.* New York: Russell Sage Foundation, 1967.

Halpern, F. C. Clinicians must listen! *Clinical Child Psychology Newsletter*, Winter 1970-1971, 9(4), 8.

Humphreys, L. Letters. *Science*, 1969, 166(3902), 167.

Jensen, A. R. How much can we boost IQ and scholastic achievement? *Harvard Educational Review*, Winter 1969, 39, 1-123.

Leary, M. E. Children who are tested in an alien language: Mentally retarded? *The New Republic*, 1970, 162(22), 17-18.

Messick, S., and Anderson, S. Educational testing, individual development and social responsibility. *The Counseling Psychologist*, 1970, 2(2), 93-97.

Moynihan, P. "Benign neglect" for issue of race? *The Wall Street Journal*, March 3, 1970, 20.

Newland, T. E. Testing minority group children. *Clinical Child Psychology Newsletter*, 1970, 9(3), 5.

Pierce, W. D., West, G. I., Dent, H. E., Rawls, J. D., and Woodson, W. B. A reply to San Francisco Unified School District Report on Special Education Classes. Report prepared by members of the Association of Black Psychologists. San Francisco, California, May 5, 1970.

Report of the Commission on Tests I. *Righting the balance.* College Entrance Examination Board, New York, 1970.

Sommer, J. Response to Robert Williams. *The Counseling Psychologist*, 1970, 2(2), 93-97.

Wechsler, D. *The measurement of adult intelligence.* Baltimore: Williams & Wilkins, 1944.

Wesman, A. G. Intelligent testing. *American Psychologist*, 1968, 23(4), 267-274.

Wikoff, R. L. Danger: Attacks on testing unfair. *Clinical Child Psychology Newsletter*, Spring 1970, 9(1), 3-4.

Williams, R. L. Black pride, academic relevance and individual achievement. *The Counseling Psychologist*, 1970, 2(1), 19-22. (a)

Williams, R. L. Letters. *Science*, 1970, 167(3915), 124. (b)

Witty, P. A., and Jenkins, A. D. The case of "B___," a gifted Negro girl. *Journal of Social Psychology*, 1935, 6(1), 117-124.

Position Statement on Use of IQ and Ability Tests

In light of the overwhelming body of scientific evidence which clearly indicates that existing group and individual tests of intelligence and group tests of scholastic ability are questionable and invalid as measures of the intellectual and the scholastic ability of black children, the Bay Area Association of Black Psychologists takes the position that:

1. The California State Department of Education declare and enforce a moratorium on the use of such tests in the psychological evaluation and assessment of black children in the State of California, by September 1, 1971.

2. The California State Department of Education enforce this moratorium by charging local school districts to utilize other psychological assessment techniques and criteria in the evaluation of black children in the State of California.

3. When a school district or a parent initiates a request for psychological assessment, the school shall inform the parent of their right to have the psychological assessment conducted and/or interpreted by a person of their own ethnic background who is competent in psychological assessment.

4. The California State Department of Education shall make intensive efforts to secure, authorize, and require the use of culturally relevant individual tests of intelligence and ability for the testing of black and other minority school children.

5. The California State Department of Education shall make intensive efforts to secure, authorize, and require the use of culturally relevant group tests of intelligence and ability for the testing of black and other minority school children.

6. Such culturally relevant individual and group tests of intelligence and ability (referred to in items 4 and 5) shall be normed and standardized on a culturally representative sample.

7. Such culturally relevant individual and group tests of intelligence and ability (referred to in items 4 and 5) used to evaluate black children shall be submitted to the Bay Area Association of Black Psychologists for their evaluation and recommendation. The California State Department of Education shall also make available to the Bay Area Association of Black Psychologists reports of the success and progress of these efforts.

8. Pursuant to Section 12821 of the Education Code: Local school districts

Reprinted by permission of the Bay Area Association of Black Psychologists.

within the State of California shall administer group (achievement) tests for the following purposes:

(a) To afford a means and procedure for evaluating the effectiveness of the public schools as shown by the competence and progress of public school pupils in basic skills and content courses.

(b) To make such evaluations available to educational agencies and the public as a basis for the correction of deficiencies in, and the improvement of, all phases of the state educational system and as a basis for research.

(c) To afford the legislature facts from which it may determine the proper allocation and expenditure of public funds for public school education, but the individual scores of all group achievement tests shall not be placed in cumulative folders and shall not be reported to the child's classroom teacher and to other faculty and administrators on the school sites. All evaluation information and research data needed to accomplish the above can and must be obtained without identification of individual children.

9. The Department of Education shall recommend to the State Board of Education for appointment to the statewide testing advisory committee persons who have expertise in test development and in minority ethnic background and experience. The State Department of Education shall endeavor to employ consultants with such experience. In selecting and authorizing tests to be administered to school children throughout the state, the Statewide Testing Advisory Committee shall consider the extent to which the testing company has utilized personnel with minority ethnic background and experience in the development of the culturally relevant test.

10. The State Department of Education shall exert leadership in the preparation and employment of black and minority psychologists and psychometrists in local school districts and on the admissions and planning committees of local districts, and as professional consultants to school districts.

11. The State Department of Education shall develop guidelines for ongoing, inservice training for personnel in the local education agencies involved in the evaluation and placement of students of diverse ethnic backgrounds in the special education programs (EH, EMR, MGM). The inservice preparation program shall be designed to prepare school personnel to understand and effectively relate to the history, cultural significants, and also the social problems of minority students and their environment. School districts shall be required to provide an inservice preparation program pursuant to said guidelines by September 1, 1971, so that those interpreting tests and evaluating psychological functioning of such pupils shall have complied with said guidelines by September 1, 1972.

12. Pupils making the transition from classes for the Educable Mentally Retarded and Educationally Handicapped (pursuant to Education Code Section 6902) to grades in the regular public school should be placed in an educational program, with children of comparable age, based on developmental, social, physical, and educational needs of the individual pupil, utilizing the persons who are most familiar with the needs of such pupils.

For pupils making the transition from classes for the Educable Mentally Re-tarded and the Educationally Handicapped to the regular grades of the public school, the regular program supplementation should include as much individual, small group, or other special attention as possible.

13. As part of the annual review and recommendation by the admission com-mittee pursuant to the Education Code Section 6902.4, continuance of minors now enrolled in programs for the mentally retarded authorized under Education Code Section 6902 should be recommended only on the basis of an evaluation in accordance with the culturally relevant criteria developed pursuant to para-graphs 4 and 5 hereof, including any necessary retesting. A report of such eval-uations, including any testing, the results thereof, and the program recom-mended for the children identified for return to the regular classes should be made to the Superintendent of Public Instruction upon completion of such reevaluating. Such reevaluating shall be a permanent feature of annual review; however, the report to be submitted to the Superintendent of Public Instruction shall be made only for the 1970-1971 school year and should be submitted to the Superintendent of Public Instruction by June 30, 1971.

14. The State Department of Education in implementing Section 2011 (b) of Title 5 of the California Administrative Code shall require districts to get statis-tics sufficient to enable a determination to be made of the members and percent-ages of minority children (black, Spanish surname, Oriental, American Indian, other nonwhite) in classes for the educable mentally retarded in the district. In the event there is a significant variance in the percentage of such minority children in a school district's EMR classes from the total enrollment of such minority students in the district, the district shall submit a written explanation of the variance to the State Department of Education which shall investigate such reports and submit its own report to the State Board of Education in each instance. The State Department of Education shall make every effort to require local districts to take the necessary action to correct the situation which created the variance in distribution of children in special classes and to bring that distri-bution in close proximity to the distribution of the total population of that district. The reports of the school districts and of the Department of Education shall be made available to the Bay Area Association of Black Psychologists and to the public upon request.

ROBERT L. GREEN

The Black Quest for Higher Education: An Admissions Dilemma

The so-called Black Revolution has finally reached major university campuses throughout the United States. During the past academic year we have observed black student alliances, United Students for Black Action, and similar groups organized on major white and black college campuses, demanding social reform and changes in academic objectives. These demands have focused primarily on the black students' thrust for a voice in the university decision-making process, curricular changes that reflect the contribution of black Americans, an increase in black faculty and black students, and, in one instance, an all-black residence hall (Black and white at Northwestern University, 1968).

The one demand that has perhaps caused the most concern among college administrators is that of enrolling greater numbers of minority youth. Black students were not aware of the fact that this demand, more than any other, has challenged structured admissions procedures of major universities throughout the country. The result has been the establishment of middle- and upper-socioeconomic student-body populations, which have formerly been essentially white. Black students who have, in the past, been able to complete their education at predominantly white institutions were not necessarily from middle- or upper-socioeconomic backgrounds, but were either themselves the recipients of an "abundant" high-school curriculum or were able to do so because of an unusually effective educationally reinforcing home environment.

Universities have reacted differently to the important admissions question raised by black college students. Some universities have actually begun to recruit minority youth on a wide scale, waiving traditional admissions criteria, while others have attempted to recruit only a very small number of minority youth, selecting only the "cream of the crop" of black high-school graduates, i.e., only those who meet the traditional criteria of major universities. Others have somewhat ignored or actively resisted any effort related to changing admissions criteria in order to admit black, Mexican-American, or other minority students. Those universities who have been most resistant to this new press have asserted that their role is not to "overcome" or "make up" for disadvantages that have been systematically built into the youngsters' prior educational background. [This] argument is also used by some high-school, junior-high, and elementary-school administrators who frequently assert that the student's disadvantaging

From *Personnel and Guidance Journal*, 1969, **47**, 905–911. Copyright 1969 by the American Personnel and Guidance Association. Reprinted by permission of the author and the publisher.

home background has produced his low educational achievement, and the school cannot be held responsible for its amelioration.

In light of new efforts that many universities are making to remove their "white only" student-body image, what considerations are important for college admissions officers if the enrollment and subsequent success of minority youth at institutions of higher learning is to be realized?

Traditional Admissions Criteria

Many universities throughout the country utilize College Board Examinations, perhaps better known as the Scholastic Aptitude Test (SAT), and similar aptitude tests as major variables for predicting college success. As indicated in the 1967 College Entrance Examination Board bulletin, the SAT has five major sections—English Composition, Humanities, Mathematics, Natural Science, and Social Science. Scores for the five areas are reported on a standard score scale ranging from 200 to 800, with a mean of 500 and a standard deviation of 100. In many southern colleges the average combined SAT score earned by black students is about 550. The North Carolina Board of Higher Education recently considered a proposal to raise the SAT minimum score to 750 or higher for admission to Negro colleges in the state. This caused much concern throughout the state since this meant that the new cutoff score would eliminate more than 50 percent of the black college population in North Carolina (Green, 1967).

Since tests such as the SAT are viewed as important predictors by many scholars in the field of measurement and more importantly by college admissions officers in assessing a student's chance for college success, it is important to examine the predictive validity of such instruments.

A brief review of prediction studies will provide information regarding the usefulness of aptitude and intelligence tests in predicting college success. Boney (1966) used several aptitude and mental ability measures to predict high-school grade point average (GPA) for 222 Negro male and female secondary students. Boney found that the predictor variables "yielded substantial correlations with high school grade point average" and stated that "it appears that Negro students are as predictable as other groups." The correlations between the Cooperative Ability Test total score and grade point average for Negro males was .66, and .70 for Negro females. The correlations between grade point average and the Differential Aptitude Test scores were as substantial.

A detailed analysis of a series of statistical reports by Stanley and Porter (1967) supports the position that academic aptitude tests predict college freshman GPA equally well for blacks and whites. Included in the review is an analysis of statistical reports from the university system of Georgia for which a preliminary study had been made by Hills (1964). Hills's data contrasting three predominantly Negro colleges with the Georgia Institute of Technology, a predominantly white college, suggest that the SAT-verbal (SAT-V) and SAT-mathematical (SAT-M) predict freshman grades equally well for these two college groups. Stanley and Porter also refer to McKelpin's study (1965) at the North Carolina College at Durham, a predominantly black college in which the SAT-V and SAT-M predictive validities for black college students were "as high as those usually reported for college freshmen. . . . " In an extension of a study by Biaggio and Stanley (1964), Stanley and Porter (1967) conclude that:

In view of the detailed analysis of the Georgia data and several related studies, it seems likely that SAT-type test scores are about as correlationally valid for Negroes competing with Negroes and taught chiefly by Negroes as they are for non-Negroes competing chiefly with non-Negroes and taught chiefly by non-Negroes.

Stanley and Porter further state that "prediction may be approximately equal for the races within integrated colleges." They cite Cleary's research (1966) as additional data which indicate that SAT-type tests are as predictively valid for nonwhites as they are for whites. Cleary studied three integrated colleges to determine if the SAT was predictively biased against nonwhite students. Again, college GPA was the criterion variable. In two of the three colleges assessed, the SAT was as predictively valid for Negroes as it was for whites. In one college, the SAT overpredicted for blacks.

In a postdictive study, Munday (1965) found "that grades for socially disadvantaged students are generally as predictive as grades for other students using standardized measures of academic ability." Munday correlated high-school grades and scores on the American College Test with college grades. Although he does not indicate the college level at which the correlations were obtained, the article suggests that total college GPA was the criterion. The multiple Rs obtained "by averaging the GPA predictions made by the optimal weighting of tests and those made by optimally weighting high school grades" ranged from .52 to .66. Munday's study concludes that "if such tests [SAT, etc.] are culture-bound, as seems likely, this feature does not appear to detract from their usefulness as predictors of academic success."

However, Green and Farquhar (1965) found later that there was essentially no relationship (−.01 correlation) between the secondary grades (GPA) of black male high-school students and their verbal scores on the School and College Ability Test (SCAT). The correlation between the two variables was significantly higher (.25) for black females on the same study. It was found that a test of achievement motivation (Self-Concept of Academic Ability Scale) correlated slightly higher with high-school grades than the verbal section of the SCAT (.36 for males and .64 for females). The −.01 correlation between high-school grades and SCAT scores for black males is of interest. McKelpin (1965), cited earlier, suggests that high-school GPA may be a poor criterion of school success for disadvantaged students, in that high-school academic programs often adjust to environmental factors. In the case of disadvantaged students this adjustment may often "preclude proper emphasis on the development of intellectual potential for many students." McKelpin further states that "this would seem to account for the relatively low correlation between SAT and HSA that is often reported for these students" (p. 165).

Morse (1963) found that for a sample of eighth-grade students the relationship between grade point average and measured intelligence was significantly lower among black students than among Caucasian students (.16 for black and .57 for white students). Morse also found that a Self-Concept of Academic Ability Scale was a better predictor of school achievement for both black and white students than IQ (.43 for Negroes and .61 for Caucasians). Morse states that the black student's self-perception "of his ability to succeed in school and his motivation to do so apparently provide a better basis for forecasting his school achievement than a measure of intelligence." Although Morse was predicting junior high-school grades, and Boney (1966) was predicting high-school grades, these studies have implications for the prediction of college achievement, since high-school GPA and college achievement (first-year GPA) are often highly related (Payne, Davidson, and Sloan, 1966).

The study by Payne, Davidson, and Sloan (1966) provides some further insights into prediction of academic success. In a study of 48 freshman students they found that the best of a set of predictors of average final work at the end of the first university year were high-school grade point average ($r = .61$) and vocabulary ($r = .41$). The personality measure yielding a significant correlation (.43) with freshman grade point average was a "measure of the tendency not to repress incompleted tasks derived from Alper's Ziegarnik experiment." The most striking finding was that the predictors of freshman grade point average—high-school GPA and vocabulary—were not significant predictors of average final examination marks at the end of the third university year.

Irvine (1966) has examined the prediction of college graduation from the university system of Georgia, where several studies cited by Stanley and Porter were conducted. Irvine found that prediction of graduation through use of high-school grade point average, SAT scores (math and verbal), number in class, and units of various subject matter courses could be made at about the .38 level of correlation. High-school GPA alone correlated .34 with college graduation. However, Irvine did find a substantial multiple correlation (.59) between first-semester GPA and a combination of high-school GPA and SAT verbal and math scores.

Lins, Abell, and Hutchins (1966), in a major study involving the entire entering freshman class at the University of Wisconsin in 1962, concluded that there is only a limited relationship between traditional aptitude tests such as the American College Testing Examination, the Scholastic Aptitude Test, the College Qualification Test, and first-semester academic performance as reflected in GPA. The correlation between SAT total score and first semester GPA was .52 for males and .59 for females. Similar correlations were found between other aptitude measures and first-semester GPA. Lins concludes that none of the scores on the aptitude tests, as sole predictors of academic success, appear to have high predictive validity.

The above data are not conclusive regarding the validity of aptitude tests for predicting college success for a range of student-body populations. It suggests that more research is needed, particularly in colleges that are integrated or are predominantely white with growing minority populations.

It is generally conceded that high-school grade point average is the best single predictor of college grade point average, and that often a substantial amount of additional predictive power can be achieved by forming a composite set of predictor variables. Additional variability may rest in more individual characteristics such as motivation, persistence, and self-perception. On the basis of recent data, university support programs may also be related to the college success of minority youth.

Programs for "High-Risk" Students

Edgerton's survey (1968) indicates that universities who have recently inaugurated programs for high-risk students are beginning to demonstrate that youngsters who did not meet traditional admissions criteria such as high SAT scores, "high" high-school grades, as well as graduation from excellent academic programs, can still survive in college if proper tutorial or support services are made available to them.

Southern Illinois University's support program indicates that proper tutorial and counseling services will assist disadvantaged students in overcoming their educational deficits. On the basis of test scores and high-school grade averages, Southern Illinois University's Counseling and Testing Office predicted at the beginning of their program in October 1966, that the high-risk group ($N = 100$) would make average grades of 2.2 (a very low "D" on SIU's five-point grading system), that 24 students would fail to make a 2.0 (D) average, and that only one student would achieve a 3.0 (C) or better. But of the 74 students still in the program, 65 have made grade averages above the figure predicted for them. At the end of the first four quarters, 30 were at or above C level, including 10 who averaged 3.5 or better and two who averaged 4.0 (B) or higher. Only five were below 2.0.

Plaut (1966) stated that the University of California at Los Angeles, New York University, and Hofstra University were admitting students with weak academic credentials and providing them with special courses, counseling, summer academic programs, and a longer period in which to graduate. Plaut noted Clark and Plotkin's data on the black student at integrated colleges, which indicated that success was possible for disadvantaged students. They studied five classes of the National Scholarship and Service Fund for Negro Students and found that "90 percent of the respondents from this very deprived group, and over two thirds of the whole group, received their bachelor's degree, against a national completion rate of less than 60 percent" (Plaut, 1966).

Similar programs for high-risk students at the University of California at Berkeley have accomplished equally good results. Of the 424 students to enter Berkeley's program, so far 74 (17 percent) have left, half of them for academic reasons. Of the 350 who remain, almost 70 percent are in good academic standing with grades of C or better. Of the 395 high-risk students at UCLA, only 13 students have been dismissed for academic reasons. At least 25 other institutions of higher learning have had success with programs for high-risk students (Edgerton, 1968). Vocational and personal counseling, as well as academic tutorial assistance, are vital aspects of each of these programs.

These recent experiences with high-risk programs suggest that students with low test performance who lack the traditional university "dressings" can succeed in major four-year colleges. These experiences also indicate that many support-program characteristics may be more highly related to college success than was previously thought. This becomes especially important when viewed in light of the recent important national concern with providing blacks and other minority groups with an opportunity for higher education.

Predictors other than aptitude tests are important because the majority of disadvantaged black students who are educated in both urban and rural communities, North and South, have experienced grossly inadequate elementary and high-school educations. The result has been that large numbers of blacks score below national norms on standardized achievement and aptitude tests. Bloom (1964) documents the fact that a deprived environment (home and school) in contrast to an abundant environment will seriously interfere with an individual's ability to perform well on academic aptitude and achievement tests. In essence, the low scores of many disadvantaged students on traditional aptitude and achievement tests result from a combination of nonacademic environmental influences. Included are such factors as low teacher expectation, the press for excellence in athletics rather than in the classroom, and, in the case of many black students, grossly inadequate public-school programs.

We should perhaps note here that among the other important aspects of one's past educational background that either facilitate or interfere with test performance is what measurement specialists refer to as "test-wiseness." There is evidence to support the point of view that many middle-class children are test-wise and that most children from very poor educational environments tend to be "test-blind." The writer can recall testing a group of black youngsters in a large, midwestern, urban high school. While completing the verbal section of SCAT, many youngsters would complete the first five or six items and, if they found item seven to be a difficult one, they would spend the remaining part of the allotted time working on that one item, rather than completing the remaining part of the test and returning to the difficult item. Behavior such as this does not facilitate performance on a given test no matter what the ability of the student involved. Such factors as these can be taken into account in tutorial or college support services.

University Standards

An examination of admissions criteria raises the question of whether the standards of the university will be lowered by admitting low-income students who do not meet "normal" admissions standards. The experience of those schools which have inititated programs for high-risk students suggests that this fear is unfounded. However, the issue of lowering standards, since it seems to be a source of consternation to many university personnel, deserves further consideration.

At many large universities the dropout rate for freshman students approximates 30 percent. Edgerton (1968) stated that at the University of Wisconsin, where more than 5,000 freshmen enroll each September, more than 25 percent drop out or flunk out by the end of the first year. Michigan State University, where the freshman enrollment in the fall of 1967 was 7,279—one of the largest freshman classes in the nation—experienced a similar attrition rate.

On the basis of the high dropout rate for many of the major colleges and universities, it would seem that present academic standards are already too high. It could be that educators are masking their exclusion policies behind the statement that disadvantaged youth should not be placed in a situation where they will fail. (Medsker and Trent [1965] found that more middle-class children with low ability are admitted into college than lower-class children with high ability.) If standards are raised high enough, the university may find itself with a relatively small student body which academically is very bright, but in the process the university will have become irrelevant to the vast majority of society.

New Admissions Criteria

To increase the relevance of the university and to make higher education available to a larger and more representative portion of our society, what is needed is not a raising or even a lowering of standards, but instead the use of a *different* set of standards which take into account motivational and attitudinal characteristics of the individual as well as the usual intellectual factor. Revised standards should take account of diverse previous educational experiences of the many black, Mexican-American, Puerto Rican, Indian, and disadvantaged white students who often come from educationally inferior backgrounds. Once these students have been admitted, special tutorial and other support services, such as educational and personal counseling, must be made available to them.

It is also important to distinguish between a more accurate set of admissions criteria and course work criteria. We may use a different set of standards to admit students, but they should not be provided a special curriculum, i.e., "a curriculum for the disadvantaged." They will still be asked to compete in the same classes with students admitted under normal standards. The major difference is that they will be given realistic and needed support services.

Summary

If we are to make an impact on the present crisis confronting this nation in terms of poverty and racial discrimination along with educating the white community regarding its own racism, we must provide black and other minority students with an opportunity for higher education. If this is to be done, traditional admissions criteria (standardized aptitude tests and high-school grades) must be carefully assessed. Although the studies completed to date suggest that aptitude tests predict college success equally well for white and nonwhite students, there is a need for further research in this area. Because of the disadvantaging school backgrounds of many black, Mexican-American, Puerto Rican, and low-income white students, these individuals will generally score below national norms on aptitude tests. But when admitted to college and given proper tutorial and counseling services (both personal and academic), their chances for success are greatly enhanced. Hopefully this new educational opportunity will allow black and other minority youth to assume greater leadership within our society. However, the foremost challenge to predominately white institutions of higher learning is to evaluate carefully and to reconsider those admissions policies of many years' standing in order to provide *all* segments of our society with an opportunity to share in programs of higher education.

References

Biaggio, A. B., and Stanley, J. C. Prediction of freshman grades at southern state colleges. Paper read at the Ninth Inter-American Congress of Psychology, Miami, Fla., December 1964.

Black and white at Northwestern University. *Integrated Education*, 1968, 6(3), 33–40.

Bloom, B. *Stability and change in human characteristics*. New York: John Wiley, 1964.

Boney, J. D. Predicting the academic achievement of secondary school Negro students. *Personnel and Guidance Journal*, 1966, 44, 700–703.

Cleary, T. A. Test bias: Validity of the Scholastic Aptitude Test for Negro and white students in integrated colleges. *Educational Testing Service Research Bulletin*, June 1966.

Edgerton, J. *Higher education for "high risk" students*. Atlanta, Ga.: Southern Education Foundation, 1968.

Green, R. L. Why the push to upgrade Negro colleges? *Southern Education Report*, 1967, 3(1), 23–27.

Green, R. L., and Farquhar, W. W. Negro academic motivation and scholastic achievement. *Journal of Educational Psychology*, 1965, 56, 241–243.

Hills, J. R. Prediction of college grades for all public colleges of a state. *Journal of Educational Measurement*, 1964, 1, 155–159.

Irvine, D. W. Multiple prediction of college graduation from pre-admission data. *Journal of Experimental Education*, 1966, 35(1), 84–89.

Lins, J. L., Abell, A. P., and Hutchins, H. C. Relative usefulness in predicting academic success of the ACT, the SAT, and some other variables. *Journal of Experimental Education*, 1966, 35(2), 1–29.

McKelpin, J. P. Some implications of the intellectual characteristics of freshmen. *Journal of Educational Measurement*, 1965, 2, 161–166.

Medsker, L., and Trent, J. W. *The influence of different types of public higher institutions on college attendance from varying socioeconomic and ability levels*. Berkeley, Calif.: University of California, Center for the Study of Higher Education, 1965.

Morse, R. J. Self-concept of ability, significant others and school achievement of eighth-grade students: A comparative investigation of Negro and Caucasian students. Unpublished master's thesis, Michigan State University, 1963.

Munday, L. Predicting college grades in predominantly Negro colleges. *Journal of Educational Measurement*, 1965, 2, 157-160.

Payne, R. W., Davidson, P. O., and Sloan, R. B. The prediction of academic success in university students: A pilot study. *Canadian Journal of Psychology*, 1966, 20(1), 52-63.

Plaut, R. L. Plans for assisting Negro students to enter and to remain in college. *Journal of Negro Education*, 1966, 35(4), 393-399.

Stanley, J., and Porter, A. Correlation of Scholastic Aptitude Test scores with college grades for Negroes versus whites. *Journal of Educational Measurement*, 1967, 4(4), 199-218.

WILLIAM F. BRAZZIEL

A Letter from the South

Sirs:

Thirteen years ago plaintiffs brought suit in Federal District Court to integrate the Louisiana public schools. The main argument of the defense attorneys and the superintendent of public instruction was that "white teachers could not understand the Nigra mind" and, therefore, would not be able to teach them effectively in integrated classrooms. The defense quoted heavily from the theories of white intellectual supremacy as expounded by Henry Garrett and Audrey Shuey.

Last week, a scant five days after Arthur Jensen made headlines in Virginia papers regarding inferiority of black people as measured by IQ tests, defense attorneys and their expert witnesses fought a suit in Federal District Court to integrate Greensville and Caroline County schools. Their main argument was that "white teachers could not understand the Nigra mind" and that the Nigra children should be admitted to the white schools on the basis of standardized tests. Those who failed to make a certain score would be assigned to all-black remedial schools where "teachers who understood them could work with them." The defense in this case quoted heavily from the theories of white intellectual supremacy as expounded by Arthur Jensen.

It will help not one bit for Jensen or the Havard Educational Review (HER) editorial board to protest that they did not intend for Jensen's article to be used in this way. For in addition to superiority in performing conceptual cluster tricks on test sheets, the hard-line segregationist is also vastly superior in his ability to bury qualifying phrases and demurrers and in his ability to distort and slant facts and batter his undereducated clientele into a complete state of hysteria where race is concerned.

Jensen and the HER editorial board will modestly admit that they have superior intellects and I am sure they realized the consequences of their actions. Questions now arise as to why they decided to raise this issue, in this way, and at this time.

Fortunately, doubts about the ability of black and yellow people to master war, finance, science, and technology are waning rapidly in both white and black minds. The imprecision of standardized testing is now clear to most literate people, and the criminal use to which they are put in schools is also becoming

Brazziel, W. F., "A Letter from the South," *Harvard Educational Review*, 39, February 1969, 200–208. Copyright © 1969 by President and Fellows of Harvard College. Reprinted by permission of the author and the publisher.

clearer. Black history has made people aware that white people did *not* give America such things as the stoplight, the shoe last, heart operations, and sugar refining, but that black people did this. That John Smith did not develop corn and tobacco but learned to grow these crops from the Indians. And the beat goes on. People are now witnessing with their very eyes the fact [that] black youth, finally given a half of a chance at education and jobs, are being able to make exotic formulas for bombs and napalm as well as anyone else. As a result of all of this, I think the present set-to might be the last go-round for white supremacy psychological theory.

I would hope the Jensenites could alter their stance and approach and try to bring some good out of this situation after all. They might work their way out of ethnic learning styles by broadening their research to include all ethnic groups. We have some rather learned men in our area who believe that English-Americans are atop the pyramid of abstract learning abilities with Welsh, German, French, Belgian, Norwegian, Swiss, Finnish, Danish, and Swedish occupying the next nine rungs in the order listed. After the top ten have been given their just due, these gentlemen give a smattering of attention to the rest of Europe and proceed to ignore the rest of the world. The Jensenites might try to clear this up in some way. They might even look into intragroup differences within the top ten. I would suspect that many would be found and that it would be healthy to make this known at professional meetings, in the journals, and in the news media.

We also have a religious wing in this group who suspect that English-American children who are brought up in Southern Baptist churches perceive things differently and might really deserve the top spot upon the pyramid. Southern-English-American-Episcopalians regard these assertions with a great deal of amusement. But who really knows? We all will if the ethnic learning line of research is extended logically to include every possible ethnic, regional, and religious stock.

Also in the status research vein, we need research on the effects of racism and caste status on learning. The Jensenites can provide this by following Robert Coles and others around in Mississippi and South Carolina to study the parasitic worm and starvation situation among black children. Autopsies of a few who died might yield valuable evidence on the brain damages wrought by malnourishment. The team could change themselves into black people à la John Griffin and run the hostility gauntlet as they tried to find some information in the local library. Or the hilarity gauntlet as they made applications for a professional or skilled job. They could fly as black men to Boston or Oakland and make the same applications to the craft union nearest the airport. Or they could try to get a tenured appointment in the Harvard Graduate School of Education, or a spot on the HER editorial board, or simply a rank higher than assistant professor among the 7,000-member Harvard faculty.

The Jensenites could give the same black injections to their children, enroll them in a different school and record what happens to them. Children learn efficiently if listening, reading, discussion, peer-group interaction, library resources, and teacher-pupil interaction are all used effectively. The investigators might be very interested in the change in quality in the last four areas for their now black offspring and to see who is to blame and how the situation can be improved. To add a spicy dimension, low IQ scores could be substituted in the transfer folders.

Creation of multiethnic and multiracial tests would also be a method of bringing some good out of the situation. If the only way to make *exactly* the same score on test items is to be of the same race, economic class, ethnic stock, and religious persuasion as the committee that developed the instrument, then we either must make intensive efforts to intermarry, redistribute income, and institute religious purges and programs in this country or we must try to integrate more multiracial and multiethnic material into the instruments. Said in the words of Dr. Nathan Wright, the Newark black-power theorist, we must try to "dehonkify" the instruments.

Or we might decide that making *exactly* the same score is not important for all races and religions and come up with an Ethnic Success Quotient for tests based on validation studies of all the hyphenated groups we are going to study. Under such a system a Richmond-born Episcopalian of English stock, from a family with an income of $12,000, would be declared below average if his Binet score was below 120. A score of 100 would relegate him to success quotient oblivion as a low normal. The Beaufort County, S.C., black children with worms might have a success quotient of 90 based upon performance of adults from this sort of situation who somehow scrambled up the ladder. A black 100 score in this county would indicate an ESQ of potential genius.

Finally, in this vein, the Jensenites might make their most important contribution if they could somehow join with Earl Schaefer of the National Institutes of Health and others at the Universities of Florida, Western Michigan, etc., who are fastening on early infant stimulation and teaching as the key to agility on standardized tests. (The problem, of course, may be in getting the Schaeferites to join with the Jensenites, given the Klan types who have embraced the latter as their own.) Schaefer has already published some fine results of efforts with black children. The logic here is simple and very much in the vein of Cronbach's rebuttal to the Jensen paper, i.e., if you want black kids to think like white kids, imprint this type of thinking habit early (5 days to 2 years of age) with simple thinking, concept cluster tasks. White teachers can enable black parents to learn how. White disadvantaged children are being imprinted in the same manner in some studies. Ethnic and religious backgrounds have not been treated as yet. There might be a problem or two here regarding people who might want to imprint their children with their own brand of thinking or who have deep affection and preference for certain racial, ethnic, or religious ways of thinking. Other parents might not want the new imprints to attend their schools on an integrated basis or live in their neighborhoods and play in their recreation centers. Something in the imprinting would thus be lost in this sort of forced isolation. But I am certain these reservations can be swept aside in the name of psychological research and the cognitive homogenizing process can progress.

Now for a closer look at some of Jensen's theories about black IQ. To begin, I received a form letter from Jensen in response to a request for clarification of his *real* stand on the implications of racial genetic inferiority that seemed to shine through the somewhat hazy statements of conclusion of his paper at the American Educational Research Association, implications which the press quickly translated into flat statements of white intellectual supremacy. His article was based on this paper and gave the same impression to the press. (See Joseph Alsop, *Washington Post*, March 11; *Virginian-Pilot*, March 12: "Yet there is no use being mealy-mouthed about it. Dr. Jensen is really saying that in *addition* to the handicaps wickedly imposed by prejudice and discrimination, the average black American begins the race of life with a detectable genetic handicap.")

Jensen's letter was addressed to the *Berkeley Daily Gazette* which he feels misinterpreted his position. The following are excerpts from the letter:

> *Obvious differences in inborn mental ability "between races"–these are a reporter's words. They certainly are not mine. The quotation marks, attributing this phrase to me, are therefore wrong. Furthermore, the statement is quite indefensible. The complex causes of objectively measurable differences in mental abilities among individuals or between different socioeconomic and racial groups are not at all "obvious."*
>
> *Although my study of the existing evidence has led me to the position that intelligence differences among individuals, social classes, and racial groups are conditioned by both genetic and environmental factors, the estimation of the relative contributions of these influences is a problem of great technical and practical difficulty for researchers in behavioral genetics, and the research so far has been inadequate as a basis for definitive conclusions about racial differences in intelligence.*

Jensen's treatment of the racial aspects of IQ in his article comes to the same point of inconclusiveness. It is very, very unfortunate that he, or the editors, failed to include a clear statement to this effect. Truth squad operations such as this letter and the rebuttals by psychologists in the HER Spring Issue will never get read.

Jensen's second error in my estimation was to lean heavily on the Coleman Report for data on black inferiority. This report has been heavily criticized for inaccuracy. The most notable criticism is contained in the Winter 1968 issue of the *Journal of Human Resources* in an article by Bowles and Levin. Sampling procedures, lack of cooperation by big school systems, failures to match black-white sample by curriculums, overreliance on administrators' contentions that black-white facilities were indeed separate but equal (black parents in Eutaw, Alabama, must have thought the research team had been smoking pot when they read the conclusions of the report), and crudeness of statistical measures were all analyzed as weaknesses which, when added to the fact that the study was made in pre-ESEA days, relegated it to the status of a 737-page, million-dollar pilot study. On page 292 of the report, the authors state similar disclaimers, especially regarding the precautions necessary in interpreting their statistics.

In regarding as law this report's conclusions that the average black kid can get no further than a ninth-grade operating level after 12 years of public school, Jensen ignores completely (or is unaware of) the record being compiled by the JOBS program of the National Alliance for Businessmen. These gentlemen take black dropouts [and] place them on the job half-time and in reading and math classes half-time; they produce a two-year gain on tests every six weeks.

Jensen's major error, I believe, was his inconsistency in following a definite line of reasoning regarding the separation of gene linkage and prepostnatal ravages of protein malnutrition. The latter is the most intensively researched thesis these days with National Institute of Health teams leading the way. Jensen did not even mention this line of research which (together with research in infant stimulation) I believe has answers for 42 percent mental retardation found in low-low (Jensen's level V) income black children and a lot of the other differences. In a half-starved brain like these kids have, how are we to really know if high or low IQ genes were linked? Jensen did not tell us how.

Jensen calls compensatory education a failure. So did reporters of the *Washington Post*, who in turn received and printed a report by the ESEA staff of the Virginia Department of Education calling their allegations inaccurate and stating that they had hard data to back their claims. In response to a request for same, I received tables for statewide pre–post testing of 10,200 pupils in 15 school districts for 1967–1968. The data show average month's increase in grade equivalency per month of 1.06 of instruction, or an average overgain in achievement of more than a half a year per pupil as a result of compensatory education. Children scoring in the lowest decile had decreased from 41 to 28 percent. In the second quartile the number jumped from 8 to 16 percent, and the dropout rate had decreased by 63 percent. The officials noted that age-grade decrement had been scotched and that they believe that they had convincing evidence that their Title I program was a success. And this from one of the more conservative states in the Union and one with a record of slow starts in educational innovations. School people, it seems, are just now learning how to run compensatory programs. Or really try to. The first report to the President of the National Advisory Council on Disadvantaged Children noted this reluctance to really plan and implement on the part of many school systems. They quoted one superintendent who stated flatly that "it was useless and a waste of money to teach those jigs anything." Let us all hope he has since initiated a good program and that he doesn't read Jensen's article.

In drawing conclusions from 200 to 300 comparative studies of black–white IQ, Jensen failed to consider that all of the pre-1948 studies and most of the post-1948 studies failed to give attention to the deprivation axioms made popular by the University of Chicago group (Davis, Eels et al.) and until recently almost no psychometrists gave attention to the fact that white examiners in a black classroom are, in many, many cases, getting an invalid test performance. Their color, voice, manner, gestures turn many kids off, and they refuse to try. *This phenomenon is growing in intensity and must be dealt with.* How are you going to have a valid test session with kids who read in black papers and magazines that white researchers are sending their kids to Harvard by overstudying the black communities with federal grants? Or with kids who received a leaflet from a community group blasting tests as an "unfair tool of colonialists who control the black community"?

I believe that Jensen is wrong and I hope he does not do too much damage. I believe the HER editorial board should publish the rebuttals in the same issue with future attacks on the Negro. Rumors abound that attacks on the Negro church are planned. This will scotch the sensationalism of the press caused by the lag in time between issues. Indeed, the rebuttals will never be read by reporters, much less printed.

Jensen failed to take into consideration the black infant mortality rate as a factor in black infant supremacy on the motoric area of the Bayley Scales. This rate is three times that of white infants. Black kids must literally undergo a survival of the fittest test to be born, once conceived, and to stay alive.

Jensen has a serious contradiction in his analysis of tests and studies of black IQ. After offering half dozen or so studies to document his thesis that black kids don't do as well on IQ tests as white kids, Jensen closes his paper by stating that IQ tests fail to measure the full potential of black kids.

Jensen failed to consider the 1969 report of the Research and Evaluation Branch of Project Head Start in writing off Head Start gains as transitory. According to this report of several studies of the maintenance of gains, the investigators concluded that the gains were maintained when the children were enrolled in first grades or kindergartens in middle-class schools. Edmund Gordon of Teachers College and John McDavid of Miami led the team which wrote this report.

Jensen, like other psychologists, is completely incapable of unraveling what would have to be unraveled in order to separate genetic from environmental influences where American black and white people are concerned, to wit:

1. If 90 percent of the black people in America have ancestors that include white people, how can we tell when black genes or white genes make for a wrong mark on a test score sheet?
2. If a large percent of white people have black ancestors, who are they? Are their samples controlled for this factor? Which genes, black or white, make for right marks on a test score sheet?
3. How can we parse out the effects of brain damage, brain stunting (due to malnutrition), and lack of early stimulation? Which accounts for a wrong mark on the test score sheet?
4. How can we parse and measure the degree of access and *welcome* of black people to cultural learnings?
5. How can we parse and measure the interest in and acceptance of the white "way of life" by black mothers and children? One can't get good scores on a "way of life" test like IQ unless one lives and accepts this life fully.
6. How can we develop indices which show comparability of school strengths, weaknesses, and emphases? The school assessment study by Tyler's group is just getting underway over loud cries from many school people.

Jensen failed to consider the learning styles of black parents and the origins of these learning styles when he made white–black comparisons on associative and problem-solving learning. If you go to many rural schools in the South today, you will find the associative type of learning proceeding as it has for many, many years—*for both races*. This is the learning heritage of most big-city black parents. They pass this style on to the kids early and it shows up in test profiles. If conceptual learning is viewed as a gradual acculturation process and offered early in school careers, these kids can be made to think. Jensen's exhortations to teachers to rely completely on associative learning might preclude this ever becoming a reality, however. Before any more articles are published, I think Jensen should do more work in the area of black history, demography, and culture and that he should try to get into the area of racism and isolation and the big role they play in differences. There really is merit in his actually taking the black injections and getting firsthand information. He would only have to be a black man for two months.

Jensen's "*g*-factor," the main basis of his claims for white supremacy, cannot be accepted as the mysterious phenomenon he postulates. Even little children now know from their television science that if something really exists, scientists will isolate it and measure it—especially before making serious conclusions about it.

I believe Jensen made two good points. One is that IQ tests don't show the full learning potential of kids who are poor and black. I was happy to learn that he had invented a test which does a better job. We should all buy it. He should make millions. The other is that intensive instruction rather than "cultural enrichment" is necessary to make these kids learn if they are locked in neighborhood schools. Unlike Jensen, I believe that they can proceed from associative learning to abstract reasoning if the instruction gradually brings them to this point. And even with this, I believe black kids will continue to think and score test items differently until full equality is achieved. Black kids screen out much of the curriculum and perceive the rest differently. Consider perceptions of Tarzan and the British Empire, for examples. Of course, some black nationalists feel that it is a blessing that black people don't think like white people. As long as they can handle modern technology, make war, manipulate stocks, etc., I don't guess it really matters.

I believe the most potent strategy in the end will prove to be a combination of early stimulation and imprinting, and integrated schools with teachers who are free of racial and social class prejudices. IQ tests will also be eliminated from the schools. This is the strategy on which Neil Sullivan based his cross-bussing operations for the Berkeley schools. This may account for some of Jensen's concerns and reservations and, perhaps, for his article. Pettigrew and others presented evidence in their work for the Civil Rights Commission that the earlier black children were placed in integrated schools, the closer they came to white norms on achievement tests. In turn, the white children came closer to perfection in their social learnings while losing no ground in test proficiency. The black children pick up the mysteries of Jensen's "*g*-factor" through association, I suppose, while the white children pick up the mysteries of "soul."

PART III

Personality and Motivation

The psychological cripple *theme is prevalent in the psychological literature concerning the personality and motivation of black Americans. Characteristically, blacks have been described as docile, acquiescent, and self-effacing in relating to whites, and as hostile, aggressive, and violent in relating to fellow blacks. In general, the black American's interpersonal relations have been described as reflecting low self-esteem, self-hatred, low achievement motivation, confused self-identity, and all manner of "marks of oppression." This* oppression neurosis *theme has frequently served as a springboard for discussions of the personality dynamics of blacks. All too often, this emphasis on identification has limited the scope of researchers. Freudian psychology has undoubtedly contributed its share of "deficit" views. There is evidence that these myopic views are changing. Racial pride, changes in identity, self-acceptance, and healthy aggressiveness are characteristic of the new blacks. Recent contributions of black behavioral scientists are documenting these changes. Articles in this section reflect these changes, develop hypotheses about their nature and origins, and point to directions for their further modification and development.*

In the first paper, "Black Youth and Motivation," Alvin Poussaint and Carolyn Atkinson identify several classes of variables that seem to have some explanatory usefulness in accounting for the motivational behavior of black Americans. In addition, the authors examine the standards and rewards of white society that have some influence upon the motivation of blacks and suggest that there is an urgent need for restructuring society. Using findings from the research literature for support, the authors identify specific areas where changes and restructuring might take place. In "Toward a Theory of the Unique Personality of Blacks—A Psychocultural Assessment," a similar and provocative kind of analysis, Doris P. Mosby views black personality development in a cultural context. The psychological effect of the new pride in blackness upon divergent cultural systems is examined.

Although one would scarcely suspect so, based on much traditional speculation and theorizing, individual differences among blacks do exist! Thomas O. Hilliard's paper, "Personality Characteristics of Black Student Activists and Nonactivists," represents one attempt at exploring differences in psychological functioning between black activists and those who passively accept racism. Early in the paper, Hilliard reviews the methodology used in studying the black personality and concludes that a principal limitation has been the absence of a social-psychological perspective. Here Hilliard touches a theme running throughout the volume—that is, any attempt to explain behavior must be undertaken within a psychohistorical and social context. The main body of the paper is devoted to an exploration of the personality dynamics differentiating black activist and nonactivist college students. Significant differences between groups were found both on test measures and on background variables.

The development of pride, racial identification, and racial awareness is one of the great psychological transformations undergone by black Americans in this century. Whether such phenomena are illusory or represent real psychological gains has not been the object of serious study. Pearl Gore Dansby's paper, "Black Pride in the Seventies: Fact or Fantasy?" is a pioneering effort in this area. In a series of studies using children in nursery-school settings, changes in racial pride, self awareness and identification were documented.

"Stages in the Development of Black Awareness: An Exploratory Investigation," the paper by William Hall, William E. Cross, and Roy Freedle, complements the Dansby work and provides a theoretical structure for the findings and related observations. The authors review incisively the literature concerning identity transformation and develop hypotheses about stages through which black Americans pass. Empirical data supporting the hypotheses are presented.

Data on the changing nature of black college students' self-image and racial identification have been published. Data on changes in the self- and racial images suggest that the racial awareness movement is also influencing the perceptions of young children, although easy generalizations cannot be made. Dansby's data on doll preferences reveal sex differences as well as socioeconomic differences in preferences for black or white dolls or black dolls with Afro or straight hair. In all of this, however, evidence from the Dansby study suggests that preschool black children, in one southern city at least, have rather high self-regard and positive racial identity. The generality of these findings is, of course, unknown.

What mechanisms lead to the development of healthy self-image and high personal regard? In the final paper of the section, "The Black Community As the Source of Positive Self-Concept for Black Children: A Theoretical Perspective," Edward J. Barnes reviews a mountain of data from social and psychological sources related to the development of the black child's self-concept and questions many of the hypotheses and findings in this area. Barnes also warns against using research based on low-income blacks as a basis for generalizing about blacks and against assuming that the generalized other to which the black child responds is synonymous with white society. Another important contribution Barnes makes is his spelling out conditions and characteristics of the black community that facilitate development of a positive self-identity in the black child. Finally, he presents the results of research supportive of certain notions advanced earlier in the paper and draws implications for educational programs, program evaluation, and research.

ALVIN F. POUSSAINT and CAROLYN ATKINSON

Black Youth and Motivation

The civil rights movement of the 1960s in America spawned a new and vibrant generation of young black people. The degree of their commitment and determination came as a surprise for most white Americans, who, if they thought of blacks to any extent, considered them to be a rather docile, acquiescent people. As the events of the early 1960s moved on with inexorable force, another, still younger generation of blacks stood on the periphery watching and waiting their turn. Their intense coming-of-age has brought still more surprise and puzzlement not only to white Americans, but to some Negroes. So busy have many been in "handling" or "coping with" the complex behavior of these young blacks, that relatively little has been done in terms of examining the basis for this behavior. This paper represents an attempt to pause in the on-going melee for an exploration of some of the factors of particular relevance to the motivation of Afro-American youth. Our analysis will focus on some of the "problem areas," so of necessity it will not detail the many strengths and positive features of the black sociocultural environment. Of primary interest in our discussion will be the areas of internal motivation: the individual's self-concept; certain of his patterned needs; and the external motivators—the rewards offered by society for satisfactory performance in any of its institutional areas.

Of obvious importance to the functioning of any individual is his concept or vision of himself. And like it or not, this concept is inevitably a part of how others see him, how others tell him he should be seen. According to Mead (1), Cooley (2), and others (3), the self arises through the individual's interaction with and reaction to other members of society: his peers, parents, teachers, and other institutional representatives. Through identification and as a necessary means of effective communication, the child learns to assume the roles and attitudes of others with whom he interacts. These assumed attitudes condition not only how he responds to others, but how he behaves toward himself. The collective attitudes of the others, the community or "generalized other" as Mead calls them, give the individual his unity of self. The individual's self is shaped, developed, and controlled by his anticipating and assuming the attitudes and definitions of others (the community) toward him. To the extent that the individual is a member of this community, its attitudes are his, its values are his, and its norms are his. His image of himself is structured in these terms. Each self, then, though having its unique characteristics of personality, is also an individual

From *The Black Scholar*, 1970, 1(5), 43–51. © *The Black Scholar*. Reprinted by permission of the author and the publisher.

reflection of the social process (4). This idea can be seen more succinctly illustrated in Cooley's suggestion of the self as a looking-glass, a looking-glass mirroring the three principal components of one's self-concept: "the imagination of our appearance to the other person; the imagination of his judgment of that appearance; and some sort of self-feeling, such as pride or mortification" (5).

For the black youth in white American society, the generalized other whose attitudes he assumes and the looking-glass into which he gazes both reflect the same judgment: He is inferior because he is black. His self-image, developed in the lowest stratum of a color caste system, is shaped, defined, and evaluated by a generalized other which is racist or warped by racists. His self-concept naturally becomes a negatively esteemed one, nurtured through contact with such institutionalized symbols of caste inferiority as segregated schools, neighborhoods, and jobs and more indirect negative indicators such as the reactions of his own family who have been socialized to believe that they are substandard human beings. Gradually becoming aware of the meaning of his black skin, the Negro child comes to see himself as an object of scorn and disparagement, unworthy of love and affection. The looking-glass of white society reflects the supposed undesirability of the black youth's physical appearance: black skin and wooly hair, as opposed to the valued models of white skin and straight hair. In order to gain the esteem of the generalized other, it becomes clear to him that he must approximate this white appearance as closely as possible. He learns to despise himself and to reject those like himself. From the moment of this realization, his personality and style of interaction with his environment become molded and shaped in a warped, self-hating, and self-denigrating way. He learns that existence for him in this society demands a strict adherence to the limitations of his substandard state. He comes to understand that to challenge the definition the others have given of him will destroy him. It is impressed upon him that the incompetent, acquiescent and irresponsible Negro survives in American society, while the competent, aggressive black is systematically suppressed. The looking-glass of the black youth's self reflects a shattered and defeated image.

Several attempts have been made to determine how this shattered self-concept affects the black child's ability to function in society, his ability to achieve, to succeed or "make good," particularly in the area of education. Though the conclusions of these varied attempts have differed on occasion, there has been general agreement as to the reality of the black child's incomplete self-image (6, 7, 8). One notable exception to this agreement, however, is the Coleman Report, a 1966 study by the United States Office of Education on the *Equality of Education Opportunity* (9). This report maintains that the black child's self-concept has not been exceptionally damaged, and is in fact virtually no different from that of a white child. The report did, however, note that the white child is consistently able to achieve on a higher level than that of his black counterpart. The Coleman Study, therefore, concluded that self-concept has little to do with an individual's ability to achieve (10). Other studies tend to disagree with these findings.

Another variation on this theme of the black child's self-concept is seen in a 1968 report on "Academic Motivation and Equal Educational Opportunity" done by Irwin Katz. Katz found that black children tended to have exaggeratedly high aspirations, so high, in fact, that they were realistically impossible to live up to. As a result, these children were able to achieve very little:

Conceivably, their [low achieving Negro boys'] standards were so stringent and rigid as to be utterly dysfunctional. They seem to have internalized a most effective mechanism for self-discouragement. In a sense, they had been socialized to self-impose failure. (11)

Katz presents evidence which indicates that the anticipation of failure or harsh judgment by adults produces anxiety in the child, and that in black children, this level of anxiety is highest in low achievers who have a high standard of self-evaluation (12). Accordingly, a black child with an unrealistically elevated self-concept often tends to become so anxious concerning his possible failure to meet that self-concept that he does in fact fail consistently.

On the other hand, Deutsch's work has shown that Negro children had significantly more negative self-images than did white children (13). He maintains that, among the influences converging on the black urban child,

... is his sensing that the larger society views him as inferior and expects inferior performance from him as evidenced by the general denial to him of realistic vertical mobility possibilities. Under these conditions, it is understandable that the Negro child would tend strongly to question his own competencies and in so questioning would be acting largely as others expect him to act, an example of what Merton has called the "self-fulfilling prophecy"—the very expectation itself is a cause of its fulfillment. (14)

Similarly, Coombs and Davies offer the important proposition that

In the context of the school world, a student who is defined as a "poor student" (by significant others and thereby by self) comes to conceive of himself as such and gears his behavior accordingly, that is, the social expectation is realized. However, if he is led to believe by means of the social "looking-glass" that he is capable and able to achieve well, he does. To maintain his status and self-esteem becomes the incentive for further effort which subsequently involves him more in the reward system of the school. (15)

These views have been confirmed in such studies as that of Davidson and Greenberg (16). In their examination of children from central Harlem, these authors found that the lower the level of self-esteem, the lower the level of achievement; while consequently, higher levels of self-appraisal and ego strength—feelings of self-competence—were associated with higher levels of achievement. For example, high achievers were more able to give their own ideas and to express basic needs, suggesting that a stronger self-concept is associated with a greater willingness to risk self-expression, an obvious prerequisite for achievement.

Certainly these various studies cannot be considered as ultimately nor unanimously conclusive. However, it is important to note that none of these reports has found any evidence of high achievement resulting from a low self-concept. Obviously the black child with such a low self-concept competes at a disadvantage with white youth in the struggle to achieve in this society.

The question then arises as to why black youth bother to involve themselves at all in this struggle. If their negative self-image handicaps them so greatly in achieving, why not simply abdicate and in fact adhere to society's definition of them as substandard? An attempted response to this question moves us into another area, that of patterned needs.

In the course of the socialization process, the individual acquires needs which motivate behavior and generate emotions. Three such needs concern us here: the need for achievement, the need for self-assertion or aggression, and the need for approval.

Among the attitudes of the generalized other which the individual in this society internalizes are the norms and values of the wider community, including, of course, the major tenets of the Protestant Ethic–American creed, i.e., with hard work and effort the individual can achieve success, and the individual's worth is defined by his ability to achieve that success. The individual who internalizes these values is motivated to act consistently with them, as his self-esteem is heightened or maintained through behaving in a manner approved by the community. Thus, the need for achievement develops in both white and black Americans. Consequently, the black youth's participation in the struggle for success is at least in part an attempt to satisfy his own needs.

This need to achieve may be very high as illustrated in the findings of Coleman [17] and Katz [18] who note the exceptionally high aspirations of Negro youth with regard to schooling and occupational choice. In addition, Katz [19] and Gordon [20] indicate that the aspirations and demands for academic achievement of the parents of these youth are also often exceptionally high. All of these sources agree, however, that the achievement of these youth is far from commensurate with either their own aspirations or those of their parents [21]. Thus, the problem does not seem to be, as some have suggested, one of insufficiently high levels of aspiration, but rather one of realizing these aspirations through productive behavior [22]. Gordon [23] and Katz [24] suggest that this discrepancy persists because the educational and occupational values and goals of white society have been internalized by black youth, but for one reason or another, the behavior patterns necessary for their successful attainment have not been similarly learned. Katz puts it succinctly:

Apparently the typical Negro mother tries to socialize her child for scholastic achievement by laying down verbal rules and regulations about classroom [behavior], coupled with punishment or detected transgressions. But she does not do enough to guide and encourage her child's efforts at verbal-symbolic mastery. Therefore, the child learns only to verbalize standards of academic interest and attainment. Their standards then provide the cognitive basis for negative self-evaluations. . . . The low achieving Negro student learns to use expressions of interest and ambition as a verbal substitute for behaviors he is unable to enact. . . . By emphasizing the discrepancy between the real and ideal performance, anxiety is raised in actual achievement situations. (25)

Thus, the black child's negative self-concept is further complicated by his internalization of white society's high-level goals, and the need to achieve them, without a true comprehension of how effectively to do so.

Further examination of the values of the Protestant Ethic leads to the conclusion that they imply that assertion of self and aggression is an expected and admired form of behavior. Through the socialization process, the individual internalizes those attitudes which reinforce his basic need to assert himself or express himself aggressively. Thus, random and possibly destructive aggression is channeled into a legitimate and rewarded avenue of achievement (26).

What happens to the black child's need for aggression and self-assertion? What has been the nature of his socialization with respect to expressing aggression? Since slavery days and, to some extent, through the present, the Negro most rewarded by whites has been the "Uncle Tom," the exemplar of the black man who was docile and nonassertive, who bowed and scraped for the white boss and denied his aggressive feelings for his oppressor. In order to retain the most menial of jobs and keep from starving, black people quickly learned that passivity was a necessary survival technique. To be an "uppity nigger" was considered by racists one of the gravest violations of racial etiquette. Vestiges of this attitude remain to the present day, certainly in the South, but also in the North: Blacks who are too "outspoken" about racial injustices often lose their jobs or are not promoted to higher positions because they are considered "unreasonable" or "too sensitive." It is significant that the civil rights movement had to adopt passive resistance and nonviolence in order to win acceptance by white America. Thus, the black child is socialized to the lesson taught by his parents, other blacks, and white society: Don't be aggressive, don't be assertive. Such lessons do not, however, destroy the need for aggression and self-assertion.

One asserts oneself for self-expression, for achievement of one's goals, and for control of one's environment. Thus, an individual's success in satisfying his need for self-assertion is to some degree determined by his sense of control of his environment. Coleman found that of three attitudes measured, sense of control over environment showed the strongest relationship to achievement (27). He further discovered that blacks have a much lower sense of control over their environment than do whites (28), but that this sense of control increased as the proportion of whites with whom they went to school increased (29). These findings indicate that for blacks, a realistic inability for meaningful self-assertion is a greater inhibitor of ability to achieve than is any other variable. These findings also suggest, however, that when blacks are interacting in a school situation which approximates the world in which they must cope, i.e., one with whites, their sense of control and achievement increases. Our emphasis here is not that black students' being in the presence of white students increases their sense of control and level of achievement, but that their being in a proximate real world suggests to them that they can cope in any situation, not just one in which they are interacting with others who, like themselves, have been defined as inferior.

Coleman's findings are supported by those of Davidson and Greenberg: High achievers were more able to exercise control and to cope more effectively with feelings of hostility and anxiety generated by the environment than were low achievers (30). Deutsch points out that black male children for whom aggressive behavior has always been more threatening (compared with black girls) have lower levels of achievement on a number of variables than do black girls (31). It is not surprising then that black people, objectively less able to control their environment than can whites, may react in abdicating control by deciding not to assert themselves. The reasons for this are clear. First, the anxiety that accompanies growth and change through self-assertion is avoided if a new failure is not risked and thus a try is not made. Second, the steady state of failure through nonachievement rather than through unsuccessful trial is a pattern which many blacks have come to know and expect. They feel psychologically comfortable with the more familiar.

However, this effort by black people to deny their need for control and self-assertion inevitably takes its toll. Frustration of efforts to control the environment are likely to lead to anger, rage, and other expressions of aggression (32). This aggression can be dealt with in a variety of ways. It can be suppressed, leading one to act on the basis of a substitute and opposing emotional attitude, i.e., compliance or docility. It can be channeled through legitimate activities—dancing, sports, or through an identification with the oppressor and a consequent striving to be like him. Aggression can also be turned inward and expressed in psychosomatic illness, drug addiction, or the attacking of those like oneself (other blacks) whom one hates as much as oneself. Or aggression can be directed toward those who generate the anger and rage—the oppressors, those whom the individual defines as thwarting this inclination to self-assertion. This final form of aggression can be either destructive or constructive: Dropping out of school or becoming delinquent are examples of the former case, while participation in black social action movements is an example of the latter instance. This latter form of aggressive behavior amongst black people is increasing in extent. The old passivity is fading and being replaced by a drive to undo powerlessness, helplessness, and dependency under American racism. The process is a difficult one for those black people who manage to make the attempt. For their aggressive drive, so long suppressed by the ruling power structure, is exercised to the inevitable detriment of still another exigency: their need for approval.

With the development of the self and through the process of identification, the individual's need for approval develops and grows as does his need to avoid disapproval (33). As we have stated earlier, the Protestant Ethic of American society approves behavior which follows the achievement motive and expresses the need for self-assertion. An individual's behavior in accordance with this ethic is often tied to a need for approval. On the other hand, for blacks in American society, the reverse is often the case, i.e., behavior which is neither achievement-oriented nor self-assertive is often approved by both blacks and whites (for different reasons), and thus, the need for approval may be met through behavior unrelated to either achievement or self-assertion.

Katz's study maintains that in lower-class homes, children do not learn realistic (middle-class) standards of self-appraisal and therefore do not develop (as do middle-class children) the capacity for gaining "satisfaction through self-approval of successful performance" (34). Accordingly, Katz suggests that achievement should be motivated and rewarded by approval not from the home, but from fellow students and teachers (35). The extent to which black children are responsive to approval for achievement in middle-class terms is, however, problematic. Some evidence suggests that lower-class black children are motivated to gain approval through physical characteristics and prowess rather than through intellectual achievement as are middle-class white and black children (36). Further, needs for approval, not often met in black children through the established institutional channels, may be met by others outside of these legitimate institutional areas. For instance, delinquent subcultures support and encourage the behavior of their members. As a result, such members are not often sensitive to the informal sanctions imposed by nonmembers of this subsociety (37). If an individual's needs are not met by others to whose sanctions he is expected to be responsive, he will be less likely to fear their sanctions for nonperformance and will seek to have his needs met by others to whose rewards of approval he will then be responsive (38). Thus, for black youth no less than others, how the need for approval motivates behavior depends in large part upon how it is satisfied or rewarded.

The rewards which the institutions of this society offer to those whose behavior meets their approval or is "successful" consist of money, prestige, power, respect, acclamation, and love, with increasing amounts of each of these being extended for increasingly "successful" behavior. The individual is socialized to know that these will be his if he performs according to expectations. Hence, these rewards act as external motivators of behavior. Blacks have learned of the existence of these rewards. They have also learned, however, that behavior for which whites reap these rewards does not result in the same consequences for them. In the various institutional areas of society, blacks are often rewarded differentially from whites for the same behavior—if they are rewarded at all. How then can such a highly capricious system motivate their behavior?

That blacks orient some aspects of their behavior to society's reward system is evidenced by the fact that many studies have shown that lower-class blacks, as opposed to middle-class whites and blacks, have a utilitarian attitude toward education, viewing it primarily in terms of its market value (39). The system provides no assurance, however, that once they obtain the proper education for a job, they will in fact be allowed to get that job. This inability to trust society to confer rewards consistently no doubt makes it difficult for blacks to be socialized to behave in terms of anticipating future reward for present activity. Thus, it is that Deutsch found that young black children are unwilling to persist in attempting to solve difficult problems. They respond to such situations with a "who cares" attitude (40). Similarly, another study showed that when a tangible reward was offered for successful work on a test, the motivation of the deprived youngsters increased considerably (41). In a New York program, young men who had been working primarily as clerks and porters were motivated to join a tutorial program for admission to a construction trade union apprenticeship program when they were promised that successful completion of the program (passing the union's examination) would definitely result in their being hired immediately at a salary often double what they were able to command previously (42).

However, motivation to achieve certain rewards may have different consequences for behavior. As Merton explained, when the goals of society are internalized without a corresponding internalization of normative means for achieving these goals, what often results is the resort to illegitimate (deviant) means to achieve the socially valued goals (43). Just as a child unable to satisfy his need for approval through legitimate channels may turn to delinquent subcultures for support and encouragement, so too might such a child, unable to gain society's rewards by legitimate means, turn to illegitimate methods in order to attain them. Such forms of behavior as numbers running, dope pushing, and prostitution effectively serve to net the rewards of society, while circumventing the institutional channels for achievement of societal rewards. That Negro children early learn that such behavior is rewarded is suggested by Gordon's study in which young (9-13) central Harlem boys were asked if they knew people who had become rich, and if so, how they thought they had managed to do so. Of those who responded affirmatively, a majority felt that they had become rich through illegitimate means or luck (44).

Consequently, for many black youth, external rewards are weak motivators of behavior, as they are discriminatorily and inconsistently given. The more immediate and direct the reward is, the stronger a motivator it is likely to be.

It would appear from this analysis that the standards and rewards of white American society simply do not work effectively to motivate productive behavior in young blacks. Clearly there is urgent need for a fundamental restructuring of the system. First, with respect to self-concept, all institutional segments of society must begin to function in a nonracist manner. To the extent that the self is shaped with reference to a generalized other, to that extent will the black child's image be impaired as long as America remains racist. The growth of black consciousness and pride have had salutary consequences for the black's self-image. But this alone is not sufficient. The operation of self-image as a motivator for behavior is like a self-fulfilling prophecy: Blacks are continuously told and some believe that they are inferior and will fail. Therefore, they fail. For the black child to be motivated to achieve in school, the school must negate everything that the society affirms: It must tell the child that he can succeed—and he will (45).

The relationship between self-concept and achievement is not clear-cut, but it appears to be a weaker motivator of behavior than the motive to self-assertion and aggression. More attention should be given to examining this dimension of personality as a motivator of the black youth's behavior than to continuing inquiries into his self-image. It has been noted that the black youth's sense of control of his environment increases as the proportion of whites in his school increases. It is imperative to keep in mind, however, that participation in all-or-predominantly-black structures need not be self-destructive if the black youth chooses rather than is forced to participate in them. For if he chooses, he is asserting control over his environment. Those structural changes being made in American society in the direction of blacks having the opportunity to be more aggressively in control of their environment must be continued and expanded. The plans to decentralize New York City schools, to develop black business, and to organize and channel black political power are significant steps in this direction.

Most of the data indicate that black youth and their parents have high educational and occupational aspirations, which are not carried through to achievement levels. The reward systems of American society are often irrelevant to the lives and aspirations of most black youth. Approval is rewarded primarily for forms of behavior in which the black youth has managed to achieve little proficiency, making him less likely to make the effort. Something is obviously wrong with any school system which permits so much young potential to be wasted simply because it cannot be developed within the confines of traditional methods. New frameworks must be developed which will enable the educational aspirations of black youth to correspond to their interests and proficiencies. With the establishment of a pattern of consistent reward, there is every possibility that intellectual endeavors would have immediate relevance to their lives.

Certainly these suggested changes are sweeping, but so too have been the dangerous effects of the maintenance of the old systems. The time for being surprised at the behavior of black youth has passed. The time for lengthy, nonproductive attempts at understanding them has too, in its turn, come to an end. The time remaining must be effectively used in action to bring about these and similar changes. America cannot afford to wait for the next generation.

Notes and References

1. George H. Mead, *Mind, self, and society* (Chicago: University of Chicago Press, 1934), Part III.
2. Charles H. Cooley, *Human nature and the social order* (New York: Free Press, 1956), *passim*.
3. *Sociological Quarterly*, Summer 1966, 7(3), entire issue.
4. Mead, *op. cit.*
5. Cooley, *op. cit.*

6. Alvin F. Poussaint, The dynamics of racial conflict, *Lowell Lecture Series*, sponsored by the Tufts-New England Medical Center, April 16, 1968.
7. Joan Gordon, *The poor of Harlem: Social functioning in the underclass*, Report to the Welfare Administration, Washington, D.C., July 31, 1965, pp. 115, 161; and Irwin Katz, Academic motivation and equal educational opportunity, *Harvard Educational Review*, Winter 1968, 38, 56-65.
8. While we recognize the limitations of many measures of self-concept and that self-concept is often defined by how it is measured, an exploration of these considerations within the scope of this paper is clearly impossible. Therefore, for the purpose of our presentation here, we are taking the measures of self-concept at face value.
9. James S. Coleman et al., *Equality of educational opportunity*, U.S. Office of Education (Washington, D.C.: U.S. Government Printing Office, 1966), p. 281.
10. *Ibid.*, p. 320.
11. Katz, *op. cit.*, p. 60.
12. *Ibid.*, pp. 61-62.
13. Martin Deutsch, Minority groups and class status as related to social and personality factors in scholastic achievement, in Martin Deutsch et al., *The disadvantaged child* (New York: Basic Books, 1967), p. 106.
14. *Ibid.*, p. 107.
15. R. H. Coombs and V. Davies, Self-conception and the relationship between high school and college scholastic achievement, *Sociology and Social Research*, July 1966, **50**, 468-469.
16. Helen H. Davidson and Judith W. Greenberg, *Traits of school achievers from a deprived background* (New York: City College of the City University of New York, May 1967), pp. 133, 134.
17. Coleman, *op. cit.*, pp. 278-280.
18. Katz, *op. cit.*, p. 64.
19. *Ibid.*, pp. 63-65.
20. Gordon, *op. cit.*, p. 115.
21. Coleman, *op. cit.*, p. 281; Katz, *op. cit.,* p. 63; Gordon, *op. cit.*, pp. 155, 160-161.
22. David P. Ausubel and Pearl Ausubel, Ego development among segregated Negro children, in A. Harry Passow (ed.), *Education in depressed areas* (New York: Teachers College Press, 1963), p. 135.
23. Gordon, *op. cit.*, pp. 115, 161.
24. Katz, *op. cit.*, p. 63.
25. *Ibid.*, p. 64.
26. Davidson and Greenberg, *op. cit.*, p. 58.
27. Coleman, *op. cit.*, p. 319.
28. *Ibid.*, p. 289.
29. *Ibid.*, pp. 323-324.
30. Davidson and Greenberg, *op. cit.*, p. 54.
31. Deutsch, *op. cit.*, p. 108.
32. Alvin F. Poussaint, A Negro psychiatrist explains the Negro psyche, *New York Times Magazine*, August 20, 1967, pp. 58-80.
33. Davidson and Greenberg, *op. cit.*, p. 61.
34. Katz, *op. cit.*, p. 57.
35. *Ibid.*
36. Edmund W. Gordon and Doxey A. Wilkerson, *Compensatory education for the disadvantaged* (New York: College Entrance Examination Board, 1966), p. 18.
37. Claude Brown, *Manchild in the promised land* (New York: Macmillan, 1965), *passim*.
38. Talcott Parsons, *The social system* (New York: Free Press, 1951), chap. 7.
39. Gordon and Wilkerson, *op. cit.*, p. 18.
40. Deutsch, *op. cit.*, p. 102.

41. Elizabeth Douvan, Social status and success striving, cited in Frank Riessman, *The culturally deprived child* (New York: Harper & Row, 1962), p. 53.
42. Personal communication (C. A.).
43. Robert K. Merton, *Social theory and social structure* (New York: Free Press, 1957), chap. 4.
44. Gordon, *op. cit.*, p. 164.
45. Kenneth B. Clark, *Dark ghetto* (New York: Harper & Row, 1965), pp. 139–148.

DORIS P. MOSBY

Toward a Theory of the Unique Personality of Blacks—
A Psychocultural Assessment

For centuries, philosophers and man have struggled with the question of determinism. Throughout humanity, man has sought to answer whether his destiny is ruled by forces within or forces without. Proponents of individual destiny feel that strong, constructive urges within the individual inspire him to actualize himself in the most positive direction. They believe in the innate goodness of man, the will to live and the ultimate triumph over environment. Those of the opposite belief maintain that man's inner urges are hedonistic (pleasure-oriented), self-centered, and destructive. They maintain that such urges, if allowed to persist, would only result in the ultimate destruction of humanity. Therefore, they argue, the environment has to undertake the character-molding and socializing of the individual for the ultimate good of the organized society.

Thus are the "lines" drawn. One view is that the individual's inner motives, behavior, and traits—his ego or selfness—exert the main influence upon the character of his life and are the main determinants of his ultimate mature personality. The opposite view holds that cultural forces distinctly mold the individual into the type of mature adult he is to become and that his personal traits have minimum influence in this molding process.

These two views of determinism are similar in that they both attempt to answer the question of emphasis in the man-vs.-environment struggle. Both agree on the direction and the importance of a force, be it the ego or the culture, upon the individual. Personality has been defined in about 50 different ways. Generally, the definitions emphasize the unique configuration of behaviors, inner dispositions, learnings, potentials, and deficits that characterizes an individual and determines his process "of becoming somebody." Culture, although defined in over 150 ways, broadly entails the influence of larger group memberships, role and status determination attendant upon being a group member, geographical adaptations necessitated by one's area of residence, and the traditional group values and behaviors rewarded in the general socialization process of one's group. "Group" can be variously defined further according to family membership, local residence, country of residence, larger geographic regions (e.g., Western vs. non-Western), and various subcultural divisions according to ethnic, racial, religious, caste, or economic differential factors of membership.

One approach to personality formation maintains "that the individual in-

Paper presented at a Universide-Wide Lecture, Texas Southern University, Houston, Texas, February 18, 1970. Sponsored by the American Psychological Association, Visiting Scientist Program. Reprinted by permission of the author.

fluences, creates, molds, and fashions his culture." This is called the "individual-istic issue" by Price-Williams (1968). The second thesis asserts "that the individ-ual is influenced, created, molded, fashioned by his culture." Price-Williams (1968) labels this the "culturological issue" (p. 88). According to the former thesis, "all large scale social characteristics are not merely the intended or unin-tended result of, but a reflection of individual characteristics" (Watkins, 1957). Thus, it is the underlying unique configuration of individual motivations, affects, beliefs, abilities, and deficits that determine the ultimate characteristic of a complex social situation, be it a city, state, nation, or the world. In contrast, the culturological view explores the effect of culture on personality traits and on psychological functions, and its ultimate modification of generalizations about human development, functioning, and efficiency.

It can be maintained that the individual cannot be "subtracted" from his culture—from his milieu—and that an external referent is always mandatory in any discussion of personality. However, one might hesitate to generalize as Popper (1900) does that "Men—i.e., human minds, the needs, the hopes, fears and expectations, the motives and aspirations of human individuals—are, if any-thing, the product of life in society rather than its creators" (p. 93). One might hesitate to propose this position for fear of advocating cultural determinism. Yet it is reasonable to state that the personality of the individual follows the form of the dominant culture. As such, the cultural or social milieu can neither be ignored nor treated complementarily by psychologists. To exclude this factor from the study of personality would omit relevant aspects of the individual's life history and the basic character of the early socialization process. Operationally, even for clinical study, evaluation, and treatment, it is not possible to conceive of the human organism in isolation from the social milieu that is significant for him or envelops him. Thus the character of the culture and the character of the individual must be delineated. In the process of that study due consideration must be accorded hereditary constitution and social environment, and their complex interaction; these factors also impinge upon the human organism.

The implications of the two varying views of personality formation are de-picted in Figure 1.

If one believes that oppressed groups differ in some important personality dimension from oppressor groups, then a theory of the unique personality of members of an oppressed group can be advanced. Furthermore, the etiology of the differential personality formation in oppressed vs. oppressing individuals can be conceptualized within a psychocultural framework. These points will be developed in support of a theory of the unique black personality.

This writer maintains that the formation of the black personality occurs mainly through culturological influence. The black person grows up on the margin of a white dominant culture, which makes him "feel inferior." The personality of the black person is molded, determined, shaped by a dominant and generally adverse cultural influence. As a result of continuous repressive restrictions and inferiority perceptions, he internalizes inadequacy, achieves at best a precarious mental balance, develops into a fragile human being. Further-

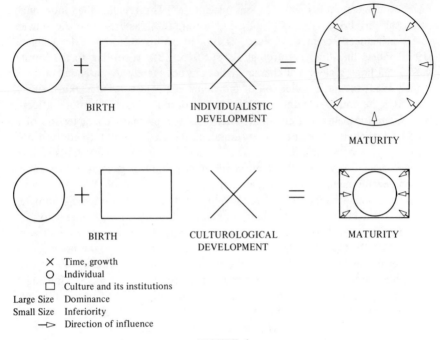

FIGURE 1
Theoretical views of personality formation.

more, this cultural influence appears to counteract and override the potentially positive factors of his innate influences and of his own subculture.

The concepts of equilibrium, divergence, and identity are important in the relations between the major and minor elements of a culture. If equilibrium, or harmony, characterizes the interactions between the dominant and marginal groups of a culture, then psychological equilibrium and an inner state of happiness should characterize all individual members of those subcultures and their interactions. But should social disorganization be more typical of such relations because the minority-group member is subjected to a position of inferiority he is not willing to accept, then individual pathology can be expected to characterize individual members of both the majority and minority groups and their interactions. The majority group may show its pathology in bigotry, rigid and pathological prejudicial attitudes, and unreasonable discriminatory practices. The minority group may show its pathology in intense fear of bodily harm, aggressiveness which is either acted out or rigidly and indiscriminately controlled, and dependent, ineffectual attitudes or behavior.

It is expected that the pathology would be generally reflected in individual subculture members, the subculture as a group, and the social structure of that subculture. This pattern appears to be reflected in the case of the black person. In the individual black, one can find a complex personality syndrome characterized by depersonalization. This trait grows out of the feeling that one lacks personal dignity, pride, and accomplishment. The lack leads to the questioning of one's ego, that which is the core of the self, that which gives continuity of personality. Usually the more pessimistic attitudes exist. Thus, the black personality may be highly loaded on negative emotionality. The individual's verbalizations and behavior appear to be influenced mostly by apathy, depression, and anxiety. These negative traits are those that have been reinforced in his interactions with culture and those he perceived to emanate from others in the socialization process. He has been subjected to the deprivation of significant or satisfying status in his life. He has been offered only menial, low-status roles which reinforce the perception of a lack of dignity and personal worth. He may even learn to hate himself as intensely as others seem to hate him. Over time, and without other positive perceptions of himself available as a referent, an identity, usually a negative one, is crystallized. Continual attempts at reassurance regarding who he is, who he wants to be, and who he is expected to be meet with discrepancy, confusion, and chaos. The real, the ideal, and the social self become cleaved from each other, rather than integrated. As a result, he may don changing hats, and play varying roles in different situations. A split rather than a whole ego may develop. Furthermore, with the personality and ego changing and lacking a continual baseline, self-actualization becomes a formidable task. The cleavage between the various aspects of the black person's ego widens rather than narrows with increasing age. This breakdown in personality is shown in Figure 2.

SEVERE   MODERATE   MILD

FIGURE 2

The breakdown of defensive layers of the black personality in interaction with cultural devaluation.

But, ultimately the individual must somehow resolve the conflict of identity. He may turn to his group. The individual finds that he shares his uncertainty with all black persons whose ancient cultural foundations of identity, stability, and adequacy have been destroyed by the *zeitgeist*, the nature of the times in which he lives. For this reason, group cohesiveness and group support of the initiation of group resources to resolve the identity conflict have, heretofore, been minimal. Therefore, when the minority group finds itself in conflict with the major culture because values are divergent and because it resists the acceptance of the roles assigned to it, then the minority group has to accept the responsibility for effecting a change to accommodate the circumstances. Thus, the group, like the individual, struggles with the same problem. Overpowered by the sheer numbers of the majority groups, the black finds that direct fighting and confrontation are inadequate resolutions. Powerless in terms of financial wealth, the black group cannot hope to buy acceptance or to change the social structure in this manner. Generally uneducated, the group as a whole cannot seek to change attitudes and their lot through the educational structure and the potential power of leadership in this area.

A realistic appraisal of what courses of action and resolution are not open to them enables blacks to place in proper perspective what avenues are open for negotiation. There seem to be two possible avenues. Blacks, as a minority group, can persist in reasserting the validity of and embracing the identity of their ancient culture, and thereby exclude all traits of the dominant culture. Or the black groups can establish a new identity commensurate with the power of the dominant culture. The first alternative is an increase in group cohesiveness by ethnocentrism. In this mode, the group unites to reject the larger and more powerful outgroup as unacceptable. The second alternative implies identity with the aggressor because one perceives it is to the best interests "to join them" if "one cannot beat them."

Specific mechanisms of the process by which a subculture works out an effective rationalization of its roles and interactions within the major culture vary. If identity with the aggressor is undertaken, one possibility is total identity. One may actually seek "to be white" in all aspects in which this is possible. Such role adoptions involve the complete destruction of all values, social systems, and structures associated differentially with the "inferior" subgroup. A second possibility is a graduated identity. This involves segmentation and selectivity. In terms of the number displayed and the roles chosen to emulate, role adoptions vary with the circumstances. However, if the minority group seeks to resolve the issue of divergent values and behavior, and in a larger sense, the issue of divergent cultures, by adamantly standing its ground, then it intensifies its embracement of all of the traditional cultural modes of its former life. This resolution is undertaken without consideration of the value of the old modes of life as contrasted with the new conditions of life. The main motives operating in this case are increased rigidity and nonconformity. This position is apt to lead to separate cultures, to limited harmonious relations, even though the two cultures are geographically proximate.

The essential point of this discourse is that the individual does not develop in a vacuum but in a complex matrix of family, social, school, personal, subcultural, and major cultural experiences. Obviously, the relative influence of such experiences varies for individuals and subgroups. As a corollary of this general theme, it is proposed that the influence of the dominant culture proves to be constructive for the individual who is a member of the white group in America. Furthermore, it is hypothesized that the same dominant culture proves to be and is categorically destructive for the individual who is a member of the largest minority group in America and thus is most influenced by its proscriptions. This minority group is the black.

More specifically, the individual white person is free to mold his ontology, or life history, within the limits imposed by his personal capabilities, deficits of ability, or essential "bargaining power" in a competitive society. For the black individual, there are covert and/or overt proscriptions placed upon the actualizing and the practicing of his basic assets. As a direct result of these limitations, the black personality is predominantly molded by a culture that relegates him to a marginal, inferior, and circumscribed position. The ultimate effect upon his ego is to produce a fragile, split, or otherwise inadequately functioning self. His personality shows maladaptive symptoms in basic self-identity, or self-image, and in emotional life, overt behavior, the level of ultimate economic and educational achievement, family patterns of organization, the social structure of the subcultural group, and in the broad social orientation. At least some and perhaps all of these maladaptive traits can be found in the personality of any black person. No one black seems to escape all of the repercussions and conflicts associated with the differential valuation based on color. The impact of the cultural influence and social proscriptions upon the process of personality development and the final, mature black personality is depicted in Figure 3. This figure also shows how the process of personality formation differs for a minority and a majority

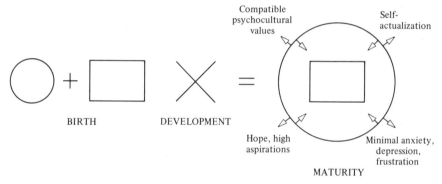

White Individual of Dominant Culture

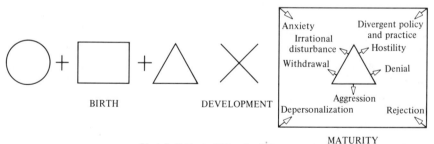

Black Individual of Minority Culture

O Black individual
O White individual
☐ Larger American culture
△ Black subculture
✕ Time, growth, interaction
+ Additive influence

FIGURE 3
A racial comparative view of personality formation.

group member, using the proposed psychocultural assessment of personality determination.

However, the devastating influence—the imprinting phenomenon—of the dominant culture upon an individual black person is not circumscribed. Rather, this adverse influence affects the entire membership of the subcultural group and all areas of psychocultural functioning. General attitudes, cognitive functioning, specific patterns of behavior, affective dispositions, life goals, control mechanisms, and defensive maneuvers are all affected. The predominance of difficulties in these areas is amply documented by research on the black personality.

The Minnesota Multiphasic Personality Inventory (MMPI), an objective measure of personality functioning, has been the test commonly used. Investigators have found that blacks score higher than white subjects on objective indications of personality deviancy and pathology. Blacks' scores show a predominance of a "psychotic pattern" (the greatest emotional dysfunction) rather than the "neurotic pattern" or "normal pattern" found among white subjects (McDonald and Gynther, 1963; Mosby, 1965). Other researchers, using individually administered projective personality techniques, have found either quite distinct areas of pathology or a general pathological level of functioning (Kardiner and Ovesey, 1949; Karon, 1958). Three of these researchers (all but McDonald and Gynther, 1963) have asserted that caste sanctions and cultural restrictions significantly predispose blacks to additional pressures which have to be resolved. These pressures differ qualitatively from those of the white person and appear to demand altered and alternative resolution attempts. Kardiner and Ovesey (1949) speak of the "psychological suicide" the black undertakes by persistent efforts to emulate the "white ideal." Karon (1958) warns of the continuing adverse influence of caste sanctions upon the black personality, even after he emigrates to the northern areas and meets less overt restrictions. The present writer hypothesizes that cultures in transition, as typified by the "borderline" states, may induce more personality pathology than either the clearly northern or southern areas.

States in transition show more ambivalence and confusion. A greater discrepancy in cultural reactions impinge upon blacks. The individual therefore internalizes more ambivalence and reflects greater pathology (Mosby, 1968). Investigations into the black personality, when they remark on sex differences, report the black male as more prone to personality difficulties, clashes with the major culture, and divergent behaviors than black females (Mosby, 1965).

The mass of pathological overt behaviors found in the black have been assembled into a profile of the black American. As a result, blacks have been labeled the "disintegrating segment of American society." (Moynihan, 1965). In general though, such capsule descriptions of "black neuroses or psychoses" neglect to consider the many diverging conflicts within the black group. These analyses omit or minimize underlying cultural clashes with the major culture as well as the personal pathos and identity conflicts. However, the descriptions maximize the overt semblance of chaos which can be "substantiated" by statistics.

This writer contends that the white person of the dominant culture is free to mold his life within the limits set by his innate individual resources to actualize himself. The black person of the minority culture is not free to mold his life within the limits set by his innate resources to actualize himself. Instead, because the black man is either grossly subjected or reduced to an inferior position, he is forced to be enveloped by a complex pattern of depersonalization and conflict in values, goals, affect, intellectual experiences, home rearing, and social situations. The ultimate result is unavoidable conflict, chaos, and condemnation. His struggle for a satisfying identity or self-image is doomed to "conflict without resolution" until death ultimately determines the end of the course and leaves the problem as a legacy for the next generation. Such a lifelong struggle in America is unique to the black Americans. The unique struggle against adverse cultural pressures necessitates a unique adaptation process which results in a unique personality. For this reason Kardiner and Ovesey, as early as 1949, spoke of "a basic personality for the Negro."

But as a colleague (Krasnoff, 1968) has pointed out, were the dominance status of the major and minor cultures reversed, a similar mechanism might repeat itself. Suppose that in one of the African countries, and Rhodesia is an example, the black group is the dominant culture and the white group is the minor one. Suppose further that the white group is reduced to a position of inferiority. It is likely that the reversed situation, with divergent cultural systems, would also result in confrontation, chaos, and identity problems. But such difficulties would afflict the white group. Krasnoff's interesting hypothesis is testable only by studying two groups: the black in America and a chosen nation in Africa. In America, the black subgroup and personality constitute the independent variable and experimental group; in Africa, the white subculture and its resulting personality constitute the independent variable and the experimental group. It is hypothesized that the experimental groups in both situations will show a significant increase in the incidence and in the intensity of identity problems.

But one does not have to replicate such a study across the continent. Some level of comparison can be made with other minority groups in America—for example, Catholics and Jews (religious discrimination), Indians and Mexicans (color and lower-class status), and poverty-striken white Americans (lower-class status). Although the available research is scant or confusing because some economic data are summarized by only white and nonwhite categories, certain trends can be observed. According to historical data, only the black group has been so pervasively subjected to general derogation, economic murder, through gross restrictions, bondage, limited housing facilities, religious discrimination, social sanctions, and overt prejudice. Others might even add to this list the psychological suicide of the young black person's mind as he has passed through the formal educational process. Although one of several of such prejudicial mechanisms is shared by black Americans *and* all the other afore-mentioned groups, it is only the black's "appearance," "overt behavior," and personality that give the semblance of total chaos. Why might this be so? Developmentally, and psychologically, "There comes a point at which quantitative development releases qualitative change" (Cox, 1965, p. 5). Too much pressure can lead to emotional or physical malfunctioning—for example, the development of psychosis or, at another level, cancer from smoking. Thereafter the human organism is distinctly different from "a normal."

Several other explanations are possible. The *pervasive nature* of the restrictions placed on the black—particularly the perception of total inferiority in all areas, which results from them—is an experience unique to the black group. Such restrictions exist on such a large scale for no other American group. Second, the *adverse influence of cultural restrictions* has been so dominant that it has neutralized and made ineffectual either the innate individual or positive subcultural influences and resources for an elevated life. Third, the black subgroup has been so *diffused* that unity behind a movement for elevation previously has not been effective. Diffusion and separation date from the early days of slavery when families were not legally defined as such and parents were not allowed to marry. At that time, family members were considered to be chattel and frequently sold as separate items of goods. Even today, many black family units consist of a female head, children, and itinerant father figures. Economic stability has been marginal traditionally. Starting in World Wars I and II, masses migrated to the North from the South and to the cities from rural areas. Many of these blacks successfully found factory jobs or adequate vocations. But for the masses of urban residents today, their life is a ghetto, a day-to-day existence dependent on welfare benefits. Thus until recently there were few emotional resources or desires for group unity or direct confrontation to change life conditions. Today, the common alphabets in the black household are not so much the ABC's as the initials which stand for various "black power" movements. These are CORE, NAACP, ABC, SNCC. Other significant movements have been the Black Liberators and the Black Panthers. The traditional sports heroes of the blacks are being replaced by those who speak the loudest for the actualization of black rights and power, by whatever means are successful. The term *black* presently connotes new pride in self and one's group. And the traditional term *Negro* is increasingly felt to be derogatory. As children who grow up, black men conceive themselves to be "Boys no more."

The Psychological Effect of New Pride in Blackness upon Divergent Cultural Systems

What psychological effect can the new movement characterized by new pride in blackness have upon divergent cultural values, harmonious intergroup relations, and the self-concept of the black? What consequence can be envisioned for the significance of the individualistic or culturological influence in the ultimate molding of the black personality?

As the black man perceives himself to have "come of age," he feels that new maturity commands new leadership, new responsibility, new behavior. This new behavior, on an overt level, means speaking up, standing tall, and thinking big.

The new black man feels compelled to break the shackles of his past dependency and to embrace a too-long delayed state of viability. But like the adolescent who seeks independence without having the obvious means for such a state, the black man cries for "power." He seeks economic security, family dominance for the male, better education and higher pay than the female—simply to be his own boss. He cries but without the visible means of actualizing those goals. And some cry simply because it is the trend of the time to cry. Yet it seems the black man's behavior and demands, in their aggressiveness and immediacy, are as much an overexaggeration or overcompensation and hence as maladaptive, as the traditional passivity in actions and pleas "to wait upon the Lord." Being opposite poles of a continuum, both approaches seem to be inappropriate. But what the black man hopes to find as a result of his advocacy for "black power" is a direct confrontation with the dominant culture. He hopes thereby to necessitate some action and to force an eventual state of reasonable and equitable integration. He asks for much that he might receive some. He does not expect to have his demands met promptly or unrealistically. He *does* seek a recognition. As his cries spread, he has successfully introduced new words to American households— "militancy," "black power," "civil rights," and "demonstrations." The black has raised the adrenalin level of many white persons, instilled fear in many urban communities, and been the topic of congressional hearings and the daily news media. For brief moments, he has even built a city to symbolize his plight and pathology, at the center of America's governmental seat. During brief moments in his struggle, he has felt a basic compassion and sharing with all Americans of all colors and stations in life. One occasion was when he had his most famous leader downed by an assassin's bullet. Others were when the Kennedy brothers, John and Robert, a President and a Senator, were likewise so downed. But most of the time the black has felt that he struggles alone.

But within his group he has cohesiveness, a new unity. Wherever he meets just one "soul brother," he knows that he is not alone. Blacks speak the same language, even without talking; they share the same affect, even subliminally; they know the same people, although their paths have never crossed. They are united in a common bond of suffering, a present state of struggle, and a future hope of success. This unity creates the confidence that together all black men "can beat" the past system and alter their destiny. Thus, the present-day black man aspires to change the relative dominance of his life pattern by culturological forces, to more individualistic self-will. He is engaged in a struggle of personal and social uplift.

This continuing struggle between culture and subculture brings into sharp relief divergent values, realistic conceptions, and misconceptions of self and the confused "other" of the outgroup. The struggle results in direct hostile confrontation and a host of negative valences.

The divergent values result from attempts by the major culture to force an alien but positively and materially rewarded middle-class value system upon the subordinate minor culture. The minor culture seeks to accommodate to middle-class values but instead finds them just slightly out of reach, no matter how high it is able to elevate through education, economic position, and the like. Thus a discrepancy becomes apparent because no matter how hard he struggles, a brown cloak prevents him from being truly integrated and accepted into the general American society. Color, particularly a devalued color, becomes an insurmountable obstacle. The middle-class black man meets such obstacles by increased compensatory efforts at organizing his own black elite class with the usual exclusion clauses for undesirables (Kardiner and Ovesey, 1949). Thus, the black individual also identifies with the aggressor insofar as he assumes the role of the rejecting authority. The traditionally passive lower-class black man shields his impotency and resorts to primitive brute force in the streets to win his battle for psychological survival. If he cannot be equal through his own constructive efforts at hard work, then he will become equal by lowering those above him to his level. Seemingly, the industrial growth of the South bears out this phenomenon, too. Where the black man has been most oppressed the white man has been demoted also.

In interracial interactions, confusion distorts the perception of self and of other. Basically, the black man and the white man view each other with mutual distrust and hostility. Both sides engage in their share of projection, that is, attributing to others traits and blame which for health's sake should be internalized and owned up to. For the black man this negative affect has been conditioned by centuries of mistreatment, economic and social curtailment, and an allocation to a hopeless social status. For the white man, this affect has been conditioned by a conscience "coming of age." Fear of retaliation that is possibly deserved retaliation fosters internal tension, a flight to the suburbs to avoid the enigma of possible reprisal, and an irrational denial of any responsibility for the plight of the black man. Guilt, fear of retaliation, and mistrust of the adequacy of internal self-control in blacks inspire this flight reaction. And the smoky, dark, smothering, charring residue in the cities attests to the black man's destructive potential. Where mutual distrust exists, there is no basis for communication: Each party is constantly on the defensive to stand his ground, protect his integrity, and remain one move up on the opponent. In this game of chess played in the real-life arena, the black man is fighting to lose the taint of being a pawn. He seeks sometime, someplace, in some circumstances to be king. The white man stands adamant in insisting only he can be king, that a pawn has never been king. The two reach an impasse. Who wins the real-life struggle for dominance has not yet been resolved for the major and minor cultures in America. But both can expect to win, although a champion may never be crowned.

As a result of the present revolt by black people, neither white nor black can expect to remain the same. Each will lose some of his traditional ground but gain in mutual understanding. Eventual integration will evolve. The black man will lose the momentum of extreme pride in an ancient African heritage. This will occur simply because an identity with African culture is too foreign and too dated for the contemporary black man. He sees in himself a combination of African traits, Indian blood, white features, and some French or Spanish descent in various degrees. To whom does he belong? Where is his cultural identity?

There appears to be no one set identity common to all black men. Each black person has to evolve a new cultural pride based in the mixed configuration of his past. He has to say "I know only how to be me." His identity has to be *more personally based.* This represents the middle of the continuum. It is not forced identification with the dominant white culture. Nor is it submissive advocacy of an alien African culture or heritage which bears no immediacy or relevancy to one's contemporary life.

It is this return to concern with conceptualizing one's individual place that the greatest psychological effect of new pride in blackness will lie. For the first time, the black American is approaching the right direction to evolve an adequate black personality.

References

Kardiner, A., and Ovesey, L. On the psychodynamics of the Negro personality. In C. Gordon and K. Gergen (Eds.), *The self in social interaction.* New York: John Wiley, 1968, pp. 259–267.

Karon, B. *The Negro personality.* New York: Springer-Verlag, 1958.

McDonald, R., and Gynther, M. MMPI differences associated with sex, race, and class in two adolescent samples. *Journal of Consulting Psychology,* 1963, 27, 112–116.

Krasnoff, A. Personal communication, 1968.

Mosby, D. P. Maternal "identification" and perceived similarity to parents in adolescents as a function of grade placement. Unpublished Ph.D. dissertation, Washington University (St. Louis), copyrighted 1965.

Mosby, D. P. Different resolutions of the inadequacy conflict in Negro adolescents and adults. Paper read at the Fifty-third Annual Convention of the Association for the Study of Negro Life and History, New York City, October 1968.

Moynihan, D. P. *The Negro family: Case for national action.* U.S. Department of Labor, Office of Policy Planning and Research. Washington, D.C.: U.S. Government Printing Office, March 1965.

Popper, K. R. *The open society and its enemies,* 4th ed. Princeton, N.J.: Princeton University Press, 1963.

Price-Williams, D. The philosophy of science and the study of personality. In *The study of personality: An interdisciplinary appraisal.* New York: Holt, Rinehart & Winston, 1968, pp. 88–102.

Watkins, J. W. Historical explanation in the social sciences. Quoted by Price-Williams, *op. cit.*

THOMAS O. HILLIARD

Personality Characteristics of Black Student Activists and Nonactivists

*When you determine what a man shall think you do not have to concern
yourself with what he will do. If you make a man feel that he is
inferior, you do not have to compel him to accept inferior status,
for he will seek it himself. If you make a man think that he is justly
an outcast, you do not have to order him to the back door. He will go
without being told, and if there is no back door, his very nature will
demand one. . . . Carter G. Woodson (1931)*

In recent years, an increasing amount of psychological research has been
generated to investigate the psychology of blacks in the United States. Implicitly, this approach conceives of a degree of homogeneity or similarity of
perceptions, beliefs, motivations, attitudes, and coping mechanisms within the
black community, which differentiates blacks from other ethnic or racial groups.
The validity of this approach is supported by sociopsychological studies of racial
differences in personality characteristics and the substantial body of literature
on slavery and racism indicating the unique nature of the "black experience" in
the United States.

However, historically, most of the psychological research has focused on the
measurement of the comparative intellectual performance of blacks and whites.
These research efforts have centered around the controversy over the alleged
innate intellectual superiority of whites. This literature was previously surveyed
by Pettigrew (1965) and more extensively reviewed by Dreger and Miller (1960)
and Shuey (1958). Howard (1970) has drawn a parallel between the intensive
and meticulous investigations of the intellectual ability of blacks in Africa and
the United States and, like Fanon (1967), identifies the role of this scientific
movement in the colonial domination of blacks.

Recently, increased attention has been focused on the personality of blacks,
although much of the work in this area has been speculative, qualitative, and
theoretical. There have been few well-controlled experimental studies of the
psychology of blacks. Further, the significance of the existing experimental
research is limited by both methodological and theoretical problems.

The most critical methodological problem is the adequacy of experimental

The present paper was written for popular consumption and, therefore, statistics and
detailed experimental procedures were minimized. Readers interested in a more scientifically sophisticated version should contact the author. Reprinted by permission of the
author.

136

controls. That is, several comparative studies of blacks and whites have failed to equate the groups for such powerful variables as region of country, education, and social class. For instance, Grossack (1957) compared northern whites with southern blacks of lower socioeconomic class. Obviously, definitive interpretations of the results were limited by the contamination of the data.

Another criticism is that tests standardized on whites have been used to measure the psychological health of blacks (Howard, 1970; Pettigrew, 1964). Other investigators suggest that separate test norms should be developed for blacks and whites (McDonald and Gynther, 1962). Hilliard (1969) suggests the frame of reference from which the test data are interpreted, not instrumentation, is the basic problem.

A principal theoretical limitation has been the absence of a social-psychological perspective. Hilliard (1969) has previously commented on the need to direct adequate attention to the historical and contemporary social forces that largely determine the black response. For, as the author explains in a critique of a book on black psychology,

> [a] major perceptual or conceptual defect is the failure to devote adequate attention to the historical and contemporary political, economic, and social forces. This distorted view then focuses on the black experience as an isolated phenomenon, omitting the societal context. Many of the blacks' alleged negative or psychopathological traits have resulted from these "psychological blindspots" and have resulted in a rather gross distortion of reality. For instance, he might not have viewed the suspiciousness and hostility as psychopathological if he had simultaneously examined the societal input of slavery, lynchings, political trickery, and such contemporary phenomena as assassinations of black leaders, "police riots" in Chicago and Detroit, and the daily exploitation of urban ghettoes. He might have conceived of such black responses as suspiciousness and hostility as appropriate means of self-protection utilized to cope with a hostile society. (Hilliard, 1969)

Grier and Cobb (1970) make a similar point in their explanation of the suspiciousness of blacks as a "cultural paranoia" which has adjustive value in adapting to society.

Howard (1970), in a paper delineating the outlines of a social psychology of colonialism, criticizes the traditional approach in social sciences toward blacks as "myopic" and terms it "victim analysis" because of its primary focus on black "casualties" and concomitant lack of appreciation of the social situation of blacks. He calls for a world view in American psychology that would point up the similarities between the psychological mechanisms of blacks in the United States and other Third World peoples, including a clear analysis of their respective social situations.

Another—perhaps the most—neglected area in the study of black psychology is the psychology underlying the current black protest movement. What causes certain blacks to resist racism and discrimination, while others passively accommodate themselves to this situation? Is this attributable to personality differences? If so, what etiological circumstances foster the development of either psychological posture? How do we account for the particular form that the protest or submission takes?

Psychological studies of black activists have, for the most part, focused on the catalyst of black protest and the relationship of black activism to personality variables such as self-concept or independence. These investigations have largely been limited to college students or college-age activists.

Maliver (1965) has tested the relevance of the concept of "identification with the aggressor" to blacks, using Sarnoff's model. His work indicates that (a) blacks with positive self-attitudes are more likely to have participated in a protest demonstration than those who have less positive attitudes, (b) membership in a black civil rights organization (primarily NAACP and CORE) is positively correlated with positive racial attitude, and (c) students with positive attitudes make significantly more spontaneous antiwhite remarks and significantly more pro-black remarks, although this might be an artifact because these subjects express more racial comments generally. Johnson (1966) indicates that a "militant" interracial group has more positive self-attitudes than the general black population. He concludes, "this study presents evidence that not all Negroes have negative self-attitudes and, therefore, further research is needed to differentiate between different segments of the Negro community in terms of racial attitudes."

However, although there has been a flurry of investigations of certain aspects of the black protest movement, the present investigator has not found a single quantitative study that compares black activists and nonactivists on a series of personality dimensions.

The goal of the present study, then, is to determine if there is a syndrome of personality characteristics associated with activism that differentiates black activists from nonactivists. There is no attempt to determine ideology, merely degree of activism. Specifically, the focus of the research will be on student activists in the total population of black activists.

Clearly, the present research should be conceived as an exploratory effort designed to identify and discover variables not to confirm clearly articulated hypotheses or theories. Essentially, this investigation will tap several different aspects of personality. The three main universes to be studied are "character," need system, and value orientation.

Method

The research population was composed of 27 activists and 25 nonactivists. All subjects were black students from a midwestern state university and from a working-class population. The groups were matched for age, sex, educational level, and social class.

Each student was administered a battery of instruments which included a scale of activism, a psychodiagnostic interview, the Edwards Personal Preference

Schedule (EPPS), the Allport-Vernon Scale of Values, and the General Information Questionnaire (GIQ). The activism scale was utilized to insure that the groups differed on the independent variable, degree of activism. The psychodiagnostic interview was conducted by the principal investigator and rated "blind" and independently by the clinical judges, two Ph.D. psychologists. The EPPS and the Allport-Vernon were scored according to the respective manuals. The GIQ was analyzed both quantitatively and qualitatively.

Results

Because each of the three personality measures taps a different aspect of personality, data from each are analyzed separately.

The data show statistically significant differences between the two groups on each of the fourteen personality variables measured by the psychodiagnostic interview. That is, the black student activists and nonactivists showed differences in self-concept, degree of independence, emotional mood, attitude of despair, and ego-strength. In summary, the black student activists were rated higher on *all* scales in the direction of greater psychological health.

The second personality instrument, EPPS, provides a measure of need system. The groups showed statistically significant differences on only two of the fourteen EPPS scales: Activists were lower on abasement and higher on nurturance than nonactivists.

The third personality measure was the Allport-Vernon Scale of Values. The six Allport-Vernon scales are Theoretical, Economic, Aesthetic, Social, Political, and Religious. The data show no statistically significant differences on any of the six scales. In fact, religion was the only subscale to approach significance (in the direction of greater religiosity by nonactivist students).

Finally, GIQ data were analyzed to determine the significance of certain demographic and background factors to degree of activism. Both a quantitative and qualitative analysis revealed no significant differences between the groups on variables such as self-description, description of parents, reported history of mental illness in family, birth order, and so forth. Only the variable parental dominance approached significance. There was a trend for nonactivists to be associated with families in which the mother "runs" the family.

An interesting incidental finding was the extent of death of parents, particularly the fathers. The fathers of 9 of the 44 subjects, or 20 percent, were dead. Four mothers had died, for a total of 13; thus 29.5 percent of the students having one parent dead. The causes of the deaths were unknown.

Discussion

Several conclusions are warranted on the basis of the analysis of the research data. First, the data clearly show that degree of activism or extent of involvement in the black movement among black college students is associated with personality functioning. That is, the black students' typical and enduring mechanism for coping, adjusting, and relating to the world is a meaningful basis for understanding the extent of activism.

Second, the results show the black student activists to be overall psychologically healthier than the nonactivists. These results, then, clearly contradict the often presented "riffraff" theory of activism. That is, there is currently a proclivity to conceive of black student activists, generally, as a group of maladjusted, impulsive, degenerate, and "anarchistic" youngsters. The treatment of the activists as criminals, then, is a logical sequel to such a conceptualization. To the contrary, these results indicate that psychological health is associated with resistance to the well-documented oppression of blacks in America. Perhaps, then, black student activism might be reconceived as a reasonable response to the reality of racism, oppression, and injustice.

More specifically, the results indicate that the personality structure of the two groups differs along several identifiable personality dimensions. First, the groups differ in terms of self-concept. Black student activists have more positive self-concepts, are more self-enhancing behaviorally, and are more aware of their motives. Conversely, the nonactivists have negative self-definitions, are more self-effacing and self-abasing, and are unaware of their motives. It is inferred, based on self-theory, that a person who conceives of himself negatively is more likely to accept social conditions consistent with his self-definition. Again, Carter G. Woodson (1931):

> When you determine what a man shall think you do not have to concern yourself with what he will do. If you make a man feel that he is inferior, you do not have to compel him to accept inferior status, for he will seek it himself. If you make a man think that he is justly an outcast, you do not have to order him to the back door. He will go without being told, and if there is no back door, his very nature will demand one.

Further, the feeling of despair of the nonactivists, also found by Maliver (1965) on the basis of a TAT analysis, is consistent with their negative self-concepts.

Succinctly, the superior ego strength of activists suggests a greater facility in coping with a wide variety of conflict and stress situations. Perhaps the ability to deal with oppression is a specific manifestation of their overall effective adaptation.

Another major personality dimension differentiating black activists from nonactivists is the degree of independence. Essentially, the research results depict the black activists as operating from a frame of reference independent of parents and reflected in the fact that their values and goals are not "introjections" from others, but are independently chosen. The personal independence of the activists corroborates the work of Gore and Rotter (1963) who found that black students involved in the "movement" had less of a need for external reinforcements. Further, the independence of activists on an individual or personal level is consistent with the overall thrust of the black movement and is reflected in the persistent demands on a social level of emerging black groups for self-determinism, self-definition, and "community control."

Further, the two groups differed in their emotional mood: Nonactivist students are both more depressed and anxious than the activists. The greater degree of depression of the nonactivists is consistent with the higher need for self-abasement, negative self-concept, and their attitude of despair.

A particular significant psychological characteristic differentiating the two groups is the level of self-abasement. According to Edwards (1959), author of the Edwards Personal Preference Schedule, abasement is

to feel guilty when one does something wrong, to accept blame when things do not go right, to feel that personal pain and misery suffered does more good than harm, to feel the need for punishment for wrong doing, to feel better when giving in and avoiding a fight than when having one's own way, to feel the need for confession of errors, to feel depressed by inability to handle situations, to feel timid in the presence of superiors, to feel inferior to others in most respects.

Thus, the greater self-abasement by nonactivists suggests that they accommodate themselves to situations, racial and others, by assuming a passive, self-effacing stance. Interestingly, the EPPS manual shows abasement to be negatively correlated with aggression. Also, such a psychodynamic process would seem to be related to the tendency toward greater religiosity by nonactivists suggested by the score on the Allport-Vernon scale of values, and more definitively established by previous studies of religion and black activism. For instance, Marx (1967) found that religiosity is negatively related to black militancy. That is, highly religious blacks tend not to participate in militant activities. These results remained regardless of whether religiosity was measured by frequency of attendance at worship services, subjective importance assigned to religion, or religious orthodoxy. Specifically, members of small sects or cults and religions with "otherworldly" approaches are least likely to participate in protest. Similarly, Howard (1968), in a pilot study of the etiology of black nationalism ideology, found that "conventional" blacks rated "religious beliefs and activities" as the most important area of their life, whereas black "nationalists" assigned greater importance to the "world of ideas."

Historically, the process of self-abasement is seen as resulting from the traditional role of religion in the black community. Frazier (1964), in his sociological study of the black church, comments on the suppression of the black masses by religious teaching such as "the meek shall inherit the earth" and "unearned suffering is redemptive" as part of the "otherworldly" orientation of black religion. Thus, a degree of pleasure is gained through the process of suffering. However, such a process can hardly be narrowly explained away as merely a masochistic desire to inflict personal pain and misery. Rather, this channeling of aggression was an ego technique having survival value, especially in slavery and during the postbellum period which involved the terrorism of lynching.

Fanon (1963) observed a similar phenomenon in North Africa, again pointing to the role of religion as a mechanism of social control manipulated by the colonial power: "All those saints who have turned the other cheek, who have forgiven trespasses against them, and who have been spat on and insulted without shrinking are studied and held up as examples." Similarly, Frazier (1964) mentions a religious chant that slave-owners in the United States often required slaves to repeat in order to maintain them in a subservient role:

> *God will reward me and indeed I have good reason to be content and thankful and I sometimes think more so than if I was free and ever so rich and great, for then I might be tempted to love and serve myself more than God. But now I can't help knowing my duty. I am to serve God in the state in which he has placed me. I am to do what my master orders me.*

Essentially, then, these examples suggest the role played by religion in the social control of behavior via the socialization or the development of the superego and ego-ideal.

It is this model of functioning that explains the attitude of many blacks toward their role in society and explains how black people have internalized negative and debilitating role and self-conceptions. For instance, many blacks believe that blacks are not "suppose" to go certain places and are, thus, wrong in a moral sense. A "live" example of this process was observed by the author in an introductory psychology class. The black students in the class were expressing their volume of experiences of racial discrimination. All students cited numerous incidents of insults and intimidation, except for one black who sat quietly in the back of the classroom. Finally, after continued provocation by the queries of other members of the class, the "sister" angrily responded that "the reason you get into trouble is that you people go places that you don't belong." Indeed, in her view, the harassment they received was punishment and rightly deserved because of their transgressions of acceptable moral and ethical standards. This internalization of the rules, standards, and roles of society is an important process; the conflict which was originally social and external between individual and society or between the slave and slave-owners becomes internal between various components of personality (id-ego vs. superego). Perhaps this is the deeper significance of Albert Memmi's (1965) statement that "the function of the superego is to rule from a distance."

In addition, the higher need for nurturance by activists is consistent with the previous discussion of the psychological health of the activists and indicates a greater degree of humanistic concern and a greater need to be generous and to help others. Perhaps, the apparent altruism in the motives of the activists is a result of their level of psychological maturity. Conceivably, then, the psychological impairment and limited ego strength of the nonactivists suggest that their psychic energy is utilized in maintaining themselves and therefore they have considerably less energy to invest in others.

The results from the GIQ indicate that generally the two groups were equivalent in terms of gross background factors. The meaning of the research finding that nonactivists tend to come from mother-run families is unclear. Perhaps activism is associated with a strong aggressive male model in the home. However, this speculation has little support and it is the burden of future studies to provide answers to such questions. Certainly the milieu and family background antecedent to activism must be studied.

The incidental finding of the high proportion of deaths of parents, particularly the father, should be pursued to determine the causes and significance of their deaths. This statistic is especially significant in view of the *alleged* absence of the black male in the black family structure. Hopefully, these results will stimulate investigations of other external forces that directly impinge on the structure and dynamics of the black family such as the disproportionately large number of black males in the prison population, the inequities of the armed forces draft system, and society's unemployment problem.

In conclusion, the present research provides scientific validation to the issue of the psychology of black protest and thus counters the often-heard public view of the psychopathology involved in the black movement. Hopefully, the present direction may lead to the identification of the psychological characteristics most appropriate to the struggle for black liberation against the forces of oppression. The present study, then, may be viewed as an initial step in the development of an independent Black Psychology—more specifically, a psychology of black liberation.

References

Dreger, R. M., and Miller, K. S. Comparative psychological studies of Negroes and whites in the United States. *Psychological Bulletin*, 1960, 57, 361-402.

Edwards, A. *Edwards' Personnel Preference Schedule.* New York: The Psychological Corporation, 1959.

Fanon, F. *Toward African revolution.* New York: Grove Press, 1967.

Fanon, F. *The wretched of the earth.* New York: Grove Press, 1963.

Frazier, E. F. *The Negro church in America.* New York: Schocken, 1964.

Gore, P. M., and Rotter, J. B. A personality correlate of social action. *Journal of Personality*, 1963, 31, 58-64.

Grier, W., and Cobbs, P. M. *Black rage.* New York: Bantam, 1968.

Grossack, M. M. Some personality characteristics of southern Negro students. *Journal of Social Psychology*, August 1957, 46, 125-131.

Hilliard, T. Unpublished letter to editor of Holbrook Press. Critique of book on black psychology. October 1969.

Howard, J. *Black students in transition.* Unpublished manuscript, University of Chicago, 1968.

Howard, J. How to end colonial domination of black America: A challenge to black psychologists. *Negro Digest*, 1970, 19, 4-10. Original paper, The social psychology of colonialism, presented at Annual Convention of the American Psychological Association, Washington, D.C., 1969.

Johnson, D. W. Racial attitudes of Negro Freedom School participants and Negro and white civil rights participants. *Social Forces*, 1966, 45(2), 266-273.

Maliver, B. L. Anti-Negro bias among Negro college students. *Journal of Personality and Social Psychology*, 1965, 2, 770-775.

Marx, G. T. Religion: Opiate or inspiration of civil rights militancy among Negroes. *American Sociological Review*, 1967, 32, 64-72.

McDonald, R., and Gynther, M. MMPI norms for southern adolescent Negroes. *Journal of Social Psychology*, 1962, 58, 277–282.

Memmi, A. *The colonizer and the colonized*. Boston: Beacon Press, 1965.

Pettigrew, T. Negro American personality: Why isn't more known? *Journal of Social Issues*, 1964, 20, 4–23. (a)

Pettigrew, T. *A profile of the Negro American*. New York: Van Nostrand Reinhold, 1964. (b)

Shuey, A. M. *The testing of Negro intelligence*. Lynchburg, Va.: Bell, 1958.

Woodson, C. G. *The miseducation of the Negro*. Washington, D.C.: Associated Publishers, 1931.

PEARL GORE DANSBY

Black Pride in the Seventies: Fact or Fantasy?

What will happen to all that beauty? For black people, though I am aware that some of us, black and white, do not know it yet, are very beautiful . . . James Baldwin (1963, p. 140).

The late sixties saw a decline on the part of blacks in interests and energies directed toward integration and assimilation with the white majority. The rallying cries "Black Power" and "black is beautiful" have been increasing in frequency and, even in power, from sheer repetition. The seventies have seen an acceleration in the decline of the usage of "Negro" and "colored." These terms have been replaced by the once despised and maligned term "black."

The popular rhythm and blues singer James Brown captured the imagination and approbation of millions with the refrain "Say it loud, I'm black and I'm proud."

Prior to this time the literature was replete with data indicating poor self-esteem and self-hatred of minority groups. Particularly prominent was Kurt Lewin's characterization of self-hatred of the minority in reference to Jewish people.

The psychoanalytic model explains this phenomenon in terms of hostility toward the oppressor being so threatening as to necessitate repression. The repressed hostility is redirected toward oneself. Furthermore, the imitation of whites as in the proliferation of cosmetics designed to make blacks more white could be subsumed under the rubric "identification with the aggressor." Social learning theory research shows imitative behavior strongest with models that appear more powerful.

Bayton (1956) described minority groups as tending to idealize the majority group thus contributing to their own self-rejection. Kennedy (1958) reported that black college students as a group accepted the racial norms of the society. The blacks sampled at that time tended to accept negative stereotypes concerning black people.

Pettigrew (1964) cites a large body of psychological research to demonstrate the power of role playing in conceptions of self. Behavior (of inferiority) that is reinforced would be predicted to increase in frequency. The black played the role of "stupid," "slow," and "inferior" to appease the white power structure to the detriment of his own self-esteem and integrity. By the same token, repetition of slogans such as "black is beautiful" and corresponding behaviors are having similar "fall out" effects on "role playing."

Reprinted by permission of the author.

In varying contexts, a diversity of black writers such as the NAACP's Roy Wilkins and psychiatrist Alvin Pouissant have cautioned against overemphasis on slogans without proper accompanying content. They warn that attempts to drill black pride in a stereotyped or isolated way may have a reverse effect or give a false sense of security. Great attention must be paid to the background of the slogans, which can be discovered through exposure to one's black heritage and appreciation for one's identity.

What data are there to document changing attitudes toward blackness? The refrain of social psychologists dealing in empirical realms is applicable here: "If we had just known one year before 'black' became a slogan, what lovely base-line data we could have had."

At Tennessee State University, the predominantly black university where the author has conducted opinion polls through her students, certain increments in changes of attitudes toward blackness since its emergence as part of the *zeitgeist* are in evidence. Indeed even as one presents such data, they are obsolete. In the past two years, the percent of students preferring to be called black has mani-fested this increment. (See Table 1.)

TABLE 1

Choice of Label of Black College Students

	1970	1971
Negro	22%	14%
Black	68	78
Afro-American	6	4
Other	4	4

Females polled as to type of hair style in the last two years showed an increase in preference for Afros, as shown in Table 2.

TABLE 2

*Choice of Hair Style of Female
Black College Students*

	1970	1971
Afro	30%	38%
Straightened	40	22
Either	30	40

Would one still expect to find self-hatred? A questionnaire administered to black college students by McDonald and Dansby (1971) had items that em-bodied antiblack stereotypes. The antiblack stereotype statements were for the most part carefully couched in justifications for undesirable behavior on the part of blacks. The questions and results were as follows:

Because of the inferior training given to black doctors, on a whole they are not as competent as white doctors.

                                                                    19% agreed

Due to the lack of business experience and equipment, black cleaners cannot do as professional a job as white cleaners.

37% agreed

Welfare makes blacks not want to work for a living.

20% agreed

Because of the lower budgets, most black hospitals cannot offer the quality of health service white hospitals offer.

52% agreed

A problem with black restaurants is their lack of courtesy to their black brothers and sisters.

68% agreed

For the most part antiblack stereotyping was an attitude of the minority of the sample. One pronounced exception was that on the question of stereotyping black restaurant personnel as less courteous. The author suspected that because the question included the possibly emotion-tinged "black brothers and sisters" it evoked either more frankness or ambivalent partisanship. To explore the possibilities, the author administered the questionnaire to another sample of students omitting the latter part of the statement: "A problem with black restaurants is their lack of courtesy." The percent that agreed declined from 68 percent to 42 percent.

Overall, there was a possibility that a minority of black college students hold some antiblack stereotypes. But it seemed safe to say that blacks have come a long way from chuckling at the old "joke," "Why do you buy your ice from Mr. Charlie (white man) instead of Luke (black man)?" "I would buy from Luke but Mr. Charlie's ice is just COLDER than Luke's."

To explore current feelings of black college students about blackness, a semantic differential test was administered. Although black and white were the target terms, the terms given the subjects to rank in order of their appearance on the list were:

1. Home	*3. Red*	*5. Moon*	*7. Weather*	*9. White*
2. Food	*4. Girl*	*6. Black*	*8. Religion*	*10. Old age*

A sample of students were pretested. When asked what the test was measuring, only one in ten of the respondents attributed any racial implication to the test. The polar adjectives were:

Soft	*Hard*	*Active*	*Passive*
Good	*Evil*	*Worthless*	*Valuable*
Weak	*Strong*	*Fast*	*Slow*
Sad	*Happy*	*Beautiful*	*Ugly*
Important	*Insignificant*		

The responses to the term *white* were neutral. The mean score of each set approximated a neutral rating. To determine if the averages were a muting of

combined extreme scores, the modal score for each term was ascertained along-
side the mean. (See Table 3.)

TABLE 3

Semantic Differential Ratings of Term White

Adjectives	Mean	Mode	Description
Soft–Hard	3.5	4–1	Neutral to soft
Good–Evil	3.9	4	Neutral
Weak–Strong	3.4	4–1	Neutral to weak
Sad–Happy	3.9	4	Neutral
Important–Insignificant	3.7	4	Neutral
Active–Passive	3.8	4	Neutral
Worthless–Valuable	4.2	4	Neutral
Fast–Slow	4.1	4	Neutral
Beautiful–Ugly	4.0	4	Neutral

The evaluations of the term *black* produced far less neutral data. The modal
scores reflected extreme scores. The term *black* was consistently scaled in
positive terms. Where the polar adjectives themselves are ambiguous as to value—
for example, "soft-hard"—the mean evaluations tend to be more neutral.
Despite pretest data, it is not impossible that this is quite consciously a response
to race, with a defensive bias operating. (See Table 4.)

TABLE 4

Semantic Differential Ratings of Term Black

Adjectives	Mean	Mode	Description
Soft–Hard	4.5	7	Neutral to hard
Good–Evil	2.4	1	Good
Weak–Strong	5.6	7	Strong
Sad–Happy	4.7	1–4–7	Happy
Important–Insignificant	2.3	1	Important
Active–Passive	3.4	1	Neutral
Worthless–Valuable	5.3	7	Valuable
Fast–Slow	2.8	1–4	Fast
Beautiful–Ugly	2.8	1	Beautiful

Another sample of black students was asked to list as many adjectives as they
could think of to describe two colors: black and white. Clarification was given as
follows:"For example, you might associate the adjective 'dangerous' with 'red.' "
Space provided for ten adjectives for each color. Students averaged five or six
adjectives for the color black; they averaged two to three adjectives for the color
white. Table 5 indicates how adjectives were grouped into clusters and gives the
percentage of responses for each category.

The adjectives most often associated with white was "pure." The category with
most frequency was the "Mr. Clean" category. For black, the modal word was
"beautiful." The category with the same frequency for "black" and "white" was
badness, with 11 percent.

TABLE 5

*Comparison of Frequencies of Categories of
Adjectives for "Black" and "White"*

Adjectives	White	Black
Quiet, peaceful	11%	0%
Evil, bad	12	11
Neutral	5	0
Cleanliness, antiseptic	35	0
Interesting, marvelous, bright	15	12
Good, holy, innocent, virginal	7	3
Dingy	5	7
Lifeless, ghostly, morbid	3	10
Pretty, attractive	5	26
Dumb, ignorant	2	4
African	0	2
Strong, tough	0	6
Intelligent	0	4
Dark, chocolate	0	16
Mysterious	0	3

The comparison of associations with "black" and "white" were then analyzed according to frequency of positive categories. The sum of percentages of adjectives in positive categories is greater for white than for black. (See Table 6.)

TABLE 6

Comparison of Percent of Positive Adjectives for "Black" and "White"

Positive categories for whites		Positive categories for blacks	
Quietness	11%	Interesting	12%
Cleanliness (antiseptic)	35	Holy (virginal)	3
Interesting	15	Pretty	26
Holy	7	Strength	6
Pretty	5	Intelligence	4
Total	73%	Total	51%

The percent of adjectives in negative categories is slightly higher for blacks than whites. (See Table 7.)

Although the "word association" for "black" was often "beautiful," there remained many connotations and categories of associations that reflected a strong residue of positive association with the word *white* and negative association with the word *black*.

The work most often cited in racial identification is undoubtedly Clark and Clark's (1939) classic study of color preference in young black children. The well-known findings were that black children thought that the white doll had a "nicer color" than the "colored" doll and was a "nicer" doll, and that they preferred to play with it. There are significant differences to be noted in the responses when analyzed by age groups. The strongest rejection of their own color occurred among four- and five-year-olds. Among the six- and seven-year-olds

TABLE 7

Comparison of Percent of Negative Adjectives for "Black" and "White"

Negative categories for whites		Negative categories for blacks	
Evil	12%	Evil	11%
Dingy	5	Dingy	7
Lifeless	3	Lifeless	10
Dumb	2	Dumb	4
Total	22%	Total	32%
Percentage of terms in neutral categories	5%	Percentage of terms in neutral categories	17%

there was a decrease in the prevalence of rejection, which suggests that identification occurred to counter the self-devaluating beliefs they had acquired.

Morland (1958) also found that black children unconsciously identify themselves with the dominant, privileged race: "The superior position of whites is emphasized to the Negro children in television, movies, magazines, books and in the pictures on the walls of their nursery schools."

Hraba and Grant (1970) used the doll preference paradigm with blacks in an integrated setting in Lincoln, Nebraska, and found that black children preferred the black doll. These results were substantially the same whether the children were interviewed by a black or by a white examiner.

Carolyn Bright (1970) executed a modification of the Clark and Clark study for her bachelor's thesis. She investigated differences in racial identification of black children as a function of socioeconomic class. The measuring instrument consisted of three 12-inch dolls. Two dolls were black—one with an Afro, the other with short straight hair. All the dolls had Caucasian features and were dressed exactly alike. An interview form was used to record each subject's response.

During the interview, which tested racial identification and preferences, females were asked, after being shown all three dolls, (1) "Give me the doll that is the prettiest"; (2) "Give me the doll that you would rather play with"; (3) "Give me the doll that you will look like when you get big"; (4) "Give me the doll that you want to look like when you get big." Males were asked only the first question.

TABLE 8

Number of Subjects Tested In Kindergarten and Day-Home Centers

	Male	Female	Class
Tennessee State University Kindergarten	15	18	Middle
Gay-Lea Kindergarten	27	28	Middle
Grace Eaton Day Home	28	27	Lower

There was a definite sex difference in response to "Give me the doll that is the prettiest." Males chose the white doll and females chose the black doll. (See Table 9.)

TABLE 9

*Comparison of Responses to Preferences
for the Prettiest Doll in Preschool Children,
by Sex*

	Black doll	White doll
Females	70%	30%
Males	42	58

Of the males who chose the black doll, there was a social-class difference in type of black doll chosen. More of the lower-class males chose the black doll with the Afro hair, whereas more of the middle-class males chose the black doll with straight hair. (See Table 10.)

TABLE 10

*Comparison of Responses to Preferences for the
Black Doll with Afro or Straight Hair
in Preschool Males, by Social Class*

	Black doll with Afro	Black doll with straight hair
Middle-class males	38%	62%
Lower-class males	58	42

There was no appreciable difference among females in preference for the Afro or straight hair style on the black dolls. However, in response to "Give me the doll that you would rather play with," more lower-class females chose the Afro doll and more middle-class females chose the black doll with straight hair. (See Table 11.)

TABLE 11

*Comparison of Responses to Doll Preferred to be
Played with, by Social Class*

	Black doll with straight hair	Black doll with Afro
Middle-class females	65%	35%
Lower-class females	40	60

To the request "Give me the doll you will look like when you get big," most females chose the black doll. However, the black identification was stronger in lower-class females than in middle-class females. (See Table 12.)

Although more females also chose the black doll when asked to "Give me the doll you want to look like when you get big," the preference was not nearly so marked. There was a tendency for a higher percentage of lower-class females to choose the black doll. (See Table 13.)

TABLE 12

Comparison of Responses to Doll You Will Look Like
When Grown up, by Social Class

	Black doll	White doll
Middle-class females	72%	28%
Lower-class females	81	19

TABLE 13

Comparisons of Responses to Doll You Want to Look
Like When Grown up, by Social Class

	Black doll	White doll
Middle-class females	65%	35%
Lower-class females	70	30

The effects of black and white teachers' influence on racial identification in black preschool children was also considered. More black females with black teachers chose black dolls when asked of "Give me the doll that is the prettiest" than did black females with white teachers. This trend was also true in males. (See Tables 14 and 15.)

TABLE 14

Comparison of Responses of Preference for Prettiest
Doll for Females, by Race of Teacher

	Black doll	White doll
Black teacher	79%	21%
White teacher	61	39

TABLE 15

Comparison of Responses of Preference for
Prettiest Doll for Males, by Race of Teacher

	Black doll	White doll
Black teacher	51%	49%
White teacher	33	67

Mary Carr (1970) compared attitudes of black students toward the black movement, hypothesizing that darker-skinned students would be more in favor. The results showed no difference for males or females as a function of color of skin of the student.

One bachelor's thesis (Brown, 1970) had the rather cynical title "Black Is Not Beautiful." This study was conducted to determine if there were behavioral indices on the part of black males to correspond with verbalizations of "black is beautiful." There were three sets of behavioral criteria: (1) College men were asked to name the three prettiest girls in a certain dormitory. (2) A sociometric device was utilized on two floors of the same dormitory with the key question being "Which girl gets the most dates?" (3) The number of times girls were asked to dance at a social in the same dormitory was recorded by two independent scores.

When girls were rated as to skin color, in all three situations girls with lighter skin tones tended to be selected more often.

Rawls Davenport (1969) used colored pictures of blacks with varying combinations of Caucasian and Negroid characteristics in terms of skin color and facial features in his investigation of black pride.

The blacks in the pictures were described as follows:

Models A—female and male = dark Negro with Negroid features (broad nose, kinky hair, and thick lips). Models B—female and male = dark Negro with white features (keen nose, thin lips, straight hair). Models C—female and male = light-skinned Negro with Negroid features (broad nose, kinky hair, thick lips). Models D—female and male = light-skinned Negro with white features (keen nose, thin lips, straight hair).

The instructions were as follows:

This is a balloting contest for you to choose your favorite male and female models. You are to choose one candidate for male and female models. First you are to choose your sex. Next, you are to place a check after the letter representing your choice. You can check only one candidate for male and female models. After having chosen your favorite female and male models, you are to fold the ballot three times and place it in the box in front of you.

The results manifested a preference for the female and male with light skin and Caucasian features. These findings are very similar to those of a series of studies at Fisk University in the forties by Charles S. Johnson (1967) and others which documented a preference for lighter skin by blacks.

A response bias to attitude questionnaires was also investigated (Myers, 1970). Questionnaires of attitudes toward blackness were given out by an Afro wearer and by a non-Afro wearer. The hypothesis that the responses to questionnaires handed to students by Afro wearers would be more militant was confirmed.

The foregoing data were gathered from blacks attending black colleges. In another study, attitudes of blacks attending predominantly black schools were compared with those of blacks attending predominantly white schools. Predictably, black students attending the predominantly white college were more militant and in addition had slightly less tendency to hold antiblack stereotypes. Both sets of students were asked, "If you had it to do over, would you go to a campus of a different racial composition (predominantly white) (predominantly black)?" Thirty-five percent of students at a predominantly white college asserted that they would. Twenty percent of students at the predominantly black college made the same assertion.

It is to be noted that all data are based on samples of black college students going to school in the South. It would be predicted that the data would be different if collected on black college students in the North, for a variety of reasons.

In the final analysis, it appeared that black college students were evidencing a heightened self-awareness and a heightened racial identification. Blacks were manifesting a more positive self-concept which has been referred to by one writer as "black arrogance" (Jarrett, 1970). Jarrett described "black arrogance" as one of the greatest spiritual achievements of all time.

The brainwashing of generations cannot be erased in a decade, even in a young population. To be sure, evidence of self-hate, self-pity, and some identification with white values remained.

Although current findings are mixed, overall, the data seem to indicate the phenomenon of black pride to be fact, not fantasy.

References

Baldwin, J. *The fire next time.* New York: Dell, 1964.

Bayton, J. A., McAllister, L. B., and Hamer, J. Race-class stereotypes. *Journal of Negro Education*, 1956, **25**, 75-78.

Clark, K. B., and Clark, M. P. Racial identification and preference in Negro children. In E. Maccoby et al. (Eds.), *Readings in social psychology.* New York: Holt, Rinehart & Winston, 1958.

Evans, P. Search for black manhood is key issue, says Samuel Banks. *The Atlanta Constitution*, 1970.

Gilter, A. B., and Yoichi, S. Color and physiognomy as variables in racial misidentification among children. *Proceedings of the Seventy-Seventh Annual Convention of the American Psychological Association*, 1969, **4**, 677-678.

Hunter, C. Black doll is "natural" success. *The New York Times*, February 20, 1971, p. 29.

Hraba, J., and Grant, C. A reexamination of racial preferences and identification. *Journal of Personality and Social Psychology*, 1970, **16**, 398-402.

Jarrett, V. Black arrogance: A key to survival. *Chicago Tribune*, October 25, 1970.

Johnson, C. S. *Growing up in the blackbelt.* New York: Schocken, 1967.

Kennedy, J. C. A study of ethnic stereotypes of Negro college students. *Dissertation Abstracts*, 1958, **19**, 376.

Marks, E. S. Skin color judgments of Negro college students. *Journal of Abnormal and Social Psychology*, 1943, **79**, 370-376.

Morland, J. K. Racial recognition by nursery school children in Lynchburg, Virginia. *Social Forces*, 1958, **37**, 132-137.

Ogletree, E. Skin color preference of the Negro child. *Journal of Social Psychology*, 1969, 143-144.

Osgood, C., Suci, G., and Tannenbaum, P. *The measurement of meaning.* Urbana, Ill.: University of Illinois Press, 1957.

Owens, J. Negro views inextricably bound to black issues. *Birmingham News*, October 8, 1970.

Pettigrew, T. F. *A profile of the Negro American.* New York: Van Nostrand Reinhold, 1964.

West, H. I. Tracing black ancestors. *Washington Post*, January 6, 1971.

Wilkins, R. Blacks and their slogans. *Los Angeles Times*, January 11, 1971.

Unpublished bachelor's theses, Tennessee State University

Bright, C. Racial identification and preference in black middle- and lower-class preschool children, 1970.

Brown, C. Black is not beautiful, 1969.

Brown, M. A comparative investigation of the attitudes of natural and nonnatural wearers at Tennessee State University and Fisk University toward Jews, whites, and other Negroes, 1969.

Carr, M. Effect of skin color on the attitudes toward the black power movement, 1969.

Davenport, R. Judgment of skin color among black college students, 1969.

Gill, D. A study of stereotyping among black and white college students, 1969.

McDonald, R. T. The degree of militancy and stereotyping in black male college students as a function of campus environment, 1971.

WILLIAM S. HALL, WILLIAM E. CROSS, JR.,
and ROY FREEDLE

Stages in the Development of Black Awareness:
An Exploratory Investigation

Since the Supreme Court decision of 1954 outlawing segregation in public schools, we have seen a change in the nature of black–white relations in America. To be sure, this change has produced many consequences, one of which has been an identity transformation among American blacks. The transformation has been from an older orientation whereby most blacks viewed themselves as inadequate, inferior, incapable of self-determination, and unable to cope with the intricacies of life in a complex society, to a new one. Through this new orientation, most black Americans view themselves as adequate, self-reliant, assertive, and self-determinative. While several discussions of this change can be found both in the scientific and the nonscientific literature, these have not presented empirical evidence documenting it in any great detail. The major focus of this chapter is the presentation of an exploratory study. The purpose of the study was to test the plausibility of a hypothesis advanced by Cross (1970) and detailed by Hall and Cross (1970) concerning black identity transformation.

Review of Relevant Research and Hypotheses

Scientific and nonscientific literature concerning an identity transformation among black Americans falls into two categories: (a) nonprocess and (b) process. The nonprocess work focuses on differences between conservative and militant black Americans in terms of traits, attitudes, opinions, and other personal characteristics. Works representing this point of view concentrate on simple before-and-after explanations in which specific and general components of the behavior of nonmilitant persons are contrasted with those of militant ones. The overall thrust of the nonprocess literature is to develop a profile of the "average" black in terms of (a) identification with black cultural values (Marx, 1967; Caplan and Paige, 1968; Maliver, 1965); (b) attitudes toward skin color (Koslin, Cardwell, and Pargament, 1969); (c) sense of personal effectiveness (Bennett, 1969; Forward and Williams, 1970; Gurin, Lau, and Beattie, 1969); (d) aggressiveness (Tomlinson, 1970; Hahn, 1970); (e) hostility toward white oppression (Tomlin-

Much of the work reported in this chapter was begun while the first author was a Postdoctoral Fellow at the American College Testing Program, Iowa City, Iowa, Summer 1970. A more technical version can be found in the *Research Reports* of the American College Testing Program, Iowa City, Iowa (in press). Reprinted by permission of William S. Hall.

son, 1970; Marx, 1967); (f) rejection of white leadership (Dizard, 1970); and (g) rejection of accommodationism (Caplan, 1970). For a more comprehensive review of the nonprocess literature, the interested reader is referred to Caplan (1970).

The process-oriented works attempt to describe each of several stages, states, or levels that a person or group traverses in identity transformation. The work emanating from this point of view emphasizes the details of what a person undergoes during the process of change. Moreover, it attempts to uncover some of the mechanisms that initiate and consolidate many of the stages. It is well to point out here that we devote more attention to the process literature primarily because we feel that this approach gives a deeper and more accurate insight into black transformations in identity.

As we turn to the process-oriented literature, it is important to bear in mind that our primary concern here is with transformations in the way that blacks see themselves as persons. Work that presents a step-by-step explanation of what has been called the Negro-to-black transformation will be emphasized. The work is by and large reported in the form of models (or hypotheses) and reflects a wide range of thought in social science. Specifically, the review here will be concerned with the work of Crawford and Naditch (1970), Wallace (1964), Sherif and Sherif (1970), Thomas (1971), and Cross (1970).

The first and perhaps most popular models created to explain the contemporary black movement were based on notions of relative deprivation and social deviancy (Crawford and Naditch, 1970). These researchers developed a rather complex model integrating concepts of social deviance, external–internal locus of control, and relative deprivation. Three stages are included in the Crawford–Naditch model. Each stage is defined by five factors: (a) ideal–real goal discrepancy or perceived relative deprivation; (b) perceived locus of control; (c) psychological content; (d) characteristics of society; and (e) behavior of the oppressed group.

Wallace (1964) has elaborated a model of culture change from the perspective of anthropology. Wallace's model, a two-pronged one, considers culture change either over long periods of time (macrotemporal), or very brief periods (microtemporal). Under the latter, he discusses "revitalization processes," which are believed by Hall (1967) to depict the contemporary black movement. Revitalization processes encompass five stages: (a) steady state; (b) period of increased individual stress; (c) period of cultural distortion; (d) period of revitalization; and (e) new steady state. Wallace (1956, 1964) suggests that two concepts are extremely important in the revitalization process: mazeway resynthesis and hysterical conversion. The former represents a "new way" of viewing old problems, while the latter typifies mass following.

A more contemporary view of the black movement in America can be found in the work of Sherif and Sherif (1970). These researchers view the black movement, particularly black unrest, as a social movement toward an emerging self-identity. Sherif and Sherif emphasize that the black movement is concerned not only with economic and environmental inequities but also with issues relating to identity. Moreover, they argue that the importance of identity is shown by two prominent patterns in the activities, functions, and rhetoric of black power advocates: (a) dissociation from white standards, institutions, and values that promote black inferiority; and (b) turning toward other nonwhite peoples in different parts of the world, particularly Africa, for a frame of reference to replace the one they have rejected.

The analysis presented by Sherif and Sherif (1970) is important because it explicitly deals with what might be called black identity issues—that is, feelings of inferiority as well as the rejection of white standards and a search for a new referent. Moreover, these researchers suggest that black pride is not created in a vacuum. Feelings of inferiority and shame lead to guilt and rage which in turn are recoded into feelings of black pride, and, if all goes well, pride is eventually internalized as self-confidence and a modified self-concept. In this sense, the *affect* underlying each of several stages appears to undergo its own systematic development.

Thomas (1971) has developed hypotheses concerning the stages through which blacks pass in working out their identity as black persons. He believes that few black people can claim that they have always been black. Moreover, he asserts that most Negroes have suffered from what is called "Negromachy" prior to the Negro-to-black identity movement. "Negromachy" is that which is ruled by confusion of self-worth and shows dependency upon white society for definition of self. Thomas believes that Afro-Americans must first withdraw into themselves before renegotiating relationships with other racial and ethnic groups.

The period of withdrawal marks but the first stage of the five that Thomas hypothesizes as depicting the steps blacks take in seeking a new racial identity. *Testifying* to all the pain previously endured in denying himself as a person represents the second stage. Another part of stage 2 is learning to express one's anxieties about becoming black. *Information processing* around black cultural heritage marks the third stage. The information processing in which the person engages leads directly into stage 4, *activity*. Here the person works through a particular group to find a link to the larger black experience. The fifth and final stage is called *transcendental*, through his unique blackness the person loses his "hangups" about race, age, sex, social class and sees himself as a part of humanity in all of its flavors.

A similar hypothesis concerning black identity is that formulated by Cross (1970) and detailed by Hall and Cross (1970). Through a careful analysis of his observations of a wide segment of the black-American community, Cross hypothesized that there exists a series of well-defined stages through which black Americans pass when they encounter blackness in themselves. Moreover, he speculates that as a result of this encounter and its subsequent resolution, the person defines himself as a black, adequate, and noninferior person. The stages have been designated as follows: (a) preencounter, (b) encounter, (c) immersion, and (d) internalization. It was the plausibility of Cross's hypothesis of these stages that was tested in the research reported below. The items depicting these stages have been listed in Table 1.

TABLE 1

Stages and Items Representing the Cross Hypothesis

Preencounter Stage

(In this stage, a person is programmed to view and think of the world as being nonblack, antiblack, or the opposite of black. Behavior and basic attitudes toward self are determined by the "oppressor's" logic.)

1. This person believes that the world is, and should be, guided by American-European concepts—i.e., the sum total of his experiences, perceptions—and dominated by a white racist orientation.
2. This person believes that to be black is to be low-down and dirty.
3. This person believes that black people came from a strange, uncivilized dark continent and that the black search for historical relevance began around 1865.
4. This person believes that the white esthetic is superior to the black one—e.g., deifies white womanhood, uses traditional white modes of expressions, etc.
5. This person believes that the white man is superior intellectually, technically mystical, and capable of understanding him.
6. This person believes that large numbers of blacks are untrustworthy.
7. This person believes that incorporation, integration, or assimilation is the black man's most effective weapon for solving his problems.

Encounter Stage

(In this stage, some experience manages to slip by or even shatter the person's current feeling about himself and his interpretation of the condition of the Negro.)

8. This person believes that the world should be interpreted from a black perspective.
9. This person believes that he should validate himself as a black person and that he has many strengths.
10. This person's beliefs make him feel guilty and anxious; consequently he is hurled into a frantic, determined, obsessive search for black identity.
11. This person feels, with great force, what being black in America means.

Immersion Stage

(In this stage, everything of value must be relevant to blackness.)

12. This person involves himself in a world of blackness—e.g., he participates in political meetings, rapping sessions, black theater, seminars, art shows, television programs, etc.
13. This person undergoes a liberation from whiteness and an involvement in blackness.
14. This person feels and behaves as if the white world, culture, and persons are dehuman—e.g., whites become honkies, pigs, devils, etc., to him.
15. This person behaves as if he feels that everything black is good.
16. This person hungrily consumes black literature and devotes much contemplation to the forms of being black—e.g., he wears dashikis, cultivates an Afro, takes on an African name, etc.
17. This person turns inward and withdraws from everything that is white.
18. This person frequently confronts the system and the man.
19. This person behaves in such a way as to indicate that he fears neither control, oppressive techniques, nor death.
20. This person feels an overwhelming attachment to all black people.
21. This person feels excitement and joy in black surroundings.
22. This person begins to see whites as just people with the strengths and limitations that this implies.
23. This person engages in a cultural analysis of black life style.
24. This person comes to accept certain factors about the black experience and drops others.

TABLE 1 (*Continued*)

25. This person behaves as if he has accepted certain factors that help explain the experience of being black in America and has incorporated these into a style of life which forms the basis for a new life style.

Internalization Stage

(In this stage, the person focuses on things other than himself and his own ethnic or racial group.)

26. This person behaves as if he has an inner security and satisfaction with himself.
27. This person behaves as if he feels a great love and compassion for all oppressed people.
28. This person actively participates in the community for the purpose of making it better —i.e., a collectivistic orientation with a commitment to the development of black power dominate the person's behavior.

It is apparent that Cross and Thomas, observing the black-American scene and working independently of each other, have formulated very similar hypotheses of racial identity. Thomas's testifying stage matches the encounter stage formulated by Cross. Immersion and activity seem highly similar, as do transcendental and internalization.

The review of the process literature is useful in the sense that it provides many ideas which can serve as a basis for experimental validation. But while the fact that a transformation in the black's self-awareness has occurred will be readily acknowledged, this does not in itself verify the discrete-stage notion nor does it verify the particular values and ideas asserted to be characteristic of each stage. Merely to list some values and ideas believed to underlie or characterize each stage gets us *closer* to the goal of empirically establishing the psychological reality of this phenomenon, but it does not finish the job. What is needed is some empirical method of attack that will allow psychologists to study the idea of "stages" with regard to blacks' recent experience and some clear statement about how the outcome of this methodology will allow us to choose among several reasonable alternative models of the process.

In the empirical research to be reported below, we do not claim to have found the best way to validate the psychological reality of black stages in self-awareness. Rather, what we present is a summary of data which explored the plausibility of one hypothesis concerning stages in the development of black awareness.

Summary of the Exploratory Investigation of Cross's Hypothesis

The chief means by which we established some empirical support for Cross's ideas was by what can be called consensual validation. To this end, three experiments were run. The purpose was to obtain empirical evidence regarding the plausibility of Cross's (1970) hypothesis that there are four stages (see Table 1) that can be distinguished by lay observers in the evolution of black awareness in America during recent years. While our main interest was to gain support for the notion that rather distinct stages of belief systems can be identified in the recent unfolding of black awareness by using black college students' judgments, we also studied the responses of white students in the same experimental setting. The purpose of this latter condition was to gain insights into the degree to which Ss who had not directly participated in the search for a black awareness may yet be cognizant of these general stages and reveal this knowledge by producing patterns of responses similar to those given by black Ss.

The 28 items suggested by Cross as representing the different beliefs and activities of the four stages were each typed on separate 3 X 5 index cards and presented to Ss for sorting. The effect of three experimental conditions on the sorting of these cards was studied (conditions A, B, and C). A brief description of these conditions follows below.

Condition A. This condition placed the fewest constraints on the Ss who sorted the cards. The Ss were instructed as follows: "On these cards you will find some items descriptive of a person—taken together many of these items form clusters. We want you to cluster the items according to whether a person would believe all of the items that are in the cluster at a particular point in his life—whereas the items in another cluster would tend to be believed by him at some other point in his life.... After sorting the items into clusters, indicate the order in which you feel these clusters occur in time." The Ss were further asked to think of a name for each of the clusters; that is, they were asked for the reason why they thought the items belonged together.

Condition B. This condition placed somewhat greater constraints on the Ss than did Condition A. Condition B started out with the same instructions as Condition A. Following this first sort, the Ss were asked if there was any meaningful way that they could recombine or group together the clusters from their first sort so that just *four* clusters remained. If the S had already produced four clusters on his first sort, the session was terminated. Following each sort, the Ss were again asked to order the clusters with respect to their temporal sequence and as well were asked to give a reason for each group of items that they produced.

Condition C. This condition placed the greatest constraints upon the Ss. Four boxes were placed in front of the S. Each box had a label placed next to it which described the nature of each of the four stages and the order in which they were believed to occur as expressed by Cross's hypothesis (see Table 1 for descriptions of the stages). The descriptions which followed each label aimed at clarifying the meaning of each stage (and hence served to remove much of the uncertainty as to what the sorting task was all about). The test session for each condition lasted about an hour.

One hundred eighty Ss were tested in all; 90 were black college students, and 90 were white college students. Within each group of 90, 30 were tested in Condition A, 30 in Condition B, and 30 in Condition C. Finally, each group of 30 was equally divided, with 15 female and 15 male students being represented. Each S was tested individually.

Results and Discussion

Conditions B and C. We present a summary of the results from Conditions B and C first because they provided us with the most detailed information regarding the distribution of the items with respect to each of the four hypothetical stages. The rank order correlations with the 28-item Cross hypothesis for each of

8 groups of Ss (male and female black Ss in Condition B, male and female white Ss in Condition B, male and female black Ss in Condition C, and male and female white Ss in Condition C) were studied. All correlations between each of the 8 groups and the Cross hypothesis were significant well beyond the .01 level.

The tentative conclusion that we reached at this point was that using just the modal response data we found significant confirmatory evidence favoring the general ideas of Cross. However, the fact that none of the correlations was perfect indicated that some differences must be occurring within each of the eight groups of Ss. It seemed to us that these differences related to how many items tended to be placed within each of the allowable four stages as well as to which particular items were placed in each of the four stages.

In order to gain further insight into the source of these differences, a more detailed comparison across items was done. This analysis focused on possible differences in black-white response patterns for each item within and across Conditions B and C. In the interest of providing a more stable response pattern base, the male and female frequency data of Conditions B and C were combined. All of the results discussed from here on were based on this pooled data.

Condition B: black-white comparisons. Of the 28 items, only item 7 produced a significant difference between blacks and whites. The blacks perceived this item as belonging primarily to the first developmental stage (preencounter), whereas the whites were equally split in believing that this item could represent an early stage or a late stage.

Condition C: black-white comparisons. This condition produced more significant differences in the item responses of blacks and whites. Item 8 was significantly different at the $p = .05$ level. Using their modal response, this item was placed in the last (fourth) stage by whites, whereas blacks placed this in the third (immersion) stage. Item 24 was significantly different at the .05 level. The whites' modal response placed this item in the fourth stage, whereas blacks revealed a bimodal response pattern by placing it equally often in the second and fourth stages. Finally, item 28 produced a significant difference at the .05 level. This difference, however, is less interesting than the previous differences found because both blacks and whites gave the fourth stage as their modal response category. The difference is presumably due to the unequal variances of the two frequency distributions.

Comparisons across conditions B and C. So far, we have concentrated on item differences attributable to different groups of subjects. One can also inquire whether significant item differences can be found when comparing across Conditions B and C. One might expect differences to occur for the following reasons: When a semantic label for each of the four stages is provided (as occurred in Condition C), this should greatly decrease whatever ambiguity there is to the sorting task. The consequence of reducing the ambiguity or uncertainty is that more subjects should agree to place a particular item into just *one* of the stages. That is to say, if a particular item *does* belong to (or is characteristic of) a particular stage, then providing information about the meaning of this stage should help to increase the number of subjects who will realize that this item matches or belongs to this particular stage. This possibility was investigated from two points of view. The first examined whether a difference in the frequency distributions of each item is significant across Conditions B and C. The second approach tested directly the implication that the modal frequency of each item in Condition C was significantly larger than its corresponding modal frequency in Condition B by using four-cluster data only.

The frequency distributions of the 30 black students in Condition B were compared with the frequency distributions of the 30 black students from Condition C, item for item. Condition B produced a modal response at the fourth stage, whereas Condition C produced a modal response at the third stage.

The frequency distributions of the 30 white subjects in Condition B were also compared with the 30 whites of Condition C. Five of the 28 item comparisons were found to be significantly different from chance. These were items 13, 15, 16, 27, and 28. Only one of these five involved a change in the modal response (item 15) where the second stage was modal for Condition B while the third stage was modal for Condition C.

Although more items yielded significant differences than could be attributed to chance, the failure of these differences to form any *systematic* pattern across conditions and across black–white comparisons suggests that most of these differences may not be very important in terms of what impact they have on the main hypothesis concerning the existence of several stages underlying the development of black awareness. The few differences found between the black and white subjects, however, may be important for reasons other than the stages hypothesis.

The second approach in evaluating differences between Conditions B and C will now be discussed. The prediction here was that the modal frequencies in Condition C would be greater than the corresponding modal in Condition B. (Only items that share the same modal category in common were considered for this test.) A sign test of this difference, using the black Ss' response across the two conditions, was significant ($p = .022$). A similar sign test using only the white Ss' responses across the same conditions was also significantly different from chance ($p = .001$). Thus this result indicates that the ability to place an item into its correct stage is significantly increased by having available a semantic label for each stage.

Results of condition A and the initial sortings of condition B. The purpose of allowing Ss in Condition A to form as many clusters as they wished upon their first sortings of the 28 items was to attempt to get some idea as to whether primarily 4 stages (clusters) would be spontaneously formed. This condition (and the initial sortings of Ss in Condition B, which placed no constraints on the number of clusters) forms the only evidence we have regarding the likelihood that these 28 items do or do not group themselves into primarily 4 clusters (stages). First, we tested to see whether the white Ss differed from the black Ss in the number of clusters which they formed out of these 28 items (this test ignored which particular items were placed in each cluster; it only counted the number of different clusters that were formed). A Kolmogorov-Smirnov two-sample test (two-tailed) showed no significant difference between the black and white students for either Condition A $(p > .05)$ or Condition B $(p > .05)$. Perhaps it will be of interest to point out the frequencies with which the different number of clusters were formed in the two conditions. In Condition A, 17 of the 60 Ss gave precisely 4 clusters in their initial sortings and 17 additional Ss gave 5 clusters. In Condition B (first sortings only) the maximum was clearly for five clusters and the second most frequent entry was for four clusters. Thus this suggests two possible conclusions. First, the hypothesis that four stages underlie the recent evolution of black awareness is *approximately* correct if we look at Condition A and more open to question if we concentrate on Condition B results. Another possible conclusion is that there may be several alternate routes or belief systems by which one can gain conviction in the search for black identity. The answer to the latter possibility will have to await a method for analyzing the semantic labels or reasons that the Ss gave for why they cluster items together. This has not been accomplished as yet.

Conclusions

1. Within the limitations of the present study, we believe that the plausibility of Cross's hypothesis concerning the existence of several stages in the development of black awareness in America has received general positive support with the data we have collected.

2. There is a pronounced tendency for white subjects to perceive these stages and the items which characterize each stage in much the same manner that black subjects perceive them. However, a few significant differences between blacks and whites in response to particular items were found.

3. There was an impressive similarity in sorting patterns across experimental conditions (Conditions B and C) which argues for the general robustness of the underlying conception—that is, the results are fairly replicable under rather different testing conditions.

References

Bennett, L. Of time, space, and revolution. *Ebony*, 1969, **24**, 31–39.

Caplan, N. The new ghetto man: A review of recent empirical studies. *Journal of Social Issues*, 1970, **26**, 59–73.

Caplan, N. S., and Paige, J. M. A study of ghetto rioters. *Scientific American*, August 1968, **219**(2), 15–21.

Crawford, T. J., and Naditch, M. Relative deprivation, powerlessness and militancy. *Journal of Psychiatry*, 1970, **33**(2), 208–223.

Cross, W. E., Jr. The black experience viewed as a process: A crude model for black self-actualization. Paper presented at the Thirty-fourth Annual Meeting of the Association of Social and Behavioral Scientists, April 23–24, 1970, Tallahassee, Florida.

Cross, W. E., Jr. Discovering the black referent: The psychology of black liberation. In Vernon J. Dixon and Baoi Foster (Eds.), *Beyond black or white*. Boston: Atlantic-Little, Brown, 1971, pp. 95–109.

Dizard, J. E. Black identity, social class and black power. *Journal of Psychiatry*, 1970, **33**(2), 195–207.

Forward, J. R., and Williams, J. R. Internal-external control and black militancy. *Journal of Social Issues*, 1970, **26**(1), 75–92.

Gerlach, L. P. *People, power, change: Movements of social transformation.* New York: Bobbs-Merrill, 1970.

Gerlach, L. P., and Hine, V. H. The social organization of a movement of revolutionary change: Case study, black power. In Norman E. Whitten and John F. Szwed (Eds.), *Afro-American Anthropology: Contemporary Perspectives.* New York: Free Press, 1970, pp. 385–401.

Hahn, H. Black separatists: Attitudes and objectives in a riot-torn ghetto. *Journal of Black Studies*, 1970, **1**(7), 35–43.

Hall, G. M. St. Malcolm and the black revolutionists. *Negro Digest*, November 1967, 4–11.

Hall, W. S., and Cross, W. E., Jr. The formation of an ego identity in black Americans: Toward a conceptualization of stages in coming to terms with self. Paper presented at the Annual Meeting of the National Association of Black Psychologists, Miami Beach, Florida, 1970.

Koslin, B. L., Cardwell, J., and Pargament, R. Which Negroes prefer what skin color? Unpublished manuscript, from Riverside Research Institute, New York, n.d.

Maliver, B. L. Anti-Negro bias among Negro college students. *Journal of Personality and Social Psychology*, 1965, **2**, 770–775.

Marx, G. T. *Protest and prejudice: A study of belief in the black community.* New York: Harper & Row, 1967.

Orum, A. M., and Orum, A. W. The class and status bases of Negro student protest. *Social Science Quarterly*, 1968, **49**, 521–533.

Sherif, M., and Sherif, C. Black unrest as a social movement toward an emerging self-identity. *Journal of Social and Behavioral Sciences*, 1970, **15**(3), 41–52.

Thomas, C. W. *Boys no more.* Beverly Hills, Calif.: Glencoe Press, 1971.

Tomlinson, T. M. Determinants of black politics: Riots and the growth of militancy. *Journal of Psychiatry*, 1970, **33**(2), 242–264.

Wallace, A. F. C. Revitalization movements. *American Anthropologist*, 1956, **58**, 264–281.

Wallace, A. F. C. *Culture and personality.* New York: Random House, 1964.

The Black Community as the Source of Positive Self-Concept for Black Children: A Theoretical Perspective

Several months ago a black graduate student asked the writer a question which served as the catalyst for this paper: "How does one rear a black child to have a positive self-concept or high self-esteem in this society?" This led to a reflection on the body of literature concerning personality development and functioning of the black child. As the writer pondered different works by various writers (mostly white), it became quite clear that those of us who are black cannot think of our children without thinking about our families. We cannot think about black children and black families without thinking about black communities. We cannot think about black children, black families, and black communities without, at the same time, realizing that this entire configuration of blackness is surrounded by a white racist society.

Two additional realizations occurred with great impact as the writer reviewed the literature: the essentially negative nature of the research, and the extent to which black children are separated from families even conceptually, and the further separation of black children and black families from the black community. But the most glaring factor concerns the separation of the black community from the surrounding white community. It is obvious that we who are concerned about the black children must think about them in relation to black families and the black community, never forgetting that this entire configuration is embedded in a society which devalues everything black.

In the past decade significant events have occurred in the lives of black Americans. The civil rights movement of the early 1960s gave birth to a new breed of black youth. As the civil rights movement gave way to the forceful thrust of the rise of black consciousness, with its demands for liberation and self-determination, still another kind of young black was born. During this period a large literature concerning black identity emerged. The bulk of this literature does not reflect significant changes in psychological attributes of blacks. It would seem that such changes would be a necessary concomitant of the new stance being assumed by blacks vis-à-vis the white society. This seeming contradiction may be explained by reference to theoretical and methodological shortcomings to be addressed later in this paper.

If the behavioral changes occurring in blacks, especially young blacks, during the past decade represent a positive change in self-concept, self-identity, and other areas, what factors made such change possible? In other words, is it possible for a black individual to develop a positive self-concept in this society, and if so, what are the contributing factors?

Reprinted by permission of the author.

The quest for self-identity is a search for answers to the questions: Who am I? What am I like as a person? Where do I fit in the world? The answers the individual arrives at are inextricably intertwined with how others see and interact with him. Leading authorities in this area (Mead, 1934; Cooley, 1956; Sullivan, 1953; Erikson, 1968; Essien-Udom, 1962) agree that the self-concept arises through the individual's interaction with other members of the society; parents, peers, teachers, and other representatives of society's institutions. According to Mead (1934), through identification and as a necessary means of communication the child learns to assume the roles and attitudes of others with whom he interacts, a posture having significance not only for how he responds to others, but also for how he reacts to himself. The continuity of the self derives from the collective attitudes of the society, or "generalized other," as Mead calls it; that is, the individual's sense of self is developed, molded, and controlled by his assuming the attitudes and definitions of others toward him. Thus, the extent to which an individual is a member of this society, its values, goals, attitudes, and norms are his. Even though each self has its unique characteristics, it is structured in terms of these societal attributes, and is, thus, also an individual reflection of the social process (1). Cooley (1956) articulated this idea by invoking the image of the "looking glass"—namely, that the self is a looking glass mirroring the three primary components of the self-concept: "the imagination of our appearance to the other person; the imagination of his judgment of that appearance; and some sort of self feeling, such as pride or mortification" (p. 184). Sullivan (1953) articulates a similar conception in his proposition that the self-dynamism of the child is a function of the reflections of significant others. The "good me" represents the approving reflections; the "bad me" represents the disapproving reflections.

Erikson's (1968) analysis of the concept gives rise to three different identities: ego, personal, and group identity. Ego identity concerns the quality of one's existence or an awareness of the fact that there is a continuity to the ego's synthesizing methods: "the style of one's individuality and that this style coincides with sameness and continuity of one's meaning for significant others in the immediate community" (Erickson, 1968). Personal identity is the perception of the continuity of one's existence in time and space and the perception of the fact that others recognize one's sameness and continuity. Group identity is the group's basic way of organizing experience which is transmitted through child training "to the infant's early bodily experiences, and through them to the beginning of his ego" (Erickson, 1968, p. 47).

Thus, regardless of whether the concept is considered from a socio psychology or from a dynamic psychology frame of reference, the nature of the child's social context is of primary significance for the development of the self-concept. What do these theoretical perspectives project concerning the possibilities of a black child's developing a positive self-concept in this society? A simple, direct deduction from these theories would suggest that such possibilities are nil. For example, for the black child, both the "generalized other" attitudes he theoretically assumes and the "looking glass" into which he gazes transmit the same message: He is an inferior human being, and because of this he is relegated to the lowest stratum of a color caste system. By accepting the values and attitudes contained in society's messages, his self-concept naturally is negative, nurtured through his contact with institutionalized symbols of caste inferiority on every hand. For example, when he looks around him, except in the spheres of athletics and entertainment, he sees very few Americans with his skin color who hold important (power) positions in the society. The mass media—especially, television—presents few black heroes. When they are portrayed, typically, they are cast in low-status roles, and until quite recently, were presented as amusingly ignorant (to whites). Observation of brutal, dehumanizing treatment of blacks at the hands of police and other law enforcement officials is commonplace. All of these communicate to the black child the lack of positive value and the negative value the society places on him. In addition to these direct negative indicators, there are indirect negative indicators such as the reactions of the child's own family who have been socialized to believe they are substandard human beings (Poussaint and Atkinson, 1970). The looking glass of the wider society reflects the undesirability of the black child's skin color and hair texture. In fact, these attributes belong to one of three categories of stigma outlined by Goffman (1963). In order to gain the esteem of the "generalized other," the child realizes that he must approximate the white ideal as nearly as possible. This means, among other things, rejecting himself and others like him.

Essien-Udom (1962) comments concerning the effects on blacks of assuming the attitudes, norms, and roles of the wider society:

> The tragedy of the Negro in America is that he has rejected his origins—the essentially human meaning implicit in the heritage of slavery, prolonged suffering, and social rejection. By rejecting his unique group experience and favoring assimilation and even biological amalgamation, he thus denies himself the creative possibilities inherent in it and in his folk culture. This dilemma is fundamental; it severely limits his ability to evolve a new identity or a meaningful synthesis, capable of endowing his life with meaning and purpose. (p. 9)

He learns that existence for him demands adhering to the role outlined by the white society. To challenge the definition assigned to him carries the risk and probability of his destruction. The Hollywood film *The Liberation of L. B. Jones* speaks eloquently to the consequences for blacks of challenging the society's definition of blacks. Dr. Martin Luther King, Jr., and Malcolm X are living testimonials to this fact (2).

Now that he have outlined some of the expected theoretical predictions, what does empirical observation reveal? Empirical findings coincide with expected findings based on theoretical projections. Findings from a variety of sources converge to indicate the black child's incomplete self-image (Rainwater, 1967; Gordon, 1965; Coles, 1965; Ausubel and Ausubel, 1963); his negative self-image and preference for things "white" (Proshansky and Newton, 1968; Rainwater, 1967; Stevenson, 1953; Goodman, 1952; Clark and Clark, 1947, Stevenson and Stewart, 1958; Radke and Trager, 1950; Morland, 1962; Landreth and Johnson, 1953); his rejection of and expressed hostility toward his own group (Goodman, 1952; Stevenson and Stewart, 1958; Clark and Clark, 1947).

If the black person feels disdain or hatred for his group, therefore for himself, and experiences himself as incomplete, as indicated above, then we can expect such factors to have negative effects on his behavior and experience.

Data brought forth in support of this hypothesis can be subsumed under two categories: "cognitive and affective status" and "achievement orientation." The black is characterized by high anxiety level (Feld and Lewis, 1967; Hill and Sarason, 1966; Sarason et al., 1960; Palermo, 1959; Caldwell, 1959); a high level of maladjustment (Rainwater, 1967; Boykin, 1957), neuroticism (Hammer, 1953), and rejection of other blacks (Yarrow, 1958); inability to delay gratification (Mischel 1966, 1961b), reportedly a critical factor in immature, criminal, and neurotic behavior (Mowrer and Ullman, 1945); low-level orientation toward achievement (Mischel, 1961c); proneness toward delinquency (Mischel, 1961b); confusion of sexual identity or sex role adoption (Burton, 1961; Hokanson and Calden, 1960; Cott and Cott, 1963; Sclare, 1953); a sense of little personal control over his environment (Crandall et al., 1965); intellectual functioning typically at the low average to borderline range (Barnes, 1969), accompanied by poor ability for critical thinking—analytical and synthetical (3). Information from the achievement orientation domain shows black youngsters as low in achievement motivation (Rosen, 1959; Mussen, 1953; Deutsch, 1960; McClelland, 1961), or as unrealistically high in aspiration levels (Katz, 1968; Ausubel and Ausubel, 1958; Deutsch, 1960; Johnson, 1941) (4).

Generally the literature paints a rather dismal picture of the black youngster from the standpoint of self-concept. Placing the black youngster within the context of the black family generates the following image. The "Negro" family is portrayed as having a life style distinct from that of all other segments of the society. More often than not the father has deserted the family; the mother, frustrated because of her own unfulfilled needs and wishes, reacts harshly and rejects the children. Her frustration generally is a "causal" factor in her having more "illegitimate" children. The children, in turn, react to this hostile atmosphere by becoming aggressive, nontrusting, and uneducable. They experience unusual difficulty in differentiating between male and female roles, and cross-role adoptions are the rule. By age three or four the black child is aware of racial differences, including a knowledge of the usual associated stereotypes, but is slow to make racial distinctions, and parents (mother) are not able to help him with questions and anxiety around black–white issues and concerns. He frequently chooses white dolls and white friends and often identifies himself as white, or shows a pained reluctance to "admitting" he is "Negro." While much of the direct manifestation of "self-hate" disappears by age seven or eight, definite indications of it still exist later—for example, "shooting" dope to escape the image, or "pimping" and having illegitimate children to deny it (5).

Both theoretical perspectives and empirical findings project little hope for the development of positive self-images on the part of blacks in this society. But do the foregoing configurations of findings and projections tell the whole story? The writer thinks not. Theory can be questioned on the grounds of its failure to account for the full spectrum of findings in the various empirical studies; for example, what about that 33 to 77 percent in Clark's (1949) studies, the

87 percent in Greenwald and Oppenheim's study (1968), and the 46 to 68 percent in Morland's (1962, 1966) studies who did not select white dolls as being "like themselves"? How does one account for Boyd's (1952) findings of higher aspiration levels for schoolwork ability on the part of black children as compared to whites when groups are matched for age, IQ, and socioeconomic status? Lott and Lott's study (1963) suggests that blacks can have high and realistic levels of occupational aspirations. It is of interest to note that when empirical results are in the unexpected direction, usually they are interpreted to be consistent with theoretical expectations. The concept of "unrealistic (high) aspiration level" seems to serve that purpose. Because the validity of a theory or conceptual system rests upon its ability to explain and predict, one has to wonder about theory-conserving operations. The history of this country is replete with instances of the creation of theories to demonstrate the inferiority of blacks—theories that can provide justification for the oppression of blacks, self-serving theories directed to maintaining the oppressor's convictions of his own superiority. Historically, biological or genetic factors have been invoked as explanatory modes to account for the status of blacks; today the vogue is to call forth environmental factors. However, as the writer has noted elsewhere (Barnes, 1969), it is of small benefit to blacks whether an environmental hypothesis is chosen over a genetic hypothesis, "if explanation remains at the level of the black individual or family and does not begin to deal with forces in the larger society responsible for creating these conditions" (p. 36). Where this observation is valid, contemporary social deprivation theories may be viewed as substituting environmental unchangeability for biologically determined immutability.

Theory, as explicitly stated and as implicitly interpreted and applied in empirical studies, gives little or no emphasis to the black community as a variable in development and functioning of the self-concept. Little emphasis is given to the black community as a processor of information and messages coming from the wider society. An implicit theoretical assumption is that the black family and child are recipients of direct impingements (messages) from the white society. Likewise, the "generalized other" in theory appears to be synonymous with "white society." This position or interpretation of theory gives no recognition to the possibility that the black community may serve as the child's social referent, thereby asserting influence as the "generalized other."

There is no place in theory or its empirical application for making a distinction between behavior emanating from role playing, on the one hand, and behavior stemming from enduring personality characteristics, on the other. This distinction is a crucial one because it is obviously important whether a given complex of behavior reflects an acting out of role behaviors, or whether it reflects enduring personality characteristics. The ability to distinguish between oneself and the role one plays may be a critical operation for blacks. Consider the lyrics that go with an old black folk song; "got one mind for white folk to see, 'nother for what I know is me" (Ames, 1950, p. 194). This is a succinct statement of the role-person distinction.

Maintaining this distinction is a task confronting each individual. The failure to distinguish between role and self, whether role is that of servility or superior being leads to trouble. Jung introduced the concept of the "persona" to describe this duality.

> *The word "persona" is really a very suitable expression for it, since persona originally meant the mask worn by an actor to signify his role. . . . It is a* compromise between the individual and society *as to the kind of semblance to adopt, what a man should "appear to be." He takes a name, earns a title, represents an office, and belongs to this or that. . . . Society expects, and indeed must expect, that every individual should play the role assigned to him as completely as possible. Accordingly, a man who is also a pastor, must not only carry out his professional functions objectively, but at all times and seasons he must play the role of pastor in a flawless manner. Society demands this as a kind of security. . . . It is therefore not surprising that everyone who wants to be successful has to take these expectations into account.*
>
> *The construction of a collectively suitable* persona *means a very great concession to the outer world. It is a real self-sacrifice which directly forces the ego into an identification with the* persona, *so that there are people who actually believe themselves to be what they present to the public view. . . . These identifications with the social role are a very fruitful source of neuroses.* A man cannot get rid of himself in favor of an artificial personality without punishment. *The mere attempt to do so releases, in all the ordinary cases, unconscious reactions in the form of moods, affects, fears, compulsive ideas, feelings, vices, etc. (White, 1948, p. 166; my emphasis)*

Undoubtedly, there is a significant difference in the dynamics of the individual who seeks to be his role, and the individual who is thrust in his role against his wishes. In the latter case, the threat of or actual punishment keeps the individual in his role; in the former case, different incentives are involved (6). Where behavior is an acting out of role definitions, it is enough for the situation to change (change in statuses and role expectations) for behavior to change. A crucial issue regards the extent to which human behavior is generated by the social contexts in which it occurs and the extent to which individuals create a "portable" reality which determines their behavior irrespective of the situation.

The theoretical position(s) and empirical studies cited do not view the black community as the highly complex, highly structured system that it is. For example, is it the case that middle-class urban blacks, living in a northeast metropolitan area, respond to messages (white racism) from the larger society in a manner identical to and with the same consequences for self-image as the nonworking lower class in the same area? We know, for example, that there are (and have been) blacks in this society who have solid, positive self-concepts and a strong sense of group belongingness. How can this be explained? Without modification and extension of current self theory, it cannot. Ralph Ellison (1967) placed this issue in perspective when asked by a group of young black writers to comment on how they might more accurately portray the complexity of the human condition, using the black experience as a theme.

Ellison, among other things, stated that the black writer would never see his subject as long as he accepted the black family as a broken one and a matriarchy, or of Harlem as "piss on the wall and blood on the stairs." Such stereotypes, as all stereotypes, have some grain of truth in them, but they do not come close to reflecting the complexity of the black condition, denying "that something else which makes for our strength, which makes for our endurance and promise" (p. 87). The concentration of the literature is on the lowest income, most oppressed black families and individuals. The findings from this group are used as an index to "understanding" and "explaining" blacks (Billingsley, 1968). The studies producing them grow out of present theory, and they feed back into theory. But obviously, to utilize information from this narrow segment of the black population as a basis for describing, explaining, and predicting for blacks is to err grossly. The practice possibly explains some of the contradictions and paradoxes in the literature regarding blacks.

We are fully aware of the many limitations in the operationalized definitions (measures) of self-concept and related dependent variables alluded to in the foregoing. The validity of the findings cited above could be questioned on these grounds; however, an examination of these considerations is beyond the scope of this paper. For present purposes we are accepting the measures of the variables at face value.

At this point we can refer to the question posed at the beginning of this paper regarding the possibilities of a black child's developing a positive self-concept in this society. That question can be translated as follows: Is it possible that the black community can and does serve as a mediator between the black child and the pernicious impingements of the white society, such that the child can develop a self-concept that is enhancing of himself and of his group, a self-concept that enables him to distinguish between who he is, his worth and value, on the one hand, and what the white society says about him on the other? An approach to answering this question requires a modification and extension of theoretical perspective—a perspective that considers the child in relation to the family, the child and family in relation to the black community, and the community, family, and child in relation to the wider society, and finally one that considers black people or the black community as a complex social system. This perspective emphasizes the interdependence of the black child and family with other levels of society and the great heterogeneity characterizing black people, as a group. It postulates the black community as social referent for the child, and as mediator between child and family and the wider society in the process of development of the self-concept. Further, this orientation shifts the focus from the behavior of individuals to recurrent interchanges between people, and may properly be called a *systems conception.*

Systems Approach to Development of the Self-Concept in Black Children

It is our intention to focus upon the social system, or the context in which social behavior takes place. We see social systems as a subclass of systems in general. As such they are subject to the principles of general systems theory (GST). According to Bertalanffy (1966), "general systems theory contends that there are principles of systems in general or in defined subclasses of systems irrespective of the nature of systems of their components, or of the relations of forces between them" (p. 708). Thus, GST is general in that it attempts to examine all types of systems. A system is an organization of elements united in a form of regular interaction and interdependence. General systems theory as an approach to organizing and looking at phenomena is, thus, applicable to the cell (biological system), to the individual (psychological system), and to groups or society (social systems). The focus of this paper is at the level of psychological and social systems.

The concept of a social system has been treated comprehensively by Talcott Parsons (1951, 1955). A social system is an aggregation of social roles or persons bound together by a pattern of mutual interaction and interdependence. It has boundaries which enable us to distinguish the internal from the external environment, and typically it is both a system for social units smaller than itself, and a subsystem for social units larger than itself.

The black family as a social system has been diagrammed by Billingsley (1968), as indicated—and grossly oversimplified—in Figure 1. As depicted the family is embedded in a network of mutually interdependent relationships with the black community and wider society. Just as the family is a subsystem of the black community, so are various patterns of interactions (*dyads:* father-son,

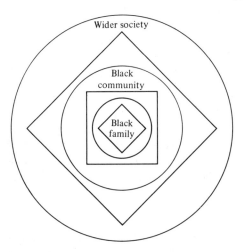

FIGURE 1

The black family as a social system. (Adapted from A. Billingsley, Black Families in White America, *Englewood Cliffs, N.J.: Prentice-Hall, 1968.)*

The family is embedded in a matrix of mutually interdependent relationships with the black community and the wider society. And there are subsystems within the family: husband-wife; mother-son; father-daughter; grandmother-mother-daughter, and so forth.

The black community includes schools, churches, lodges, social clubs, funeral societies, organized systems of hustling, and other institutions.

The wider society consists of major institutions: value, political, economic, health, welfare, and communication subsystems.

mother–daughter, brother–sister; *triads:* grandmother–mother–daughter, etc.) subsystems of the family, which for them is a social system. The individuals in these various patterns, in turn, are subsystems to the larger interactive patterns (dyad, triad, etc.) within the family.

A key consideration in all of this concerns the mutually interdependent relations existing between the family and its members, on the one hand, and the family and the black community, on the other. It may be that, among other things, the nature of the relationship of the family to the black community is a key factor in development of the child's self image.

Primary among the subsystems of the larger society having a direct impact on the black community, and through it, the family and family members are the communications, political, economic, educational, and values subsystems. Blacks have been systematically excluded from participation in these subsystems, while being gravely influenced by them. It is our contention that the nature and intensity of this influence varies differentially as a function of community characteristics and relation of families to the community.

A second major feature of this theoretical orientation concerns the conception of blacks as the highly complex heterogeneous, diverse people that they are. Even though, in this country, black people are viewed as a group apart from other people, and as showing common intragroup attributes, behaviors, and conditions, great variations are also obvious. Billingsley (1968) offers the concept "ethnic subsociety" as a means of capturing this duality. This concept was taken from Milton Gordon's theoretical work *Assimilation in American Life* (1964). An ethnic group is a relatively large configuration of people with a "shared feeling of peoplehood." In this society such groups are organized around race, religion, national origin, or some combination of these. Gordon (1964) states that, common to the ethnic group

> is the social-psychological element of a special sense of both ancestral and future-oriented identification with the group. These are the "people" of my ancestors, therefore, they are my people, and will be the people of my children and their children. With members of other groups I may share political participation, occupational relationships, common civic enterprise, perhaps even an occasional warm friendship, but in a very special way, which history has decreed, I share a sense of indissoluble and intimate identity with this group and not that group within the larger society and the world. (p. 29)

This conception seems to reflect the reality of the existence of black people. It also reflects the growing black consciousness or awareness of our peoplehood, which is evolving at a rapid rate in black communities throughout the country. While we are one, as members of a color caste system, and by virtue of our common peoplehood, we are not a homogeneous mass. Billingsley (1968) has depicted the black community as an ethnic subsociety, as indicated in Figure 2.

Billingsley's conceptual model makes use of three dimensions in describing the black community as an ethnic subsociety. They are social dimensions on which members within an ethnic group vary—namely, social class, rural or urban resi-

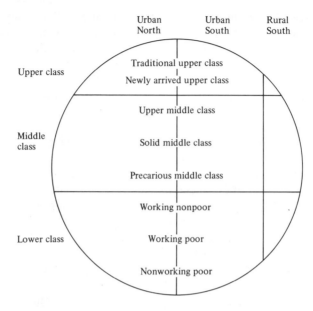

FIGURE 2

The black community as an ethnic subsociety. (Adapted from A. Billingsley, Black Families in White America, *Englewood Cliffs, N.J.: Prentice-Hall, 1968.)*

This figure is conceptual and does not reflect the exact social and geographic distribution of the black population. In 1966, about 50 percent of all black families lived in the urban North, 25 percent in the urban South, and 25 percent in the rural South.

If income is used as the index of social class, about 50 percent of all black families fall into the lower class, about 40 percent in the middle class, and about 10 percent in the upper class.

dence, and region of the country lived in. For our purposes then, black groups not only are blacks to be compared or contrasted with whites, they also may be upper class, middle class, or lower class, with northern, southern, or western residence, with urban or rural backgrounds, and significantly they may be meaningfully compared and contrasted with each other.

As indicated by Billingsley (1968), the significance of social class is not to be able to make statements such as "middle-class whites and blacks have more in common than do middle- and lower-class blacks." Such a formulation obscures more than it reveals, and fails to make a distinction between the different types of identities people share. Gordon (1964) conceptualizes two types of identities people share: historical and participational. The ethnic group is the locus of a sense of historical identification. The intersection of ethnicity and social class is the locus of participational identification.

With a person of the same social class but of a different ethnic group, one shares behavioral similarities but not a sense of peoplehood. With those of the same ethnic group but different social class one shares the sense of peoplehood but not behavioral similarities. The only group which meet both these criteria are people of the same ethnic group and social class. (Gordon, 1964, p. 53)

As Billingsley (1968) suggests, even though social class lines among blacks are less rigid than among other groups, social class distinctions within the black community do provide a distinct basis of differentiation which helps to condition the lives of blacks. Hence, we would expect differential responses to white impingements by people located at different positions in the structure, differential responses that have implications for black children's developmental status.

Developing Black Consciousness or Sense of Peoplehood

Considering the mutual interdependence of the black family and the black community, it is of critical importance to assess the status of black people in terms of extent of group unity, identification, sense of peoplehood, or what you will. Changes in the community have implications for changes in the family and in the units of which it is comprised. A growing pride, sense of peoplehood in the one, should be accompanied by a similar change in the other, along with the implications such changes carry for development of a positive self-concept in the child.

Carmichael and Hamilton (1967) argue for the development of a black norm by means of which black people must redefine themselves, set forth new values and goals, and organize around them. Barbara Sizemore (1969) and Barnes (1970) mount similar arguments, pointing out that for the black man to support the norms and values of the larger society means to support his own inferiority. It seems clear that the definition of what is "good" and "desirable" and what is "bad" and "undesirable" for a society is primarily in terms of the interests of those who hold the power in that society. The most cursory examination of the current status of blacks today and historically in this country reveals conclusively that the value structure and normative patterns of the society work in the interest of its whites and against the interests of blacks. In a word, the white society imposes a racist authoritarian ethic upon blacks. The black community must define what is "good" and desirable and what is "bad" and undesirable from the standpoint of its own interests and conditions of its existence. Sizemore (1969) points out the undesirable implications of supporting the norms and values of the larger society. The support of this norm by a black means to support his classification as a stigmatized being. For the stigmatized individual who cannot "pass," he must decide to assume responsibility for the sin, thus shifting the burden from society to the victim, or to alienate himself from the community of the sinner. Obviously, a stigmatized status cannot provide a basis for development of a positive self-concept. The latter alternative of alienation (regroupment) allows for developing those conditions for self-determination.

Talcott Parsons (1965) observes the need for collective and mutual support on the part of black people, particularly at the level of the family and local community, and suggests that the healthiest line of development for the black man would be toward group solidarity and cohesion and the sense that being a black man has positive value.

Erikson (1968) argues that self-determination is an integral part of ego identity:

For the American, group identity, supports an individual's ego identity as long as he can preserve a certain element of deliberate tentativeness, as long as he can convince himself that the next step is up to him and that no matter where he is staying or going he always has the choice of leaving or turning in the opposite direction. (p. 67)

He also states that a strong ego, secured in its identity by a strong society, does not need artificial inflation, for it tends to test what feels real, to master what works, to understand what proves necessary, to overcome the morbid and to transmit its purpose to the next generation for the creation of a strong mutual reinforcement with others in the group.

What is the status of black people with respect to the various imperatives outlined above? While blacks have always been aware of connections with other blacks in this country and others, they have not felt free to act on it. It was not until after World War II that blacks again embraced the theme put forth by Marcus Garvey and others, that blacks have a common history, a common position vis-à-vis the white world, and a common destiny. Developments over the last decade indicate a sharp rise in the number of black people who recognize the need for blacks to assert their own definitions, to reclaim their history and culture, and to create their own sense of community and togetherness. Throughout the country, middle- and upper-class blacks are turning to explicit recognition of a common destiny shared by blacks (Billingsley, 1968). There is no civil rights or protest activity that does not have privileged blacks in leadership positions. The ghetto uprisings of 1965, 1966, and 1967 in more than 100 cities had substantial support from middle-class blacks.

In many ways the group identification process shows itself—for example, growing resistance to school desegregation and to breakup of black communities through urban renewal, blacks quietly moving back into the ghetto and others refusing to move out, organization of black student groups at secondary and postsecondary levels, discussion groups focusing dialogue around the blacks' common destiny and potential for change.

Salient examples of group solidarity occurred around the election of black mayors in Cleveland, Gary, and Newark, feats made possible by blacks voting in large proportions and in a bloc for the black rather than the white candidate. Further moves toward self-determination and definition are reflected in rejecting the term *Negro* and replacing it with *Afro-American*, *African American*, and *black*, and the development of black esthetic norms, as reflected in the natural hair style and "dress." All of these recent behavioral manifestations of a participational identification indicate an increase in magnitude of those dimensions of ethnic similarity.

Carmichael and Hamilton (1967) comment on the end significance of this process:

When we begin to define our own image, the stereotypes—lies that the oppressor has developed—will begin in the white community and end there. The black community will have a positive image of itself it has created. (p. 37)

This view suggests that the black community, through a process of group solidarity, self determination, and definition (development of black norms), can serve as a filter to sort out or attenuate the pernicious impingements from the larger (white) society, a process which should have a facilitating or enhancing effect on the development of the self-concept in black children.

The Black Muslim organization is instructive regarding one approach to developing a black norm. In doing so, the founder, Mr. Muhammad, deals with negative identities: social definition or the definition of Negro, ego identity, quality of one's existence in the face of significant others, and personal identity, individual name, or identity peg. The new social identity is born out of the community of Islam, an international brotherhood of Asiatics (Africa is a part of Asia). A new name, given by Allah, is substituted for the slave name, giving the individual a new identity peg. The quality of one's existence is enhanced by certain teachings. Arabic is taught in the school, as well as the civilization and religion of the black man. Members of the organization are encouraged to obey rules and regulations surpassing the Protestant Ethic in stringency. However, Mr. Muhammad does not expect his followers to accept the blame for their victimized status at the hands of society. He places the blame directly on society and further charges that such a society must be one of beasts and devils. This is his black norm. It serves not only as a source of positive identification for his followers, but also as a mode for delegitimizing (7) messages from the white society.

Hence, in response to the question posed at the beginning of this paper, we can postulate that it is possible for a black child to have or develop a positive, actualizing self-concept in this society, under certain conditions. These conditions are that the black community containing the child and family be characterized by a sense of peoplehood, group identification, or black consciousness, or pride, and that the family be identified with or experience a sense of belonging to the community. It is postulated that when these conditions prevail, the black community, interposed between the family and white community, serves as a filter against the harmful inputs from the latter. In social system terms, the black community either rejects such messages as input or in its transformations of them renders them innocuous. Or to paraphrase Carmichael and Hamilton (1967), the stereotypes and lies of the oppressor will begin within the white community and die at its borders.

The theoretical perspective advanced here can also begin to explain some of the contradictions and paradoxes in the literature. Consider the complexity of the ethnic subsociety composed of the following classes: the lower class, which can be divided into nonworking poor, working poor, working nonpoor; the middle class, which can be divided into the precarious middle class, solid middle class, upper middle class; and the upper class, which can be divided into recent-arrived upper class, and old families or traditional upper class. It would be unimaginable to think that individuals and families in such diverse life circumstances would respond uniformly to certain kinds of experiences, such as white racism. No doubt, the sense of peoplehood experienced with reference to blacks differs with different life experiences; children are differentially shielded from the ravages of such diseases as racism. The cases in the various studies cited that do not fall in the categories predicted by theory may be explainable with an adequate description of the populations from which the samples came, rather than merely being described as "Negro." The excess of negative findings, among other things, may be explainable on the basis of the location of the subjects, for those studies, in the ethnic subsociety. The generation of adequately defined samples of blacks would also make possible comparisons between blacks, probably the most crucial comparison anyway, if understanding, explaining and programming are primary goals of studies.

A social systems orientation assumes an interactive process among elements of the system: consequently, the relationship between black community, family group, and child is not conceptualized as reactive in nature. The child does not merely respond to the larger family group and the family group to the community. The relationship is one of interaction, which means that the input into each subsystem is transformed into output which is accepted as input by another system, and both become subsystems of a more general system. Thus, the nature of the relationships established between systems may be related to characteristics of the subsystems or systems. Consideration of some of them lead to certain propositions which can be subjected to empirical test: (a) The degree of identification of the family with the black community (ethnic subsociety) is a factor in its capacity to serve as a filter against harmful impingements from the white society; (b) the degree to which a black community can develop its own norms is contingent upon the degree to which its members perceive of themselves as sharing a common "peoplehood"; (c) families that perceive themselves as more centrally located (greater sense of belonging with respect to the ethnic subsociety) are more effective filters against racism; (d) families at different levels in the ethnic subsociety differ in degrees of identification with the subsociety; and therefore differ in their effectiveness as social filters; (3) input from family members is accepted as such by the children to a greater extent in those cases where the relationship defined by the parent–child subsystem is stable and consistent.

Some Observations on Methodology

Implicit in the foregoing discussion is the concept of communication process. As indicated in the postulate regarding a social system, the units are bound together in a pattern of mutual interaction and interdependence. Hence, the study of the self-image in the black child, or more properly of the processes by which white racism is absorbed, deflected, denied, combated, succumbed to, and overcome by blacks, requires a methodological approach appropriate to the analysis of communication. Communication as a process can be divided into three levels: (a) action, (b) transaction, and (c) interaction (8). Analysis of the communication process at the action level focuses on the content of the message and the occurrence of events in a regular fashion. This level of analysis is exemplified in a study of self-concept where one of its components is conceptualized as independence or autonomy, operationalized as problem-solving behavior (putting a puzzle together), carried out independently of an adult present in the child's setting. The investigator might count the number of times the child directs verbalization to the adult and classify (categorize) the content as "help seeking" or "other." The important factor here is that no attempt is made to establish causal connections. The method is observation and categorization of actions. The appropriate statistical approach to handling data involves simple counting operations.

The communication process at the transaction level involves a unidirectional channel of communication between two systems. For example A's output is accepted as input by B, but B's output is not accepted by A or any other system as input. The focus at this level is on the isolation of cause and effect or antecedent and consequent sequences. Most of the investigations of the self-concept are at this level.

The following section reports the findings of a study carried out by the writer, which illustrates this methodological approach. It also represents an initial step in the explanation of some of the implications of the theoretical perspective propounded in this paper.

Illustrative and Exploratory Investigation

The question posed concerned the relation between black consciousness (group identification, or sense of peoplehood), on the part of parents, and self-image, or self-concept, on the part of their children. Casual observations of friends, students, acquaintances, and their children suggested such a relationship. At the time this information was obtained, the writer was directing an evaluation of a year-long inservice training program for school personnel in the Dayton, Ohio, Model Cities schools. Eight elementary and two high schools were involved in the inservice training program.

The two variables studied, group identification and self-concept, are considered as states of the individual (hypothetical constructs), and as such give rise to observable behavior, such behavior being accessible to observation by technique designed for that purpose. Group identification and self-concept are defined as indicated in the body of this paper.

Sample. From the total population of eight Model Cities elementary schools, four were chosen with the intent of maximizing socioeconomic differences, two schools in the most economically depressed areas and two in the least economically depressed Model City area. From the total population of kindergarten and first-grade classes in each school, a more or less random sample of 50 students was drawn. Samples of 50 subjects for kindergarten and first grade, respectively, were chosen randomly within limits of cooperation from a parochial Catholic school. This school was not located in and did not draw youngsters from the Model Cities area. All subjects in both groups were black. Samples within grades within schools were stratified by sex. For each group of 50 children at each class level, parents of 30 children, randomly selected from their group of 50, were tested. The majority of parents tested were female. Our children sample consisted of 250 males and females, and the adult sample consisted of 300 parents or caretakers, with a sex distribution of 100 fathers and 200 mothers.

Average socioeconomic status for children attending school in the badly depressed areas was slightly lower than those attending school in less depressed areas, and both of the latter were lower than the Catholic school sample.

The questions investigated concerned the relationship between aspects of children's self-concept and achievement-test scores (reading readiness and reading), and parents' sense of "group belongingness" (identification), individual-system blame, racial militancy-race ideology, sense of personal control, and individual–collective action.

The instrument utilized with the children was labeled Ethnic Pictures Test (EPT). The subject's task was to choose pictures in response to verbally presented questions designed to tap friendship preferences, social valuation, and color preference or racial identification. Parents (both when present in the household) were tested after the children were tested, but before analysis of the latter's responses was undertaken. Parents responded to self-report techniques (opinions, knowledge, self-ratings, and self-definitions). Parents also responded to a data form providing for information on income, educational level, occupation, organizational memberships, names of neighbors, and frequency of social contacts with them, father's occupation at time respondent was 25 years of age, father's educational level, political affiliation, and last time voted.

A full analysis of the observations made is not presented here. Only some of the more salient findings bearing upon the parent's perception of their relationship and orientation to the black ethnic subsociety and children's self-attitudes.

Preliminary data analysis reveals a significant relationship between SES level, using income and education as indices, and level of political activity; conception of term *black power* in political or militant terms; feeling strongly that Black History and an African language should be taught in the early grades. Higher SES parents responded in the directions indicated to a greater extent than lower SES parents. Lower SES group had more frequent contacts with and named greater number of people as neighbors. When the overall group was classified on level of political activity, conception of "black power," and social contact with neighbors, significant differences in children's responses to EPT emerged. Regardless of SES, the EPT scores of children whose parents indicated a high level of political activity (attending and participating Model Cities Citizens Meetings, voting in the last national and local elections, voting for black candidates for city council and school board) indicated greater ethnic identification, as indicated by positive social valuation of group, friendship choices, and racial or color identification. The same held for degree to which "black power" was conceptualized in political and militant terms, as well as for social contacts with neighbors, with a frequency of four or more times a month. And finally a positive relationship was found between parent measures on individual-system blame, individual-collective action, race ideology and children's EPT scores, when analysis was based on a dichotomous socioeconomic classification.

The relationships for higher SES groups were stronger. Given this fact, the child whose parents tended to blame the system for the conditions of blacks as a group and to endorse collective and militant action as an approach to the solution of the problems of blacks tended to score more favorably on the EPT. In this investigation, measures of group identity or black consciousness are provided by the instruments tapping the following dimensions: conception of "black power," political activity (voting for black candidates for local, state, and federal offices, etc.), racial militancy, individual-system blame, and individual-collective action (9).

These findings support the notion that parental involvement in the black community and specific beliefs, attitudes, and orientations toward the conditions of one's group, defined as indices of black consciousness, or sense of peoplehood, is associated positively with more positive self-concepts in children. They also support the importance of recognizing the complexity of the black ethnic subsociety in designing studies. The number of variables in this preliminary study is large, and the number of relationships still to be examined is large. Chi square statistical procedures have been utilized.

The following resumes the general discussion of communications process.

Analysis at the level of interaction focuses on bidirectional channels in communication, the type of interaction and nonlinear patterns that characterize human communication and social behavior. For example, in a triadic group consisting of father, mother, and son, there are three bidirectional channels of communication: (a) father–son; (b) mother–son; (c) father–mother; (d) son–father; (d) son–mother; (f) mother–father. Hence, there are six directions in which communication can flow. The kind of analysis outlined in the transaction level of analysis, while used in studies of reactive, nonsymbolizing elements, is not adequate to handle interactive (social) relations.

Research methods utilized to study human interaction processes are clinical impression and description, interview and questionnaire methods, experimental approach, and systematic analysis of ongoing interaction process through observation or categorization of records of such processes.

Each method is associated with its own strengths and weaknesses; however, they do not present uniform attributes in this regard. The systematic analysis of ongoing interaction through observation or categorization of records of such processes appears to offer the greatest advantages. In the writer's judgment, the patterns in human interaction processes are not fully accessible to clinical description, no matter how informed or skilled the clinician; nor is it felt that complete and accurate information about such processes is evoked by interviews and questionnaires. The experimental method raises the issue of representativeness or comparability of laboratory languages to that used in "natural" social interaction. Experimentation provides a new medium of interaction; however, media not only contain messages but also constrain messages (McLuhan, 1966). Thus, the most promising approach appears to be quantitative analysis of stored interaction process data—written, taped, and filmed records of interaction. In this approach each communicative act is evaluated and coded along a number of dimensions derived from conceptual frameworks considered to be significant in the study of interaction.

The possible advantages of quantitative analysis are several. By working with stored interaction process data, the same data may be subjected to repeated examination. Data can also be analyzed on the basis of multiple categorization over time. The significance of this is that the most skilled observer is limited in the scope of his observations—for example, he can work with only one category system at a time. Utilizing stored data also allows one to change the size of the unit under study as he proceeds.

Some disadvantages concern cost when data are stored by means of audiovisual tape. When audio tape is utilized, important visual aspects of the communication are lost, and when data in written form are utilized, all nonverbal aspects of communication are lost. Another problem is presented by the necessity of developing category systems with the accompanying difficulty of defining categories, the unitization of the interaction process, and the problem inherent in sampling the interaction process. Finally, there is the problem of getting at highly complex interaction patterns—for example, interaction of mother, father, and child, or teacher, parent, and child simultaneously.

What is the proper statistical method for the analysis of interaction patterns? While there are mathematical models extant that can be applied to this complex interactional data, its application to the kind of data has not been worked out, a task feasible only for the specialist, highly sophisticated in the field of mathematics (Clark, 1971). Up to this point in time, the usual statistical methods available to the social scientist (parametric and nonparametric statistical techniques) have been utilized. Taking into consideration this fact plus the lack of clearly developed methods for observing and coding complex human interactive patterns, it is concluded that methodology for the analysis of human interaction is in an embryonic stage of development.

Nevertheless, this does not prevent our moving toward a new methodological perspective, a perspective that stresses open-ended, naturalistic, observational strategies. This orientation also emphasizes a shift in focus—from the child alone to the child in interaction with others in the classroom, on the playground, in the home, and in the community. Multiple measurement techniques including self-report methods and observational methods are necessary to register the full range of phenomena, from internal states (subsystems, in GST language, or attitudes, beliefs, values, etc.) to external behavior. As Mills (1963) observes, the disparity between talk and action constitutes the central methodological problem of the social sciences. Neither alone provides a complete picture.

Implications for Education Programs, Program Evaluation, and Research

The perspective advanced here has specific implications for programming, as well as for evaluation of programs within the school setting, and for research into the educational process in the school conceptualized as a learning environment. The main thesis advanced regards the role of the black community as a resource for positive self-concept for its members. The community is comprised, among other things, of its institutions, including its schools. The schools have access to all the children in the community for some interval of time, and quite early in the child's life when the self-system is still developing and is most pliable. Given this, we can assume that it plays a role as "significant other" in the development and maintenance of the self-concept. It is, thus, imperative that the school face this responsibility and consciously plan its curriculum and select and train its personnel with this view in mind.

Educational Programs

A central implication of the perspective proffered here is the necessity for redefinition of early childhood education programs to include a total developmental approach. Every aspect of the child's environment and living experiences must be considered in the educational process. Thus, the school is recognized as a part of the child's community and as such plays a mediating role between the child and parent, on the one hand, and the larger society, on the other. Its effects in this role may be largely positive or negative for the child's self-concept. Thus the school can no longer afford to define its responsibilities to involve only the cognitive domain of the child; it must expand the concept of objectives to include the affective domain, and especially the self-concept, because it appears that its status has implications for other significant areas of human functioning: achievement motivation, aspiration levels, expectancy, fate control, and so forth. The assumption can no longer be made that a positive self-concept will automatically follow successful academic achievement—even though, no doubt, the two go together and mutually reinforce each other.

If the foregoing is accepted, then it follows that the classroom as a subsystem of the school, and the various subsystems within the classroom, are significant focal points. The classroom environment should be such that it facilitates joy in working and learning. Thus, the interaction of peers is a critical factor. For example, arrangements promoting individual competition rather than individual cooperation and intergroup competition should have implications for the students' self-concept (esteem).

The student–teacher subsystem is also critical. Because the teacher controls reinforcement (rewards and punishments), he plays a "shaping" role with students. Thus, teacher values assume import in interaction with students. So long as the society places differential value on characteristics such as hair texture and skin color, the fit, with respect to these dimensions, between teacher and child will be critical. Teachers in the positively valued group present the child in the negatively valued group with Promethean difficulties regarding the process of identification. For a black child to identify with a white teacher means to accept at least some of the white society's negative evaluation of himself and his group—a destructive act. This is to say that the white teacher cannot be a source of positive identification for the black child in this society today. Thus, the racial composition of the teaching staff is crucial. When the school is viewed as a subsystem of the large community and reflects this fact in the characteristics of those selected to participate in the educational process, this difficulty is easily surmounted. The observations made regarding the classroom also apply to the school as a whole. The child should have sufficient opportunities to identify with members of his group who hold top authority positions in the school setting.

Because the school is a critical subsystem of the child's community, the relationship between school and parents is of paramount importance. So long as the school and parents view each other in mutually hostile, suspicious terms, the child will be more or less unable to make a commitment to academic learning, with the result that he is retarded in those skills necessary for successful performance. The school must work toward creating a learning environment that is part of and supportive of the child's community.

If, as indicated above, all aspects of the child's environment and living experiences are to be considered in the educational experience, then the curriculum must reflect this fact in materials and content of instructional media, in teaching methods and approaches, in wall art, concepts, and so forth—all of which have implications for self-concept, directly or indirectly. Thus, follow-through programs should plan specifically for generating and maintaining positive self-concepts. The curriculum should include those experiences and exposures directed toward that end. The Black Muslim school can be instructive on this point.

Program Evaluation

If, as the position here has it, the school is a part of the child's community, and if a total developmental approach is the appropriate one, then program evaluations must cover noncognitive as well as cognitive change, which must be assessed. The evaluation has the responsibility of assessing changes in both domains even if the author of the program failed to explicitly spell out objectives in the two domains. In other words, both intended and unintended effects should be assessed. If the underlying concept of an activity is growth, then certain questions must be asked regardless of the stated intent of the program. From the perspective of a developmental or "aggregate" model as contrasted with the "mental health" model of change, success in school would be defined, in part at least, in the child's pride in himself and the ethnic group to which he belongs, his academic achievement motivation, the development of his creative potentials and intellectual promise. Evaluation should focus upon the effectiveness of a given program in creating an environment that is part of and supportive of the child's community.

Findings of evaluations are increasingly used by those who make or influence policy. Thus, those who undertake the evaluation of any social action program have a responsibility for making their findings as comprehensive, explicit, and valid as possible. This means viewing the whole person in a social context and not as a fragmented being separated from his surrounds. The evaluator should remember that, in a sense, the power to evaluate is the power to decide, a fact based on the consideration that evaluation is designed to yield conclusions about the worth of a program, and in so doing affects allocations of money on which the program's existence depends.

Research

Under this heading, one implication of the perspective developed in this paper concerns new methodologies and techniques—those consistent with a social system concept of the school and the educational process, and those based on a new model, reflecting a change from a "mental health" concept to a developmental or aggregate concept of pupil change. A detailed consideration of this implication is presented in the earlier discussion of communication analysis.

A second implication is the necessity for research that is directly concerned with understanding and resolving social problems to be more explicit about its underlying assumptions, values, and goals. Laboratory-based research may be able to remain at the level of "pure knowledge," but research into programs concerned with understanding and resolution of social problems cannot. The developmental model offered by the writer incorporates growth as its base value, with self-concept offered as a significant aspect of growth. Can growth serve this end? MacKinnon and Maslow (1951) were of the opinion it could:

> *Most import for motivation and value-theory is the introduction of a positive force to supplement the Freudian pessimism and the neo-behavioristic relativism motivated by avoidance of punishment, the relief of tension, and the seeking for a few physiological pleasures, e.g., food, sex, etc., and by whatever can be learned on this basis. . . .*
>
> *What such a positive concept can do for psychology is seen in the numerous writing of [Carl] Rogers . . . and his students, in which the concept of "growth" (indistinguishable from self-actualization) assumes more and more a central and essential role. This can be equally so for a psychological theory of democracy, of interpersonal relations, of social improvement, of cross-cultural comparison, and of a scientific system of values. With its aid there is no reason why cognition, conation, and affection should not be tied together once again, i.e., the contrast between individual and social, between selfish and altruistic, between instinctive and rational, and many other such false dichotomies can be resolved. (p. 646)*

Research on a particular problem area, thus, should not be concerned only with a narrowly defined approach, such as the evaluation of pupil cognitive change as a function of being exposed to a program of compensatory education, but should take into account wider experiences which influence growth negatively or positively. Researchers will then be in a better position to assess and interpret their findings (for our purposes, that being with respect to the education of young children) to the wider community. After all, it is the wider community that provides sanction for further action.

The perspective propounded here leads one to new data domains, a shift from the pupil centered to the interactive process. The interactions of focus are those involving subsystems within the home (child and parent) and within the school (child and parent and school; child and peers; child and other functionaries within the school, etc.), and those between subsystems—family, school, and other significant institutions in the community.

The act of viewing group and individual behavior from a social systems perspective, in addition to contributing to an understanding of personal characteristics, also contributes to an understanding of event properties and bridging variables (interactive) as well. Today, bridging concepts that explain the interaction of person and event variables in interpersonal interaction are in a rudimentary stage of development. This is the case despite the fact that the very core of self-theory is based on the interactive notion.

And finally, this paper argues for the extension or modification of self-theory, such that social referents in the developmental process are specifically defined in theory and its application. Sound programs designed to enhance self-concept can be erected only if we have a fair knowledge of those forces in the child's environment involved in its development. We need to know more about the family as mediator between child and its surrounds, and about the community as mediator between the family and the larger society.

Conclusions

Blacks are threatened with the specter of white racism from the cradle to the grave. Yet many escape the worst features of oppression, and many have shown an incredible capacity to survive, achieve, and conform in the face of impossible odds. Nevertheless, all blacks are members of a color caste system in this society and are subjected to ruthless oppression. We need to know more about the oppressor—his self-concept, factors in its development and maintenance, and the like. Surprisingly little is known to date. We need to know more about the dynamics of racism. We need to trace its dynamics and learn how it is transmitted. Thus, we need to study white families. We also need to study black families, but for a different set of reasons and from a different perspective. We need to study them as subsystems of the larger white society. Black children are at the center of our reasons for suggesting this study of black families. We need to study the process by which racism is absorbed, deflected, denied, combated, succumbed to, and overcome by particular black families and individuals.

This paper represents a modest attempt to articulate a beginning perspective consistent with these objectives and concerns. However we realize that more important than papers and studies, we need strategies of action to combat the insidious limitation on the ability of blacks to care for their children. Perhaps if we can delineate the process whereby societal racism is transformed into personal terms, we will be in a more propitious position to structure those strategies necessary to save the children.

We have concluded with a hypothesis in need of immediate testing, namely, that a primary factor in developing strategies to save black children is the power to define and determine one's group, roles, and values. He who has power to define is the master of the situation.

Lewis Carroll (1947) understood this:

"When I use a word," Humpty Dumpty said in a rather scornful tone, "it means just what I choose it to mean—neither more or less."
"The question is," said Alice, "whether you can make words mean so many different things."
"The question is," said Humpty Dumpty, "which is to be master—that's all."
(p. 196)

Notes

1. As indicated by H. Cantril [*The psychology of social movements* (New York: John Wiley, 1963), pp. 11–14], individuals, families, and communities do not adopt norms of the society without modification. Each of these units acts as a selective or transforming agent vis-à-vis behavioral and expectancy norms of the society. Such transformations or interpretations are influenced by a variety of factors both psychological and sociological. Consequently, it is not enough to be knowledgable of the value structure, norms, etc., presented to a community or group to be able to know about what is interiorized, one must also have knowledge of community and group characteristics, one must guard against oversimplification of this process. A shortcoming of self theory concerns its failure to isolate specific social referents involved in the development of self-concept. For example, does the community of the black child play a role in his self-concept and its development?

2. For a lucid treatment of the relationship between status and role, and the social process involved in forcing and maintaining role enactments for ascribed and achieved status, see T. R. Sarbin, A role-theory perspective for community psychology: The structure of social identity, in D. Adelson and B. L. Kalis (eds.), *Community psychology and mental health* (San Francisco: Chandler, 1970), pp. 88–113.

3. E. Barnes [*Cultural retardation or shortcomings of assessment techniques*, *Selected convention papers* (Washington, D.C.: CEC, 1969)], criticizes recent relevant literature in this domain from the standpoint, among others, of the status of the black community, family, and individual within society. The criticisms brought to bear in this article are relevant to other dimensions of functioning covered in the current paper.

4. Conceptualizations by B. C. Rosen (Race, ethnicity, and the achievement syndrome, *American Sociological Review*, 1959, **24**, 47–60) and E. Epps (Correlates of academic achievement among northern and southern urban negro students, *Journal of Social Issues*, 1969, **25**, 55–70) point out the weaknesses of conceptualization in the areas of achievement motivation and aspiration levels. Epps's concepts of "hope for success" and "perceived probability of success" make for greater precision in studies of achievement motivation and provide a basis for clearer distinction between this concept and that of as-

piration level. Rosen's conceptualization advances the concept of achievement motivation by specifying these factors upon which achievement motivation depends in this society. These three factors he labels collectively as "achievement syndrome." The factors are (a) McClelland's "achievement motive," a personality characteristic; (b) achievement-value orientation, which involves a concern with social mobility and behavior patterns instrumental in pursuing long-term goals; and (c) educational and vocational aspiration, which concerns the levels of academic and occupational achievements desired by parents for their children and by the children themselves.

5. For a representative article providing a general picture based on research findings of development and functioning of blacks, individual and family, see Lee Rainwater, Crucible of identity: The Negro lower-class family, in T. Parsons and K. B. Clark (eds.), *The Negro American* (Boston: Beacon Press, 1967), pp. 160–204.

6. For a detailed and systematic treatment of this process, see Sarbin, *op. cit.*, pp. 101–110.

7. C. Clark, in Social change and the communication of legitimacy: The case for Dispute settlement (*Journal of the Developing Areas*, 1971, 5, 577–588), defines and analyzes this concept, its operations, and application from the standpoint of relations between black and white groups.

8. C. Clark, in General systems theory and black studies: Some points of convergences, in C. Thomas (ed.), *Boys no more: A black psychologist's view of community* (Beverly Hills, Calif.: Glencoe Press, 1971), provides a systematic analysis of the communication process and types of communication.

9. It is assumed theoretically that black consciousness, or sense of peoplehood, or group identification, conceived as a complex psychological state, is reflected in certain attitudes, feelings, and behaviors which are amenable to observation by means of appropriate techniques. The techniques are given the names of the behavior, attitudes, and feelings which, theoretically, reflect black consciousness, or sense of peoplehood. These instruments are (a) conception of "black power," (b) political activity scale, (c) racial militancy scale, (d) individual–system blame scale, and (e) individual–collective action scale. The racial militancy, individual–collective blame, and individual–collective action scales are specially constructed internal–external control scales. For an account of how they were constructed, and examples of items, see Patricia Gurin et al., Internal–external control in the motivation dynamics of Negro youth (*Journal of Social Issues*, 1969, 75, 29–54). The race militancy factor "poses alternative forms of collective action for the respondent to choose. One is preference for protest and pressure activities; the other is a preference for less militant approaches such as relying on conversations and negotiations of Negro and white leaders on biracial councils (Gurin et al., p. 45)." The individual-collective action factor contrasts individual effort and mobility with group action as the best way to overcome discrimination (Gurin et al., p. 45). The individual–system blame factor refers to the individual's explanation for the plight of the black's condition—political, economic, social, and cultural—in this society.

The political activity scale taps the respondent's report regarding actual behavior in voting for issues, candidates, etc., having significance for black people, as well as participation in neighborhood and local political actions—e.g., attending Model Cities meetings, serving on citizens committees, attending open school board meetings, etc.

The "black power" factor refers to the extent to which the concept is viewed favorably and the extent to which it is defined in militant and political terms. D. Auerbach and L. Walker, in a study carried out in Detroit, found that southern-born blacks were less likely to interpret the term in militant terms and were less likely to have a positive attitude toward it. See their meaning of black power: A comparison of white and black interpretations of a political slogan. Paper presented at the meeting of the American Political Science Association, Washington, D.C., 1968.

See Nathan Caplan, The new ghetto man: A review of recent empirical studies (*Journal of Social Issues*, 1970, 26, 59-74), for psychological characteristics of the young black militant. The characteristics outlined are polar to those traditionally associated with a negative self-concept and weak group identification, as reflected in black individuals. Outstanding are his changed conception of himself vis-à-vis the world around him, the acceptance of blame for the victimized status of the group, increased social insight into social barriers to realization of potential and aspirations, and a heightened sense of personal effectiveness.

References

Ames, R. Protest and irony in Negro folksong. *Social Science*, 1950, **14**, 193–213.

Ausubel, D., and Ausubel, P. Ego development among segregated Negro children. In A. H. Passow (Ed.), *Education in depressed areas*. New York: Bureau of Publications, Teachers College, Columbia University, 1963, pp. 109–131.

Barnes, E. J. Cultural retardation or shortcomings of assessment techniques. In *Selected convention papers*. Forty-seventh Annual International Convention, Denver, Colorado, April, 1969. Washington, D.C.: The Council for Exceptional Children, 1969, pp. 35–43.

Barnes, E. J. *Counseling the black student: The need for a new view*. Pittsburgh: University of Pittsburgh Press, 1970.

Bertalanffy, L. Von. General system theory and psychiatry. In S. Arieti (Ed.), *American handbook of psychiatry*, vol. 3. New York: Basic Books, 1966, pp. 705–721.

Billingsley, A. *Black families in white America*. Englewood Cliffs, N.J.: Prentice-Hall, 1968.

Boykin, L. L. The adjustment of 2,078 Negro students. *Journal of Negro Education*, 1957, **26**, 75–79.

Burton, R. J., and Whiting, J. W. M. The absent father and cross-sex identity. *Merrill-Palmer Quarterly*, 1961, **7**, 85–95.

Caldwell, M. G. Personality trends in the youthful male offender. *Journal of Criminal Law, Criminology and Police Science*, 1959, **49**, 405–416.

Carmichael, S., and Hamilton, C. V. *Black power: The politics of liberation in America*. New York: Vintage Books, 1967.

Carroll, L. *Through the looking glass*. New York: Doubleday, 1947.

Clark, C. General systems theory and black studies: Some points of convergence. In C. Thomas (Ed.), *Boys no more: a black psychologist's view of community*. Beverly Hills, Calif.: Glencoe Press, 1971.

Clark, K. B., and Clark, M. Racial Identification and preferences in Negro children. In T. M. Newcomb and E. L. Hartley (Eds.), *Readings in social psychology*. New York: Holt, Rinehart & Winston, pp. 169–178.

Coles, R. Its the same but it's different. In T. Parsons and K. B. Clark (Eds.), *The Negro American*. Boston: Beacon Press, 1967, pp. 254–279.

Cooley, C. H. *Human nature and the social order*. New York: Free Press, 1956.

Crandall, V. C., Katkovsky, W., and Crandall, J. J. Children's beliefs in their own control of reinforcements in intellectual academic achievement situations. *Child Development*, 1965, **36**, 91–109.

Crayton, H. R. The psychology of the Negro under discrimination. In A. Rose (Ed.), *Race prejudice and discrimination*. New York: Knopf, 1951, pp. 276–290.

Deutsch, M. *Minority group and class status as related to social and personality factors in scholastic achievement*. Monograph No. 2. Ithaca, N.Y.: The Society for Applied Anthropology, Cornell University Press, 1960.

Ellison, R. A very stern discipline. *Harper's Magazine*, March 1967, 76–95.

Erikson, E. H. *Identity, youth, and crisis*. New York: Norton, 1968.

Essien-Udom, E. U. *Black nationalism*. New York: Dell, 1962.

Feld, S., and Lewis, J. The assessment of achievement anxieties in children. Unpublished manuscript, Mental Health Study Center, National Institute of Mental Health, 1967.

Goffman, E. *Stigma*. Englewood Cliffs, N.J.: Prentice-Hall, 1963.

Goodman, M. E. *Race awareness in young children.* Cambridge, Mass.: Harper, 1952.

Gordon, J. *The poor of Harlem: Social functioning in the underclass.* Report to the Welfare Administration. Washington, D.C.: U.S. Government Printing Office, July 31, 1965.

Gordon, M. *Assimilation in American life.* New York: Oxford University Press, 1964.

Greenwald, H. J., and Appenheim, D. B. Reported magnitude of self-misidentification among Negro children—Artifact? *Journal of Personality and Social Psychology*, 1968, 8, 49–52.

Hammer, E. F. Negro and white children's personality adjustment as revealed by a comparison of their drawings (H-T-P). *Journal of Clinical Psychology*, 1953, 9, 7–10.

Hill, K. T., and Sarason, S. B. The relation of test anxiety and defensiveness to test and school performance in the elementary school years: A further longitudinal study. *Monographs of the Society for Research in Child Development*, 1966, 31 (whole no. 2).

Hofanson, J. E., and Calden, G. Negro–white differences on the MMPI. *Journal of Clinical Psychology*, 1960, 16, 32–33.

Johnson, C. S. *Growing up in the blackbelt.* New York: Schocken, 1967.

Katz, I. Academic motivation and equal educational opportunity. *Harvard Educational Review*, 1968, 38, 57–66.

Landreth, C., and Johnson, B. C. Young children's responses to a picture and inset test designed to reveal reactions to persons of different skin color. *Child Development*, 1953, 24, 63–79.

Lott, A. J., and Lott, B. *Negro and white youth: A psychological study in a border-state community.* New York: Holt, Rinehart & Winston, 1963.

Mead, G. H. *Mind, self, and society.* Chicago: University of Chicago Press, 1934.

McClelland, D. C. *The achieving society.* New York: Van Nostrand Reinhold, 1961.

McLuhan, M. *Understanding media: The extensions of man.* New York: New American Library, 1966.

Mills, C. W. Methodological consequences of the sociology of knowledge. In I. L. Horonitz (ed.), *Power, politics and people: The collected essays of C. Wright Mills.* New York: Ballantine, 1963, pp. 453–468.

Mischel, W. Delay of gratification, need for achievement and acquiescence in another culture. *Journal of Abnormal and Social Psychology*, 1961, 62, 543–552. (a)

Mischel, W. Father-absence and delay of gratification: Cross-cultural comparisons. *Journal of Abnormal and Social Psychology*, 1961, 63, 116–124. (b)

Mischel, W. Preference for delayed reinforcement and social responsibility. *Journal of Abnormal and Social Psychology*, 1961, 62, 1–7. (c)

Mischel, W. Theory and research on the antecedents of self-imposed delay of reward. In B. Maher (Ed.), *Progress in experimental personality research*, vol. 3. New York: Academic Press, 1966.

Morland, J. K. Racial acceptance and preference of nursery school children in a southern city. *Merrill-Palmer Quarterly*, 1962, 8, 271–280.

Morland, J. K. A comparison of race awareness in northern and southern children. *American Journal of Orthopsychiatry*, 1966, 36, 22–31.

Mowrer, O. H., and Ullman, A. D. Time as a determination in integrative learning. *Psychological Review*, 1945, 4, 187–201.

Mussen, P. H. Differences between the TAT responses of Negro and white boys. *Journal of Consulting Psychology*, 1953, 17, 373–376.

Palermo, D. S. Racial comparisons and additional normative data on children's Manifest Anxiety Scale. *Child Development*, 1959, 30, 53–57.

Parsons, T. *The social system.* New York: Free Press, 1951.

Parsons, T. Full citizenship for the Negro American? In T. Parsons and K. B. Clark (Eds.), *The Negro American.* Boston: Houghton Mifflin, 1965.

Parsons, T., and Bales, R. F. *Family socialization and interaction Process.* New York: Free Press, 1955.

Poussaint, A., and Atkinson, C. Black youth and motivation. *Black Scholar* 1970, 1, 43–51.

Radke, M., and Trager, H. G. Children's perceptions of the social roles of Negroes and whites. *Journal of Psychology*, 1950, **29** 3-33.

Rainwater, L. Crucible of identity: The Negro lower-class family. In T. Parsons and K. B. Clark (Eds.), *The Negro American*. Boston: Beacon Press, 1967, pp. 160-204.

Rosen, B. C. Race, ethnicity, and the achievement syndrome. *American Sociological Review*, 1959, **24**, 47-60.

Sarason, S. B., Davidson, K. S., Lighthall, F. F., Waite, R. R., and Ruebush, B. K. *Anxiety in elementary school children*. New York: John Wiley, 1960.

Sclare, A. Cultural determinants in the neurotic Negro. *British Journal of Medical Psychology*, 1953, **26**, 278-288.

Sizemore, B. A. Separatism: A reality approach to inclusion? In R. L. Green (ed.), *Racial crises in American education*. Chicago: Follett Educational Corporation, 1969.

Stevenson, H. W., and Stewart, E. C. A developmental study of racial awareness in young children. *Child Development*, 1958, **29**, 399-410.

Sullivan, H. S. *The interpersonal theory of psychiatry*. New York: Norton, 1953.

White, R. W. *The abnormal personality: A textbook*. New York: Ronald Press, 1948.

Yarrow, M. R. (Ed.) Interpersonal dynamics in a desegregation process. *Journal of Social Issues*, 1958, **14**, 3-63.

PART IV

Counseling Blacks

Repeatedly, black youth have been advised by white counselors, and others, to lower their sights and goals, and to be realistic. Such advice has, of course, shaped and influenced the self-concept, outlook, and future orientation of many a black youth, and it has contributed to black genocide. Increasingly, blacks have come to suspect that counseling practices have been instruments of racism. Papers in the present section develop and elaborate this theme. In the first, "The Neglected Client," Martin H. Jones and Martin C. Jones highlight concerns of black professionals regarding the counseling situation. Central problems relate to textbooks on counseling, the fact of the great preponderance of white middle-class workers in the counseling enterprise, the culture-bound nature of tests used in the counseling situation, and inadequate training given to counselors, particularly those who would work with black youth. Careful examination is undertaken of the consequences of these factors for counseling blacks.

The fact of failure of counselors to understand and appreciate cultural differences is a theme running throughout papers reported in this section.

In "The Black Client and the Helping Professionals," William M. Banks, like Jones and Jones, points to the fact that race and social factors have been ignored in the counseling relationship with the result that the conceptual framework from which most counselors work is dysfunctional for black clients. Banks summarizes important counseling psychology literature which buttresses this view. He cautions, however, against assuming that all of the client's problems are racially inspired, and suggests that new approaches to psychological theory may be needed to clarify issues in this important area.

Edward J. Barnes's "Counseling and the Black Student: The Need for A New View" argues that counseling must be rooted in an understanding of what it means to be black in white society. The role of values in the counseling of blacks and appropriate counseling goals are also addressed. Perhaps most interesting in the paper is a treatment of the issue of the white counselor in the black institution. Most writers have stated categorically that white counselors must go. The reasons for such a recommendation are well known: White workers simply do not possess sufficient understanding of the black culture and show little likelihood of developing such understandings. Moreover, many blacks will not accept a counseling relationship with whites. It is unlikely, given limited personnel resources, that all white counselors will be removed from all black institutions. In the light of this possibility, Barnes's description of alternative roles for white counselors who work in black settings may prove useful.

William A. Hayes and William M. Banks, in "The Nigger Box or A Redefinition *of the Counselor's Role," suggest that counselors must move away from the deficiency hypothesis about black behavior. An alternative based upon the experimental analysis of behavior (EAB) is suggested. The role of the counselor following the EAB paradigm is to understand the mechanisms by which the behavior of blacks is controlled. Drawing analogies from laboratory psychology, Hayes and Banks show how the behavior of black Americans is controlled, the role played by counselors in maintaining control of black behavior, and the implications of such an analysis for the modification of counseling practices.*

In the final paper of the section "Black Economic and Cultural Development: A Prerequisite to Vocational Choice," Willie S. Williams takes up the problem of occupational choice for blacks. Williams indicates that given the racist nature of our society, vocational choice and vocational satisfaction as dealt with in current theories and concepts are not applicable to black Americans. The basis for understanding vocational choice he suggests is rooted in economic considerations, black cultural solidarity, and the black condition in America.

MARTIN H. JONES and MARTIN C. JONES

The Neglected Client

Meaningful knowledge of blackness does not exist because the great majority of student and academic personnel are from the white middle class. They have not lived in black communities; they are aware of black problems only superficially. It is not unfair to say that their awareness is mainly of the fact that great problems exist rather than of the problems themselves. The chief problem, of course, is the economic deprivation of blacks, but this misfortune is deeply rooted in psychological and sociological problems within the ghetto culture as well as the patterns of black-white interrelations which have been three centuries in the making. True insight leading to meaningful solutions can only come by thoroughly knowing and feeling the black person's point of view, and such knowledge can only come from an intimacy of association with the hard-core ghetto and the ghetto culture. Such association is not customarily available to the middle class, or at least they do not seek it out.

Later we were to find, most dishearteningly, that even when the opportunity to see, hear, and feel exists, many whites are unable to take advantage of it because of rigid, preformed views and because of bureaucratic structures to which they are attached. While a student, my awareness was chiefly of the great gap between the good intentions and any realistic store of knowledge possessed by white students and teachers.

This basic ambivalence, which ultimately has such a great effect on black people, is well illustrated by college teaching and texts. On the positive side are general principles of attitude and action set forth in counseling theory, such as Rogers' concept of unconditional positive regard for the client. Such a concept is certainly ideal, but its observation in practice is also conducive to the most effective practical results, as my experience has shown.

The principles of counseling, which are both practical and ideal, are universally applicable to all people in Western culture, black and white, and probably to people everywhere. As principles of human relations they extend far beyond the realm of counseling. If they had been learned and applied by the world leaders who make international policies, we would not now be faced by the dilemmas of neocolonialism and spheres of influence, and by the embattled color consciousness that pervades the world.

If the counselor (or physician or government official) does not recognize the person whom he faces as a fellow human being and does not listen to him as such, he cannot relate to him in any meaningful way. He cannot act construc-

From *The Black Scholar*, March 1970, 5, 35–42. ©*The Black Scholar*. Reprinted by permission of the authors and the publisher.

tively toward the person, nor expect the person to act constructively toward him.

For minority and ghetto groups, the negative side of this ambivalence lies in the practice of counseling as opposed to theories of counseling. As mentioned, the overwhelming majority of college teachers and textbook authors are from the white middle class. When it comes to the specifics of applying counseling theories, the application is necessarily bound up with the background and unconscious attitudes of these people. The illustrative cases in texts and journals are white middle-class people with white middle-class problems. When the cases do happen to be blacks or other minority people, it will generally be found that their problems are of white middle-class types. The actors are different, the plot remains the same.

This means that students are not trained to cope with the problems of people from the black culture. An individual is in constant psychological and sociological interchange with his environment. It is this interchange that determines personality and attitudes, and the person cannot be considered apart from it. Those trained in counseling, those who teach counseling and write about it, do not have an instinctive, internalized knowledge of ghetto culture as they do of middle-class culture. Nor is a realistic opportunity to learn provided them. The student or counselor who wishes such knowledge must find his own way to acquire it, which takes unusual determination and initiative. The blandness of good intentions must be replaced by a truly crusading spirit.

Thus the average counselor, when faced by a black or other minority person, often finds himself at a total loss. If he applied the basic acceptance of counseling and were willing to listen receptively, interaction might conceivably take place, but instead he attempts to project his innate middle-class orientations on the client. The cultural barrier becomes an immediate block to communication. The client perceives that he is not being heard or understood and mentally withdraws.

Aware that communication does not exist, the counselor resolves his frustration and bafflement by rejecting the client. He has decided that if the client cannot interact on his terms, no interaction will take place. This paranoid self-righteousness and rigidity solves the counselor's internal dilemma so that he does not feel "alone and afraid in a world he never made," but it arouses powerful negative emotions in the client. The client feels, and rightly so, that he is not being helped, and that no honest effort is being made to help him. He is the neglected client, and he knows it.

Two theoretical considerations help to throw light on this type of disrupted client-counselor communication. The first is the classic case of the Freudian concept of penis envy as a prime neurotic factor in women, which illustrates how valid psychological principles of universal scope may be invalid when reduced to certain specific corollaries which are culture-oriented. The second is the concept of libidinal diffusion, a structural theory of culture-bound human reactions as discussed by Slater (1965), Benne (1961), and James (1950).

From observing himself and his clientele, Freud made deductions which revolutionized psychology; without which, in fact, modern psychology as we know it would not exist. In broadest terms, his essential discovery was the fact that many actions of people are motivated by hidden needs of which they are not consciously aware. As a general principle, this applies to people of all cultures. When it comes to the derivation of specific subconscious motivations, however, culture plays an essential role, a fact that was not realized by Freudian psychologists for quite a long time, and even today is not as well understood by counselors as it should be.

Because of the social structure of Vienna, most of Freud's clientele were upper middle-class Jews. From facts that emerged in analysis, the keystones of the application of Freudian theories were built. One of these keystones was the concept of penis envy. Freud found that most, if not all, of his female patients had strong feelings of inferiority and suppressed envy and hostility toward their husbands, fathers, and brothers. In delving into this, Freud found that Viennese women identified the male sex organ with the strongly authoritarian position held by males in that culture. Subconsciously, and often consciously, the women felt that they had been "castrated" as infants, and thus deprived of their rights as self-determining human beings, a privilege obviously enjoyed by their fathers and brothers, who were judged to be sexually "complete."

In the Vienna of Freud's day the concept of penis envy was a valid deduction. The twentieth-century United States, however, is not a patriarchal society where the father plays the role of absolute monarch and the lowliest brother takes precedence over all sisters. For many years psychologists struggled to apply this imported concept of penis envy to their female patients, until it was finally realized that it is minor in this culture rather than being the primary cause of female neurosis. In black ghetto culture, in fact, because of the economically engendered matriarchal structure, it is the young males who are frustrated by the absurd futility of trying subconsciously to identify with their mothers rather than, as in Vienna, young females who are frustrated in being shut out of the enviable father–brother roles.

Factors of futility, despair, mistrust of hope, play a major role in ghetto culture just as penis envy did in Viennese culture. But these are not major factors in white middle-class United States culture and therefore do not appear as momentous, neurosis-producing problems in the literature of psychology and counseling, which in the main devotes itself to the problems of an essentially more leisured and economically secure class. Ghetto people have problems which stem from lack of money and life choices; middle-class whites often have problems which stem from too much money and a confusing multitude of choices.

Marijuana use provides an example of the dichotomy between textbook theory and the realities of ghetto life. The literature on marijuana has traditionally treated its use as a subconscious desire of the individual to withdraw, to escape, to turn his psychic projections inward and wreak social and personal suicide on himself. This view stems from middle-class attitudes, which see any deviation from the idealized norm as a withdrawal from society (that is, the business-military world) and a threat to it.

A University of California team sent into the East Oakland ghetto to study marijuana use at first hand discovered just the opposite. Among young ghetto people, marijuana is a social cohesion factor. It is used in conjunction with the group; to use marijuana is to belong, and its use is a factor in group acceptance. Thus it is exactly the opposite of an escape or a withdrawal, and the findings of this team contradict the traditional literature and attitudes on the subject.

This proves the value to the counselor of exerting himself to learn ghetto problems openly and intimately. When he does, he may discover new concepts diametrically opposed to standard theory and practice. At the least he will have to unlearn many textbook "facts" that have been written from the middle-class point of view, and he will have to reorient himself to a world that is bigger, more complex, and more difficult than the middle-class environment in which he supposes he finds psychological safety. However, the example of the ostrich indicates that hiding the head in the sand is the most dangerous, not the safest, thing to do.

Counselors who fail to recognize the conditional factor of acculturation in psychological concepts, the basic role of the socioeconomic environment in the psychology of the individual, cannot help ghetto people. It is probable that they cannot help anyone.

The second operative factor in this type of aborted client–counselor relationship is libidinal contraction. From Freud's several definitions of libido, the one considered here is libido as the sum total of psychic forces. Libidinal contraction is the constriction of these forces within some group with which the individual identifies for purposes of immediate self-interest and the security of clinging together. Libidinal diffusion means that the affective cognitions are directed outward toward objectives and toward persons without extreme preferential selectivity. The libidinally contracted person is socially crippled and is paranoid to some greater or lesser degree. The libidinally diffused person can, with wisdom, find in himself the resources to cope with the structural complexities of modern society and to help others.

By the very definition of the ghetto as a forced in-group structure, the ghetto person is, to a greater or lesser extent, libidinally contracted. It is the counselor's duty to help him break out of this shell psychologically and economically. If the counselor, too, is libidinally contracted, with his psychic forces frantically directed toward the traditional values of middle-class society, it will be like two billiard balls striking. Two glassy surfaces will bounce off each other, and both counselor and client will react negatively to their meeting.

The counseling situation should be like a truck tire connected to a bicycle tire. With its resources of experience and its knowledge of counseling principles, the truck tire gives the bicycle tire the air it needs to make its own way. The diffused libido of the counselor has streamed some of its own attitude and energy into the client. Like the truck tire, the counselor is continually replenished.

Very often all the client needs to diffuse his own libido and feel himself a man in this world is a job. The counselor with diffused libido, which embraces the conditionality of circumstances, will see this and will work actively for the client in that direction. The counselor with contracted libido will dispense advice and information, largely negative, which are neither helpful nor meaningful to the client, and affect him adversely. An example of this is the counselor who tells the client how limited he is as a person, that he cannot possibly handle the job or profession he wants, and then removes the burden from his own shoulders by shunting the client off to a battery of tests coached in libidinally contracted, middle-class terms.

Simultaneous operation of the two factors—culture-bound concepts accepted as general principles, and libidinal contraction—is illustrated by the occupational interest inventories which are so widely used and misused by private and public agencies.

It was not until the beginning of this decade, when the Minnesota Vocational Interest Inventory was introduced, that the authors of these inventories took serious notice of any occupations outside of the highly paid professions. Since many counselors feel they need something to go on besides their own libidinally diffused good sense, these tests have been used indiscriminantly on the presumption that they embody general principles which by extrapolation are applicable to all. In truth, they are culture-bound by the unspoken postulate that only persons educationally prepared for middle-class status occupations are worth serious concern: All others can take their chances.

Tests confined to status occupations exhibit the libidinal contraction of highly placed professors and researchers who see value in thorough investigation of professions akin to their own, but not in the great spectrum of ordinary occupations which employ the great majority of people.

The strictly limited scope of these tests gave the libidinally contracted, middle-class oriented counselor the opportunity to express his hidden needs and fears by flatly telling a client that his occupational choice had to be much narrower than he thought and hoped. Such misuse of these tests against minority clients has been and continues to be widespread.

This is not to say that such tests are not valuable when correctly used. The test literature specifically states that the tests indicate only the interests the testee has in common with the measured interests of norm groups representing a limited number of occupations. Because there is no proven theoretical connection between these interests and the occupation (the correlation is merely statistical), extrapolation to supposedly related fields is not reliable. Nor do the tests measure success potential; it is admitted that motivation is the prime success factor. The tests are not designed to make the counselor's job easier by giving him a mechanized decision-making process or to provide authority for his prejudices.

The authors have served as counselors at a public employment agency and at an industrial high school. In both places we found operative all the negative factors mentioned above. We were shocked at the great gap between counseling theory and practice. There was a nearly total lack of empathy for ghetto people and no real knowledge of their situation. Nor was there willingness and desire to learn; the people of these agencies are apathetic and often actively hostile to the needs of their clients. They collect their paychecks for appearing at work each morning and going through the day with the least possible disturbance to themselves. More social good would be done if they were paid for staying home.

There are, of course, heartening individual exceptions to this dismal picture, but on the whole, negative employee attitudes are condoned by supervisors and reflect tacitly understood, although not official, agency policy.

The taxpayers' money is not being spent constructively, in the manner intended by the legislature. Perhaps the extreme example of this disregard for human and legal values is the lady who tears up an application and throws it in the wastebasket when the applicant in some small way displeases her.

Outside of negative attitudes, the chief barrier to efficient operation of this public employment agency is the departmentalized fragmentation of its basic service, which is supposed to be finding the client a job. The applicant is shunted from employment or placement interviewer to counselor to testing service, and frequently to some time-wasting irrelevance such as watching a reading improvement course on TV. Specific instruction in the valuable techniques of filling out employment test forms and applications is not given, nor, for youth who have not had previous employment, is there instruction in what the employer will expect of them or in the social and psychological difficulties they are likely to encounter on the job.

Neither initial interviewing, job placement, nor follow-up is adequate for the client's needs. The special problems of ghetto people cause little concern and receive little understanding, although this area is supposed to be a primary objective of the agency.

During our tenure as counselors at the employment agency, we were fortunate in securing approval to experimentally apply the concept of a one-package client service. This involved both placement and counseling interviews, job development using a variety of community resources, the active seeking of suitable placement, and follow-up. The family situation always received attention as did interviews with the employer both before and after placement. When difficulties arose, such as the new employee not appearing for work or not functioning in the job, inquiry was instituted, which usually led either to a satisfactory solution in that situation or re-referral to a more suitable job.

It is my opinion that this agency could be put on a decently efficient functional basis by a two-step program. First, a training program in the principles of counseling should be instituted for the employees who deal with the public, particularly those older employees who began their employment before professional training was required. Much higher standards of agency expectation must be set: The supervisory staff must demand professional standards of conduct and attitude from all employees, and must demand that there be an active, aggressive attempt to place every applicant.

No applicant can be given up for lost. My experience was that a place could be found for even the dimmest prospect if a thorough attempt were made. One case was that of a mentally retarded, illiterate youth who was brought to the agency by his pastor and could only tell us about himself: "I want a job." After investigation and talks with his family, and an initial error in placement, he was put in a job suitable to his needs and talents and to the employer. Another case was that of a Vietnam amputee further handicapped by deep discouragement. It was first proved to him that there were many good paying jobs, such as teletype operator, that he could do without the strain of having to be on his feet all day. He was then helped to employment and to enter college.

Second, the package system of one counselor or qualified agency employee handling all aspects of a case should be adopted. The only exception would be formal testing when necessary. Because of the much higher placement rate, this system would be more efficient and less wasteful of time and money than the present departmentalized specialization. The client would be provided many personal benefits of attention and understanding he is not now receiving. The mass-production methods of Henry Ford are good for automobiles but not necessarily for black people.

Always the expressed ideals, needs, and ambitions of the client must be of serious concern to the counselor. Because motivation is the most important factor in job success, openly expressed attitudes are often much more valuable in placement than any number of hidden attitudes uncovered by formal testing. It is up to the counselor to strike the balance most beneficial to the client. To do this for black people requires intimate knowledge of the ghetto situation and a more than usual depth of understanding. When faced with frank descriptions of ghetto problems and needs, which were offered in the spirit of helpful information, the supervisory personnel of this agency demonstrated bafflement, frustration, and unwillingness to cope with reality by either withdrawing into the shell of libidinal contraction or reacting with open hostility. Neither objectivity nor the desire to help others as a prime motivation could be accepted.

The vocational high school followed much the same pattern of a tired bureaucratic structure following a rutted, timeworn path. Although educational facilities and the teaching staff are excellent, counseling as such, truly a great need for many minority and ghetto youths in this school, was nonexistent. There was no individual counseling, and only one counselor who could even be described as semiliberal. The assistant principal was the chief counselor, and his idea of counseling was discipline. He expected this type of performance from the one adequate counselor, who felt he was in a very difficult situation. Although the assistant principal maintained that there were no problems in the school, it appeared that he was disliked by a large proportion of students, and the student with problems had nowhere to turn for help or advice.

For example, there was a black math teacher in this school who realized that one of his black students was perfect college material although the boy had been recommended to a trade school. Fortunately he was able to intervene on the boy's behalf, but there seems no doubt that numerous others go down the drain. The individual loses his best opportunity in life and our society loses the best contribution he could make.

Thus the neglected client is the individual, all too often a black or other minority person, who finds himself helpless in the face of rigid, entrenched, self-serving attitudes; who receives neither help nor acceptance because of the preformed prejudices and unbending structure of dehumanized bureaucracy; and who, through lack of adequate help and understanding, is unable to find the job he needs or to make his life valuable to himself and society.

If members of the black community, as well as other ethnic groups, are to be a visible part of the mainstream, they must not be castrated members of a society. They must in turn be treated with utmost courtesy and diplomacy. In a counseling relationship individuals must not be put into a said frame of reference (i.e., slow learners, underachievers, misfits).

In a therapeutic relationship these people must be understood with clarity by knowing their culture, idiom, and jargon which is not a part of the everyday counseling setting. The counselor must be thoroughly exposed to the environmental conditions from whence his client came. In addition, there must be family consultations in the areas of school, colleges, etc. The knowledge of the family brings about the knowledge of the client and his role within the family setting. If a counselor does not meet his client on the real level, he is ineffective in his establishment of rapport. For example, "Hello, Brother, what's going down?" brings the counselor down to the real level instead of intellectual plane. Therefore, the counselor must exempt himself from formal greeting to make the therapeutic conditions comfortable.

The counselor must always bear in mind that counseling is a feeling relationship, that his effectiveness is in direct ratio to the amount of warm, positive feeling generated between him and his client. Thus counseling relations are most effective as intellectual activity *decreases*. The counselor's intellect must always be active, of course, but as an instrument for feeling, for sensing his client's emotions and needs. Too often counselors establish "intellectual fences" between themselves and their clients. These fences may take the form of preconceived theories brought to the counseling situation about the client ("Well, according to Moynihan, he's . . . " or "His records show . . . " or "The Skinner hypothesis maintains that . . . "). Or, they may take the form of highly verbal activity on the part of the counselor, which can be a form of one-upmanship. The student may walk away with his head ringing, saying, "Man, that cat's bad"—and with no effective counseling having occurred.

Effective counseling occurs with the ear—and the voice. The client must be heard and what he is *truly* saying must be heard, not filtered through what the counselor *thinks* he is saying. Most important in counseling is the pitch and tone quality of the voice. The voice tells as much as the face. It should be a soothing, friendly voice, that gives the client reassurance that he has been heard, listened to, with warmth and regard.

The black counselor should invoke and always use his knowledge of the black community. He must realize that many youngsters have been on the streets at an early age, as their families have struggled to make ends meet. Sometimes called "keychain babies," such youths have a starvation for real relationships, which can result in an intense dependency when the youth makes such a connection with his counselor. The counselor will hear statements such as, "I wish my daddy was like you," or, "I sure enjoy being here," or, "I'm glad we've got a black counselor."

In group counseling situations, black sensitivity groups can be effective. But the counselor must bear in mind that many blacks are wary of sensitivity training. Very rarely has sensitivity training been done from a black perspective, in blackness. Too often the encounters have been mixed, which creates a different kind of group content—the race problem itself, with focus on white guilt and black anger. Such encounters, while having a limited usefulness, do not provide effective counseling or therapy for the black client's deeper problems. Generally speaking, the white client has different group interaction needs than the black client; the need to touch, to feel, are not particularly black needs, nor do blacks need training in how to directly express anger to each other. Group counseling and sensitivity work can bring excellent results for black students, provided they are done from a black perspective, with an ear to particular black needs.

With the increase of black students and students of other ethnic backgrounds on college campuses nationwide, it is of the utmost importance that black counselors or counselors of other ethnic backgrounds bridge the gap for clear and direct communications. For the student it is very important that he has a counselor of his own ethnic background.

Blackness as a counseling factor avoids the time-consuming efforts of the client in testing his counselor with reference to a real, true counselor–client relationship. The client will not "shine the counselor on."

Community involvement is a function that counselors, psychiatrists, psychologists must be a part of. They should be available for talks at various churches, schools, and social organizations. This makes the community at large aware of their experts and their relationship toward their community. Community involvement also serves as a level of sensitizing the professional elite. New values and norms have to be prescribed for this individual in order for him to communicate.

In conclusion, to make a therapeutic relationship more adoptable and acceptable to black people and members of other ethnic groups, high schools, colleges, universities should adhere to the need for direct communication. For example, the hiring of more minority counselors, psychiatrists, psychologists, etc., and professional counseling programs of colleges and universities at the master's and doctorate levels should attend to the needs of the neglected client by having more ethnic faculties. At these levels courses of relevancy should be taught which make it possible to bridge the gap of disturbed communication.

Black counselors must form an association of black counselors to exchange methods and ideology with reference to the neglected client. As I envision it, such an association would be an adjunct of the National Association of Black Psychologists, with emphasis not only on counseling in academic situations, but in industry, on the job, and in the black community itself.

References

Benne, Kenneth D. The uses of fraternity. In Warren B. Bennis (Ed.), *Interpersonal dynamics*, Homewood, Ill.: Dorsey Press, 1964.

Buscaglia, Leo. Major address "Can you hear me?" and "Your words get in your eyes," at the convention of the California Personnel and Guidance Association, San Diego, February 1970.

Clark, Kenneth B. *Dark ghetto*. New York: Harper & Row, 1965.

James, John. Some elements in a theory of small groups. In Robert W. O'Brien (Ed.), *Readings in general sociology*, Boston: Houghton Mifflin, 1964.

Lewis, Oscar. *La vida*. New York: Random House, 1966.

Segal, Ronald. *The race war*. New York: Bantam, 1969.

Thomas, Charles W. Ph.D. in psychology; past President of the National Association of Black Psychologists and Director of Education and Training at the University of Southern California's Watts Health Service. Professor of Urban and Rural Studies, University of California, San Diego.

Washington, Kenneth S. Director of the Educational Opportunity Program for the California State College System. Author of the article Black Power—Action or Reaction?

Wells, Teresa Twyla. Teaching Assistant in the High Potential Program at UCLA. Author of the article The effects of discrimination upon motivation and achievement of black children in urban ghetto schools.

West, Gerald. Ph.D.; Assistant Professor in Counseling at San Francisco State College.

White, Joseph. Ph.D.; Counseling Psychologist and Director of Black Studies at University of California, Irvine.

WILLIAM M. BANKS

The Black Client and the Helping Professionals

Research efforts concerned with the particular experience and problems of black people have been conspicuously absent from the literature of the helping professions. Researchers ignore race and social factors in client–counselor interactions. In fact, attention seems to be focused away from the potent, although complex sociocultural determinants of client and counselor behavior. The absence of serious research in this area reflects an astonishing naivete or benign neglect of the findings accumulated in the literature of social psychology and race relations. Being white or black in America virtually assures the individual a set of perceptions relating to his own and the opposite racial group. In spite of overwhelming data supporting this thesis, counseling researchers rarely explore or even reflect on the interaction between counselor and client of different racial groups. Apparently, many persons feel (or hope) that within the confines of the counselor's office, individuals will shed their racial attitudes and behaviors and embark on the kinds of individualistic forays that most theoretical counseling models encourage. In the search for "universal" models and techniques, researchers ignore the documented potency of racial and cultural variables in the interaction between client and helper.

The black client population served by the helping professions is acutely aware of the problems they experience with helping professionals. Kendrick and Thomas (1969) write: "We think it is important to say here that in our experience, members of disadvantaged minorities are extraordinarily bitter about failures of both admission and commission by guidance personnel." Undoubtedly, there are several sources of the described disillusionment. I contend, however, that the conceptual framework of the vast majority of professional counselors is inappropriate and even dysfunctional when counseling poor black clients. The individualistic orientation of most therapists and counselors (via their graduate training program) in effect minimizes the importance of very real psychosocial factors operating on the black client.

The counseling literature has long insisted that acceptance of and respect for each person as an individual is crucial to positive movement in interpersonal relationships. There is wide agreement that in American society persons belonging to a particular race or group acquire certain stereotyped attitudes about their own group and members of the "other" group. Through the family, and other sources, the individual, black or white, acquires social attitudes that influence his response to persons with whom he comes in contact. Frequently, the learned attitudes prevent the consideration of persons as individuals, which, as stated earlier, is a core assumption of traditional counseling strategies. (Regarding inter-

Reprinted by permission of the author.

racial contacts, many black intellectuals are insisting that recognition and respect *as black people* is as important to blacks as the individualistic orientation offered by most theorists. Such a "collective identity" emphasis of blacks and other minorities is incongruent with most counseling models popular today.) Although the directionality of a stereotype or prejudice may vary considerably (i.e., strongly positive to strongly negative), the fact that the attitude is not a function of the considered individual makes such attitudes, and more importantly resultant behavior, potentially negative forces in counseling relationships.

The Clients

The majority of published papers concern themselves with the problems that the black client brings to the counseling session. Vontress (1971) laments the fact that blacks tend to feel hostile toward whites. Such attitudes, he claims, impede the establishment of rapport so necessary in the therapeutic encounter. In the same paper, Vontress contends that "Negro Americans" should be considered in terms of three distinctive subgroups, "Black," "Negro," or "Colored." He writes that all Americans of African descent fall within one of the three groups. The groups are characterized by differential responses to white society; blacks representing the most assertive response, colored the most accommodating. Presumably, by assigning the black clients to one of the three groups, white therapists would be better able to facilitate constructive personality changes. Black counselors (such as Vontress) might be expected to demonstrate a greater sensitivity to the dangers of "classifying" blacks. It is clear that in today's atmosphere of increased racial awareness, most black people are constantly examining and modifying their responses to the majority group. The responses and behavior of the individual black may reflect tendencies toward aggression or accommodation, depending on the particular situation. The mistake is made when theorists propose labels that suggest certain fixed personality traits when the behavior is so often a function of a specific situation. White researchers for years fostered the illusion of the "happy-go-lucky" black. Recent studies and observations strongly suggest that what was thought to be a fixed personality trait was actually a behavior designed to achieve specific or general ends. By continuing the unfortunate habit of labeling black people (rather than describing behavior in context), Vontress obfuscates rather than illuminates the complex question of race as a variable in the therapeutic process.

English (1957) is concerned about the responses of black people to white counselors. In 1957, he seemed surprised that blacks still held negative feelings about whites and about themselves. English felt that even if certain discriminatory barriers were removed, blacks would still be characterized by poor self-esteem and generally withdrawn behavior in the presence of whites. He suggests that the solution to the dilemma is the enhancement of self-concept through the incorporation of black-oriented content in the school curricula. Many blacks have, for some time, expressed amazement at how certain behavioral scientists expect overnight and radical changes in the attitudes of the oppressed, but are unquestionably pessimistic about the potential of "attitude change" in the majority group. Many scholars are genuinely concerned about the dilemma of white counselors trying to deal with clients who resent the counselor for what are traditionally called "irrational reasons." It seems difficult for white researchers to see any psychological validity in the negative perceptions of whites held by black people. From a purely statistical standpoint, the number of negative emotional experiences blacks have with white far exceeds the number of emotionally positive encounters. Given this reality, it seems evident that black people are responding normally in their negative perceptions of whites. To expect neutral or positive feelings toward whites is to expect an unquestioning tolerance that runs counter to basic principles of social learning. Black people, after all, are governed by the same psychological principles that operate in all humans. People tend to respond positively to stimuli that they perceive as rewarding and develop negative attitudes about stimuli that have been associated with negative experiences. A recent study by Banks (1970) documents an increasing degree of antiwhite attitudes among students.

Three well-designed experimental studies support the thesis that black clients have difficulties in responding positively to white therapists. Banks, Carkhuff, and Berenson (1967), in a controlled study, found that type of training and orientation was an important factor in the acceptance of white counselors by black students. Banks et al. summarized the findings:

In a counterbalanced design, an inexperienced Negro and three white counselors of varying degrees of experience saw eight Negro counselees and were assessed on the dimensions of counselor empathy, positive regard, genuineness, concreteness and depth of client, depth of self-exploration by tape-ratings and inventories filled out by the counselees. The Negro counselor and the two inexperienced white counselors, all trained to attend to the conditions of the counseling relationship, functioned significantly higher than the experienced white Ph.D. trained in a traditional trait-and-factor orientation. All of the Negro counselees indicated that they would return to see the Negro counselor, and none indicated that they would return to see the experienced white Ph.D.

When data from all black counselees were considered, it emerged that two-thirds would not return to see a white counselor.

Research by Carkhuff and Pierce (1967) in a mental hospital with schizophrenics found that therapists' race and social class difference had a retarding effect on client movement in therapy. Black and white high-school students reported a greater degree of rapport when counseled by racially similar persons according to recent research by Banks (1971). In addition to the self-report of the clients, trained raters rated client self-exploration significantly greater when the client and counselor belonged to the same racial group.

The Helpers

Hollingshead and Redlich (1958) found that therapists reported greater ease of communication and more positive assessments of clients who were white and middle class. They speculate that therapists were indeed more responsive to persons from their own social class whose attitudes, values, and behavior were most familiar to them. Lesse (1965), in the *American Journal of Psychotherapy*, raises a pointed question:

> *Can such individualistically oriented psychotherapists effectively empathize with patients from other socioeconomic milieu whose motivations, aspirations, sources of security, and defenses may be at great variance with those of the therapist . . . How often have therapists heard patients from a depressed socio- economic environment say in effect, "Doctor, you're a smart man, but you just don't understand my background."*

Bloch (1968) discusses the problem of countertransference of the white coun- selor in helping black clients. She suggests that hypersensitivity, sympathy, and class differences all affect the countertransference of the white counselor. Unless white workers actively examine their own feelings relative to race, they are likely to be ineffective in helping black clients, Bloch argues. Vontress (1970), too, sees the problem of countertransference and points out a number of general responses and tendencies of white counselors that make for ineffectual counsel- ing.

A study by Lane (1968) found that therapists tended to rate black male clients "process" (withdrawn, or aggressive toward others) rather than "reactive" (ag- gressive toward oneself). She hypothesizes that therapists' bias is a significant source of effect in the observed outcome. A number of other studies have supported the thesis that black mental patients are generally regarded as more severely disturbed than white clients and receive less in terms of therapy. The fear and racial feelings of diagnosticians undoubtedly is a factor in the differen- tially severe assessment of black clients. Kleiner (1960) agrees, and suggests that mental disorders of blacks are usually classified as paranoid or schizophrenic because these categories represent extremes in behavior. Kleiner encourages pro- fessionals to pay more attention to the social barriers that often prevent blacks from achieving their goals. Friedman (1966) writes that the literature on racial factors in psychotherapy is woefully inadequate. He recommends the use of current fiction to understand and better relate to the psychodynamics of black people. A case study is described, where the therapist utilized the work of James Baldwin to gain insight into a client's problem.

Helping Models

The counseling process itself is criticized by Calia (1967) in terms of its appro- priateness for culturally different clients. He criticizes currently held views re- garding (1) sedentary talk as a medium for client–counselor interaction; (2) un- conditional positive regard as an essential therapeutic element; (3) the goal of counseling as the facilitation of self-exploration; and (4) self-referral as a neces- sary prerequisite for effective counseling. Calia urges a much more action-oriented and externally focused approach to the difficulties of culturally different clients, and recommends new conceptualizations about the role and functions of counselors.

Frantz Fanon, the Algerian psychiatrist whose more political works have become must reading for many black intellectuals, developed several novel approaches to the cultural dimension of therapy as a result of his experience with hospitalized patients during the French-Algerian war. Fanon observed that while the European patients responded favorably to therapeutic measures adopted by the hospital staff, the Moslem natives sank further and further into depression, and refused to cooperate with the hospital staff. He finally concluded that the hospitals' egalitarian approach to psychotherapeutic treatment was inappropriate for the Moslems. In effect it demanded that the Moslem natives respond to a mode of therapy that did not take into consideration their culture and life experience. After Fanon and his colleagues took the time to study Moslem society, they proceeded to develop procedures and treatments that acknowledged and respected the sociological realities of Moslem life. Fanon had ordered cafés set up for the patients, but Moslems did not frequent them. Later Fanon concluded that the Moslem men did not frequent them because women were allowed, and similarly women would not enter a café where men were present. Such male–female intermingling is inconsistent with the mores of traditional Moslem culture. After Fanon provided separate facilities for the sexes, Moslem patients responded favorably. Fanon (1954) describes other therapeutic innovations designed to integrate the Moslem personality into Moslem realities rather than the European experience.

The question of training as a way of helping counselors bridge the gap is largely unexplored. A number of graduate programs are publicized as being directed toward "counseling the culturally deprived" or the "inner-city" youth. We are unaware of data that suggest that such programs result in gains in trainee functioning that are translatable into positive benefits derived by racially different clients. We suspect that most programs are more concerned with documenting process than with outcome (in terms of client benefits). Carkhuff (1971) and his colleagues are making significant inroads into the whole question of race-relations training. Their consistent focus on translatable benefits is likely to result in more solid data regarding the training process.

In recent years, many persons have proposed group training sessions as a way of sensitizing helpers to the attitudes and values of black people. Frequently, anecdotal support for such measures appears in the literature. It is difficult to generate much enthusiasm for the group dynamics approach at this time because of its proponents' failure to offer empirical evidence as to its effectiveness. Bancroft (1967) perhaps recognizes the somewhat artificial nature of the group dynamics approach and encourages helper trainees actually to experience the black clients' social milieu. In the same article, he expresses pessimism about the likelihood of whites' voluntarily submitting to such an experience. Vontress (1970), too, urges a type of intern experience that would require counselor-trainees to live and work in poor black communities. One can only speculate

about the communities' response to such culturally different persons moving in
with their strange way of speaking and behaving.

Summary and Implications

The research and literature cited throughout indicates that black clients are
not well served by the helping professionals, particularly white professionals.
Several writers suggest that the inability of whites to transcend the parameters of
their own cultural reference points is the main problem. Other scholars suggest
that black clients must change their attitudes if counselors are to be effective.
The implication is that when black clients are able to submerge their negative
feelings about whites and to perceive each prospective helper as an individual,
better counseling interactions will occur. Still other writers minimize the race
variable and insist on an egalitarian approach to therapy. They insist that human
beings reflect a core of universal feelings and intrapsychic phenomena, which can
be handled by any competent therapist regardless of race, color, or class. In
order to bring some clarity to the overall question, and to avoid the either/or
stance, new approaches to psychological theory appear necessary. Certainly,
blacks are subject to the same intrapersonal psychological dynamics as non-
blacks. Grier and Cobbs (1971) caution against a type of therapeutic effort that
attributes all of a client's problems to race. They describe a type of professional
who tends to interpret all of the black client's behavior in racial terms. Such a
strategy ignores the possibility of mental deterioration for reasons specific to the
client's own functioning. Ellison (1970) writes eloquently of the perils in assuming that the black man's life is simply a series of reactions to white oppressions.
The intrapersonal variables must be considered in the context of "reality factors" in the client's experience. Dimensions of the social system such as race,
class, and powerlessness interact with intrapsychic variables to produce behavior
that is clearly a product of both factors.

Training Strategies

At this point in time, the research evidence suggests that in terms of the effectiveness of the one-to-one interview, the attitudes and behavior of the white
helper constitute a serious detriment to a positive interpersonal relationship.
Unfortunately, training programs to correct or modify the negative aspects of
counselor attitudes and behavior are virtually nonexistent. Much work needs to
be done to identify counselor behaviors that are particularly detrimental to
blacks. Once identified, training programs might be designed to eliminate certain
behaviors. Training programs have traditionally focused on similarities in the
human experience rather than considering differences (and the therapeutic implications of differences). The work of Andrew Griffin and Robert Carkhuff in
Springfield, Massachusetts, suggests that through careful selection and training,
helpers can function more effectively with the black poor. Richard Kelsey at

Ohio State is currently experimenting with a number of curricular changes designed to broaden the experimental base of counselor trainees.

Even a training program that encourages the perception of differences still may produce helpers who are a part of the problem rather than the solution. The fact that a counselor "understands" the alienation felt by a black high-school student toward the school experience is not in itself sufficient. The counselor must, after "understanding" the problem, make a decision concerning who or what is to be the focus of his efforts. At this point, the orientation of the overwhelming majority of professionals encourages them to zero in on what they consider are problems of personal disorganization within the black student. Volumes and volumes have been written documenting the thesis that minority (and increasingly majority) youth view schools as being oppressive and insensitive to their needs. Given these perceptions, one should expect behaviors and attitudes consistent with the perceptions. Rather than examining and modifying the situations that produced the perceptions, counselors demonstrate a myopic tendency to focus on the "normality" of the individual. The emphasis of professional counseling overwhelmingly has been on helping the clients to "adjust" to the given state of affairs, despite occasional scholarly rhetoric to the contrary. The tendency for counselors to presume personal disorganization rather than societal or institutional dysfunctions is particularly detrimental to the black client.

There are no formulas for the transformation of white or black helpers into humane, sensitive, and empathic persons when dealing with a member of the opposite group. Research previously cited indicates that within the context of traditional counseling interviews, black clients are best served by black helpers. Obviously, being black does not insure the success of a helper in working with a black client. Banks (1971) obtained data that confirm "helper accurate empathy" as a more significant single variable in the counseling process than racial similarity alone.

What perhaps is needed is a move beyond analysis of, and intervention with, the victim. As a matter of emphasis, counselors and therapists might begin to pay more attention and exert more energy at the level of social and environmental change. When many of the environmental restrictions that retard the development of black people are removed, it is likely that the adaptive responses that evolve from the restrictions will become obsolete. The many forms of behavior that served to insure the viability of the black psyche and person will no longer be necessary.

References

Bancroft, J. Counseling the disadvantaged child. *School Counselor*, 1967, 14(3), 149–156.
Banks, G., Berenson, B., and Carkhuff, R. R. The effects of counselor race and training upon counseling process with Negro clients in initial interviews. *Journal of Clinical Psychology*, 1967, 23, 70–72.
Banks, W. The changing attitudes of black college students. *Personnel and Guidance Journal*, 1970, 48(9).

Banks, W. The differential effects of race and social class. *Journal of Clinical Psychology*, 1972, **28**(1), 90–92.

Bloch, J. The white worker and the Negro client in psychotherapy. *Social Work*, 1968, **13**, 36–42.

Calia, V. F. The culturally deprived client: A reformulation of the counselor's role. *Journal of Counseling Psychology*, 1966, **13**(1), 100–105.

Carkhuff, R. *Helping and human relations*, New York: Holt, Rinehart & Winston, 1969.

Carkhuff, R., and Pierce, R. The differential effects of therapist race and social class upon depth of self-exploration in the initial interview. *Journal of Counseling Psychology*, 1967, **19**, 632–634.

Carkhuff, R., and Griffin, A. Selection and training of functional professionals for concentrated employment programs. *Journal of Clinical Psychology*, 1971, **27**(2), 163–165.

Ellison, R. *Shadow and act* New York: Random House, 1964.

English, W. Minority group attitudes of Negroes and implications for guidance. *Journal of Negro Education*, 1957, **26**, 99–107.

Fanon, F. and Azaulay J. La Sociothérapie dans un service d'hommes musulmans. *L 'Information Psychiatrique*, 1954, **9**, 349–361.

Friedman, N. James Baldwin and psychotherapy. *Psychotherapy: Theory Research and Practice*, 1966, **3**, 177–183.

Grier, W., and Cobbs, P. *Jesus bag*. New York: McGraw-Hill, 1971.

Hollingshead, A., and Redlich, F. *Social class and mental illness*. New York: John Wiley, 1958.

Jones, M. H., and Jones, M. C. The neglected client. *The Black Scholar*, March 1970, **5**, 35–42. [See also this volume pp. 195–204.]

Kendrick, S. A., and Thomas, C. Transition from school to college. *Review of Educational Research*, 1970, **40**(1), 151–174.

Kleiner, R., Tuckman, J., and Lovell, M. Mental disorder and status based on race. *Psychiatry*, 1960, **23**, 271–274.

Lane, E. The influence of sex and race on process—Reactive ratings of schizophrenics. *Journal of Psychology*, 1968, **68**, 15–20.

Vontress, C. E. Racial differences: Impediments to rapport. *Journal of Counseling Psychology*, January 1971. **18**(1), 7–13.

Vontress, C. The black militant as a counselor. Paper read at the Annual Meeting of the American Personnel and Guidance Association, Atlantic City, April 1971.

EDWARD J. BARNES

Counseling and the Black Student: The Need for a New View

Today, counseling faces a challenge which strikes at its very foundation—the challenge to address itself to needs of black folk in a meaningful and positive manner. We have examined the theories, principles, and practices of counseling and have found them wanting. Time and again, black observers from many quarters have sounded the need for new social forms—forms responsive to the needs and experiences of black people. Counseling, also, does not escape this judgment.

The purpose of this paper is to show the need for a new view in the counseling of blacks—the need for an approach that explicitly recognizes the special place and meaning of black people in this white society and the implications of these realities for counseling.

But some might object and say that counseling is neutral in this regard, that it makes no distinctions between whites and blacks, that as a process it is not in the service of any color, race, or social class, that it focuses on the individual, and that its overall goal is the person's optimal development and functioning.

These are laudable claims, to be sure, but they do not tell the whole story, as a brief analysis will reveal.

"Counseling" is a term covering many functions, done by persons with varieties of training, occupying diverse roles—teacher, psychologist, minister, social worker. They interact with members of different populations—children, adults, married couples, "disadvantaged" families. A constant against this shifting background of disciplines, roles, and populations is the notion of goals and objectives, and a formulation of what it is about when one wishes to do something.

It is fairly evident that goal setting involves choosing certain alternatives over others, and it is also evident that making a judgment regarding the meaning of a behavioral event requires a standard against which to measure or judge that event. Thus we arrive at the notion that counseling as a process and as a system of ideas is an expression of values; choosing and judging obviously invoke values. While it is no longer fashionable to deny the place of values in counseling (e.g., in choice of counseling method, technique, selection of population), it is by no means agreed that values enter into the very process itself—goal determination, judgments as to the meaning of a behavioral event, which provide the focus for counseling, and labeling that event (e.g., "problem," "abnormality," "deviancy," "aggression"). Values also enter into the process of labeling the population from which the individual comes (e.g., "culturally deprived," "intellectually slow,"

This paper was presented at Dayton, Ohio, Model Cities Educational In-Service Training Program, January 31, 1970. Reprinted by permission of the author.

"disadvantaged"). The significance of the labeling process lies in the fact that the label attached to an event subtly influences the analysis and problem-solving strategies brought to bear on that event. Words are definitions, definitions are assumptions, and assumptions structure our perceptions and thoughts. Witness the evolution of the status of those designated "emotionally ill." Labeling psychotic individuals "sick" rather than "madmen" or "lunatic" was accompanied by raising their status from that of persons doing evil, mischievous deeds to that of persons suffering against their will (Deutsch, 1949). The problem-solving strategy changed from brutal treatment to humane care.

Counseling as a nomological system as well as a process rests on the values and norms of the society in which it is conceived. By values, we refer to general conceptions of desirable social ends. These conceptions legitimize and rank into hierarchies certain classes of social events. Any attempt to identify the value structure of this society is rendered difficult by the duplicity and hypocrisy of the system—by the discrepancy between what is preached and what is practiced. For example, it is said that the values of this society are peace, equality of men, worth of the individual, justice before the law, democracy, equality of opportunity, and so forth. However, observation of societal practices suggests the "real" values of the society to be authoritarianism rather than democracy, private property rather than worth of the individual, discrimination and oppression rather than equality of opportunity, superiority of white European over black rather than equality of man, war rather than peace . . .

By norms, we refer to the implementation of values in concrete interactive settings—that is, they are specific prescriptions and proscriptions directed to supporting the "real" value system. A body of social science findings suggests that the core of the socialization process in any society is to have the young learn the ways of that society (Davis, 1953; Benedict, 1953). This includes internalizing its values and normative patterns. If this is a valid conclusion, then those who function in a counseling capacity are also carriers of the values and norms of their culture, and these values and norms necessarily come into operation when activities requiring goal setting, formulation of problems, or diagnosis of other conditions are undertaken.

The answer to the question of what is good and desirable and what is bad and undesirable for a society is determined primarily in terms of the interests of those who hold the power in that society. The most cursory examination of the current status of black people and of their 400-year history in this country reveals conclusively that the value structure and normative patterns of the society work in the interest of the white people and against the interests of black people. In other words, the white society imposes a racist, authoritarian ethic upon blacks.

Now, any theory or approach that proposes to address itself to blacks in this society must explicitly face and deal with this social reality. This is precisely because counseling theories, methods, and conceptions are based primarily on white interests. This is not surprising because it is generally the case that creations typically serve the interests of their creators. I am unaware of any black person's writings that have influenced the area of counseling to any great extent. One white writer (Kincaid, 1969) who has attempted to come to grips with this issue states that "therapeutic efficacy, independent of theory and process, is primarily a function of a central core of facilitative conditions that include empathic understanding, positive regard, genuineness, concreteness, self-disclosure, spontaneity, flexibility, confidence and openness . . ." (p. 888). She concludes that these conditions are independent of racial origin and experience. I contend that establishing these very conditions as well as maintaining them are influenced by what one feels, believes, and thinks about another, dispositions that are, at once, based on one's values and standards. My main thesis is that any approach to counseling black people must explicitly recognize the fact that black people exist in a society that does and has victimized them for 400 years, a society that keeps the mass of blacks in an oppressed state economically, educationally, politically, and socially, a society that asserts in countless ways that blacks are inferior, a society that uses the brutal, dehumanized conditions it creates as evidence for its claims and justification for its position. What are the implications of these observations for counseling?

For one, it is patently obvious that any approach that counsels blacks to "adjust" to the existing set of social arrangements or to "cope" with them is insane and would play a grim joke on black people. Any counseling concept appropriate for black people must, first and foremost, be directed toward the liberation of black people—liberation from beliefs and feelings that kill the spirit, liberation from lies about their worth, abilities, and potentials—toward infusion of new values and principles leading to feelings of being in control of one's own destiny, of being the locus of control of one's life, toward the development of social insight into the position of blacks in white America, toward recognition that privation, discrimination, segregation are not their burdens and creations, but are placed upon them by a white racist society. Any other posture is merely another means of perpetuating the slavery of both blacks and whites—blacks to their victimized status, and whites to their illusions of superiority. Counselors who do not operate with a full awareness and knowledge, and take into account the meaning and status of black people in this society are in the role of gatekeepers for the status quo.

If we cannot accept the values and norms of the larger society with respect to counseling goals, then neither can we accept them with respect to definitions of behavioral events as "normal" or "healthy" or "abnormal," "deviant," or "pathologic." To embrace the norms of the larger society in this regard is to embrace death, because to do so means to subscribe to systems calculated to perpetuate our victimized status. Definitions of what is normal, healthy, deviant, pathologic, must relate to the conditions of our existence, to our interests, and to what we conceive as socially desirable and socially undesirable. Acceptance of white definitions of "health" and "pathology" leads to the ironical situation Barbara Sizemore (1968) so ably formulates in her A/B conception. The paradigm is as follows: A creates a set of conditions for B. If B is to survive, he must respond in those ways having survival value, but A defines this behavior as sick or abnormal, but, in fact, B's response is natural and appropriate to the conditions. A response that A would call normal would not have survival value for B. Blacks and whites do not live in the same social reality. That which is deviant behavior for a white might be healthy for a black and vice versa. Rosa Parks's refusal to sit in the "proper place" on that bus in Montgomery in 1955 was problem or deviant behavior from the vantage point of whites. How would you define the behavior of a bright thirteen-year old living in one of the more dehumanizing housing projects in Chicago, who almost daily during the school week had the choice of fighting or running, and who chose to fight? This child was referred to me with the complaint of being overly aggressive and hypersensitive to provocation. Clearly, the healthy response in this situation was not running—that is, if we are concerned about the youngster's self-esteem, and psychological survival.

It is precisely with respect to the goals and objectives of counseling and to judgments regarding the meaning of behavioral events that counseling concepts must be modified. Modifications must be in ways and along dimensions alluded to in the foregoing, if they are to begin to address themselves to the needs and interests of the black community.

Of critical significance to the contemporary counselor is the drive by the black community, especially young black people, for self-definition and self-determination. What modifications in the counseling process does this trust demand? What modifications are called for in the counselor's role with black students? How can the counselor work with students who might view the school system, as presently constituted, as irrelevant or hostile? What are the implications for the white counselor in the black inner-city school?

Because the school counselor is concerned with the full psychological and social development of the student, he should welcome the student's identification with the "Great Black Awakening," particularly in view of the implications such involvement has for healthy psychological functioning: heightened self-esteem, increased positive group identification, and increased feelings of control (Proshansky and Newton, 1968; Solomon and Fishman, 1964; Pettigrew, 1964; Seasholes, 1965). The counselor should be concerned about any factor that influences the student's affective functioning, whether it is within or without the classroom. The counselor is or should be well aware that the pupil's cognitive growth is not independent of his affective status.

Growing black consciousness is giving birth to a new breed of young black. He is alert and aware, and he is beginning to challenge those institutions (especially the schools) that hitherto have not been responsive to the needs of black people. He is becoming more aggressive in the pursuits of those rights that are his. In the pursuit of these rights, he is dedicated neither to violence nor to nonviolence. Nevertheless, he is resolved to pursue his goal at all costs. He will strike back if attacked, and will strike back hard if sufficiently provoked. He is likely to manifest behavior that, in the past, surely would have been labeled "problem" behavior.

In judging this behavior, it is imperative that the contemporary counselor place it in proper context, utilizing a new standard for judging, a standard based on the needs and conditions of black people, thereby determining whether given behaviors are a normal reaction to an abnormal situation. It seems clear that traditional standards for judging the acceptability of black students' behavior are obsolete. We can expect black students to make demands never made before on the school system, and furthermore, stand ready to back up their demands with actions. They may reject the curriculum as meaningless, demand courses more relevant to their lives and experiences, demand black personnel at all levels in the organizational structure—in general involve themselves in ways that shake the very foundation of the school. How will the counselor interpret such behavior—as manifestations of social-personal difficulties, problems with authority, aggression, or hypersensitivity, or as normal behavior?

The counselor has to understand that such behavior represents a microcosm of what is occurring in the society outside the classroom. It represents a healthy demand that education be relevant to the black student's life and circumstances. Rather than viewing it as maladaptive behavior, the counselor should view it as a sign of healthy personality development and functioning.

The student who remains passive under the covert violence done him by the racism inherent in the institution of the school may be the one manifesting pathology. Kenneth Clark (1965) addressed this issue when he observed that "in a very curious way the ghetto delinquent's behavior is healthy, for at least it asserts that he still has sufficient strength to rebel and has not yet given up in defeat. This youngster is more healthy than the one who is passive in the face of his conditions and resigned to his third-class status in the jungle of his existence (p. 88).

In short, the school counselor must be prepared for increasingly greater numbers of black youths, utilizing as a mode of reaction to oppression "moving against" the oppressor (Horney, 1937), and for greater direct expression of anger and resentment toward, and rejection of, the school. Even under these conditions the counselor has the responsibility of helping the student utilize his anger in a positive, effective, nonself-destructive manner. The counselor who has some understanding of the black man's history of oppression, and who is able to relate it to the current black revolution, need not be frightened or defensive in the face of these attitudes and behaviors, nor need he feel constrained to respond with counterhostility. The counselor who does not have this knowledge, understanding, and orientation will not be able to establish a working relationship with the black militant student, nor will he be able to achieve the goal of helping him channel his energies into positive achievements.

The counselor has to keep abreast of the latest developments in the struggle of black people to liberate themselves, if he is to distinguish personal-social problems from behaviors indicative of identification with and involvement in the black revolution.

It is almost certain to be so if he uses traditional terms and definitions, if he identifies with white middle-class norms as an index of healthy adjustment.

Even prior to the burgeoning of black consciousness, many black students viewed many white counselors with suspicion, a condition making difficult the establishment of the quality of communication necessary for an effective counselor–counselee relationship. The history of black Americans has taught us to keep our anger and hostility toward whites closely guarded as a survival strategy. Blacks became adept in telling the white man what he wanted to hear, such that today, even in the face of the growing black awareness, many blacks still wear communication "masks" in their interaction with whites. This situation has held for white counselors in black inner-city schools, and is even more salient given today's social context. Black students at both the college and high-school level frequently articulate a refusal to interact with white counselors. White counselors should be prepared for this difficulty; in many instances they should be prepared for total rejection. Such seems to be a logical expression of the move toward organizing on the basis of separatist and collectivist values and moving away from the melting-pot individualistic values, an orientation that has not worked for blacks. When black people establish their own power base from which they can bargain effectively from a position of strength with the larger society, communication of a genuine open nature between whites and blacks in this country may be a possibility, for the first time.

The white counselor working with members of the black community almost inevitably will face value conflicts. He finds himself in the unique position of having to view the society, of which he is a part, through the eyes of its victims. He must give support to a choice of goals and objectives that may contradict or clash with those of the majority society. The main thrust of the black movement is toward personal freedom and identity. This model is based in part, at least, on a rejection of white values. A genuine commitment to the black person's freedom requires accepting this fact, and assuming the task of helping him understand the discrepancy between his values and those of the white society, and to make choices based on his own values free of the threat of disapproval for "wrong choices" by the counselor. To assert that this is likely to be a difficult task for the white counselor, a middle-class professional with middle-class values, is an understatement.

Counseling is rendered difficult to impossible when one does not understand and therefore appreciate or respect the subculture of the student. Language is an expression of culture, and a language barrier is likely to exist between those from a white middle-class background and those from the black subculture.

If communication between the white counselor and black client is to be possible then the counselor must become sufficiently acquainted with the subculture to understand the black idiom and nonverbal modes of communication (facial expressions, gestures, body movements). The middle-class counselor placing emphasis on verbal fluency is likely not to perceive the counselee's nonverbal messages and perhaps label him "uncommunicative," "silent," "nonverbal." Value conflict may also manifest itself in the counselor's selectively responding to expressions congruent with his own values, and ultimately attempting knowingly or unknowingly to move the student toward a position desirable to and approved of by the counselor.

The contemporary counselor must be particularly mindful of his role as a resource person. He can help the counselee gain a meaningful perspective of his strengths and weaknesses, and knowledge of educational and vocational opportunities. As a resource person the counselor is instrumental in increasing the counselee's options. The counselor should be mindful of "advice giving or making decisions for" the counselee and thereby actually diminishing options. Much damage to and waste of human resources have resulted from counselors sitting in judgment on students' career and college choices.

White counselors in black schools have been particularly guilty of these practices. However, black counselors operating from a white middle-class frame of reference cannot be completely exonerated of these practices.

A poignant example of this practice is related by a colleague and friend, Dr. Donald H. Smith (1967)—that of Ted, a black youngster, who was advised against making application to Harvard even though he was valedictorian of his class. It was the counselor's judgment that his language scores were too poor to consider a first-rate college. Ted accepted this verdict. It was only with the persistent urging of Dr. Smith that he applied to Harvard. Harvard too was concerned about his low language scores but suggested a way around this barrier at their own expense. This story has a happy ending. Ted graduated from Harvard in June 1968. Whether the account to follow has a happy ending I leave to your judgment.

I am sure all of you are familiar with the case of Malcolm X (1965). In his autobiography he relates how as a young boy he aspired to be a lawyer and how a white English teacher whom he trusted and admired dashed his hopes by declaring he would do better to abandon his thoughts about the legal profession and aspire to a more realistic educational-vocational goal—that of becoming a carpenter or a plumber. We know the rest of the story of Malcolm's life.

I can think of no circumstance in which a counselor should operate in such a way as to circumscribe the student's choice. Even when a counselor limits and circumscribes out of a desire to spare the student "future frustration," to inform him of the nature of the "real" world, he is doing the student a grave disservice. Such a position serves the status quo, advocates a defeatist, fatalistic outlook, serves the interests of a racist social system, and presumes the ability to foretell the future. A message to the black youth to lower his level of aspiration communicates a belief that he is not capable of higher achievements. Rosenthal and Jacobson (1968) have presented evidence to the effect that the performance of youngsters can be largely determined by what significant others expect of them.

Black students need black counselors whether at the elementary- and secondary-school or college level. The black counselor is not far removed experientially, culturally, and psychologically from the student and does not necessarily present a conflictual model. If we are to take seriously what we know about the process of psychological identification, we must inevitably conclude that the white counselor contributes to the identity crisis of the black student. Identification, in this instance, is an act of denial of self because it means identifying with the "enemy" in the person of the white counselor, a symbol of the oppressive system. A black counselor who shares a common experience with his counselee, and who has not rejected his own personal history, presents an appropriate figure for identification and is most able to inspire a feeling of confidence and a sense of hope in his black charges.

The white counselor in the black community should begin to reassess his position. He is the farthest removed psychologically, sociologically, economically, and culturally from his counselees, and is more intimidating to black youth than even before, given the increased struggle for black freedom. The white counselor who remains should carefully examine his motivations for doing so. He should seek to determine whether his motives involve, for example, seeking out a "power role," undertaking the task out of guilt, seeking affection and gratitude, or seeking to establish a position of dominance. Counselors with these motivations have no place in the black community. The white counselor who remains must seek to define new roles in working with the black community. What are some possibilities? He might serve as a referral agent, directing black students to local community leaders and nonprofessionals who can serve as models for identification and as sources of hope and inspiration. Another role concerns the use of pupil personnel data. Typically, a large amount of such data is collected but remains uninterpreted to teacher and student. The development of methods of involving teachers with these data so that they become meaningful parts of interaction with and planning for students is crucial. Even this role requires of the counselor a reevaluation of attitudes concerning the black youngster, his abilities, potentials, interests, and perceptions, and the interaction of these with his life conditions.

A third role, and perhaps the greatest challenge to the white counselor, is his willingness and ability to fulfill a role as interpreter and change-agent in the white community where he is subject to the sanction of his peers and more often looks upward rather than downward at his clients.

It is apparent that counselors as a group seem to carry little influence with those in decision-making positions. Counselors in a given area should organize to become a recognized force. Such a group could form a coalition with parents and other community groups to push for the dismantling of barriers to full development of black youth in the school setting. This group could also give its weight to student demands which relate to their interests and welfare in the school setting.

Many counselors, both black and white, may feel that a social-action orientation is outside of their roles as counselors, but a body of literature is beginning to develop which suggest that counselors must become agents of social reconstruction (Williamson, 1965; Riccio, 1968). This role also requires that the counselor be sensitive to and knowledgeable of the sociological, historical, and cultural backgrounds of blacks and that he has (if he is white) systematically studied his own cultural background.

The counselor who would work with black folk must be knowledgeable of the typical family pattern of most poor black youngsters, and of the nature of the demands and impingements on its adults. It should be recognized that parent conferences and PTA meetings have different priorities for these family members. A parent or working member who cannot afford to miss a day's wages for a parent conference chooses survival first.

Parent-Teachers Association meetings are for those who understand their importance and who subscribe to the help they can give. The PTA typically has been participated in by and benefited the more articulate parents, and those who have been members of families who have found this activity beneficial. For the family new to the neighborhood, a family whose working members are tired at the end of the day, a family that has had little previous experience with this activity, either as a student or as a participant family member, PTA meetings are of little significance.

Counselors, therefore, need to bring the school to the home at times convenient to the home. Efforts need to be made to communicate with the family, in language it can understand and accept, about programs, opportunities, and advantages available in the school setting. Interpretation of grades and the responsibilities and needs of children, parents, and school, and the arrangement of parent-teacher conferences and interactions are part of the total responsibility of the counselor who works with black children. Encouragement of family involvement in some of the adult programs offered in most communities would encourage more participation in the long run in those activities specifically devised for students of these families. Some follow-through programs sponsored by the U.S. Office of Education are experiencing success utilizing this model. These contacts can prove valuable resources for later changes. Once parents are organized and experience some success in extracting needed resources from the community they can become a group "to reckon with."

The counselor should be thoroughly knowledgeable about the shortcomings of standard assessment techniques as a means of evaluating black folk. Nevertheless, many counselors insist on using the results of such instruments in an uncritical way to make judgments about and to make programs for black people. Such practices result in great harm. We are all aware of the relationship between test scores and the attitudes and expectancies of those responsible for using them in programming and teaching.

Children with low scores are not expected to do much, not expected to learn, and generally this expectancy is borne out. The work of Rosenthal and Jacobson (1968) indicates that this result may have little to do with the child's intellectual ability, but rather may reflect what the teacher expects of the child.

Counselors should never use tests in a perfunctory, indiscriminate manner; for a variety of reasons, a test might not assess what it purports to assess. "Achievement" tests, for example, do not necessarily measure what an individual knows, when he comes from a subculture in which achievement is not "academically oriented" but "survival oriented." His performance would be quite different on tests that defined achievement in terms of "survival." This points out that all tests reflect the culture of their creators (remember man is made in the image of

God) and are inappropriate for anyone from a different culture. The only viable plan for developing tests appropriate for poor black people in this society is to move away from the idea of "culture fair" to "culture specific" tests.

Use of a standardized measure with any person must satisfy the following conditions:

1. The child must have had the same opportunity to learn, whatever the measure, as the normative group;
2. He must be equally motivated, and
3. He must have had equal practice in taking such tests.

At best, current tests imperfectly meet these conditions for members of the black subculture, a fact which invalidates their test performance as a basis from which to argue their abilities, achievements, and the like.

The counseling responsibilities and activities I have alluded to are not the sole domain of the professionally trained counselor. The classroom teacher also engages in counseling. This becomes quite clear when the term *counseling* is used to apply to interactions where one person takes the responsibility for making his role in the interaction process contribute to the other's full social and psychological development and functioning.

What are some of the counseling functions the classroom teacher can and does perform? (1) A counseling function is performed (a) when the teacher presents and interprets grades and their implications for future directions and programming to family members; (b) when conferences are held with family members and/or other members of the guidance team and observations of behavior, hypotheses based on observations, and child's needs are presented with a view to facilitating social and psychological development and functioning; (c) when the teacher identifies the child's guidance needs and makes referrals and provides necessary information and follow-up to insure appropriate action; (d) when the teacher arranges the child's experiences to develop a sense of accomplishment (e.g. providing opportunities for more success than failure in the school setting); (e) when self-esteem is approached by providing the child who needs it with special status-giving roles (e.g. board erasing, plant watering, pet feeding, etc.); (f) when the teacher attempts to help the child understand his motives with a view toward facilitating positive development and functioning (e.g., classroom disrupting behavior stemming from feelings of not being important to anyone); (g) when the teacher believes the student can learn and expects him to do so; (h) when models from the black community are provided who may serve as inspirational sources and level-of-aspiration raisers, and who may contribute to pupils' learning experiences by discussing and describing their vocational and avocational skills, interests, and achievements, thus making learning smart, respectable, and attainable. Dr. Donald Smith (1967) has written a fascinating account of a project in which he provided speaker models for his class of eighth-graders several years ago. The significance of this experience in the lives of his students is attested to by comments he has received from them over the years.

The foregoing are only a few examples of possible teacher counseling activities. I am sure that each of you can think of many more. The significant observation I hope to convey is that the teacher is as much involved in the development of the total child as anyone on the guidance team, and in many ways may be more significant in that the teacher's contacts with the student are more frequent than anyone else's in the school setting. This means the teacher is or should be more accessible for the daily exigencies and concerns of the student. If this is the case, the classroom teacher will probably be the first person to whom these concerns are expressed. His-her response could be a critical factor in determining the student's future directions, motivations, and aspirations.

It seems to me that I have spoken rather lengthily today, but not out of a need to be before an audience, but because the topic is vital to me. Counseling has a vital role to play in the lives of our children. Whether it will, remains to be seen. If it decides to accept the challenge, it must catalyze some profound changes from within.

Such changes must go to the very bottom of its foundation—changes that demand that the practitioner be in some ways a social worker, in some ways a PR man, and in some ways a catalyst for social change.

To be sure, there will be those who will resist—those who will continue to define their roles in terms of functions instead of in terms of needs of people. But there is still hope. Hope has brought me here today. Nevertheless, lest we grow weary, we should be mindful of the question put forth by Langston Hughes when he asks:

What happens to a dream deferred?
Does it dry up
like a raisin in the Sun?
Or fester like a sore—
and then run?
Does it stink like rotten meat?
or crust and sugar over—
like a syrupy sweet?
Maybe it just sags
like a heavy load—
Or does it explode?

What shall the answer be: Watts, Newark, Detroit—or a creative turning to human needs?

References

Benedict, R. Continuities and discontinuities in cultural conditioning. In C. Kluckhohn, H. A. Murray, and D. Schneider (Eds.), *Personality in nature, society, and culture*. 2nd ed., New York: Knopf, 1953, pp. 522–531.

Clark, K. *Dark ghetto: Dilemmas of social power*. New York, Harper & Row, 1965.

Davis, A. American status systems and the socialization of the child. In C. Kluckhohn, H. A. Murray, D. Schneider (Eds.), *Personality in nature, society, and culture*. 2nd ed., New York: Knopf, 1953, pp. 567–576.

Deutsch, A. *The mentally ill in America.* New York: Columbia University Press, 1949.

Horney, K. *The neurotic personality of our time.* New York: Norton, 1937.

Hughes, L. Harlem, from *Selected Poems of Langston Hughes.* New York: Knopf, 1959. Copyright 1951 by Langston Hughes. Reprinted by permission of Alfred A. Knopf, Inc.

Kincaid, M. Identity and therapy in the black community. *Personnel and Guidance Journal,* 1969, 47, 884–890.

Malcolm X (Assisted by Alex Haley). *The Autobiography of Malcolm X.* New York: Grove Press, 1965.

Pettigrew, T. A. *Profile of the Negro American.* New York: Van Nostrand Reinhold, 1964, pp. 159–177.

Proshansky, H., and Newton, P. The nature and meaning of Negro self identity. In M. Deutsch, I. Katz, and A. R. Jensen (Eds.), *Social class, race, and psychological development.* New York: Holt, Rinehart & Winston, 1968, pp. 178–218.

Riccio, A. C. The counselor as a social actionist. *Guidance Journal,* 1968, 4, 353–364.

Rosenthal, R., and Jacobson, L. *Pygmalion in the classroom.* New York: Holt, Rinehart & Winston, 1968.

Seasholes, B. Political socialization of Negroes: Image development of self polity. In W.C. Kvarceous et al. (Eds.), *Negro self-concept: Implications for school and citizenship.* New York: McGraw-Hill, 1965, pp. 52–90.

Sizemore, B. Separatism: A reality approach to inclusion? In R. C. Green (Ed.), *Racial crisis in American education.* Chicago: Follett, 1969, pp. 249–279.

Smith, D. H. A speaker models project to enhance pupils self-esteem. *Journal of Negro Education,* 1967, 35, 177–180.

Smith, D. H. The white counselor in the Negro slum school. *The School Counselor,* 1967, 4, 268–272.

Solomon, F., and Fishman, J. R. Youth and social action: II. Action and identity formation in the first student sit-in demonstration. *The Journal of Social Issues,* 1964, 20, 36–45.

Williamson, E. G. *Vocational counseling.* New York: McGraw-Hill, 1965.

WILLIAM A. HAYES and WILLIAM M. BANKS

The Nigger Box or A Redefinition of the Counselor's Role

The problems in counseling black students have been cited by several writers (Kendrick and Thomas, 1969; Jones, 1970; Vontress, 1970). While the source of the problems does not follow strict racial lines, it is becoming increasingly clear that white counselors counseling black students contribute disproportionately to the problems. Whites' ignorance of black history, sociology, and psychology, their apparent inability to identify with blacks, their lack of experience in black schools, and their unfamiliarity with black slang have been posited as explanations of this phenomenon (Smith, 1968). It follows that the training of white counselors in, for example, black history and psychology, helping whites to identify with blacks, and increasing the interaction of whites with blacks would be seen as solutions to the problems. Other solutions range from an increased desire and commitment on the part of the counselor (Smith, 1968), to the removal of white counselors from the black ghetto and into the white community where their function should be the eradication of prejudice (Kincaid, 1969). While the posited causes of the problem may, at one level, appear to be intuitively sound, they seem to oversimplify the nature of the problem and lead to solutions which, at best, attempt to treat cancer with an aspirin and, at worst, are detrimental to the future functioning of black youth. One can argue that these posited causes are mere reflections of a more fundamental cause. The present paper suggests a more fundamental cause for whites' ineffectiveness in counseling blacks and presents an alternative conceptual framework upon which more realistic solutions can be based.

Counselors are placed in the peculiar position of being advocates for their clients *and* the institution to which the clients are responsible. Often, services necessary for the ultimate well-being of the client are incompatible with the needs of the institution. The problem is exacerbated when the counselor is faced with black students as clients. Almost as if it were an unconscious effort to combat the cognitive dissonance which may result from the apparent contradiction in roles, counselors have adopted the deficiency hypothesis, which focuses on the students' real or perceived intellectual, academic, or motivational deficiencies. Thus, counselors have adopted an approach to counseling which is incompatible or renders unnecessary the examination of their own behavior and their role and responsibilities to the institutions that contribute greatly to the structure of the environment in which blacks must function. We suggest that this inability or unwillingness of whites to examine their own behavior and the

Reprinted by permission of William A. Hayes.

effects of their behavior on the behavior of their black clients is the fundamental problem from which other problems arise in the counseling of black students. While the subscription to the deficiency hypothesis is only one outcome of the fundamental problem, its role is so central to the outcome of the counseling sessions that its nature and consequences must be considered before we present an alternate conceptual framework for the counseling of black students.

Deficiency Hypothesis

The conceptual framework of the vast majority of professional counselors is inappropriate and even dysfunctional when counseling blacks. The average counselor's work with black clients seems to be individualistic in its orientation and predicated on the deficiency hypothesis. The deficiency hypothesis assumes that black people have underlying deficiencies, attributable to genetic and/or social pathology, which limit the probability of achieving successful academic and/or social adjustment. This assumption dissuades white counselors from objectively examining their own behavior and minimizes the likelihood of their considering important psychosocial factors which determine black behavior.

Volumes and volumes have been written documenting the thesis that minority youth view society as oppressive and insensitive to their needs. Rather than examining the experiences that produced the perceptions, counselors demonstrate a myopic tendency to focus on the "abnormality," "peculiarity," or "deficiency" of the individual client. Despite occasional scholarly rhetoric to the contrary, emphasis is placed on counseling the client to adjust to the given state of affairs—while the behaviors of whites and the role they play in creating and maintaining psychologically oppressive environments in which blacks must function are ignored. The tendency of counselors to presume personal disorganization rather than societal or institutional dysfunction is particularly detrimental to the black client.

It should be noted that the tendency to assume personal deficiencies or disorganization is a phenomenon which is not peculiar to counselors. It seems to be characteristic of American whites in general. The President's Commission on Civil Disorders (1968) put it this way:

> What white Americans have never understood but what the Negro can never forget is that white society is deeply implicated in the ghetto. White institutions created it, white institutions maintain it, and white society condones it. (p. 2)

Like most white Americans, white counselors either naively ignore or fail to understand the critical functional relationships which operate between the races. Instead of naively wishing that such relationships did not exist (Rousseve, 1970), the counselor must be aware of these functional relationships and the effects they have upon his client. Moreover, the counselor must be as willing to help modify his own behavior and the environment in which blacks function as he is to counsel students directly.

A major consequence of the deficiency hypothesis has been a flurry of research efforts and service programs designed to identify and correct the presumed deficiency—while the existing environmental conditions that created the presumed need for these programs are allowed to persist. The research efforts have resulted in a list of characteristics of blacks including inferior intelligence, inability to delay gratifications, fearfulness of parental authority, poor motivation, low achievement, low level of aspiration, low self-esteem, and poor educability. The vast majority of these research efforts have succeeded more in documenting the effects of living and learning in environments structured by racists and cultural imperialists than in contributing to the understanding of black people. They have succeeded in at least two other ways. The current emphasis has provided a fertile field for many researchers who operate under the rule of "publish or perish." From the black community's point of view, more of these researchers, when faced with that choice, should give more serious consideration to the latter. These research efforts have established the black man as the most frequently used research animal since the white rat. During a recent conversation, a perceptive colleague remarked, "It has provided an attractive alternative to study of the real white rat."

Current research suggests that service programs predicated on the deficiency hypothesis provide few lasting rewards (Klaus and Gray, 1968; Baratz and Baratz, 1970). These programs have promised much and delivered little, save unfounded enthusiasm and unrealistic expectations for their success and accomplishments. The most widely known program of this sort, Project Head Start, may be considered as illustrative of the orientation and problems inherent in this class of "intervention" programs. That such programs subscribe to the deficiency hypothesis is evidenced by the selection of the intervention method, with the focus almost entirely on the children, as opposed to attempts to alter the kinds of environments that produce "culturally disadvantaged" children.

The early enthusiasm generated by Head Start and the anecdotal support derived from early efforts have overshadowed the fact that the data collected so far from intervention studies do not support the efficacy of such programs. Where gains have been shown, they have been found to be temporary. Educators and psychologists subscribing to the deficiency hypothesis accepted as a challenge a problem created by racism and oppression, but paid only lip service to environmental factors. Furthermore, questions regarding the adaptive function of certain behaviors in the home environment of black youth were seldom raised. Researchers were so busy looking for deficiencies that they overlooked or ignored obvious strengths in the cultural characteristics of ghetto youth. Instead of intervening efforts to make the black child adopt middle-class traits (which may be dysfunctional in the home environment), more attention should be given to effecting revolution in the nature and character of public education, particularly at the early levels (Silberman, 1970).

In a very real way, these preschool programs are a disservice to the poor and black people in America. These programs have discouraged investigation into the real causes of the educational problem while supporting the belief that a correction factor could be developed in the form of educational intervention programs to fill the alleged gaps left by oppressive social environments. These programs have failed to admit that the psychological, sociological, and educational problems of the disadvantaged are only symptoms of the isolation, segregation, and different kind of interaction of the disadvantaged with the mainstream of American culture. In their treatment of the symptoms, interventionists have institutionalized preschool programs by establishing thousands of jobs whose existence is contingent upon the existence of a class of children called *culturally disadvantaged*. The probability of effective preventive programs is probably inversely related to the increasing numbers of service and research interventionists with vested interests in cultural deprivation (Hayes, 1967).

Counselors, personnel managers, and psychologists can be of service to black people only if they have the courage and are willing to look beyond the black client to the barriers and structure of the environment in which blacks function. If counselors and others persist in considering blacks and their behaviors as aberrations from a normal social system, they are harmful to black people in that their only contribution is to help people adjust to an unjust system. We abhor this form of psychic violence and support all attempts to eliminate the perpetrators from black communities.

Beyond the Deficiency Hypothesis

Clearly, there is a need to go beyond the treatment of victims of an oppressive and racist society if progress is to be made. Fortunately, at least two approaches suggest that alternatives to the deficiency hypothesis are being considered. One alternative is found in the experimental analysis of behavior (EAB). Illustrative of this approach is the case of a three-year-old girl who spent 75 percent of her time at a nursery school either crawling or sitting on the floor. The teacher's response to seeing the child on the floor was to approach her with friendly and warm attention. A psychologist suggested that off-feet behavior be weakened by withholding attention while the child was off her feet, and providing the warm attention when the child was standing or walking—somehow on her feet. After a one-week period the percentages of time on and off feet reversed. The reinforcement contingencies were shifted again so that attention was not given when the child was on feet and continuous attention was given when she was off feet. After two days under this contingency, the child spent 82 percent of her time at nursery school off her feet. Finally, the reinforcement contingencies were reversed again. After about two hours the child was almost steadily on her feet (Harris, Johnston, Kelley, and Wolf, 1964).

The child probably benefited more from the psychologist's counseling and modifying the teacher's behavior than she would have from direct contact with the psychologist. It was not necessary for the psychologist to assume personal disorganization or to make assumptions about the "causes" of the unusual behavior to change it. Rather, the psychologist observed the child's behavior in relationship to the consequence of her behavior. This demonstrated to the

teacher that her behavior was an important component of the child's environment and that there was a functional relationship between her behavior and the
child's behavior.

A second alternative to the deficiency hypothesis is the work initiated by
Rosenthal and his associates on teacher expectancy. Rosenthal and Jacobson
(1968a, 1968b) presented data to support the contention that teachers' expectancies are functionally related to student achievement. The Rosenthal thesis is
further supported by the research of Rist (1970), who also describes the behaviors that contribute to the documented result. Rist appears to understand the
social implications of his findings:

> *Through ridicule, belittlement, physical punishment, and merely ignoring*
> *them, the teacher was continually giving clues to those in the high reading*
> *group as to how one with high status and a high probability of future success*
> *treats those of low status and low probability of future success. To maintain*
> *within the larger society the caste aspects of the position of the poor vis-à-vis*
> *the remainder of the society, there has to occur the transmission from one*
> *generation to another of the attitudes and values necessary to legitimate and*
> *continue such a form of social organization. (p. 446)*

The experiments of Rosenthal and Rist both reversed the deficiency hypothesis and assumed that some degree of deficiency might be in the schools and in
the expectations and behaviors of teachers. The results suggest that counselors
should consider looking beyond the "deficiencies" of the student, particularly
the black student, to the learning environment, including teachers and administrative structure. In fact, there is need to go beyond education to examine the
myths perpetuated by the industrial society. Matlin and Albizu-Miranda (1968)
point to the contradiction that modern industrial society is demanding more
schooling of its job applicants as it requires less skill to do its work. In fact, the
simplification of the job is the main selling point of machinery manufacturers.
Psychologists, counselors, and personnel managers have helped foster the myths
about the difficulty of the industrial society's jobs. They are among those whom
Matlin and Albizu-Miranda accuse of confusing the complications of the industrial society's machines with the complications of its jobs while failing to distinguish between requirements for getting a job and the requirements for holding a
job.

The Nigger Box

To be effective counselors for black students, counselors must understand the
mechanisms by which the behavior of blacks is controlled. This approach demands a close examination of the students' environments and the events in the
environment that maintain the students' behavior. Because the counselor is a
part of the students' total learning environment, the approach demands that he
examine his behavior as an integral part of the students' environment. It is

extremely important that serious counselors understand that the real issue is the control of black behavior and recognize the different methods of control and the effects of these methods on the behavior of black people.

One of the best places to illustrate the control of behavior is in the experimental psychology laboratory. Most labs are equipped with a Skinner box. The Skinner box is literally a box with a retractable lever which can be manipulated to obtain food, a foodwell where the food pellets are dropped, and grid floors which, along with the walls, can be wired to provide electric shock to the animal. The subject most often used in this kind of Skinner box is a rat.

The experimenter can create any of several kinds of environments for the rat. For example, he can expose the lever to the rat or he can take it out; he can program the apparatus so that the rat must respond (press the lever) one time to get a pellet of food, or he can require 100 responses; he can turn on the shock and require the rat to press the lever to turn it off; he can require the rat to respond so that it can avoid shock; and so on. The point is, the experimenter creates the environment for the rat to fit his own research purposes or needs. He has complete control over the rat's environment; therefore, he has control over the rat's behavior. To maximize this control and increase the probability that the rat will respond, the experimenter keeps the rat in a state of food deprivation so that the rat continuously wants and needs food.

The number of responses required to get a pellet of food and the time schedule on which the food is dispensed is called the *schedule of reinforcement*. Each schedule of reinforcement produces a different pattern of response, and within each class of reinforcement schedule the rate of response will be determined by the time or number of responses required by the experimenter. For example, the experimenter may require 2 or 200 responses on the fixed ratio schedule, but in general a low ratio (2) produces a higher rate of response than does a high ratio (200). It is possible for an experimenter to require too much work, say, 600 responses, to get 1 pellet of food. Under these conditions the rat will stop responding. The experimenter has strained the schedule.

Imagine a special kind of Skinner box which dispenses five-dollar bills. Imagine further that the responses made by the rat resulted in consequences greatly desired by the experimenter. For example, the rat could keep the lab clean, feed the other laboratory animals, wash and iron the E's lab coat, . . . by pressing the level on a fixed ratio schedule. Because the money is valuable to E, chances are he will try to get as much work out of the rat for as few five-dollar bills as possible. In fact, he is likely to strain the schedule, resulting in no work from the rat. Under these conditions, the E's mental condition would be highly suspect if he begins to label the rat or this strain of rats "lazy," "good-for-nothing," or "genetically inferior." We would also be suspicious of his mental state if he embarked upon a program to train abstracting ability or delay of gratification so that the rat would be able to appreciate this 600-to-1 schedule. Emotionalism may drive the E to punish the rat by withdrawing the lever to assure the rat that he will never get another five-dollar bill from that Skinner box, or by turning on the shock under a contingency in which a response must be made before the shock is turned off again. Shock can also be used to suppress any attempt to escape the box.

We contend that the predicament of black youth in American institutions is not unlike the plight of the rat in the Skinner box. American society goes to great lengths to insure that a state of deprivation exists among black youth. From the minute they enter school, black students are made to feel that they are intellectually and socially inferior. By the time they reach the secondary level, most have become optimally receptive to the misguidance that so often comes from white counselors. Through devices such as standardized tests the counselor justifies certain of his own attitudes about black inferiority. The very bright student is counseled to go to college, but too often with the suggestion that he seek a "better" education by enrolling in a white college or university. He is informed that an "A" in a black college is equivalent to a "B" or "C" in a white school. The black is then sent on his way—feeling inferior and feeling that black schools are inferior.

Upon his arrival on campus, the black student encounters well-meaning white folk whose behavior help to maintain the feeling of academic and intellectual deprivation. He learns that his test scores did not meet the standards set by the college but the college accepted him anyway (for which he should be eternally grateful). Thus, he finds himself in a special education program identified as a "high-risk student." During the days of the first week, he listens to white instructors and counselors relate how much they understand the conditions from which he is a product and how important motivation is. At night he is entertained by soul music groups located by the college officials in a frantic attempt to make him feel at home.

Once the black student is in the box, he is expected to respond at the same rate as his white classmates. To put it another way, he is expected to be as motivated as white students in spite of the fact that he knows that, unlike his white classmates, he will face a postgraduation world which will present obstacles for him and his people far greater than those encountered by his white classmates. While he may not be able to quote the exact figures relating to the differential in expected earnings of blacks and whites, he is aware of the fact that things are not getting better for black people, especially from the economic point of view. It will not be until after graduation that he will fully realize that economic deprivation of blacks is basic to the white society's neurotic need to control black behavior. For white society to reinforce blacks at the same rate as whites would be incompatible with the need to keep the blacks in an economically deprived state so that their behavior can be easily controlled.

Counselors play a subtle yet critical role in the structuring of the Nigger Box. They are utilized by institutions to mollify and dull the sensitivities of blacks concerning their status as members of an oppressed group. Youth are encouraged to forget they are black, and the implications of that fact, and to adopt, quickly, the cultural characteristics of the white majority. The quicker this happens, the quicker they will win "acceptance." Above all, the emphasis is on the individual. Counselors are far from admitting that being black insures a number of experiences usually not related to any characteristics of the individual. To concede such would seriously weaken the ideological base from which they operate. A redefinition of mental illness, and a new focus of treatment might emerge; treatment that would focus on the sickness of society, rather than black reactions to that sickness. We are pessimistic about the prospect of white people ever seriously examining their behavior and attitudes, and even more pessimistic about their ever seeking treatment.

References

Baratz, S., and Baratz, J. Early childhood intervention: The social science base of institutional racism. *Harvard Educational Review*, 1970, **40**, 29–50.

Harris, F. R., Johnston, M. K., Kelley, C. S., and Wolf, M. M. Effects of positive social reinforcement on regressed crawling of a nursery school child. *Journal of Educational Psychology*, 1964, **55**, 35–41.

Hayes, W. A. Education of the culturally disadvantaged. Unpublished manuscript, George Peabody College for Teachers, Nashville, Tennessee, 1967.

Jones, M., and Jones, M. The neglected client. *Black Scholar*, 1970, **1**, 35–42.

Kendrick, S. A., and Thomas, C. Transition from school to college. *Review of Educational Research*, 1969, **40**, 151–174.

Kincaid, M. Identity and therapy in the black community. *Personnel and Guidance Journal*, 1969, **47**, 884–890.

Klaus, R. A., and Gray, S. W. The early training project for disadvantaged children: A report after five years. Monograph. *Society for Research on Child Development*, 1970, **33**.

Matlin, N., and Albizu-Miranda. Some historical and logical bases for the concept of cultural deprivation. Paper read at the International Conference on Socio-Cultural Aspects of Mental Retardation, George Peabody College for Teachers, Nashville, Tennessee, 1968.

National Advisory Commission on Civil Disorders. *Report of the National Advisory Commission on Civil Disorders.* New York: Bantam, 1968.

Rist, R. Student social class and teacher expectations: The self-fulfilling prophecy in ghetto education. *Harvard Educational Review*, 1970, **40**, 411–451.

Rosenthal, R., and Jacobson, L. F. *Pygmalion in the classroom: Teacher expectations and pupils intellectual development.* New York: Holt, Rinehart & Winston, 1968.   (a)

Rosenthal, R., and Jacobson, L. F. Teacher expectations for the disadvantaged. *Scientific American*, 1968, **218**, 16, 19–23.   (b)

Rousseve, R. Reason and reality in counseling the student-client who is black. *School Counselor*, 1970, **17**, 337–344.

Silberman, C. *Crisis in the classroom.* New York: Random House, 1970.

Smith, P. M., Jr. Counselors for ghetto youth. *Journal of Personnel and Guidance*, 1968, **47**, 279–280.

Vontress, C. Counseling blacks. *Personnel and Guidance Journal*, 1970, **48**, 713–719.

WILLIE S. WILLIAMS

Black Economic and Cultural Development:
A Prerequisite to Vocational Choice

Existing theories of vocational choice lack applicability to blacks. Osipow (1) gives the following broad classification of theories: trait-factor theories, sociology and career choice theories, self-concept theory and vocational choice and personality theories. When one attempts to apply these theories to blacks, he must consider the black experience in the United States. As a result of racism, many occupations are closed and other occupations have quota systems.

It now becomes necessary to develop both a new method of understanding vocational choices and a new economic base which will provide occupational and social mobility for blacks. The occupational and social mobility may be provided through a "developing-nation" program. While this developing-nation program will receive extensive treatment later in this article, a brief summary of the concept follows: The inner-city or black community should receive economic support from the federal government and private institutions in order to develop its resources. To deal effectively with the developing-nation concept, as it applies to vocational choices, a comparison of an agrarian and an industrial society will be presented.

Agrarian Society

During the early years of our national development, occupational choice presented little, if any, difficulties. The agrarian nature of society required minimal production of goods and services outside the family unit. Clothing, soap, and other household needs came by way of family production. Consequently, it was only necessary for boys to learn little more than how to clear the land, till the fields, and make adequate provisions for their families.

The impact of slavery, however, thrust the overall job market of the American South into a peculiar position. Whites with means spent most of their time in management positions or leisure-time activities, while slaves provided the labor. Those whites who lacked the financial means to own slaves eked out a living as farmers or overseers on the large plantations. A limited number of jobs outside the field of agriculture existed prior to the Industrial Revolution around 1800.

Blacks were forced as slaves to perform certain jobs which served the convenience of the masters. These jobs frequently required great skill and intellectual comprehension. Other jobs required only brute strength. In either case, the slave had no choice except to perform at a level acceptable to the slavemaster.

Reprinted by permission of the author.

The imposition of certain types of jobs on blacks did not end with slavery. In the North, as well as in the South, certain jobs developed for blacks only and certain other jobs developed for whites only. The conjuring up of black-only jobs has fluctuated with the labor needs. When a job shortage occurred, although these jobs usually consisted of service or unskilled labor, whites replaced blacks. Job labeling and placement of the type described set the stage for the lack of vocational choice by blacks to be discussed later.

Industrial Society

Following the Industrial Revolution, people began to leave the farms and move to the cities. A greater need for services resulted from the close compacted living of city dwellers. Fire protection, police protection, and utilities are but a few of the services required. The businesses and factories demanded employees to fill jobs ranging from common laborers to top executives. Numerous vocational choices then became available to whites in a very short time.

Employers bent on the profit motive demonstrated more concern for profits than for welfare of the workers. This lack of concern for the welfare of workers inadvertently created occupations for those persons who were concerned about the worker, his rights and his benefits. Thus, an expanding industrialized society introduces new jobs as a by-product of employment conditions. While regulatory agencies developed within the firms for quality control and improved working conditions, regulatory agencies outside the firms developed in government for quality control of consumer products and protection of workers.

These situations stimulated the work of Frank Parson and others to the development of the field of vocational education or guidance. Our society had become affluent enough to instigate a strong concern for the satisfaction one would get from his work. Ginsberg has stated . . . "ours is a country characterized by affluence, which means that men should be able to gain more than a living for their work. They should be able to derive many other satisfactions from working." (2) This statement of Ginsberg epitomizes the concern of people in the vocational guidance movement for the affluent society of white America, but its relevance for black America is absent.

While white America can deal in affluence, black America remains in the squalor of the rural South and of the ghettoized North. Even though our society is highly affluent, blacks live in a sea of poverty, destined to remain there as a result of the racist nature of the American society specifically and Western society in general. Vocational choice and vocational satisfaction have not been concepts that have been at all applicable to the black Americans.

Developing-Nations Concept

Now, there is hope for the plight of black America. The hope lies in the way that American government, business, and industry commit themselves to the development of black communities throughout this country. Contributions of both seed and operational capital for a developing-nation program of black inner cities become emminently necessary.

By providing for business and industrial development of the inner city, a basis for "achievement motivation" arises within the black community. David McClelland writes in the *Harvard Business Review* that "the need for achievement is an essential ingredient for entrepreneurial success" (3). He feels that learned drive determines the desire for achievement. The conclusion that South Americans, East Indians, poor from other countries, and black Americans lack this drive, which is tantamount to lacking achievement motivation, is highlighted in McClelland's article. Still, it is both necessary and possible, according to McClelland, to produce drive and consequent need for achievement within groups or nations that lack achievement motivation. While, on the one hand, McClelland has inadvertently placed the above-mentioned groups in an inferior position, on the other hand, he has a positive view as contrasted to most authorities in the field of entrepreneurship for developing nations.

Achievement motivation may be germane to the successful development of business and industry if the model presented by McClelland is appropriate to the black community. Yet, we may recognize the ingenuity demonstrated by blacks in communities, which are in a constant state of economic depression, as a positive orientation from which we can build a cadre of black entrepreneurs. This black entrepreneurship will enhance black vocational development in a way not otherwise possible. Without the model of black entrepreneurship, black vocational development will be a rubric rather than a reality. It is only through employment of blacks in black-owned and black-operated business that we can expect meaningful job opportunities to become available to large numbers of blacks. Labrie very adequately analyzes the problem this way:

> . . . the linkages drawn between the ghetto structure and black employment problems rest primarily upon the fact of expanding job opportunities in the suburbs, to which most blacks lack access because of their concentration in the central city. These expanding job opportunities are a product of both new suburban job growth and large-scale outflow of older industrial and commercial firms from the central city to the suburbs. It is well known among urban analysts that a multitude of commercial and industrial business have accompanied white residents in their mass movements to the suburbs over the past couple of decades. These movements and new suburban employment growth have led to both an absolute and a relative decline of available jobs in the central city. Naturally, it is assumed that this decline has had a depressive impact on job opportunities for blacks remaining in the central city, but very little empirical research on the problem has actually been done. (4)

Obviously, the existing racist structure of the business community will deny blacks the necessary job opportunities.

In trying to recoup economic losses resulting from the flight of businesses to the suburbs, black communities find themselves in several double-bind situations. One of these double binds which confront black economical development is stated by Browne as follows:

Attempting to chart a rational but effective economic development path for black people in America is a peculiarly difficult task because of the double inequalitarianisms of American society. On the one hand, income and wealth (and inevitably, of course, power) are so inequitably distributed in America, irrespective of race, that a powerful case can be made, indeed, must be made, for a total restructuring of the economy as a necessary precondition for genuine black economic development. On the other hand, the society is so ridden with racial inequality and racial prejudice that astute black people are rightfully skeptical about blindly supporting any of the numerous movements for revolutionary economic change in America. Such movements are inevitably led and financed by whites, so even should they prove successful in bringing about revolutionary economic change, they offer no guarantee that white socialism would be any more free of racism than is white capitalism. (5)

Browne also points out that we should be clear about what we mean when we discuss black economical development. He provides these options: (a) raising median family income, (b) closing the gap between median family income of blacks and whites, or (c) securing for blacks an equitable share of the nation's income—its wealth and its power. Although the first two have high priority, the third has the most wide-reaching short-term, as well as long-range, benefits.

A very strong rationale for black economic development comes from this statement of Browne's:

There is wide unity on the need for a massive transference of assets to the black community. . . . these assets can only come from the public treasury, a fact which dramatizes the necessity of a black political/cultural thrust as a pre-condition to effective economic development for black America. Whether entitled reparations or disguised by another name, resources on a scale paralleling those dispersed in Vietnam will have to be transferred to the black community, if we expect to correct existing inequities. A significant sum will be required merely to counter the enormous raids on the public treasury being perpetrated by white America's establishment in its own behalf. I refer here to oil depletion allowances, agriculture subsidies, public utility privileges, cost overruns, and other financial shenanigans conspired in by big government and its favored defense contractors, political supporters, etc.—to say nothing of rectifying our exclusion from the nineteenth-century welfare programs like the Homestead Act and the celebrated giveaways to the railroads and other establishment institutions of white America. (6)

Attitudes

The controversy rages between those who feel that the attitudes of whites in labor unions and government toward blacks are favorable and helpful, and those who feel that the actions of whites in labor unions and government are racist. Moynihan and Hampton attempt to present cases to show favorable union attitudes toward blacks, yet the net effect of the efforts of labor unions places blacks in an unfavorable position (7). Hill's report on the activities of labor unions is representative of those who feel that unions are racists:

> *AFL unions and the railroad brotherhoods used their extensive power to eliminate or limit Negroes as a group from competition in the labor market by a variety of methods. Among these were: (1) exclusion from membership by racial provisions in union constitutions or ritual by-laws; (2) exclusion of Negroes by tacit agreement in the absence of written provisions; (3) segregated locals; (4) "auxiliary" locals; (5) agreements with employers not to hire colored workers and other forms of collusion; (6) separate racial seniority and promotional provisions in contracts, limiting Negro workers to menial or unskilled jobs; (7) control of licensing boards to exclude Negro workers from craft occupations; (8) refusal to admit Negroes into union-controlled apprenticeship training programs; (9) negotiating wages and other terms of employment affecting Negroes while denying them admission into the collective bargaining unit; and (10) denial of access to union hiring halls, where such hiring halls are the exclusive source of labor supply. (8)*

Besides the activities of unions reported by Hill, Rowan reports on the lack of representation of blacks and other minorities in the top 150 positions of the 15 Post Office Department regions and the top 24 positions of the 6 Post Office Department regional data centers (9).

Although the federal government may demonstrate its willingness to hire blacks and other alienated minorities, it fails to provide adequate representation in positions of responsibility. One can only assume that these alienated groups—that is, blacks, Chicanos, and Indians—are not qualified because they do not score high enough on the Civil Service examinations. But, as psychologists, we know that most existing tests are not valid for these groups.

While Art Fletcher, a top-ranking black in the Nixon Administration, attempts to bring about more jobs in the building trades industries by forcing the unions to admit more blacks (10), the attitudes of whites within and without the unions concerning blacks will remain the same. They have said that standards must be lowered for blacks and that they are inherently inferior. Only the enlightened whites and the progressive blacks recognized that during slavery blacks were used in all levels of the skill trades to build houses, roads, and edifices, some of which stand today as monuments to the antebellum South. No selection tests were used then for screening purposes. Empires were built in the past and cities are built today in Africa using black skilled laborers at all levels to perform the many tasks. So it is obvious that when labor unions and state certification boards use written criteria that systematically and illegitimately exclude certain segments of our society from these jobs, some sinister scheme is operating.

Basic attitudes of whites, as defined by Guttman (11), at the action level create situations that can be changed only when blacks have economic options equivalent to whites. If a black wishes to open a restaurant or a hotel in a black neighborhood, the economic or financial power base of the neighborhood must support and sustain it. Presently, most large black neighborhoods lack this financial base, and small neighborhoods cannot begin to consider it. Therefore, if we wish to provide blacks with vocational choices, support must come from business, industry, and government for black entrepreneurship. Only when blacks gain economic independence will substantial attitude change come about.

Peoplehood

The concept of peoplehood will be presented here from the standpoint of a developing nation for Afro-Americans. In order for English-Americans, German-Americans, Russo-Americans, Israeli-Americans, Chinese-Americans, and other-nation-Americans to have a unifying base from which they could develop a psychological, social, economic, and religious frame of reference, they possessed a dimension of peoplehood.

While peoplehood has eluded blacks in the past, it can now be developed. Peoplehood enables a group with certain national or ethnic ties to unite and work toward a common goal as a result of their culture, music, languages, homeland, literature–poetry, native food, and economic base–job entrepreneurship. Although the specific development of each component of peoplehood is beyond the scope of this chapter, a comment on each of the components follows:

Culture. Blacks in America have exhibited a strong humanistic quality which portrays a sense of brotherhood. The friendly speech patterns demonstrated by blacks toward each other on campus and in public gatherings show to some extent this brotherhood. In fact, when one black fails to return the greetings to another the question arises "Why is he so stuck up?" or "Who does he think he is, somebody special?" Organizations on campuses such as the United Black Association usually have as a primary goal the maintenance of strong personal relationships among all blacks on campus.

The creative rhythmical dances performed by blacks illustrate another aspect of their culture. Steps are frequently impromptu and can readily be learned by other blacks. Black music, to be discussed later, has the same creative, often impromptu quality. The dances are expressive and usually require very complex movements of all parts of the body.

Other aspects of culture important enough to be considered separately in the concept of peoplehood are music, art, literature–poetry, and language.

Music. Since the chants of slaves chained to ships sailing the Atlantic expressed the anguish of their dire plight, folk music of black Americans has had a unique quality. Songs and music of oppressed blacks expressed their desire to be free. The desire for freedom expressed in the spirituals also described routes to freedom for slaves. Songs today such as "Young, Gifted, and Black" express the surging feeling of the near victory or the near freedom over oppression. Another example of the expressive impromptu creative music is jazz. The music has the

African beat, sometimes with strong Western overtones. Frequently, it is adapted into Western styles of music without getting due credit.

Language. As colleges and universities begin to accept modern African languages as equivalent, at least for credit, to other languages, a strong base for the development of language ties arises. Swahili has more popular appeal than most other African languages; consequently, it may serve as the language to unite blacks with the homeland. Aside from the development of an African-based language for ties, the special language patterns in this country are a condition which can be used in the language development. For instance, blacks speaking in street talk are able to "get over on whitey" in much the same way that foreigners exclude others by speaking in their native language.

Homeland. Although African countries cannot absorb large numbers of blacks from other lands, the recognition and acceptance of Africa as a mother country is essential. The kind of diplomacy displayed by E. M. Debrah, Ambassador to the United States from Ghana, exemplifies the stance needed for better relationships with Africans and blacks from other countries.

Debrah feels that, as an African, he wants to help American blacks find their roots. He does this by going out among his American brothers and sisters and spreading the word. He has traveled to most of the fifty states and spoken to hundreds of primarily black audiences. He has dined with VIPs as well as average black Americans in order to operationalize his philosophy of closer association between African and black Americans.

Since the advent of many independent nations in Africa, the relationship of black Americans to African countries has become multinational. Because the exact origin of black Americans cannot be clearly determined, it is necessary to identify with blackness alone. By so doing it will be much easier to establish and maintain good working relationships with most of the African nations. The homeland then will consist of a continent rather than a nation.

Literature–poetry. The will to be free comes out strongly in black literature. As in the lyrics of black music, prose and poetry surge with the feeling of control over one's own destiny.

While James Baldwin and Leroi Jones show black awareness and success in writing novels and plays, respectively, the heralded Nikkie Giovanni and Sonya Sanchez show the same awareness and success in poetry writing. Their language and style appeal to the college students as well as grass-roots blacks.

Art. It has been reported by black art historians that some of the masters during the Renaissance and post-Renaissance periods used black artists and art form in their work. More recently, Pablo Picasso has admitted that he borrowed from African art in developing some of his artistic creations.

Until the 1900s African art was looked upon as a curiosity by Western artists and art critics and it was placed in ethnological museums. In the course of the development of contemporary art a search for boldness and freedom occurred. The boldness, freedom, and conceptual qualities searched for was highly evident in art forms of Africa. They were subsequently recognized and incorporated into Western art.

The visual art form has many artists who are searching for a black (Afro-

American) esthetic. As have their brothers and sisters in music, literature, and other aspects of black culture, artists have begun to ignore reviews of critics from the mainstream of American and Western society. They use African art forms as a criterion for the development of the black aesthetic. The strength of this position epitomizes the new militancy in blacks. It also provides an association with a culture or homeland that the concept of peoplehood requires.

Native food. Native foods for American blacks did not originate in Africa. Blacks were forced to part from their native diets and placed on sustenance diet of flour, fat back, beans, and greens during slavery. Many of the foods and eating practices have come about as a result of the indignities of slavery. At the present time, "soul food" serves as the native food acclaimed by blacks. It may be that as ties with black nations grow stronger native African dishes will demand greater prominence.

Economic base—job entrepreneurship. This concept has received in-depth treatment throughout this paper.

The development of peoplehood has a very important role in the developing-nation model. A camaraderie or unity among blacks can be produced which will eliminate most of the negative stereotypes and negative ways of life which exist in the black community. This unity and camaraderie will also reduce another one of the double-bind situations of the black community. That is the great tendency for blacks as they become leaders, professionals, and businessmen to move from the inner city to the suburbs. If the developing-nation process is to succeed, it is necessary for more of the indigenous experts to remain in the black community.

A new socialization and value structure can come about as blacks are indoctrinated with and exposed to peoplehood. Young and old alike must establish a relationship built on mutual trust, understanding, and acceptance. The stereotypes as well as the realities of crime, violence, and property destruction may be explored and corrected through this exposure to and indoctrination with peoplehood. Blacks may recognize ties to a heritage and culture built on a life of peace and harmony among their people in Africa.

Vocational Choice

In order for the psychological dimension of identification, imitation, and role modeling to function in vocational choice of blacks, they must have positions in the many fields and levels of vocations. Sometimes this will come through working for governmental agencies and existing business and industry. Most of the time, however, this will come about as a result of positions obtained through a developing-nations program.

The concept of peoplehood along with black entrepreneurship will provide the medium through which identification, imitation, and role modeling may be developed. At the present time, most employed blacks are in lower Civil Service grades or in positions equivalent to common laborers or domestics. Consequently, we have limited and often inappropriate role models. From the black perspective, a need exists for extensive research on the effects of identification, imitation, and role modeling in vocational choice; these dimensions will not be dealt with further here.

While the developing-nations program provides the basis for incorporating large numbers of blacks into many fields and levels of vocations, a strong need also exists for inclusion of blacks in existing business and industry at other than menial jobs. Approximately, 40 percent of America's trillion-dollar GNP is controlled by government and a few large industries; therefore, blacks must develop expertise in the operations of big government and big businesses. By obtaining expertise and positions in big government and in big business, several concerns may receive attention. First, a means of coordinating the economic aspect of the developing-nations program is obtained. Second, the personnel will be available to provide an efficient integration of blacks into the mainstream of the American economy. And, finally, blacks will have access to more vocations.

Theories

In order to counsel blacks, the existing vocational choice theories need revision in terms of the black experience, because under the present conditions blacks receive advice instead of counseling. Osipow attempts to relate the theories to blacks by dealing with the so-called cultural-factor aspect of vocational choice. He states, "The process of career choice is so deeply imbedded in cultural and economic factors that it is unreasonable to try to develop a theory of vocational development without including those variables" (12). The fact that some ethnic groups are denied entry into certain occupations has little importance, when viewed from this perspective. So, when he goes on to point out that most (if not all) career theorists deal with the impact of cultural change upon career choice and behavior, it is quite clear that he thinks the need to include everyone in theory is greater than the reality of exclusion of certain groups from the field of theory.

Because choices available to blacks now mirror the economically depressed black community, vocational theory can neither describe nor predict black vocational choices adequately. The following operational model is presented, however, as a guide for vocational counselors who work with blacks. Before providing vocational advice, the counselor should understand the special employment problems and assist the client in understanding and solving them. Although the counselor may have a middle-class orientation which makes him believe that in order to get a job all one needs to do is to qualify, he must understand the restrictions placed on vocational opportunity by the subtleties of institutional racism and by the flagrance of overt racism.

It can be seen in Figure 1 that most blacks are excluded from the mainstream activities of the larger American society. Exclusion from employment has caused

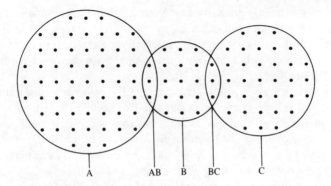

A   Larger American society
B   Successful blacks
C   Black society

FIGURE 1
Value cluster created by social conditions and employment situations in America. (Adapted from a lecture presented at Michigan State University by William E. Gardner and Willie S. Williams, 1969.) Clusters may be used to afford satisfactory vocational choice or career planning.

counselors to advise blacks to go into jobs grossly beneath their realm of inter-ests. An analysis of sections AB, B, BC, and C in Figure 1 may help the coun-selor in working through problems of vocationally guiding black students.

Those in section AB are physically and/or psychologically caught up in the mainstream of American life. They may look, act, feel, and/or think white. Their goals and objectives will be centered around activities of total integration and rugged individualism, without seeing the internal contradictions of the two. For the AB group, existing counseling theories may function within limits. Limits are set by their abilities, aggressiveness and political savvy on the one hand, and by the extent to which pressure is applied to an oppressive structure, on the other. Examples include many politicians and junior executives in big businesses, and government.

That portion of group B outside of A and C constitute what E. Franklin Frazier calls the black bourgeoisie. They set up a microcosm of the white social structure and proceed in a manner similar to that of the oppressor. This group includes a number of professionals, small-business owners, skilled laborers, and others in the lower-middle-income brackets. They move about their own social structure with some financial security.

Vocational choice for this portion of group B, and for BC as well as C, does not fit into any of the traditional theories. Forces operating to determine the vocational choices of these groups come from group A. Most existing theories assume that the choices come from the individual as a result of his personality development, yet the luxury of this position is obvious from the forgoing dis-cussion. Moreover, this author feels that the social system approaches and Hol-land's theory have the greatest potential for use with blacks. Holland theorizes that "personal and environmental factors are conducive to vocational achievement" (13). To a lesser degree he is concerned with personal development and personality. In a somewhat different vein:

> *The sociological approach is fundamentally based on the notion that elements beyond the individual's control exert a major influence on the course of his entire life, including his educational and vocational decisions. Supporters of this view suggest that the degree of freedom of occupational choice a person has is far less than might at first be assumed and that a man's self-expectations are not independent of the expectations society has for him. Society, in its turn, is assumed to present occupational opportunities in a manner related to class membership, a matter which has been extensively studied by interested sociologists. (14)*

Even the theories of Holland and of the social system advocates cannot perform adequately at this point, primarily because they assume the wrong research posture. As a means of testing the effectiveness of the theory, research should deal with the systemic forces—that is, the forces set in motion by political, social, and economic systems, operating to prevent mobility of blacks.

So, for the counselor working with groups B, BC, and C the most effective technique will be to work toward removal of any obstacle placed in the path of these persons. For example, demand the elimination of testing when it is used as a means of screening out blacks from jobs and educational opportunities. The counselor may also encourage people from these groups to explore the occupational literature in areas of expressed interests. Then he should assist the client in developing techniques for gaining entry or acceptance into a given occupation by an employer. Obstacle removal may take two other directions. One is to deal with the student who probably has a low level of aspiration. Because low aspiration usually results from fear, often at a subconscious level, that he will not be granted entry into high or prestigious positions, the counselor may help the student develop an awareness and eliminate the fear. Sometimes this low aspiration may come as a result of the parents position and/or status. For example, a gifted youngster may live in a home where the mother, who works as a domestic, is the only parent present. He may need extensive assistance from the counselor in developing goals and objectives that allow optimum use of his talents.

A systematic approach to counseling is the other direction which obstacle removal may take. To understand and operationalize the systemic approach to counseling the counselor must recognize that personal problems are caused by a societal press—that is, the system or subsystems that control political, social, economical, and educational activities. An individual or group that has been relegated to an inferior position by a selection process or other processes within the system can do little to change his relative position. Consequently, the counselor, if he is to help the client, must become active in bringing about the necessary change within the system. Or put another way, the counselor should spend less time dealing with the client's acceptance of or adjustment to unjust situations, and spend more time helping the client bring about changes in the system. Then, if the counselor is an agent of change, he is an agent of system change more than personal change.

Continuing the analysis of Figure 1, group BC remains intricately interwoven with the masses of the black communities in spite of having become economically, educationally, or politically successful. They are the ones who will at the outset by responsible for the entrepreneurships of the developing nation.

The remainder of Group C operates inside the black community on meager resources. They have much hope of rising above their existing conditions. The constant frustration of hope and desire led to riots of the 1960s. A realization of this hope through meaningful choices by way of a developing nation can begin in the 1970s.

A successful developing-nation program that would eventually allow blacks to operate within the mainstream of American society (Group A), as other national or ethnic groups do, must make use of all four subgroups—AB, B, BC, and C. While a gradual merger of the four subgroups takes place, a gradual merger of blacks into the "melting pot," the mainstream, of America will also take place.

Summary

The odious nature of discrimination lurks deep into economic and social practice of our society. No rational person tries to deny its deleterious effects on minority groups, especially blacks. Because of the existing racist socioeconomic structure the special problems of economic advancement for blacks require a new economic structure. Black entrepreneurs living and operating businesses in the inner city are imperative.

Once these entrepreneurs are developed, occupations will become available to blacks at many different levels. Subsequently, a choice of occupations will become available.

Through the developing-nation program, government, as well as the private sector of our economy, can participate in raising standards of living of the often and long neglected black populace. Occupational and social mobility will be clearly available when this type program is put into operation.

Conclusion

A need for blacks to obtain positions of power in the existing business-industrial complex significantly parallels the need for blacks to secure entrepreneurships. In the long run, this will allow America to realize its creed of one nation under God—justice and equality for all men—and equal interpretation of laws and theories with reference to every individual.

References

1. S. H. Osipow, *Theories of career development* (New York: Appleton-Century-Crofts, 1968), pp. 10-11.

2. E. Ginsberg, Vocational education is the answer, *Phi Delta Kappan*, February 1971, **LII** (6), 369.

3. D. C. McClelland, Achievement motivation can be developed, *Harvard Business Review*, 1965, **43** (6), 6.

4. P. Labrie, Black central cities dispersal or rebuilding, Part 1, *The Review of Black Political Economy*, **1** (2), Autumn 1970, 7.

5. R. S. Browne, Barriers to black participation in the American economy, *The Review of Black Political Economy*, Autumn 1970, **1** (2), 57.

6. *Ibid.*, p. 64.

7. A detailed discussion of the positions of Moynihan and Hampton is beyond the scope of this paper. However, the reader is referred to D. P. Moynihan's article The Presidency and the press (*Commentary*, March 1971) **51**, 41-52. R. E. Hampton's address Testing and equality of career opportunity, in *Psychology and the problems of society* (Washington, D.C.: American Psychological Association, 1970), may also be of interest to the reader.

8. H. Hill, The racial practices of organized labor, in B. N. Schwartz and R. Disch (eds.), *White racism* (New York: Dell, 1970), p. 327.

9. C. Rowan, On postal reform, *Cincinnati Enquirer*, May 20, 1971, p. 7.

10. V. Riesel, Big move on to get blacks into higher paying crafts, *Cincinnati Enquirer*, May 16, 1971, p. 36.

11. L. Guttman defines attitudes as a "delimited totality of behavior with respect to something" [The problem of attitude and opinion measurement, in S. A. Stouffers (ed.), *Measurement and prediction* (Princeton, N.J.: Princeton University Press, 1950), pp. 60-90].

12. N. J. Osipow, *op. cit.*, p. 235.

13. J. L. Holland, *The psychology of vocational choice* (Waltham, Mass.: Blaisdell, 1966), p. 1.

14. Osipow, *op. cit.*, p. 200.

PART V

Educating Blacks

During 1969–1970, there were more than 600 racial incidents reported in the nation's high schools, ranging from mild confrontation through severe and disruptive confrontation leading to injuries among participants in many cases, and in one instance, death. If there were ever a question, it is apparent now that black youth and their elders are dissatisfied with the schools and the education being received in them. Their concerns include ability grouping which frequently relegates blacks to the lowest tracks, or far worse, into special classes for the mentally retarded; racist teachers and administrators (or those actually perceived to be so); proportionately few minority teachers and administrators; a curriculum which fails to give attention to the history and culture of black Americans, and is focused upon white middle-class values based on the Protestant ethic; and the sheer isolation of black students from the mainstream of school activities. There is good reason to believe that these factors have taken a heavy toll on the psychological health and well-being of the black school child. It is possible for a black student to complete twelve years of formal education with virtually no knowledge of black literature and scanty knowledge of the history of black Americans and their contributions to this country. He learns little of black culture. And almost daily he has some experience in the schools that reinforces the view of black Americans as undervalued people.

Consider curriculum materials. In one survey of black curriculum materials available in 1968-1969, Smith (1970) found that of the 50 states and the District of Columbia, only 28 had some type of material available (limited to bibliographies in some instances); 19 states had neither available material nor plans for developing any in the near future; 4 states were developing materials or had established what type of material would be needed. In a number of districts, a black studies curriculum was used only in schools enrolling sizable numbers of blacks. Such materials are, of course, needed in these schools. It is apparent, however, that the need is just as great in schools with predominantly white enrollments.

Consider now blacks as portrayed and discussed in public school textbooks. In 1949, a committee of the American Council on Education (ACE) found that blacks most often were referred to almost exclusively in history textbooks only. Content was usually limited to slavery and the Reconstruction period. Slaves were typically depicted as happy, contented, and well treated. Africa was treated as a continent of strange, backward people whose primitive culture was very much different from that in America. For the most part, blacks in contemporary America were ignored as were problems related to discrimination in housing,

247

voting, jurisprudence, education, and public accommodation (Banks, 1969). A 1961 investigation of the treatment of minorities in the most widely used junior and senior high-school social studies textbooks (Marcus, 1961) revealed that few changes had occurred since the 1949 ACE report. The most obvious shortcoming in the newer textbooks was the absence of the current struggles and changing status of blacks. Few textbooks mentioned the achievement of contemporary blacks, and blacks were portrayed either as simple, childlike slaves or as uneducated bewildered freedmen.

Now consider establishment "priorities." The school systems have focused on deficiencies possessed by blacks, which make them "poor risks" for conventional school programs. Seldom, if ever, is attention given to factors within the educational system which perpetuate—if not create—the very problems needing remediation. Data about the school performance of black children are well known. Also well known are speculations about the causes of the educational deficiencies. Most often the problems are hypothesized to be attributable to the black child's background, his motivational makeup, his subaverage intelligence, and in a host of other variables all residing in the child himself or correlated with his family and life circumstances. Research and speculation in this area constitute a vast literature.

From a black perspective, racist middle-class-oriented teachers who expect and receive poor performance from black children, lily-white curriculum materials, irrelevant and inappropriate tests, too few black teachers and administrators who could serve as models for black children, inadequate guidance and counseling, and racist students are factors all "contributing" to the black child's educational performance.

The papers which follow do not focus on the black child's deficiencies. Rather, the concern is with the manner in which the various services are offered to black children, and with the effect of such services on the black child's psychological adjustment and school achievement. The perspectives offered here obviously do not exhaust the range of concerns held by black social and behavioral scientists regarding the consequences of educational programs and practices for the psychological health and well-being of black Americans. They do, however, represent significant concerns, and importantly, those that have been given insufficient attention in the planning of educational programs for black children. Several additional educational issues—for example, those related to the use of psychological tests in the assessment of black children, considerations in modifying and understanding personality and motivational phenomena in black children, and counseling needs and practices—are presented in other sections of the volume (Parts II, III, IV).

In the first paper, "The Black Revolution and Education," Price Cobbs, a black psychiatrist, presents a brief history of racism in education as background to the black rage now being directed against the schools. Current activity and demands for changes in school policies and practices are viewed as healthy evidence of the profound psychological changes black Americans are undergoing.

Edward Weaver, in "The New Literature on Education of the Black Child," points to several key black concerns about the schools and those responsible for *programs in them. First is the fact that most of the literature on educating the "disadvantaged," and particularly compensatory education for black ghetto children, has been written by whites and thus is unlikely to have a black perspective. Weaver, in addition, highlights the fact that many of the special programs for blacks merely cover up the poor quality of education, that deprivation theory places the blame on the black child and his family, and that white racism is a factor influencing inadequate educational provisions for blacks. Moreover, compensatory programs are based on theories of colonialism, dependency, and power. Psychological consequences for the black child of the various new programs are highlighted.*

Thomas Gunnings looks at the "Psychological, Educational, and Economic Effects of Compensatory Education Programs on Blacks." He calls attention to the fact that many programs were developed without sufficient input from those knowing poverty first hand, and that the onus of the problem is placed on the victim. Four deficit models—inadequate socialization, constitutional inferiority, environmental deficit, and cultural inferiority—are disavowed as adequate to explain the educational problems and behavior of black children. Gunnings gives considerable attention to a description of various government programs designed to improve the education of lower-class children. Evaluation of these programs— particularly Head Start—has been an area of some controversy. Additional items related to Head Start and other preschool programs, and to some of the evaluative issues involved, are listed in a special bibliography presented at the end of this section.

Reginald Jones, in "Labeling Children Culturally Deprived and Culturally Disadvantaged," looks at the consequences of this practice, including children's perceptions of themselves, their affective and cognitive responses to such terms, the effects on school attitudes and performance, and teacher expectations associated with the labels. Jones concludes that the use of deficit labels must be abandoned.

John Johnson, in "Special Education and the Inner City: A Challenge for the Future or Another Means for Cooling the Mark Out?" calls attention to special education in the inner city and suggests that the overall educational system for blacks be overhauled, with blacks themselves determining the direction of the system. Moreover, like Jones, he argues against describing black children as deviant, deprived, retarded, and disadvantaged, and suggests the need for new programs for the education of black children based upon psychological and cultural considerations. The psychological and educational implications of educational programs based upon black self-determination, black pride, and black consciousness are examined.

References

Banks, J. A. The need for positive racial attitudes in textbooks. In R. L. Green (ed.), *Racial crisis in american education*. Chicago: Follett Educational Corporation, 1969, pp. 167– 185.

Marcus, L. *The treatment of minorities in secondary school textbooks.* New York: Anti-Defamation League of B'nai B'rith, 1961.

Smith, W. L. Critique of developments at the secondary level. *Journal of Negro Education,* 1970, 39, 239–261.

Bibliography on Early Childhood Educational Programs

American Institutes for Research. *Academic preschool. Champaign, Illinois.* U.S. Department of Health, Education, and Welfare, Office of Education. Washington, D.C.: U.S. Government Printing Office, 1970.

American Institutes for Research. *The ameliorative preschool program. Champaign, Illinois.* U.S. Department of Health, Education, and Welfare, Office of Education. Washington, D.C.: U.S. Government Printing Office, 1969.

American Institutes for Research. *Early childhood project, New York City.* U.S. Department of Health, Education, and Welfare, Office of Education. Washington, D.C.: U.S. Government Printing Office, 1970.

American Institutes for Research. *Learning to learn program, Jacksonville, Florida.* U.S. Department of Health, Education, and Welfare, Office of Education. Washington, D.C.: U.S. Government Printing Office, 1970.

Baratz, S. S., and Baratz, J. C. Early childhood intervention: The social science base of institutional racism. *Harvard Educational Review,* 1970, 40, 29–50.

Bloom, B. *Stability and change in human characteristics.* New York: John Wiley, 1964.

Caldwell, B. M. The effects of psychosocial deprivation on human development in infancy. *Merrill Palmer Quarterly,* 1970, 16, 260–277.

Cicirelli, V. C., Evans, J. W., and Schiller, J. S. The impact of Head Start: A reply to the report analysis. *Harvard Educational Review,* 1970, 40, 105–129.

Datta, L. *A report on evaluation studies of project Head Start.* U.S. Department of Health, Education, and Welfare, Office of Child Development. Washington, D.C.: U.S. Government Printing Office, 1970.

Deutsch, M. Social and psychological perspectives on the development of the disadvantaged learner. *Journal of Negro Education,* 1964, 33, 232–244.

Deutsch, M. Facilitating development in the preschool child: Social and psychological perspectives. *Merrill Palmer Quarterly,* 1964, 10, 249–263.

Gordon, I. J. Stimulation via parent education. *Children,* 1969, 16, 57–59.

Gray, S. W., and Klaus, R. A. The early training project: A seventh year report, *Child Development,* 1970, 41, 909–924.

Greenberg, P. *The devil has slippery shoes: A biased biography of the Child Development Group of Mississippi.* New York: Macmillan, 1969.

Hunt, J. McV. *Intelligence and experience.* New York: Ronald Press, 1961.

John, V. P., and Goldstein, L. S. The social context of language acquisition. *Merrill Palmer Quarterly,* 1964, 16, 265–275.

Karnes, M. B., Teska, J. A., Hodgins, A. S., and Badger, E. D. Educational intervention at home by mothers of disadvantaged infants. *Child Development,* 1970, 41, 925–935.

Kirschner Associates Inc. *A national survey of the impact of Head Start centers on community institutions.* U.S. Department of Health, Education, and Welfare. Office of Child Development, Project Head Start. Washington, D.C.: U.S. Government Printing Office, May 1970.

Klaus, R. A., and Gray, S. W. The early training project for disadvantaged children: A report after five years. *Monographs of the Society for Research in Child Development,* 1968, 33(4), Serial No. 120.

Powledge, F. *To change a child: A report on the Institute for Developmental Studies.* Chicago: Quadrangle, 1967.

Smilansky, S. *The effects of sociodramatic play on disadvantaged preschool children.* New York: John Wiley, 1968.

Smith, M. S., and Bissell, J. S. Report analysis: The impact of Head Start. *Harvard Educational Review*, 1970, **40**, 51–104.

Spicker, H. H., Hodges, W. L., and McCandless, B. R. A diagnostically based curriculum for psychosocially deprived, preschool, mentally retarded children: Interim report. *Exceptional Children*, 1966, **33**, 215–220.

U.S. Department of Health, Education, and Welfare, Office of Child Development. *Project Head Start 1968: The development of a program.* Washington, D.C.: U.S. Government Printing Office, October 1970.

Weikart, D. P. *Preliminary results from a longitudinal study of disadvantaged preschool children.* ERIC Document Ed 030-490, 1967.

Weikart, D. P. A comparative study of three preschool curricula. Paper presented at the meeting of the Society for Research in Child Development. Santa Monica, Calif., March, 1969.

Williams, W., and Evans, J. W. The politics of evaluation: The case of Head Start. *The Annals of the American Academy of Political and Social Science*, 1969, **385**, 118–132.

PRICE COBBS

The Black Revolution and Education

*"Black people have always felt implicitly that getting an education
could somehow make them a little less black. . . . Recently, however,
many black people have come to the realization that education has been
used to prevent them from attaining full citizenship.*

Education used to be thought of as such a quiet and sedentary profession. Now in these turbulent times, it is almost impossible to believe that only a short while ago people were accused of going into a career in teaching so they could avoid the real world. In fact, the change has been so drastic that I did not know whether to come to this meeting wearing a bulletproof vest, or looking as if I was carrying a Molotov cocktail.

These are perilous times in which to speak. If a person speaks too passionately about the problems of his time, he is labeled as alienated from the society and, therefore, unqualified to speak critically about it. On the other hand, if he does not raise his voice in at least some anger, there is another voice saying that he is not involving himself in the struggle, that he has no moral integrity—that he has sold out.

With everyone, including educators, saying that they do not know why schools have become such a focus for the Black Revolution, I think it is time to spell out in some detail what has happened, as I understand it. I should like to analyze why the Black Movement has rushed into the halls of academia.

Why have groups of people who have heretofore been labeled friends now been labeled enemies? What has been the process by which the teacher and school administrator now find themselves in the eye of an increasingly mounting storm? As always, we must look to history, recent and remote, to better understand that which is happening around us.

Americans, including educators, are reluctant to took at the past. We are a nation of fast movers, of future seekers, and to look back, even under the cover of scholarship, is at times to invite charges that one is not forward-seeking.

The end of 1968 found me, along with countless other Americans, enveloped by melancholia. Americans demonstrated during that year that they still were not ready to solve our pressing social problems. We saw the war in Vietnam continue to go on, reminding the world of our immorality. During 1968, black people continued to press their demands and continued to feel that too little was

From the *National Association of Secondary School Principals Bulletin*, 1969, **53**, 3–18. Reprinted by permission of the author and the publisher.

being done. During 1968, we saw our noble black advocate, Martin Luther King, assassinated. He had counseled patience and faith and his voice was stilled by the very violence that he sought to prevent. We saw the assassination of Robert Kennedy, who, whatever his deficiencies, was attempting to align himself with the forces of change. During 1968, we saw black students from college to elementary school confronting teachers, administrators, and school boards and asking for an education that was relevant to their lives. And, with all of this, the majority of people kept talking about the law and order and adhering to the status quo.

But if we are to truly understand 1968, we must take a look back into our recent past. Black people have for over 100 years been asking for change. Now we see black people and their oppressed allies turning to the institutions of education and asking for change. And people look at each other and ask why they are doing this.

Education—A Fickle Mistress

Few bewildered and angry white Americans seem to know that education has long been a fickle mistress to black Americans. The institutions of education, from elementary school to graduate programs, have promised so terribly much and delivered so painfully little. Because of great promises, education has been spared when other institutions of this country have come under scrutiny. There was always the frequently acknowledged feeling that somehow an education, any kind of education, would help that painful transformation into full Americans.

Black people have always felt implicitly that getting an education could somehow make them a little less black. More than a little magical thinking has been behind the belief that to get an education was to be cleaner, more responsible, and less like the stereotype of a black person. Along with so many endeavors in the life of black Americans, getting an education became also the moral and virtuous thing to do. The black man thus needed an education so that he would be ready to prove his responsibility and thereby attain full citizenship.

Education for Slavery

Recently, however, many black people have come to the realization that education has been used to prevent them from attaining full citizenship. The process began during slavery when the education of bondsmen quickly became yet another tool for dominating them. Early slavemasters quickly learned that to provide a slave with an education, however meager, was to stir a dormant curiosity which could lead to hopes and yearnings for freedom. In order to prevent this possibility, education became a very practical and utilitarian instrument in the institution of slavery, and the educating of slaves could no more be left to chance than any other aspect of their existence.

If a slave needed to read and write to carry out the business of his master, he was taught to read and write just to that extent. Book learning was parceled out to few slaves and only to the extent that it saved the master from an unpleasant or tedious chore. The same was true for other aspects of knowledge. If the job of a particular slave demanded the understanding of elementary addition and subtraction, then what could be taught was just elementary addition and subtraction. The rudiments of an education could be received, but only to the precise point that it had maximal value to an owner and not one step further. Beyond that precise point lay the danger that an education would have more value to the slave than to the master, and a mind might be unshackled only to begin plotting escape.

Those caught in the cruel institution of slavery evolved their own method of education. Information was passed on by a vast apprentice system which functioned from generation to generation. This system of apprenticeship began when the slave was born, and became crucial at the age of five or six when the child went out to the fields or into the master's home. The odious chores of slavery were learned by doing, and to survive physically and psychologically the young child had to learn a great deal in a very short time. To be a slave and not learn all the nuances of one's job at an early age was to invite death. That many young slaves lived and worked refutes the popularly held white idea that black kids can't learn.

The use of education as a tool to control black people continued as the prime model when slavery ceased. The Emancipation Proclamation purported to free the slaves, but it sharpened a dilemma for white Americans. Frantically waiting to take their places as citizens were several million ex-slaves who were like helpless pawns in a game of someone else's choosing. Whatever means the white man chose for deliverance and, hence, assimilation would surely indicate whether freeing the slaves was an act that had resulted from the outraged conscience of America or had occurred because slavery was outmoded and too expensive. To be apprenticed into the halls of business and finance would have demonstrated a much different commitment than being allowed to remain as sharecroppers and tenant farmers. The intermediate step of entering growing industries as skilled and unskilled workers would have revealed some intention of white Americans to truly share some of the fruits of this society with black Americans. But the solution to the dilemma was delayed to the present, and the white American betrayed the shallowness of his commitment by turning to the education of blacks not as a primary task but as the only task.

A Society Reflected in Its Schools

One needs no evidence to prove that the freed slaves were ignorant and in need of an education. Over 200 years of bondage had prepared them for survival in a cruel system but had hardly prepared them to flourish. There is no doubt that schools were among the basic needs of newly freed slaves. But if there is truth in the dictum that one sees a society, its magnificence and flaws, reflected in its schools, then the postslavery schools established for blacks were harsh mirrors. The proliferation of segregated black schools introduced a jarring note of reality that white America was committed—if not dedicated—to a segregated society. The formation of Negro colleges and other educational institutions in the Reconstruction period laid bare the fact that only the visible institution of slavery was dead. The thought processes and rationalizations which allowed slavery to endure were turned to new tasks.

Of all the jobs needing attention, why the focus on education and education alone? Few businesses were started and subsidized, and the little land that was apportioned was quickly retaken by force. Any pathways by which black Americans could ultimately join the rest of America were blocked. The sad truth is that the black schools of the nineteenth century taught millions of black Americans to read and write and, once beyond that, the educational effort became a means to try to make blacks somehow more respectable and serviceable to white Americans. The foundation of Negro education was reinforced by the belief— held to this day—that white people are inherently superior to black people. That there have been profoundly dedicated teachers, white and black, who have tried to alter this belief and could not only serves to remind us of the tenacity of this belief.

The history of this country demonstrates that no sizeable group of immigrants has risen to power, either economic or political, solely via the educational route. Since these are the two main constellations of power in this country, the decision to focus on education for the ex-slaves was, underneath, a decision to keep them powerless.

Washington and DuBois

Generations of Americans, black and white, have castigated Booker T. Washington as a hopeless Uncle Tom. But the hindsight of history teaches that the villains are few who do not exploit thoughts and feelings present in the majority of the population. Washington was truly a man of his time who had a finely tuned antenna, listening for what whites wanted to hear and then feeding it back. Whites wanted blacks to stay to themselves, teach themselves, and receive ample training to be of service to whites. What better way to insure this and have a minimum of agitation than by a control on the philosophy and direction of the education of blacks? Those few blacks who understood this and raised their voices to prevent it were in no position to effect a change, and there was scant white support from which they could draw allies. The virtues of a classical education may have been apparent to all, but these virtues have continued to be of little use to most black Americans. That Washington seemed to feel the same way about a classical education certainly demonstrated that he was shortsighted, but the negative labels might more appropriately be applied to his white supporters. He may have been guilty of too vigorously enforcing the mandates of white men, but he can hardly be accused of having misread the currents of his time. Many of those who now cry loudest that Booker T. Washington was a flagrant sellout to his race forget that white America was not at that time, nor at this, ready to truly educate its black citizens. The same educational establishment which later tried to disinherit him was previously only too glad to have him as a stalking horse.

W. E. B. DuBois will ultimately be rewarded well by history for his many scholarly contributions, but he remains for black Americans their most visible symbol of the failure of education. He took a route that white America had decreed the avenue by which all unfortunate blacks could attain equality. He possessed a superb mind, and he used it to secure an education. Starting from a poor background, he obtained a classical education with a doctorate from one of America's foremost universities. He possessed the qualities that black people were exhorted to strive for: He was respectable, urbane, and responsible, and his skin color was light enough to make him almost acceptable to whites.

As if this were not enough, DuBois studied in Europe and became even more whitened. He became a connoisseur of good food and fine wines and a devotee of the theater and opera. During all this time, he was honing his intellect and using it in serious and scholarly studies as did few of his contemporaries. Upon returning to his native land, he must have felt somewhere inside a personal triumph in breaking barriers and in the feeling that he would be personally accepted. What a shock this magnificently educated man must have felt when he was rejected by those very institutions of education which had previously encouraged him. He had done all they said to do and had done even more, but still they rejected him because he was black. That he continued to have a productive career after the trauma of such a primary rejection speaks probably of a mind that through the ages has had few equals.

During his career, DuBois continued to experience the occupational misfortune of the visionary by being ahead of his time. Just as he had secured an education and had exploded the myth that America would then accept him, he advanced ideas about his people that few were willing to accept. He drew from the infant discipline of sociology and showed how black Americans were the unfortunate victims of history and an oppressive society, and were not the lazy and indolent primitives so dear to the minds of racists. He made the mistake of proposing an intellectual aristocracy of black people when the country was scarcely prepared to tolerate an intellectual aristocracy of whites. But, ultimately, DuBois may have fallen victim to his own soaring intellect and scholarship. He must have known that the earliest schools taught the children of nobility to wage war and to govern, and the schools established to teach blacks did neither.

In whatever direction his inquisitive mind took him, he found blocks to himself personally and hypocrisy about professed American ideals. We can only speculate that his later disenchantment with the American system was in partial response to his disillusionment in ever being such an idealist as to think that American schools were truly interested in the education of black people.

Black Idealism and Disillusionment

Every perceptive study of education repeats in some manner the truism that schools are designed to train the children of a society to participate in the work of that society. They serve less to impart knowledge about a nation than to impart attitudes about that nation. Schools serve to teach some that they are perpetual followers and to teach others that they are ordained leaders. In post-bellum America, they were ideally suited to help black Americans repeat idealistic slogans about democracy but never share its fruits.

The wrenching and constricting idealism so characteristic of black Americans has been reinforced by the school experience. Birthdays of American heroes who have borne no relationship to black people have been celebrated, while authentic black heroes have been forgotten. Black children have learned of the birth of this country, the early settlers, the magnificent currents of American history without even a footnote about the contributions of their forebears. They have been offered courses of instruction that, once moving beyond the rudiments of simple reading, writing, and arithmetic, have borne not the slightest reference to anything in their lives or the lives of those around them.

Black people have suffered greatly in the schools of this country. They have suffered most in schools, because it has been in them that the greatest unkept promises have been made. Many times, an education has done little more than open yearnings which this country is not yet prepared to satisfy.

But American education for whites has not been static and has responded and changed as the needs of the country altered. As the nation became more industrial and immigrants poured to these shores, it fell to education to Americanize the new arrivals. This was no altruistic decision dictated by starry-eyed patriots, but a necessary response to an emergency situation. The rapidly growing industries of the country needed American workers with American attitudes and American skills for American profits. The educational directives may have been differently phrased, but this necessity underlay the cry that went out. Expanded schools, night hours, classes in English, apprentice programs in an endless variety of trades, all attest to the response to a challenge. And in studying this period in American education, we can see why education for black people has failed so miserably up to this time.

In this society, the demands of business and commerce have determined to a large extent the direction of education. Education in this country achieved its finest hour when called upon to fill the factories and plants of an expanding economy. For all this moralizing and pretense, every captain of industry has known that education in this country is an appendage which can be directed and controlled by outside forces. That blacks came so belatedly to this realization once again points out that they remain the most idealistic of Americans.

In the period of this country's greatest industrial expansion, white America demanded workers—white workers—and it got them. In contrast, the response of America to its uneducated blacks was at first to establish agricultural and mechanical schools and later to act as if the education offered by these schools was adequate. In the South of the Reconstruction era, commercial interests demanded that blacks remain as docile and unobtrusive as possible so as not to hinder profits; the education of blacks throughout the nation today continues to reflect this policy.

Education–A Means of Deliverance

As the country has grown, blacks have continued to focus on education as a means of deliverance. As the population shifted from rural to urban and from southern to northern, the demand for an education remained unchecked. This demand would not seem so curious if the same amount of energy had been expended by both blacks and whites for better housing, black industries, and voting power. It was as if a great store of feeling had to be directed toward something innocuous, much as a priest or minister is called to talk to a man about to jump from a building. And always the black American continued with his idealism mixed with optimism, undergirded by cynicism and depression about his chances of ever making it into the mainstream.

In the face of a reality that pointed in a different direction, black people have been admonished always to continue seeking deliverance by getting educated. Whatever their problems, they have been told that an education would solve them. The two world wars should have convinced all with eyes to see that the black man's fixation on education was diversionary. Wars bring out the best and worst in the front-line soldier and in the people on the home front.

In the society at large, the excitement of an emergency has a way of stripping away much pretense. Jobs that blacks had been repeatedly told were not theirs because of educational inadequacies were suddenly available, and they were filled by blacks. Uneducated black men and women poured into major cities and began working on assembly lines in aircraft factories and in shipyards. And all of this happened without benefit of the very education that black people had been told was such a deficiency. In other instances, training programs were set up to prepare workers quickly for a particular task. Whereas black people had been told that to perform a certain job required years of preparation and training, they discovered that training could be finished in a matter of weeks. Whereas blacks had been rebuffed and told they needed years of preparation to perform a simple task, they were literally pulled off the streets and cajoled into performing. In the services, the same thing was happening. So-called white occupations were suddenly blackened when it was discovered that the only people around to fill them were black.

An old black woman recalled her years at a defense plant during World War II. She moved from the South to a large city, uneducated and looking for work. She quickly went to a defense plant, expecting to be placed in the cafeteria, and found herself in a training class for riveters. After a minimum of training, she found herself on the assembly line placing rivets in airplanes. Everytime she read or heard of a plane crash, there would be a curious mixture of feeling.

She would first experience an intense personal guilt; then she would begin laughing and thinking, "Serves them white folks right for trying to make a riveter out of black-assed me."

Effect of World War II

The end of World War II may have finally begun the process of dissipating the fantasy of the black American that an education would make him free. Black soldiers returned home as eagerly as anyone else, and the GI bill allowed them to go to school in greater numbers. Then the message began to seep in, that few changes were going to be made. The endless rhetoric about democracy that was needed to prepare a people to wage war had been more for enemy consumption and was again ignored on the home front. At some point during this time, with many minds still freshly wrung by the horrors and trauma of war, a scrutiny of education was begun.

Previous generations of college-educated blacks had privately joked about a black person in college taking chemistry or business as a major; but after a war in which large numbers of blacks fought and died, the jokes became even more hollow. The safety valve of turning to teaching became increasingly useless as black college graduates attempted to find jobs outside the South. There was always a certain fatalism present when there was the knowledge of being the last hired and first fired, but the anger moved much closer to the surface when it became more evident that there were fewer jobs for which to be hired.

Black people have a sure wisdom nurtured by centuries of oppression: Whenever neighborhoods are ravaged, jobs are abolished, and when experiments in human engineering collapse, they know long before anyone else who the victims will be.

Empty Promises Recognized

During the decade following the World War II, some of the empty promises of education began to lose their ability to placate even a patient people, and the anger nurtured by long-suppressed reality began to emerge. This anger began to rise with the long-denied realization that there had been a massive hoax. It was a hoax that began early in slavery and continued on to plague black Americans: the indoctrination of black people to believe that education would qualify them for full acceptance as Americans. Black Americans with an education finally began that painful process of looking at themselves and seeing that a cynical America had played a cruel trick on them. In their idealism and faith in this country, a certain blindness had been created which prevented them from observing that which was around them. For much of the life of this country, the schools of this country took European immigrants and called them imperfect Americans. They accepted this designation in the hope that the process of education would transform them into Americans. This worked for most, and after one or two generations of attending American schools and eliminating Old World customs and names, the process was complete.

But black people, including those with an education, continued to stand outside waiting to be invited in. A rage began to rise—increasingly directed at education—as blacks came to see the obscene discrepancy between America's treatment of the European immigrant and its treatment of them. Where the immigrant was viewed as an imperfect American, the black American was characteristically seen by the educational establishment as an imperfect white person. Going to school could Americanize, but it could not change pigmentation and did not change the thought that white is inherently superior to black. Once the veil began to be lifted, the black American started to see that a major aim of the educational process was to make him more white—an impossibility. At times, the frenzied search for an education became as suicidal as a moth's repeatedly crashing into a incandescent light. One could get an education and more education and more education, but to the majority of the population you were still a nigger.

Casualties on the Altar of Education

The lore of black life is filled with instances attesting to the numerous casualties on the altar of education. Post offices throughout the country are filled with educated black men and women with higher degrees than their white co-workers —many of them cynical and despondent after the long years of being unable to find the work they had spent years educating themselves for.

The boy recalled a peculiar incident. His physician father had many friends who would occasionally stop by. They would be in the city for a convention or vacation or just passing through. On one occasion, a man visited who was "running on the road." This meant that he was a dining car waiter, a high calling for depression-era blacks. The boy recalled that the man had a particularly reticent and distraught quality. As he sat and talked, the physician father kept referring to the man as a classmate—although this seemed strange, for the man clearly did not work at his chosen calling. After a rather hurried dinner, the man looked at his watch, gave thanks, and left. His leaving seemed to trigger a strange gloom in the boy's father. Years later when the boy had grown to manhood and had chosen the calling of his father, the incident became clear. The young physician was seeing a patient who kept muttering, "There but for the grace of God go I."

The time immediately after the war was a period of awakening for vast numbers of blacks. Deteriorated buildings, overcrowded classrooms, and inexperienced and underpaid teachers all pointed to the sad conclusion that white people had never been serious about the education of black children. Hand-me-down textbooks borrowed from white schools across town, if they did nothing more, pointed out a certain system of priorities. And as more and more Americans scrutinized school systems, they found that blindness and sterility had affected all schools—white and black alike. Looking at schools finally resulted in the discovery that they were often a joke for white students as well as black students. What at one time had at least been a place of refuge had never really educated, and now had ceased even to comfort.

Then on May 17, 1954, the Supreme Court of the United States ruled on "separate but equal" education. After close to a century of justifying the travesty of black education, the dam, it was thought, had been cracked. And if the speed of the needed changes did not satisfy the early ebullience, it was still a landmark decision which continues to affect American education. Black and white parents for the first time began to look at the schools attended by their children, and their vision became more clear.

Education Has Condoned Inhumanity

Now blacks are directing rage at schools with the same intensity as that formerly reserved for bus stations in dusty southern towns. The startling and frightening realization has come that they are both the same. If society promises a man a job and then reneges, in his anger he turns to the streets to burn and loot and take what he feels is his. That innocent victims are in the way shows how we all share, however passively, in the inhumanity of society. And the institutions of education have been surpassed by none in condoning that inhumanity. Where the police department has been a repressive force for keeping blacks in line, the educational establishment has been a tranquilizer for lulling them into a foolish sense of security.

Just as the unemployed laborer eventually settles on his enemy, the school child and his parents are now settling on their enemy. The battlefield has shifted, but the underlying anger is the same. Many black parents are now saying this school which has stood so imposing and remote, which has promised my kids that it would transform them, has lied to me. These teachers who have grinned at me and patronized me and insulted me have lied to me. And now, I will be lied to no more.

First in college, and now even in elementary school, black students are also saying that they will be lied to no more. They at last realize the duplicity of the American educational system, and the intensity of their reaction can be likened to that of a scorned and discarded lover.

Yet, people in the educational establishment look up with bewilderment and protest their good faith and intentions. We are trying, they say. Give us time. But young black Americans are now repaying their eternal mistress education for all her past indiscretions and infidelities.

Now we have reached a historic moment in the life of this country. Education is being assaulted by those who are asking for change. For those of you who revere the American Revolution and, yet, incongruously feel that America is forever sealed off from change, I have a message: Right now, in the midst of modern-day America, we are experiencing a major social revolution. Black Americans are undergoing psychological changes of the most profound implications, and the wonder is that up till now it has been so peaceful.

If truth is the goal of any scholarly inquiry, we must honestly, though sadly, conclude that too few white Americans are really changing their fundamental attitudes and beliefs. Many of our leaders, including those in education, who are now talking about violence, are in reality causing the very violence they profess to deplore. To tell one portion of the population to remain static while the other part is changing is to invite a holocaust. The way to avoid violence is to appeal to the instincts for change—to facilitate change rather than to resist it. If there is a streak of violence insinuated into the national character, it is there because there have always been elements in this country which have set themselves in opposition to change. To resist necessary and healthy change in America today is to incite violence and riots, the blame for which will probably then be laid at the feet of black militants.

Powerful Forces Unleashed

Black Americans are now responding to their moment in history and can no more be stopped than can an overflowing stream. We have been bred with the words of freedom, but immersed in bigotry and oppression. The winds of change are adrift in the minds of black Americans, and they are as powerful as the forces at the Alamo which directed men to fight to the death. We, who have been rebuked and scorned, are now fighting our battles and they are not in Khe Sanh, but in the schools of America.

Black people and their oppressed allies have finally joined a revolution. When we ask for black studies, black curricula, black faculty, more black students, we are asking that this primary institution of our culture speak directly to the needs of the black community, as it has to other communities.

We must have a revolutionary change in the national character of this country if black people are to survive, and the educational establishment must participate in this. We must immediately change the way Americans perceive themselves and others. Black survival demands that, either willingly or unwillingly, institutions of education reflect our heritage, our contributions, our pride. Black survival, and perhaps the survival of this country, demands that black be exalted in this country—that white people and white institutions reflect that Black is Beautiful.

Finally, the American Revolution has been joined by black people. And we now intend to force America to make good its promise to be a melting pot where all are respected and honored. In resolving the issues of the day, we realize at long last that the piecemeal approach can no longer serve us.

I am asked to renounce black anti-Semitism—and I do—fully and with no reservations, but the equation does not stop there. What about those of you who personally and professionally have never renounced white anti-Semitism and white racism?

We Must Change the National Character

We must now ask that educators join the revolution and demand that the institution of education—the keeper of tradition—move on to the truly revolutionary task of a radical mutation of the American national character. We must ask that educators renounce curricula and teachers who follow too closely the racist traditions of this country, and that they renounce governors who get elected by exploiting educational and racial unrest and then talk of keeping schools open by bayonet. We now ask you to attack the superpatriots who demand repression and, yet, have never responded to any demands, however mild, for change. And I ask that you listen carefully to college presidents who now advocate law and order, while referring to legitimate black voices as kooks and yahoos.

The lesson of Ocean Hill, Brownsville, San Francisco State College, Columbia, Berkeley, and Prince George's County is that we must change the national character of this country from its original white Anglo-Saxon Protestant outdated model to something that reflects all America. Anything less is to repeat the lessons of history's losers and not survive. We must radically alter the national character of this country so that when one thinks of an American he will no longer think just of a white American, but also of a black American, an oriental American, a Mexican-American. Educators at this very convention can start this process by asking that the birthdays of Martin Luther King and Malcolm X be national and school holidays.

I wish that there was some way I could offer a tranquilizer and say that change is not needed, but by doing so I would be untrue to my people and my profession. I wish that I could come to you as "a responsible Negro" and tell you that everything is going to be all right, but there are now few in our ranks who can honestly say to anyone that everything is going to be all right. There is an emergency in this land.

In this season of change, with a new Administration in Washington, the institutions of education can side with oppressed people and ask for very specific things. We can ask that Brotherhood Week be changed to "Racial Confrontation Week." We must no longer dread the confrontation but push it, so that people can be transformed. The educational process must be shifted in school so that every class at every grade level will discuss feelings, starting with feelings about race. We must make this nation one vast encounter group, dedicated and committed to immediate change—to a radical transformation of the national character. All schools such as those where you work should devote an entire semester to discussing nothing but race. Business and commerce must show change by dropping all barriers and admitting black people into their ranks.

There are no more psychological tricks blacks can play upon themselves to make it possible to exist in dreadful circumstances—

no more lies to tell themselves
no more dreams to fix on
no more opiates to dull the pain
no more patience
no more thought
no more reason

—only a welling tide risen out of all those terrible years of grief, now a tidal wave of fury and rage, and it's all black, black, as night.

"For unless man puts an end to this damnable sin,
He will put the world in a flame—
What a shame."

EDWARD K. WEAVER

The New Literature on Education of the Black Child

During the 1960s a "new" literature emerged based on a concern for the education of the disadvantaged, and especially compensatory education for black ghetto children. This literature has been written mostly by whites and, to some extent, is directed toward white audiences. Funding for the programs and projects has come from both private and public sectors, and the programs are usually directed by white professionals. The purpose of this article is to try and answer the following questions:

1. Are the books about the education of the black ghetto child too hurriedly written? Do they have overall value?

2. Why is the problem of educating black ghetto children being brought to the public at this time if, as implied by the "new" literature, the condition has existed for thirty or more years?

3. Does what is presented in these books reflect a form of planned retardation for black ghetto children on the parts of boards of education?

4. Inasmuch as these books were written about the education of the black ghetto child in the northern urban ghetto, should comparative studies be made of the black child in the North as against the South?

Attempts to answer these questions will be in a holistic frame—that is, all four questions will be dealt with at once. At the end of the analysis, specific answers will be given for each question. The following assumptions operate as hypotheses or biases in the remainder of this article.

1. Compensatory education (education of the disadvantaged, for the culturally deprived) is a "cop-out" of educators to cover up the poor quality of education and the inadequately staffed and housed schools which have been afforded low-income and minority-group children.

2. The deprivation theory, proposed in the "new" literature, and the programs for black ghetto children place the blame on the black children and their parents and thereby free the school systems, the communities, and the society from sharing the responsibility.

3. The history of neglect of the education of low-income pupils and of superior provisions for the advantaged has frozen low-income pupils into social classes, and handicapped them for life.

4. Cultural deprivation has been a conscious policy and is still a major factor excluding black children and youth from appreciating, gaining, or becoming able

Reprinted by permission of the author and *Freedomways* magazine, Vol. 8, No. 4, 1968, published at 799 Broadway, New York City.

to utilize the full potentials of public education—the major factor perpetuating this situation is white racism as applied to the black poor.

5. The compensatory education programs for the black ghetto child are too little, too late, and are based on theories of colonialism, dependency, power, and have been inordinately influenced by the conditions which private and public funding agencies stipulate as bases for obtaining grants. Very little funding comes directly from the public school systems themselves.

6. Many of the programs are segregated (Educational Improvement Programs, Head Start, Follow-Up, and the like) and are designed as a sop to black people. They are artificially induced and die when funds cease.

7. Compensatory education programs for black ghetto children help to salve and ease the conscience of white citizens by making them believe that something significant is being done for black people.

In 1492 Columbus sailed the ocean blue and "discovered" America—that is, white Europeans first learned that an America existed. In less than four centuries these white Catholics and WASPs (white Anglo-Saxon Protestants) had stolen the land from the red "savages," driven them onto the reservations, brought millions of black slaves from Africa, and turned the South into the biggest brothel in the history of mankind. In the 1960s the black ghetto child was "discovered" and a "new" rapidly advancing specialized field of education was invented—compensatory education for the disadvantaged. A rash of books and articles, mostly written by whites, emerged. The wretched, the black poor, the black alienated, the black misfits had been "discovered."

For purposes of this article some 75 books and more than 250 articles were reviewed. Only a few, prototypes, will be specified. The overall reaction to the "new" literature is that it is full of debate about unclarified issues. Much of the debate is about the proper designation of the area (the deprived, the disadvantaged, the alienated, the wretched, the poor, or, as one individual puts it, the depraved). Another persistent issue is whether the education of black ghetto types should be considered as a separate area of specialization within the broad spectrum of education or whether it should be considered as a problem which resides within each of the already well-established areas or fields of concern and interest in education.

This article will not deal with the universe of controversial problems that educators now begin to call problems of the education of disadvantaged children and youth. Special problems of disadvantage which groups such as Mexicans, Indians, poor whites, and others encounter in the American democratic society will not be dealt with. For a central thesis of this paper is that solution of the problems of the black people in the United States and elsewhere will, at the same time, solve the problems of all the oppressed and exploited peoples in the United States. When black Americans are free and equal and have been liberated, all Americans will have freedom, equality, and liberty. For the United States has become a racist and separatist society—separate for black and separate for white.

The black people in the United States have been studied and manipulated more than any other group of Americans. Most masters and doctoral studies conducted by black scholars have dealt with aspects of the "Negro problem." Thousands of books and articles have been written about the black people in the United States. Much of this literature was produced by black sociologists, anthropologists, economists, social workers, historians, psychologists, and educators such as W. E. B. DuBois, Horace Mann Bond, Charles S. Johnson and his colleagues, Carter G. Woodson and his colleagues, Ira De A. Reid, E. Franklin Frazier, Hylan Lewis, Lawrence D. Reddick, Ralph Bunche, Rayford Logan, Doxey A. Wilkerson, St. Clair Drake, Herman Long, Preston and Bonita Valien, Allison Davis, Mozell Hill, Kenneth B. Clark. The essential point here is that the "new" literature on the education of the black ghetto child ignores this literature. It also ignores literature and research such as the Carnegie Corporation-sponsored comprehensive study of the Negro in the United States, which Gunnar Myrdal, a Swedish social economist, summarized in *An American Dilemma*. The "new" literature, in ignoring this vast scientific literature about the black people, has no roots, and indeed, sets out to be "new" by deliberately operating as if it is a new field.

When the "new" literature is read, then one who is already sophisticated in the problems and proposed solutions for the black people concludes that the "new" literature is for uninitiated whites who must be convinced that it is now necessary to do something about the poor quality of education for black children. One feels somewhat like Kenneth B. Clark whose perceptive comment before the National Advisory Commission on Civil Disorders (the Kerner Report) stated: ". . . in candor . . . a kind of Alice in Wonderland—with the same moving picture reshown over and over again, the same analysis, the same recommendations, and the same inaction."

On the other hand, there are some serious studies and reports which seek to deal directly with the past literature and the present situation. The work of Kvaraceus (*Dynamics of Delinquency*), of Frost and Hawkes (*The Disadvantaged Child*), of Bereiter and Englemann (*Teaching Disadvantaged Children in the Preschool*), of Riessman (*The Culturally Deprived Child*), and even the Kozol documentary (*Death at an Early Age*) of "the destruction of the hearts and minds of Negro children in the Boston Public Schools" are clearly and forcefully written, and one reads these with a sense of ease and familiarity, and of identification with the material. It is almost as if one already knows or has experienced this and the book merely synthesizes or sharply specifies—or as if one has read this somewhere sometime before. Only a very, very few of the white writers of the "new" literature have the insight, capacity, or creativity to write in this way. To repeat, the "new" literature is new only for the uninitiated, the newcomer, the still uncertain white.

More basic and more useful are the works of Arthur Pearl and Frank Riessman (*New Careers for the Poor*), based primarily on the study and research at the Howard University Institute for Youth Studies, of Edmund W. Gordon and Doxey A. Wilkerson at Yeshiva University (*Compensatory Education for the Disadvantaged*), and of Harry L. Miller (*Education for the Disadvantaged*). *New Careers* is potentially one of the most provocative, sophisticated, and significant books to emerge from the plethora of the "new" literature in its specification and demonstration of what can be done, efficiently and quickly. The Gordon-Wilkerson book is the most comprehensive analysis and evaluation of programs and practices in compensatory education from preschool through college which is available at this time. Yeshiva also publishes the IRCD Bulletin (Information Retrieval Center on the Disadvantaged), which with ERIC (Education Retrieval and Information Center) and some other potential sources makes possible consideration of cognitive and affective dimensions of behavior as a single process. The Miller book, *Education for the Disadvantaged*, is one of a series intended to cope with the information explosion affecting all of the arts and sciences and is a substitute for a bibliographical guide to the current literature—it is one of the more comprehensive analyses of current issues and research on education for the disadvantaged.

One of the factors involved in the rash of "new" literature on the education of the black ghetto child is the dilemma of the white missionary type. Peace Corps, Vista Corps, and Teacher Corps now attract the middle-class white youth who are dedicated and consecrated, and they have increasingly supplanted the WASP missionary types who are not quite as welcome in the Near and Far East, in Latin America, in Africa, or in the slums. What is left for white professionals? The education of the black Americans. "Discovery" of the black ghetto child and proliferation of a special educational enterprise for the disadvantaged is a financially attractive endeavor, for very large sums of money are now available from both the public and private sectors for the compensatory education of the black ghetto children and youth. Moreover, the Education Professions Development Act (EPDA) will make even larger sums available for educating disadvantaged at all levels.

The following is indicative of this kind of concern. The Atlanta Constitution under the general headline for a series "Educating the Disadvantaged" stated under the headline (August 12, 1968) "Project Headstart Lifts Slum Children":

> *Modern educators have decided the best way to attack the problems of educating the disadvantaged child is* with preschool programs designed to eliminate the causes of his deprivation. Leading the field in the race to educate children before the ravages of poverty become irreversible is the federal government's massive Project Headstart. *(Emphasis mine.)*

On August 13, 1968, under the head "City to Test Learning in Pre-School Years," the following appeared:

> *Atlanta school officials have decided the time has come to institute programs designed to measure the effects of preschool education on disadvantaged youth.* As a result the city school system this year will participate in the federally sponsored Project Follow-Through, *an attempt to give deprived children in the primary grades the same specialized care provided by the summer Head Start Program (Emphasis mine.)*

In passing, it should be indicated that only 225 of the thousands of children who will attend the Atlanta Public Schools (preschool, early childhood, kindergarten, and first grades) will be given this follow-through treatment. It was stated that school officials indicated that the school system will not have the funds itself to accomodate all of the city's disadvantaged children and the project will be regarded as in the "pilot stage" and take place in two "Negro" elementary schools. The objectives of this program, typical of hundreds all over the United States, are:

1. To help each child develop intellectually by providing programs designed to compensate for his deprivation.

2. To help each child develop socially by relating the contents of subject matter to attitudes and behavior.

3. To help each child avoid losing the benefits of his education by including parents as active members of the educational program.

4. The main purpose is to help each child (to teach each child) to be an independent learner. The model for the sequential program of instruction is that developed by Dr. Lassar G. Gotkin of New York University.

Miller, in *Education for the Disadvantaged*, indicates that programs for the disadvantaged may be criticized on the grounds that they do not emphasize what should be emphasized, and they are uncreative. However, the reviewers go further and state that this does not constitute the most serious charge which may be leveled against them. Educators tend to become concerned with outcomes (changes in behavior?) which are long delayed or even unmeasurable. The "new" literature and the programs they describe, such as the Educational Improvement Projects funded by Ford, are so anxious to see success for their expensive efforts and to justify the millions of dollars which are involved that the directors and advisory committees become strongly committed to whatever the project or program is alleged to be about. Moreover, the agency personnel responsible for the large grants are also strongly desirous of success for efforts and for results which may be interpreted as successful. Consequently, glowing reports are written about the effectiveness of the programs for the disadvantaged, but very little data are collected or published which specify how changes in behavior are induced or even the actual changes which accrue to the children as they participate in the program. Changes are reported in general mass data based on tests which may or may not be germane to the children, or their ghetto experience.

Moreover, very few teachers and even fewer administrators are prepared to believe that the one-group procedure, which is so consistently used, should be abandoned. This procedure gives such very poor evidence of program effectiveness. The result is that the "new" literature presents, as yet, very, very few reasonable grounds for the many claims and allegations of causal connections between improvement and procedure. There is an alarming lack of the classical required and necessary effort for control and comparison in the "new" literature and in the programs for the disadvantaged. Dr. Doxey A. Wilkerson, in *Education for the Disadvantaged*, identifies this deficit this way:

The research evaluation of any program of compensatory education would seem to require (a) precise description of the educational experiences involved, (b) clear formulation of hypotheses concerning the effects of specified and controlled pragmatic activities, (c) definition of appropriate tests of such hypotheses, and (d) collection and interpretation of relevant data through technically adequate procedures. Most of the studies here reviewed do not satisfy any of these requirements, and their infirmities are less pronounced than those of many other investigations not selected for review. As a consequence, currently available research in this field typically reports ambiguous outcomes of unknown or amorphous educational variables.

The result is that much of the "new" literature and, perhaps many of the programs for the disadvantaged, are based on naive, perhaps even intuitive, decisions and programming. This possibly accounts for many of the contradictory and premature conceptual bases and trends which the "new" literature reflects. It is also quite likely that, since a very, very few of the programs and/or projects are directed at the decision- and policy-making level by black professionals, some of the contradictory and premature aspects of education for the deprived are due to inadequate experience, identification with, or insightful understanding of the victims of compensatory education.

The most pervasive and significant of the influences on education for the black ghetto child now appears to be due to the changes which black people are making in themselves, and which they are introducing into the society. The white racists have believed that white is right and that whites can do anything they choose. The white racists still believe that they have the right to spoil things or make things right. It is this arrogance which black people now challenge, and more and more it is stated that this arrogance is what had led us into Vietnam, and is responsible for what has been done to the liberation movements all over the world, and to the liberation movement of black people here at home. Today more and more black people believe that there is no real desire or sincere program for basic social change.

Most black people cannot understand why so many white people do not accept the Kerner Report which said that the United States is a racist society. More and more black people dislike the fact that black people are still being asked to side with white people who think that if the blacks went a little slower or if they didn't express their anger, more would be accomplished. And all those cliches bug black people, like "We did it, why can't you?" or "What do you people *really* want?" When white people say "Hasn't there been a great deal of progress in the past few years?" the black man says, "Yes, there has been a little. But I don't have to settle for a little."

So, perhaps the most significant factor influencing present concern over the education of the black ghetto children and youth is now coming out into the open. For some, the summer programs and swimming pools and other activities are seen as not only a "cooling down" operation, but also as a blind alley, a kind of miasma or form of planned retardation, and as a sop to the conscience of whites. Martin Luther King, Jr., and now Ralph Abernathy, Stokely Carmichael, H. Rap Brown, LeRoi Jones, Malcolm X, the hippie movement growing out of white youth participation in SCLC in Mississippi, Resurrection City, and the black nationalist movement have all made the white man aware. A large part of this awareness is the explosion of the 400-year-old myth of the "good nigger." It also is due to discovery that many black people don't even have pity for the white racists.

There is, then, very little question but that the "discovery" of the need to compensate for the disadvantage of the black ghetto child is largely response to the black nationalism sweeping the nation. While some white racists continue to say that all black people know is to burn, loot, snipe, kill, and be a "tool of the communists," some other whites are turning to compensatory educational programs "designed to eliminate the causes of deprivation" before "the ravages of poverty become irreversible."

Hence, the "new" literature postpones to another generation any real solution of ghetto problems. It also places the burden for change upon the shoulders of the black child. For it is the black ghetto child who must be changed, not the centuries-old conditions which have perpetuated disadvantage. Many black people find these programs much less than thrilling, as having not too much potential, and as a delaying tactic.

The "new" literature has been written too hastily. The problem of educating black ghetto children is being brought to the attention of our people at this time partially as a cover for the poor quality of education which has long been the fate of low income and minority group children. The deprivation theory places the burden on the black children and the effort to denigrate the black family, and especially the black mother, is a systematic effort to free the school systems from accepting responsibility for the miseducation of black children. The present and prior history of neglect of the children and youth of the poor and to provide superior education, facilities, and opportunities for white middle- and upper-class children and youth still continues. This means a widening gap between the black ghetto child and middle- and upper-class white children, and results in a lifelong handicap to the black child by freezing him into low class status. Cultural deprivation of the black people has been a conscious policy of the white racists and their dupes and stooges on the boards of education for more than a century. Cultural deprivation is still the major factor in the education of the black child.

Compensatory educational programs are too little and too late. Many of these programs are based in (1) a power field which does not yet involve parity for black people; (2) a content field which does not identify the kinds of changes in behavior to be induced in blacks other than as a condescending approach to the culture of the black people with no effort to structure dignity for the life-style, linguistic habits, and behaviors of black people, but rather designed to produce white middle-class conventional behaviors; (3) a reward system oriented toward a racist society, rather than integration of black and white people, providing for development of individual self-respect and self-control and identity with the society and culture—a reward system which develops in each individual respect for the heterogeneity of culture and cultures, a sense of responsibility for other people, and development of the capacity to make things happen; and (4) rejection of the field of colonialism and dependency for a field of relevancy. That is, insofar as the education of the black ghetto child, or indeed for that matter the education of any child, must be in a field wherein the cognitive, affective, and psychomotor domains are relevant to the lives of the children, youth, and educational personnel. Do the program philosophy and content and the methodologies go beyond the current myths of the social and behavioral sciences and does the educational program face the present national crisis and does education see itself as a major force for social change for humanism and what is, in fact, education for survival? It is also true that this education must reflect serious and basic concern for the poor and wretched, for lawlessness in our society, for the degradation and attempt to destroy the cultures of people, and for increasing use of aggression, money, and war to solve conflict.

The "new" literature not only sets out to bring the ghetto school up to par with the middle-class school, it fails to take its content from the ghetto itself. It closes its eyes to that passionate cliche of American educators "the study of the life situation" and, while it "steals" much of the format and arrangements from the progressive education movement and its successors, it does not yet have a rationale, philosophy, or conceptualization. It does not have research or other data to account for change which the reading and writing and speaking and listening and problem-solving will induce.

One concludes, then, that the goal of the "new" literature and the programs which derive from it is to educate the black ghetto child so that he will become a black "Anglo-Saxon." It postulates that a black "Anglo-Saxon" can or should escape from the ghetto. It ignores the real estate, industry, and financial controls which conspire to block any significant outward movement from the ghetto. Its obsession that black ghetto children and their teachers must be held to the same standards as white middle-class children and teachers is based on the dogma that the black ghetto child must look forward to that tenuous future when, as a black "Anglo-Saxon," he will leave the dependent environment for the white world. Verily, the "new" literature proposes that the black ghetto child become a superchild, lifting himself through reading and language skills to a nobler and greater world of the future.

THOMAS S. GUNNINGS

Psychological, Educational, and Economic Effects of Compensatory Education Programs on Blacks

Early in 1964, the nation was awakened to the inadequacy of the existing educational system for poor, disadvantaged, economically deprived American children. Black Americans, particularly, had aroused the nation's conscience to the deprivations and injustices they were suffering. Partly as a conciliatory effort to appease a group that would not let this nation relax, as a therapeutic process to relieve the nation's guilty conscience, and as a commemorative gesture to a slain President, the War on Poverty was instituted. The immediate result was the enactment of legislation, particularly the Economic Opportunity Act of 1964, which provided for the establishment of certain community action programs. These programs were aimed at the children who were going to be or had been losers in the regular school program. The purpose of these programs, compensatory in nature, was established as the improvement of the social, psychological, economical, and educational welfare of the participants. While the objectives have been carefully laid out by government specialists and meticulously guarded by experts, these programs have not enjoyed the success that was predicted.

Attention will be focused here on three widely instituted compensatory educational programs—Head Start, Follow Through, and Upward Bound. The specific government act under which these programs were authorized will be related, the general purposes of each will be stated, and the psychological, educational, and economic effects on black participants will be discussed.

Governmental Guidelines for the Establishment of Head Start, Follow Through and Upward Bound

The Federal government supports various programs in an effort to effect a permanent increase in the ability of individuals, groups, and communities afflicted with poverty to improve their own conditions. One group of such programs is called CAP—community action programs. In some communities a community action agency (CAA) exists and it receives and disperses funds for the administration of various programs. In communities where no such agency exists, funds are given directly to the nonprofit public or private organization operating a program under the general principles of community action—participation of the poor, mobilization of resources, and targeting of programs to the

Reprinted by permission of the author.

273

poor. Title II of the Economic Opportunity Act, "Urban and Rural Community Action Programs," authorizes the establishment of the programs whose specific purposes are to promote, as methods of achieving a better focusing of resources on the goal of individual and family self-sufficiency,

the strengthening of community capabilities for planning and coordinating Federal, State, and other assistance related to the elimination of poverty, so that this assistance, through the efforts of local officials, organizations, and interested and affected citizens, can be made more responsive to local needs and conditions;

the better organization of a range of services related to the needs of the poor, so that these services may be made more effective and efficient in helping families and individuals to overcome particular problems in a way that takes account of, and supports their progress in overcoming, related problems;

the greater use, subject to adequate evaluation, of new types of services and innovative approaches in attacking causes of poverty, so as to develop increasingly effective methods of employing available resources;

the development and implementation of all programs and projects designed to serve the poor or low-income areas with the maximum feasible participation of residents of the areas and members of the groups served, so as to best stimulate and take full advantage of capabilities for self-advancement and assure that those programs and projects are otherwise meaningful to and widely utilized by their intended beneficiaries; and

the broadening of the resource base of programs directed to the elimination of poverty, so as to secure, in addition to the services and assistance of public officials, private religious, charitable, and neighborhood organizations, and individual citizens, a more active role for business, labor, and professional groups able to provide employment opportunities or otherwise influence the quantity and quality of services of concern to the poor. (1)

Upward Bound, Head Start and Follow Through are Office of Economic Opportunity (OEO) community action programs established under the above mentioned purposes or guidelines. Title II of the Economic Opportunity Act, Sec. 222 (a) specifically authorizes the establishment of Head Start, Follow Through, and Upward Bound.

A program to be known as "Project Head Start" focused upon children who have not reached the age of compulsory school attendance which (A) will provide such comprehensive health, nutritional, education, social, and other services as the Director finds will aid the children to attain their full potential, and (B) will provide for direct participation of the parents of such children in the development, conduct, and overall program direction at the local level. (2)

A program to be known as "Follow Through" focused primarily upon children in kindergarten or elementary school who were previously enrolled in Head Start or similar programs and designed to provide comprehensive services and parent participation activities, which the Director finds will aid in the continued development of children to their full potential. Funds for such program shall be transferred directly from the Director to the Secretary of Health, Education, and Welfare. (3)

A program to be known as "Upward Bound" designed to generate skills and motivation necessary for success in education beyond high school among young people from low-income backgrounds and inadequate secondary school preparation. Projects must include arrangements to assure cooperation among one or more institutions of higher education and one or more secondary schools. They must include a curriculum designed to develop creative thinking, effective expression and attitudes toward learning needed for postsecondary educational success, necessary health services, and such recreational and cultural and group activities as the Director determines may be appropriate. (4)

The Office of Economic Opportunity draws specific attention for Upward Bound support to other government and private agencies. Specific attention is drawn to the following:

Public Law 89–10, The Elementary and Secondary Education Act of 1965, which offers assistance to programs for the education of children of low-income families.

Public Law 88–452, The Economic Opportunity Act of 1964, which establishes the Neighborhood Youth Corps under which Upward Bound high-school students should be eligible for paying jobs while in high school.

Public Law 88–329, The Higher Education Act of 1965, which contains Federal scholarships for needy college students which may be conditionally committed to high school students.

Numerous other programs designed to respond to the disadvantaged high-school-age student supported by private foundations and other sources. (5)

General Purposes of Head Start, Follow Through, and Upward Bound

Project Head Start, a part of the War on Poverty, was initiated in 1965 to benefit the economically disadvantaged preschool child. It is based on the philosophy that:

1. *a child can benefit most from a comprehensive interdisciplinary attack on his problems at the local level, and*
2. *the child's entire family, as well as the community, must be involved in solving his problems. (6)*

Each Head Start center theoretically provides a comprehensive program of parental involvement, nutritional, medical, dental, psychological, and social services. These programs are generally tailored to the local needs of the families of each community, but some broad goals of Head Start Child Development Programs are:

Improving the child's health.

Helping the child's emotional and social development by encouraging self-confidence, self-expression, self-discipline, and curiosity.

Improving and expanding the child's ability to think, reason, and speak clearly.

Helping children to get wider and more varied experiences which will broaden their horizons, increase their ease of conversation, and improve their understanding of the world in which they live.

Giving the child frequent chances to succeed. Such chances may thus erase patterns of frustration and failure and especially the fear of failure.

Developing a climate of confidence for the child which will make him want to learn.

Increasing the child's ability to get along with others in his family and, at the same time, helping the family to understand him and his problems—thus strengthening family ties.

Developing in the child and his family a responsible attitude toward society and fostering feelings of belonging to a community.

Planning activities which allow groups from every social, ethnic, and economic level in a community to join together with the poor in solving problems.

Offering a chance for the child to meet and see teachers, policemen, health, and welfare officers—all figures of authority—in situations which will bring respect and not fear.

Giving the child a chance to meet with older children, teenagers, and adults who will serve as "models" in manners, behavior, and speech.

Helping both the child and his family to a greater confidence, self-respect, and dignity. (7)

The Follow Through program was established by the U.S. Office of Education in collaboration with OEO to support and build on the gains made by children in Head Start programs and other preschool programs funded by the government. The broad objectives of Follow Through involve meeting the physical, psychosocial, and educational needs of children in a comprehensive program that establishes a relationship between each participating community and the resource institution acting as a program sponsor for the program approach chosen by that community. The guidelines of Follow Through state that the community must give clear evidence that it will implement and support processes leading to

the direct participation of the parents of Follow Through children in the development, conduct, and overall direction of the project;

the involvement of agencies, organizations, and other community resources that have a concern for the poor;

the creation of a climate in which communication between the poor and nonpoor can be achieved and in which a partnership between the school and community can be realized. (8)

Upward Bound is a precollege preparatory program for secondary-school students aimed at keeping these students college bound. In addition to being from low-income families, Upward Bound participants have been handicapped by economic, social, and educational deprivations. The program seeks to rescue the participating students from inadequate secondary-school preparation, and awaken within the student the potentials, skills, and motivation necessary so that the student's talents and energies may be used constructively toward acceptance and success in a college environment.

Upward Bound, begun in 1965, aspires to these guidelines:

Activities should be proposed which will enhance the personal effectiveness of Upward Bound students. Activities should be designed to develop abilities to organize, to persuade, and to cooperate. A sense of personal responsibility, self-discipline, and other leadership qualities are important goals for Upward Bound.

Specific plans for cultural enrichment must be a part of every project.

Recreational and physical activities should be a part of the summer phase of every Upward Bound project.

The overriding goal must be to prepare students in the essentials of success in college. The curriculum should be aimed, therefore, toward these objectives: critical thinking, effective expression, and development of positive attitudes toward learning. (9)

Psychological, Educational and Economic Effects on Blacks

Compensatory programs were designed specifically to "compensate" for something that has been missed. In this instance, they are an attempt to compensate for an inadequate education. Compensatory education programs, particularly Head Start, Follow Through and Upward Bound have not attained the goals for which they were designed. One of the fallacies of these programs is that the guidelines and purposes were set forth by the wrong persons who asked the wrong questions. The federal government hired what it terms "experts" to develop a set of guidelines for each poverty program. These so-called experts had never truly known poverty from experience. Their idea of experiencing poverty was to ride through Harlem or the backwoods of Mississippi in air-conditioned limousines and shake their heads at the dreadfulness of the situation. There is no better expert on poverty than those who have lived in the rat-infested ghettos or those who have experienced hunger and unemployment. In order to solve poverty in the United States, the persons living in poverty must be involved in political decisions concerning poverty and a new set of guidelines must be instituted. It is not suggested here that only the poor can be involved in the establishment of criteria for a poverty program, but it is necessary to have the thinking and experience of the poor reflected in the guidelines. If a successful poverty program is to be established, the expertise is needed that only the people in poverty can bring; also needed is the expertise and knowledge of the economic and political arena that the professional person should be able to bring. The main task of the latter should be that of consultant or advisor, not policy maker. The poor do not generally possess the awareness of all the political and economic aspects to be encountered and will need the professional's aid in unlocking the many doors that must be opened in order to make changes in the system. In other words, any meaningful poverty program must reflect the joint undertakings of the poor and the professional or expert.

That compensatory education guidelines were developed by persons not experienced in the feelings and attitudes of the poor is evidenced in the basic assumption upon which these programs were conceptualized. The formulators of the purposes and guidelines took the clinical approach which puts the onus of poverty on the people in poverty. It was, and still is, assumed that there is something wrong with poor people, that all the problems are caused by the poor, disadvantaged child and his family and that we need to work on improving him. Then, if the poor people do not welcome these programs with open arms, they are accused of not accepting help. These compensatory education programs force the poor to accept as valid the four deficit models—inadequate socialization, constitutional inferiority, environmental deficit, and cultural inferiority. These theses depict the cause of poverty as being individual or family oriented. However, the disadvantaged person is not the problem or even the cause of the problem; it is the system in which we live that forces certain segments of our society to be unemployed, poorly educated, in poor health, and residents of dilapidated housing. Poor people can learn and are willing to learn if their worth is considered and they are not made to feel inferior. Compensatory education programs do not treat the causes of societal ills, but merely treat the symptoms that attest to an ailing system. Therapeutic programs should be aimed at the system and not at the people who are merely manifestations of the system's evils. The system must begin to act as though it is the cause of the problem and come up with strategies to modify its own behavior.

Compensatory education programs are analogous to penicillin or drug treatments for the common cold. A stuffed nose and headache (symptoms) may be temporarily relieved by an aspirin or an antihistamine, but these medicines do not cure the common cold because they only treat the symptoms, not the cause. Until the cause or causes of the common cold are determined and a suitable treatment is developed to arrest the cause, man will continue to be plagued by this discomfort. So, we can continue to treat the symptoms of our societal ills with compensatory education programs, but until we examine the cause and penetrate this evil these symptoms will recur. Some of the societal ills that must be treated are (a) the insistence of a white middle-class life style model for all; (b) the perpetration of racial injustice and prejudice; (c) the suppression of morals and values that do not concur with traditional, staid standards; and (d) the failure to recognize the existence and merits of a culture that does not contain pure American white influences. It is obvious that there is something very wrong with a system that must have a Head Start, a Follow Through, and an Upward Bound program.

The purposes of the various programs are evidence that the clinical approach is used to eliminate poverty rather than the systemic approach. For example, one Head Start purpose is to increase the child's ease of conversation and improve his understanding of the world. This purpose as stated is really telling the child that there is something wrong with the way he speaks. When you take any person out of a familiar setting which has already been labeled as inappropriate, it is to be expected that his mannerisms will be different from those in the new environment, but nothing is done in the new environment to allow for different cultural patterns to become a part of the accepted standards. Denial of the child's cultural patterns in the new environment deprives him of part of his existence. As far as understanding the world, blacks have a clear understanding of how the world is operated. It is whites who pretend that the world operates differently from the way it actually does. Perhaps what is needed is a program in which blacks teach whites what this world is all about.

Another purpose of Head Start is to "develop a climate of confidence for the child which will make him want to learn." How does one develop confidence in a system that does not include him in the first place? If one does learn in Head Start, he will see the irrelevancies of the system and the inconsistencies of those who teach him. What is really meant here is that the child should learn to keep his place as a second-class citizen and that white is right and black is wrong. The child in Head Start may want to learn but he may not want to learn what he is being taught.

Another aim of Head Start is to help strengthen the child's family ties. It is assumed here that the black family is not a tightly knitted family, but there are no data to substantiate this erroneous assumption. This program forces him to deny his family at one level and to try to get along with his family at another level. This is a paradox. The aim here should be to get teachers to understand and accept a variable other than the white middle-class family. This means that white teachers must be reeducated, or educated for the first time.

The purpose of bringing together people from different ethnic, social, and economic levels does not aid in solving problems, but creates frustration on the part of the poor minority and a false security role on the part of the more affluent ones. What is labeled as problem solving is really problem causing.

One other purpose of Head Start is to teach the child to respect the authority figures of teachers, policemen, and health and welfare officers. Why should the child respect any figure that does not respect him, that only rapes his mind and body? Seeing these people in positive authority roles is only teaching falsehoods.

A Follow Through purpose is to develop a partnership between the school and the community. No partnership can be developed unless there is equal input from both partners. The school, which by structure has the greatest input, is in fact seen by the community as the authority figure. No true partnership exists under these conditions.

The overriding goal of Upward Bound is to prepare students for success in college. For a black to be successful in college he must be white-erized. Preparing to be successful is preparing to be white. The overriding goal should be to work with colleges to deal with people from a pluralistic point of view. Upward Bound is also educationally unsound because it is geared only toward those students who have shown that, if treated properly and taught, they may be successful in college. It clearly omits those students who have shown no promise of remediating deficits and being taken in by society's value system. Then, even if a student successfully completes Upward Bound, there is no assurance that he will be admitted to college. It is a program of false hope for many.

The student who successfully completes Upward Bound and is lucky enough to find a college to admit him faces still another problem. The lily-white college students in many instances resent and question his mere existence on campus. The affluent students attempt to determine whether the Upward Bound student belongs in the dormitory or whether the stipend he receives is fair. No mention is made of the scholarships and fellowships the affluent students receive. Some students complain that the Upward Bound student brings down the standards of the university or college. The Upward Bound student is no longer pampered and given extensive individual supportive services, but is pitted against an educational system that is more likely to fail him than give him a chance to succeed.

Compensatory education programs have failed for many reasons other than inappropriate guidelines. Another cause of the failings of these programs is pointed up by evaluation surveys conducted for Head Start by the Bureau of the Census and fourteen university-based Evaluation and Research (E&R) Centers in 1967–1968. The E&R evaluation, based on data collected on 260 Head Start classes, points up the ethnicity of the teachers, while the Census survey gives the ethnicity of the children (10).

Children	Teachers
24% White	55% White
51% Black	40% Black
25% Other minorities	5% Other minorities

These surveys show that while less than one-fourth of the children are white, more than one-half of the teachers are white. White teachers are put in the Head Start programs to teach children of minority races. This is that white middle-class value model to which our education system ascribes. The white teachers who work in these compensatory programs are usually those who have failed to be successful in the regular school program. White teachers supposedly possess the personalities, characteristics, and culture traits the black child must try to imitate. This is the type of thinking supported by social scientists such as Henry Garrett and Arthur Jensen who believe that blacks are constitutionally inferior because of genetic differences. Supporters of this thesis would surely feel that the white teacher would be more effective with black children than the black teacher. This ethnic imbalance of teachers and students cannot be supported because research does not point up the superiority of the white race. The white teacher who has never experienced racial injustice and poverty cannot relate to black children better than a black teacher who has similar life experiences, mainly because people relate more efficiently to those of their own kind. Certainly, in a program where about half the children are black, half the teachers should be black.

Another fault in community action programs is that they do not involve the parents and other family members at a meaningful level. It was mentioned earlier that the federal guidelines call for the "direct participation of the parents of the children in the development, conduct, and overall program direction at the local level." While this statement would cause one to believe that parents are involved in all phases of the programs, the actual level of involvement is not meaningful. Parents are usually placed in some peripheral position from which they cannot have too much of an affect on the operation of the program. Typical of the attitude of the menial involvement of the parents is the statement by Annie May Murray, an East Carolina College educator who reported at the end of the 1965 Head Start year that

> *Teachers and administrators need to know the value of using parents and the ways in which they can render service, such as in transportation, food services, altering donated clothing, and contributing in the planning of programs. (11)*

Note that the roles in which parents are cast are those that do not involve any sort of critical thinking or any real contribution to the programs. Other evidence of the meaningless involvement of parents is reported in the 1968 Head Start report from the Office of Child Development, which shows that only 4 percent of the paid staff in 1968 were parents (12).

Some centers evade the parental involvement clause in the federal guidelines by placing a token number of parents on planning boards. These are sometimes parents who have been or can be coopted to agree with the ideas of the other board members who are the actual policy makers. Then, even if the parents cannot be coopted, they are usually too few in number to have any sort of collective power. The planning and governing boards are generally politically imbalanced in favor of the white power structure.

The denial of meaningful involvement of parents in compensatory programs has negative effects on both the child and the parents (family). Parents who have no intricate relationship to the program in which their child is placed usually have guilt feelings because of this forced inadequacy role, and the family security base becomes unstable. Parents are given the feeling that they do not have the intellect to speak in the best interest of the child and thus their self-image is lowered. In addition to these psychological effects on the parents, the child is given the feeling that his parents are inferior and cannot help make meaningful decisions concerning his life. The child loses faith and trust in his parents' ability and therefore, he concludes that he cannot get any psychological gratification from them because they are in powerless positions. It is here that the early seeds of white supremacy are planted.

Another fallacy of the compensatory education programs is that they attempt to change completely the child's attitudes, behavior, interests and motivational aspirations without respecting the attributes and characteristics the child already possesses. This reinforces the environmental and cultural deficit theories and instills within the child the feeling that he is no good and that in order for him to be "somebody" he must become an entirely different person. This is the principle of self-denial, and it implants in the child a feeling of worthlessness and inferiority. The child's environment is ignored and downgraded, yet it is this environment to which he must return at the end of the day. He returns not necessarily by choice, but he returns to a fate dictated by a circumstance of birth. This is an inadequate foundation upon which to build any program.

Head Start, Follow Through, and Upward Bound are perpetuators of schizophrenia. Schizophrenia is a psychotic disorder characterized by:

> the splitting off of portions of the psyche, which portions may then dominate the psychic life of the subject for a time and lead an independent existence even though these may be contrary and contradictory to the personality as a whole. (13)

The late psychiatrist, Harry Stack Sullivan, referred to schizophrenia "not as a disease but a way of life." Schizophrenia, while it may take many forms, is a manifestation of social as well as individual disorders. A child in these compensatory programs is constantly compelled to change not only his behavior but also his basic personality as he is shifted back and forth between school environment and home environment. Each place demands markedly different behavior from him. The child must be careful to display all the rigid traits in the right place. For example, if he attempts to use impeccable manners and speech at home, he immediately becomes a threat to his siblings. He is ridiculed and made to feel that he does not fit into the family structure. In school, if he uses the slang language of the street, he is quickly corrected and he begins to withdraw and become afraid to articulate his ideas for fear of embarrassment and rejection. Suddenly, the child does not belong anywhere—not at home, not in school. With all this attention focused on him, this child could be the loneliest person in town.

The aforementioned criticisms of the compensatory education programs all have dramatic psychological effects on the child and his family, but there also are educational faults with these programs. While Follow Through is geared to build upon what the child has learned in Head Start, there is no linkage between Head Start, Follow Through, and the regular public school educational program. If it is assumed for one moment that Head Start and Follow Through are successful, it would be obvious that the "self-confidence, curiosity, broadened horizons, and chances of success" are quickly thwarted as the child tries to matriculate through the primary grades. He is no longer that special person who deserves individual attention and encouragement, but he now becomes simply nobody. Dr. Joseph S. Roucek expresses the importance of the linkage.

If these children are really to have a head start, the changes, or the adjustment, will have to be provided by the schools, so that programs are no longer run on the false assumption that all children come to school with the same values and attitudes and experiences common to the white middle-class child in our society. (14)

Compensatory education programs also have an economic effect on the poor and disadvantaged. While the budgets for individual programs look enormous, an itemized statement of the typical program's budget will show that a great deal of the money goes to the white-collar workers, not the poor. For example, the *New York Times* reported that Model Cities officials requested $126,300 per year in expense money to cover such services as babysitters, telephone calls, transportation, meeting attendance, and vehicle expenses. Also included was the sum of $25.00 per month for board members who cannot attend meetings because of illness (15). The poor people who really need the babysitters, telephones, and cars were not considered.

It was mentioned previously that there is only token representation of parents who are paid staff members in these programs and they have menial jobs that do not pay much more than welfare—and some do not pay as much as welfare. Psychologically, these people are off welfare, but economically they have made no progress. Parents who work in these programs are forced to choose between a lousy job or welfare. Compensatory programs lock poor people out of the mainstream of the economy and place them in a controlled welfare economy. Poverty can only be solved when poor people are given options. They must be able to have job choices. The employment problem can only be solved when there is more work available than there are people. This will force the system to compete for people rather than having people compete with the system for employment. Once people are fully employed, they can become politically involved in decisions that affect their lives.

Summary

Poverty in the United States has become big business and big politics. It is advantageous to the people in power that poverty should continue to exist. Poverty has become a means by which directors of poverty programs, other high officials, and politicians use the unfortunate plight of others to their financial and political gain. Federal legislation on poverty only passed when it became convenient and politically wise for lawmakers to come out against deprivation.

The type of education one receives will determine the type of job he will get. The type of job he gets will determine how much money he will earn, which in turn determines where he will live and the type of politics he will get involved in. So, a poor person must receive a good education if he is to have any chance at all to escape from a life of deprivation.

Head Start, Follow Through and Upward Bound, while they are feeble attempts to provide better education for the poor, will always face problems because they are organized around the philosophy that there is something wrong with the child. This clinical approach is inappropriate because it does not treat the cause of the problem—the system. The systemic approach means treating the societal system; it would be aimed at the attitudes, characteristics, and misconceptions of an unfair system. Until this is done, a program such as Head Start will only be a false start.

Clearly defined goals of education must be established and strategies for implementing these goals must be instituted. We are living in times when education is being challenged by those who have supposedly been the recipients of all the benefits this system can offer. White students today are rejecting the values and mores that compensatory education programs are trying to instill in blacks. Blacks are being taught skills that will further frustrate them and add nothing to their growth and upward mobility in this society. Those who have waited outside the doors of opportunity for years truly need an education, not a promise. Compensatory education programs only offer a promise, not an education.

Notes and References

1. U.S. Statutes at Large, 1965, Economic Opportunity Act of 1964, Sec. 201 (a).
2. U.S. Statutes at Large, 1967, Economic Opportunity Act of 1964, Sec. 222 (a) (1).
3. *Ibid.*, Sec. 222 (a) (2).
4. *Ibid.*, Sec. 222 (a) (5).
5. Office of Economic Opportunity, *Upward Bound guidelines*, December 1965.
6. U.S. Department of Health, Education and Welfare, Office of Child Development. *Head Start child development programs: A manual of policies and instructions*, September 1967, p. 1.
7. *Ibid.*, pp. 2-3.
8. Draft of Follow Through Program Guidelines, February 24, 1969.
9. Office of Economic Opportunity, *op. cit.*, pp. 8-9.
10. Office of Child Development, *A report on evaluation studies of Project Head Start*, 1969, pp. 8-9.
11. Department of Elementary-Kindergarten-Nursery Education and National Association of Elementary Instructional Service Leaflet, *What we learned from Head Start*, 1965.
12. Department of Health, Education, and Welfare, Office of Child Development, *Project Head Start 1968: The development of a program*, October 1970, p. 26.
13. L. Hinsie, and Robert J. Campbell, *Psychiatric dictionary* (New York: Oxford University Press, 1970), p. 678.
14. J. S. Roucek, What is Head Start? *College Journal of Education*, March 1969, **XIII**.
15. The *New York Times*, May 23, 1971.

Labeling Children Culturally Deprived and Culturally Disadvantaged

The current descriptive term for the child of low socioeconomic background, usually of black or other minority status, is *culturally disadvantaged* or *culturally deprived*. Many textbooks and articles describe the "deprived" and "disadvantaged" child's presumed cognitive, motivational, affective, demographic, and background characteristics. Like other exceptional children he is portrayed as missing something necessary for successful school performance. Seldom have the consequences of the labels used to describe the child been explored. The present paper takes up this task and deals with the following questions: Do children of whatever socioeconomic background label themselves culturally deprived or culturally disadvantaged or accept such labels? What are the consequences, in terms of school attitudes, motivation, and self-concept associated with the acceptance of the labels? What affective responses to these labels? What cognitive understanding of the terms? What consequences in terms of teacher and counselor expectations? What consequences for student performance? These are some of the questions that must be dealt with as we attempt to explore the effects of labels on the child.

That the terms are felt keenly by blacks is indicated in a recent paper by Kenneth Clark (1969), first black president of the American Psychological Association:

Although I reveal a certain cynicism by this, I find myself constantly thanking God that when I was in the Harlem public schools nobody knew that I was culturally deprived. I'm afraid that if they did know I would not have been taught on the grounds that being culturally deprived I wouldn't be able to learn. (p. 36)

Similarly Johnson (1969), a black special educator, has written:

When we speak of inner city, or ghetto or core area and when we use euphemisms such as educationally disadvantaged, culturally deprived, and poverty-ridden, we are really talking about black people or Afro-Americans. . . . I am suggesting that education has failed in its responsibilities to black Americans. What then about special education which has long been involved in educational endeavors in the inner cities?

Its black clientele has been labeled delinquent and retarded, thus helping the general educational enterprise to avoid some of the responsibility for its failure to adapt to individual and collective needs. Basically this labeling process imputes a lack of ability or a lack of values which are acceptable to the schools.

285

The rule of thumb for black children is: IQ below 75 = learning problem or stupidity; and IQ above 75 = behavior problem or crazy.

Children's Perceptions of Themselves as Culturally Disadvantaged and Culturally Deprived

A survey of one large metropolitan school district in the midwest was undertaken in which some 7,252 children, in grades 4, 6, 8, 9, 10, and 12, were requested to give a variety of self-perceptions—e.g., Do you see yourself as culturally disadvantaged? Do you see yourself as middle class? Do you see yourself as lower class? The subjects represented the entire school system and included 934 students in grade 4; 772 in grade 6; 1,339 in grade 8; 1,803 in grade 9; 1,028 in grade 10; and 1,376 in grade 12. Significant numbers of black and lower-class students were represented permitting analyses on these dimensions. Such analyses were unnecessary, however, because most students at all grade and socioeconomic levels rejected such labels as descriptive of themselves. Thus in schools where excessive numbers of mothers were receiving Aid to Dependent Children and where virtually all children were lower SES blacks, the labels were rejected by as many students as was the case in predominantly white middle-class schools. Most students of whatever social class perceived themselves as middle class. Insofar as the validity of responses was concerned, the subjects' self-descriptions were unrelated to a measure of social desirability. Using biserial correlations, no significant relationships were found between social desirability scores and self-descriptions at any grade level. Confidence in the validity of the responses then is quite high.

The results are clear. Regardless of socioeconomic or grade level, children reject the labels culturally deprived and culturally disadvantaged as descriptive of themselves. The independence of the responses from measures of social desirability was confirmed. A related methodological question, however, concerns whether the respondents were familiar with certain of the terms used in the study—for example, culturally deprived and culturally disadvantaged, among others. The concern is particularly relevant for our elementary-school respondents. Did they know the meaning of these terms? Could they give satisfactory definitions of them?

A small study involving 259 students in grades 5 and 6 in several classrooms was undertaken in which the children were requested to give definitions of some 20 terms including key items of interest in the present investigation. Prior to a content analysis of responses the subjects were grouped into high, average, and low ability groups based on group-intelligence test scores recorded in school records and into low- and middle-class backgrounds based on teacher reports. Such measures proved unnecessary, however, because virtually none of these young subjects could give satisfactory responses to the key terms culturally deprived and culturally disadvantaged.

Content analyses of these same terms, and others, were also carried out using some 2,397 students in grades 9 and 12 in 24 junior and senior high schools. The results were remarkable, particularly with respect to omissions and tangential remarks given by subjects in some schools. Many older subjects could give reasonably satisfactory responses to these terms. A curious finding, however, was the tendency for many omissions and irrelevant or defensive terms to be given in certain schools. A clinical interpretation would lead to the conclusion that there was more defensiveness among the students in these largely black schools in responding to the terms culturally deprived and culturally disadvantaged.

Affective Responses

It seemed reasonably clear that the younger respondents were unfamiliar with the terms culturally deprived and culturally disadvantaged. But what of affective responses to the terms? Do the terms hold certain denotative (affective and attitudinal) meanings for the children in spite of their inability to give satisfactory connotative or conventional definitions? It was suspected that at some level young elementary children are familiar with the terms and do have feelings about them. Test of this notion was undertaken using 49 black children in grades 3 through 6 in a small midwestern community. The subjects responded to a number of questions related to their affective perceptions of various labels—for example, If someone called you culturally disadvantaged, would that be good or bad? The subjects responded to 19 different socioeconomic and class descriptive terms. As data in Table 1 reveal, the respondents perceived the terms culturally disadvantaged and culturally deprived as essentially negative descriptions with, respectively, 78 and 76 percent of the respondents indicating "bad" if the terms were used as descriptive of themselves. Additional data in Table 1 confirm previous suspicions about affective responses to certain other special education terms. Thus it is good to be gifted (agreed to by 74 percent of the respondents) but bad to be a slow learner or mentally retarded (agreed to by, respectively, 96 and 92 percent of the respondents). Other data were confusing—for example, the perception of the label *black* as bad, and the label *colored* as good. It has been assumed, based on current sloganeering (e.g., black is beautiful) and the changing times, that a more favorable affective meaning would be attached to the term black than has been the case heretofore. Evidence exists that this is the case with older blacks (Dansby, 1971). Further exploration of the meaning of the findings for younger black populations should be the focus of additional work in this area.

Acceptance of Deprivation Labels and School Attitudes

It is one thing to know that children reject the labels culturally deprived and culturally disadvantaged. A more important question relates to the consequences of acceptance or rejection of the labels and school attitudes. Do children who label themselves culturally disadvantaged or culturally deprived hold lower school attitudes than those who see themselves, regardless of objective circumstances, as middle class? Using biserial correlations, one study of 1,706 children

TABLE 1

Student Reactions to Certain Socioeconomic and
Class-Descriptive Terms (N = 49)

Term	Percent of Ss responding "good"	Percent of Ss responding "bad"
Black	22	76[a]
Culturally deprived	30	68
Culturally disadvantaged	16	78
Deprived area (lived in)	16	82
Colored	74	24
Head Start	34	64
Inner city (lived in)	66	28
Poverty	32	64
Lower class	6	92
Mentally retarded	6	92
Middle class	66	30
Negro	76	22
Poor	4	94
Rich	94	4
Slow learner	2	96
Slum school	2	96
Upper class	94	4
White	10	88
Gifted	74	24

[a]Percentages do not add up to 100 because of omissions and rounding error.

in grades 4 and 6 revealed reliably lower school attitudes (i.e., attitudes toward teacher–pupil relationships, other pupils, the school plant, general feelings about school, etc.) for those who labeled themselves culturally deprived or culturally disadvantaged as opposed to those who labeled themselves middle class. The finding held across schools of varying socioeconomic classes and was independent of social desirability response sets (Jones, 1971).

Labels and Performance—Two Experiments

There has been no work that supports the belief that deficit labels actually affect the behavior of those labeled. If labels have the deleterious effects hypothesized by many, it should be possible to demonstrate that learning and performance proceed more slowly or inefficiently under a deficit label than under a neutral or a positive label. The present section presents the results of experimental investigation of this hypothesis (Jones, 1970b).

Two studies on the effects of having black college students perform a digit symbol substitution task under various label conditions were undertaken. In the first, the subjects (who believed the digit symbol task to be a measure of psychomotor intelligence) completed the forms with one of three labels at the bottom of each page: (a) Study of Culturally Disadvantaged College Students; (b) Study of Black College Students; or (c) Study of College Students. No attention was called to the labels in the instructions, and subjects under the three conditions were randomly assigned to the treatments within classrooms. The subjects were 243 black college students in 3 predominantly black colleges—2 in the South (Ns of 63 and 120) and one in the Midwest ($N = 60$). The data from each school were treated separately. The hypothesis tested was that digit symbol performance would be highest for the Black College Student condition and lowest for the Culturally Disadvantaged condition.

One-way analyses of variance of total number of symbols correctly translated revealed no reliable differences ($p < .05$) in mean performance for subjects in the three conditions at any of the three schools, thus providing no support for the hypothesis (Fs of 2.63, df 2/57; .54, df 2/117; and .26, df 2/60). A small follow-up pilot study revealed that few subjects could actually recall the labels.

A follow-up study utilized 100 different black students in two predominantly black midwestern colleges. It was designed to mirror in a rigorous experimental fashion practices currently followed in schools—for example, a student is identified as having an educationally related deficiency and is placed in some special program to remediate the deficiency. The possibility that placement may itself stimulate a decrement rather than an improvement in performance has not been the object of serious investigation. The subjects were first given the digit symbol substitution test (said to be a measure of learning ability) under a nonlabel condition. About one week later the subject was informed via personal letter that he scored in the high group and that he would be given the advanced exercises to permit further improvement of his performance, or that he had scored in the low group and hence remedial exercises would be given—all to be followed by an immediate posttest to determine the effectiveness of the remedial or advanced exercises. To heighten awareness of the experimental variables, the content of the letter, letterhead, and signature line attempted to call attention to the treatments which were: (a) Study of Culturally Disadvantaged College Students ($N = 25$); (b) Study of Black College Students ($N = 25$); (c) Study of College Students ($N = 25$); or (d) Project Accelerate ($N = 25$). These labels were also placed at the bottom of each page of the intermediate (remedial or advanced) tests which were identical for the four treatments but a more difficult form of the digit symbol task than the pre- or posttest. A posttest (identical to pretest) followed the intermediate exercises.

No reliable differences ($p < .05$) in pretest performance were found. A one-way analysis of variance of posttest scores revealed no reliable differences in digit symbol performance as a function of exposure to the treatments ($p < .05$). There was, however, a reliable tendency for those who had been told that their pretest performance was good (Project Accelerate) to believe that they had done well on the posttests.

Several possibilities may account for failure to support the hypothesis: (a) dependent measures were not sensitive to treatment effects; (b) a confirmed failure of subjects to attend to the labels; and (c) the subjects were college students, a somewhat homogeneous group, who may have been impervious to the suggestion that they possessed learning deficiencies. The need obviously is to carry out similar investigations using more heterogeneous public school populations.

Teacher Expectations and Labels

Teacher expectations about the performance of children can serve a self-fulfilling prophecy. Such a possibility was demonstrated in a dramatic way by the research of Rosenthal and Jacobson (1968). The methods and conclusions of this study are by now well known and hence can be summarized briefly. A group of elementary-school children were pretested with a standard nonverbal test of intelligence, the test being represented to the teachers as one that would predict intellectual blooming or spurting. Approximately 20 percent of the children in grades 1 through 6 were randomly identified as potential spurters. These children and others not so identified were retested with the same nonverbal IQ test after one semester, and after one and two academic years. The results were remarkable: Students in the control group made some significant gains in IQ (19 percent gained 20 or more IQ points); 47 percent of the special children, however, gained 20 or more total IQ points.

The Rosenthal studies have been faulted on many methodological grounds (Barber and Silver, 1968a, 1968b; Thorndike, 1968). However, the results of related investigations suggest that teachers *do* hold low expectations for certain classes of students and that such expectations *do* relate to the ways in which teachers interact with their pupils.

Herriott and St. John (1966), on the basis of interviews with a national sample of teachers and pupils in urban public schools, report that the lower the socioeconomic status (SES) of the schools, the smaller the proportion of teachers who held favorable opinions about the motivation and behavior of their pupils. (It will not escape the reader that a large majority of low SES schools in urban areas contain substantial numbers of "disadvantaged" students.) Moreover, these same teachers were less likely to report that they had personal loyalty to the principal, that they desired to remain at their present school, or that they enjoyed their work. The finding concerning work satisfaction is particularly important because there is evidence indicating that reported satisfaction in teaching is directly correlated with pupil school morale (Jones, 1968). Pearson product-moment correlations between eight indices of school morale and reported teacher satisfaction for 34 randomly selected teachers and their fourth-grade students in 34 urban classrooms revealed significant correlations between reported satisfaction with teaching and (a) attitudes toward other pupils ($p < .01$), (b) pupil–teacher relationships ($p < .05$), (c) general feelings about school ($p < .01$) and (d) general school morale ($p < .05$). Similar analyses were carried out with 28 sixth-grade classrooms. However, no significant correlations were found between reported teacher satisfaction and any of the morale subscales. The results are clear: For young children, teacher satisfaction is related to pupil satisfaction. Unfortunately, it is not possible to know which group influenced which. Perhaps perceived poor pupil attitudes led to lowered satisfaction in teaching; or the situation could have been reversed, with pupils responding to perceived poor teacher attitudes. Regardless of the order of development of the attitudes, it seems reasonably clear that lowered satisfaction in work with young children is very closely tied to pupil satisfaction with school. Apparently, teacher satisfaction is more reliably related to pupil morale in the early grades. Implications of these findings for the placement of teachers in classrooms for work with black children, and others, are significant.

The Mediation of Expectancy Effects

What happens to the "culturally disadvantaged" child in the classroom? If expectancy effects are operative at all, how are they mediated? Several studies have now examined the mechanisms through which expectancy effects become translated into actual teacher behavior. The first was that of Beez (1968). This experiment showed the effects of teacher expectation on pupil performance. Subjects were 60 teachers and 60 pupils in a Head Start program. Teachers taught each child the meaning of a symbol. Half the teachers had been given the expectancy that, based on a psychological appraisal of the child, good learning would occur; the remaining half were led to expect poor learning. The results were remarkable. Seventy-seven percent of those alleged to have good intellectual prospects learned five or more symbols, whereas only 13 percent of those alleged to have poor prospects achieved at this level. Moreover, teachers who had been given favorable expectations about their pupils actually attempted to teach more symbols than those teachers who had been given unfavorable expectations about their pupils.

Expectations not only cover subjective forecasts of pupil ability and motivation but extend to school attitudes as well. Expectations regarding the school attitudes of a "culturally disadvantaged" child held by a group of college students were investigated in a social cognition experiment (Jones, 1970a). Subjects were 119 female undergraduate students who volunteered to participate in a psychology experiment as part of an introductory psychology course requirement. Approximately 75 percent of the participants were prospective teachers. Seventy-five of the subjects (experimental group) were given the following instructions:

Social cognition experiment
This is a study to determine the way in which individuals make certain kinds of predictions about the responses of others.

Please fill out the enclosed inventory according to the instructions in the booklet. However, instead of answering the questions as you normally would, answer as you think the person described below would respond.

A twelve-year-old culturally deprived boy in the sixth grade in an inner-city school.

Remember, you are to answer as you feel this person would.

Please answer every question, even though you may sometimes find it difficult to make a decision.

A second group of 44 respondents (control group) received instructions identical to those above except that the boy in the vignette was not described as inner city or culturally deprived. All subjects completed the School Morale Inventory (Wrightsman, 1968), an inventory designed to measure student feelings about school in a number of important areas, according to the directions given above. The inventory was scored in the conventional manner and the subtest scores given under the set to simulate the culturally deprived child compared (using t tests) with those given under the set to simulate the nondeprived child. The results were unequivocal (see Table 2): The deprived child was pre-

TABLE 2

School Attitudes Attributed to Culturally Deprived and Nondeprived School Children

Attitude subscale	Predicted attitudes of deprived ($N = 75$; mean)	Predicted attitudes of nondeprived ($N = 44$; mean)
School plant	3.15	6.37[a]
Instruction	2.36	4.77
Community	1.95	6.57
Administration, regulations, and staff.	2.56	5.01
Other students	4.63	7.44
Teacher–student relationships	4.00	6.53
General school morale	3.31	5.50
Total morale	21.89	45.52

[a] All differences were significant at less than the .01 level. The maximum score for individual subscales is 12; total morale, 84.

dicted to have reliably lower morale on all subscales of the School Morale inventory—for example, (a) morale about the school plant, (b) morale about instruction and instructional materials, (c) morale about administration, regulations, and staff, (d) morale about community support of schools and parental involvement in school, (e) relations with other students, (f) morale about teacher–student relationships, (g) general feelings about attending school, and (h) total school morale.

The study was replicated with a group of experienced teachers and counselors who had completed a year of study in an institute devoted to preparing counselors of "culturally deprived" youth. The responses of these specialists were identical to those given by the undergraduate students: The school attitudes held by the "culturally deprived" were predicted to be reliably lower than those held by the "nondeprived." For both counselors and undergraduate subjects the cognitions given for the "deprived" child were considerably more discrepant than those actually given by children who could be so labeled.

No pretests of counselor cognitions were obtained. It is difficult therefore to know the extent to which any changes took place in counselor attitudes toward the "deprived" as a function of the year-long institute. It is entirely possible that counselor attitudes were even more negative than those found at the end of their training. Obviously, it is not now possible to obtain this information. All that can be said is that following a full year of training devoted to the "culturally deprived," counselors held very negative and very stereotyped views of this group. If the program for counselors referred to above is any good at all, it suggests that prospects for modifying negative attitudes toward the "deprived" through formal training (including considerable fieldwork) are not at all bright.

The results of investigations reported here reveal that children do reject the labels culturally deprived and culturally disadvantaged as descriptive of themselves. Acceptance of such terms as self-descriptive has been found to be associated with lowered attitudes toward school. Moreover, teachers and counselors hold clear stereotypes about characteristics and attitudes of children so labeled. Unfortunately, most of these characterizations and stereotypes are negative. The specter of the self-fulfilling prophecy is ever present.

What changes then do the results suggest? The need for modification of labeling practices in this area is clear, for as Clark (1969) observes:

> . . . the most serious of all the obstacles which must be overcome is the tendency to label these youngsters, to name-call them, and to embark on the self-fulfilling prophecy of believing them to be uneducable by setting up social science and educational jargon which justifies this belief, setting up procedures and approaches which make education almost impossible, and then proving all of it by demonstrating that these children are retarded. If we are going to educate these children, this, I believe is the significant obstacle. (p. 37)

And finally, Mackler and Giddings (1967):

> . . . We must purge ourselves of the concept of cultural deprivation and all its derogatory implications. If a concept is needed, then we must seek a more accurate, authentic, and honest term. If we conclude that no term is needed, perhaps that will be all the better. (p. 397)

References

Barber, T. X., and Silver, M. J. Facts, fiction, and the experimenter bias effect. *Psychological Bulletin Monograph*, 1968, 70, (6, pt. 2), 1–29. (a)

Barber, T. X., and Silver, M. J. Pitfalls in data analysis and interpretation: A reply to Rosenthal. *Psychological Bulletin Monograph*, 1968, 70, 48–62. (b)

Beez, W. V. Influence of biased psychological reports on teacher behavior and pupil performance. In *Proceedings, Seventy-sixth Annual Convention of the American Psychological Association*. Washington, D.C.: The Association, 1968, pp. 605–606.

Clark, K. B. Learning obstacles among children. In A. L. Roaden (Ed.), *Problems of school men in depressed urban centers*. Columbus, Ohio: College of Education, Ohio State University, 1969.

Dansby, P. G. Black pride in the seventies: Fact or fantasy? This volume, pp. 145–155.

Herriott, R., and St. John, N. H. *Social class and the urban school*. New York: John Wiley, 1966.

Johnson, J. L. Special education and the inner city: A challenge for the future or another means for cooling the mark out? *The Journal of Special Education*, 1969, 3, 241–251.

Jones, R. L. Student attitudes and motivation. In Ohio State University Advisory Commission on Problems Facing the Columbus (Ohio) Public School, *A report to the Columbus Board of Education.* Columbus, Ohio: Ohio State University, June 1968, pp. 272–300, 313–332.

Jones, R. L. Labeling black college students culturally disadvantaged: A search for behavioral correlates. Unpublished paper presented at the Annual Convention of the Western Psychological Association, Los Angeles, April 1970. (a)

Jones, R. L. New labels in old bags: Research on labeling blacks culturally disadvantaged, culturally deprived, and mentally retarded. Unpublished paper presented at the Annual Convention of the Association of Black Psychologists, Miami Beach, September 1970. (b)

Mackler, B., and Giddings, M. G. Cultural deprivation: A study in mythology. In E. T. Keach, Jr., R. Fulton, and W. E. Gardner, *Education and social crisis.* New York: John Wiley, 1967, pp. 393–398.

Rosenthal, R., and Jacobson, L. *Pygmalion in the classroom.* New York: Holt, Rinehart & Winston, 1968.

Thorndike, R. L. Review of R. Rosenthal, and L. Jacobson, Pygmalion in the classroom. *American Educational Research Journal*, 1968, 5, 708–711.

Wrightsman, L., Nelson, R. H., and Tranto, M. The construction and validation of a scale to measure children's school morale. Unpublished paper, George Peabody College for Teachers, 1968.

JOHN L. JOHNSON

Special Education and the Inner City: A Challenge for the Future or
Another Means for Cooling the Mark Out?

The recent call by the National Advisory Committee on Handicapped Children for "Program Development for Handicapped Children in Inner City Areas" represents, on the surface, a new challenge—an invitation for special education to become involved in the solution of one of the major crises facing America in the next decade. Education in the inner city is now in a state of crisis and will not improve unless massive changes are brought about in a creative fashion. The committee's stated need for "special studies" and "identification and determination of needed diagnostic and remedial services" (pp. 37-39) challenges every specialized segment of our profession. Certainly, a problem orientation comes to the fore when "inner city" is suggested as the geographic designation for any professional intervention.

Equality of educational opportunity is a pressing problem in all metropolitan areas, and recent legal decisions have amplified the problem all the more. Specialized and segregated tracking systems and discriminatory intelligence tests can no longer be justified when the basic rights of the individual are at stake. Because of the issue of equality of educational opportunity, an extremely serious problem has developed within the American educational establishment. It has to do with the role to be taken by special education within the total revitalization of education in metropolitan areas. Lloyd Dunn's (1968) condemnation of the practices and procedures of special education has essentially gone unanswered, and Donahue and Nichtern's (1965) findings that teacher-moms can help public-school disturbed children have been scoffed at and ignored by special educators.

The general body of special education is proceeding along the course of "special education and programs for disadvantaged children and youth" (Tanenbaum, 1968) with assistance from 15 percent of Titles I and III, all of Title VI, P.L. 88-164, and more recently from EPDA. These efforts have the clear support of the special education establishment.

In spite of research and clinical evidence which show that current models of general education are less than successful, efforts continue to be directed toward the establishment of a parallel and separate school structure called special education. The indictment against the general educational enterprise includes special education, for it is both passive and active in perpetuating the present conditions

From *Journal of Special Education*, 1969, **3**, 241-251. Reprinted by permission of the author and the publisher.

of inequality, failure, and the rendering of impotence, especially in the inner city.

The inner city itself is a problem which is deeply imbedded in America, but for no one is the problem more severe than for professional educators. Education, and special education in particular, faces a major challenge in the coming decade. Whether to take up the challenge or to continue business as usual is the major question to be considered in this paper. This question has political, social, psychological, and educational ramifications.

Whom and What Are We Talking About?

When we speak of inner city, or ghetto, or core area, and when we use euphemisms such as educationally disadvantaged, culturally deprived, and poverty-ridden, we are really talking about black people, or Afro-Americans. While Puerto Ricans, Indians, and poor whites may be included, at the heart of the matter is the fact that inner city means black. Based upon 1965 estimates (Clark, 1968, p. 119), black Americans constitute 66 percent of the total population in Washington, D.C.; 44 percent in Atlanta; 34 percent in Detroit; 31 percent in Philadelphia; and 22 percent in Kansas City. The school-age population for these cities—which are among the 15 having the largest percentages of blacks—are even larger: for instance, the school population in Washington, D.C., is more than 90 percent black and in Chicago it is more than 70 percent black. This is mainly because of one pervasive reason: Blacks are forced to live in the inner city, mainly in depressed, ghetto conditions. The Kerner Report (1968) has clearly cited the cause for this condition:

> "What white Americans have never fully understood—but what the Negro can never forget—is that white society is deeply implicated in the ghetto. White institutions created it, white institutions maintain it, and white society condones it." (p. 2)

What is most distressing is that in spite of what is termed a massive effort to improve the conditions under which black Americans live, they appear to be worsening in both intensity and extent. Clark's chapter, "The Negro and the Urban Crisis," in the Brookings Institutions Papers (Gordon, 1968) amply documents the problem. He stated:

> The fact of the ghetto—the involuntary restriction of the masses of Negroes to a particular geographic area of the city—underlies every other aspect of the problem. The ghetto results in de facto school segregation, which affects middle- and low-income Negroes alike, and the inferiority in education that is invariably related to it. Inferior education, in turn, reinforces the overriding economic fact of disproportionate Negro unemployment and underemployment. (pp. 119–120)

America's history of slavery, segregation, discrimination, and bigotry against blacks comes to focus in the inner city, and in particular in its inferior education. The Kerner Report (1968) cites the role of the school as an institution:

The bleak record of public education for ghetto children is growing worse. In the critical skills—verbal and reading ability—Negro students are falling further behind whites with each year of school completed. The high unemployment and underemployment rate for Negro youth is evidence, in part, of the growing educational crisis.

One can conclude that public education bears a large share of the responsibility for the miserable condition of the black inner-city resident. There are two pathologically symbiotic reasons for the conclusion, one having to do with the overall values of education in America and the other having to do with education for blacks.

First, as a transmitter of culture and a force which liberates men by providing them with truth, American education has failed. It has offered only a form of technological mind-shaping which permits its products to understand and to develop the great theories of nuclear fission, to recite the philosophies of Hume and Locke, and to master economics and business, while remaining almost totally unable to comprehend and act upon the simple words of 20,000,000 men, women, and children who are saying:

I want to be free; I want equal opportunity in a country which was founded upon this very premise; I want to determine the course of my own future; I am human.

Thus, we find all around us liberal intellectuals who can eloquently articulate the concepts of democracy and equality, but who have little commitment to carrying out these ideals. In essence, our schools have transmitted to an entire generation values of passivity, acquiescence, exploitation, and omission, instead of integrity and social responsibility.

The schools have also produced an increasingly vocal group of bigots who would systematically relegate entire segments of this society to lower status position, largely on the basis of color, although differences in physique, economic status, and religious preference are also favorite targets for their seething prejudice. The large majority of our schools avoid teaching truth and sensitivity about race, physique, economic status, and culture, instead fostering a system in which an increasing number of students learn bigotry, discrimination, and segregation. The root cause of America's major social problem is the value system which permits racism and exploitation to exist, which in turn is the result of the educational establishment's failure to transmit concepts of human dignity, brotherhood, equality, and democracy to its charges.

Secondly, the educational system's overt practices of segregation and discrimination, feckless fostering of programs upon entire populations without so much as a cursory consideration of their culture, values, and heritage, and its dehumanization of students through corporal punishment and rejection simply because they do not present themselves as "ideal clients" (Becker, 1952), have resulted in oppression of its black students. This results in large numbers of young people who, until recently, had no other method of gaining success and attention than through such self-defeating mechanisms as sex, violent confrontation with the images and agents of white society, or narcotics.

The increased racial hostility and the rising suicide rate in the ghettos are, to a great extent, the consequences of the white educational establishment's failure to provide viable programs which make social, educational, and economic opportunity a reality for blacks. Instead, a set of panaceas has been offered which represents a commitment to system maintenance rather than to the clientele the system purports to serve. As long as there is not too much threat to the model which has precipitated the failure, then attempts to find causes for the obvious facts are encouraged. A number of the panaceas, for instance, involve the assumption that quantitative inputs will affect qualitative outputs. Thus, one finds sincere attempts to fight cancer with corn plasters. The proponents of this view hold that we must sensitize the teachers, inject Negro history, reduce class size, and add some new services (but only when substantial outside pressure to do so is exerted). Where these initial attempts to patch up the system fail, schools can always fall back upon the processes of labeling and stigmatizing inner-city children as deviants either culturally, socially, or emotionally, and thus placing them in "special" or "compensatory" programs. Then, the children can be blamed, rather than the racism which permeates our educational institutions.

What Role Has Special Education Played?

It must be crystal clear by now that I am suggesting that the educational system has failed in its responsibilities to black Americans. What, then, about special education, which has long been involved in educational endeavors in inner cities?

Its black clientele has been labeled delinquent and retarded, thus helping the general educational enterprise to avoid some of the responsibility for its failure to adapt to individual and collective needs. Basically, this labeling process imputes a lack of ability or a lack of values and behavior which are acceptable to the school. Recent sophistication in labeling has added such terms as learning disability, slow learner, learning and adjustment problem, and conduct disorder to the more shopworn phrases such as mentally retarded and emotionally disturbed. The rule of thumb for black children is: IQ below 75 = learning problem or stupidity; and IQ above 75 = behavior problem or crazy.

The latest attempt at system maintenance is the generation of data to show that blacks may actually be genetically less intelligent and therefore less able to learn. Most of this psychometric data rests upon classical controlled variable research but has absolutely no ecological validity. Special education is implicated, for it has cheerfully accepted the charge with little or no scrutiny of either the faulty concept upon which IQ is grounded or the sociocultural environment of its clientele. Special education has continued blithely initiating special classes, work–study programs, resource rooms, and other stigmatizing innovations which blame the poor, black child for the failure of the dominant educational system. Are we to assume that the new challenge for special education will be handled differently? The research evidence from within the field suggests that current efforts in special education are "obsolete and unjustifiable from the point of view of the pupils so placed (Dunn, 1968, p. 6)." We must, also, consider that the efficacy research on special classes for the retarded shows that children who are placed in special classes achieve no better than those who remain in regular classes, and that those who remain in regular classes learn more social skills than special-class children (Goldstein, Moss, and Jordan, 1964). Research evidence on therapeutic educational provisions for behavior problem children has not been productive, and research on special-class achievement is also sparse and conflicting (Glavin and Quay, 1969). Where evidence is available, it has been obtained largely from white-majority populations. Thus, we must pose the question: If special education placement, as currently operating, is questionable for white children, what makes it any more valid for blacks? There is direct evidence to document its ineffectiveness (Clark, 1965; Shulz, 1969; Tyler, 1968), on top of the fact that placement out of the mainstream of education and other forms of tracking are illegal and racist-motivated. Thus, if special education becomes involved in this new effort in the inner city, then we will be operationalizing bigotry, discrimination, and segregation.

How Did All This Come About?

The current plight of the black is, in fact, a direct result of the regular school's failure to cope with individual and collective differences in learning and conduct of an increasing number of pupils. Regular schools have been the major force for accommodation of the "regular" blacks, and special education receives the "hard to break" blacks. It is an unwritten pact between the two.

Goffman's (1952) concept of "cooling the mark out" is relevant to blacks when consideration is given to the relationship between special education and the general educational system. Goffman has analyzed adaptation to failure and the methods by which one individual can aid another who has failed by helping him to build a new framework for judging himself. This process is called cooling the mark out.

General education, by definition, is supposed to be capable of teaching all children, but when confronted with inner-city black children, it has failed. Given traditional methodology and most crash programs, both white and Afro-American teachers have found themselves impotent when it comes to educating increasing numbers of black children. One method by which these individuals and the school can preserve their identities is by cooling the child out. Special programs are mandated on the basis that the new placement is helping the child. In essence, he is given a seemingly better provision in hopes that he will stop putting up a fuss. It is easier for all to cool out the child and to find him a new place than it is to change the system for his benefit.

Special education is part of the arrangement for cooling out students. It has helped to erect a parallel system which permits relief of institutional guilt and humiliation stemming from the failure to achieve competence and effectiveness in the task given to it by society. Special education is helping the regular school maintain its spoiled identity when it creates special programs (whether psychodynamic or behavioral modification) for the "disruptive child" and the "slow learner," many of whom, for some strange reason, happen to be black and poor and live in the inner city.

Some systems are already involved in programs for the "emotionally disturbed" and "socially maladjusted," which are no more than euphemisms for aggressive, black, male children.* For instance, a past issue of *Instructor Magazine*, a classroom teachers' periodical, featured an article on a "special education program for emotionally disturbed children" in a city where more than 75 percent of the school-age population is black and resides in massive ghetto areas. An extensive "therapeutic program" including entire schools for "disturbed" children is described. There is a subtle connotation of sickness or craziness. The schools involved are able to co-opt not only special education, but psychiatry, psychology, and social work (including indigenous paraprofessionals) in a direct fashion, and to effectively invalidate the cultural experiences of a select group of black children (Laing, 1969). The perpetrators of this type of cultural invalidation are products of the white racist value system spoken of earlier.

What Are the Social-Political Implications?

It is obvious that black people cannot sit idly by and watch white conceptions of normality and abnormality, or appropriateness of school behavior, foisted upon their children. Black professionals are, of course, implicated in this insidious practice by virtue of their white educations and ideologies, but a growing number have "come home" and are helping to formulate a challenge to the system of racist values which now permeates our schools.

This is the heart of the inner-city problem for special education. Left to whites and to special education, blacks have a choice: Be labeled crazy or unable to learn and get cooled out, or submit to a far worse plight—loss of their own black identity and integrity by permitting themselves to be integrated and thus con-

---

*When black "deviant" children are rated by white teachers, there is a tendency for their behavior to be classified more often as aggressive and acting out (cf. Quay, 1966; Rich, 1969).

vinced that the white man's values are the ones which must be adopted—the very values which created the condition in the first place.

What Is to Be Done?

I have grave doubts that anything can be done within the present system. I reject the assumption that the basic model of age-graded education as we know it must be preserved, even in view of the patching that is being attempted. It is not a model for blacks, it has failed blacks, and it is dominated by white values and methods. It is incompatible, even in its special forms, with black culture.

The first step toward solution is straightforward: *Black Self-Determination*. Blacks, as a people, must define themselves in a way that is meaningful to them. We will determine our identity, not as culturally deprived or Negro, but as black and Afro-American, if we so choose. We will determine what is in our best interests in this country, culturally, socially, economically, politically, and educationally. We will develop ourselves through institutions which support feelings of self-pride and attitudes of racial dignity, social responsibility, and human dignity.

The essence of this social-political implication lies in the *power* to carry out the task in the inner city. There is no doubt that it is the black American who has the most stake in the inner cities and their institutions. Blacks *are* the inner city and therefore they must determine its course. Institutions which serve blacks must become accountable first to blacks and then to the rest of society.

The new spirit of the inner city reflects this ideology. Black self-determination, black pride, and black consciousness are the values which inner-city schools must teach. The new way of "taking care of business" involves black people from all walks and persuasions coming together to decide what is in their best interest; this necessitates a temporary withdrawal until we know our brothers and until we awaken all of them to the need for enhancing Afro-American culture in this country—not a culture that is physically separate, but one that is of our collective mind and one in which we can determine the course of our existence without white interference, domination, exploitation, or classification. Certainly, whites must be involved, but only at the operational level. The planning and leadership levels will be for blacks. Whites may be consulted, but decisions about blacks cannot be made by whites and then followed by blacks.

Most of all, we have to preserve the integrity of our culture. Cultural preservation is our goal, not integration toward whites. The achievement of soul is important, soul being the "conscious release from white values determined without black participation. It is a freedom from shame imposed from without" (Scott, 1969, p. 19).

In our minds, the preservation of Saturday night, CPT, Sounding, our emotional styles, our free sharing, our natural hair styles, telling it like it is, the way we listen, our postural gestures, and the noise we make are important. Integrated education which would make us "copies" of the quiet, white, racist middle class, therefore, from our point of view, would really mean cultural deprivation. There is a definite, traceable, and positive Afro-American culture which contains its own products and reflects certain psychological processes. This culture must be reflected in schooling and education in the inner city.

A first operational step is the process of social regeneration for blacks by blacks. The recognition of a positive heritage, the building of community, and the defining of goals by blacks are the initial steps for destigmatization and for the building of positive self-identity. Education is a central force in any movement for cultural preservation, and this force must be directed toward goals determined by black communities. It is obvious, then, that such concepts as cultural deprivation, mental retardation, and emotional disturbance are bankrupt, and have little place in the new schema for building viable educational programs to serve Afro-Americans.

What Are the Psychological and Educational Implications?

Political and philosophical rationales based upon black self-determination and black pride must determine the goals of child-rearing and socialization, within which education has a role. What becomes "special" about education is the manner and force with which it understands the saliencies of Afro-American culture and then seeks to serve that culture rather than to accommodate it.

One of the most critical areas of concern is child development and the need for the establishment of a positive pedagogy for Afro-American children. Considerable attention is now being given to "cognitive development" and "socialization" for inner-city children, based upon the presumed effects of social deprivation. There is in this, first, a tacit assumption that most, if not all, of the early experiences and later development of black children is negative and deprived. Secondly, there is an assumption of black-inferiority/white-superiority typical of the subtle supremacy argument: "What you need is to be like us because white is right!" In essence, Afro-American children can then be subjected to "cognitive stimulation," "language development," and "behavior modification" programs, all based on the assumption that they have neither a unique cognitive style nor a language which is expressive and communicative, and that their behavior is obnoxious. The extensions of this inferiority argument reach into other domains, including the imputation of family instability and the application of Victorian views of sexual behavior, to name two.

The fact of the matter is that there is little precise ecological data about child-rearing practices and socialization processes for any cultural group, and the little that is available for Afro-Americans was generated from a social order which perpetuated unconscious racism and a purposively negative view of the Afro-American experience in this country. Essentially, the pedagogical descriptions of black children have been negative, emphasizing intellectual retardation, maladaptive and delinquent behavior, self-derogation, and hopelessness. What have been systematically ignored are (1) the spontaneity, problem-solving ability, and creativity which exist and grow even under severe environmental limitations, (2) the nature and effect of peer collectives, which are the major socializing agent for the urban black child, and (3) the development of acute social perceptiveness, particularly the cognitive and affective styles which permit the development of extensive nonverbal communication processes (Johnson and Wilderson, 1969).

There is mounting evidence that the Afro-American child develops normally and positively within the dimensions of his own cultural and social environment. What must first be ascertained is, just what is the environment in which many black children live?

Living conditions for many black children are such that their primary referents are black and all other persons are intruders into the values and culture of the ghetto and thus are viewed as hostile agents of the other (white) America. To blacks, the other America is all that is not within the black community. There is an especial "black norm" of life that must be understood (Grier and Cobbs, 1968, p. 149). We need to devote attention to understanding the socialization of the black child in his black community. We need to understand and remove the black norm from any thoughts of treatment for so-called psychopathology or determination of behavioral disorders. We need to explicate their unique cognitive styles before we dare classify black children's "learning disorders." We need to build and support models of the nonverbal and verbal communications which exist in the black community.

An important task within the next few years becomes clear: *Time and knowledge must be turned toward understanding the course of socialization and affective development of Afro-American children, with black self-perceptions being the dominant focus.* The time has ended for describing Afro-American children as deviant, deficient, deprived, retarded, or disadvantaged. The development of a positive pedagogy, in terms of black self-determination, is the pressing order of business, rather than more regular and special education. Until the establishment adopts a positive perspective of blacks and builds educational programs which are special for blacks, determined by blacks, then blacks have little alternative except to reject what is offered as racist, stigmatizing, and helping to maintain a vast number of children in good and bad "nigger roles." Education must support our culture as we determine it, as it can do in a multisocial, pluralistic, technological, and humanistic society.

Education: Special or Regular in the New Conception of Urban America?

There is little doubt that the role and process of education in the cities must be based upon conceptions which are acceptable to blacks. The new environment for man in the metropolitan areas of America cannot permit conceptions which label and stigmatize its children or condone an extensive and separate educational system for special, compensatory, or supplementary concerns. The main concern of the new education must be in the form of Haworth's (1963) *The Good City*: It must include power, freedom, and community, with community being the main force for creating independence and a nexus of voluntary associations. In this conception, education must be the central force. Its goals for blacks at all levels must include more than the learning of basic subjects and the development of social and vocational skills. Education must emphasize the development of knowledge, cooperative attitudes, positive black self-identity, and an ideology of black self-determination.

What is in order is a careful determination of goals and objectives of community development for the future. We will have to develop new institutions to support these goals. One of them will be the education-centered community (Melby, 1959), in which all the forces of voluntary associations and extensive peer collectives will be directed toward education. In this institution, community involvement, leadership development, and civic participation are needed. All other structures—newspapers, radio and TV, churches, etc.—have a role to carry out, as has the school. As Melby (1959) has stated:

> At the education-centered-community level of development, schools are not only doing things for people; they are involving people in the process of building both themselves and their communities and thus adding a new dimension of power to their activities. (p. 49)

Another institution of the future might well be the child care community, suggested by John R. Platt (1969). He has proposed a new "self-maintaining social institution" based upon the functions of child rearing and child care. The basic model is of a group collective or self-help organization in the form of an entire neighborhood or large apartment building:

> Such a child care community might be organized with as few as 10 to 20 families, or 50 to 100 adults and children. Larger communities, with 50 to 100 families, or a total of 200 to 500 persons, would probably be able to afford more professional managerial services and a better teaching staff, with separate teachers for different age groups; the quality and efficiency of the dining services would probably be better as well. (Platt, 1969, p. 18)

We will have to look also at changed conceptions of schooling and the concepts and roles which will be required for the future. Head Start, store-front schools, individualized instruction, and team teaching are well-known and certainly must continue. However, in the black community, the development of preventive educational planning may also be a necessity. Such preventive planning would include teams of educators and social scientists, contracted by a community, who would move into that community and begin to develop educational programs for students who are not yet born and for those who are about to make a transition to a new level of schooling. Once their target population becomes available, the team would carry out the schooling and a new team would begin planning for a new population. The demands of decentralization, pedagogical integrity, and accountability could thus be met. Schooling would remain flexible and person-centered, yet achieve the goals of community development.

New structural arrangements may have to be developed, but within a set of nonmaterialistic values that will not permit large, expensive physical structures to determine the course of education. Schooling might take place in school-homes for children from the ages of three to six, the school being essentially an extension of the child's home and neighborhood. These units could be established in available but especially designed spaces, including learning laboratories and other environments which evoke explorative responses and provide immediate feedback of results. The next stage might be school-units organized upon principles of group development rather than by grades. Such a unit would provide for continuous progress and task-oriented group work. A no-retention policy would be in effect. Another structure might be the satellite school, attached to a central core. There might be a number of satellite units and one technologically advanced core. The satellite school would house 300 to 500 pupils, while the core would contain services shared by a number of satellites, including computer-assisted instruction, instructional modulation centers, closed-circuit TV production capacity, and electronic information retrieval, all formulated into an individually prescribed instructional format.

New roles, obviously, will be required. Child-development specialists who have been trained in ways of managing the child's milieu and in the techniques of causal teaching, psychoeducational assessment, and life-space interviewing will be essential. Prescription teachers with competency in criterion-referenced assessment, the specification of behavioral objectives, and programmed learning will also be required. Finally, group interaction teachers, who possess the ability to mobilize group forces and whose everyday content will be the teaching of emotional skills and strengths, will be necessary.

Above all, the new roles in this conception of education must include a commitment to the goals of the Afro-American community and attention to administrative and instructional behavior which will respect the right of self-determination. The new education must create a force for learning in which form and function are congruent.

Summary and Conclusions

One might ask, How does special education fit into all this? How will "deviant" children be dealt with? Better questions might be: Will there be a need for special education? Will there be special classes in education-centered communities? Will child-rearing communities produce disturbed children? Will any satellite school child who can achieve 90 percent success on all educational tasks be disruptive? Will any black child who is taught by persons committed to the goals of his community suffer racial dis-identity? The problem at hand is neither the reshaping of what is now called special education nor a thrust into the gradual changing of a failing, racist institution. The goal must be the establishment of a revolutionary process of education, in which no child is labeled special, in which self-enhancement, not mental health, is an objective, and in which community is the force for learning. Where "special education" fits into this revolutionary process is up to special education.

The message is clear: Special education in our inner cities suffers from obsolete, racist conceptions of deviance and unjustifiable ways of cooling out children. If special education as a way of producing self-enhancement can agree to the new black ideology and work within it, then it has a place in the new conception of education.

If not, then it falls to special education and those of us in the field to answer the question, Special education and the inner city: A challenge for the future or another means for cooling the mark out? Black Americans are not to be cooled out any longer.

References

Becker, H. S. Social class variations in the teacher–pupil relationship. *Journal of Educational Sociology*, 1952, 25, 451-65.

Clark, K. B. *Dark ghetto*. New York: Harper & Row, 1965, chap. 6.

Clark, K. B. The Negro and the urban crisis. In K. Gordon (Ed.), *Agenda for the nation*. Garden City, N.Y.: Doubleday, 1968.

Donahue, G. T., and Nichtern, S. *Teaching the troubled child*. New York: Free Press, 1965.

Dunn, L. M. Special education for the mildly retarded–Is much of it justifiable? *Exceptional Children*, 1968, 35, 5-24.

Dunn, L. M. Emotionally disturbed children: Whose fault? Whose responsibility? *Instructor Magazine*, August/September 1967, 77, 22-25.

Glavin, J. P., and Quay, H. C. Behavior problems. *Review of Educational Research*, 1969, 39, 83-102.

Goffman, E. On cooling the mark out: Some aspects of adaptation to failure. *Psychiatry*, 1952, 15, 451-463.

Goldstein, H., Moss, J. W., and Jordan, Laura J. The efficacy of special class training on the development of mentally retarded children. Cooperative Research Project 619, U.S. Department of Health, Education and Welfare, Office of Education, 1964.

Grier, W. H., and Cobbs, P. H. *Black rage*. New York: Bantam, 1968.

Haworth, L. *The good city*. Bloomington: University of Indiana Press, 1963.

Johnson, J. L., and Wilderson, F. B. The Institute for Research on the Social and Emotional Development of Afro-American Children. Manuscript proposal. Syracuse, N.Y., March 2, 1969.

Kerner, O., et al. *Report of the National Advisory Commission on Civil Disorders*. New York: Bantam, 1968.

Laing, R. D. *The politics of experience*. New York: Ballantine, 1969.

Melby, E. O. *Education for renewed faith in freedom*. Columbus: Ohio State University Press, 1959.

Platt, J. R. Child care communities: Units for better urban living. *Urban Review*, 1969, 3, 17-18.

Quay, H. C., et al. Some correlates of personality disorder and conduct disorder in a child guidance clinic sample. *Psychology in the Schools*, 1966, 1, 44-57.

Rich, H. L. An investigation of the social-emotional climate in a class of disturbed children. Unpublished doctoral dissertation, Syracuse University, 1969.

Schulz, D. A. *Coming up black*. Englewood Cliffs, N.J.: Prentice-Hall, 1969, pp. 158-161.

Scott, B. *The coming of the black man.* Boston: Beacon Press, 1969.

Tanenbaum, A. J. (Ed.). *Special education and the programs for disadvantaged children and youth.* Washington, D.C.: Council for Exceptional Children, 1968.

Tyler, R. W. Investing in better schools. In K. Gordon (Ed.), *Agenda for the nation.* Garden City, N.Y.: Doubleday, 1968.

PART VI

Perspectives on Racism

Racism is the nation's most serious disease. It affects the lives of millions of Americans, black and white alike. Within recent years the wide presence of racism has been highlighted on a grand scale by various high-level governmental task forces, yet curiously, there appears to be little significant psychological research and programming devoted to this critical problem.

The investigator or student interested in psychological perspectives on racism who consults Psychological Abstracts *will be disappointed, for the term* racism *did not occur in the index during the period 1966–1971. While this observation does not indicate categorically that psychologists are not working in this area, it does suggest that the work on racism has either not been sufficiently noteworthy or that it has not been profuse enough to catch the eyes of the* Psychological Abstract *indexers. However, some work can be considered relevant to the topic of racism—for example, studies or attitudes toward "Negroes," psychological studies on prejudice, and the like. A content analysis of* Psychological Abstracts *for a three-year period was revealing. Abstracts of several hundred research studies reported in* Psychological Abstracts *during the years 1950, 1960, and 1970 were examined to determine the kinds of work being reported concerning black Americans. Virtually all the writing could be categorized into attempts to understand some correlates of deficiencies in blacks or to explore differences between blacks and whites. Only a handful of studies concerned modification of presumed deficiencies and fewer still alluded to factors leading to the deficiencies of the individual and his family. The study of racism and racial attitudes and their modification were not topics which occurred with great frequency.*

In the first paper, James P. Comer, a black psychiatrist, traces the development of white racism in the United States, outlining the functions it has served and its transmission from one generation to the next. Given the great racial awareness and pride characterizing contemporary blacks, Comer concludes that without a significant reduction in white racism now, black reactions can only be intensified and form the basis for a "more widespread and malignant form of black racism."

Charles B. Wilkinson, in "The Destructiveness of Myths," examines beliefs, attitudes, and hypotheses that have been "formulated into 'scientific' documents, thus perpetuating fallacies found in myths." Among others, Wilkinson addresses the myth of the "Negro" past, the myth of the sociopathological basis of black inferiority, and the myth of disintegration of family structure in the black community.

J. H. Howard's "Toward a Social Psychology of Colonialism" presents a "world view" on the psychological effects of racism and oppression. The point of the article is that a number of behaviors thought to be uniquely descriptive of blacks—for example, "self-hatred," intellectual inferiority, paranoia—are shared by colonized people the world over. If black psychologists understand these phenomena and their universality, they will be able to plan how to end "the colonial relationships between the black community and white America"— another dimension of a Black Psychology.

The late Lloyd Delany's "The Other Bodies in the River" views white racism as classic pathology. Using examples from past and contemporary history, Delany examined the acting out, denial of reality, projection, transference of blame, disassociation, and justification components of white racism. This classic paper has received acclaim from a wide array of sources.

In the final selection, "Psychological Aspects of the Black Revolution," Roderick W. Pugh examines contemporary black responses to the sickness of racism. While acknowledging that the black revolution has economic, cultural, and political ramifications, the thesis is advanced that psychological factors are at the core of the black revolution. Pugh presents and elaborates psychological processes hypothesized to constitute the basis of the black revolution.

JAMES P. COMER

White Racism: Its Root, Form, and Function

After the *Report of the National Advisory Commission on Civil Disorders* (11) implicated white racism as the major cause of black and white conflict and violent civil disorders, responses ranged from angry rejection of the notion to serious calls for corrective action. One of the weaknesses of the report was that it failed to demonstrate the psychological roots, forms, and functions of racism and their direct relationship to interracial conflict and violence.

Racism is a low-level defense and adjustment mechanism utilized by groups to deal with psychological and social insecurities similar to the manner in which individuals utilize psychic defenses and adjustment mechanisms to deal with anxiety. In fact, the potential for a racist adjustment is rooted in personal anxiety and insecurity. A given society may promote and reward racism to enable members of the group in control to obtain a sense of personal adequacy and security at the expense of the group with less control. Racism is manifest in at least four major forms and in a racist society is transmitted from generation to generation as a positive social value similar to patriotism, religion, and good manners.

Racism cannot be explained on a here-and-now basis, nor can it be understood as a function of any single social condition of the past such as slavery. As evidence, Caribbean, Central, and South American countries with a history of slavery are less overtly racist today than most of the United States. Racism has a history peculiar to the specific social context in which it occurs. White racism in America grows out of the social conditions of sixteenth-century Europe and Africa and was shaped by forces specific to the formation, religious and political ferment, geography, and economics of this country.

The Reformation and the Justification of Slavery

Prior to the Protestant Reformation, which took root in sixteenth-century Europe, the exploitation of one group by another group to achieve economic, social, and psychological security did not have to be justified. Every race of man was subject to slavery, and the enslavement of women for sexual exploitation is as old as the institution of slavery itself. William Graham Sumner, a political and social scientist, wrote of Roman slavery: "The free men [Romans] who dis-

From *The American Journal of Psychiatry*, volume 126, pp. 802–806, 1969. Copyright 1969, the American Psychiatric Association. Reprinted by permission of the author and the publisher.

cussed contemporary civilization groaned over the effects of slavery on the family and private interest, but they did not see any chance of otherwise getting the work done" (14).

The Protestant Reformation spawned the belief in man's direct accountability to God, implying personal dignity and rights unrecognized before. From that point on, particularly so because the Reformation was characterized by fanaticism and extremism, it was necessary to demonstrate that the slave was a different kind of man—indeed, less than a man. That same Reformation served as a stimulus to the rise of capitalism and European expansion.

With the discovery of the new and rich land overseas, hands and bodies were needed to exploit it. But because of religious precepts that were deeply ingrained by the seventeenth, eighteenth, and nineteenth centuries, it was necessary to devalue the man who would be used to exploit the new land. No less than Her Majesty Queen Elizabeth was burdened with the awesome decision between religious values and personal greed. She said of the activities of the capricious slaver Captain John Hawkins, "It is detestable and will call down vengeance from Heaven upon the undertakers." English historian Daniel P. Mannix pointed out that Hawkins showed Her Majesty his profit sheet; she not only forgave him but became a shareholder in his second slaving voyage (10).

The highly religious early American handled the conflict with equal aplomb. Historian Basil Davidson wrote, "If European attitudes toward Africans in these early times [fourteenth and fifteenth centuries] displayed a wide range of contrasts, they were generally uniform in one important respect. They supposed no natural inferiority in Africans, no inherent failure to develop and mature" (4). But when necessary it was relatively easy to reduce the black African—different in culture, appearance, and religious practice—to the picture of a savage beast suitable for enslavement.

Because of the revolutionary ferment, with much rhetoric about freedom, rights, and representation, it was particularly necessary to show the black man as an "unfit." A determined and prolonged propaganda campaign was waged in the press, by the politician, from the pulpit, and among the populace. It established the notion that slavery was not only just but beneficial. The slaver and slaveholder viewed themselves as agents of God bringing religion, light, and civilization to black heathens. These rationalizations "poisoned" the social atmosphere of America toward blacks and firmly established the notion of white superiority and black inferiority (8).

Patterns of Adjustment to Slavery

The effect of slavery on the slave served to reinforce the rationalizations for the institution. Most of the stabilizing aspects of African culture were destroyed. Families and kinsmen were often separated. The African kinship system, economic system, government system, work, recreation, and religious systems were not permitted. Only those elements of the culture like music, the dance, and other nonthreatening features were permitted. Far from home, easily identified, socially disorganized, and despised throughout the populace, it was fairly easy to force the black African into a subservient, powerless position of forced dependency, exploitation, rejection, and/or abuse relative to an all-powerful white master and in a degraded position relative to the entire white population (2).

A range of adjustments to varied conditions of slavery was made by blacks with varying consequences (1). Identification with the master and aggressor was a frequent adjustment mode. Imitation, emulation, and acceptance of the master's values and style were a frequent consequence of this adjustment pattern. When the master was extremely paternalistic, severe dependency and infantilization frequently occurred through this mechanism. Many slaves utilized religion and personal skills to develop a relatively positive self-concept and life style independent of the master, in spite of the conditions of slavery. At the opposite pole was the slave who rejected and/or rebelled against the master and his values and style.

While many, using this pattern, made satisfactory adjustments through other mechanisms, it often led to an unstable existence. There was no longer an African culture that cherished and reinforced values and relationships leading to a delay of gratification and the development of attitudes of respect for the self and responsibility toward other people. The culture of slavery, with no real opportunity for manhood or adequacy, independent of the church and the master, often fostered the immediate gratification of sexual and aggressive impulses. It was to this group of slaves, reacting as could be predicted, that the apologists and rationalizers pointed to justify the slave system. All circumstances of slavery—from house to field, from a relatively humane to an animal-like existence—resulted in consequences that ranged from severe, disabling psychic, emotional, and social trauma to moderate impairment such as low self-esteem and group esteem.

Economic exploitation was only one benefit of slavery to whites. (There was economic advantage in slavery for poor whites in that it kept blacks off the better job market.) J. D. B. DeBow, editor of the most influential pre-Civil War periodical in the South, *DeBow's Review*, pointed up another benefit. He wrote, "The poor white laborer at the North is at the bottom of the social ladder, whilst his brother here has ascended several steps and can look down upon those who are beneath him [black slaves], at an infinite remove. . . . No white man in the South serves another as a body servant, to clean his boots, wait on his table, and perform the menial services of his household" (5). Social distance or higher status over blacks was a way in which poor whites, often living under difficult circumstances and coping with life's tasks quite poorly, could view themselves as relatively adequate.

But the psychological benefits for whites were even more extreme. Prior to the middle of the twentieth century, America was a land of rigid religious doctrine coupled with the laxity that rapid expansion, wealth, and an individualistic frontier spirit fosters. Thus man sinned, but he could not see it. It had to be denied or seen in others. Nobody was more vulnerable to the "projection of evil" or psychological exploitation than the black man.

Projection of "Bad Impulses"

Until relatively recently, the wish or expression of normal sexuality and normal forms of aggression have been viewed as bad . . . sinful . . . wrong. To reduce guilt and anxiety, the wish or desire for expression of these impulses was often projected onto blacks. Louis Jolyon West, a psychiatrist wrote, "In spite of the historical fact that for more than 250 years in North America whites were often raped, enslaved, and slain by Indians while the Negro was the white man's helper, it is still the Negro who appears in the white Oklahoma maiden's dream as the ominous rapist, and the sight of a Negro boy dancing with a white girl still moves Oklahomans to feelings and acts of violence" (15, p. 647). Charles Pinder-hughes, a psychoanalyst, gives a likely explanation (13). He points out that if a group is different in appearance, culture, and behavior—particularly when a low value is given the specific differences—the group can be associated with low things—the bottom, buttocks, genitals, and sexuality.

The apologists for slavery had made their case well and such an association was quite possible. The average white American, until recently, knew little of the black kingdoms of Ghana, Mali, and Songhay (3) or the highly ordered societies of the Yoruba, Ashanti, or Ibo (6). The myth was that the African was a naked, lustful savage running loose in the jungle before he was rescued by the white man. The Indian, while different, was an enemy to be destroyed, not to be exploited—a noble savage. Thus rationalization and debasement did not have to be carried as far in that case.

A United States Congressman from South Carolina presented the viewpoint of many in a poem written in 1837; it is short of being a classic but revealing nonetheless. He wrote:

In this new home, what'er the negro's fate—
More bless'd his life than in his native state!
Instructed . . . in the only school
Barbarians ever know—a Master's rule,
The negro learns each civilizing art
That softens and subdues the savage heart,
Assumes the tone of those with whom he lives,
Acquires the habit that refinement gives,
And slowly learns, but surely while a slave,
The lesson that his country never gave. (7)

This picture, combined with the fact that slavery left many without a purpose or opportunity beyond the gratification of basic human drives—sexual, aggressive, survival—rendered blacks as a group vulnerable to the projections of "bad impulses." The fact that the black man could not defend himself against physical, social, or psychological abuse without fear of extreme repression did not help the situation.

Skin color differences in the racist American milieu had an impact that they did not and do not have in other places. This characteristic, perhaps more than any other, facilitated the projection of "evil" sexual and aggressive impulses onto blacks. Psychoanalysts have repeatedly found among their patients a psychic association of blackness with darkness, fear, evil, danger, sexuality, and aggression. West wrote, "For man, daytime is a good time, the safe time, the healthy time, when he can see what is going on and make his way in the world. The daydream is aspiration; but the nightmare is consummate terror. . . . Night is the time of secret, mystery, magic, danger, evil; and the man of the night is black" (15, pp. 646-647).

It should be added that night is also the time when father sleeps with mother and the young child or adolescent attempts not to hear what is going on while being tempted by a guilt-provoking wish and the ultimate sin—incest. Malcolm X, the slain black leader, wrote that during his days as a hustler the most frequent sexual exhibition request he received from whites was to observe a black man having sexual intercourse with a white woman (9). One can speculate that the observers probably gained pleasure by watching their own forbidden, repressed sexual desires acted out by the evil black who seduced the good, beautiful, white, pure mother . . . even though she was a whore. Thus the need to project evil, sexuality, and aggression onto the black man added to the case against him and formed another root cause, along with economic and social exploitation, for white racism.

The Transmission of Racist Attitudes

In a reciprocating fashion, racist attitudes helped to establish racist social policy, and racist social policy became the basis for the establishment of racist attitudes. White parents often openly and inadvertently transmitted racist attitudes and adjustment techniques to their children. The racist message from a loved and meaningful adult, coupled with the racist institutional and/or societal message—from schools, mass media of all kinds, segregated theaters, ball parks, water fountains, etc.—made it difficult for a child growing up in America to develop anything other than a racist attitude, ranging from benign to malignant. The white Mississippi youngster who heard the late Senator Theodore Bilbo declare in a public speech that he did not want an egg from a black chicken or milk from a black cow, emphasizing his antagonism toward blacks, received preparation for the establishment of an extreme racist attitude. The suburban white child who pointed to a black youngster in the city and said, "Look Mommy, there is a baby maid" had received preparation through isolation for a benign but nonetheless racist attitude.

In the heat of the current attack on racists and racism, the distinctions between the varying forms of racism are often blurred or ignored. I. A. Newby, in his book *Jim Crow's Defense* (12), described three different forms of racism or three major groupings of racists—extremists, moderates, and reformers—all racists but of different degrees and advocacies. Extremists are described as openly hostile and endorsing repressive policies to maintain white superiority.

Moderates are also convinced of the innate inferiority of blacks but urge understanding and reason. The reformer, consciously and unconsciously, accepts the concept of black inferiority but explains it away as a product of environment. He usually supports the extension of basic rights to blacks—the ballot and economic opportunity—as long as white supremacy and control can be maintained. Newby was describing the period between 1900 and 1930. To this classification probably should be added a group that acknowledges racial differences without a value judgment and favors equal opportunity but occasionally manifests racist responses as a result of growing up in a society that has sanctioned, promoted, and transmitted racist attitudes.

All forms of racism from the benign to the malignant are harmful—to blacks, whites, and the society. Again there is a parallel between the psychic and social defense and adjustment mechanisms. A low-level or inadequate psychological defense mechanism may lead to personality disturbances, difficult interpersonal relationships, and mental illness. Racism, a low-level defense and/or adjustment mechanism utilized by groups in a social context, leads to intergroup conflict and a malfunctioning society.

Prior to the past few years a positive racial identity was not widespread or sustained among black Americans. As a partial result, expressions of white racism often were not met with anger and rebellion. Today black awareness and pride are pervasive, even affecting very young children. Without a marked reduction in white racism, black reaction can only be expected to become more intense and form the basis for a more widespread and more malignant form of black racism. Such a development threatens the continued existence of the society.

References

1. B. A. Botkin, *Lay my burden down*, Chicago: University of Chicago Press, 1945.
2. J. P. Comer, Individual development and black rebellion: Some parallels, *Midway*, 1968, 9 (1):40–46.
3. B. Davidson, *The lost cities of Africa*, Boston: Atlantic-Little, Brown, 1959, chap. 3.
4. B. Davidson, *Black mother*, Boston: Atlantic-Little, Brown, 1961, p. 5.
5. J. D. P. DeBow, The interest in slavery of the southern non-slave holder, in E. L. McKitrick (ed.), *Slavery defended: The views of the Old South*, Englewood Cliffs, N.J.: Prentice-Hall, 1963, p. 174.
6. J. L. Gibbs, Jr. (ed.), *Peoples of Africa*, New York: Holt, Rinehart & Winston, 1966.
7. W. J. Grayson, *The Hireling and the Slave, Chicora and other poems*, Charleston, S.C.: McCord & Co., 1856.
8. W. D. Jordan, *White over black*, Chapel Hill: University of North Carolina Press, 1968, part 3.
9. Malcolm X, *The Autobiography of Malcolm X* (with the assistance of Alex Haley), New York: Grove Press, 1966, p. 120.
10. D. P. Mannix, and M. Cowley, *Black cargoes*, New York: Viking, 1965, p. 22.
11. National Advisory Commission on Civil Disorders, *Report of the National Advisory Commission on Civil Disorders*, New York: Bantam, 1968, p. 2.
12. I. A. Newby, *Jim Crow's defense*, Baton Rouge: Louisiana State University Press, 1965.

13. C. A. Pinderhughes, Understanding black power: Processes and proposals, *American Journal of Psychiatry*, 1969, **125**, 1552–1557.
14. W. G. Sumner, *Folkways*, New York: Dover, 1959, p. 294. (Originally published in New York by Ginn, 1906.)
15. L. J. West, The psychobiology of racial violence, *Archives of General Psychiatry*, 1967, **16**, 645–651.

CHARLES B. WILKINSON

The Destructiveness of Myths

As we have heard of the "myth of the Negro past" (7), we hear now of the "myth of the Negro present" (1). If national and local action programs to improve the black person's plight are based on unconsciously or consciously perpetuated myths, and if the myths are derived from erroneous formulations, such programs cannot be anything other than destructive. Interpretations of disparities between black and white family life and educational achievement may be based on false premises, developed so as to appear authentic. Well-intended plans made to eradicate these disparities may prove to be destructive instead. Such are the contradictions that can arise from myths.

While the word *myth* connotes fictitiousness to most persons, myths can be vital to history and to the strengthening of tradition. According to Toynbee (16) there are three techniques of viewing and presenting the objects of thought in which the phenomena of life inherently exist. The first of these, history, is based on the determination and recording of facts. The second is scientific: Comparative studies of determined facts produce series of general laws. In the third technique, the facts are re-created in an artistic fashion and are presented in the form of fiction or drama.

Despite this classification into three categories, the boundaries are not necessarily distinct. History and fiction particularly draw upon and have recourse to each of their respective methods, and history also makes use of scientific laws. Of significance is the realization that history, and consequently fiction, has roots in mythology.

Myths spring from history. At some point a story or a statement of primeval reality begins, and from that moment it provides a means of orienting oneself to reality by supplying a pattern woven of moral values, sociological order, and magical belief:

Myths are stories which, however marvelous and improvable to us, are nevertheless related in all good faith, because they are intended, or believed by the teller, to explain by means of something concrete and intelligible an abstract idea or such vague and difficult conceptions as creation, death; distinctions of race or animal species; the different occupations of men and women; the origin

From *The American Journal of Psychiatry*, volume 126, pp. 1087–1092, 1970. Copyright 1970, the American Psychiatric Association. Reprinted by permission of the author and the publisher.

of rites. . . . Such stories are described as etiological, because their purpose is to explain why something exists or happens. (9)

Myths can program the writing of history.

Freud in *Totem and Taboo* (5) resorted to myth in presenting the basis for paternal authority and the maintenance of civilization. He never indicated his belief or disbelief in his legend, stating that whether it actually happened or not was unimportant since it corresponded to the myths and dreams of all of the human race (15). Similarly, it does not matter whether the saga of Adam and Eve in the Garden of Eden is or is not a historically confirmed fact. What is important is that this myth presents a picture of the birth of human moral consciousness that has truth and meaning assumedly for all people of all ages and religions (10).

Myths, then, are vital ingredients of civilization in that they help develop social structure and cultural products. They strengthen tradition and endow it with value and prestige by attaching it to both a higher and more supernatural basis than exists in contemporary society. But myths not only may disclose the truth, they can also serve to disguise truth.

Modern man, like his primitive predecessor, is beset by fears and complicated situations that may appear insoluble. Although primitive man's fears were more naturalistic than his present-day successor's, the threats to both individual and group security are no less severe in the current technological age. Occurrences and events beyond immediate comprehension, conflictual situations, and unexpected sudden changes are some of the external crises that threaten individual and group security and create anxiety. Threats originating from internal sources relating to feelings of inadequacy, failure, guilt, repression of undesirable impulses, etc., similarly produce anxiety, which may be enhanced or precipitated by external pressures. The immediate responses are usually defense reactions that tend to minimize the disturbing unrest. A frequent defensive maneuver is the use of the myth. When man has available a means of providing himself with an apparently rational answer to seemingly insoluble problems, regardless of its validity, he then has a readily available defense for his anxiety.

In a nation in which a series of myths has been built up with their bases rooted in a difference in skin color, one segment of the country, commonly termed "the white majority," has a readily available source of beliefs that it may use to relieve its anxiety. White Americans can thus use myths to buttress for themselves as valid their view of black Americans as being different and inferior. It is not uncommon both in daily life and in psychiatric practice to observe a direct relationship between degrees of belief in prejudices (and their accompanying myths) and fluctuations in levels of anxiety. During times of inner peace prejudices may lie quiescent, but when security is disturbed, they erupt with renewed intensity (6).

Some of the myths underlying prejudices are that blacks are morally inferior to whites, who by implication become very moral, and that blacks are childish,

irresponsible, and given to the pleasure of the moment; also, they are supposed
to be sexually overresponsive.

Myth of the Negro Past

The mythology that has evolved about the Negro is in part traceable to the
failure of the scholars who have assumed the task of investigating the Negro past.
In these investigations, errors have been flagrant, scholarship shoddy, and research efforts slovenly. Believing that nothing of Africa could have remained as a
functioning reality in the life of Negroes in America, students have repeatedly
relied on assumption rather than fact, and this has served only to compound the
original series of errors. In summarizing these failings, Herskovits has formulated
them into what is known as the Myth of the Negro Past (7), a condensed version
of which follows:

*Negroes are by nature of childlike character and both readily and happily
accept and adjust to the most unsatisfactory of social conditions. Those Africans enslaved and brought to the new world consisted only of the poorer
stock, the more intelligent having evaded captivity. Those enslaved came from
all parts of the African continent, thus differing in language and custom. Their
loss of tribal identity through their wide dispersal throughout the new world
was of no great consequence since there would have been no common basis for
understanding or communication if placed together. Even if enough Negroes of
a given tribe would have had the opportunity of living together and continuing
their customary mode of behavior, the culture and way of living was savage
and so low on the scale of human civilization that the obvious superiority of
European customs would cause them to give up their pristine traditions rather
than preserve them. The Negro is thus a man without a past.*

To accept this myth requires overlooking now historically documented facts
that challenge the validity of these statements. The area that suffered the greatest losses to the slave traders of the Western World was a relatively small section
of the African continent, an area in the coastal belt of West Africa (principally
the Gold Coast and Ghana) and a part of the Congo. The major tribes in these
areas were large and had achieved a complex political, economic, and social
organization. Except for local differences, they were remarkably similar in language and culture.

There was no selectivity in slavery. This is particularly evident when the two
principal means of procuring slaves are considered: kidnapping and capture in
warfare. In the former instance, slavers would set out by boat from the mouth of
a river and simply take by force anyone whom they encountered. In the latter, a
victorious tribe could rid itself of enemies captured in conflict at a profit. Also, a
local ruler could dispose of intratribal political enemies. As a result, the slaves
who were exported to the New World covered a wide socioeconomic range.
Records reveal that slavery was not endured as passively as written American

history would have us believe. There were innumerable revolts—aboard ship as well as in the Americas. In addition, suicide, mass suicide, infanticide, running away, massive work slowdowns, destruction and loss of tools, etc., were other means by which the African black resisted slavery (18).

While the acceptance of the erroneous myth of the Negro past was an error on the part of scholars, it was a blessing for the practical American, for it provided him with a rational basis for the entire dehumanizing process of slavery. Once the black's position was clearly defined as genetically or inherently inferior, a certain group of responses by the slave owner had a logical and justifiable foundation. He could be sympathetic and treat all his slaves as children regardless of age; or he could be cruel, subjecting his chattels to beatings, overwork, and family separations; or he could be indifferent and treat his possessions as simply objects to further his own economic cause. Moreover, after the black's inferior status was established, his responses to this kind of treatment could be labeled categorically. These stereotypes formed the basis for how whites were to relate to blacks and also established the white person's means of understanding black persons. Since no other kind of alternative was permitted, the responses became self-fulfilling, thus further fixating the stereotypes.

Although slavery as an institution is a thing of the past, the myths and accompanying stereotypes remain. Since the doctrine of racial inferiority was responsible for many of the laws as well as our nation's code of ethics that separated whites from blacks, it is apparent how destructive a myth can be when it does not convey the truth.

While there is no denying the viciousness of slavery and of the discrimination and economic deprivation that followed Emancipation, it is apparent that considerable distortion exists in the interpretation of their effects.

Sociopathological Basis for Inferiority

Recent years have produced a growing change from the belief in the inferiority of black people on a genetic basis to a belief in the inferiority of black people on a sociopathological basis. This is founded on the fact that the trials and tribulations undergone during years of legal subjugation, followed by a freedom of sorts, have created a set of complexes that have produced behavioral and adjustment patterns that deviate from those of the white majority. Measurement for this societal deviation is based on a white middle-class yardstick. Statistics have been accumulated pertaining to the lack of conformity of the black person to "normal" standards. This portrayal of the black as a "sick white man" has moved Baratz (1) to call this "the myth of the Negro present."

Scholars of the eighteenth and nineteenth centuries erred by failing to investigate and analyze objectively the culture and social background of blacks imported from Africa and hence failed to see that a large group of people were being forced into an alien cultural mold. Scholars and behavioral scientists of the twentieth century are erring by making judgments of ghetto blacks based entirely on an idealized norm that may not only be alien for many blacks but probably is also apocryphal.

A few of the erroneous and uncertain aspects of the existing myths pertaining to blacks and whites are offered for consideration at this point.

Foremost in the sociopathological tangle are the treatises on the disintegration or lack of family structure in the black community (11). Perhaps the most popular of these themes is that the black community has been forced into the model of a matriarchal family structure, which is labeled as being out of line with the rest of American society (2). It is explicit in this statement that some other type of family structure prevails as the norm in American society. Indeed it does, but it is questionable whether the patriarchal structure that is held in such esteem and taken for granted is really the norm of white middle-class America. It is noted with considerable frequency in the white middle and upper middle classes that often the father's business and executive responsibilities keep him out of the home to such a degree that he is rarely with his family (17). Despite the fact that the reason for his absence differs from that of his black counterpart, the bulk of the child rearing, as in the black family, requires a heavy input on the part of the mother.

Findings from investigations into family roles in white suburban communities directed by Schneider (13) reveal that rather than the family being father-centered, the husband and wife are actually coequals. Interestingly, the study reports that the initial response of the wife to the question about who is head of the family always produced an answer in favor of the husband. However, further inquiry made it clear that the wife had equal responsibility in all of the major decisions; it was expected that things would be done together; the husband was frequently active in child care roles usually designated as women's work. On occasion during reinterview in the husband's absence, the wife was found doing work about the house that one would expect to be done by a man. In one instance, a wife explained that she was repairing the roof because her husband became dizzy with heights. One may wonder if the marked emphasis placed upon a matriarchy in the black community is in reality a result of the projection of the anxiety of the white male community. These fears could be a result of the insidious slipping away of the system of patriarchy, which nevertheless is clung to tenaciously as an ego-strengthening need.

That a large number of black family households are headed by women is undeniable, but this finding is also present in diverse peoples in many parts of the world, many of them without a history of slavery. The common feature in practically all of these instances is poverty (8). Although it is readily admitted that female-directed households, common-law marriages, and illegitimacy are found among the poor regardless of ethnicity or geographical location, their occurrence in this country is more often found in the black minority than in any other group. Thus methods and programs that attempt to rectify these situations all too often become intermingled with racial rather than poverty issues and can result in confusion around the original goals.

Most of the emphasis in research on black families has been on the matriarchal structure; studies of the intact ghetto family are rare. An exploratory study by Schulz (14) was too small to permit conclusions to be drawn but nevertheless introduced pertinent features for further exploration. These families, despite the openness to life on the street, were amazingly cohesive. The father was not found to be simply subordinate to his wife. His family status was dependent upon several things—his ability to earn a living and share it with his family, to deal with the harsh realities of the ghetto, to adhere to the norms of a monogamous marriage, and to be a "pal" to his children. In cases where there was no hope of upward mobility, the ability of the family to cope with the environment as it existed was the decisive factor that held the family together as a unit.

This brief study is important because the author, instead of labeling his subjects and drawing comparisons with time-worn norms, made an effort to understand the adaptive devices the family utilizes in order to survive.

Another important area in which much has been written pertains to the failure of the black underprivileged child to achieve in school. Middle-class culture has molded the school, its educational techniques, and its theory. According to Deutsch (3) it is not only the Negro child but all children from impoverished, marginal social and economic conditions who are ill prepared when they enter the school situation. This is because their socializing process is different from what is demanded of them by the school. The living conditions of the families of these children are often characterized by the presence of a large number of siblings, affording no opportunity for privacy, and an environment in which there is a scarcity of objects that could serve as stimuli as well as a means of providing familiarity with the tools and equipment made use of in school. Although the environment is noisy, it is not meaningful to the child but instead is an unavoidable and ever present background, contributing to his inability to maintain attention. Moreover, the home is not verbally oriented, so there is little or no practice in auditory discrimination or feedback from adults, which would permit a correction of grammar, pronunciation, and enunciation. The net result is a youngster whose achievement level decreases by the time he reaches the fifth grade due to underdeveloped language and to cognitive difficulties.

In addition to these deprivations, Deutsch finds the Negro child to be the victim of special circumstances. A prominent feature is the broken home due to the absence of the father. As a result, the lower-class Negro child entering school has had no experience with a successful male, nor is he provided with the psychological framework through which he can feel that the use of effort will bring the possibility of achievement.

Several years later the same author, after observing black children in Head Start programs, stated that achievement in school did not require the father to be in the home (4). The decisive factor appeared to be the presence of two adults in the household, but the sex of the second person did not make a difference. The adults could be the mother and an aunt or grandmother, or even an older sister. It would appear that what the young student needs is to observe and hear the planning of adults within the home. This also offers him the probability of participating in an adult verbal exchange, which is an opportunity that is not available when there is only one adult in the household. The fact that children not only achieve but adapt appropriately to the classroom when there is more than one adult in the home is also corroborated by Schiff (12) in a first-grade project in the Woodlawn area of Chicago.

The Linguists' Approach

Considerable attention has been focused on such language and cognitive deficiencies in lower-class black children principally by three major professions: educators, psychologists, and linguists. The educators, working under the assumption that there is a single correct way of speaking, described these children as essentially verbally destitute and noted that when they did talk, their speech was deviant and filled with errors. The psychologist reaffirmed this inability to talk and further considered it to be a deterrent to cognitive growth. Linguists, however, are interested not in the "correctness" of the speech but in the function and structure of an utterance. They also work under the assumption that any verbal exchange utilized by a community that has a well-ordered system with a predictable sound pattern fulfills the requirement of a language. By these criteria no language is better than another. Furthermore, the linguist feels that children learn a language in the context of their environment—this is not simply because the father is in the home or that the mother reads books to them, but rather because the language they speak is the one they hear constantly. This is the language to which people in their environment respond (1).

The linguists have taken a different and perhaps more workable approach than the educators and behavioral scientists. It has a distinct advantage in that it does not attach a label of illness to the clientele with whom they work. It is based on the simple premise that if ghetto children have a language of their own at the time of entry into school, they can be taught English as a second language.

Needless to say, the myths of male inferiority, racial abnormality or inadequacy, deviance, or illness have had their effect on America's Negro population as well as on the white. Much misinformation has been absorbed as truth and perpetuated by blacks, thus compounding the difficulty of designing appropriate ameliorative measures.

Summary

Myths are vital ingredients of civilization. The fact that myths may disguise the truth as well as they may disclose truths makes them potentially destructive, particularly when their legends become institutionalized. This is exemplified by early American myths which held that black persons were inherently inferior to whites. In present-day America, this genetic basis for inferiority is being replaced by the belief in an inferiority with a sociopathological basis caused by the oppressiveness of slavery and the failure to rectify the ills that followed this subjugation. The fallacious aspects of some of these present-day myths as they pertain to black and white families, poverty, and social achievement were briefly examined. The important issue is that action programs that are supposed to improve the black person's plight may be based on these erroneous judgments and formulations.

Undoubtedly there are many more beliefs, attitudes, and hypotheses that have been formulated into "scientific" documents, thus perpetuating the fallacies found in myths about black people. Those presented represent several prominent ones. Some of these, through further and more intensive investigation, can be exploded, which can help destroy the damaging and destructive uses of myths. Such corrections could help give impetus to new myth formations and symbols that can be particularly important in helping black persons establish a sense of worthwhileness for themselves; American society as a whole would then no longer project evil under the delusion of myths.

References

1. J. C. Baratz, Language and cognitive assessment of Negro children: Assumptions and research needs. Paper read at the annual meeting of the American Psychological Association, San Francisco, Calif., September 1968.
2. Department of Labor, Office of Policy Planning and Research, *The Negro family*, Washington, D.C.: U.S. Government Printing Office, March 1965.
3. M. Deutsch, The disadvantaged child and the learning process, in H. Passow, (ed.), *Education in depressed areas*, New York: Teachers College Bureau Publications, 1963.
4. M. Deutsch, personal communication, October 1968.
5. S. Freud, *Totem and taboo*, vol. 13, J. Strachey (trans.), New York: Norton, 1914.
6. Group for the Advancement of Psychiatry. Report No. 37, *Psychiatric aspects of school desegregation*, vol. 3, New York, May 1957, pp. 16-25.
7. M. J. Herskovits, *The myth of the Negro past*, Boston: Beacon Press, 1958.
8. O. Lewis, The culture of poverty, *Scientific American*, 1966, 215, 19-24.
9. B. Malinowski, *Magic, science and religion*, New York: Doubleday, 1954.
10. R. May, The significance of myth for mental health. Read as the Roy A. Roberts Visiting Scholar Lecture, Rockhurst College, Kansas City, Mo., February 2, 1969.
11. T. F. Pettigrew, *A profile of the Negro American*, New York: Van Nostrand Reinhold, 1964.
12. S. Schiff, personal communication, October 1963.
13. D. Schneider, personal communication, October 1968.
14. D. A. Schulz, Variations in the father role in complete families of Negro lower class, *Social Science Quarterly*, 1968, 49, 651-659.
15. D. Stafford-Clark, *What Freud really said*, New York: Schocken Books, 1965.
16. A. J. Toynbee, *A study of history*, London: Oxford University Press, 1956.
17. F. E. Wawrose, personal communication, October 1968.
18. C. B. Wilkinson, Racism, Paper read at the Rights of Man Series, Augustana College, Sioux Falls, North Dakota, October 1968.

J. H. HOWARD

Toward a Social Psychology of Colonialism

It is well known that few of the psychological and sociological studies of Afro-Americans have been done by blacks themselves. However, what is perhaps more significant, few of the studies by black scholars have reflected a world view clearly different from that of their white counterparts. This brief essay is an attempt to suggest what the foundations of such a perspective or frame of reference may be.

Our efforts to create a productive and clear frame of reference are impeded by the fact that there is little if any meaningful theoretical work being done in American psychology and indeed in American social science in general. The "system maintenance" connotations of Parson's so-called *Theory of Social Action* is clearly antithetical to the interests of the black community, in addition to being needlessly unintelligible. It has been, nevertheless, the only serious attempt to give coherence to an otherwise unrelated aggregate of studies. The only unifying themes discernible have been a reification of logical empiricism as method and as Frantz Fanon has said, a unilateral declaration of the "normative value" of Western culture.

The "Minnesota empiricist" approach to the universe is both myopic and, most importantly for our purposes, ahistorical. This is to be expected in a country more concerned with social engineering than with human development. The study of the so-called Negro American, which has become so fashionable among white scholars in recent years, has suffered because of the narrow definition of psychology and because of the provincial insistence that the study of the black man in the Americas can only be undertaken within the national boundaries of the United States. Consistent with this point of view has been the definition of the Afro-American and other Third World peoples as a "minority problem." This myopia may be a perceptual defense against the fact that the white population is a minority on the planet by approximately four to one, even if one excludes the intermixtures.

To correct this situation we must look beyond the narrow conception of psychology and beyond the boundaries of the black community in America. A small but suggestive body of literature supports the enlargement of our view. Hopefully more thorough analysis and experimentation in the future will confirm our brief and tentative suggestions.

When a sister or brother fries his hair or bleaches his skin, this has traditionally been called "self-hatred" behavior following the work of Kurt Lewin (1948). In the current resurgence of black nationalism, this is referred to as the "Oreo" phenomenon. It is likely that such a person will be referred to as "Negro" rather than "black." But when the wife of General Nguyen Cao Ky has plastic surgery done on her eyes to make them less slanted, as some 200,000 Asian women do annually (1), it is scarcely noticed in the black community. Both of these attempts to become more "beautiful" are of the same order of phenomena, for they are both attempts to become more European looking. Both are manifestations of what my colleagues and I call the "colonized mentality."

There are many similarities in the behavior of Third World people which have not been given as much attention as the differences. There have also been consistent approaches to the study of "minority" peoples which invite our reinterpretation. Undoubtedly nothing has been so thoroughly studied as the "intelligence" of non-Western people. Contained in Shuey's (1958) survey and other reviews of the literature on Afro-Americans (2) are hundreds of measurements of black "IQs." Not until Klineberg's well-known study in 1935, did American psychologists begin to tire of attempting to validate the myth of black mental inferiority.

What is significant about these numerous, ethnocentric, and futile efforts is that, at the same time these studies were being done, the mental abilities of thousands of Africans were being meticulously measured in all parts of colonial Africa. An annotated bibliography by Andor (1966), compiled for the South African government is filled, like Shuey's, with numerous studies seeking to establish the mental incapacity of Africans.

In both the American and African research, the Europeans have frequently debated the intellectual ability of blacks. As interesting as this debate has been, we will decline to review it since none of this activity has changed the history of colonial domination. In fact, this research has helped to maintain colonialism both here and in Africa by asserting the "native's inability" to determine his own destiny. In Zimbabwe, or Southern Rhodesia as the Europeans call it, for example, there were in 1958 twenty-three secondary schools for 300,000 Europeans and two for 3,000,000 Africans (3), as the "scholarly" debate continued over whether or not the African had a brain.

The search for the black man's mind has been almost as old a quest in Western social science as the search for his "soul." Second in number to the intelligence studies, have been a series of "personality" investigations in both America and Africa. The often quoted psychiatric study of Kardiner and Ovesey (1951), *The Mark of Oppression*, and the Thematic Apperception Test (TAT) study by Karon (1958), *The Negro Personality*, both found massive amounts of suppressed hostility and low feelings of self-esteem. Both of these feelings, Kardiner argued, led to fear which may be manifested as self-abnegation, caution, and "apologetic" behavior. Kardiner goes on to say that blacks become depressed because of the inability to express their anger at the source of their frustration. Karon also found that blacks make frequent use of denial, and fear the direct expression of aggression. They often had the "idea that some one is making trouble for you" (4). According to Kardiner and Ovesey, blacks compensate their feelings of inferiority by use of denial, humor, flashy dressing, drinking, "vituperative gossip," disparagement, gambling, and "explosive spending" (whatever that means). They conclude their portrait by saying "he tends to live from day to day because of an inability to plan" (5). Without commenting upon the rather familiar ring of their findings, the assumption inherent in psychoanalytic theory, that somehow the fault lies inside the individual, should not be missed.

Although Kardiner and Karon's findings are familiar, what are not so well known are the findings of De Ridder in his *The Personality of the Urban African in South Africa* (1961). In a TAT-type investigation sponsored interestingly enough by Shell Oil of South Africa, it was found that (a) the African personality is characterized by strong feelings of anxiety and insecurity; (b) the African frequently turns to crime, in particular he joins the so-called "tsotist" gangs which feed parasitically off the African ghettoes or townships; (c) the urban African personality is a personality with strong, latent aggression and insufficient moderation and control; (d) there is a strong American influence on the slang language of the gangs; (e) there are trends toward exhibitionism, a feeling of "being discriminated against," general suspicion of Europeans, outspokenness, and criticism of urban policy (6). Although it is not difficult to imagine that the African in South Africa feels "discriminated against" since he lives on reservations called Bantustans, must carry a pass at all times, and is subject to indefinite arrest, it is hard to imagine De Ridder's surprise at his own findings when he says that these "urbanized communities seem to develop a being 'discriminated against type of complex,' with the result that their general perception has become so biased that in many instances they apperceive well-meaning European motives in a totally wrong light" (7).

As interesting as the South African study is, what is more remarkable are the findings on other colonized people in widely different parts of the world. Studies by Doob (1954–1957) found considerable hostility and resentment toward Europeans among the Luo, Ganada, and Zulu peoples of Africa as well as in Jamaicans. Doob noted that this tendency was particularly pronounced among the more educated "natives."

Studies of American Indians by Havighurst and Neugarten (1955), Kluckhohn and Leighton (1946), and Leighton and Kluckhohn (1948) found great discontent and hostility. So-called acculturation studies of other Indian groups such as the Ojibwa (Hallowell, 1955; Caudill, 1949), the Chippewa (Barnouw, 1950), and the Wisconsin Menomini (Spindler, 1955) consistently show the negative impact of Western culture on the personality dynamics of these people as revealed by projective tests. For example, Cheyenne children tended to see the external world as hostile (Alexander and Anderson, 1957).

Furthermore, studies of native and foreign-born Chinese by Abel and Hsu (1949) showed that American-born Chinese display a high incidence of adjustment problems and greater anxiety when compared to those born in China. One of Doob's conclusions was that the less the contact between non-Western people and Europe, the better the impact upon the natives, an important exception being where the indigenous culture is similar to the invading colonizer.

One of the most provocative findings in the Kardiner and Ovesey study was the Rorschach analysis done independently by Goldfarb. He found that 88 percent of the blacks studied tended to perceive mutilated human bodies or parts of bodies in the ink blots (8). These findings were the same as those of DeVos and Miner (1959) in a sample of Algerians. It should also be noted that Algerians who lived in the city of Casbah, thus having more contact with the French, showed this type of projection with much higher frequency than the portion of the sample living in the countryside. Similar findings have been noted in the samples of Japanese immigrants to America also studied by DeVos (1954). Although there may be deeper levels of interpretation, these findings again point to the existence of massive amounts of suppressed rage (9). The findings may also suggest the projection of feelings about the mutilation of the ego under condition of domination.

How can we account for the universality of these findings in such widely scattered places and among such culturally and racially different people? Clearly, the genetic explanations so favored by racist sectors of the scientific community past and present are ruled out by the wide genetic differences among the samples. It is unlikely also that the members of the samples all have the same personality. Therefore, the explanation must lie in the similarity of the social situations in which each of the peoples studied find themselves and the devastating impact that those social relations and processes have upon their being. This impact produces the "colonized mentality" which was formerly said to be the "self-hatred" phenomena in "minority" groups. Obviously, dominated men hate their oppressors as well as themselves.

An important question in all this is how the massive amount of hostility and resentment is handled by the personality and by the social institutions of the "native." These responses are perhaps most clearly seen among those who have been more colonized than anyone else, those who have physically survived the most brutal system of slavery in the history of man—black people in America.

We have tended not to look at black history as the history of resistance to colonization because it appeared that slavery was a relationship "between individual slaveholders and slaves or landlords and sharecroppers, rather than essential social relations between metropolitan white society and colonial black society in which the rapid development of the former society occasioned the veritable destruction of the latter society" (10). Colonialism is the aggression at all levels, physical and cultural, by one society or group of societies upon another, such that the existence of the colonized is subjugated to the survival of the colonizer. It is a system, as Fanon says, of "organized domination," where racism is but the most visible aspect of the "systemized oppression of a people" (11). Our former "culture, once living and open to the future [became] closed, fixed in the colonial status. . . . The social group, militarily and economically subjugated, is dehumanized in accordance with a polydimensional method" (11). To accomplish this, of course, the colonized must be removed from history, not just from the historical records published in metropolitan Europe, but from the process of history itself.

This removal from history, as Memmi likes to say, is "the most serious blow suffered by the colonized. . ." (12). The result is the destruction of the native's own systems of reference, and he attempts, because nothing else is left, "to immitate the oppressor and thereby to deracialize" himself. This is the deeper meaning of "self-hatred," self-doubt. As Clark (1958) and Frazier (1962) have often noted, blacks express their feelings of inferiority by overidentification with the white society and the rejection, or perhaps more accurately, the negation of themselves. The overdriven quest for status, ambivalence about personal identity, the creation of social and religious myths (14), supermasculinity or the swaggering bravado I like to call the "pimp syndrome"—all of these are attempts to deal with the severe ego destruction undergone by colonized man.

These compensations are, of course, by no means confined to the American black man. For example, the popular press recently noted that General Ky changed his appearance in order to win over more of his own people: "Gone is the dashing Captain Midnight look, the tailored black flying suit, violet scarf, pearl handled .38," now there are Mao-styled suits (15).

Often these various ego compensations are unsuccessful, and the result may be severe aberrations of the personality such as schizophrenia. Note in light of the previous remarks the productions of the following psychotics studied by Myers and Yochelson (1948):

R. E. is a nineteen year old who had an acute schizophrenic reaction after being inducted into the Army. "I am not black or white but I am red. . . . I am John J. Anthony's son. I am white (looks at his hands). No, black, black, used to be white—tried to bleach myself burning my skin with a flame thrower in Tokyo."

J. W. was hospitalized when he persistently reported dreams to the police in which he saw "colored women having white babies with wings." He maintained that he was born in Germany and that he had no Negro blood in him. . . . he claimed people had put camphor and asafetida in his blood and caused him to turn black.

A patient whom I tested, diagnosed as a severe neurotic, gave the following response to the blank white card number 16 on the Thematic Appreciation Test. After some hesitation she said:

This is a special white board and it has special powers. And if you touch it, you can become the same color as the board. And it's meant for people who don't like the color they are. If you touch it, it not only changes your skin color, but also your eye color and hair color. So if you're Puerto Rican, or a Negro, or a Chinaman, you can touch this board and be a blond, blue-eyed, Caucasian.

There is often continuity between so-called normal and pathological cases. One is able to see perhaps more clearly in the extreme cases the tendencies latent in more organized personalities. For example, note this comment by a schizophrenic black male. In speaking about his peers in the hospital, he said, "some of their mothers must have been direct descendants of an uncivilized section of darkest Africa" (16). Weaver (17), in studying "normal" black children, recorded how these children recollected having first discovered that they were Negroes.

Child 1
I can remember when I was real small how children would be drawn away from me by their mothers and told that I was a black African cannibal, and that black was evil.
Child 2
A small child came over and called me a nigger. Having lived in an all-Negro town all my life, I had never been called a nigger like that before. I thought something terrible had happened to me. Of course, I knew that I was another color but I was proud of our people until that time.

These comments by children remind us of the terrible impact which the school as an institution makes upon black children. Grier and Cobbs (1968) are very correct when they say that the school evaluates the entire being of the black child when he enters and not just his competence. To a black child all intellectual activity is thus alien to him. The severest impact is upon the black male, for it must be remembered that the colonized male is very much the target of the colonial system. A number of studies have shown that the black male is failed more often, and tends to be encouraged out of the school system with much greater frequency than the black female (18). It it little wonder then that the black school children protect what is left of their egos by calling anyone who succeeds academically a sissy.

So much for descriptions of what is and what has been. The only reason for describing what the outlines of a psychology of colonialism may be is to call for the participation of black psychologists to help end the colonial relationship between the black community and white America. We must begin to do experiments to find out the best ways of developing black people on their own terms rather than to continue to use the instruments of the colonizer to describe what colonization has done to us. We must end the tradition of what one of my colleagues likes to call the "victim analysis" type of research and begin to do reconnaissance research on every colonizer. The history of lynching, which is not over, would be a useful starting place since it reveals deep fears which have helped to produce the long history of hatred and aggression against us. I might suggest that lynching is an early sample of "overkill" requiring both a political and psychodynamic approach to understand it.

The current notions of a psychology of adjustment as psychological health are inappropriate to our struggle. As Albert Memmi says, "the colonial condition cannot be adjusted to; like an iron collar, it can only be broken" (19). Thus, if there is to be therapy for black people, it must be a therapy of struggle. If it is the condition of colonized people to be torn from their past, then the struggle must involve a poignant sense of history. If the colonized culture is "closed to the future" as the master psychologist of colonialism, Frantz Fanon, suggests, then we should see this manifested in individuals as fatalism. Note the theme of powerlessness in another TAT fantasy from the patient mentioned earlier:

Card 11

Well this is heaven, what heaven really looks like. It's ruled by six people and these are standing here. (center detail) They are looking down on the world and they rule everybody's life like puppets on a string. They can do what they like with people below and the funny thing is that out of all these people, not one of them is good. They just have a lot of cruel fun with people on the earth. I guess they just make life one big joke. . . .

This severe fatalism brings out nicely the essence of the colonized world view. Colonized people do not seriously deal with their own existence.

We must begin to educate our children without transforming them into white Anglo-Saxons in black skins, to borrow a phrase from Nathan Hare (1964). (Nobody, not even white folks, seems to be pursuing *that* any longer.) We must end the use of testing designed to contain and control our existence. We must take the notion of nation building seriously as a crucial stage in the creation of a new world. We must think of black people as a whole because, although we think as individuals, we are treated as a whole. Black professionals must undergo a process of decolonization so that we can think as social scientists and not continue to be defined externally as psychologists, anthropologists, et cetera.

Finally, a wider point of view is needed if we are to learn the bitter lesson of South African blacks who protested in the early sixties for nationalism and "community control" and got it in the form of the Bantustan reservations where they are now captive. Perhaps the best warning from Nazi-style South Africa can come from the words of De Ridder, a European "liberal," reflecting upon some of the "uppity" brothers and sisters in his study.

The educated African must be given an outlet. He has become educated to increase his earning potential and if he cannot do so, he will turn either to crime . . . or become disgruntled, frustrated, and an agitator.

The urban African tends toward immature attitudes and an exhibitionistic approach, but such functions in no way imply that he will not respond to understanding and tactful handling. He has still much to learn, especially in the spheres of emotional moderation and control. His ideas are rather egoistically biased and education tends to make him feel disproportionately superior—but he is learning.

The problem which the European in South Africa must face is what to do with those Africans whose learning has given them ambitions beyond the industrial color bar. Ambitions need outlets if their latent energies are not to be diverted by continual frustration into antisocial activities (15).

Perhaps, we can begin to see the booming "black studies *business*" in light of the South African experience!

Notes

1. *Time Magazine*, December 23, 1966, 88, 24-25. (According to the article, Madame Ky wanted to be "more charming to my husband." As Dr. Jiro Menagawa, head of the Menagawa Cosmetic Clinic in Tokyo, said, "girls come in and go out much as they go to the beauty salon to have their hair done.")
2. For surveys of this literature, see E. W. Miller, *The Negro in America: A bibliography* (Cambridge, Mass.: Harvard University Press, 1966), esp. pp. 25–33, and T. F. Pettigrew, *A profile of the Negro American* (New York: Van Nostrand Reinhold, 1964).
3. W. V. Brelsford (ed.), *Handbook of the Federation of Rhodesia and Nyasaland* (London: Cassell, 1960), p. 479.
4. B. Karon, *The Negro personality* (New York: Springer-Verlag, 1958), pp. 160–169.
5. A. Kardiner, and L. Ovesey, *The mark of oppression* (New York: Norton, 1962), pp. 325–326.
6. J. C. De Ridder, *The personality of the urban African in South Africa: A Thematic Apperception Test study* (London: Routledge & Kegan Paul, 1961), pp. 153–168.
7. *Ibid.*, p. 67.
8. Kardiner and Ovesey, *op. cit.*, p. 324.
9. G. De Vos and H. Miner, Oasis and Casbah, in M. Opler, *Culture and mental health* (New York: Macmillan, 1959), pp. 333–350.
10. R. Rhodes, and A. Montero, Papers on colonialism, 1968–1969. Unpublished.
11. F. Fanon, *Toward the African revolution* (New York: Grove Press, 1967), p. 33.
12. A. Memmi, *The colonizer and the colonized* (Boston: Beacon Press, 1965), p. 91.
13. Fanon, *op. cit.*, p. 38.
14. Compare, for example, the Nation of Islam described by E. U. Essien-Udom (*Black nationalism: A search for an identity in America*, New York: Dell 1962), with the international analysis of messianic cults by V. Lantemari (*The religions of the oppressed: A study of modern messianic cults*, New York: Knopf, 1963).
15. *Time Magazine*, Creation of Uncle Nguyen, June 21, 1968, 91, 27.
16. J. E. Lind, Color complex in the Negro, *Psychoanalytic Review*, 1914, 1(404), 43.
17. E. K. Weaver, How do children discover they are Negroes? *Understanding the Child*, 1955, 24, 108–112.
18. M. Deutsch, Minority group and class status correlated to social and personality factors in scholastic achievement, *Society for Applied Anthropology Monograph*, No. 2, 1960, p. 12. Also see P. Moynihan, *The Negro family: The case for national action*, U.S. Department of Labor, Office of Policy and Planning and Research (Washington, D.C.: U.S. Government Printing Office, 1965), p. 77.
19. Memmi, *op. cit.*, p. 28.
20. De Ridder, *op. cit.*, p. 172.

References

Abel, T. M., and Hsu, F. L. Some aspects of personality of Chinese as revealed by the Rorschach test. *Rorschach Research Exchange*, 1949, 13, 285–301; and *Journal of Projective Techniques*, 1949, 13, 285–301.

Andor, L. E. *Aptitudes and abilities of the black man in Sub-Saharan Africa, 1784–1963: An annotated bibliography*. Johannesburg: National Institute for Personnel Research, South African Council for Scientific and Industrial Research, 1966.

Barnouw, V. Acculturation and personality among the Wisconsin Chippewa. *Memoirs of American Anthropological Association*, 1950, No. 72.

Caudill, W. Psychological characteristics of acculturated Wisconsin Ojibwa children. *American Anthropologist*, 1949, 51, 409–427.

Clark, K. B., and Clark, M. P. Racial identification and preference in Negro children. In T. M. Newcomb and E. L. Hartley (Eds.), *Readings in social psychology*. New York: Holt, Rinehart & Winston, 1947, pp. 169–178.

De Ridder, J. C. *The personality of the urban African in South Africa*. London: Routledge & Kegan Paul, 1961.

Doob, L. *Becoming more civilized: A psychological exploration*. New Haven, Conn.: Yale University Press, 1960.

Frazier, E. F. *Black bourgeosie*. New York: Crowell Collier and Macmillan, 1962.

Grier, W. H., and Cobbs, P. M. *Black rage*. New York: Basic Books, 1968.

Hollowell, A. I. *Culture and experience*. Philadelphia: University of Pennsylvania Press, 1955.

Hare, N. *Black Anglo-Saxons*. New York, Mangani and Mansell, 1965.

Havighurst, R. J., and Neugarten, B. *American Indian and white children*. Chicago, University of Chicago Press, 1955.

Kardiner, A., and Ovesey, L. *The mark of oppression*, New York: Norton, 1951.

Karon, B. P. *The Negro personality*. New York: Springer-Verlag, 1958.

Kleinberg, O. *Negro intelligence and selective migration*. New York: Columbia University Press, 1935.

Kluckhohn, C., and Leighton, D. *The Navajo*. Cambridge, Mass.: Harvard University Press, 1946.

Leighton, D., and Kluckhohn, C. *Children of the people*. Cambridge, Mass.: Harvard University Press, 1959.

Lewin, K. *Resolving social conflict*. New York: Harper & Row, 1948.

Myers, H. J., and Yochelson, L. Color denial in the Negro, *Psychiatry*, February 1948, **11**, 39–46.

Parsons, T., and Shils, E. S. *Theory of social action*. New York: Harper & Row, 1951.

Shuey, A. M. *The testing of Negro intelligence*. Lynchburg, Va.: J. P. Bell, 1958.

Spindler, G. D. Sociocultural and psychological processes in Menomini acculturation. *University of California Publications in Cultural Sociology*, 1955.

LLOYD T. DELANY

The Other Bodies in the River

The Mississippi River flows murky and slow through the state of Mississippi. And the Pearl River winds a snake's course into the main stream. In 1964, when an honest search began for three missing civil rights workers, it was natural to drag the rivers.

James Chaney, Andrew Goodman, and Michael Schwerner were found. Shot, and then buried in a pit. But there were bodies in the rivers. Two were found in the Mississippi, and a couple more in the Pearl before the graves of the murdered civil rights workers were uncovered. Then the dragging of the rivers ceased. There was no investigation about those other deaths. No one really knows why the bodies were in the river, or really who they were, or how many more remain in the mud. Kipling wrote of "the great, grey, green, greasy Limpopo River." It is a terrible temptation, when speaking of the Mississippi, to add the word *deadly*.

As a nation, we do well what Freud termed *the work of mourning*, a task he described as necessary to assuage feelings of loss and guilt after facing a death. We have mourned the death of Martin Luther King, Jr., very well, indeed.

White America is shocked frequently by such violence. There is mourning in varying degrees—depending on how well-known the victim is. And we float down the River Styx while as a nation we drown the memory of violence over and over again.

For there is a sickness in our society. White racism. It is classic pathology with the usual destructive behavior: acting out, denial of reality, projection, transference of blame, disassociation, justification. The sickness of racism runs deep in the history of this nation, and no institution in society is immune.

Acting Out

The National Advisory Commission on Civil Disorders has just released its report after a lengthy study, and the report traces the history of violent acting out through many yesterdays:

Cincinnati Riot of 1829: "White residents invaded Cincinnati's 'Little Africa,' killed Negroes, burned their property and ultimately drove half of the colored population from the city."

Reprinted from *Psychology Today*, June 1968. Copyright ©Communications/Research/Machines, Inc.

New York Riot, 1863: "The crowd refused to permit firemen in the area, and the whole block was gutted. Then the mob spilled into the Negro area, where many were slain and thousands forced to flee town."

New Orleans Riot, 1870 (quoting General Sheridan): "At least nine-tenths of the casualties were perpetuated by the police and citizens by stabbing and smashing in the heads of many who had already been wounded or killed by policemen. . . . It was not just a riot, but an absolute massacre by the police."

The Commission report documents scores of such examples in decade after decade. Pathological acting out of hate also can be found in lynching statistics. The authoritative *Documentary History of the Negro People in the United States*, edited by Herbert Aptheker (Citadel Press) proves that 3,426 blacks are *known* to have been lynched between 1882 and 1947. The National Association for the Advancement of Colored People found that between 1892 and 1918, a black man, woman, or child was lynched every three and one-half days somewhere in this country.

As the President's Commission on Civil Disorders traces the patterns of racial conflict, it becomes apparent that up to and including World War II, acting out involved white racists physically attacking, destroying, and burning blacks and black property. Following World War II, and to some extent during it, the pattern of racial conflict shifted. Black violence emerged, almost entirely in attacks on property *within* the black community. Few whites were physically attacked in these disorders.

This is crucial in the context of today. For whites cringing at the prospect of black violence, it should be comforting to note that the Commission finds that all of the 1967 disorders, including those listed as the eight major areas—Buffalo, Cincinnati, Detroit, Milwaukee, Minneapolis, Newark, Plainfield (N.J.), and Tampa—involved primarily destruction of ghetto property. Almost all the serious injuries and deaths involved blacks killed by law enforcement agents.

Violence, black violence, has meant burning their own black neighborhoods, looting local stores, destroying property within the ghetto areas. These are attacks on the *symbols* of ghetto oppression. (Editor's note: The antonym of symbolic is diabolic and the American people are not a diabolic group. Perhaps this answers the question of so many whites—Why are the fires in the ghettos? It is because the attacks are symbolic. They are attacks on the *symbols* of exploitation, degradation, anger, frustration, and despair.)

Recent pathology involving law enforcement agents is familiar: State troopers with tear gas to halt the march to Jackson, Mississippi, in 1966 following the shooting of James Meredith; the National Guardsmen who shot into Newark riot area stores which had remained untouched last summer [1967] because they bore signs indicating black ownership.

No one has made this pathology as clear as Dick Gregory, the actor and active civil rights worker, in an interview in the Long Island newspaper, *Newsday*, this past March 9. Here is part of what he said:

"You ought to try to integrate those schools like we did in Greenwood, Mississippi. Spent a whole summer talking to colored folk, trying to get them

to commit their kids. Had to lie to them, tell them the government was going to protect them, but we knew damn good and well we were all going to get killed. And you finally get 12 black kids committed, but the morning school is open, you only get eight. Maybe you've got to feel what its like to be walking down the street with that little black kid's hand in your hand. And your hand is soaking wet from your sweat, because you know what's going to happen. But the kid don't. And as you approach those steps to that school, not only are you attacked by the white mob, but also by the sheriff and the police. . . .

"The next thing you know, you're knocked down in the gutter with that cracker's foot on your chest and a double-barrelled shotgun on your throat. And he's saying 'move, nigger, and I'll blow your brains out.' Which is interesting because that's the only time that cracker admits we got brains. . . .

"Maybe you have to lay in that gutter, knowing it's your time now, Baby, and then look across the street . . . laying down in that gutter, from that gutter position and see the FBI standing across the street taking pictures. . . .

"And then as you lay there in that gutter, man, it finally dawns on you that that little five-year-old kid's hand is not in the palm of your hand anymore. And that really scares you. . . .

"And you look around trying to find the kid. And you find him just in time to see a brick hit him right in the mouth.

"Man, you wouldn't believe it until you see a brick hit a five-year-old kid in the mouth."

Denial

California's State Superintendent of Public Instruction, Max Rafferty, spoke against the new Civil Rights Bill on April 11, by evading the issue. The *San Diego Union* article about his speech in that city reported:

Rafferty said the Bill is "superfluous and redundant" and would have a wicked result raising false expectations. "There are four things causing American sickness," Max Rafferty told the group, "and I think that everyone will agree there is a sickness." Rafferty listed them as violence, pornography, law breakers, and tolerance for drug users and addicts. Rafferty said he would have voted against the Civil Rights Bill "because it will not do any good."

The Jackson, Mississippi, *Clarion-Ledger* used both denial and disassociation in a 1964 editorial before the bodies of the murdered civil rights workers were found.

If they were murdered, it is by no means the first case of such disposition by Communists or their dupes to insure their silence. However, the careful absence of clues makes it seem likely that they are quartered in Cuba or another Communist area awaiting their next task. There is no reason to believe them harmed by citizens of the most law-abiding state of the Union.

After the assassination of Martin Luther King, Jr., Georgia's Governor Lester G. Maddox, reported by United Press International, demonstrated both denial and what, as a clinician, I can only call *thought disorder*. Maddox said:

> *"Could it be the Communists had decided that he, Dr. King, had lost his effectiveness, and this was a way to revitalize their efforts? Or was this only to pass the Bill (Civil Rights Bill)... I believe they done him in, and I will continue to believe that until they apprehend the killer or prove otherwise. I hope I am wrong, and the guilty person is apprehended."*

This Communist-connected form of denial is particularly dangerous, for it denies not only white citizen responsibility, but it takes the race problem right out of this country. Should this projection of the race problem onto Communists continue, it could discredit both whites and blacks who are working together to end a national shame. In addition, it will further disillusion and alienate American youths of both races, young people who seek a better future.

Denial must end, because it will take all the cooperation citizens of this country can summon to cure the sickening results of racism. Black nationalists certainly are guilty of denial, but they are hardly a threat. Everyone knows they are playing games with their dreams of separate communities. Before his murder, Malcolm X gave up the whole business of separatism and shifted toward working with both white and black elements of the community.

Martin Luther King moved from being a black civil rights worker into working for a total civil peace. He rose through the ethnocentric viewpoint to the broader vision of economics and peace.

What a symbol it is: King went into Memphis over a strike of *garbage* collectors. A strike by the lowest paid men in our society.

Certainly a current, shocking example of denial is the persistent rumor that Martin Luther King arranged for his own martyrdom, that he was somehow involved with his assassin. Obviously, he knew he was in danger when he went to Memphis. He lived with danger.

It should not have been necessary for Martin Luther King to stage marches in Montgomery, Birmingham, Selma, or to go to jail 30 times trying to achieve for his people those rights which people of lighter hue are entitled to simply by being born.

The Commission on Civil Disorders clarifies the pathology of denial: "What white Americans have never fully understood, but what the Negro can never forget, is that white society is deeply implicated in the ghetto. White institutions created it. White institutions maintain it, and white society condones it."

This sickness, which the Commission has once more diagnosed, has been explained many times and many ways. Two black men, commenting 74 years apart, spoke typically and similarly about the pathology of denial. Frederick Douglass, the leading Negro abolitionist from the early 1840s until his death, wrote in 1892:

> *Where rests the responsibility for the lynch law ... not entirely with the ignorant mob ... they are simply the hangmen, not the court, judge, or jury.*

They simply obey the public sentiment . . . the sentiment created by wealth and respectability, by press and pulpit.

Dr. Benjamin Mays, retired president of Morehouse College, said in his eulogy to Dr. Martin Luther King, Jr.:

"Make no mistake, the American people are in part responsible for Martin Luther King's death. The assassin heard enough condemnation of King and of Negroes to know that he had public support. He knew that there were millions of people in the United States who wished that King were dead. He had support."

The roots of denial are as old as the nation itself. They go deep into our foundations. Thomas Jefferson, author of the Declaration of Independence, wrote the words: "All men are created equal, . . . endowed by their Creator with certain unalienable Rights, that among these are Life, Liberty and the pursuit of Happiness." Jefferson held in bondage 106 men, women, and children—slaves. On August 26, 1814, in a letter to a friend, Edward Coles, he wrote:

Nothing is more certainly written in the book of Fate than that these people are to be free. Nor is it less certain that the two races, equally free, cannot live in the same government. Nature, habit, opinion, have drawn indelible lines of distinction between them.

Too little of our denial in thought and emotion has changed with time. White society has suffered from a long illness.

Disassociation

The process of disassociation is far more sweeping than that of denial, for in disassociation, large segments of one's actions are treated as though they have never existed. Reasonable Americans now realize they disassociated when they forgot about those three murdered civil rights workers. And it is becoming politically popular to point to our disassociation with the misery of the American Indian.

But few Americans remember the internment in the United States in virtual concentration camps of 72,000 American citizens during World War II—Japanese-American citizens. Except for the weaker parallel of Indian removal in President Jackson's day, there was no precedent in American annals for a mass internment without evidence of disloyalty, and with race as the sole determining factor. More than 30,000 families were imprisoned.

There had been a long history of strong racism directed at Japanese residents on the West Coast. As early as 1906 students of oriental background were segregated in San Francisco schools. Japanese immigrants fared exceedingly well as farmers and, beginning in 1913, land ownership laws were passed specifically to limit Japanese land holdings in California. Limits on Japanese immigration to this country became more and more stringent over the years.

Earl Warren, Chief Justice of the U.S. Supreme Court, was California's Attorney General at the beginning of World War II. That very different man led the movement to send Japanese, citizens and aliens alike, to internment camps.

War is an emotional time, but color counts. German-American citizens kept their homes and their jobs. The racial composition of Hawaii differs from that of California. There was no*such internment in Hawaii. In a speech to a convention of California district attorneys and sheriffs shortly after Pearl Harbor, Warren explained the total absence of fifth column and sabotage activities on the part of Japanese-Americans as a "studied effort to hold off until zero hour." There are no recorded cases of Japanese-American spy activity during World War II.

The scholarly book, *California*, by John W. Caughey (Prentice-Hall) describes clearly what happened after President Roosevelt signed executive order 9066, giving the War Department authority to act on *enemy aliens*.

General J. L. DeWitt then ordered "voluntary departure" of Japanese from designated coastal areas, an 8 P.M. to 6 A.M. curfew... and on March 27, 1942, evacuation of all Japanese–citizens and aliens alike. Some 110,000 persons were subject to this order, two thirds of them American citizens. Japanese Americans of western Washington and Oregon and southern Arizona were included, but the main body to be evacuated was from California....

The evacuees were transferred to more distant relocation centers, two of them on the eastern margin of California, the other eight scattered as far east as Arkansas. These were called Relocation *rather than* Concentration *camps. Barbed wire fences and armed guards gave the opposite impression.*

Some youths were released from the centers through enlistments or the draft, many of the young men went off to the battlefields in Europe and later in the Pacific, where they performed with extraordinary valor. A few were released to go to guaranteed jobs outside General DeWitt's prescribed area. Late in the war, a few were permitted to come back to California. Most were kept in camps until after V-J Day, and the Centers were not closed until January 1, 1946.

Transference of Blame

Racism, among other things, is a chronic blaming process, a process which requires self-fulfillment. The person who needs to blame the ghetto man for living in squalor, who claims that the Negro is incapable of being educated, or that the Negro doesn't really want to work, must, by the nature of the blaming process, perpetuate that which he deplores. Less than one week after the assassination of Martin Luther King, Jr., Congressman George Bush (R) Texas, submitted a bill under which persons convicted of breaking the law during civil disorders would be prevented from either keeping or getting federal jobs. The National Commission on Civil Disorders carefully explains that the dearth of jobs is a basic cause for disorders in the ghetto.

Transference is a defense mechanism by which an individual evades responsibility for his own acts by placing blame elsewhere. Perhaps no characteristic of racism is more common in this nation.

Negroes are getting tired of being blamed for living in substandard housing, for being unemployed and underemployed, and for "not taking advantage of" educational opportunities.

The Commission on Civil Disorders says:

Pervasive unemployment and underemployment are the most persistent and serious grievances in minority areas. They are inextricably linked to the problem of civil disorder. . . . Despite growing federal expenditures for manpower, development, and training programs, and sustained general economic prosperity and increasing demands for skilled workers, about two million—white and nonwhite—are permanently unemployed. About 10 million are underemployed, of whom six and a half million work full time for wages below the poverty line.

About housing, the Commission reports that

. . . nearly six million substandard housing units remain occupied in the United States. The housing problem is particularly acute in minority ghettos. . . . many ghetto residents simply cannot pay the rent necessary to support decent housing. In Detroit, for example, over 40 percent of the nonwhite occupied units require rent of over $35\frac{1}{2}$ per cent of the tenant's income.

Second, discrimination prevents access to many nonslum areas, particularly in the good suburbs where good housing exists. . . . The Federal programs have been able to do comparatively little to provide housing for the disadvantaged. In the 31-year history of subsidized federal housing, only about 800,000 units have been constructed. . . . By a comparison of a period only three years longer, FHA insurance guarantees have made possible the construction of over 10 million middle and upper income units.

About education, the Commission states that

. . . education in a democratic society must equip the children of a nation to realize their potential. . . . For the community at large, the schools have discharged this responsibility well, but for many minorities, and particularly for the children of the racial ghetto, the schools have failed to provide the educational experience which could help overcome the effects of discrimination and deprivation.

Projection and Justification

The Negro in our society is the victim of one of the most commonly employed devices used by individuals to avoid dealing with deep-seated inner conflicts. Projection lets a man attribute to others characteristics of his own which he knows or fears are unacceptable to others. James Baldwin, in *The Fire Next Time*, comments on how well white racists use this device:

If one examines the myths which proliferate in this country concerning the Negro, one discovers beneath these myths a kind of sleeping terror of some condition which we refuse to imagine. In a way, if the Negro were not here, we might be forced to deal within ourselves and our own personalities with all those vices, all those conundrums, and all those mysteries with which we infest the Negro race. . . . The Negro is thus penalized for the guilty imagination of the white people who invest him with their hates and longings, and the Negro is the principal target for their sexual paranoia. . . .

We would never allow Negroes to starve, to grow bitter and to die in ghettos all over the country if we were not driven by some nameless fear that has nothing to do with Negroes. We would never victimize, as we do, children whose only crime is color. We wouldn't drive Negroes mad as we do by accepting them in ball parks and on concert stages, but not in our homes, not in our neighborhoods, not in our churches.

Justification is fairly obvious. It is racist. And it is sick. Like a letter to the editor published in *Newsday* last month [May 1968]:

I am a white middle-class American who along with tens of millions of other middle-class Americans, both black and white, has been roundly criticized and condemned as a "racist" by the President's Commission on Civil Disorders.

I am a white middle-class American who served his country in World War II, who managed via 22 years of hard work and initiative to pull himself and his family out of the slums of Manhattan to life in a middle-class community in a house which will require 19 more years of labor to pay for.

I am tired of hearing Whitey blamed for all the plights and ills of the Negro in Harlem and elsewhere, and I am sick and tired of the "get Whitey" slogans of the black extremists who would rather take what Whitey possesses rather than working for it like this Whitey has.

Yes, I am a white middle-class American, tired but proud of my accomplishments and heritage, proud of the community in which I now reside. . . . If this be labeled racist by the learned gentlemen of the President's panel, I shall wear this label with pride. (Editor's note: The letter was signed, we withhold the name here.)

A reprint by the group for the Advancement of Psychiatry describes the adverse psychiatric effects of attitudes in whites in which

. . . a feeling of superior worth may be gained merely from the existence of a downgraded group. This leads to an unrealistic and unadapted kind of self-appraisal based on invidious comparison, rather than on solid personal growth and achievement. . . . And even encourages the expression of hostile or aggressive feelings against whole groups of people.

It forces a distortion of reality and provides a target in the lower status group for the projection of painful feelings from one's self or from the significant people in the immediate environment onto members of the segregated group. Anxiety springing from unrelated personal problems may thus be com-

batted by inappropriate displacement of the constrictual feelings to the area of race relations. Such displacement impedes direct and mature facing and dealing with the actual anxiety-arousing conflicts.

There should be pride of race in every man. The white man who justifies his prejudice refuses to accept reasons for blacks' pride. And the Negro in our culture suffers from lack of both white and black acceptance of black dignity and honor in our history. Take a few examples: that black men were with Columbus—one of them a ship's pilot; that Estevanico, a black man, discovered and explored the Southwest; and the Negro, Du Sable, founded Chicago.

Since the man who wrote to *Newsday* fought in World War II, his life may have been saved by a Negro. Dr. Charles Drew established the method for preserving blood plasma. After Dr. Drew developed this method, blood plasma was given according to race, contrary to all scientific fact that there is no difference. This irrational practice since has been discontinued.

Men like the letter writer forget that the first man to die for this nation's independence was Crispus Attucks, that 5,000 other black men fought in the American Revolution. Blacks fought with Jackson in the War of 1812; 186,000 of them in the Civil War; blacks rode with Teddy Roosevelt's Rough Riders in the Spanish-American War; black units in World War I won special commendations for gallantry. Black men fought German racism in a *segregated* army in World War II, and black men are now dying in higher proportion than whites in Viet Nam.

Certainly racism and bigotry are not limited to the United States. They are universal. In the Sudan, the Muslim North commits genocide on the African South. In India, the Hindu is directed against the Dravidian of the South. The Hottentots regard themselves as the Khoikhoin—the chosen people. The Chinese culture is highly racist; the Chinese look down on everybody else.

But our own racism is our own pathology. And we must face it. The recent rash of civil rights laws often is cited as an example of our progress. Yet these laws actually contain little that the Civil Rights Act of 1875 does not contain.

A critical question about the kind of society we are is answered by Dr. Kenneth Clark. Called to testify before the President's Commission on Civil Disorders, he said:

"I read the report of the 1919 riot in Chicago, and it is as if I were reading the report of the investigating committee of the Harlem Riot of 1935, the report of the investigating committee on the Harlem Riot of 1943, the report of the McCone Commission on the Watts Riot.

"I must say in candor to you members of this commission—it is a kind of Alice in Wonderland, with the same moving pictures shown over and over again. The same analysis. And the same inaction."

RODERICK W. PUGH

Psychological Aspects of the Black Revolution

*Our past is not our future, only a part of its foundation.
Our past has been made. Our future must be made by us.
Hare (1971, p. 37)*

What Is the Black Revolution?

We are now experiencing one of the most significant and far-reaching social developments of modern civilization. It is a social development born out of the American black man's will to survive, and beyond that, his will to overcome the effects of radical oppression and to achieve self-realization. It is a social development that is highly complex and many-faceted. It has come into being in a particular historical context, is influenced by and in turn influences processes of national and world history, and must be properly understood from a historical perspective. It is a dominant factor of national and international politics, of local and of world cultural evolution. Its central and essential features are, however, psychological. This social development is the Black Revolution.

Because this movement is highly complex and many-faceted, it can be viewed and interpreted from multiple vantage points, all of which have a certain validity. The revolution is often described in terms of specific group goals such as social, educational, economic, and political enhancement in local and world society. These are its practical end-purposes, and these goals are variously given different priorities by different factions of the national black community. Otherwise, the Revolution is sometimes characterized according to its tactics, strategies, or advocated methods for achieving its goals. It is described as violent, nonviolent, or disposed to employ "whatever means necessary" to achieve its practical goals. Such descriptions are likely to reflect the degree of militancy of the particular advocate.

Chrisman (1970), for example, takes the following popular interpretive stance regarding the Revolution:

The black revolution is both a cultural revolution and a political revolution, and each enforces the other. Politics is a cultural act and culture is a political fact. For culture is the collective thrust of a people and it encompasses the economic, political, social, and esthetic conditions of their existence. (p. 6)

This is a revision of "The Black Revolution: The Psychology of Self-reclamation," in R. W. Pugh (ed.), *Out of the Black Experience: A Symposium by Black Psychologists*, in preparation. Used by permission of the author.
344

This is a statement emphasizing the rather broadly political and cultural processes which characterize the Revolution, with mention of the economic, social, and aesthetic factors which they encompass. One can hardly argue with the general validity of this as a descriptive statement, but one might take issue with its emphasis if one is seeking a postulate of the essential elements of the Black Revolution as a process of human behavior.

Psychological Factors Are Central to the Black Revolution

It is the thesis of this essay that the essential factors of the Black Revolution are psychological because they explain the individual and group processes of evolving experience, awareness, understanding, sense-of-self, sense-of-self in relation to others, motivation, goal direction, and action, which taken together globally characterize the Revolution. There will be an attempt here to identify and to assess the principal psychological factors which are seen as basic to the Revolution as a process of human behavior.

One of the earliest published statements which grasped the psychological essence of the Black Revolution was the following by Carmichael and Hamilton (1967):

Black people must redefine themselves, and only they can do that. Throughout this country, vast segments of the black communities are beginning to recognize the need to assert their own definitions, to reclaim their history, their culture; to create their own sense of community and togetherness. There is a growing resentment of the word "Negro," for example, because this term is the invention of our oppressor; it is his image of us that he describes. Many blacks are now calling themselves African-Americans, Afro-Americans, or black people because that is our image of ourselves. When we begin to define our own image, . . . the black community will have a positive image of itself that it has created. (p. 37)

Nathan Hare (1971) makes a restatement of the above principles which reflects the trend since 1967 toward a more militant and nationalistically political stance by an increasingly large segment of the black community:

I am an African: I am the exotic quintessence of a universal blackness, an unbreakable link between my past victimization and the inevitable resurgence of an ancient and glorious history, an eternal pastness. I have lost by force my land, my language, my life. I will seize it again, so help me, but this will never be fully accomplished until I have restored the integrity of my race. (p. 35)

Morris (1969) defines revolution as "an assertedly momentous change in any situation" (p. 1113). The Black Revolution is the "assertedly momentous change" in the American black people's reassertion of themselves as persons and as a people. It is the relatively sudden emergence of changed attitudes and behavior which result from a reintegration of a sense-of-self which has been painfully long in the making.

Black people collectively are now rejecting the most insidious and debilitating effect of more than three hundred years of racial oppression in this country. *This has been a deeply instilled sense of self-devaluation and inferiority, with its accompanying pervasive insecurity and inhibition of self-actualizing assertion.* Black people are wresting for themselves again a legitimate self-concept and sense of self-esteem. The *revolutionary* impact of this development on black people as well as the overall society derives not merely from the nature of this reintegrative process per se, but most importantly from the *degree of dedication* to it. Although it is toward life that they strive, black people have demonstrated to themselves and to the world that they are, if need be, willing to put their lives on the line in order to insure authentic life for those who will survive. They no longer passively submit to the noose of the lynch mob nor to any of the less obvious but more insidious evidences of white racism. Thus, these two psychological processes are hypothesized as constituting the basis and essence of the Black Revolution: (1) a reintegration of self-concept (individual and group); and (2) a high degree of motivation (drive, dedication) toward achieving concrete goals at every level of living which support self-actualization and a constructive reintegration of self-concept.

When Was the Black Revolution Born?

Perhaps it is not entirely rhetorical to ask when did the Black Revolution begin? Again, a designated point in time for its realization might depend largely on one's principal frame of reference, whether historical, economic, political, or psychological.

The seeds of the Black Revolution were planted in the early seventeenth century on the day the first slaves were sold to traders on the west coast of Africa. From then it developed from a long evolutionary network of inter-related, supporting, and reactive processes. However, on the basis of the present thesis that the central factors of the Revolution are psychological, one might ask when was it that the psychological factors of the Revolution coalesced, thus heralding the recognizable birth of the Revolution. The Revolution was born on August 28, 1963, in the nation's capitol. The event was The March on Washington.

The March on Washington of 1963 is selected as symbolizing the psychological birth of the Black Revolution because no other single event is so responsible for the coalescing of a national sense of black unity, identity, pride, and dedication to a commonness of purpose.

It was a day to be remembered.

It was a day of sunshine and hope, of good will and of solemnity. It was a day of pride and of dignity. It was a day of rededication to the struggle for freedom now. It was an historic day. (A Day to Remember, 1963, p. 466)

Even though The March was an integrated (multigroup, multiracial) effort, the leadership and superstars of the demonstration were outstandingly black. This fact alone was history-making. Blacks had never before so proudly and impressively asserted their own leadership for all the nation and the world to witness. From that day on it was unmistakably evident that American blacks would drop the passive stance and pursue their own destiny as a people under their own leadership. In spite of the superleader of the day, Martin Luther King, Jr., and his "I have a Dream" speech which captured the emotional revival of that historical moment, it was also evident that the leadership was not ultimately centered in one person or vested in one faction.

The March on Washington was a surprise success to most American blacks. Had most blacks dreamed that it would be the success that it was, the demonstrators might have numbered two to three times the 250,000 (A Day to Remember, 1963) who were actually present. Until that day, blacks were still laboring under the self-debasing stereotype that they could never depend on each other to cooperate in any massive effort for their mutual benefit, so many did not want to go all the way to Washington to participate in a flop ("You can never count on niggers to work together or to do anything right!"). However, this notion had been progressively undermined in the minds of blacks by the success of such organized efforts as the Montgomery bus boycott of 1955, the sit-ins of 1960, the freedom rides of 1961, and the black–white confrontations in Birmingham of 1963. In addition, the heroic, self-sacrificing bravery and dedication to cause of such individuals as Rosa Parks of Montgomery, the black students of Little Rock, and above all James Meredith and Medgar Evers of Mississippi had moved every black in the country to begin reassessing his notions about his own people and his identity and dedication to the common cause of his people. A sufficient number had been so moved that they went to Washington and created on that August day in 1963 perhaps the greatest single corrective emotional learning experience for a people in all history.

The Black Revolution and Black Liberation

A few weeks ago a white colleague asked in all sincerity what it means when Negroes nowadays talk about "liberation." He said he was puzzled by this because obviously, as bad as things might still be for Negroes, certainly they were no longer slaves in need of liberation! This reaction was all the more meaningful because it came from a knowledgeable white person with extensive exposure to people and conditions in both the South and the North, who is "liberal" in his thinking and in his politics, and who rejects racism. Yet, because he views the situation from the white perspective and not the black, it is not easy for him to understand that in reality black people are still unliberated.

Black people are not yet liberated in this country because the psychological processes basic to the Black Revolution have not achieved closure: The reintegration of self-concept is not yet complete for the totality of the national black community, and the drive toward achieving support for this reintegration at every level of experience has not been satisfied. The self-actualizing goals of the Revolution, summarized by Carmichael and Hamilton (1967) as black people achieving "full participation in the decision-making processes affecting the lives of black people" (p. 47) are far from being realized. These are minimum requirements for liberation.

Otherwise stated, liberation is the freedom to be one's self fully as a human being with all aspects of one's developmental, educational, social, political, and cultural experiences supporting that freedom. When black people can fully embrace a sense of identity and self-acceptance based on criteria emanating from blackness rather than from whiteness, and when they can be essentially in charge of their own lives and free from a controlling and oppressive dependency in society, then they will be liberated. When and by what means this ideal will be achieved is yet another question.

A Summary Look at the Case History

History and Behaving Individuals

In recent years, under the impact of the Black Revolution, there has been a renewed interest in the history of blacks in this country. Over and above biologically endowed characteristics and capacities, people are made by their history. The history of a people consists of the collective ongoing experiences of the group as well as of the individual members of the group.

People are products of their history; but as they live, grow, and act they in turn influence their history or experiences. Therefore, there is an interesting interaction between ongoing experience (history) and the acting, behaving person. The less knowledgeable people are about the circumstances in which they find themselves and the less power they have in those circumstances, the less likely they are to influence their experiences (history) in the directions they might desire. For example, the experiences of an infant are largely determined by adults with power, and the adult with greater comprehension and power is in a much better position to determine the nature of his own experiences. But, in turn, the adult is most likely to influence his ongoing experiences in ways largely determined by what he has learned from his past experiences.

Blacks were transported to this country under conditions which determined that at first they had little comprehension of Western civilization in the process of industrialization, and of the total circumstances of their slavery. In addition, they were completely powerless. Suicide was about the only power option left to the individual slave. Therefore, in those years after the first slaves landed in 1619, the directive influence that blacks had on their own experiences was relatively insignificant. It was not until two centuries later that directive influence on their own experiences as a collective group had grown relatively more significant as evidenced by the lives of Nat Turner, Charles Remond, the first prominent black abolitionist, and Frederick Douglass (Bennett, 1962).

Although from the beginning there was sporadic overt resistance against slavery on the part of individual blacks and small groups, by the first half of the nineteenth century black resistance was beginning to be more sophisticated and threatening. Some blacks were beginning to show meaningful knowledgeability about the alien culture and the circumstances of their bondage. This led to rudimentary attempts at the development of power—attempts at systematic, organized resistance.

At that stage of history, however, only a relatively small number of blacks were openly involved in such action. A large percentage of blacks, out of ignorance, fear, and an adaptive inferiority, believed that their plight was no more than they should expect or even deserve (!); so they were basically accepting of their condition. There was generalized identification with the aggressor, and the form of resistance, when present, was largely passive.

Anxiety Conditioned to Blackness

Until the black revolution took form, hardly any experience of a black person in this society authentically supported his sense of self-worth *as a black person.* Some experiences may have supported his sense of worth as a good nigger slave, as a preacher, as a cook, as a school teacher, as a pimp, as a hard worker, as an athlete, as an entertainer, as a student, or as a parent, but not as a *black person.* One was a "good this" or a "good that" *in spite of* being black. One's blackness was always there to detract from a feeling of complete well-being and congruence of self. It was always there, either at a conscious or unconscious level, demanding to be dealt with. It was there decreasing one's personal acceptability because that was the constant feedback blacks received from the white majority from the beginning of their mutual history in this country. In this, this was the feedback blacks learned to give themselves as if to confirm a self-fulfilling prophecy.

What was the nature of the original black experience—the nature of the first feedback? It is now very difficult to conceive of how total the exploitation of blacks was during slavery. A slave was presented with only two alternatives: life under conditions of total exploitation—physical, sexual, and emotional—or death. Many blacks chose death; and those who chose life did so at *extreme psychological expense.* Grier and Cobbs (1968) present a brilliant elaboration of the psychology of the black experience in their book *Black Rage* which, in the opinion of this author, is "a giant step toward a definitive psychological interpretation of the relationship between black and white in this country (Pugh, 1969, p. 296)." Grier and Cobbs emphasize that the despising of blacks has been a unique element in the national character of this country, and that because of this "the overriding experience of the black American has been grief and sorrow and no man can change that fact (p. 209)."

Until very recently, blacks in this country have been considered fair game in a twelve-month open session. I can still recall the helpless dread I felt as a small child when the Ku Klux Klan paraded in my hometown, Richmond, Kentucky, and burned their huge crosses draped with rubber tires. We stood transfixed in rigid silence as they marched by, realizing that our lives depended on the whim of any single one of them, for we were without recourse. Any notion of equal protection under the law was a mockery. We were governed daily by the knowledge that the "penalty for misjudging a situation involving white men—[would be] death" (Grier and Cobbs, 1969, p. 208).

The era of lynching, which stretched essentially from the emancipation to the 1920s, was a reign of terror for black people. Bennett (1962) cites a report by W. E. B. DuBois that "1,700 Negroes [were] lynched between 1885 and 1894 [and that while] he was at Atlanta University, an average of one Negro was lynched every week" (p. 280). This was around 1901. Katz (1967, p. 344) confirms this latter count by stating that between 1892 and 1901, lynchings occurred at the rate of three to four per week. In 1892, there were 161 lynchings (Kerner, p. 216). By 1913, the estimate had dropped to 79, was down to 38 in 1917, but rose to 83 by 1919, the year after World War I. In that same year, eleven different Negroes were burned alive in six different states (Bennett, 1962). Of those lynched during the year after the "war to save democracy," a "substantial number" were black soldiers not yet out of uniform (Kerner, p. 219).

In the minds of blacks one thing and one thing only was responsible for their being terrorized, slaughtered, segregated, and oppressed—their blackness. *Anxiety was conditioned to one's blackness.* This was a simple and easy association for people to make who were exposed to few contradictory experiences and who had been held by law to illiteracy, ignorance, and superstition as slaves. One cannot minimize the force of ignorance, nor forget how painstakingly slow the first blacks began to acquire significant education and sophistication after the precedent of laws forbidding the education of slaves. Corrective emotional learning regarding blackness and anxiety associated with blackness is still in progress in 1971.

Adaptive Inferiority

Personality theory, especially that of Carl Rogers (1961), stresses the necessity of achieving congruence if one is to be a fully functioning and well-adjusted individual. A state of congruence exists when all "systems" of personality organization are "go," so to speak. This means that all aspects of personality organization are functioning well in a mutually supportive way. If there is an aspect or factor of personality which does not fit well with, function well with, or contribute constructively to the overall personality organization, then the functioning efficiency of the personality is decreased or perhaps even seriously disrupted.

Under these circumstances, the individual has two kinds of solutions available to him, broadly speaking. One kind is only a quasisolution: It is to institute some psychological stopgap measures which at best minimize or compensate for the lowered functioning. Or such psychological stopgap measures will merely ease the anxiety and unsettling feelings which accompany disrupted functioning. The other kind of solution is truly corrective: It solves the problem at its source by modifying the disrupting factor in ways that restore the congruence of the self-system and promote the full functioning efficiency of the personality.

Adaptive inferiority, identification with the aggressor, the color-caste system, and the be-like-white success formula are all psychological stopgap measures. They are sham, quasisolutions which at best placate and momentarily reduce anxiety, but they solve no problems at their source nor resolve any conflicts definitively.

Adaptive inferiority is a psychological defense which, under stress so extreme that survival itself is threatened, allows for relative intactness of functioning within a seemingly valid structure of experience. Identification with the aggressor is a similar defense. Adaptive inferiority is an easily instituted defense when there is no precedent for "equality" with the dominant group. It is much less likely to occur when there has been such a precedent.

In the seventeenth century and even now, "equality" was all too easily gauged on the basis of the most superficial and immediately evident status and power criteria such as number and size, facility with a particular culture and its language(s), material possessions, and military–political power and influence. Therefore, the black man, being on the low end of all these criteria, was easily brainwashed into believing that this was evidence for his natural inferiority, especially when he had experienced no precedent of equality with the white American majority. Likewise, the white man, because of the reverse of these conditions for himself, believed that his natural superiority over the black man was proven.

Adaptive inferiority served to reduce the impact of the black man's inner conflicts and frustrations. If one's inferiority is accepted as valid by nature, then domination by the "superior" as well as one's lessened lot in life are much more easily rationalized and accepted. One's experiences then make more sense, and the intactness of one's functioning can be relatively maintained within the context of one's experiences.

When I was an undergraduate at Fisk University in Nashville, Tennessee, the white president of the university once expressed to some of us his puzzlement as to how we managed so well psychologically under circumstances of segregation and oppression. His attitude seemed to say, "I don't think I could do it; I don't think I could tolerate it." Possibly he could not have, because he viewed the situation from a background and precedent of experienced equality. We had never had such a background. (Niggers were niggers, and white folks were white folks; and niggers just had to accept their lot in life!)

The "We-ain't-ready" Syndrome and Other Examples of Adaptive Inferiority

As recently as the mid-1960s, it was common to hear one black person proclaim on witnessing, for example, some negative stereotypic behavior on the part of another: "You see, we ain't ready!"—meaning not ready "to be treated like white folks" and to share equal rights with them. Or another example of the "we-ain't-ready syndrome" was illustrated when one black professional exclaimed with joking irony to another upon his moving into a newly available (to blacks) luxury high-rise apartment building: "Now you know no niggers need to live like this!"—meaning, as well as white folks live.

During the height of interest around the pending 1964 civil rights legislation, a near-illiterate black male, recently migrated from the South to the North, was asked about his reaction to the civil rights push in Congress. His reply in a long, slow drawl was, "I don't pay no 'tention to dat. I don't need no civil rights. That's only for people with money!" In addition to his adaptive inferiority, this man expressed some significant insight into the meaninglessness of the *right* to enjoy certain privileges without the money to afford them.

In the early 1940s, the present author conducted one of the first objective studies of the comparative psychological adjustment of black students in integrated and separate schools. The same study also attempted to assess the attitudes of blacks toward themselves (Pugh, 1941). Other early objective or semi-objective studies focusing on the psychological adjustment of blacks were those of Crowley (1932), Davis (1937), Gandy (1938), Gregg (1938), and Frazier (1940), the latter being one of five studies sponsored by the American Council on Education in Washington, D.C. All of these studies, this author's included, provided ample evidence of the negative, self-rejecting attitudes on the part of blacks toward themselves as individuals and as a group. However, *the strength of such attitudes varied and tended to be most deep-seated among the most oppressed.* Those whose oppression had been balanced by some positive experiences and opportunities for self-enhancement seemed much more *ambivalent* toward themselves and "the Negro." As a result of certain corrective experiences, their adaptive inferiority had been undermined to that extent, and consequently they were more noticeably in conflict. They were also more inclined to take further corrective action.

A reexamination of the most differentiating and the least differentiating items of a scale entitled "Attitude of Negroes Toward Negroes" which was used in a study by this author (Pugh, 1941, 1943) will serve to illustrate some of the specifics of the self-rejecting attitudes and the ambivalence of blacks toward themselves as of the early 1940s. The most differentiating items on a scale are those that tend to generate the greatest division of opinion. For example, a significant number of subjects will say "yes" to such items, but also a significant number will say "no" to the same items. The least differentiating items on a scale are those that generate no meaningful division of opinion. Although the sample on which this particular questionnaire was used was small (122 black students drawn from both integrated and all-black high schools in Dayton and Columbus, Ohio), it was considered fairly representative of the black high-school population of that time and geographical section of the country. The sample was restricted because several school principals (white) refused to allow their black students to take the questionnaire.

The five most differentiating items out of sixty were:

31—We are inferior to white people because our forefathers were earlier savages and later slaves.

54—I have often felt inferior because I am a Negro.

28—We ought not to say anything whenever one of our race is killed illegally for fear of making the white man mad.

7—Because of differences in skin color and quality of hair, prejudice within the race is to be expected.

57—I feel more self-conscious when in the presence of important white people than when in the presence of important Negroes.

In 1971, one would hardly expect these items to generate a division of opinion among black high-school students anywhere in the country.

The following were among the least differentiating items out of sixty, that is they tended to generate no significant division of opinion. The usual answer is indicated in parentheses following the item.

8—Negroes are more outstanding in sports than whites as proved by Joe Louis, Jesse Owens, and Henry Armstrong. (YES)

14—Because comedians like "Rochester" attain wide popularity among whites, they should be considered Negro leaders. (NO)

27—It would be a disgrace to the Negro race if Paul Robeson married a white woman. (YES)

34—The inferior members of our race bring down the prejudice of the white man against all of us. (YES)

5—We should expect full-blooded Negroes to become leaders of our race. (YES)

A comparative examination of these most differentiating and least differentiating items would suggest a sharp ambivalence toward "the Negro" and, therefore, toward themselves on the part of these black high-school students. While a good number felt inferior to whites because their "forefathers were earlier savages and later slaves," almost all agreed that blacks were more outstanding in sports than whites. This latter negation of felt inferiority would seem to be directly responsive to the specific corrective experience of identifying with the outstanding athletic achievements of Louis, Owens, and others. It is suggested that while there was still a generalized feeling of inferiority to whites (items 31, 54, and 57), in specific areas there was significant contradiction of this, such as in athletics.

A division in group identity is strongly suggested. The response to item 34 suggests that certain blacks were considered more inferior than others. It is also suggested that many of these students felt that wherever there were differences in "skin color and quality of hair" (item 7), even within their own race, there would be prejudice. This feeling was directly related to the existence in fact of a color-caste system among blacks at that time which was tacitly recognized and supported by many whites. The widespread attitude on the part of many blacks and also many whites was that the closer a black approximated being white, the more acceptable he was. The ultimate hitch there was that in order to be *completely accepted* one had to be *completely white*! Therefore, the be-like-white success formula was no success formula at all. The great promise held out to blacks by whites, especially those most responsible for and interested in black education, turned out to be an empty promise indeed. This was the prevailing promise to blacks until after World War II. It was this promise that supported the color-caste system and which was largely responsible for the schism that arose between the black "haves" and the black "have-nots." The correction of the schism between the more educated and affluent blacks and the more oppressed black masses is one of the primary goals of the Black Revolution.

Interestingly, just as there was relative solidarity regarding the black man's greater athletic ability over whites, there was equal solidarity in rejecting any overt endorsement of white-influenced leadership or of white criteria (items 5, 14, and 27). Last but not least, one has to point out the *fear* of the white man, which is suggested here as a very significant factor in the behavior of blacks even until the early 1940s. The responses to items 28 and 34 indicate that considerable anxiety was associated with the possibility of increasing the white man's ire to any degree and that many of these black students were inclined to avoid doing so, even to the extent of hesitating to protest an illegal murder (lynching) of a black person.

This has been a loose but, nevertheless, meaningful reexamination of one kind of data from one of several studies which attempted some objective assessment of the self-concept of American blacks in the 1930s and early 1940s. The interpretations drawn here are in general agreement with the findings of the studies as a whole.

The Black Revolution and Black-White Relations

Relationships between people achieve a certain mutuality and balance in terms of role expectancies. In stable relationships, role expectancies tend to support and reinforce each other. If one party of a relationship begins to change his role and the concept of himself in that relationship, this disturbs the mutuality and balance which the relationship had achieved in the past. Therefore, if the relationship is to maintain mutuality and balance, a role change on the part of one party forces an accommodating role change on the part of the other. Put another way, the self-concept of one party in a relationship will be affected by changes in the self-concept of the other party. During times when role and self-concept changes, and accommodations to role and self-concept changes, are being worked through by parties of a relationship, anxiety, tension, and friction within the relationship may be significantly heightened.

Whites in this country have related to blacks from a role concept of assumed superiority. Adaptive inferiority in blacks not only is seen to be reactive to assumed superiority in whites, but also it has served to support and perpetuate it. In other words, the self-concept of whites to some degree has been organized around how they have seen themselves in relation to blacks. It is hypothesized, therefore, that the basic process of the Black Revolution consists in fact of two self-concept effects: (a) there is a reintegration of self-concept on the part of blacks, which entails the assumption of a positive sense of self-esteem and a rejection of adaptive inferiority; and (b) there is a forced reintegration of self-concept on the part of whites, which undermines their assumed superiority to blacks. This forced reorganization of self-concept, which negates the assumed superiority of whites, is very threatening and anxiety-provoking to many whites and results in various kinds of "backlash" and resistance against change. Nevertheless, the Black Revolution gains much of its significance not only because it is a push toward self-realization on the part of blacks, but also because it forces the white majority toward a truly sound basis for self-realization devoid of defensive measures such as assumed superiority. The Black Revolution may likely prove to be the most healthy psychosocial development to this time in the history of man. It is a truly corrective solution aimed at modifying the conflict over blackness at its very source.

References

Bennett, L., Jr. *Before the Mayflower: A history of the Negro in America 1619-1962.* Chicago: Johnson Publishing Company, 1962.

Carmichael, S., and Hamilton, C. V. *Black power, the politics of liberation in America.* New York: Vintage Books, 1967.

Chrisman, R. The formation of a revolutionary black culture. *The Black Scholar,* 1970, **1,** 2-9.

Crowley, M. R. Cincinnati's experiment in Negro education: A comparative study of the segregated and mixed school. *Journal of Negro Education,* 1932, **1,** 25-33.

Davis, T. E. Some racial attitudes of Negro college and grade-school students. *Journal of Negro Education,* 1937, **6,** 157-165.

A day to remember—More on the Washington march. *The Crisis,* 1963, **70** (8, whole no. 606), 466-467.

Frazier, E. F. *Negro youth at the crossways: Their personality development in the middle states.* Washington, D.C.: American Council on Education, 1940.

Gandy, J. M. A study of racial attitudes of Negro college students. Unpublished master's thesis, Ohio State University, 1938.

Gregg, H. D. Non-academic and academic interests of Negro high school students in mixed and separate schools. *Journal of Negro Education,* 1938, **7,** 41-47.

Grier, W. H., and Cobbs, P. M. *Black rage.* New York: Basic Books, 1968.

Hare, N. Wherever you are. *The Black Scholar,* 1971, **2,** 34-37.

Katz, W. L. *Eyewitness: The Negro in American history.* New York: Pitman, 1967.

Kerner, Otto (Chairman). *Report of the national advisory commission on civil disorders.* New York: Bantam, 1968.

Morris, W. (ed.) *The American Heritage dictionary of the English language.* New York: American Heritage and Houghton Mifflin, 1969.

Pugh, R. W. A comparative study of the adjustment of Negro students in mixed and separate high schools. Unpublished master's thesis, Ohio State University, 1941.

Pugh, R. W. A comparative study of the adjustment of Negro students in mixed and separate high schools. *Journal of Negro Education,* Fall 1943, **12,** 607-616.

Pugh, R. W. Review of W. H. Grier and P. M. Cobbs, *Black Rage. Contemporary Psychology,* 1969, **14,** 296-297.

Rogers, C. R. *On becoming a person.* Boston: Houghton Mifflin, 1961.

PART VII

Psychology and Psychologists in the Community

How is the black psychologist to relate to the black community? Should he remain outside the struggle? Does he have skills and perspectives which can be of value to problems facing black Americans? How most effectively can his skills and perspectives be used? These, and others, are problems discussed in this section.

His existence scarcely acknowledged only a few years ago, the black psychologist is today in demand. From the growing militance of blacks, their insistence that only blacks can understand and treat the psychological problems of blacks, and white recognition of their inability to understand and cope with the new blacks have sprung new roles for the black psychologist. Problems associated with this activity at the community level are examined in two papers. In the first, "The Black Psychologist: Pawn or Professional?," Jesse J. Johnson rejects the notion that the black professional has nothing to contribute to the struggle and, indicates specific ways in which black psychologists can help repair the schism between the black professional and the black community. Complementing Johnson's analysis is Ferdinand Jones's "The Black Psychologist as Consultant and Therapist." Jones elucidates the inner dilemmas faced by the black psychologist himself who is forced to face the fact that his "grail," the credential "Ph.D.," itself bespeaks a certain establishment orientation. But he, no less than a client, is struggling with his blackness. He must be given to understand that the society in which his personal and professional success was achieved exists simultaneously in a personally destructive context. Through many examples from clinical practice, Jones highlights issues and dilemmas faced and resolved by the black psychological consultant.

Charles W. Thomas, in "Psychologists, Psychology, and the Black Community," looks at the role that white psychologists have played in the black community and concludes that such activity has been wanting. Consistent with a theme running throughout this volume, Thomas makes the point that psychologists must understand the cultural context in which the behavior occurs. Factors that impede understanding of black Americans are highlighted, and the need for psychologists to move beyond their "parochial teachings" is stressed. Thomas presses the case for the black ethic as a social science model.

The remaining papers take up various problems related to the mental health of black Americans. In "Drugs in the Black Community," William M. Harvey re-

357

minds us that the drug problem has had a long existence in the black ghetto. Its elevation to problem status, however, has come only with its entry into the white middle-class suburbs. The article is educational beyond merely providing information about the background and social and psychological consequences of drugs in the black community. In addition, Harvey provides clarification of confusing terminology in the drug area and information about the classes of drugs and their effects. Finally, details of a treatment program for black addicts are presented.

William D. Pierce, in the final paper, "The Comprehensive Mental Health Programs and the Black Community," examines the context in which comprehensive mental health programs must operate in the black community as background for structuring such programs. Attention is given to such variables as community attitude toward emotional disturbance or mental illness and its consequences for treatment programs, the establishment nature of the agent first responsible for forging a link between the disturbed person and the treatment facility, the role of religion, and the kinds of professional personnel available in the black community. The case is made that a community mental health program existing within the black community should function as a social change agent.

JESSE J. JOHNSON

The Black Psychologist: Pawn or Professional?

When the Association of Black Psychologists first issued a call for participants on this panel, I reported that I was involved in a school situation in a northern Westchester community and that my experiences might be pertinent. There was no way of anticipating the continuity of my involvement and I proposed that if it was not sufficient for a paper in its own right, that I would write a general paper on this question. The situation was the following: A racially tense atmosphere existed in a rather large high school where blacks constituted about 13 percent of the population. There had been several recent incidents, and there were many who were apprehensive that a major explosion was imminent. A number of blacks were regarded as "not deriving maximum benefit from the school opportunity," and it was felt that if a black person were brought in to counsel them, the situation might be improved. It soon became apparent that what was really wanted was someone to "quiet the natives" and that much more importance was attached to considerations of "law and order" than the needs of the students. In this situation I clearly felt I was a pawn. There was a long list of blacks who had either been on the verge of expulsion or had actually been recommended for removal. I soon began receiving communications of the following variety: "Dr. XYZ, the school psychiatrist, was wondering if perhaps you might not think that Mamie Jones is too disturbed to function in the environment of this school and whether if, in fact, you thought she might be better situated in a setting for the emotionally disturbed." But I also felt something of a pawn of the students. They were quick to perceive that attendance at weekly sessions with me afforded them some degree of immunity from immediate expulsion from school. Any additional motivation for coming was not apparent to me. When I insisted to the administration that the students not experience a sense of coercion and advised the students that the sessions were entirely voluntary, attendance dropped sharply and the project was eventually terminated.

I suppose that there may be some value in devoting the time allotted to me to an analysis of the factors that contributed to the failure of this project. It is my conviction that a much better purpose would be served by sharing with you my subsequent reflections on the necessity for an organization such as the Association of Black Psychologists and establishing some broad outlines as to how I feel its members can make maximum contribution to the black's struggle for human dignity. For me, two things are abundantly clear. There is an inverse relationship

Presented at the Annual Meeting of the Eastern Psychological Association, Philadelphia, Pa., April 1969. Reprinted by permission of the author.

between the black psychologist's degree of involvement in the struggle and the extent to which he is a pawn of the establishment. Here I simply mean those who have power over the lives of others. There is no historical precedent for any group ever voluntarily surrendering its position of advantage to the less advantaged. Any deviation from the status quo has to be on the terms of the power group. Hence the black psychologist who has a contribution to make to the struggle on his own terms, but who has been maneuvered into a position of minimal involvement by either blacks or whites, is clearly, in effect, a pawn of the establishment. The second conviction seems to me implicit in the first—that is, it is extremely doubtful that any significant contribution can be expected from anyone acting as an agent of the established order. This order I feel is all too comfortable in the present hierarchical arrangement and has no real motivation for any other. Many in the vein of Martin Luther King have attempted to engender some discomfort via "pricking the conscience of America" or stirring guilt feelings in the manner of Grier and Cobbs. However as Ken Clark points out in his review of *Black Rage*, this type of activity has been in abundance since the thirties, but the evidence for any resulting fundamental structural change is hardly overwhelming. As psychologists we know that probably the least recommended way of motivating anybody to anything is by creation of feelings of guilt.

Let us recall that I alluded to the black psychologist's being rendered a pawn by the black community. I am in complete agreement with the observation that there is a substantial component of self-hate in all blacks. This has been discussed extensively by such writers as Malcolm X. It is my contention that the present estrangement of the so-called "black bourgeois" from the black community is clearly a form of self-hate on the part of both groups. It seems to me that E. Franklin Frazier was clearly playing into the hands of the establishment with his classic attack, and the cleavage is being perpetuated by his present-day disciples in the likes of Nathan Hare, a black. Hare's account of his personal experience with black intellectuals is must reading for all would-be racists. I submit that we can hardly afford to respond in kind to the venom of the militant who accuses us of having "sold out." Some may have sold, but none are out. Those who think they are, deceive themselves. All must come to recognize that self-hate may have had some survival value for us at an earlier period as it did for those in concentration camps. However, it has no place in the present struggle. Our first order of business is to understand the dynamics of the rejection that we will probably encounter as we attempt to close the ranks. It is imperative that we work this through as we, like it or not, are all in this thing together and can ill afford to withdraw or become indifferent.

The question of how to close the ranks calls to mind one of Hare's criticisms that I consider valid and that could be leveled at many black psychologists whom I know personally. The criticism is of our seeming reluctance to take to the printed page. I, a single offender, exhort my black colleagues to join me in my resolve to publish as extensively as I possibly can, immediately. I do not intend the type of publication that enhances one's professional career, as for an example articles in the APA journals. The messages that I have in mind are intended primarily for black consumption and hence should appear in places that provide maximum exposure to blacks—*Journal of the National Medical Association*, *Ebony*, *Liberator*, *Freedomways*, *Amsterdam News*, for example. I feel that there are three broad areas about which we as professionals can provide scientific substance to the black struggle. I feel that these efforts will contribute significantly to bridging the schism between the black professional and the black community.

The first broad area pertains to the self-concept. It seems to me that the militants appear to be the principal blacks who have a real grasp of the existential dictum that existence precedes essence and as human beings blacks have subject qualities. Sartre distinguishes between a subject and an object in the example of a table. A table, he argues, has an "essence" which precedes its existence in that it is man-made. The concept existed previously in the mind of man and can be evaluated in terms of the fulfillment of the essence of "tableness" which one may define in advance. Sartre continues that man exists before he has an essence and it is man himself who eventually defines himself. Thus man is a subject in that he defines himself through his own activities, while objects are defined by the activities of subjects. The behavior of the black man in America has been more that of an object as he appears to have accepted a definition of himself that was provided him by those who would exploit him. The militants seem to be saying, "White America, I no longer accept your definition of me. I reject it categorically. I am free to define myself and I have the capacity which I will exercise forthwith." The militants need to be reassured in their self-definitional pursuits because there are many forces operative which are calculated to interfere with these efforts. Of equal importance is the necessity to get this message to the segment of the black community which seems to resist this freedom. The reasons are quite complex, but it is mandatory that they exercise this freedom lest someone, not of good-will, exercise it for them.

The second broad area might be labeled "Psychological Testing Revisited." I submit that psychological tests have been, in fact, a most effective weapon of the powerful and the privileged, to preserve the existing hierarchical arrangement. Blacks have been led to believe that an inferior performance is reflective of an inequality created primarily by nature. The story goes "heredity sets the limits beyond which the environment cannot go." This arrangement was consoling to the favored who felt that nature intended them to be entitled and the less fortunate were expected to resign themselves to a position of disadvantage. Intellectual inequality is a fundamental assumption of the American way of life. The fundamental requirements of democracy are assumed to have been met if equal opportunity for competition exists among people who are genetically unequal. The American educational system assumes unequal capacity to learn and has developed an extensive armamentarium of psychometric techniques for identifying those thought to be more highly endowed. It is obvious that if, in fact, people have inherently equal capacities, our system is grounded in quicksand and reinforces arbitrary privilege. Boyer Walsh recently reviewed the four types of evidence typically offered to prove that people are innately different in their capacity to learn. The following were their conclusions:

Studies of innate intelligence, then, have not produced conclusive evidence to justify the claim for an innate difference in individual intellectual capacity. Equally there has not been conclusive evidence that the innate potential between people is equal. The research is heavily marked by the self-serving beliefs of the researchers. Psychologists have usually created 'intelligence' tests which reflect their own values, predetermining that their own scores will be high. When they have discovered they are high they have often proclaimed such tests to be indicators of innate superiority.

Assumptions made about blacks on the basis of their performance on these tests have created their own self-fulfilling prophesies. We know as professionals that we aspire to *creating ability, increasing intelligence,* and *developing interests.* We know that we can help an individual to learn by changing his self-concept, his expectations of his own behavior, and his motivations, as well as his cognitive style and skills. It is imperative that we as black psychologists get this message to the millions of blacks who are fraught with frustration and despair and who have a deeply ingrained sense of incompetence. With their new-found awareness of their actual potential they will be a much more potent source of pressure for a change in the social system. The elite will no longer be able to console themselves with the validity of their processes of exclusion.

The third broad area might be labeled "Psychological Invalidism." If the black community were to take seriously the preachments of the writers of the Kardiner and Ovesey ilk, with their concept of the mark of oppression or their present-day counterparts such as Kenneth Clark (*Dark Ghetto*) and Grier and Cobbs (*Black Rage*), they could only conclude that that black community abounds with psychological cripples. I doubt seriously if the blacks in this room feel that they recognize themselves in the portraits that have been presented of them by these writers. I feel that I can compare ghetto experiences on the west and southsides of Chicago and Jefferson Avenue, in St. Louis, Missouri, with any of the people that these writers describe, but I do not feel that my self-concept could have been derived from their conclusions. I insist that we, as black psychologists, must get the message to the black masses that they can choose whether they will view themselves as having been scarred for all eternity. I have seen reviews of Claude Brown's *Manchild in the Promised Land* which dismissed the work as the type of a hustler. I am not convinced. This is exactly the kind of option I am talking about.

From the above remarks, it is obvious that I reject the conclusions of Grier and Cobbs who state "the black intellectual must accept his exclusion from this battle." I have conviction that with continuing messages of the three types I have mentioned, the black community will cease to view us as "outsider" and eventually we will be able to meet *the man* together—singing . . . if you like . . . not "We shall overcome" but "I aint gonna be your low down dog no more!!"

FERDINAND JONES

The Black Psychologist as Consultant and Therapist

The black clinical psychologist is increasingly called upon to perform services with the expectation that his blackness makes his service special—a valid expectation according to many black clinicians. An examination of some of the elements of that specialness is the intent of this discussion.

The rise in black awareness and the accompanying realization of the inevitable limitations of traditional social science and white-dominated theoretical positions account in part for the current urgency to employ the black psychologist. There has also been an emphasis on the development of community-based and community-controlled mental health programs. These kinds of programs are growing rapidly and stimulate experimentation with innovative ideas. They also challenge the traditional concepts of what mental health is and what treatment of "mental illness" is. One of the questions resulting from these critical perspectives is what qualifies one to deliver what services. The black psychologist, because he is a part of the challenging, reevaluative force, emerges as the sought-after professional person.

On an almost-daily basis, the black psychotherapist is referred black individuals with psychological problems who will not consult anyone white. The individuals who seek help exhibit the entire range of diagnostic pictures. They also invariably display all of the effects of being victims of white racism, which complicate and expand whatever interpersonal and emotional struggles they are having (Grier and Cobbs, 1968, pp. 154-180). They tell the therapist that they could not feel comfortable talking to a white person about their problems; they do not feel that a white therapist will understand them; they cannot be convinced of the white therapist's interest in them; they feel too angry with whites to be able to focus on anything else.

The black clinician in so much demand and legitimately needed by so many people and organizations must examine himself. He is required to reevaluate much of his training and much of his thinking about psychology and black people. He does this in the same spirit of racial awareness that is involving all blacks. Critical introspection is not easy, particularly for the kind of ambitious, achievement-inspired person who usually winds up being a psychologist these days. It involves a challenge to both what he often struggled to attain and the understandable commitment to that which he has learned. What is demanded in this kind of personal reevaluation is particularly difficult because it includes social, emotional, and cognitive as well as self-image dimensions. This necessary process is also paradoxical. On one hand, the black clinician is in the business of promoting self-examination and therefore is well-equipped to use it himself. On the other hand, this very kind of inner-viewing is part of what is often criticized by many in the black community as an avoidance of dealing with exploitative social and economic realities. It is perceived as a luxury we cannot afford. But the black clinician is unquestionably in need of such review in himself. For him it is no luxury. He knows what effects internal conflicts can have on behavior; and he has conflicts. He is black and oppressed like his brothers everywhere, but he often enjoys enough environmental comforts to be able to think that he escapes the full effects of oppression some of the time. His effectiveness with community agencies, black patients, and clients depends on how successful he is in dealing with these conflicts. He has to establish fundamental goals for himself in the light of which clearer perceptions and decision-making can take place. The black clinician must see that the society in which his personal and professional success was achieved exists simultaneously in a personally destructive context. His identification with all black struggle should be obvious. Fortunately, the nature of his work fosters this process in him. The black patients and community groups he works with and the climate of the times for all blacks stimulate the personal questioning and review he requires to be capable of performing his tasks. At least two elements of the black psychologist's specialness have been implied in the discussion so far. He has the capacity for providing services in innovative community mental health situations. This capacity exists because he is as devoted to the kind of overall challenge of the usual ways of thinking and doing things as the communities he is serving. He is also engaged in the inner personal struggles with his own blackness with the individuals he is helping, and can help them more comprehensively by being familiar with this. What else is special? At this point it might be clearer to discuss consultation and psychotherapy separately because of the psychologist's different skills, procedures, and roles in the different contexts.

The Black Consultant

One of the major reasons the black psychological consultant is uniquely valuable to black community-based agencies and programs is that he knows the setting. Not merely because he is likely to be either a product of similar neighborhoods or at least have some kind of direct personal experiences with them, but also because he is black and can understand the essentials of black life wherever it is in most of this country. This is not to imply any mysterious qualities to blackness; there are certain common cultural factors we all understand and are able to appreciate. The main point, however, is that the black consultant cannot easily maintain the kind of tunnel-vision of black life which dominates much of · social science: "The best studies of blacks are by black scholars (Billingsley, 1970, p. 138)." Similarly, the black consultant does not have the psychological need to distort the reality of black life, as is the unfortunate condition of his white counterparts. It is to the average white person's most basic, intimately personal advantage not to understand the black person's condition. Sadly, the white psychologist is no exception, generally speaking. Efforts on the part of whites to change this fact for themselves are understandably difficult. And, at least at this time, only a few seem to recognize that there is even a problem for them. Kovel (1970), Delaney (1970), Billingsley (1970), Butts (1968), and others write convincingly of the vital dependence of whites upon a definition of blacks which requires that blacks remain "the problem." It seems to be possible for the white psychologist to gain some understanding of this psychological phenomenon in personal terms only if he is unusually motivated and if he is an unusually sensitive individual. The black psychologist, however, has every motivation to maintain clear senses in this regard and is therefore definitely at an advantage.

The writer was a consultant to a storefront mental health unit in a poverty area of New York City which employed community residents as community mental health workers. He participated one day with a worker in interviewing a desperate mother. She had come in because of a "housing problem." She was living with her eight children in a three-room apartment. She had never been married. She was about to be evicted for not paying the rent. She was also scheduled to go into the hospital the coming week to have a hysterectomy. The writer went through a personal inner process which involved an effort to achieve "professional" detachment from this emotionally painful material and to offer "objective" advice. He also felt the pull to identify with the woman and her problems and to feel all of her despair, anger, and hopelessness with her. Another part of him wanted to get angry with her and to see her as the irresponsible, promiscuous stereotype of the hard-hearted black woman. The community worker, who was an expert at dealing with the reality problems the woman presented, began to handle them. He set about trying to find someone to watch over her children while she was in the hospital. He investigated better housing possibilities, etc. The consultant, aware of the mixture of reactions in himself, could eventually gain enough perspective to contribute an appropriate understanding of that part of the woman's problems which involved her concept of herself as a person and as a woman. He could help to connect these aspects of the situation with the others. His tendency to become detached and to see the client as a stereotype represented conflicts in himself. He had to get himself together. The situation aided this process. The worker expected that the consultant would be helpful. There was no mistrust of motives or commitments because of a sharing of many things apart from academic preparation, e.g., growing up in similar neighborhoods, interest in black music, involvement in political struggles in the community and political struggles in the program itself. The client, although initially guarded with both worker and consultant, nevertheless seemed to expect an understanding of her situation. She showed this by her openness and frankness. All of this positiveness served to help the situation to be constructive. For the consultant it propelled his working through an unquestionably complicated and not entirely perceptible psychological dilemma. He was free to offer what understanding he could on the basis of his psychological training as well as his knowledge of the social and reality forces which produced the problems he was helping with. The major point, however, is that the context for the black consultant was positive in the direction of achieving undistorted perception, while for most whites it would probably be the opposite.

It is the experience of many black psychological consultants to spend a great portion of their time listening to and talking with staff members in the programs they are consultants to. The consultant is very valuable in this respect. These on-the-spot raps can be about anything, including relationships with other staff members, hiring and firing issues, family and personal subjects, and so forth. This kind of service is not exclusive to the black consultant to community agencies, but in many instances the dimension of black-white is significant.

The black director of one program felt perplexed about her decision to fire an incompetent black staff member. A very excellent white staff member was the logical replacement. It was useful to go over some of the implications of her dilemma—both in personal terms and in terms of the program. The black consultant could readily understand the kind of struggle she was undergoing. He had similar questions himself in many instances. He could be of immeasurable help to her. He also understood the realities of the program's setting and its goals in the context of the community it served. The director finally decided to hire the white replacement and could feel secure in her decision after having reviewed the whole thing with the consultant.

The black consultant can sometimes gain entry into situations closed to whites. His actual acceptance requires more than his obvious racial membership, however. If it is clear to him and to his clients that he is as committed as they are to the necessary changes for blacks, he can do much toward supporting feelings of unity together with whatever else he does. Because he often has been both educated in white graduate programs and "schooled" about whites, he knows how to relate to white institutions and can often be a help in facilitating communication with whites when this is necessary.

Some years ago a neighborhood association in Harlem waged a campaign to get the city to provide more health services. It was necessary to educate the residents to the urgency of the situation and the need for action. Large numbers of individuals had to be organized to apply pressure on the city government. The black consultant helped in interesting a Madison Avenue advertising agency to donate materials and staff for one aspect of the campaign. This meant working with the advertising agency to ensure that it provided what was needed without trying to exercise any authority over how the campaign was being conducted. He also helped the community group to understand that the advertising agency could be controlled and useful in this particular project.

The black consultant can apply his understanding of psychological processes toward the development of pride in blackness with individuals and agencies he serves. Again, if he has gained in his own internal struggles, he can be effective in aiding others. The ways this can be accomplished are numerous.

A social worker of mixed racial heritage in a community mental health program was accused by some of her colleagues of being an "Aunt Tomasina." The black consultant had many talks with her about her despair over this. Her rightful membership in the black community was stressed and her own positive feelings about that identification emphasized. She was an extremely competent worker. With her strengthened sense of herself and her blackness, she could be freer to use her good skills and sensitivity to cope with the many aspects of her dilemma.

Is the patient sick or are his seeming suspiciousness and paranoia justified reactions to white racism? This kind of question is often put to the black consultant. Here the limitations of some white clinicians are obvious. Their handicap is represented in their difficulties in communicating adequately with black patients in making a diagnostic appraisal and often further illustrated in a lack of understanding of the black condition. But at least there is enough awareness for the question to be raised. The black consultant can answer the question. He can also try to do some teaching about racism and its effects on its victims and its beneficiaries.

The black consultant cannot be peripheral to the thrust of the forces for change in the communities he works in. He has to get involved both psychologically and physically. At times his contribution may have little to do with his skills as a psychologist. He should seek, however, to find ways to contribute as a psychologist. He needs to provide as much as he can; this logically means that his most developed skills should be employed. His usefulness depends on his ability to be thoughtful and to have as broad a perspective on the issues he is confronted with as possible. He then draws on his training, his experience, his knowledge of black life, and his commitment to change to come up with methods, ideas, and interpretations that can be employed by those who consult with him.

The tensions that are inevitable between black and white staff members in community programs are also often the province of the black psychological consultant, both formally and in his informal contacts. He must avoid being seen as the person who can "cool it" or sweep things under the rug. He knows that the tensions have justifiable origins. But if the whites are going to be in the program because of the realities of organization, funding, and so on, he cannot join in a move to oust them. These decisions depend on his sensitivity to the climate, mood, timing, and history of the setting. He can help to interpret and focus on the important goals and to help others to do so as well. The whites are inevitably in need of guidance in understanding the black's hostility. The implications of this lack of understanding are enormous, of course. Ridding numbers of whites of deeply ingrained distortions regarding blacks and themselves is not realistic for most programs. Some efforts at least to acquaint them with the superficial aspects of their position can be made, however. In some instances profound changes can be brought about; but these are not typical, unless there is a program set up to aim for profound change (Jones and Harris, 1971). The blacks also need to be helped to deal effectively within realistic boundaries. If the whites are going to be there, they need to be helped to deliver what they can deliver at the same time that the blacks are demonstrating leadership in terms of goals and tasks. The black consultant can be a resource for both groups.

In one community mental health program in which the writer worked, the small group of blacks in professional positions formed a Black Professionals' Committee. When this group was mentioned in a general staff meeting, an angry black staff member, who was not professionally trained shouted, "What's this professional shit?"

Professionalism represents so much of what is destructive in our attempts to be unified in the struggles for black definition and direction. It emphasizes artificial differences, and the black consultant is very occupied in most community-based programs working with the tensions among the black staff because of various frictions. Professionalism is a good example of the kind of issue that creates barriers. It implies the acceptance of standards blacks have not participated in setting up. These standards require review; they may not be germane to our conditions. These standards also stress a social and economic hierarchy which depends on the maintenance of the status quo when what is so urgently needed is an overhauling of existing systems for delivering services to people. This becomes another area of conflict the black consultant has to deal with in himself too. It involves again a challenge and sometimes a threat to what may be very basic to the consultant's image of himself and what he has tried to accomplish in his life. It includes his standard of living both in a financial sense and in terms of his personal style and manner. Much distance can be felt between people if such issues get to mean too much. Avoiding this gulf is possible if the consultant can get his priorities structured in accord with general standards of real humanity. This means an acceptance of the fact that one's own comfort and personal advancement is ultimately seccondary to the progress and advancement of the masses of black people. This does not necessarily mean the acceptance of less than the common fees for his services or his moving into a slum apartment (although such decisions may be desirable in some instances). It refers rather to a personal emphasis on what is valuable. This posture will dictate how specific decisions about one's life will be made.

This examination of the role of the black consultant has implied that the psychologist has a clinical background. However, it merely represents the experiences of this writer. Consultants with other kinds of backgrounds may draw other conclusions from their work. The issues of inner conflict regarding blackness and status and the issue of a challenging perspective on psychological problems plus the broader implications of both of these sets of factors are probably to be found in most situations black consultants are involved in. What is to be stressed is an attitude, a perspective, an identification, and a direction in which the consultant and those blacks who employ his services concur. The black consultant who is effective is a participant and a facilitator in a process of enormous significance for black people. He can aid that process with the appropriate use of his skills and understanding as a psychologist. In defining the stance he assumes, he must personally and professionally parallel the forward movement of the people and the programs he serves.

The Black Therapist

The following discussion will not deal with many issues which appropriately belong—for example, referral patterns and problems or the many factors involved in interracial therapy. The focus will be on what unique qualities characterize treatment of black individuals by black therapists. This is still an enormous subject which could be approached from many directions. Here the writer, based on his experiences, will attempt to highlight what appear to be factors common to the experience of other black therapists. However, this is a discussion about psychotherapy in general wherever it takes place—private offices, clinics, in-patient settings.

As mentioned earlier, it is certainly true that a growing number of black individuals are deliberately seeking black therapists. We must necessarily think about what it is we have to offer that cannot be found in treatment with white therapists. This raises the first very crucial question: Is it really true that there is something in the black treatment situation which cannot be duplicated in the interracial one? The answer is certainly affirmative. The next questions then are "What is that quality?" "Is it necessary to the goals of treatment?"

The individual seeking a therapist's help is in trouble. He wants the earliest possible alleviation of his distress. During the course of treatment, other goals are sometimes agreed upon. These generally involve changing situations or a personality which has been established over a long period of time. In terms, then, of short- and long-range goals, the dimension of black can vary. It also varies in individual patients or clients. And the differences among therapists will certainly influence the effects of the black dimension. It becomes clear that this is a most complex subject, further complicated by all of the hazards of subjectivity common to most discussions of psychotherapy.

Most clinicians agree that effective treatment begins with the most adequate possible assessment of the presenting problems. The black therapist with his inevitable familiarity with black life is in a position to evaluate these problems in the context of the black patient's environment. He has a natural facility and is thus significantly superior to his white counterpart with comparable clinical skills. He also has other assistance in assessing the black individual's problems in the relative readiness of the help-seeker to inform about himself. Because anxiety about communication will be logically lowered, misunderstandings based on language and style will be minimized. (There are certainly class and regional factors involved here too. Regional differences among blacks in speech, customs, etc., impress this writer as far more significant than class differences, although such distinctions are recognized.)

In the usual initial contact, the black therapist can more readily assess the meaning of the problems presented to him in the context of a life with which he is familiar. The individual's way of expressing himself is less likely to be misunderstood. He is more inclined to allow the therapist to know him. The usual kinds of protective guises present in beginning interracial relationships will be absent. The black therapist is therefore in the position to make a quicker, more comprehensive diagnosis than his white counterpart. This advantage is important in terms of speed of distress relief and in terms of fostering the therapeutic relationship which must be developed in order for effective treatment to take place.

A very intelligent black professional woman sought help because of extreme anxiety and depression. She related how miserable she was most of the time and how she had no satisfying relationships with people. She focused on her strong hatred of white people. The black therapist could see that her isolation from people was very comprehensive. He could also appreciate, however, what was special and realistic in her feelings toward whites and not dismiss them as part of her general suspiciousness. The woman had been in treatment with white therapists and had not been helped. Her work with the black therapist went very well. He could accept her in the way she needed to be accepted, provide an identification for her, understand the meaning of her hatred for whites from all sides in a way she could trust and not be handicapped by any defensiveness about race.

The therapeutic relationship which is of such importance in treatment can certainly be fostered when both therapist and patient or client are black, as we have begun to document. There are also instances, however, in which blackness is an obstacle. Because of the history of black-white relationships in this society, there are, of course, many blacks who feel that the white professional is likely to be a better trained, more competent person. The black therapist working with this handicap in his patient's thinking has to be sensitive to it and secure enough in himself to be able to help him see it for what it is. This master-slave remnant is demonstrated in many ways, and the black patient is often unaware of the contempt he harbors toward blacks. His abuse of the therapist can often bring this to the surface. His self-hatred can then be interpreted and worked on.

The advantages in the black treatment relationship are greater than such hindrances. Indeed, the working out of conflicts about one's racial identity is of the utmost importance, and references to conflicts about blackness are to be seen in many facets of all black patients' lives. It is rewarding to achieve the feeling of kinship in therapy. The establishment of that foundation depends very much on the effective handling of the inner struggle regarding blackness on both the therapist's and his patient's part. Conflicts about blackness are impossible for the white therapist to deal with sufficiently, and this is a pivotal area in the black patient's psychological life.

A black man sought help from a prominent white therapist for rather common problems regarding his marriage and other personal problems. He was initially very depressed. The therapist expertly guided his patient towards the resolution of the acute problems. His depression lifted and he felt healthy again.

When attention was drawn to the personality factors which set the stage for a lot of his acute difficulties, the issue of his blackness and conflictual feelings about it loomed very large. The therapist could recognize how important these issues were for his patient but couldn't really understand them enough to aid in their resolution (He could fortunately admit this.) The patient found it impossible to get into this area with the therapist even though he had been genuinely helped with his initial symptoms and felt positively toward the therapist. They both agreed that he should see a black therapist to work on the blackness issue.

The pervasiveness and complex depth of white racism is not yet recognized by establishment psychology or the mental health field in general. Consequently, white therapists do not learn to appreciate the racist distortions in themselves and in the rest of the American society. They cannot handle the blackness dimension in their treatment of black patients even with the most human intentions and the most proficient skills. The very sensitive white therapist can become knowledgeable about racism and its effects. He is unusual if he does, but when he does, he begins to see the limitations of his own capacities to deal with the questions surrounding blackness in black patients.

The black therapist is capable (but not always developmentally ready) to guide the black individual toward the resolution of his conflicts about his blackness. This is not to minimize the importance of other psychological conflicts, but blackness is a powerful dynamic much neglected in considerations of the personality development of black individuals. We need to know conceptually infinitely more than we do about black identity development and black family life. We do know that most of the social science literature demonstrates the distorted views of whites who were unable to know that their scholarship is as biased as it is.

"What does being black mean?"
"How black is black?"
"What do I have in me that's white?"
"Should I be ashamed of my white friends?"
"Should I be ashamed of my white spouse?"
"Do I have more in common with the whites on my job than the blacks who are doing different tasks?"
"Do I really want revolution?"
"Should I teach my child to hate whites?"
"Does wearing a wig mean I'm not black enough?"
"How can I work with them and still distrust them?"
"I've always used 'Negro,' why do I have to start saying 'black'?"

Time will probably tell us that the essential of "real" blackness is unspoiled humanness and the tenacious ability to express that humanness which black people have manifested in spite of their oppression. In very general terms, therapy should be directed toward the emphasis on the return to humanness in individuals. For black individuals in psychological trouble, self-concept improvement and the resolution of conflicts about what is important in one's life are goals he has in common with most other individuals. The difference for blacks is that a pivotal portion of an image of ourselves has been damaged by the basic inhumanity of the larger society, and we have to contend with that reality as well as with the specifics of our personal situations. Further, those standards of life which the larger society defines as desirable are contaminated with antihuman qualities such as greed, unscrupulousness, and selfishness. The black individual's behavior when viewed against the backdrop of diseased standards can be distortedly perceived. For these reasons, the many stereotypes about blacks flourish. Black laziness, passivity, stupidity, childishness, supersexuality have meaning only in a setting characterized by ruthless competition, an overemphasis on form and quantity, too much of a premium placed on control and superficiality, and a denial of natural impulses and feelings. The therapist who is black is capable of an undistorted view of his black patients' behavior in this regard. He is in the position to help them not only to see themselves more realistically, but also to see the society in a clear light. This can be a very significant and health-producing experience in the most real sense. This also invariably involves questions of political activity and other actions toward altering that which is so destructive to people. The black therapist logically encourages these actions.

In some instances, the black therapist might suggest that his black patients or clients involve themselves in appropriate political movements. Such direct guidance and other deviations from passive, psychoanalytically modeled psychotherapy illustrate the natural inclination for the black therapist to expand the boundaries of treatment. What actually helps people in psychotherapy is one of the most debated issues in clinical psychology. This writer seeks all kinds of techniques to employ to help people who come to him and is frustrated because he is not more creative about it. The verbally centered traditional psychotherapies seem too limited—especially with lots of black people.

It seemed to make sense to have therapy sessions in the home of one black family where the parents' severe marital disputes took place. The children could participate in the therapy sessions and the family in their own living room provided a natural setting for observing and interpreting the interaction between various family members.

A psychotic, alcoholic mother separated from her husband and trying to raise three children on public assistance required a great deal of active intervention, in addition to office visits. The therapist kept close touch with the workers from several agencies involved with the family coordinating the services the family required and building the relationship with the black mother.

A young black youth was in a destructively dependent relationship with a good but possessive mother which resulted in his trying to commit suicide. The therapist in the hospital actively assisted him in getting into a college where he could use his excellent intellect, be away from home in an acceptable way, and continue his treatment.

The black mother was the primary patient, but the black therapist found it appropriate to see her children for varying lengths of time to discuss the kinds of difficulties the husbandless mother could not deal with. The benefits for the whole family were tremendous.

The black therapist needs to be broad in his expectations of what such terms as *healthy* or *well adjusted* or *normal* mean. He needs to be critical of the medical model as the only way of understanding an individual's attempts to cope with life. Clearly the interaction of the black person with his environment involves the very real fact of "sick" America and judgments about blacks have to include this very significant phenomenon.

A talented black teacher sought help for a phobia which handicapped her movements. She was a highly respected churchgoing member of her community. As therapy progressed and the many conflicts she was trying to resolve with herself became apparent, she became more conscious of that part of her she had been taught to hold in check, but which she could identify as her blackness. Her style, her dress, and her priorities began to change. She found herself less liked by many of the people who previously admired her. Her own parents deplored her "militancy." But she was happier with herself and felt that she had more parts of her personality together. She ended treatment with the phobia diminished in intensity and significance. She'd made huge changes in her personality and in her pride in herself as a black woman.

Conclusion

The black clinical psychologist should be in the forefront of expanding and refining definitions of psychological problems and psychological treatment. This involves many things but seems to begin with an attitude which challenges much of what has been inaccurately attributed to the black condition by the society at large and, therefore, reflected in academic teachings. This is, therefore, the same spirit with which all blacks are beginning to view their world and themselves. The specifics of what psychological help for individuals, families, groups, or agencies will be in the future cannot be envisioned now. The main objective of the black psychologist at this time is keeping open in our understanding of the situations our black brothers and sisters in trouble bring to us, to give proper weight to the dimension of the truly diseased world in which we all strive to live, and to be as creative and unfettered as possible in offering our skills as psychologists.

References

Billingsley, A. Black families and white social science. *Journal of Social Issues*, 1970, **26**(3), 127–142.

Butts, H. F. White racism: Its origins, institutions, and the implications for professional practice in mental health. *International Journal of Psychiatry*, 1969, 8(6), 914–928.

Delaney,L. T. The white American psyche-exploration of racism. In B. Schwartz and R. Disch (Eds.), *White racism, its history, pathology and practice*, New York: Dell, 1970.

Grier, W. H., and Cobbs, Price M. *Black rage*. New York: Basic Books, 1968.

Jones, F., and Harris, M. W. The development of interracial awareness in small groups. In *Encounter: Confrontations in Self and Interpersonal Awareness*. L. Blaugh, G. Gottesgen, and M. Gottesgen (Eds.), in press.

Kovel, J. *White racism: A psychohistory*. New York, Pantheon Books, 1970.

CHARLES W. THOMAS

Psychologists, Psychology, and the Black Community

It is not entirely by accident that ghettoized people are saying, more and more, words to the effect, "Psychologists, take your psychology and go home." This growing development does not seem to disturb many men of science in psychology. If anything, research, educational, and service functions appear to be maintained by self-serving interests, as based on philosophical and scientific parameters nourished by a cover-up for a failure to see the human condition as it exists. It is around this basic flaw that psychology, in my opinion, has yet to achieve recognition as an extraordinary science that would in fact "promote human welfare in the broadest and most liberal manner." On the other hand, it would seem not only ethical but efficient to simply state that for some, the human condition will be promoted; for others, their human condition will be used to contain them. The problem is not really one whereby psychologists need to see the circumstances, for example, of ethnic minority people, but to simply see their whole society and their place in it as it is. Should that occurrence take place, they might see among other things how psychologists are sustained by and have contributed to those white racist values of society deemed too good to give up. Under the present conditions, changes will not come easily for a different fixation on scientific scrutiny, and certainly not before the traditional, cultural value system has had a more honest arrangement. The latter is difficult to achieve due, in part, to the proliferation of studies which seek to justify those social orders that reinforce the plight of those who do not fit into the dominant social group. So often the data accumulated give the curious aura of providing impressionistic confirmation which, according to Guthrie (1969) and K. B. Clark (1965), stems from the fantasy of aristocracy.

Another source of resistance to change can be seen in maintaining the meaning of too many conventional concepts. In conjunction with that reality, several implications have to be considered. As most of us know, theory is an important tool of science, which can be used in many ways. It is this mechanism, for example, that enables an analysis of structure or permits a description of a state of conditions as well as defining the major bearings of a discipline (Goode and Hatt, 1952). Of course, there is the circular condition also, in which theory

Invited address presented to the Division of Psychological Aspects of Disability at the Annual Meeting of the American Psychological Association, Washington, D.C., September 2, 1969.

375

predicts facts. The resulting circumstance is often more of the same in a more refined manner, and the best illustration of this can be seen in a review of the research findings about Afro-Americans, whereby the great majority of studies conclude that we are not only different but deviant or inferior.

The doctrine of white supremacy in social and behavioral sciences has been around for some time and has been useful in both explaining and justifying the dehumanized treatment of nonwhites (Garcia, Blackwell, Williams, and Simpkins, 1969). Conversely, it is also the use of a tradition of racism in scientific activities that maintains the testing business, publishing, and government commissions. These activities tend to promote racial tensions and by implication, at this point in time, to indicate that social scientists want to assume responsibility for destroying society. As long as psychologists omit the resonance of experiences and desires of the oppressed as well as the oppressors, they cannot have experimental modes that legitimately deal with the nature of scientific problems.

Withdrawing, or otherwise retreating from crucial social problems, will not contribute to the advancement of psychology as a science. Psychologists have not been the pacesetters of history. Rather, they fled from, or denied, the occurrence of most of the great social crises, only to merge at a later time, following the garden variety of people, but armed with some artificial distinctions made in the scientific enterprise. Professional activities have, in this connection, a significant way of repeating what society wants to hear. This situation appears to be a result of that peculiar cognitive world in which the professional has his existence; namely, "What a man sees depends both upon what he looks at and also upon what his previous visual-conceptual experience has taught him to see" (Kuhn, 1962). Along these lines, results of studies involving racial comparisons are illustrative.

Among Afro-Americans race itself is almost invariably cited as the factor that limits the human potential in some innate way. While conclusions based upon that assumption have come in for increasing criticism, as can be seen in the most recent case of the Jensen report (1969), the more subtle variations on the same theme can be observed in the work of those who have environmental orientations. With respect to the latter, one finds that attitudes, values, and patterns of social organization are learned, but little attention is devoted to the sociopolitical arrangements that determine the very special cultural behavior of those who are disengaged from the white, Anglo-Saxon, Protestant norm. Differences reported in sex roles, identity formation, child-rearing practices, social skills, and a variety of interpersonal functions have been extensively documented by a large variety of scholars. In one report, by way of illustration, David and Pearl Ausubel cited 130 different references by 114 professionals. Yet, the typical report seems to have two serious limitations. One is the orientation of psychology in the direction of pathology. The other involves an almost total lack of recognition of institutionalized racism as a basic factor influencing the life styles and particular motivational patterns of so-called disadvantaged minority people. In a mutually reinforcing manner, these two assumptions have contributed to sustaining racial attitudes and the formation of laws and general social practices. At the least there are some notions about changing the individual to fit the existing social and legal structures (Ausubel and Ausubel, 1963).

Under these limitations those facts uncovered have not been particularly revealing of the nature of various personal-social arrangements found among ghetto people. If anything meaningful has been achieved, it seems to be the direction of reducing the scope of problems around behavioral response sets, while increasing the accuracy of maintaining ghetto residents not only as different, but inferior and hopelessly deviant as well.

Racism: A Dilemma for Psychologists

For many social scientists, this is no easy dilemma to resolve. Racism, in its overt and latent manifestations, has been a part of their adjustment mechanisms throughout life. In addition, their education did not contain significant exposure to historical parameters as an important factor in referential processes and the latter's impact on behavioral response sets. Hence, one might state simply that social scientists are equipped neither by temperament nor by training to consider anything other than the universality of white cultural norms. In this connection, there has been no significant change in the community of psychologists that would alter the constellation of facts, theories, and methods. Scientific activities continue to be limited in both scope and precision with respect to extending knowledge of those facts inherent in the social system upon which experimental models are constructed.

A real discovery of the human condition of those who are socially disengaged by virtue of age, sex, race, or social class requires an awareness of how the demographic variable in and of itself does not account for more than a suggestion of a relationship between the variable and some personal-social circumstances. In actuality, however, it is not infrequent to find explanations of sociocultural patterns based on a personal trait. Normative differences in society, at the present time, would seem to require a revolution in conceptual schemes. Should that condition obtain, it would encourage new questions about old data as well as the formulation of new conclusions from the existing evidence. Behavioral response sets would become the indices of social efficiency instead of the static, psychodiagnostic classifications that have little bearing on immediate social realities. No amount of humanistic disguise in the way of a social penalty for being too old, nonwhite, female, or having low test scores will lessen the trauma for receiving treatment at an infrahuman level. Nor will the continued use of the tools of science to sustain such circumstances serve the best interests of society. Kuhn (1962) stated it very well when he wrote, "Assimilating a new sort of fact demands a more than additive adjustment of theory, and until that adjustment is completed, until the scientist has learned to see nature in a different way, the new fact is not quite a scientific fact at all" (p. 53). Hence, the prevailing distinction of many behavioral activities has been not simply a focus on isolated events but isolated effects in a repeated social structure. Facts, theories, and methods assembled in the name of science are no better than the men of that science. Some will recoil from the indictment that in psychology as a whole, the actualization of institutionalized racism is quite apparent in the determination of significant facts, the matching of facts with theory, and the articulation of that theory.

A Challenge for Psychologists

The challenge to be confronted lies in working through that professional vanity which does not allow for radical social-scientific changes in treatment, organization of services, or expectations based on a single choice that is virtually impossible to pursue. Significant improvement in the applied, human-centered areas of psychology will come in direct proportion to the extent that findings from ethnological research are incorporated into the spectrums of psychological paradigms. Anthropological studies have underscored the importance of understanding the cultural context of relationships and have shown that behavior regarded as abnormal in one culture can be socially acceptable in another.

The same observations appear to hold with subcultural groups. Research involving Afro-Americans, for example, most often reflects interpretations that do not consider the cultural and social patterns within which behavioral events take place. Issues concerned with personality integration, role occupancy, communication processes, or motivation overlook normative prescriptions that are peculiar to the referential processes of Afro-Americans. Ignorance of the latter not only perpetuates normlessness as a myth but fails to appreciate developmental progressions that are critical to the total efficiency of distinctive behavior patterns in the matters of age-related expectancies or sex-related roles.

To the person outside a culture it is almost impossible to understand that the cues, feedback, and reinforcement of life styles within the culture are designed to assist the members of that culture in actively mastering their social environment. Within this context the established social order fosters differences in developmental experiences, differences in role responsibilities, and differences in standards of beliefs and behavior. Confusion surrounding these issues seems to come from those who lack training in dealing with psychocultural data (Leites, 1948). Then, there are the myths as expressed in the notion, "The Negro is only an American and nothing else. He has no values and culture to guard and protect" (Glazer and Moynihan, 1963). The latter denies, among other things, that the national character of our society has not changed significantly with respect to the treatment given Afro-Americans. Such value orientations also overlook the relation of personality to the functioning of major political and socioeconomic institutions (Inkeles, 1956). An understanding of these circumstances has not only some far-reaching implications but also helps to firm up some rather specific functions for the psychologist who would be engaged in those activities that pertain to Afro-Americans.

In an ideal sense, the psychologist who becomes involved in the humanity of Afro-Americans would have an education in the broad array of social sciences as well as specific experiences to equip him for dealing with the social realities of life in the ghetto. Under this arrangement, I believe one would see the clear interdependency of the diverse physical, social, political, cultural, and psychological features of the community. By contrast, there would be a rejection of the dependency syndrome in professional activities that has a way of furthering pathological accommodations. In this same vein, C. Clark (1969) has written,

> White [largely liberal] thinking has brainwashed us all into believing ... for example, if education is increased, better housing will ensue, etc. Such thinking is strongly dependency-oriented, and while it lends itself neatly to prepackaged programs to "help the disadvantaged," it cannot deal with social reality. The fact of the matter is that the problems facing black Americans are infinitely more complex and are related to systemic social forces and not due to a group of elements which operate independently of each other. To adequately deal with these forces necessitates a radical break with traditional modes of thinking. (p. 5)

Accordingly, one might begin with a problem in education, but the solution becomes sterile unless education as a subsystem is related to the larger social system.

Meanwhile, it is virtually impossible for advocates of community psychology in the ghetto to be dissociated from the black movement which, in all of its parameters, involves primary prevention of identity confusion and the advancement of positive behavioral patterns. Furthermore, current mental health activities with common roots in the concepts and approaches to public health are congruent with significant aspects of the new black ethic. As a consequence, the organization and delivery of mental health services in the Afro-American community must be responsive to and accepting of the new black consciousness. Along these lines, the therapeutic community cannot be simply a treatment center with concerns around demographic characteristics at the expense of a sense of significance. This means that the primary goal must be directed toward the unfolding of creative powers to be used in such matters as a reduction of cognitive dissonance, the resolution of community disorganization, an elevation of self-esteem, and the promotion of changes in those social practices of life that have created and maintained pathological interdependency.

To do anything less would render such concerns as irrelevant to the most critical social issues. This approach is not only as it should be, but it is necessary if the humanity and sensitivity of social progress are to be achieved smoothly. Moreover, this is the only way that the transformation of conventional nonsense in the way of methods, techniques, and philosophy can be fused into an anthem that signifies significant reform.

This frame of reference makes the assumption that the treatment of Afro-Americans is directly tied in with the fate of society generally. It also recognizes that progress in various health, social welfare, educational, and political areas has its antecedents for change in the new black consciousness as a model for improving the quality of life.

In Afro-American communities, the psychologist is challenged to mobilize his vast body of knowledge, new and old, so that his consumers can be assisted in dealing with their environment more effectively. On the surface it would appear that this premise is not too different from what one might expect elsewhere. Yet, the reality is that neither psychology nor psychologists as a whole can be given that responsibility freely. This is especially critical since the context and definitions of the functional group have not been incorporated into the training of psychologists. Thus, the value of psychologists must be handled on an individual basis.

With aggressive assertion, seeking changes in social arrangements and content, the black man is no longer content with his lot as the end. Instead, he has cast his plight as the means for transforming society into one governed by truth and justice. Therefore, the basic goal centers around the unfolding of his creative powers and his becoming increasingly reactive to the choices available. A psychologist can make a significant contribution to changes in patterns of self-defeating behavior *if* he has a clear appreciation of the nature and properties of what is being changed. Likewise, it is no small matter to know how he arrived at the response to the challenge of working in the Afro-American community. In short, why is he paying his dues in this manner? Looking at the situation from the opposite point of view, if the psychologist has "paid his dues," so to speak, and is "doing his thing," he understands that the realities involve the following alternatives for Afro-Americans: (a) an acceptance of defeat by withdrawing; (b) an escape from the horrors of life through the use of alcohol, or drugs, or by suicide; (c) an acceptance of the expected, conforming mode of behavior; (d) a refusal to recognize defeat by adopting the values of the dominant group; or (e) a refusal to retreat from biosocial realities by searching for new meanings as expressed through blackness. The conceptual and behavioral contexts within which these choices arise are somewhat easy to recognize. Possible solutions and resources require another level of realization.

Social progress and conflict resolution, complex though they might be, if engaged in as they should be by the community psychologist, will take him to those necessary arenas beyond his parochial teachings. His life space will embrace participation, mobilization, communication, and confidence of the community people. These activities might include problems concerning (a) whether police departments are needed as they are presently organized to preserve law and order, (b) the social gains to be derived from decentralized schools, (c) the pathological dependency fostered by the welfare system, (d) the kind of social research needed, (e) whether developmental programs are responsive to community needs, or (f) coming to grips with some of the other by-products of racism. These conditions hold for psychologists of any ethnic group. However, as matters now stand, these activities appear to have more significance for the white psychologist because he is more readily identified as being from the Establishment.

This particular state of affairs cannot be managed successfully without a consideration of the facilitating, institutionalized social actions and circumstances. It is at this junction that the psychologist must be prepared to deal with his own values and social distinctions in terms of what Erikson (1968) has called the "wider identity" of the Afro-American. In much the same manner, the agent of change must firmly understand whether he is, in the words of Keniston (1968), "promoting another way of controlling deviant behavior under the disguise of community mental health." Conversely, one must know if he is influencing the course of events with new coping patterns that challenge existing structures. The achievement of that goal is dependent upon technically sound but socially productive programs that incorporate the interdependent effects of social class and ethnicity.

Implications of the Black Ethic for Social Science

As a social science model, the new black ethic holds promise, because it is based upon psychocultural factors involving racial awareness, identity, and pride that nurture biosocial acceptance in Afro-Americans. While somewhat limited in precision because it is still being articulated, there are several reasons that can substantiate the black ethic as a paradigm that offers more successful empirical propositions for productively stimulating human development than either the *bioasocial* or social deviance models.

The bioasocial or genotypic orientation, at best, seeks to maintain the brutality and inhumanity of society at the expense of actualizing the Afro-American's human potential. Studies involving cognition seem to use this type of model, and as Downs (1969) has pointed out, the results do not assess racial inheritance as much as they rank the social structure of the United States.

The social deviance model conceptualizes the Afro-American family as a pathological socializing agent transmitting cultural malignance. Studies involving our families have almost nothing to say about the resourcefulness and ingenuity that exist; and one also finds a conspicuous absence about the need for changes in the larger society that would foster a different type of family organization.

Perhaps the most compelling reason for the use of the black ethic as a social science model is its mental health implications. To this extent, it can be considered as a functional theory whereby Festinger's cognitive-dissonance in social psychology would be illustrative of what is being suggested. Both are based upon constructive explanations that allow for motivational determinism in a social definition of reality. Socially valued objectives and socially provided means to establish and pursue goal-directed activities are derived from the reliance on opinions of the group's functioning.

A healthy personality according to Jahoda (1958) actively masters his environment, shows a certain unity of personality, and is able to perceive the world and himself correctly. By comparison blackness is the manifestation of a specific form of behavior that enables the Afro-American to enhance his self-determined mastery over those political and socioeconomic institutions that would grossly impair his socially relevant behavior. For this reason Afro-Americans who have internalized their blackness tend to be seen not only as persons of high self-esteem but also as less susceptible to pernicious influences of the dominant group. The internalization of membership in their racial group may also be seen as a type of creative experience coming from adaptable deviance.

Social competence based upon biosocial acceptance would be more congruent with cognitive needs and seems to serve in the reduction of ambiguity between ideals and achievement. It strengthens the capacity to meet new challenges because confrontation with the self brings about or sustains a more authentic self-concept. The action patterns or motivational systems are characterized by the black man's aggressiveness, independence, and at times hostility, in dealing with groups and institutional failings that would maintain him as a passive, dependent, self-defeating person.

> *Life experiences inconsistent with self-awareness of the black man have been the basis for intergroup tensions on the one hand, and self-defeating behavior on the other. This conflict could not change in any meaningful way until there was an acceptance of self. . . . As a result of his commitment to blackness, the Afro-American thinks, feels, and sees himself as a member of a society in which he is no longer a passive onlooker. (Thomas, 1969, p. 11)*

The willingness among Afro-Americans to commit themselves to a more competent sense of self and to seek the essence of collective manhood is related to centuries of symbolic childhood.

Two other circumstances around the use of the current black ethic as a theory are important. First, it can be viewed, to paraphrase Simon and Newell (1963), as a theory of man that takes into account his characteristics as an information-processing system. Next, "all theory," according to Marx (1963),

> *tends to be both a tool and a goal. This statement means that theory is seen to be useful as an aid, sometimes perhaps as essential aid, in directing empirical investigation (the tool function) and also to be something valued as an object in its own right (the goal function). (p. 5)*

These conditions constitute the challenge that must be faced by those professionals who claim scientific interests and who require scientific status.

Conclusion

To strive for security or completion as an individual allows response sets that are no longer productive for personal-social constancy to drop out. In other words, if through psychological processes Afro-Americans internalize their blackness and cease to survive by clinging to a thread because they are confused about their worth as humans, benefits will also accrue to those who overtly or otherwise have been caught up in the historical assemblage of this same process. In short, it is not simply Afro-Americans who gain in mental health, because upon becoming black the black person also forces white people to respond in terms of some reaction formation that should promote a healthier meaning within whites. With respect to the latter, there is considerable doubt that any such essay on personality will gain widespread currency.

In different words but on the same theme, Murphy (1947) and K. B. Clark (1965) posed the question about who was to do what in making clear what the sense of fulfillment was in the individual himself, and, at the same time, understand implicit meanings in the social order.

Psychologists are in serious need of a reexamination of their philosophical commitment. The last few years have become increasingly characterized, not so much by a quest for truth, as by a search for power. Meanwhile, the social revolution has caught social scientists in the wilderness resting on a cot of science for science's sake, with their proverbial pants down.

References

Ausubel, D. P., and Ausubel, P. Ego development among segregated Negro children. In H. Passow (Ed.), *Education in depressed areas*. New York: Teachers College Press, 1963.

Clark, C. On racism and racist systems. *Negro Digest*, 1969, **XVIII**, 4–8.

Clark, K. B. *Dark ghetto dilemmas of social power*. New York: Harper & Row, 1965.

Downs, J. F., and Bleibtreu, K. K. *Human variation: An introduction to physical anthropology*. Beverly Hills, Calif.: Glencoe Press, 1969.

Erikson, E. *Identity, youth and crisis*. New York: Norton, 1968.

Goode, W. J., and Hatt, P. K. *Methods in social research*. New York: McGraw-Hill, 1952.

Glazer, N., and Moynihan, P. *Beyond the melting pot*. Cambridge, Mass.: Harvard University Press, 1963.

Garcia, S. J., Blackwell, A., Williams, C. F., and Simpkins, G. Research in the black community: A need for self-determination. Paper presented at the meeting of the Western Psychological Association, Vancouver, B.C., June 1969.

Guthrie, R. V. The psychopathology of white folks. Paper presented at the meeting of the Western Psychological Association, Vancouver, B.C., June 1969.

Inkeles, A. Some sociological observation on culture and personality studies. In C. Kluckhorn and H. A. Murray (Eds.), *Personality in nature, society, and culture*. New York: Knopf, 1956.

Jahoda, M. Toward a social psychology of mental health. In M. J. E. Benn (Ed.), *Symposium on the healthy personality, Supplement II: Problems of Infancy and Childhood*. New York: Josiah Macy, Jr., Foundation, 1950.

Jensen, A. R. How much can we boost IQ and scholastic achievement? *Harvard Educational Review*, 1969, 39, 1–123.

Keniston, K. How community mental health stamped out the riots. *Trans-action*, July/ August, 1968, 5(8), 21–29.

Kuhn, T. S. *The structure of scientific revolutions*. Chicago: University of Chicago Press, 1962.

Leites, N. Psycho-cultural hypotheses about political acts. *World Politics*, 1948, 1, 102–119.

Marx, M. *Theories in contemporary psychology*. New York: Macmillan, 1963.

Murphy, G. *Personality: A biosocial approach to origins and structure*. New York: Harper & Row, 1947.

Simon, H. A., and Newell, A. The uses and limitations of models. In M. Marx (Ed.), *Theories in Contemporary Psychology*. New York: Macmillan, 1963.

Thomas, C. W. On being a black man. Voice of America Presentation, February 1969. (Mimeo.)

WILLIAM M. HARVEY

Drugs in the Black Community

The nation is currently experiencing an epidemic of promiscuous drug use by its young people. This crisis has been developing for several years; however, general awareness of the scope of the problem is of quite recent origin. Why now? Most observers feel it is because the "drug problem" is no longer restricted to the black ghetto, but has hit the suburbs and is affecting white middle-class and upper middle-class youth. College, high-school, and even grade-school youngsters in large numbers are experimenting with drugs; and some are getting hurt.

People in positions of power now want to "do something about the spreading problem of drug abuse." Stricter control of prescription drugs, liberalization of the marijuana laws, antidrug campaigns by the media, widespread drug education programs in the schools are all indications that white society considers the drug problem a serious threat to the country's survival.

The black community is also gravely concerned about drugs. However, unlike the situation with the society as a whole, this concern does not date back just a few years. Rather, the black community has been plagued with this problem for a long, long time. Ironically, had the larger society chosen to exert half the effort it is beginning to muster in dealing with illicit drug use when the problem was essentially confined to the ghetto, we might well have had no problem in either community now. Even today, one gets the impression that the black community is being slighted in the attention it receives. This is particularly the case in terms of financial support for treatment and education programs.

There are a number of reasons why drug addiction is such a serious menace to the black community. To start with, there is the physical, psychological, and social harm to the addicted individual. Typically, he gets caught up in the drug scene during his late teens and remains a victim the better part of his adult life. Dropping out of school is the usual result, followed by the embarking upon a career of "hustling" and "making it" in the street by using one's wits. A narcotics habit increases in cost the longer one has it. The ten-dollars-a-day habit grows to forty or fifty dollars in a matter of months, and it is not infrequent for the addict to spend 75 to 100 dollars a day for heroin. Fantastic amounts of energy, creativity, and intelligent planning are devoted to getting money to pay for one's habit. Most often this involves illegal pursuits. Many sell drugs to others as a way of making money. The addict "turning" drugs does quite well economically, but, unfortunately, most of what he makes goes into his own arm.

Contrary to a widely circulated myth, most addicts are brighter than normal—they have to be to survive. Nevertheless, most eventually do get caught and

Reprinted by permission of the author.

periodically serve time in prison. The psychological toll in prison is severe: gang rape, forced homosexuality, loss of confidence, and schooling in becoming a more proficient criminal are but some of the consequences. A disproportionately large number of black men are in the nation's prisons. A number of factors related to the unequal way in which the laws are enforced contribute to this. However, some credit must be given to narcotics; as many as 50 percent of the prisoners have a history of drug involvement.

The mortality rate for narcotics addicts is several times higher than that for the general population. Death from overdoses, hepatitis from dirty needles, and general neglect of the body—making it more susceptible to all kinds of diseases—are all too frequent occurrences.

In addition to himself the addict hurts his family. He literally drains them of their financial resources, lies to them, disappoints them. If small children are involved, they may be severely neglected, even though the addict consciously is usually very concerned about his or her children. However, if the choice is between milk for the baby and a fix, the fix wins out.

Confusing Terminology

Before proceeding further, it is well to define some terms. Presently, there is a great deal of confusion surrounding the way terminology in this area is used, even by experts. Narcotics addict, drug abuser, drug-dependent person, dope fiend, junkie—all are terms used to describe someone with a drug habit. They have, however, different connotations depending upon the context. Even the word *addiction* is used in different ways. One hears, for example, that a particular drug is not addicting or that you cannot get hooked on it, whereas others insist that the same drug *is* addicting and you can get hooked on it.

Part of the difficulty lies in the fact that there are two ways in which a person can be addicted to a drug: physically and psychologically. When someone has become physically addicted to a drug this means that should he stop taking it, his body will react violently and he will become very ill. Severe cramps, nausea, diarrhea, insomnia are among the most frequent symptoms. These symptoms will persist several days and are sometimes referred to as the withdrawal syndrome. The addict himself often refers to the experience as "kicking" (his habit). Physicians frequently are able to make this withdrawal experience less painful by giving the individual other drugs (medicine), and gradually reducing the amount of the drug he is trying to kick. If the addict simply stops taking the drug without benefit of medication, he is said to kick "cold turkey."

Psychological addiction refers to the existence of a strong desire or craving for the drug and an inability on the part of the person to discontinue its use, even when he consciously desires to stop. Should the person who is psychologically addicted be prevented from taking the drug, he would become very uncomfortable, but not get "sick" with the withdrawal syndrome. Most drugs possess the capacity to produce psychological addiction; but only a few are physically addicting. In actuality, the current vogue is to substitute the term "dependency" for "addiction."

Many people question the wisdom of attaching too much significance to the distinction between physical and psychological dependency. The heroin addict will tell you that overcoming the psychological dependency is far more difficult than overcoming the physical part. He feels this way because, if he has been in the drug subculture for an extended period, he has usually kicked his physical habit several times. Often it is involuntary as when he gets arrested. After he gets over being "sick," he is physically free of the drug. Yet, he invariably begins using again and within a short time is physically hooked once more.

Four Classes of Drugs

Although there are almost an endless number of drugs being abused, the most common ones fall into four basic categories: narcotics, sedatives or depressants, stimulants, and hallucinogens. The most commonly used representatives of each category will be described.

A narcotic drug is one that relieves pain, puts one in a drowsy nod, wipes out worry and concern, and generally creates a feeling of well-being. Long time use, however, decreases the drug's positive benefit and creates a situation wherein the person simply feels less bad with than without the drug. Narcotics refer to opium, opiate derivatives, and synthetic opiates. Until 1970, federal law classified marijuana and cocaine as narcotics; but, on chemical grounds, these drugs should not be so classified.

Opium is the dried juice of the oriental poppy plant. A hot and dry climate is necessary for the production of opium. When a pod or the poppy flower is cut open, a heavy milkish juice appears. With exposure to the air, it gradually hardens and turns brownish black. In this form it can be eaten or smoked, and, usually, this is the way raw opium is consumed in other parts of the world.

In this country, it is mainly the derivatives of opium that are used. Chemical refinement of opium can produce morphine. Morphine, which is stronger and more addicting than raw opium, is primarily used by physicians as a pain killer. During the second half of the nineteenth century, large numbers of white Americans were morphine addicts. Thousands of soldiers on both sides became addicted during the Civil War. Today, however, relatively few people are morphine addicts; the drug of choice for 90 percent of the narcotics addicts over the past 50 or 60 years has been and continues to be heroin.

Heroin is derived from morphine, but it is quite a bit stronger and more addicting. That it is so much stronger accounts for the fact that heroin can be "cut" many times to the point where that sold on the street is only about 5 percent pure. Available in powder form, the color varies from brown to white, depending on what substance has been used to cut it. A tablespoonful may cost $150. If the person buying this amount judges the heroin still to be fairly strong, he may cut it further to increase the amount he has to sell. He then packages small amounts either by partially filling No. 5 gelatin capsules or placing it in small pieces of aluminum foil to be sold for $4 or $5 each.

Heroin can be sniffed or snorted, but this is unsatisfactory over the long run. The user much prefers to inject directly into the vein. After he has "copped" (bought the quantity needed to satisfy his habit), he normally places it in a spoon or bottle cap, adds water, and heats it with a match. This "cooking" is done both to liquefy and to boil off impurities. In order to shoot the drug into his arm, the addict needs proper equipment, which is called an "outfit." The outfit may be a hypodermic needle and syringe or a medicine dropper. Often a small piece of cotton is used as an added strainer. Repeated injections over time cause scars, or "tracks," on the person's arms, and he begins to use other areas of the body: back of his hands, feet, fingers, inner thigh, wherever he can find a vein.

The sale, possession, or production of heroin is illegal. Nine out of ten narcotics addicts use heroin; however, necessity and other factors occasionally bring about the use of other narcotics such as codeine, paregoric, Demerol, or Dolophine (methadone). Codeine is a so-called exempt preparation, which means it can be sold under certain conditions. Not as strong as heroin or morphine, the main medical use of codeine is cough suppression, although it has some painkilling properties. Many cough syrups, therefore, contain codeine. When times are hard, some addicts use it temporarily to stave off the withdrawal symptoms.

Cough syrups, which also contain alcohol, are more a problem for the young adolescent than the adult addict. There is usually one or more unsavory drugstore operator in every section of the ghetto who will sell Robitussin AC or some other exempt narcotics to the kids with full awareness of their abuse intentions. While this is by no means the case with the majority of druggists, it points up one of the added reasons for ridding the ghetto of those white businessmen whose concern for the residents ranks far below their desire to make a big profit. Just to give an example, a $2 bottle of cough syrup will be sold for $6 or $8.

The physical effect of narcotics on the body generally is to slow things down. The central nervous system is depressed, blood pressure and respiration rate are reduced. Dulling of the senses, loss of appetite, and severe constipation are all associated with continual use. The female addict's menstrual cycle is often disturbed, and both sexes lose interest in intercourse. Further, a host of physical ailments afflict the heroin addict because his overriding preoccupation with getting the drug usually causes him to neglect his health.

A second major class of drugs is the depressants or sedatives. Alcohol and barbiturates are the most prominent members of the class. The devastating effect of alcohol on the social well-being of the black community is well known. A disproportionate number of liquor stores are found in the ghetto. Often they stay open later at night. Through the years, many a senseless homicide in and outside of taverns or at dance halls has occurred in a setting of excessive alcohol consumption. Approximately half of auto fatalities can be traced to one party's driving while intoxicated.

Alcohol is unique as a drug of abuse because of its legal status. Practically everyone uses alcohol on a moderate basis, with most not becoming addicted. Physical dependence, when it does occur, takes a lot longer than with narcotics. Only about 6 or 7 percent of alcohol users can be classified as alcoholics. It is estimated that about 1 in every 14 drinkers eventually becomes an alcoholic. A big problem is that the person seldom will admit that he is slipping deeper and deeper into complete dependence. He progresses through several stages: nonrecall of some of his activities while drunk, immediate loss of control after one drink, and regular morning drinking.

Physicians prescribe barbiturates to people with insomnia or to those needing mild sedation, as well as for the treatment of epilepsy. At higher than normal doses, tolerance is easily developed and physical dependency becomes quite a problem. Over the last few years, barbiturate abuse has become a steadily rising problem among black teenagers in or out of school. Nicknamed yellow jackets, red devils, or Christmas trees (because of the color of the capsules), barbiturates are extremely plentiful in the ghetto. Instead of the calming, sleep-inducing effect that occurs with moderate dosage, when taken in large amounts a state of arousal and exhilaration is produced in the young person, although drowsiness and stuporous behavior gradually set in. The possibility of lethal overdose is high, particularly if alcohol is also consumed. The confused mental state that is brought about frequently leads to accidental death in that the person may not remember how many pills he has already taken. That one does not "throw up" as when drunk from alcohol further increases the danger of overdose.

Behaviorally, the teenager on barbiturates is considerably more dangerous to those around him than is the case from other drugs. The likelihood of his physically attacking even close family members is great. It is best, therefore, not to try to constrain or "talk to" a young person in this condition, but rather, if possible, to wait until the effect of the drug has worn off. When he is more himself again, the family must persistently attempt to get him into a treatment setting.

The third major class of abused drugs is the stimulants. The primary group in this category is the amphetamines. Synthesized in the twenties, they are produced in several forms, the main ones being amphetamine sulphate (benzedrine), dextroamphetamine sulphate (dexedrine) and methamphetamine hydrochloride (methedrine or desoxyn). They are effective in combating fatigue, providing energy, curbing appetite, and treating sleeping sickness. Forms of amphetamine have become very popular as diet pills and highly controversial in the treatment of the so-called hyperactive child.

Tolerance builds rapidly with amphetamine abuse, but it is currently not thought to be physically addicting in the same sense as narcotics and barbiturates. That is, one does not get the violent physical withdrawal syndrome. The person who has been taking large amounts over a long period does show a type of withdrawal reaction, and certainly an intense and persistent psychological craving for more of the drug. While some take it orally, injection into the veins is more usual when the person really "gets into it." It appears, however, that amphetamine is even more physically damaging to the veins than heroin. Veins rapidly get hard, the user looks for others, and finally may resort to injecting into the penis or the side of the tongue. Hepatitis is a big problem here. It is not just the dirty needles; it may also be that the amphetamine itself is having an effect on the liver that is similar to hepatitis.

The term *speed* to refer to methedrine and other amphetamines was popularized by the young white drug-using subcultures of San Francisco and Los Angeles during the late sixties. However, serious amphetamine abuse in the black community began ten to twelve years earlier. Some addicts were fond of mixing heroin with amphetamine to make "speed balls." In addition to "speed," words such as "splivin," "rhythm," and "splash" were used to describe amphetamine.

"Splash" was introduced by a black St. Louis addict during the fifties and began to see heavy use around 1960, when many heroin addicts switched over. One reason for the switch was the stiff penalties being handed out and the step-up of law enforcement efforts during that period. Heroin became temporarily less available and the addict found he would stand less risk of going (or going back) to the penitentiary if caught with amphetamines than with heroin. Subsequently there developed two distinct drug-using subgroups: splash users and heroin users, who tended to look down on one another. (David Smith of San Francisco has noted that a similar development occurred between stimulant and psychedelic users in Haight Ashbury.) Amphetamines could easily be obtained for a mere fraction of the cost of heroin. All one had to do was go in and tell the doctor he (or she in most cases) wanted something to help lose weight. Most physicians would not, of course, continue to cooperate, but unfortunately there would always be one or two that the addict subculture knew it could use. Recently, because of the wide publicity of white middle-class involvement with "speed," it has become more difficult to obtain amphetamine even in the ghetto. There is, in fact, a movement to ban or greatly limit the manufacture of all amphetamine.

Hallucinogens, or psychedelics, constitute the fourth major class of drugs. Mescaline and LSD belong to this group, along with a number of other synthetics with abbreviations such as DMT and STP. Mescaline is extracted from the peyote cactus that some Indians in the Southwest use as part of their religious ceremonies. As such, mescaline is thought of as a "natural" psychedelic. LSD, however, is by far the most popular as well as most powerful of the "heavy" psychedelics. LSD, or "acid," as it is frequently called, has no color, taste, or odor, and requires a fantastically small amount to create its effect. In fact, it is estimated that a shot glass full would be enough to make 400,000 doses.

As a rule, black people shy away from LSD and drugs of this type. They are generally afraid of them. "I don't try it, 'cause it messes with your mind" reflects the most prevalent attitude. Another reason is the supply routes are different than with the more traditional drugs: England, the West Coast, the college campus, amateur chemistry labs. Unfortunately, however, there are signs that some of the more educated brothers who are doing the integrated thing are beginning to "drop acid."

The hallucinogens, or psychedelics, have the capacity seriously to distort one's perception of reality. They bring about heightened sensitivity such that stimuli are experienced as much more intense: colors appear brighter and more saturated, sounds seem louder, touch feels stronger. It is not just the intensity dimension that is distorted; the qualitative meanings attached to stimuli are exaggerated. The subjective appreciation of beauty is greatly enhanced and one becomes significantly more suggestible. Commonplace objects take on fascinating interest. Events that are somewhat amusing may be perceived as hilarious. However, by the same token, events that are somewhat sad or scary may become profoundly sad or terrifying. The latter is probably the basis of many of the so-called "bad trips." A bad trip is one wherein the user becomes uncontrollably upset and panicky. Undoubtedly, the upset stems from the individual's interpretation of the events going on around him and in his head.

Marijuana, the last drug to be dealt with, is in many ways the most troublesome. Some experts classify it as a mild hallucinogen, while others see it as being more properly described as a hypnotic sedative. Marijuana comes from the plant *Cannabis sativa*. It grows in many parts of the world, including the United States. A hot, dry climate is most conducive, however, and that which grows in this country is of very weak potency as compared with that grown in Mexico or India.

Usually marijuana is greenish in appearance, consisting as it does of leaves, flower stems, and seeds, explaining in part the popular names of "grass" and "weed." Of course, there are many other terms for marijuana such as "reefer," "pot," or "tea." The most recent trend among black youth is to call it "smoke." The active ingredient thought to be responsible for producing the high effect is tetrahydrocannabinol, or THC. The THC content of the flowers and leaves is greater than that of the stem and seeds. The climate condition under which the plant grows is also a factor in determining the THC content. Often dealers will "treat" relatively inert American variety marijuana with chemicals to give it more "kick." Formaldehyde is often used in the ghetto. Marijuana sells for about $20 an ounce, depending a great deal on supply and demand factors and the amount of heat being exerted by law enforcement officials. And, like most other commodities, the quality is poorer and the price is higher in the ghetto.

There is a stronger form of *Cannabis* known as hashish, or simply hash. Hashish comes from the resin obtained from the flowers of the hemp plant and contains considerably more THC. The effects are closer to those of the stronger psychedelics. Hashish comes in a solid form and frequently is eaten or smoked in a special pipe. Marijuana is most often rolled in cigarette paper as a "joint" and smoked. Joints are smaller and flatter than regular cigarettes. They are smoked with a lot of fanfare: sucking deeply both air and smoke, and holding the mixture down as long as possible.

Because of the wide range of potency, it is impossible to make flat statements about the effects on the individual of marijuana. If the person smokes too much, he may become nauseous and feel badly for a while. If this happens, it generally occurs in the inexperienced smoker. With experience, the individual learns to gauge how much he should smoke. The social conditions under which the person first gets started are very important. What he has heard about the way it affects people, his subconscious fears, and the way those around him are currently behaving all influence the way it will affect him. Subjective awareness of physiological and psychological changes begin shortly after smoking and reach full force 30 to 45 minutes later. The total "high" normally lasts about four hours.

Among the more prominent features of the "high" are a sense of relaxation, light headedness, and a dreamy state of mind, heightened interest in food, particularly sweets, enhanced appreciation of music, release of inhibition, and exaggerated laughter. Because most regular smokers do so for pleasure, it is not surprising that many of the usually reported effects are positive in tone. Other effects, which are not necessarily pleasant, also occur. Some of these include mild attention and concentration difficulty, losing track of one's train of thought, time and space distortion, blocking or temporary impairment of short-term memory, increased suggestibility, and mild paranoia, usually regarding the possibility of being caught and punished. Some individuals "freak out" on marijuana in a fashion much resembling that observed with the "bad acid trip." While the marijuana "freak out" is the exception rather than the rule, it does occur often enough to cause concern.

Combating the Drug Problem

There are three major approaches to dealing with the drug problem: law enforcement, treatment and rehabilitation, and preventative education. Neither of these approaches works well alone, as each has serious limitations. Over the years more effort and money have been devoted to law enforcement than to the other two. One reason for this is that educators and medical and social scientists have amassed less hard data to support their theories than have the law enforcement people. Another reason is the public demand for simplistic answers to complex social problems. To many it seems like the easiest thing in the world would be just to "arrest the pushers and cut off the supply." On the contrary, control of the illicit drug traffic has proved one of the most difficult tasks of the century.

Many people are unaware of the fact that the proportion of addicts relative to the total population is quite a bit less today than was the case 50 and 60 years ago. Again, statistics in this area leave much to be desired, but approximately one in every 400 persons was thought to be addicted in 1914. Today that ratio is more like one in every 7,000. The invention of the hypodermic needle and the widespread use of morphine as a pain killer during the Civil War resulted in thousands of addicts in the late 1800s. The fact that many patent medicines contained large amounts of narcotics further added tq the ranks of the addicted. Heroin was introduced in 1898. Ironically, it was originally hailed as a cure for morphine addiction because it prevented the occurrence of the withdrawal syndrome. For several years, heroin was thought to be nonaddicting. Ultimately, however, word was circulated among the medical practitioners that it was even more addicting than morphine.

In 1914, legislation was passed greatly restricting the importation, manufacture, sale, and distribution of narcotics. Subsequent laws tightened those restrictions and made possession and/or distribution of heroin illegal even for physicians. There are many who feel that enforcement of the antinarcotic laws is responsible for most of the social problems associated with drug addiction. Leading spokesman for this group is sociologist Alfred Lindensmith who has repeatedly asserted that the high cost of maintaining one's habit because of black market control of supply forces the addict into a life of crime. His notion is that addiction is a medical problem rather than a legal one and is best handled by avoiding the complications associated with criminalizing the addict.

Opponents of this view hold that strict control laws and vigorous enforcement are essential lest the problem get completely out of hand. They point out that when law enforcement efforts are increased, there is a corresponding reduction in the number of addicts coming to the attention of authorities. Further, they argue that both treatment and education entail a long-range approach and require time even if perfectly planned. In terms of the immediate practical problem they see no substitute for effective law enforcement.

Few would dispute that the heroin traffic is controlled by the underworld. Although there are some encouraging signs recently, it would appear that the top figures here are still in the "untouchable" class. Certainly, in most instances, it is the small fry pusher who serves time in jail for drug offenses. Nine times out of ten this person has a habit himself and makes just enough to keep his own habit going. In other words, there is an inverse relationship between the amount of profit made in the narcotics game and the likelihood of serving time in jail. The majority of narcotics addicts today are "nonwhite" and live in economically depressed sections of large metropolitan areas. Conversely, virtually all of the big dealers are white and live in suburbia.

The relationship between illicit drug use and crime is complex. That most heroin addicts eventually resort to illegal behavior to get money for their habit is an uncontested fact. The extent to which this holds true for the nonnarcotic and less expensive drugs of abuse is more open to argument. The great majority of black people who have become narcotics addicts appear to feel that they got started on the illicit drug route with marijuana. This fact does not necessarily mean that marijuana smoking leads to heroin. In order to determine if there is a connection, one must phrase the question differently. How many of those who smoke marijuana graduate to heroin? The answer to this question depends upon several factors: the personality of the user, how often and under what conditions he smokes, his set of friends, the interpretation he and those who have influence on him place on his smoking, and whether he comes to "lean on" marijuana as a relaxant or tension reducer. Many ghetto youths who get started and continue to smoke marijuana soon become immersed in the drug-using subculture, whose existence is illegal by definition. At the very least the drug user must begin to take precautions against getting caught. Often this includes forming alliances with others who are in violation of the law; and he soon develops an antilaw orientation.

Very few members of the black community have used illicit drugs consistently over a length of time without being arrested. In part this is a function of the high probability of a black man being stopped for questioning by the police. Often if two or three black men are walking down the street or driving around in either a "beat up" or shiny new car, they are, in the opinion of many a police officer (and a significant number of private citizens, for that matter), "suspicious persons," and there then "exists grounds for stopping and searching them." Owing to deep-seated feelings of prejudice toward or fear of the subject, the tone and content of the language used by the inquiring officer is frequently hostile, aggressive, and insulting. This, of course, leaves a bad taste and reinforces an expectancy of unfair, hostile treatment from authorities. By the same token, however, some of the many who are stopped in this fashion actually have drugs with them and many narcotics arrests are made this way. In the vernacular of the drug-using subculture, to have drugs on you when you are stopped by police is to be "caught dirty." In addition to being in a most unfortunate legal predicament, this is also a source of extreme embarrassment and prestige loss among one's friends.

Once a man has been arrested for a narcotics violation, a vicious circle is begun. He becomes known to the authorities and is stopped for questioning more often. It is said to be virtually impossible to deal in drugs or commit any major illegal operation without the police becoming aware of it. It is now rather freely admitted that blacks, the poor, and other members of the American underclass do not obtain an equal break under our justice system. The black narcotics offender has been perhaps the most dispossessed of the second-class citizens. The society as a whole tends to see him as incurably evil, dangerous, and a menace. He is unlikely to get the best legal counsel, and when he does get a "good lawyer" he has to resort to the same sort of illegal behaviors to obtain money for the lawyer's fee which may be higher than normal because of the addict's poor risk potential. The circle widens. Note the instances in which newspaper accounts assail "liberal judges" for granting bond to someone committing a crime while waiting to come to trial for another. Often this is not because he is such a habitual criminal and has always to be stealing. He must take on this risk to get money to pay the high-priced lawyer to get him off.

The young black woman who winds up dependent on drugs is usually brought into contact with the ghetto drug-using subculture by her boyfriend or husband. Many insist that they were unaware their young man was using drugs until they had become extensively involved emotionally with, or even married to, him. When she does find out, she may do her best to persuade him to stop, but this is typically of no avail. All too frequently, she may, out of a sense of frustration and continual exposure to his "turning on," decide to join him. The female addict is more or less forced into prostitution to support her habit.

An overriding thought with most narcotics addicts is how to acquire money as quickly as possible with minimal risk. He tries hard to avoid committing crimes where weapons are involved, and greatly prefers not to come into direct physical contact with his victims. Favorites are check forgings, shoplifting, burglarizing apartments when the occupants are away, or executing a confidence game. Even when he is stealing items, say, from a large department store, he will tend to take three articles at different times each with a market value of just under fifty dollars rather than one worth $150. This is because the penalty for stealing over fifty is much more severe than is the case for under fifty. Nonetheless, as his habit continues to grow, and as he gets deeper and deeper involved in debt, he gets more desperate and begins to take greater risks including perhaps mugging and armed robbery. Eventually he gets caught.

Traditionally, the courts have dealt harshly with narcotics offenders. In large part, this is a function of the fact that the laws governing drug-related offenses are generally strict and leave little latitude for the judge to exercise discretion. In evaluating legislation in this area, one may concern himself primarily with protecting the individual user or with protecting society from the user. To date, the emphasis has been primarily on protecting society. This has been attempted by making the drugs hard to obtain and illegal to possess, and giving long sentences to those convicted of violation. Unfortunately, however, most of those convicted and sent to prison are the low men on the totem pole, and most often, people who themselves are addicted. They go to jail, get released, reacquire their habit, and start the whole cycle over again. If any progress is to be made, ways must be found to rehabilitate the narcotics offender.

During the early twenties, the notion of giving narcotics to the addict at a medical clinic was experimented with for a short time. Some abuses and certain political considerations led to the abrupt closing of these clinics. Ten to fifteen years later, the government established two large hospitals for the treatment of narcotics addicts at Lexington, Kentucky, and Fort Worth, Texas. These hospitals were primarily for addicts convicted in federal courts. They could choose straight prison or one of these two hospitals for the purpose of seeking to rehabilitate themselves. It was possible for someone with a narcotics habit voluntarily to commit himself for treatment. The treatment programs within these institutions were slow in developing. Opportunity for a meaningful exchange of views between the designers of the treatment and the people receiving that treatment was very limited. The result was that the therapeutic agents had little real understanding of the addict as a person, and the addict tended to see the staff and the institution as just another example of the "system" going through the motions, but really not being responsive to, or even caring about, his needs. These hospitals are now being phased out.

A highly significant development in treatment for addicts occurred in 1958 with the establishment of Synanon. Synanon was started on the West coast by an ex-alcoholic whose philosophy was that people do better when they can manage to help themselves. The founder, Chuck Deterich, who is gifted with charisma and a forceful and persuasive personality, was able to succeed where others had failed. The notion he implemented was the setting up of a therapeutic community of ex-addicts who would live, work, and introspect together. Synanon pioneered the development of "attack therapy," "encounter groups," and sensitivity training. The basic idea of the therapeutic approach is that the drug addict (or dope fiend as they prefer to call one another) is an immature person who has not learned attitudes of responsibility to others. Their brand of therapy is designed to strip the addict of his false sense of self-satisfaction, his selfish orientation, and to develop insight into his behavior toward others. By being rewarded for constructive communal behavior and punished for selfish acts, he comes to recognize the necessity for group acceptance.

The Synanon approach has become the model for a number of ex-addict led therapeutic community treatment programs funded by the government. One of the first was Daytop Lodge in New York. Others are Gateway House in Chicago and Archway House in St. Louis. The overall philosophy of these programs is similar to that of Synanon. The distinction is that more professionals are involved and there is a much greater emphasis upon research. The ex-addict leadership has responsibility for the running of the therapeutic community, but not the overall administrative control of the program. In fact, the tendency now is for the therapeutic community to be but one of several components of a multi-faceted treatment program.

A most encouraging development in the treatment of narcotics addiction has occurred in St. Louis during the past few years. There, Don Mitchell, a black ex-heroin addict, has managed to start—and obtain widespread community support for—a self-help rehabilitation center known as NASCO. The full name of the organization is Narcotics Service Council. For the most part, NASCO is an "on the street" rehabilitation program. The *striver*, as the participating addict is called prior to his graduation from the program, lives at NASCO house initially for about a month, and again for short periods should a relapse or crisis occur. The emphasis, however, is upon getting him a job and having him return to the community as soon as possible. He returns to NASCO house four or five times a week for therapy, "rap" sessions with other strivers, committee assignments, and the like. The underlying theory is that he must overcome his addiction and make a new life adjustment in a setting similar to the one in which he originally acquired his addiction, and to which he is eventually to return. The staff represents a merger of ex-addict and professional talent. But unlike most other programs in the country that tend to underemphasize the decision-making participation of one or the other, NASCO is built around the concept of equal input.

Group therapy augmented by individual counseling is the hub of the treatment program. However, extensive emphasis is placed on what they describe as "comprehensive assistance." That is, the hard-core heroin addict has a lot more going against him than the fact that he is dependent on drugs and has personality problems. Virtually every aspect of his life has been adversely affected. He needs, for example, extensive and continuing legal help. Usually he has incurred large debts, has "married" several times, and has violated in one form or another some court order. While he is still in the throes of addiction, the addict need give little concern to matters of this sort. However, as soon as he begins to show signs of pulling himself up, all sorts of old claims are lodged against him. The recovering addict also needs a tremendous amount of assistance and patient understanding in landing and maintaining employment. Finding decent jobs for black men is difficult enough under the best circumstances. When the situation is compounded by the candidate having a police record *and* a history of narcotics abuse, the problem becomes extremely serious. Also complicating matters is the fact that many addicts are used to making (through illegal channels) more money in one day than their first legitimate job will pay in two weeks. Constant attention to the striver's social needs is a NASCO strong point. The psychotherapists there long ago learned that a man finds it very hard to concentrate on therapy when he is worried about pressing social and economic problems.

The therapeutic philosophy of NASCO differs from Synanon or Daytop mainly in rejecting the necessity for making a frontal attack on the ego defensive structure of the recovering addict. Rather, the technique at NASCO is to strengthen and build upon positive aspects of the personality. The assumption is made that particularly for an addict who has lived in the ghetto all his life, it is crucial to improve his self-esteem and to offer an approach that allows him to get himself together with *dignity*. In addition to the other therapeutic efforts, the striver is required to devote a significant amount of time each week to working with youngsters in his neighborhood who seem to have a good chance of ending up dependent upon drugs if no intervention occurs. In fact, it appears that the best indication of whether a striver will make his rehabilitation stick is the extent to which he becomes involved with helping others.

Becoming drug free is a goal of many programs. Unfortunately, however, many addicts fail to demonstrate the motivation and stamina necessary to negotiate this ideal.

A great deal of attention and publicity has been given recently to a medically oriented treatment of narcotics addicts known as methadone maintenance. Methadone is itself a synthetic narcotic, less potent than pure heroin, but certainly having the capacity to produce physical dependency. Methadone when given in high enough doses will prevent the withdrawal symptoms which occur when the addict stops shooting heroin. Advocates admit that methadone does not cure addiction and, in fact, substitutes one narcotic for another. They hasten to add, however, that methadone does not make the addict as "high" as heroin does and allows him to work and function effectively. The big plus is removing the necessity for trying to raise the money to pay for a heroin habit. Methadone is cheap and the amount given can be carefully controlled. Most attempts to get the addict off methadone have resulted in his going back to heroin, and the idea at present is to maintain him indefinitely. Many programs, however, are experimenting with gradual reduction.

The reports publicized so far have been very encouraging, and many state programs are adopting this approach. Methadone, of course, is not a panacea and caution in interpretation is necessary until more data are available. A methadone program works best in combination with a meaningful group or individual psychotherapy plan, and most programs realize this. Unfortunately, there often is a tendency merely to give lip service to the necessity of seeing to it that the addict being maintained has some opportunity to work through some of his personality problems with a therapist.

Because most of the people on methadone today are black, the black community should demand assurance that history is not allowed to repeat itself as when heroin was introduced at the turn of the century as the cure for morphine addiction. Being dependent upon methadone (or worse, those who control its distribution) is not a permanently satisfactory state of affairs. At this point, no one has a full answer, and all of the programs mentioned deserve support. The community, however, must demand that practitioners and researchers not be content with partial answers. The government must be forced to fund private community-based programs at a level commensurate with the way it funds well-established state- and university-operated programs.

Unfortunately, there is little to report in the area of preventative education as far as the black community is concerned. The thrust of most of the programs presently funded is toward the young, white, middle-class drug abuser and potential drug abuser. There is growing evidence, however, that positive forces are at work within the black community to counteract the high status drug use has enjoyed over the past thirty or forty years. As black pride and consciousness increase more and more, indications emerge that there is realization of the tremendous harm and destruction drugs have brought to the black community. Young militant groups, such as the Panthers, have begun to give notice that pushers and drug peddlers are enemies and exploiters of black people and that their continual existence will not be tolerated. Churches and radio stations that beam toward the black community have begun to wage strong antidrug campaigns. Entertainers and jazz musicians are beginning publicly to disavow drug use. To be sure, it is not enough to provide information on the effects of the specific drugs. Rather, adults and youngsters alike must consciously wage an all-out propaganda campaign to give low status to drug use. Of course, the use of hard-line scare tactics will not succeed. The message that drugs are "uncool" has to be couched in positive terms. The fact that one cannot possibly hope to make a meaningful contribution to the struggle for liberation if he is "stoned" most of the time has compelling logic for young people. Their (the young people's) cooperation and enthusiastic participation must be obtained before any massive preventative education effort can have a chance at succeeding.

References

Brown, C. *Manchild in the promised land.* New York: Macmillan, 1965.

Chein, I., Gerard, D., Lee, R., and Rosenfeld, E. *The road to H.* New York: Basic Books, 1964.

Clark, K. B. *Dark ghetto.* New York: Harper & Row, 1965.

Cohen, S. *The drug dilemma.* New York: McGraw-Hill, 1969.

Helay, P. F., and Manak, J. P. (Eds.) *Drug dependence and abuse resource book.* Chicago: National District Attorneys Association, 1971.

Jones, K. L., Shainberg, L. W., and Byer, C. O. *Drugs and alcohol.* New York: Harper & Row, 1969.

Lindeman, R. R. *Drugs from A to Z.* New York: McGraw-Hill, 1969.

WILLIAM D. PIERCE

The Comprehensive Community Mental Health Programs and the Black Community

The mood and the atmosphere that exists within the black community is indicative of a posture of self-assertion, self-direction, and self-determination. External manifestations of more deep internal transitions within the black community should be vivid and clear to those either looking on or directly experiencing the intensity of the black movement. The contemporary social situation in our country, which demonstrates urban crises, racial discord and an overall moral failure of an old social order in response to black Americans, has generated the demand for change and has given birth to new, more relevant ideology. New ideology and demand for change along with social action is a response of a people—a people committed to change.

The impetus for change, for transformation, for revolution is ridding oneself of an existing condition, alleviating an intolerable state of affairs. Indeed the basic issue is revolution from something. Revolution from what? Black people are clear on the issue revolution from what—from the experience of existing under certain conditions and knowing damn well that this manner of existence does not have to be. Black people eagerly and urgently set about the task of changing the conditions under which they exist. Revolution, yes! Revolution to what—to something different, much different than what now exists.

The reaction of the American majority to this black posture ranges from defining the direction of the black movement as realistic self-determination, to cultural pluralism, to polarization, to separatism, to, and by some strange, esoteric logic, reverse racism. However seen and defined, the changes are real and are indicative of meaningful departure and growth from previously established patterns. Social change, social action is the reality and the necessity.

If comprehensive community mental health services in the black community are going to be, indeed, part of the community they serve, if community mental health programs are to be, indeed, community relevant, then the transitions taking place within the black community have important implications and agendas for these programs.

Let us then focus our attention, briefly but seriously, on the role of comprehensive community mental health programs within the black community in terms of the social-environmental-attitudinal context in which services of whatever nature are provided.

Reprinted by permission of the author.

398

Attitudes Concerning Mental Health

When thinking about and attempting to make some sense out of mental health and the black community, one is confronted with the task of unraveling and isolating numerous interacting variables. On the one hand, there are variables that are operative within the black community, and on the other hand, there are variables operative in the provision of mental health services. In terms of the community mental health approach wherein a basic tenet is to take into consideration that behavior is a function of the individual and attributes of his environment, his milieu, his community, the complexity of the interaction of many factors becomes unavoidably more clear and one must maintain a healthy respect for these complexities.

Let me first comment on the community's attitude and operative definition of emotional disturbance or mental illness. Though generally throughout the society there is a negative value attached to mental illness, there appear to be some specific factors operating in the black community which further influence the already functioning negative attitude. It is a common opinion that the black community tolerates or absorbs a greater degree of "deviant" behavior. Because of the multiple problems that exist and are perpetuated, the community has adjusted to a certain level of chaotic and socially disruptive behavior. Hence the expectable environment is defined by a greater degree of disruptive activity. Thus behavior that is considered disturbed or "crazy" would have a greater disruptive intensity in order to be viewed as outside of the norm or abnormal. So for the community or agents in the community to recognize that something is wrong with someone and to react to him, the behavior has to be visibly bizarre or the functioning severely impaired. A result is that being mentally ill takes on the negative and threatening connotations associated with a crisis situation. Another result, as some studies have suggested, is that black people clinically appear more acutely or severely disturbed on admission to a psychiatric facility (Dreger and Miller, 1960). This finding leads the naive observer to a false conclusion— that black people become more sick or are more severely disturbed. The issue is at what point within the community is mental illness recognized and at what point is there contact with a treatment facility. Take, for instance, a person who indeed may be severely depressed, not communicating much, not active, or not working. Because it is not unusual within the environment to be out of work and inactive, the person is not highly visible until his symptoms become so severe or his functioning becomes so impaired as to be disruptive or such a burden on those who may be caring for his needs; he remains unnoticed and therefore untreated.

The traditional lack of availability of psychiatric services and the lack of exposure to knowledge about emotional disturbances, of course, are in large part responsible for this state of affairs. Needless to say, the state of affairs—remaining unnoticed and untreated—presents a somewhat unique but indeed important problem that must be dealt with, especially in the design of effective programs of primary and secondary prevention—that is, minimizing the causal factors of emotional and mental disturbance and the early recognition and early treatment of disturbances once they do occur.

Another important factor influencing a negative attitude toward mental illness is that in a majority of cases the agent who intervenes and is responsible for making contact between a disturbed person and a treatment facility is a police-man, social worker, welfare worker, school counselor or teacher—in short a member of the "establishment." The intervention many times results in a court commitment to a hospital. The implication is a punitive, oppressive, discrimina-tory situation where black folks are involuntarily taken and put away in terrible places.

It is realized, of course, that there is reality to this implication many times. However the point is that this phenomenon influences a negative attitude toward not only mental illness but also the treatment of mental disorders. Comparative studies of different racial groups validate this attitude of black people. Once admitted to an inpatient psychiatric facility, mainly state hospitals, black people are kept longer. They are not released at a comparable rate as whites and final release rates are lower than for white patients. However, when blacks are released, they are received with more support and acceptance within the black com-munity than white ex-patients are within the white community. But, black ex-patients are accepted much less when the overall social structure is taken into consideration (Maas, 1967). Thus, in the society at large, in other words outside of the black in-group, black ex-patients not only have the negative stigma of an ex-mental patient, but by being black in a racist society all of the indignities, insults, and limitations inherent to the racist system must be dealt with also.

Finally, in regard to attitudes about treatment, the relative importance of the role that religion plays in the black community deserves comment. The position or point of view that one's suffering is a result of, or in large part a result of, his sinfulness or evilness, or that one is "full of the devil," suggests that one's suffering has come out of something he has done or has not done, and thus, provokes guilt and designates blame for one's suffering. Likewise, the position that one's suffering is only alleviated by getting to the Promised Land can be interpreted to mean that nothing can actually be done. I by no means intend to be sacreligious or point the finger at the church, for certainly it has been a major therapeutic and survival force in the black community—there when nothing else was there, or cared enough to be there. Nevertheless, the factors I have men-tioned are found to be operative.

There is another interesting and important treatment implication involved here; that is, that through prayer one can take his suffering to God. Hence, to make an analogy, the church becomes the referring agency and God becomes, of course, the therapist. The implication is that there is no other valid treatment route and if taken to mean this, no other avenue is sought.

Again, the variables I have briefly commented on are by no means compre-hensive and all-inclusive; they are among those that appear to be of relative significance in terms of the black community and community mental health. In regard to my last point, the analogy of God's being the therapist as opposed to the doctors, at times when I look at where we are and what we do, I am not so sure that I want to try and figure out who is the most successful.

Community Mental Health Program and Social Action

A community mental health program that exists within a black community and that provides services to a black community, on the basis of where and why it exists, should be functioning as a social action program. In both direct and indirect services, social change, relevant change has to have the same priority and the same sense of urgency to the program as it has to the people of the community which it serves.

Black people are in the process of changing their state of affairs and hence the black community is in transition and is changing. Therefore, institutions and programs in the black community are inextricably connected to and involved with this change. This is particularly important for community mental health programs in terms of the broadening definition of mental health and its broadening arena of responsibility. From prenatal care to child development, through education, housing, employment and on to concern about our senior citizens, there are variables, issues, and problems that fall within the community mental health program's "conceptual catchment area." This "conceptual catchment area" reflects the battlegrounds of social action and change within the community.

The important aspect is a particular program's relationship with the change in the community. What stances does the community mental health program take in reference to change? Several alternatives come to mind:

1. The program can stand in either covert or overt opposition to change, resisting innovation and attempting to maintain the status quo.
2. The program can maintain a stance of cautious neutrality; a "don't rock the boat mentality" that directs the program to just be cool and wait until the dust settles so it can be sure of what hook it should hang its hat on.
3. The program can stand in support of and in sympathy with change but not actively participate in any social action to bring about change.
4. The program can be part of the dynamic processes of the black community, an active, assertive and aggressive participant in social action, an active part of the black movement.

This last stance is the only justified relationship between a community mental health program and the black community. It must exist as part of the black movement; it must be committed to social action and change.

Being part of the movement requires that the mental health program have a functional relationship with those elements of the black community that are operating as mechanisms and vehicles for change and social action. Community action programs, Head Start programs, Upward Bound programs, skills and job development programs, housing programs, and various other programs that deal with youth, education, employment, job training, and police and legal problems are examples of operations that are attempting to implement change. I am not merely referring to the traditional "War on Poverty" and "Urban Crisis" programs but also to the various independent black organizations and groups with the black community that have been born out of the womb of the black revolution. These programs and organizations are down front attempting to deal with the social problems and social issues that are relevant to black people. They are struggling with the problems and issues that make up the intolerable state of affairs that the black community is revolting from. Not only are these programs, groups, and organizations concerned with change but also they are concerned with removing and eliminating factors that cause and perpetuate the unnecessary human suffering that has been imposed upon black people. Hence these groups, organizations, and programs operating within the black community are not just curative and/or remedial but they are also preventative; they are concerned about making sure that the future will not duplicate the past—that black tomorrow will not be like black yesterday.

In community mental health jargon this is referred to as primary prevention. If comprehensive mental health services can become part of the community movement and community social action, primary prevention programs can be implemented by grooving with these elements of the black community that are mechanisms and vehicles for change and social action.

So often in community mental health programs primary prevention is just a nonfunctional concept. It does not become functional by merely programming into the grant a community consultation and education component. There must be a functioning relationship with the black revolution. There must be reciprocal consultation and education between the mental health program and the black community. The mental health program is going to have to get "hip" to what is going on and it is going to have to go where the social action is!

Essentially this discussion has to do with the general mandate that community mental health programs be relevant to the community and be responsive to the needs of the community that it serves. It is important to realize and understand that basic to being relevant and being responsive to needs of the community, the mental health program must maintain the same philosophical posture and orientation of the black community. The mental health program must act out of the same framework that is existent in the black community. The mental health program and the black community must be "coming out of the same bag." A primary prerequisite is that the mental health program and the black community have their "heads in the same place." The actions and reactions to each other must be syntonic. This primary prerequisite should be fulfilled as the initial response and commitment of relevancy to the black community, and if not, conflict should be expected.

If this initial and basic need is sincerely fulfilled, then direction and clarity are given to the manner in which the other mental health needs of the black community are met, not only in the indirect services subsumed under primary prevention as discussed above, but also in the provision of direct services (inpatient, outpatient, partial hospitalization, and emergency).

Needless to say, one of the overwhelming needs in the black community is the increase of the quantity and the quality of direct services. The black community is concerned not only with having more mental health services but also with the quality of services rendered and their relevance in both content and style of delivery. As mental health professionals, we generally are aware of the need to provide services to those segments of the population which previously have been denied or shortchanged. Yet there are problems with the quality of services which we seem reluctant to attack and which are important to the black community specifically.

The issue I am about to deal with has been touched upon by William Schofield (1969). He recognizes the need by writing "current concern is with the establishment of mechanisms to assure that no segment of the population will be without access to adequate health services. This effort involves two components: creation of a sufficient pool of skilled health personnel and assuring that their services are made efficiently available to the public." With this important recognition of need that should lead to an arrangement of priorities, Schofield lays bare the painful truth. He reports that in a survey of 19,027 psychologists nearly two-thirds saw their service as related to the field of mental health. Schofield reports, and I quote:

Of the clinical and counseling specialists, only 41 percent and 33 percent, respectively, reported engagement in direct service as their primary (not necessarily full-time) activity. Of the total sample of psychologist, only one-fourth are primarily engaged in direct service activities as clinicians or counselors.

How are these figures to be appraised? They indicate that a majority of American psychologists see their primary activities as germane to at least one sector of health, that is mental health. They reveal that an appreciable but very much smaller number are engaged in rendering direct clinical services to people with problems.

Schofield goes on to suggest: "The more socially oriented psychologist may feel that we are making an insufficient contribution to the psychological needs of the population if less than one-half of the clinicians and counselors report direct services as a primary activity."

Regarding the black community's demand for an increase in relevant, skilled, and quality services, this is most definitely an understatement. As mental health professionals, let us try to be more honest about what is happening in terms of service in many of the "high risk areas," the new term that connotes the black community. In too many instances university departments and medical center complexes are utilizing their students and trainees of the mental health professions to provide services to the black community and feeling satisfied that they are making the significant contribution. It is a community or social-action orientation, but only for the students and trainees who have the minimal experience and skills, not for the professionals who do have needed expertise and skills, who send the trainees. Indeed we need to increase the number of mental health professionals, and this means training of personnel. Yet it becomes an important issue when we only use students and do not make available to the black community the maximum skills and expertise available, and this means the professionals that do exist. It is also an important issue for the black community when it realizes the paucity of blacks that are among this student and trainee contingent. It is important in view of the need for quality and relevant services in the black community. I daily face this issue in the community mental health center where I function. The need for both quality services and a black orientation is demonstrated when increasing numbers of black brothers and sisters walk in seeking to talk with a black therapist. When they ask for black they mean black, and when they ask for a therapist they expect to talk to a skilled, relevant, and experienced professional. It is going to take time to increase the numbers of black mental health professionals. But we can do more when it comes to providing the community with the most experience, skills, and expertise that is available.

We cannot be satisfied by attempting to resolve the demand for blacks by merely increasing the number of indigenous nonprofessionals. Although this is an important step, the role of the indigenous nonprofessional has limits and in many respects perpetuates old inequities because in terms of employment it is a low entry-level job with low power and no mobility.

The issue and the sad fact of the matter is that in too many black catchment areas most of the direct services provided by the community mental health program are being rendered by preprofessionals or nonprofessionals—that is, by psychology interns or students, psychiatric residents, social worker trainees, and indigenous personnel. This means that direct services are being rendered to the black community by those with the least amount of professional experience and expertise. Although the indigenous personnel may stay when the trainee or student, who is usually white, completes his training and gains professional status, he keeps right on stepping out of the black community to return later as a consultant, supervisor, or possibly an administrator. He returns in a capacity that does not provide direct services. Meanwhile, the quality of direct services offered the black community does not change. This is exploitation!

In community mental health we are going to have to make better sense out of the training-service issue if we are going to respond to the need of the black community for quality direct services. This means we are presently going to have to make better sense out of the use of the professionals that we now have. Just as the philosophy of the black community points out, we are going to have to change. Surely, as the black community becomes more exposed to the mental health area there will be heightened concern with the quality of professional services offered.

As Schofield's article shows, too many psychologists with clinical skills and training are not making their skills available. I think an outmoded criterion of professionalism is, in part, the cause. Unfortunately, professional progress is now measured in the direction of supervisory or administrative positions. These positions carry with them more professional prestige, authority, and compensation—

things which certainly appeal to all of us. Nonetheless, attaining one of these positions usually means that one is giving less and less direct service, the very thing in the black community that is needed most. It just does not make sense for those professionals who are providing direct services to have less professional authority and to receive less compensation in the program in which they serve. Independent of who the directors or administrators are or what their talents may represent, the effectiveness and success of a community mental health program is dependent on the quality, level, and scope of the services it provides. We, as black people, cannot afford to continue this subtle but strong orientation away from the most urgent needs in the mental health professions. If we do, in the black community, we are going to find ourselves in conflict with the community.

In conclusion, let me state again that community mental health programs and the black community are going to have to be "coming out of the same bag." The actions and reactions to each other must by syntonic. If comprehensive community mental health programs are to be an integral part of the dynamic social processes of the black community, then they must immediately begin to acknowledge the validity and seriousness of the "black phenomenon" and not only be directed by it but also be encouraged to participate and function within it.

The response to inequity and deprivation is a move for power, control, and self-acquisition; the response to submission is a move for autonomy; the response to resistance is further alienation, rejection, and conflict; the genuine commitment to social change is a response of ACTION.

References

Dreger, R. M., and Miller, K. S. Comparative psychological studies of Negroes and whites in the United States. *Psychological Bulletin*, 1968, **70**, 1–58.

Hollingshead, A. B., and Redlich, F. C., *Social class and mental illness.* New York: John Wiley, 1958.

Maas, J. P. Incidence and treatment variations between Negroes and Caucasians in mental illness. *Community Mental Health Journal*, 1967, **3**(1), 61–65.

Pierce, W. D. The black community and mental health. Paper presented at the Conference on Medicine in the Black Community, sponsored by John Hale Medical Society, San Francisco, 1969.

Pierce, W. D. The comprehensive community mental health movement and the black community. Paper presented at Symposium "Social Action and Clinical Views in the Comprehensive Mental Health Movement," Annual Convention of the American Psychological Association, Washington, D.C., 1969.

Schofield, W. The role of psychology in the delivery of health services. *American Psychologist*, June 1969, **24**(6), 565–584.

CAROLYN ATKINSON is a lecturer, Department of Sociology, Columbia University.

WILLIAM M. BANKS is Assistant Professor of Ethnic Studies at the University of California, Berkeley. Formerly he held faculty appointments at Federal City College and Howard University, both in Washington, D.C.

Dr. Banks completed his undergraduate work at Dillard University. In 1967, he was awarded a Ph.D. in counseling and guidance from the University of Kentucky. While in graduate school, he developed an interest in the problems of minorities in the counseling and therapeutic professions.

Since 1967, he has been active in research and publications regarding the black client, as served by helping professions. In 1969, he led a black caucus at the American Personnel and Guidance Association national convention. The outgrowth of the caucus was the establishment of an Office of Nonwhite Concerns within APGA.

Presently, he is involved in teaching and writing. In progress is a text on counseling black students and a volume on the current status of black studies programs.

EDWARD J. BARNES is Associate Dean, College of Arts and Sciences and Director of University-Community Educational Programs at the University of Pittsburgh. Previously he was Associate Professor of Psychology and Director of Counseling at the Center for Inner-City Studies, Northeastern Illinois State, Chicago. He has held faculty appointments at Northwestern University School of Pediatrics and Department of Psychiatry, and was staff psychologist and director of internship training, pre- and postdoctoral, at the Children's Memorial Hospital Child Development and Child Guidance Clinics.

Dr. Barnes is a native of Oakland, California, and received a B.A. degree summa cum laude in psychology and sociology from San Francisco State College in 1954, a M.S.S. in psychiatric social work and social service administration from the University of California in 1957, and a Ph.D. in clinical psychology from Michigan State University in 1963.

He has authored several papers, theoretical and empirical in nature, including factors in psychological assessment of black individuals, required modification in perspectives, principles, and practices in the counseling and therapy process as it applies to members of oppressed minority groups, and a social systems approach to development and maintenance of the self-concept in the black child. One of the papers included in this volume reflects this latter focus, and is an aspect of an ongoing research project. He recently authored an instrument, Childrens Cultural Awareness Scale, currently utilized by Stanford Research Institute in the National Follow-Through evaluation. His *Learning to Letter* was published in 1964 (New York: Harper & Row).

Dr. Barnes has presented papers and been a symposium participant at the annual meetings of the American Psychological Association, the American Orthopsychiatric Association and the International Council for Exceptional Children. He is a frequent speaker and leader at in-service training endeavors, focusing on teacher-learner interactions and learning outcomes, and the counseling and learning process at the elementary, secondary, and postsecondary level.

He has a strong interest in evaluation research, especially as it applies to educational and mental health programs, and believes that the value base of evaluation research must be explicitly examined. His paper, "The Utilization of Behavioral and Social Sciences in Minority Group Education: Some Critical Implications," presented at the Seventy-ninth Annual Convention, Washington, D.C., September 3-7, 1971, brings the issues into focus. Some empirical data relevant to the proposed perspective are undergoing analysis. Much of his consulting activity has revolved around the issues raised in that paper. He is currently a U.S. Office of Education consultant for Head Start and Follow Through, the Stanford Research Institute, Menlo Park, California; the Social Science Research Council, subcommittee on compensatory education of the committee on learning and the educational process. During 1970, he was a member of the Presidential Task Force on Child and Family Care.

WILLIAM F. BRAZZIEL is Professor of Higher Education at the University of Connecticut. He is a specialist in undergraduate education and college teaching. His research interests include the development of theoretical models of undergraduate programs based on the developmental aspects of adolescents and young adults.

Dr. Brazziel served as Director of General Studies at Virginia State College-Norfolk for a decade. He has also held teaching posts in developmental psychology and education at Southern University and Central State College of Ohio. In 1968, Dr. Brazziel served as a Visiting Professor at the University of Wisconsin.

Dr. Brazziel holds degrees from Central State College of Ohio (1948) Pennsylvania State College (1949), and Ohio State University where he received his Ph.D. (1956). He has authored 50 publications in the areas of development, measurement, and curriculum. He is a member of the American Association for the Advancement of Science, the National Council on Measurement in Education, and five honorary societies. Dr. Brazziel serves as an advisor to the Tennessee Valley Authority, and the U.S. Offices of Education and Child Development. He has completed research under the sponsorship of the latter as well as for the Office of Manpower Automation and Training.

CEDRIC CLARK received a B.A. from Trenton State College (N.J.) in 1962 and spent the years 1962-1964 as a Peace Corps Volunteer in West Africa

(Nigeria). He received a Ph.D. from Michigan State University in 1968 and held a postdoctoral fellowship at the University of Pennsylvania prior to his appointment as an Assistant Professor of Psychology and Communications, Stanford University.

Dr. Clark's most recent work, "The Concept of Legitimacy in Black Psychology," is part of a general theoretical work which attempts to provide a general systems framework for the analysis of the Black Experience. He recently returned from a six-months' stay in East Africa (Kenya) where he was conducting research into African conceptions of space and time. The paper appearing in this volume represents Dr. Clark's interests in identifying the distinctive orientations, of Black Psychology.

PRICE COBBS, M.D., is Consulting Psychiatrist at the University of California Medical Center.

JAMES P. COMER is Associate Professor of Psychiatry, Yale Child Study Center and Associate Dean, Yale Medical School. He has been a member of the Yale faculty since 1968. Previously he was a member of the U.S. Public Health Service (1961-1968) and was assigned to the National Institute of Mental Health from 1963 through 1968.

He received an A.B. from Indiana University in 1956, an M.D. from Howard University in 1960, and an M.P.H. from the University of Michigan in 1964; he trained in psychiatry at the Yale Medical School (1967-1968).

He has editorial appointments with several scientific journals and been a consultant and advisor to a number of governmental agencies and commissions.

His first book, *Beyond Black and White*, was published in Spring, 1972 (New York: Quadrangle Books).

WILLIAM E. CROSS, JR. received an A.B. in psychology from the University of Denver in 1963. He is currently a graduate student in Developmental Psychology at Princeton University.

PEARL GORE DANSBY is Head of the Department of Psychology at Tennessee State University, Nashville. Formerly, she was Assistant Professor of Psychology at the University of Illinois, Urbana. She has held appointments as Clinical Psychologist in the Pediatrics Department of Meharry Medical College in Nashville, the Columbus State School for the Mentally Retarded in Ohio, and the Emma Pendleton Bradley Home in East Providence, Rhode Island.

Nashville, her birthplace is where she received a B.A. from Tennessee State University in 1949. Her M.A. and Ph.D. degrees in clinical psychology were awarded by the Ohio State University in 1951 and 1962.

During 1971, she served as Director for the Southeastern Region encompassing ten institutions of higher learning of a U.S. Office of Education sponsored project to develop a new "professional" in the area of pupil personnel services.

She has conducted several research projects that have appeared in the *Journal of Pediatrics*, *Journal of Personality and Social Psychology*, and others. She has presented several papers at the meetings of the American Psychological Association and the Southeastern Psychological Association. She holds membership in both organizations.

LLOYD T. DELANY, late clinical psychologist and certified psychoanalyst in private practice in New York City, was also Associate Professor at Queens University. He received a B.A. from City College of the City University of New York, an M.A. from the New School for Social Research, and a Ph.D. from New York University. He completed his psychoanalytic training at the William Alanson White Institute.

ROY FREEDLE received an A.B. from Roosevelt University, Chicago, in 1957, and a Ph.D. from Columbia University in 1964. He has been a Research Scientist at the American Institutes for Research, and is currently a Research Psychologist, Educational Testing Service, Princeton, New Jersey. Dr. Freedle is interested in psycholinguistics, choice theory, and learning theory.

ROBERT L. GREEN is Professor of Educational Psychology, Assistant Provost, and Director, Center for Urban Affairs, Michigan State University. He is currently involved in teaching undergraduate and graduate courses in educational psychology, and structuring, implementing, and evaluating programs related to urban social problems.

From September 1965 to September 1966, Dr. Green was Education Director of the Southern Christian Leadership Conference in Atlanta, Georgia. His primary responsibility was related to structuring educational programs for Southern urban and rural blacks. Problems of illiteracy, communication, consumer education, and community organization were integral aspects of this program.

Dr. Green received a B.A. in general psychology in 1958, an M.A. in school psychology from San Francisco State College in 1960, and a Ph.D. in educational psychology from Michigan State University.

Dr. Green has published *Racial Crisis in American Education* (Chicago: Follett, 1969), and is co-author of the *Famous Negro American Series*. He has also produced many papers and articles of various problems related to the education of black Americans.

THOMAS S. GUNNINGS is Associate Professor of Counseling and Psychology at Michigan State University. He is Director of the multiethnic counseling component at Michigan State University.

Dr. Gunnings is a native North Carolinian; he received a B.S. in education from Winston-Salem State University at Winston-Salem, North Carolina in 1958. He received an M.Ed. in guidance and psychology from Oregon State University in 1967, and a Ph.D. in counseling psychology from the University of Oregon in 1969.

Dr. Gunnings taught in the public schools of North Carolina for eight years and at present serves as consultant to various public-school systems and universities as an expert in crisis prevention and management and counseling minority students. He is also a visiting scientist for the American Psychological Association.

He has published articles in *The School Counselor*, *The Counseling Psychologist*, and various other educational journals. His interests are in the areas of counselor confidentiality and the systemic approach to counseling. His writings and speeches reflect his belief that most of the problems of our society are caused by the societal system, not be the minorities and the poor who are victims of the system.

Dr. Gunnings is a member of the Kappa Delta Pi Honorary Society and is a certified psychologist in the State of Michigan. He has served as Midwestern Coordinator for the Association of Black Psychologists.

WILLIAM S. HALL is Jonathan Dickinson Bicentennial Preceptor, Assistant Professor of Psychology at Princeton University. He has been an Associate Research Fellow at the Metropolitan Applied Research Center, New York, under the direction of Hylan Lewis, as well as a Postdoctoral Fellow at the American College Testing Program, Iowa City, Iowa. He received a Ph.D. from the University of Chicago in 1968.

Hall is currently preparing a book entitled *Development, Poverty, and the Cities.* His current research includes language and cognitive functioning, "social deviance," and the black experience. A member of the American Psychological Association, he is chairman (1971) of the New York Area Chapter of the Association of Black Psychologists.

WILLIAM M. HARVEY took his undergraduate degree at Tougaloo College (Tougaloo, Mississippi) in 1954. He received a Ph.D. degree from Washington University in 1966. He is currently Director of Research and Psychological Services for the Narcotic Service Council (NASCO). He was previously the director of the Clinical Psychology Service of St. Louis State Hospital.

Dr. Harvey considers himself a clinical-social psychologist. In addition to drug abuse, his research interests include delinquency, development of more appropriate assessment techniques for minority groups, and problems of the hard-core unemployed. He is the author of several articles related to narcotics and drug use and a forthcoming monograph series (with Harry Triandis) on subjective perception and the hard-core unemployed.

Dr. Harvey is chairman of the Commission on Equal Opportunities for Psychologists for the American Psychological Association and was instrumental in organizing the Association of Black Psychologists.

WILLIAM A. HAYES is Assistant Director for Research at Westside Community Mental Health Center in San Francisco. He was formerly Associate Director of the Center for Health Care Research and Assistant Professor of Family and Community Health at Meharry Medical College in Nashville, Tennessee. He has also held faculty appointments at Fisk University, Tennessee State University, as well as a research appointment in the John F. Kennedy Center for Research on Education and Human Development, George Peabody College in Nashville.

A native of Chattanooga, Tennessee, he received a B.A. in psychology from Dillard University in 1963, an M.A. in psychology from Fisk University in 1964, and a Ph.D. in psychology and mental retardation from George Peabody College in 1969.

In 1969–1970, he was a Visiting Scientist and Southern Regional Representative for the Association of Black Psychologists and the president of the Nashville chapter of the Association of Black Psychologists. He also has served as consultant to the Epidemiologic Branch of the National Center for Health Services Research and Development. He has published papers on learning by animals and retarded children in *Psychonomic Science* and the *American Journal of Mental Deficiency* and has authored other relevant papers in the areas of health and the low socioeconomic status individual.

THOMAS O. HILLIARD currently is a Visiting Lecturer at the University of California, Berkeley, and is a Clinical/Community Psychologist at the Westside Community Mental Health Center, San Francisco. Prior to his present positions, he held a variety of clinical and academic positions. The clinical positions were as Clinical/Community Psychologist in the black community in Chicago, and more recently in Miami, Florida. The faculty positions were at the city colleges of Chicago and the University of Miami. Also, he has functioned as a psychological consultant in a number of governmental and private agencies.

Dr. Hilliard, a native of Tyler, Texas, received a B.A. in psychology from Hampton Institute (Va.) in 1963 and "captured" the Ph.D. in clinical psychology at Illinois Institute of Technology in 1970. He completed an American Psychological Association-approved internship in clinical psychology at Illinois State Psychiatric Institute, and a six-month community psychology internship.

Finally, he has co-authored with R. Roth and D. Hershenson, *The Psychology of Vocational Development* (Boston: Allyn & Bacon, 1970) and is presently completing *Black Psychology: A Study of the Social Psychology of Oppression.* Dr. Hilliard's other articles and papers were written in the areas of academic underachievement and black psychology.

JOSEPH H. HOWARD, III is a Ph.D. candidate in human development and clinical psychology at the University of Chicago. He has lectured at University of California, Berkeley; Meritt College, Oakland; Malcolm X College, Chicago; and elsewhere.

He is completing dissertation research on the political socialization of grammar-school children. He is a native of Chicago and received his formal education at Berkeley and San Francisco State College.

JESSE J. JOHNSON provides consulting services to industrial organizations. A lecturer at Briarcliff College, he is Adjunct Associate Professor of Psychology at the State University of New York, Purchase. "The Psychology of the Black Experience" is a special program that he conducts at that Institution.

He is a regular consultant to the U.S. Department of Health, Education and Welfare on recruitment and utilization of minority group members.

The consulting corporation of which he is president has representation in the ten largest cities of America. Clients include the International Telephone and Telegraph Corporation, the General Electric Company, Cornell University School of Industrial Relations, and the Fairchild Camera and Instrument Corporation.

From 1961 to 1967, Dr. Johnson served as Supervisory Psychologist for the Veterans Administration Hospital in Montrose, New York. While there he also functioned as Deputy Equal Employment Opportunity Officer. Upon leaving the Veterans Administration, he established a private psychoanalytic practice, conducting group, individual, and family psychotherapy.

Dr. Johnson received a B.S. in science from Dillard University in New Orleans in 1946. After serving internships at Michael Reese Hospital and Illinois Neuropsychiatric Institute, he received a Ph.D. in clinical psychology from Northwestern University, Evanston, Illinois in 1951. He is certified in psychotherapy and psychoanalysis by the Postgraduate Center for Mental Health in New York City.

Professional associations include the American Psychological Association, American Group Psychotherapy Association, Association of Black Psychologists, Eastern Group Psychotherapy Association, and the New York State Psychological Association. He is a member of the New York Organizational Development Network.

New Madrid, Missouri is the place of his birth, and he currently resides in Croton-on-Hudson, New York.

JOHN L. JOHNSON is Associate Superintendent for Special Educational Programming, Washington, D.C. Public Schools. Formerly, he was Assistant Provost and Director of Afro-American Studies at Syracuse University, holding the rank of Associate Professor. He has also held a faculty appointment at Michigan State University, and has been a consultant to the Urban Studies Center at Wayne State University.

He received a B.S. in special education in 1959, an M.Ed. in educational psychology in 1962 from Wayne State University, and an Ed.D. in special education from Michigan State University in 1965. His special areas of professional interest are special education for emotionally disturbed children, educational psychology, and group dynamics. His more recent interest and professional preparation has been in humanistic education and achievement motivation training.

He has authored numerous papers and articles including studies of learning problems in children, design of teacher education programs, affective education, participant observation, and racism. He has been an invited speaker at workshops on classroom management throughout the country.

He has served as a consultant to the U.S. Office of Education, serves on the Policy Commission of the Council for Exceptional Children, and holds membership in the American Orthopsychiatric Association, the Society for Research in

Child Development, and the American Political Science Association. In 1970, he was appointed delegate to the White House Conference on Children.

The paper included in this volume is widely read in special education and is regarded as a social commentary which points out a direction for the future in mental health of black children.

FERDINAND JONES was born and raised in New York City. He received an A.B. degree from Drew University in 1953 and a Ph.D. from the University of Vienna in 1959. He has been associated with several mental health clinics and hospitals in the New York City area. From 1962 to 1967 he was Chief Psychologist with the Westchester Community Mental Health Board. He is currently a member of the Psychology and the Black Social Change faculties at Sarah Lawrence College and consulting privately in and out of his offices in Hartsdale. He is a member of numerous professional associations and was president of the Westchester County Psychological Association from 1967 to 1969.

In recent years Dr. Jones has been primarily interested in the use of clinical methods to understand the intricacies of white racism. He is devoted to the application of that understanding toward the advancement of black people. The paper in this volume and the paper on groups written with Myron W. Harris and cited in the bibliography are the first published reflections of this preoccupation.

Father and son *MARTIN H. and MARTIN C. JONES* are known throughout the black community as a dynamic counseling team. Within the community, college campus, and on the yard, they are known as Jones and Jones. Originally musicians from New Orleans, they have performed with Ernie K'Doe, Fats Dominoe, Aron Neville, Smiley Lewis, Lloyd Price, and many other top-knotched New Orleans musicians. At present they are managers and bandleaders. They have a band called "Calvin Jones and His Deans of Rhythm," in which the father plays bass viol and the son plays alto sax and vocalizes.

Jones and Jones began their studies at Southern University, and attended Loyola University of New Orleans, the University of San Francisco, and completed their graduate work at San Francisco State College, with M.A.s in counseling, and are currently working on Ph.D.s in community psychology at the California School for Professional Psychology in San Francisco.

Jones and Jones began their counseling careers by analyzing attitudes of various musicians' behavioral patterns and by observing collective attitudes of sex deviants. Since then they have been employed as counselors in various settings: the Hospitality House of San Francisco, the West End Nursery School of Oakland, and the Gateway Montessori School. They also have conducted workshops in counseling in prison communities, and have been employed in black counseling at San Francisco State and held the positions of Chairman and Co-Chairman of the Black Studies Department during the academic year 1970-1971.

Jones and Jones are currently assistant professors of black studies at San Jose State College, teaching in the areas of black counseling and prison community.

They are authors of the book *The Neglected Client* (in press) and Executive Director and Director of the Neglected Client Counseling Center which is community based, affiliated with the "Help Us" corporation, and equipped with a total problem-solving process which includes a 24-hour hot-line service.

REGINALD L. JONES is Chairman and Professor of Education at the University of California, Riverside. He is also research specialist, Research Center for Mental Retardation, Pacific State Hospital. Formerly, he was Professor of Psychology and Education, and Vice Chairman, Department of Psychology, The Ohio State University. He has also held faculty appointments at UCLA and at Miami, Fisk, and Indiana Universities, and appointments as a clinical psychologist in state and military hospitals.

A native of Miami, Florida, he received an A.B. degree cum laude in psychology from Morehouse College in 1952, an M.A. in clinical psychology from Wayne State University in 1954, and a Ph.D. in psychology from The Ohio State University in 1959.

He has edited three other books and has authored more than 100 papers, reviews, technical reports, and research articles in the areas of psychological measurement, applied learning, and the psychology and education of exceptional children. The paper included in the present volume reflects his interest in the correlates and consequences of labeling black children culturally disadvantaged and culturally deprived, and is part of a large-scale research program.

During 1970, he was a member of a Presidential Task Force on the Mentally Handicapped. He has also served as a consultant to NIMH and the U.S. Office of Education. He has held editorial appointments with *Contemporary Psychology*, the *American Journal of Mental Deficiency*, the *Journal of School Psychology*, the *Journal of Social Issues*, *Rehabilitation Psychology*, *Professonal Psychology*, and the *Journal of Black Psychology*, now being planned. A fellow of the American Psychological Association, he is National Chairman (1971-1972) of the Association of Black Psychologists.

DORIS P. MOSBY, formerly Assistant Professor of Psychology at the University of Missouri, St. Louis, is Associate Professor of Psychology (in child clinical) at Georgia State University in Atlanta, Georgia. Prior to university affiliations, she served as Clinical Psychologist for the Jewish Hospital of St. Louis and the St. Louis Board of Education. She has served as consultant to various child agencies for blind children and emotionally disturbed in-patient children, and to federal programs for Head Start, and Parent-Child Center activities. Consultations include service to school systems experiencing racial upset for in-service training, evaluation, and research.

Born in Starkville, Mississippi, she has lived since infancy in St. Louis, Missouri. All schooling was in St. Louis; she received an A.B. cum laude from Washington University in 1960; and the same year was initiated into Phi Beta Kappa. In addition, she earned a Ph.D. in clinical psychology (child) from Washington University in 1965.

Mrs. Mosby has authored about twenty papers, reviews, articles, and book chapters in the areas of psychological functioning of black persons, personality theory, psychotherapy, and the effects of the sociocultural system upon personality adequacy. The papers included in the present volume reflect her interest in establishing a view that individual differences in personality functioning follow racial lines as well. It is part of research into black family functioning. The result of this is an unpublished manuscript on the black psyche.

During 1969–1970, she was a member of the American Psychological Association's Visiting Scientist Program. She currently is a member of APA's Committee on Assessment. Other activities include membership and offices in the St. Louis chapter of the Association of Black Psychologists, American Psychological Association, and the Missouri Psychological Association. She holds state certification in Missouri and lectures extensively on black psychological problems to local groups and via presentations at national meetings.

WADE W. NOBLES, a native of Roxbury, Massachusetts, received an A.A. degree in social science from Meritt College, Oakland, California, in 1967, a B.A. in psychology from San Francisco College (where he organized a group of black faculty and students into the Black Psychology Students Association) in 1969, and, in 1971, an M.A. in psychology from Stanford University where he is currently a doctoral candidate. At Stanford he has assisted in developing courses in the psychological dimensions of the black experience and for the 1970–1971 school year he was a member of a team of black psychologists evaluating the effectiveness of primary educational systems and curriculum programs in relation to black self-concept.

His professional experience includes working for the Opportunities Industrialization Center (OIC) as a testing technician and as program coordinator for North Oakland's Neighborhood Youth Corps and summer youth programs; consultant for Merritt College's Afro-American Studies Department, where he later worked as an instructor in Afro-American Psychology.

Wade Nobles has been interested in the area of Black Psychology for several years. He believes that black people are African by philosophical definition as well as by place of origin. In his pursuit for information and evidence, he has written a research grant (and received funding) to study for a summer (1971) in Africa. The paper presented in this volume reflects his orientation in building Black Psychology on a philosophy which is in accord with the most basic definition of black people: WE ARE AN AFRICAN PEOPLE.

Brother Nobles belongs to the African Heritage Studies Association and is a member of the Bay Area Association of Black Psychologists. He is also the Western Regional Coordinator (1971–1972) for the Black Students Psychological Association.

WILLIAM D. PIERCE is an Assistant Director of Westside Community Mental Health Center in San Francisco. He is also a Visiting Lecturer in the Department of Psychology, Psychology Clinic, University of California, Berkeley. Formerly,

Dr. Pierce was on the staff of the Department of Psychiatry, Mt. Zion Hospital and Medical Center, San Francisco.

Raised near Pittsburgh, he received a B.S. from the University of Pittsburgh in 1962 and then attended Ohio State University where he received an M.A. in 1965 and a Ph.D. in clinical psychology in 1967. In 1967-1968, he was a National Institute of Mental Health Post-doctoral Fellow at Mt. Zion Hospital, Department of Psychiatry, and Stanford University, Department of Psychiatry.

Dr. Pierce has published and presented papers and has research interests in community mental health, psychotherapeutic process, and development of black identity in black children and adolescents. He has served as a member of the American Psychological Association, Visiting Psychologist Program Committee and as a member of National Institute of Mental Health Region 9 Community Mental Health Grants Review Team. Dr. Pierce was the Western Regional Representative for the Association of Black Psychologists from 1969 through 1971.

ALVIN FRANCIS POUSSAINT is Associate Professor of Psychiatry and Associate Dean of Students, Harvard Medical School, Boston, Massachusetts. He is also Associate Psychiatrist, Massachusetts General Hospital, Boston. He has been a member of the Tufts University Medical School; Director of Psychiatry, Columbia Point Health Center, Boston; and during 1965-1966, was Southern Field Director, Medical Committee for Human Rights, Jackson, Mississippi.

Born in East Harlem, New York, he received a B.A. from Columbia University in 1956, an M.D. from the Cornell University Medical College in 1960, and an M.S. from the University of California, Los Angeles, in 1964. He has published a number of papers on psychological aspects of the black experience and first came to national attention in the early 1960s when, as a young psychiatrist writing in leading scholarly and popular journals, he exposed the sexual conflicts between black and white female civil rights workers in the South and their impact on the movement, an impact which was to result in a growing nationalism and the "black power" thrust. Later, on the faculty of Tuft University's Department of Psychiatry, Dr. Poussaint was a pioneer in the study of the ego-mortifying effects of assimilationist ideals on the black psyche.

RODERICK W. PUGH is Associate Professor of Psychology at Loyola University of Chicago, and is in the private practice of clinical psychology. Until 1966 he had spent most of his professional career at Hines Veterans Administration Hospital, Chicago, where he was variously Chief of the Clinical Psychology Section and Coordinator of Psychological Internship Training.

He finished high school in Dayton, Ohio, and received a B.A., cum laude, from Fisk University in 1940, an M.A. from The Ohio State University in 1941, and in 1949, a Ph.D. in psychology from the University of Chicago where he was elected to Sigma Xi. He is a Diplomat of the American Board of Professional Psychology and appears as a board examiner in the film on its procedures which the Board will release soon.

Dr. Pugh is currently a consultant to the Veterans Administration Training

Program in Psychology, is on the Juvenile Problems Research Review Committee of the National Institute of Mental Health, and is secretary of the board of trustees of Fisk University, where in 1966 he was a visiting scholar in psychology. He is a member of the American Psychological Association and the Association of Black Psychologists, among others.

He has traveled extensively in the Orient, India, the Middle East, Europe, Scandinavia, and Africa. His professional interests are psychotherapy, interpersonal theory, training in clinical psychology, and the psychology of the black experience. In 1970, he organized and chaired a Symposium by Black Psychologists at Loyola University, and he is currently editing a volume based on this symposium.

CHARLES W. THOMAS completed his undergraduate work in 1951 at Morgan State College, and received an M.A. from John Carroll University in 1955. He was awarded a Ph.D. from Case Western Reserve University in 1961.

He has been a self-employed psychologist who worked as an Urban Problems Consultant and now is Professor, Urban and Rural Studies, Third College, University of California, San Diego. He has been a lecturer in the Black Studies Programs of The Claremont Colleges and University of California, Irvine. He has also been a faculty member or lecturer at University of Oregon; John Carroll University; the Medical School, University of Southern California; Arizona State University; California State College, Los Angeles and Dominguez Hills. In 1969, Dr. Thomas was a Visiting Distinguished Lecturer at Michigan State University.

He is the National Honorary Chairman of the Association of Black Psychologists and was conferred the title "Father of Black Psychology" by the Black Students Psychological Association.

Dr. Thomas is 1971-1972 Chairman-elect of the Education and Training Board of the American Psychological Association and also serves as its Chairman of the Task Force on Masters Level Education. He is a member of the Board of Governors of the California Professional School of Psychology.

Dr. Thomas is listed in *Outstanding Personalities of the Midwest and West*, and has numerous commendations and awards for his work in the black community. Dr. Thomas's many publications include *Boys No More: A Black Psychologist's View of Community* (Beverly Hills, Calif.: Glencoe Press, 1971).

EDWARD K. WEAVER is Dean and Professor of Education at Atlanta University, Atlanta, Georgia. Formerly he was dean at seven black institutions, vice-president of one, and served in eight other black institutions of higher education throughout the South. He served as a British Colonial Servant in Nigeria (1959) and on the Nkrumah Commission for implications of science and technology for education up to the university (1964-1965). He was a guest of the Israeli Government in 1966 to observe and study the impact of Israel on Africa South of the Sahara and has directed two Peace Corps Training Programs for Ghana. He has also worked as a State Department Consultant in West Africa, and his last sabbatical was spent as a Visiting Professor at Cornell University.

Born in Lampassos, Texas, and raised and educated in Oklahoma, Kansas, he received a B.S. from Langston University, an M.S. from the State University of Iowa, and an Ed.D. from Teachers College, Columbia University in 1947.

He has authored more than 100 papers, edited science education journals, made technical reports, and conducted researches on the implications of science, and its methods, for the development of democracy. Within recent years, his broad administrative experience, his international understandings, and his work with peoples in urban settings here and overseas, have led him into serious identification with brown, red, yellow, white, and black poor all over the world, and exposure of the current social and behavioral science mythologies about the poor, the disadvantaged, and the depraved.

For the immediate past, he has been involved in a consortium of Ford Foundation funded institutions for the training of adminstrators. The Atlanta University program is designed to train black superintendents for the key urban districts where black people are in a majority and to utilize their knowledge to change not only the schools but the city.

Dr. Weaver was a member of the Trainers of Teacher Trainers national advisory committee. He has served as a consultant to various components of the Office of Education and is on several advisory boards, including *Science Education.* He is a fellow of the American Association for the Advancement of Science (formerly Committeeman-at-Large and on the President's Commission), the National Association for Research in Science Teaching, Life Member of NEA, and the like. In 1947, he was honored at the World Federation of Democratic Youth in Praha for his contribution to the plenary sessions.

JOSEPH WHITE is Professor of Comparative Culture and Psychology at the University of California, Irvine. Prior to the current academic year, he served as Assistant to the Vice Chancellor of Academic Affairs as special advisor for Affirmative Action on the Irvine Campus. He also served as Director of the Black Culture Program, within the Program in Comparative Culture since its inception in July 1969. Dr. White was formerly Dean of Undergraduate Studies at San Francisco State College. Previous to that he was Director of Educational Opportunities Program and a counseling psychologist at Long Beach State College.

Dr. White received an A.B. cum laude from San Francisco State College, in 1954, an M.S., also from San Francisco State in 1958, and a Ph.D. from Michigan State University in 1961—all in the field of psychology. He was a U.S. Public Health Fellow in 1960-1961, and the recipient of the Jesse Smith Noyes Foundation Fellowship in 1959-1960.

His article in *Ebony* (September 1970), "Toward a Black Psychology," has evoked inquiries from all over the United States; the same is true of *The Black Scholar* article, "Guidelines for Black Psychologists." Dr. White's areas of expertise include in-service cultural awareness (in black experience), training for teachers, counselors, and administrators; and black curriculum development in higher education.

Though he is presently devoting his energies to teaching, he retains his certificate as a clinical psychologist and plans to return to counseling in the future.

CHARLES B. WILKINSON, M.D., Assistant Dean of Curriculum and Professor of Psychiatry, University of Missouri at Kansas City School of Medicine, is also the Executive Director of the Greater Kansas City Mental Health Foundation, a position he has held since 1969. Prior to the appointment, he served as Acting Director of the Foundation for the period 1968–1969. He was recently elected to the Board of Trustees of the APA (and is a member of its Executive Committee) and to the Group for the Advancement of Psychiatry.

Dr. Wilkinson obtained a B.S. from the Virginia Union University in 1941, an M.D. from Howard University College of Medicine in December 1944, and an M.S. (psychiatry) from the University of Colorado School of Medicine in 1950. His career consists of a variety of experiences in the field of medicine and psychiatry.

From 1950 through 1955 he was a member of the Division of Neuropsychiatry at the School of Medicine, Howard University, attaining the rank of Assistant Professor. In 1955 he entered the U.S. Army, serving in the United States and Europe, and was discharged in 1958 with the rank of major.

He is a member of the Governor's Advisory Council on Mental Retardation and Community Mental Health Centers for the State of Missouri; Examiner, American Board of Psychiatry and Neurology; the Governor's Advisory Council of the National Association of Mental Health. In addition, he served as a member of the National Advisory Council of the National Institute of Mental Health from 1966 through 1970. He served as a member of the Mayor's Commission of Civil Disorders in 1968, which investigated and reported on the civil upheaval that occurred that year in St. Louis.

In the area of scientific publications, Dr. Wilkinson has written articles in the field of mental health and medicine, ranging from commentaries on the social scene to family therapeutic intervention.

ROBERT L. WILLIAMS is Director of Black Studies and Professor of Psychology at Washington University, St. Louis, Missouri. Formerly, he was Chief, Psychology Service, Jefferson Barracks Veterans Administration Hospital in St. Louis, an NIMH Mental Health Consultant in Region IX, San Francisco, and Executive Director of a Hospital Improvement Project in Spokane, Washington.

A native of Little Rock, Arkansas, he received an A.B. (cum laude and distinction in the field) from Philander Smith College in 1953, an M.Ed. from Wayne State University in 1955, and a Ph.D. in clinical psychology from Washington University in 1961.

Dr. William's major research interests are in the areas of early education and intellectual and cognitive development of black children. He is currently developing a Black Intelligence Test of Cultural Homogeneity (BITCH) under an NIMH grant. The article included in the present volume reflects his concern with the dehumanizing effects of biased intelligence tests on black children in particular. He has written numerous articles in the general area of the misuse and abuse of testing black children.

He is a past president of the National Association of Black Psychologists

(1969–1970) and a current member of NIMH Personality and Cognition Review Committee.

WILLIE S. WILLIAMS is Executive Secretary, Center for Minority Groups Mental Health Programs, National Institute for Mental Health. Formerly he was Assistant Professor of Psychology and Director of Minority Groups Counseling Service at the University of Cincinnati. He also served as psychologist for the Cincinnati Police Department. Formerly, he was a secondary-school counselor in the Cincinnati Public Schools.

After graduating from high school in Cincinnati, Ohio, he received an A.B. degree in chemistry from the University of Wichita in 1958, an M.Ed. in educational administration from Xavier University, Cincinnati, in 1960, and a Ph.D. in counseling with a cognate in psychology from Michigan State University in 1970.

He has published articles and presented papers at national conventions on racial attitudes of police, education of low-socioeconomic status persons, and the development of counseling services for minority groups. The paper presented in the present volume reflect his interests in vocational choice and the economic development of blacks.

INDEX

Abel, T. M., 328
Abernathy, Ralph, 270
Acculturation factor in psychological concepts, 198
Achievement motivation, 235
"Acid," 389
Acting out, 335-337
Activists, black
  psychological studies of, 138
  student, 136-143
Adaptive inferiority, 350-351
Addiction. *See* Drugs, Narcotics
  physical, 385
  psychological, 385-386
Adolescents. *See* Youth
  black, 34, 35, 36, 37-38
  compared to white, 40
  and mothers, 38-40
  Northern male compared to Southern male, 41
Affective responses
  to term culturally deprived, 287
  to term culturally disadvantaged, 287
AFL unions, 237
African art, 239
African (black) Psychology, 26
African ethos, 26
African languages, 26, 239
African tribes, 19
"Africanism" in the New World, 28
Afro-American communities, 379-380
Aggression, 119
Aggressive assertion, 380
Agrarian society, 233-234
Aid to Dependent Children, 286
Alcohol, use of, 387-388
Allport Vernon Scale of Values, 139, 141
American College Testing Examination, 98
American Council on Education, 247, 352
American Dilemma, An, 267
American Educational Research Association, 107
American Indians, 328
American Journal of Psychotherapy, 208

American Psychological Association, 285
Ames, R., 170
Amphetamine abuse, 388-389
Amsterdam News, 361
Anastasi, A., 79, 80
And Then We Heard the Thunder, 47
Anderson, S., 78, 79, 90, 328
Andor, L. E., 327
Antiblack stereotyping, 147
Anxiety conditioned to blackness, 349-350
Apprenticeship system, 254
Aptheker, Herbert, 336
Archway House, 395
Artists, black, 239
Ashanti, 25, 27, 29, 314
Assessment technique, 71-72
Assimilation in American Life, 174
Association of Black Psychologists, 77, 78, 84
Associational learning, 69
Associative learning, 110
Atkinson, Carolyn, 111
Atlanta Constitution, 268
Attack therapy, 394
Attitude change, 207
Attitudes, 236-238
  concerning mental health, 399-401
Attucks, Crispus, 343
Ausubel, D., 168, 376
Ausubel, P., 168, 169, 376

"Bad impulses," projection of, 314
Baldwin, James, 239, 341
Bancroft, J., 209
Banks, William M., 193, 205-211, 225-232, 248
Bantu languages, 26
Baratz, J. C., 82, 227, 321
Baratz, S., 82, 227
Barber, T. X., 290
Barbiturate abuse, 388
Barnes, Edward, 61, 62, 112, 166-190, 193, 213-223
Barnouw, V., 328
Bay Area Association of Black Psychologists, 62, 92-94

77 78 79 80   10 9 8